SOUTH DAKOTA CRUSADER

Also by Stephen L. Wilson

Advising Chiang's Army: An American Soldier's
World War II Experience in China

Answering the Call: With the 91st Infantry Division
in the Italian Campaign During World War II

SOUTH DAKOTA CRUSADER

FRANCIS CASE'S ROAD TO CONGRESS

STEPHEN L. WILSON

JOYCLIFF PRESS

South Dakota Crusader: Francis Case's Road to Congress
© 2024, Stephen L. Wilson. All rights reserved.
Published by Joycliff Press, Saint Paul, Minnesota
steve.wilson.wwii@gmail.com

Publisher's Cataloging-in-Publication
(Provided by Cassidy Cataloging Services, Inc.)

Names:	Wilson, Stephen L., author.
Title:	South Dakota crusader : Francis Case's road to Congress / Stephen L. Wilson.
Description:	Saint Paul, Minnesota : Joycliff Press, [2024] | Includes bibliographical references and index.
Identifiers:	ISBN: 978-0-9789600-1-8 (paperback) | 978-0-9789600-2-5 (eBook) | LCCN: 2024900798
Subjects:	LCSH: Case, Francis H. (Francis Higbee), 1896-1962. | South Dakota--Biography. | Case family--Biography. | Newspaper editors--South Dakota--Biography. | Politicians--South Dakota--Biography. | Legislators--South Dakota--Biography. | Legislators--United States-- Biography. | Black Hills (S.D. and Wyo.)--Description and travel. | LCGFT: Biography. | BISAC: BIOGRAPHY & AUTOBIOGRAPHY / Editors, Journalists, Publishers. | BIOGRAPHY & AUTOBIOGRAPHY / Political. | HISTORY / United States / State & Local / Midwest (IA, IL, IN, KS, MI, MN, MO, ND, NE, OH, SD, WI)
Classification:	LCC: E748.C25 W55 2024 | DDC: 328.73/092--dc23

Without limiting the rights under copyright reserved above, no part of this publication may be reproduced, stored in or introduced into a retrieval system, or transmitted in any form or by any means (electronic, mechanical, photocopying, recording or otherwise whether now or hereafter known), without the prior written permission of both the copyright owner and the above publisher of this book, except by a reviewer who wishes to quote brief passages in connection with a review written for insertion in a magazine, newspaper, broadcast, website, blog or other outlet in conformity with United States and International Fair Use or comparable guidelines to such copyright exceptions.

This book is intended to provide accurate information with regard to its subject matter and reflects the opinion and perspective of the author. But ensuring all information provided is entirely accurate is not possible. Therefore, the author and publisher accept no responsibility for inaccuracies or omissions and specifically disclaim any liability, loss or risk, personal, professional or otherwise, which may be incurred as a consequence, directly or indirectly, of the use and/or application of any of the contents of this book.

Publication managed by AuthorImprints.com

For Jane Case, and in
memory of Phillip Saunders

In the final analysis, the term "crusader" probably fits Case better than any other man in political life in the state. He prides himself on conducting a clean campaign, scorning off-color personalities, but he packs a stiff wallop and repeats it at every opportunity—unbending and uncompromising.

—John A. Bailey, Editor
Aberdeen American-News

CONTENTS

Prologue 1
1. Early Life in Iowa 3
2. Move to South Dakota 23
3. College Career at Dakota Wesleyan Before America Entered the World War 47
4. Dakota Wesleyan After War Declared 75
5. Becoming a Marine 101
6. Return to Alma Mater 117
7. Graduate School and Trade Paper Job in the Windy City 139
8. Rapid City Newspaperman and Involved Citizen 169
9. Hot Springs Newspaperman and Black Hills Promoter—the Early Years 199
10. Hot Springs Newspaperman and Black Hills Promoter—the Later Years 237
11. Back to the Newspaper Business, and Pursuit of Other Interests 269
12. If At First You Aren't Elected, Try, Try Again 315

Epilogue 363
Photos, Maps, and Other Images 393
Acknowledgments 441
Notes 451
Index 553

PROLOGUE

Francis Case was a sophomore in college when he entered a national oratorical contest in the spring of 1916. That event was held in Mohonk, New York. He took a train from Mitchell, South Dakota, to get there. After the contest concluded, he travelled to Washington, D. C., and met with students who had been in his father's Sunday School class and were now serving as assistants (known as "pages") to congressmen in the House of Representatives. After that visit, Francis "left with the ambition to be a representative some day." That ambition stayed with him throughout his life as a college and graduate-school student, teacher, newspaperman, civic leader, Black Hills promoter, political reformer, and eventually a candidate for representative in the U. S. Congress. The goals of this volume are to describe that life in detail and show its impact on the development of Western South Dakota.[1]

CHAPTER 1

EARLY LIFE IN IOWA

I tell you there is a picnic with him. Wide awake fellow.
—Mary Antoinette Case

In May 1837, Francis Llywellyn Case and Mary Antoinette Davidson were born on adjoining farms in Chautauqua County, New York. "Frank" and "Mary A." grew up there and were married on March 25, 1858. Six years later, they and their two-year-old daughter Hattie migrated to Cedar Falls, Iowa, in a prairie schooner. Cedar Falls is situated in the northeast quadrant of the state. When the family moved there, the town's population was about 3,000. In 1867, son James Francis was born. Much to the young family's sorrow, he died in infancy.[1]

The next year, Frank purchased a farm near Mason City— about 58 miles northwest of Cedar Falls. While he and Mary A. lived on their farm, two more sons were born: Herbert Llywellyn in 1871 and Duwane Davidson in 1877. Tragedy struck the family again, as Duwane also died while he was an infant.[2]

In 1881, the Case family moved to a house in nearby Clear Lake, a town "named for the large lake on which it is located." There, Frank "practiced as a veterinary surgeon." He also sold or gave away liniment to friends, neighbors, and relatives—a remedy he "originated... to relieve himself of the sciatic rheumatism, contracted while riding in all kinds of weather." Mary A. looked after the house, prepared the family's meals, and spent significant time reading the Bible. Their daughter Hattie, by now married to Warren Brown, lived in nearby Mason City and often visited them. Herbert regularly attended school. On most Sundays, the Cases could be found praying and listening to a sermon at the local Methodist Episcopal Church.[3]

In the spring of 1889, 18-year-old Herbert was "authorized to hold meetings for prayer and exhortation subject to the rules... of the M. E. Church for the term of one year or so long as his conduct becometh a Christian of such position." This "License" was "subject to renewal by the District Conference." He thereafter "began his ministry" by "riding circuit in the rural areas of the Northwest Iowa Conference of the Methodist Episcopal Church."[4]

After finishing high school, Herbert entered Upper Iowa University at Fayette. In mid-June, 1893, he graduated with a bachelor of arts degree. His father Frank took the train from Clear Lake to Fayette to attend the graduation ceremony, but his mother was feeling "so miserable" and "poorly" that she had "to stay at home."[5]

The twenty-second session of the Methodist Episcopal Church's Northwest Iowa Conference convened at Sioux City, Iowa, in late September 1893. During those proceedings, Herbert and 17 others were "admitted on trial" to the Conference. "Brother Case" was described as "a full case of good things, active and true." His first appointment was as pastor of the M. E. Church at Ledyard, Iowa—a small town located about 44 miles northwest of Clear Lake. Herbert's appointment began in October 1893.[6]

During the first half of 1894, Herbert made three trips to Clear Lake to visit his folks. On July 3, he made yet another visit. This time, "Miss Grannis" and a married couple with two children "came and stayed all night from Ledyard." The next day, additional "young folks" joined the group to celebrate the 4th with a dinner that Mary

A. prepared. The guests left on July 5 after they "all went across the lake in [a] sailboat."[7]

THE "MISS GRANNIS" REFERRED TO above was twenty-six-year-old Mary Ellen Grannis. Her father, Samuel Higbee Grannis, was born in 1839 in Claremont, New Hampshire. In 1853, he and his parents headed west to Wisconsin. Seven years later, Samuel moved to Vernon Center, Minnesota, where he took up farming and carpentry. He also acted as a "Minute Man" in the 1862 Sioux uprising, and in early 1865 he and his brother Henry enlisted in a Minnesota artillery regiment to serve in the Civil War. After the war, he "developed a grain business... with [a] line of elevators in southern Minnesota and northern Iowa." In 1867, Samuel married Armenia Jane Lewis. He was 27 years old; she was "just past 16." Mary Ellen ("Mary E.") was born on May 15, 1868, and the couple would go on to have five more children.[8]

The Grannis family moved from Vernon Center to Mankato in 1887, where Samuel engaged in "grain and coal business." There, Mary E. was "awarded a diploma in 1890 from Mankato State Normal School, and in 1891 was the first graduate of Mankato Commercial College." She then taught school at Willow Creek and Worthington, Minnesota. Mary was described as "a woman of keen intelligence, high ideals, and firm religious beliefs." She met Herbert in Ledyard during the winter of 1893, where she worked in a store owned by her father. Mary and Herbert fell in love and decided to get married.[9]

In late July 1894, Herbert visited Mary E. in Mankato, where the couple finalized their wedding plans. Then in early August, Herbert returned to his folks' home in Clear Lake. The next day, with the thermometer reading 108 degrees in the shade, they "all got ready and went to Mason City" where "Herbert bought himself a new suit of clothes [that] cost 25 dollars." The new suit was likely purchased so Herbert could wear it at his upcoming wedding.[10]

On August 27, Herbert, Mary A., Frank, Herbert's grandma Patty Fairbanks Case, and two friends boarded the eleven o'clock train to Mankato. They arrived in the evening and stayed overnight there. The next day, the group attended Herbert's and Mary E.'s wedding. The morning ceremony was performed "in the old Grannis home at 528 South Front Street." Later that day, Herbert and his new bride accompanied the elder Cases and their friends on the return trip to Clear Lake, where the group arrived at 7:00 p.m.[11]

In the days that followed, Mary A. had a "tea" for the newlyweds, Herbert and Mary E. attended prayer meetings and church, and Herbert introduced his wife to several Case family friends. In some instances, the young couple stayed overnight at the friends' houses. On September 11, Herbert and Mary E. "started for Ledyard," and Mary A. became "awful lonesome."[12]

In October 1894, Herbert's ministry assignment was changed from Ledyard to Renwick, Iowa. He apparently also had a brief assignment at Klemme, Iowa, in early 1895 before resuming the pastorate at Renwick that summer. On July 4, the Cases' first child—named Joyce Armena—was born and "Grandma Grannis was there to help welcome her." Four hours after the birth, Herbert wrote to his parents that "this morning a little girl weighing 7 or 8 lbs. . . . took up her abode at the M. E. Parsonage. . . . the little one was welcomed & the 4th of July declared to be Most Important day in the year." Nine days later, Frank and Mary A. went to Renwick to meet their new grandchild, whom Mary A. described as "a real pretty babe."[13]

Herbert was awarded his Master of Arts degree from Upper Iowa University sometime in 1895. In addition, on October 6, one of the bishops in the Methodist Episcopal Church "set apart Herbert L. Case for the office of a Deacon" in the Church after the Northwest Iowa Annual Conference determined that he "was well qualified for that work." As a Deacon, Herbert was "recommended . . . as a proper person to administer the ordinance of Baptism, Marriage, and the Burial of the Dead, in the absence of an Elder, and to Feed the Flock of Christ . . ." In addition to becoming a Deacon, Herbert was also reassigned to a new pastorate at Lake Mills, a growing community located about 20 miles north and west of Clear Lake.[14]

HERBERT CONTINUED HIS MINISTRY IN Lake Mills until October 1896. He was then reassigned to Everly, Iowa, "where they needed a new parsonage." Like his previous assignments at Ledyard, Renwick, and Klemme, Everly was a small town with less than 400 people. It is about 100 miles west of Clear Lake. While the Everly parsonage was being built, the Cases rented a "corner house North of the Church." Francis Higbee Case was born there on December 9, 1896. There was no doctor present at the birth, and Herbert "ushered" Francis "into the world alone." Herbert later recalled that Mary E. was "as brave as a lion" during the birth, and "she seemed to think I could do as well as a Dr." Mary A. recorded the event in her diary by stating "Herbert had a boy this morning. Glory Hallelujah."[15]

In March 1897, Mary E. and her two "babies" went to see her parents in Mankato, while Herbert visited Frank and Mary A. in Clear Lake. Two months later, Herbert sent them baby pictures. Upon receiving the photos, Mary A. observed that "Joyce looks very natural but the other on[e] I don't know."[16]

The Northwest Iowa Annual Conference met at Ida Grove, Iowa, in late September, 1897. During that meeting, Herbert was selected to become an elder in the Methodist Episcopal Church. In that position, he was designated "as a proper person to administer the Sacraments and Ordinances and to Feed the Flock of Christ." He was to remain a deacon "so long as his spirit and practice are such as become the Gospel of Christ, and he continueth to hold fast the form of sound words, according to the established doctrines of the Gospel." Herbert was formally ordained as an elder in a ceremony held at Ida Grove on Sunday, September 26. Frank joined Herbert the day before and attended the ceremony. Mary A. had house guests and did not make the trip. But on that Sunday, she ruefully remarked: "I wish I was to Ida Grove to see Herbert ordained today."[17]

On February 6, 1898, 14-month-old Francis was "baptized... according to the Discipline and usages of the Methodist Episcopal Church." The Reverend John B. Trimble, who was the presiding elder of the Sheldon District at the time, performed the service.[18]

Herbert's family made an eight-day visit to Clear Lake in mid-May, and they were all present for Mary A.'s 61st birthday. In early October, she learned that Herbert had been transferred from Everly to Wesley, and she was glad he was "so near now to us." Indeed, Wesley is 31 miles west of Clear Lake.[19]

GIVEN THE CLOSE PROXIMITY BETWEEN Clear Lake and Wesley, frequent family get-togethers occurred in late 1898 and 1899. Herbert's family would come to Clear Lake, and Mary A., Frank, and sometimes Hattie, would visit the younger Cases at Wesley. In early February, 1899, with the temperature at 40 degrees below zero, Hattie and Mary A. "went up to Wesley to see Herbert... [and] found him & his family well." During that visit, Mary A. proudly noted that "Herbert's baby [Francis] kneels down beside his Papa's knee and says his prayers... before he goes to bed." She thought this act was a "lovely sight." Several back-and-forth visits continued throughout 1899. And in August, Mary E. took Joyce and Francis to Mankato to visit the Grannis grandparents. In late September, Herbert was informed that he would continue his assignment at Wesley for another year.[20]

On May 3, 1900, Mary A. got a letter from Herbert that stated the family "have moved" and was "getting ready to increase." Leland Davidson Case arrived on the 8th. Several years later, he joked that when he was born in Wesley, he "increased the population of that town by one percent." On July 4, Herbert and his family travelled to Clear Lake to celebrate the holiday and Joyce's fifth birthday with the elder Cases, Hattie, her daughter Inez Durr, and her son-in-law Ora Durr. In early October, Herbert was told he was reassigned to Swaledale for the coming year. His mother's reaction to that news: "Praise the Lord he is so near us." Swaledale was another small Iowa town—only 12 miles south of Clear Lake.[21]

On Saturday morning, October 6, Herbert and his family arrived in Clear Lake after driving their horses and buggy all night from Wesley. At noon, they took the train to their new home in Swaledale. Later that month, Mary E. and her three children went to Mankato to see Mary's parents, and in late November the entire family made another trip to Mankato. They briefly stopped in Clear Lake on their way back home. From there, Mary E. and the children took the train—and Herbert drove his horses and buggy—back to Swaledale.[22]

The Case families held an early Christmas celebration on December 21 at Clear Lake. Herbert gave his mother a diary and his father "four kerchiefs." Mary E. gifted a necktie to her mother-in-law. On Christmas Eve, Frank gave his wife "a new Bible for... [her] Christmas present," which was "just lovely" because "now I have [a] Bible of my own to read."[23]

Herbert and his family's first trip to Clear Lake in 1901 occurred on March 7. They arrived at noon, and shortly thereafter Leland became sick. Mary E. "took him up to let Dr. Wright see him." There is no suggestion that any diagnosis was made. Leland showed no improvement the next day, and the Case family ended their brief stay because the "baby is real sick" and Mary E. "wanted to get home with him." His illness continued through March. Finally, on April 4, Mary A. gladly declared that the "baby is better so good." But sickness visited the family again in 1901, as Joyce and Leland contracted the measles in early July.[24]

Herbert and his family continued to see the elder Cases throughout the year—both at Clear Lake and at Swaledale. The pattern of frequent visits continued during 1902. In mid-July, Herbert's family also went to see the Grannis family in Mankato. They then stopped at Clear Lake on the way back to Swaledale. Their mode of transportation made an impression on Mary A., who noted in her diary: "Herbert & his family came here from Mankato. Drove through with his team one hundred and 25 miles. What a drive."[25]

During yet another visit, his parents and grandparents took Leland to a "Memorial Sabbath" in Clear Lake on October 5. At that service, Bishop J. W. Hamilton ordained "19 ministers into the Methodist Church." He also baptized Leland. Herbert, Mary E., and Leland stayed in Clear Lake until the following Tuesday, when "they went back to Swaledale for another year."[26]

A STORM STRUCK SWALDALE LATE at night on April 11, 1903. Mary E. was about to give birth to her fourth child, and Herbert decided she needed the town physician—Dr. Cogswell—to assist her. Cogswell was in Burchinal at the time—a small village located eight miles away. So, Herbert hitched up his team; and he asked a man named Seth Wellman to drive it to Burchinal and bring Dr. Cogswell back. After Mr. Wellman left but before he returned, Mary E. gave birth to Caroline Mary at 2:30 a.m. on Easter morning. Herbert assisted her in the delivery—just as he had done when Francis was born. And grandma Armenia Grannis "was present at that fine event to usher in our Easter Carol."[27]

Soon after Carol was born, a family friend named Charles Young offered (in jest) to trade six-year-old Francis a "farm & Shetland pony" for his "baby sister." Francis came home and told his dad he "did not know but what it would be a pretty good trade" because then he "could have a Shetland pony to ride." But after further consideration, Francis decided he "would keep ... [his] sister and when ... [he] got big could buy a farm." After recounting this tale to Francis on the day before Carol's 18th birthday, Mary E. rhetorically asked: "Wise decision, eh?"[28]

Early Life in Iowa

FRANCIS STARTED SCHOOL SOMETIME in January 1903 at Swaledale. He showed early signs of being a diligent student—evidenced by a framed Certificate of Award given to him on May 14, 1903. The Certificate states in part: "This Certifies That Francis Case of School District Swaledale of Pleasant Valley Township Cerro Gordo County, Iowa, was awarded this Certificate for being NEITHER ABSENT NOR TARDY during four months of school." It is signed by his teacher (Mary Woodward) and the County Superintendent of Schools (P. O. Cole).[29]

Francis made a solo four-day visit to his Case grandparents' home in July. On the first day he arrived, Mary A. remarked: "I tell you there is a picnic with him. Wide awake fellow." During the time he spent there, Francis saw Mary A. and Frank begin each day with "Bible reading and prayer." Members of the Herbert Case family made additional brief trips to Clear Lake that summer. The first mention of Caroline being among them occurred on September 23, when the entire family came for the day.[30]

In October, Herbert was assigned to preach at Sanborn, a town located 115 miles west of Clear Lake. Its population was 1,247 according to the 1900 census. This assignment meant that Herbert's family was now farther from Clear Lake than they were during any of his previous pastorates. That bothered Mary A., who later admitted that she was "very lonely since Herbert went away."[31]

After the Herbert Cases moved to Sanborn, Herbert, Joyce, and Francis came to Clear Lake on December 29. The next day, Herbert left for Mankato to join his wife and attend the wedding of Alice Grannis (one of Mary E.'s younger sisters). On New Year's Eve, Frank "went up to M. E. Church to [a] watch meeting," and Mary A. "stayed with the children." The three celebrated the New Year by having popcorn and playing dominos. Their celebration continued on New Year's Day, 1904. Guests came over for tea, and one of them "played the organ for the children," who had "a high time." On January 2, "Frank went to the train with Joyce and Francis," who "started for Sanborn [and] got there all right."³²

Neither Herbert nor any member of his family made additional visits to Clear Lake in 1904. Toward the end of January, Leland and Carol were infected with whooping cough. Both had the disease for at least a month. Further serious illnesses would follow.³³

Frank's veterinary practice was quite busy that year. Mary A.'s diary contains several entries on that subject. For example, she noted occasions when he "lost [a] sick horse," "had to doctor two cows and 5 horses," "went to . . . doctor [a] pig," and "dressed some horses teeth." He also honored at least three requests to provide his home-made liniment to relatives and friends.³⁴

In early October, Herbert learned that he would stay in Sanborn for another year. The following month, Frank and Mary A. made their first visit to Herbert's family home there. They arrived on Saturday, November 19. The next day, Mary A. and Frank saw Herbert "preach two excellent sermons . . . to a full house" at his church. While at Sanborn, the elder Cases read the Bible and prayed with Herbert's family every day, and Mary A. met with some local people. She and Frank returned to Clear Lake on the day before Thanksgiving. After they got back home, Mary A. remarked that "we had a fine time on at Case house: Sanborn, Iowa."³⁵

WILLIAM ASHLEY "BILLY" SUNDAY WAS born near Ames, Iowa, on November 19, 1862. His father died of pneumonia five weeks later, and his widowed mother was left with three small children. She later remarried and had two additional children. When Billy was about 12 years old, his "impoverished" mother sent him and his older brother George to an orphanage in Glenwood, Iowa. By age 14, Billy left the orphanage and "found work as a stable boy for Colonel John Scott in Nevada, Iowa." Scott and his family "provided Sunday a supportive home environment and the opportunity to attend Nevada High School."³⁶

Billy left high school before he graduated and moved back to Ames "to play on the baseball team." Shortly thereafter, in 1880, he moved to Marshalltown, Iowa, where he worked at odd jobs and played baseball for both a fire brigade team and the town team. Three years later, Adrian "Cap" Anson—a "Marshalltown native and future Hall of Famer"—was persuaded to come to Marshalltown to watch the young outfielder play. After doing so, Anson recommended to A. G. Spalding—president of the Chicago White Stockings—that he sign Billy to play for "the defending National League champions."³⁷

As a professional baseball player, "Sunday's speed was his greatest asset, and he displayed it on the base paths and in the outfield." Moreover, his "personality, demeanor, and athleticism" made him popular with his teammates and the fans. In 1887, he became Chicago's regular right fielder, but an injury limited his playing time. That winter he was sold to the Pittsburgh Alleghenies. In the ensuing 1888 season, he became Pittsburgh's starting center fielder. During that season and the next, Sunday "performed well in center field" and was "among the league leaders in stolen bases," although he played on a losing team. And the following year, when Sunday became the team's captain and star player, Pittsburgh "suffered one of the worst seasons in baseball history." By August, the team was broke, and Billy was traded to the Philadelphia Phillies "for two players and $1,000 in cash."³⁸

In March 1891, Sunday decided to quit professional baseball. During his eight-year career, he appeared in 499 games. He was "never much of a hitter" and was an "exciting but inconsistent fielder." Not surprisingly, Sunday was best known as "an exceptionally fast runner." He had a total of 92 stolen bases—second only to Ty Cobb's record of 96.³⁹

On a Sunday afternoon in Chicago during the 1886 or 1887 baseball season, Billy and his teammates had imbibed alcoholic drinks and were wandering around the city on their day off. A preaching team from the Pacific Garden Mission was singing on a street corner, and the baseball players stopped by to listen. Sunday was "immediately entranced" as the group performed old gospel songs that his mother used to sing. After that encounter, he began attending the mission's services and was told he needed to accept Christ as his savior. Once he did so, Sunday immediately stopped drinking and began attending Jefferson Park Presbyterian Church on a regular basis. Two years later, he married Helen Amelia "Nell" Thompson, who would later become known as "Ma Sunday." The couple would go on to have four children.[40]

Sunday left baseball in 1891 to become "'Assistant Secretary'" with the Young Men's Christian Association (YMCA) in Chicago. That position involved "a great deal of ministerial work" and "provided him with valuable experience for his later evangelistic career." In 1893, he became J. Wilber Chapman's full-time assistant. Chapman was "one of the best-known evangelists in the United States at the time." Billy learned much about evangelistic preaching from Chapman—both by listening to him preach and by receiving detailed critiques of Sunday's own attempts to deliver a sermon. After Chapman returned to a pastorate in 1896, Billy continued to preach on his own. He began with meetings in Garner, Iowa, a small town 12 miles west of Clear Lake. For the next 12 years, Sunday preached in approximately 70 communities, mostly located in Iowa and Illinois. In 1903, he was ordained as a minister in the Presbyterian Church.[41]

In 1908, Nell and Billy hired a nanny to look after their four children, so Nell could manage her husband's revival meetings and the couple could spend more time together. Nell turned out to be a very capable and astute manager. She transformed Billy's seat-of-the-pants organization into a "'nationally renowned phenomenon.'" By 1910, Sunday began to conduct meetings in small cities like Youngstown, Ohio, Wilkes-Barre, Pennsylvania, South Bend, Indiana, and Denver, Colorado. Between 1915 and 1917, his meetings moved to

Early Life in Iowa

major cities, including Philadelphia, Detroit, Boston, Buffalo, and New York City. The large crowds who attended those meetings made financial contributions (also known as "love offerings") to the Sundays' operation. They earned over a million dollars between 1908 and 1920. During that same time period, the average worker earned less than $14,000.[42]

Billy did not hesitate to take a stand on the important political issues of his day. He vigorously supported America's entry into the World War and the Prohibition movement. Regarding the former, he stated: "'I tell you it is [Kaiser] Bill against Woodrow, Germany against America, Hell against Heaven.'" With respect to temperance, he said, "'I am the sworn, eternal and uncompromising enemy of the Liquor Traffic. I have been, and will go on, fighting that damnable, dirty, rotten business with all the power at my command.'"[43]

Sunday's preaching style delighted his audience. It has been aptly described as follows:

> At a given meeting, Sunday would wait until the moment felt right, and then would launch into his message. Sunday gyrated, stood on the pulpit, ran from one end of the platform to the other, and dove across the stage, pretending to slide into home plate. Sometimes he even smashed chairs to emphasize his points. His sermon notes had to be printed in large letters so that he could catch a glimpse of them as he raced by the pulpit.

Some journalists criticized these antics, but Sunday's followers "clearly enjoyed them."[44]

Sunday's popularity declined after the World War. His revivals were forced to compete with the rising popularity of radio and movie theaters. His and Nell's health deteriorated as well, forcing them to cut back on their tour schedule. Death took their nanny in 1930, their daughter in 1932, and their oldest son in 1933. In 1935, Sunday suffered a mild heart attack. Ignoring his doctor's advice to "stay out of the pulpit," he preached his last sermon at a Methodist Church in Indiana in late October. Less than two weeks later, he died of a heart attack. Death came on November 6, 1935—just days short of what would have been his 73rd birthday.[45]

MARY A. FIRST MENTIONED BILLY SUNDAY in her 1904 diary. There, in a passage dated February 27, she noted that "Billy Sunday, the ex-ball player who is now an ordained minister, recently converted over 600 people in the town of Marshall, Minn. whose population is only 2000." In mid-January the next year, Frank went "to Mason City to hear Billy Sunday in his revival" and met Herbert there. Five days later, Mary A. accompanied Frank to the Billy Sunday meeting, and the couple made another visit on January 22 to hear "Rev. Evangelist Sunday" give a sermon titled "The hour is come." Shortly thereafter, Mary A. noted "B Sundays meetings are in a flourishing way now to do some good." The next day, Frank made his fourth January trip to the Sunday revival meeting in Mason City.[46]

Throughout the spring of 1905, Mary A. followed newspaper accounts of Billy Sunday's revival meetings at Dixon, Illinois, and discussed him with her relatives and a friend. She frequently expressed admiration for him and his work, noting on March 30 that "his meeting[s] are fine everywhere he goes. Praise the Lord for Billy Sunday." At the end of her 1905 diary, she listed several "Sayings" of "William Ashley Sunday." These were among them: "Heaven is a place not a state"; "Don't pin your hope of salvation on a church membership"; and "I would rather have standing room in heaven than all the money."[47]

IN MID-JUNE OF 1905, the elder Cases received word from Herbert that "Carol is ... sick." A few days later, they learned that Herbert's family was "quarantined for diphtheria," and "Carol had it the worst."

Early Life in Iowa

In a subsequent letter, Herbert described Carol's treatment, which was summarized in Mary A.'s July 2 diary entry. There, she noted that "Carol has had a silver tube in her throat 12 days to breath[e] through diphtheria."[48]

Twenty-eight years later, Herbert still had vivid memories of Carol's struggle with that disease and the family's joy at her recovery. Those recollections were captured in a letter he wrote to Carol in 1933:

> Then those twelve days when night and day 24 hrs in each day the Nurse sat on one side of the bed and I on the other and every 3 minutes by the tick of the watch dropped one drop of salt water into the tube in your throat. And every minute of the time when you were awake you held onto my hand with a death like grip. I can feel that grip of your hand yet.
>
> * * *
>
> How well I recall that first Family altar after your sickness and you were perfectly alright again. My how grateful to our Father in heaven we and each of the children felt. Our family circle was complete and how we were so happy.[49]

Herbert was reassigned once again in early October—this time to Plover. It was a small village situated 67 miles southwest of Clear Lake. The family moved from Sanborn to Plover that month, where they found an eight-room house to live in. Francis celebrated his ninth birthday there, and Frank gave him a watch for his birthday present. Herbert managed one quick visit to Clear Lake in mid-December. He and his family spent the Christmas holidays in Plover.[50]

In early 1906, Mary A. continued to follow Billy Sunday's meetings and comment favorably on his ministry. She read newspaper accounts about his January revivals in Burlington, Iowa, and a month later she learned he was holding meetings in Princeton, Illinois. After Sunday had spent about two weeks preaching in Princeton, she noted that he had 3,000 converts "out of [a] ... population of 4,000." And later that spring, she stated that he "had 1,388 conversions [at] Austin, Minn."[51]

Herbert and his entire family made one visit to Clear Lake in 1906. They arrived on July 25 and returned to Plover on August 3. In the fall of that year, Herbert and Mary E. added to the family's transportation methods and procured a bicycle (which they referred to as a "wheel"). The three older Case children—especially Francis—showed great interest in it. Mary E. described their interest in a letter to her folks: "When we came home Francis was trying the wheel. He is hardly tall enough to stride the wheel and would make you laugh to see him get on." As for Leland, he "wants to ride badly but is too short." Finally, "Joyce says she is going to put on bloomers and learn to ride." After Herbert took the bicycle for a spin by the house, Mary stated that "it pleases the boys to see their papa ride." She concluded this discussion by declaring "A great time we have here," but "Francis is so afraid something will happen to the wheel that he keeps it in the dining room."[52]

On July 4, 1907, Mary A. and Frank got a card from Herbert that indicated "he wants to come down here visiting soon." It had been "almost a year since we saw" him, which "seems so long." Three weeks later, Herbert, Francis, and Leland arrived at the elder Case home. Herbert preached in the afternoon on July 27. Mary A. declared he did "fine" and it was "good to have him home again." The next day (a Sunday) the five Cases attended three separate "camp meeting[s], and all three were "wonderful." The following Tuesday, "all went up [and] heard Billy Sunday." Mary A. expressed her typical unabashed approval of Sunday's performance: "God bless the Boy. He is working for the master. Bless God." On August 1, "Herbert and the Boys started for Plover this morning." Upon their departure, Mary A. spoke to her diary: "So sorry Herbert had to go back so soon[.] But such is life[--]here a minister then gone."[53]

Herbert was transferred to Marathon, Iowa, on October 3 to take over its pastorate. Mary A. regarded this reassignment as a "better appointment" and was "glad" to hear of it, even though Marathon is further from Clear Lake than Plover is. Shortly after the Case family made that move, Francis got a job selling the *Saturday Evening Post* magazine. Early in his career as a *Post* "agent," he won a watch fob for "stimulating the market." In late 1907, he was photographed holding the December 14, 1907, edition of the *Post* in his right hand and the watch fob in his left. That *Post* edition contained a political article that said "the big news of the moment in Washington is the Republican presidential booms (for nomination in June) of President Roosevelt, Speaker Cannon, Taft and Governor Hughes," while "the Democratic candidates are /sic/ William Jennings Bryan."[54]

On December 20, "Herbert's baby girl was born at 9:00 a.m. this morning." She was named Esther Josephine, and upon her birth, the Herbert and Mary E. Case family was complete. Mary A.'s reaction to the news: "Hallelujah for the Case race."[55]

Mary A.'s early messages to her 1908 diary heaped continued praise for Billy Sunday. On January 5, she noted that his "meetings closed in Muscatine, Iowa," the total number of converts at those meetings was 3,579, and those "converts came from all classes [--] doctors lawyers dentists insurance agents business men, mechanics, factory hands retired citizens" who "all came to the altar." The next month, she recorded that at Sunday's revival in Bloomington, Illinois, "his converts number over 4,000" and "he has addressed 400,000 persons in five weeks breaking all records." In March, his meetings in Decatur, Illinois, produced 6,206 converts. There, the thankful "people of Decatur" awarded Sunday with a "freewill gift" in "the handsome sum of $10,379.52." Mary A. summarized her thoughts on Sunday's performances by writing, "I wish there were more Billy Sundays then we would have better times. Glory for Billy Sunday meetings."[56]

Herbert and his entire family arrived at Clear Lake in the evening on March 23. When the family gathered the next morning, Francis read the Bible, and Frank led the group in prayer. Mary A. "was so glad to hear Herbert's oldest boy read the 'Scripture lesson' this morning, and all the children start in on the Lord's prayer when we say it .... The good work for the Master is going on reaching out."[57]

Wednesday, March 25, 1908, was Frank and Mary A.'s "Golden Wedding" anniversary. They celebrated 50 years of marriage by having dinner at the Methodist Episcopal Church in Clear Lake. Herbert's family, Hattie's family, and 130 guests joined them. After dinner, the Herbert Case and Hattie Brown families "all went and had our picture taken in a group." That group consisted of the guests of honor, their two children and spouses, nine grandchildren and two of their spouses, and two great grandchildren—a total of 19 people. Following the photo session, "Rev. Maynard Baptized Herbert's Baby[,] Frank Brown's Baby and Inez's girl Daphne so two great grandchildren [and] one grandchild were Baptized." Mary A. was very pleased with the celebration. She told her diary that "we all had the best time of our life."[58]

Two days later, "Joyce and Francis went home to Marathon." Herbert and the rest of his family followed them there the next day. Before he left, Herbert gave his parents "5 dollars in gold coin for our wedding." They also received gifts from other family members and friends who attended the Golden Anniversary dinner.[59]

Francis's photo as a *Saturday Evening Post* salesman, taken in late 1907 and referred to above, was used to make a picture postcard. On April 4, 1908, he sent this card to his grandpa Case. On the front of the card underneath his photo, Francis wrote: "Hello Grandpa Have a Post? See my fob in the picture. How are you all? My Banty rooster got through allright. Your grandson Francis H. Case. P.S. We are all well." The banty rooster referred to in the card "got through ... a train ride in an express car; Francis had a banty hen and Grandpa sent her a

Early Life in Iowa

husband." On the other side of the card, Francis said: "Have been going to school this week. Mamma went to Plover to attend a funeral."[60]

During that summer, Herbert and his family attended a Chautauqua meeting in Storm Lake. In mid-September, Mary A. and Frank made a quick trip to Marathon. The first day of their visit, Mary A. wrote that Herbert was in a "hurry hurry hurry" to get ready for the annual Northwest Iowa Conference meetings; that "Joyce Francis Leland & Caroline go to school now"; and that "we have seen the city of Marathon." About a week after they returned home, they got a letter from Herbert telling them he was "sent back to Marathon" for the next year.[61]

THAT FALL, MARY "READ IN the Marshalltown Times that Billy Sunday talks of holding a meeting at that place," and she "wish[ed] we could have him here." A week later, she reported that "we have Tafts red Button now for a badge," and Frank went "uptown to vote for Taft" on November 3. On the 7th, after Republican William Howard Taft defeated William Jennings Bryan for the presidency, Mary A. proclaimed: "hurrah for Taft."[62]

A week before Christmas, Mary's diary stated that Herbert's "baby can walk some [al]most one year old will be [on]Sunday." She also noted that baby Esther "walked down to the altar and put her one penny in the box all the other children did according to their age. Big one to do one year old, one penny."[63]

Billy Sunday did make good on his stated plan to hold a revival in Marshalltown in 1909. In mid-May of that year, "nearly 15,000 attended meetings," and a "total of 327 [were] led to Christ in two days." On May 18, "people gave Sunday over six thousand dollars," and 39 were converted at the "farewell meeting for men." Finally, on May 23, "there were 20,000 people at the Sunday meeting ... with 200 conversions." Attendance at this gathering was increased because "the Iowa Central excursion trains brought many saint and sinner to the meetings." Mary A. followed the progress of these revivals and commented to her diary: "How I do wish I was there."[64]

In the spring or summer of 1909, Herbert attended a Laymen's Missionary Conference. When he returned home, a letter from Dr. Robert H. Dolliver was waiting for him. Dr. Dolliver was Superintendent of the Methodist Black Hills Mission at the time. His letter urged Case to come to western South Dakota's Black Hills, serve as a "Home Missionary" of the Methodist Church in Sturgis, and "ride circuit on the countryside." Since this request was unsolicited, Herbert considered it to be "a call from God." He decided to answer that call. So, after getting married, preaching at ten different pastorates in the Northwest Iowa Conference over the past 15 years, and fathering five children, Herbert chose to leave Iowa and move 600 miles west to the largely untamed Black Hills.[65]

CHAPTER 2

MOVE TO SOUTH DAKOTA

Now there are, always have been and always will be, two important classes of people in this world, viz; the people who lead and the people who follow, the people who dare and the people who dare not, the people who blaze the trail and the people who follow the trail. The trail followers have occupied little space comparatively speaking either in or out of history.

—Francis Case

On August 31, 1909, Mary A. and Frank received a card from Herbert that notified them he was "going to Black Hills." In preparation for this journey, he sold a horse for $125 and used the money to buy railway tickets for himself and his family. His ticket was for an "'emigrant'" car, which was "a boxcar that the railroad made available at special rates to people moving in the new territories." The rest of the family acquired coach tickets for a passenger car that would go to Sturgis after Herbert had arrived there. After buying the tickets, Herbert got access to his boxcar and loaded it with "everything he and Mary felt was worth moving." These items included "two young horses, Dolly and Queen; their cow and some chickens; farm and shop tools; bedding, clothes, and kitchen utensils; their golden oak bedroom set and their new Epworth piano, a mahogany beauty that

Joyce was learning to play." Once the boxcar-loading operation was complete, Herbert "climbed in himself" and set off for South Dakota's Black Hills "to begin his ministry and to prepare for the rest of his family."[1]

Herbert sent at least two postcards to his parents while he was en route to Sturgis. They received the first one on September 9, which reported that he was at Westerville, South Dakota, and "on his way." One day later they learned that he had reached Miller, a town located in the east-central portion of the state. Finally, on September 17, a third card told them that Herbert "has got to the City." When he arrived in Sturgis, he "found the town overflowing with homesteaders." Since his church's former pastor was still occupying the parsonage, Herbert sought to rent a room or even just a chair to sleep in at a hotel. Having no success in that effort, he "went back to the boxcar and slept in the bed his farmer friends in Marathon had fixed up for him." Using a ladder to enter and exit the boxcar, he milked the cow each day and exercised the young horses. In his first sermon at the Methodist Church—given before his family arrived—Herbert began by saying, "'Most charges wish their pastor to come into the pulpit looking as if he had stepped out of a bandbox, but, unable to hire a room or even a chair, I come out of a boxcar."[2]

Mary E. and the Case children's train trip took two full days. Although kerosene lights in their passenger car stayed on all night, they did manage to get some sleep. The family—especially Francis and Leland—spent most of their waking hours "craning out the windows to see the West." Their food supply came from a basket packed by their neighbor in Marathon. By the second day, it had about run out and had to be rationed. When at last they pulled into the Sturgis train station at dusk, Herbert was there to meet them. He had brought a baby carriage from the parsonage (which the former pastor had finally vacated), and "they piled things into the carriage and put baby Esther on top." While Joyce made sure her youngest sister did not fall out, "the family trudged down the boardwalk and through the evening light to their new home."[3]

The parsonage, located next to the church, turned out to be more than adequate. After the former minister departed, Herbert put a new galvanized roof on it. There were two bedrooms upstairs. Francis and Leland occupied one of them; Joyce and Carol took the other. Mary E. and Herbert had the "'best'" bedroom downstairs, where Esther stayed as well. There was also a separate sewing room downstairs. That room was "important because the family got most of their clothes out of missionary barrels." These barrels typically contained "'seconds' from Sears and Roebuck, as well as 'hand-me-downs' that folks back east sent to the mission fields." Mary E. "became an expert at reworking dresses and blouses for the girls, shirts and pants for the boys, underwear and pajamas for them all—just about everything the family needed."[4]

Herbert quickly settled into his new ministry. Some of the homesteaders in the area "were in his congregation 'almost every Sunday... from forty to a hundred miles.'" Reflecting on his early days in Sturgis, he said: "I doubt if we ever found a parsonage in our years in the ministry where we were given a more joyous welcome."[5]

Despite the warm welcome that Herbert received from his congregants, Leland described Sturgis as "a pretty rough town." In a 1973 interview, he brought up two incidents that illustrated this point. First, he recalled hearing and seeing a large crowd gather in front of the mayor's downtown law office. He joined the crowd and soon learned that the "mayor... had been shot by an Irish customer." Second, he remembered that his dad was stopped by somebody "who might have had it in for him" for an unknown reason. Tom Cook—a Civil War veteran and a "quick-triggered gentleman and friend"—was present in the room where this confrontation occurred. Mr. Cook went to the opposite corner and "loitered" in the doorway "to make sure that there wouldn't be an attack on the preacher." Herbert also took steps to protect himself. Leland kept a reminder of this fact in his study: "the brass knuckles that his father had carried in his pocket for emergencies."[6]

Although no records have been located, it appears that the Case children (except for Esther) enrolled in the Sturgis public schools that fall. Francis was a freshman in the high school, and Joyce was a sophomore. In the spring of 1910, "Francis won the silver medal in oratorical debates." He would continue to win numerous similar awards throughout his remaining high school and college careers.[7]

BECAUSE SOME OF HERBERT'S CONGREGANTS were travelling considerable distances to hear him preach, he selected two schoolhouses to use as "additional preaching stations." These were located six and thirteen miles from Sturgis. Herbert also decided to move out of town to a place from which "the triangular parish could more easily be handled by horseback, spring wagon, or buggy." He chose an area ten miles northeast of Sturgis and one mile north of Bear Butte—a 1,200-foot-high mountain formed from volcanic rock and regarded as a sacred place by Native American tribes.[8]

At his selected site, Herbert acquired a 120-acre plot of land (instead of the usual 160 acres) as a "relinquishment." This meant that someone had previously filed a claim to the plot. But since the prior claimant had not completed the technicalities necessary to obtain permanent title, the land had reverted to the U.S. government. Herbert paid a small amount of money—perhaps $75.00—for this land.[9]

There was no house on the property when Herbert bought it. Instead, he acquired an "unusually substantial claim structure" from the adjoining property. It was a small house covered with "red-brown rusted tin" that was "embossed like brick." With help from his friends, Herbert "skidded" the house over to his site. Those friends also helped build a foundation for the home, using "stones that were picked up from old teepee rings scattered along this ridge."[10]

The Case family moved out to their new home—which they interchangeably referred to as the "claim," "homestead," or "ranch"—in the summer of 1910. The house had two rooms. One was divided by a curtain. Mary E. and Herbert took one half for their bedroom, and the girls took the other. Francis and Leland slept on a couch in the other room, which also contained the piano and "the rest of their simple furnishings." Some of the better household items, including the golden oak bedroom set, were left in the Sturgis parsonage. Although the claim became the family's primary residence, they continued to maintain the parsonage, would return to it on an infrequent basis, and would eventually use it as a guest home for future visitors.[11]

The Cases celebrated Joyce's 15th birthday and Independence Day on July 4, 1910. Although they had recently moved to the claim, they were back at the parsonage on that day. The Sturgis townsfolk had organized several activities to celebrate the Fourth, and soldiers from nearby Fort Meade "helped out in the sports." Those "sports" included "sword drill, pyramid race, and a potato race by boys under 14." Francis entered the potato race and won it. He was awarded the first-place prize of five dollars and "was pretty proud of that." The July 4 celebration also included "lots of drinking." Mary E.'s comments about it indicated her disapproval: "Many a poor fellow will be put where he can cool off. My there is a lot of drinking here and the poor soldier boys are among the victims. Those who are not are a small number." The family returned to the claim the next day.[12]

The year 1910 turned out to be a very dry one in western South Dakota. Rainfall was below normal and "everything... was drying up." Crops died and livestock suffered, as the animals were driven "'several miles to water in the ponds of a creek that had stopped flowing.'" The claim had a well on it, but "the alkali water took some getting used to." Herbert's neighbor (the Ezra Bovee family) had "sweet water" on their land and generously allowed the Cases to fill up their milk cans with it. When water was scarce, they would use the same potful to boil a meal, then make the coffee, and then wash the dishes. They dug another well on the property, but it turned out to be dry. Years later Francis remembered that 1910 and the next year gave him "'an early education in South Dakota's greatest economic problem—Water! I have not forgotten it.'"¹³

All the children were given chores to do. Joyce, Carol, and Esther helped with the cooking and house cleaning. Francis "helped dig wells, string fence, gather fuel, plant gardens, and field crops[.]" Leland milked the cow with Carol's assistance. He also used the plow to clear a six-foot wide fire break around the house and recently constructed cowshed. The boys provided meat for the family by shooting pigeons with a BB gun, pinning frogs to the ground with a pipe (for fried frog legs), and fishing in the creek. It was also their job "to get the chickens ready for the pot when that was on the menu." And Leland trapped jackrabbits—again with Carol's help—for another meat source.¹⁴

For recreation the boys played baseball on a team whose games were held on the Bovee property. The Case and Bovee children also took part in "'hide and seek' and 'fox and geese' on the sparse-covered ground." In the evenings, the Case family played carrons, checkers and dominos. They also worked on jigsaw puzzles made from pictures that were taken from old magazines, glued onto a thin piece of wood, and then cut into pieces. The family enjoyed singing hymns and modern songs. Joyce would often accompany them on the piano. She went into town every two weeks for a piano lesson and "loved to play" at home. On most Sundays, the family went to church at the May Schoolhouse. It was situated east of Bear Butte and was one of the additional locations where Herbert held services to better serve his parishioners.¹⁵

Herbert was often away from the claim for several days at a time while he tended to his church duties throughout his large, sparsely populated circuit. He typically drove the family buggy "while making his rounds." The inadequate or nonexistent roads "made his trips hard" and "took a lot out of him." His father's difficult travels made a lasting impression on Francis, and dealing with the "paucity of decent roads" became one of his major goals while he served in Congress.[16]

Herbert hired an itinerant photographer to come out to the claim and take the family's picture in front of their house. It was framed as follows: Mary B. sat on her chair in the middle, while Esther stood by her mother's knee and held her favorite doll. Joyce stood directly behind Mary B. Carol was on her mother's far right with her doll. Francis stood beside Carol with his hands on his hips. Leland stood to his mother's immediate left, and the family dog Peggy was by his side. Finally, Herbert was next to Leland—wearing a coat and tie. In later years, this photograph became a visual symbol of the Cases' life on the claim, and Francis often included it in his campaign literature when he became active in politics.[17]

Given the remote location of the claim, the Case children did not attend school when it began that fall. But they continued to learn on their own and with their mother's assistance and encouragement. She "helped with lessons" and "they all read a lot." Leland taught Carol how to read "at such an early age, she could hardly remember a time when she did not read." As he looked back, Francis commented that missing this year of school "did a great deal of good . . . but would have been better had it come between grade school and high school."[18]

THE DROUGHT CONDITIONS THAT PLAGUED western South Dakota in 1910 "grew worse the following year." Crops failed on several homesteads, and the bank failed at Sturgis. Herbert "distributed 60 barrels of clothing that year to needy Methodist families;" and "altogether he helped over 500 individuals who needed support." The continuing drought caused many homesteaders to leave their farmsteads during the late summer. Those who stayed "learned to adapt themselves to the region." Despite these harsh conditions, the Case family continued to enjoy living on the claim. Herbert "proved it up" and acquired title to the 120-acre plot. His family did not see themselves as being poor and "felt sorry for other people who had less than they had."[19]

On May 31, Mary A. recorded in her diary that "Herbert came... tonight from Sturgis to see our old home. God bless the boy. I am so glad to see him." During his seven-day stay at the "old home," he visited a friend with his parents, took a ride around town with his dad, and "preached in... Church" on Sunday morning. On June 6, Mary A., Frank, and Herbert left Clear Lake in a Milwaukee passenger railroad car bound for Sturgis. They went "from one town to another" and "had a big time trying to sleep on the car's seats." Arriving in Sturgis at 11:00 a.m. the next day, they "found the family well" and were glad Mary B. had dinner ready for them. Mary A. described their trip as "a tired journey."[20]

The elder Cases spent 16 days visiting South Dakota. They became guests at the parsonage in Sturgis, and various members of Herbert's family made trips to and from the claim (which Mary A. consistently referred to as the ranch) to see them and do things with them in town. On their first Sunday there, Mary A. and Frank heard Herbert preach twice in town, and Frank "went out in [the] country" to hear him a third time. The next day, they went to the ranch and got a good look at the Black Hills and Bear Butte. While there, they visited a "dog town" (probably a reference to a prairie dog town) and heard coyotes howling and barking. Mary A. compared that sound to "men fighting." At mid-week, Herbert drove his mother back to the parsonage, while Frank stayed at the claim to help dig another well.[21]

During the following week, Frank worked in the garden at the parsonage. Mary A. prepared meals for any Case family members who had come into town from the ranch. On two occasions, members of the Bovee family were also guests for dinner or supper. That Sunday, Mary A. and Frank attended two of Herbert's services in Sturgis and one at the May Schoolhouse. The next day, Herbert and Mary E. took them to Lead, South Dakota, and its close neighbor—Deadwood City. At Lead, Frank and Herbert "went up to the gold mines [and] saw some of the gold that they were digging," while their wives "took in the sights in the City" and "saw the kindergarten school." Three days later, Herbert and Frank were back at the ranch continuing to dig a well in 100-degree heat. Mary A. informed her diary that "they don't strike water very fast though."[22]

On June 23, Herbert took his parents to the train station in Rapid City and wished them well on their way back to Clear Lake. Upon their departure, Mary commented that leaving Herbert "makes me lonesome but it is his doing not mine. God knows I would have it otherwise if I could." On their return trip, the Cases saw South Dakota's Badlands, which Mary A. noted "are rightly named." When they arrived home the next day, Mary A. declared that the journey to and from Sturgis was "a long one . . . and a good one."[23]

THE CASE CHILDREN CELEBRATED JULY 4, 1911 with the Bovee children and their father Ezra. He "loaded them all into his big wagon" and they drove into Sturgis to see the fireworks show. After it was over, Mr. Bovee took his charges to a hamburger wagon and "ordered big ones for everybody." This was a special treat for the Cases. They knew that if they were with their parents, they would have had to share fewer hamburgers and would not have been allowed to each have a whole one.[24]

In September, Herbert learned that he would spend another year in his current assignment at Sturgis. The Case family moved back into the parsonage—probably because Herbert and Mary E. decided their children should resume their formal education. Classes at Sturgis High School began in the fall. The Case and Bovee families had a student in each of the four classes. Myrtle Bovee was a senior, Joyce a junior, Francis (who had grown five inches taller during the year he was out of school) was a sophomore, and Esther Bovee a freshman.

Their class sizes, respectively, were 14, 13, 12, and 22. The senior, junior, and freshman classes had about an equal number of girls and boys. But Francis's class consisted of ten girls and only two boys. Five members made up the faculty. The superintendent and principal were men, and the principal taught science. The three remaining faculty were women. Collectively, they taught mathematics, Latin, English, German, and music.[25]

In mid-November 1911, the sophomores entertained the seniors at sophomore Berniece Bauer's home. Three faculty members attended and "quite willingly joined in the games." A "dainty luncheon" was served later, and as the faculty guests left, they expressed "hearty appreciation for a most enjoyable evening." The senior class reciprocated by entertaining the sophomores in early 1912. Senior Ethel Hansen hosted that party at her house. It featured "new games, a "delicious oyster supper," and a vaudeville act by three senior boys."[26]

On Friday March 22, a large crowd gathered in the Assembly Hall to watch and listen to the annual declamatory contest. It was held to determine who would represent Sturgis High School at the regional contest the following week. The latter contest would take place at Spearfish Normal—a teacher's college in the northwestern part of the state. It would choose a student from a Black Hills high school who would compete in the state oratorical contest at Vermillion—located in the state's southeastern corner. Francis and four other students entered the Sturgis contest. His presentation was titled "Spartacus to the Gladiators," which he "rendered with ease and force." After all the students made their presentations, the judges awarded first place to Francis. When their decision was announced, it "was approved by the audience." One week later, Francis gave his oration to an audience at Spearfish Normal, along with high school students from Lead, Rapid City, Hot Springs, and Deadwood. The student from Deadwood won this round and the right to go to Vermillion. Francis was awarded second place. Along with a silver medal, he was presented with three silver dollars for his performance.[27]

Francis also joined the track squad in the spring of his sophomore year. The 14-member team had its photograph taken for the yearbook. The manager, standing directly behind the coach, appeared in the middle of the picture. Both were wearing a coat and tie. Half of the team was sitting or standing on their left, and the other half on their right. The boys were all wearing singlets and shorts. Francis was seated on a box in the front. When Mary A. received a copy of this photo from Herbert, she described it as "Francis' picture in a bunch of boys with just short breeches pants not pretty." The team finished second to Deadwood in "the athletic championship of the Black Hills" held at Spearfish in late May. Lead, Belle Fourche, Hot Springs and Spearfish Normal also had entries. A press report about this meet listed the events and top three (or in some cases top two) finishers in those events. Francis's name did not appear on that list.[28]

IN AUGUST, 1912, HERBERT WAS APPOINTED as "Superintendent of the Cheyenne River District of the Dakota Conference of the Methodist Church." This district covered a large area that extended from the Black Hills to the Missouri River. He moved his family to Mitchell, a town in southeastern South Dakota, about 70 miles east of the river. Its population—according to the 1910 U.S. census—was 6,515. Although he visited whenever he could, Herbert did not live with Mary E. and the children in Mitchell. Instead, he "stayed behind" and set up headquarters at Philip—a small town in the west-central part of the state about 94 miles south and east of Sturgis and 180 miles west of Mitchell. From that location, he "rode the train, rode horseback, hitched rides and walked" to cover his vast territory and establish "little Methodist churches throughout." In addition to those duties, Herbert continued his pastorate at Sturgis until his replacement was found that fall. He also served as pastor at Midland and Capa—two small towns that were close to Philip.[29]

When the Case family first arrived in Mitchell, they rented a house on Pennington Avenue. They then moved to a large house on South Edmunds Street. It featured a unique "prairie schooner porch on the second floor" and a small yard. Mary E. rented rooms to two Englishmen who were studying to become ministers. She also took in a young girl about Joyce's age, who shared a room with Joyce and helped do some of the housework. Harold Card—who was Francis's high school classmate during the 1912-13 school year and would later become his college roommate, business partner, and life-long friend—lived with his parents about a block and a half down the street from the Cases. One of his earliest memories was seeing Francis "ride up and down the street on his pony" and admiring the way Francis rode and handled his horse.[30]

Herbert decided to move the family to Mitchell in 1912 so the older children could attend Dakota Wesleyan Academy. Dakota University was founded in 1885 and located in Mitchell. In its early days, the university had three regular departments—College, Preparatory, and Normal. The Preparatory Department provided a general high school education. Dakota University changed its name to Dakota Wesleyan University in 1904. During that same year, the Preparatory Department "officially distinguished" itself from the college and named its first principal. Three years later, the Preparatory Department changed its name to Academy. It introduced a four-year high school program that included courses in languages, history, mathematics, and science. It also offered a four-year high school commercial course.[31]

In the fall of 1912, Dakota Wesleyan's program "had three major divisions: The College, the Academy, and the School of Music." The school's enrollment records confirm that Joyce entered the first term at the Academy as a fourth-year student and Francis entered there as a third-year student. In addition, Carol entered "in Music Department and was in Piano Class." This class's formal name was the Children's Primary Piano Course, and it was one of six courses offered by the School of Music. It was "designed to meet a need often felt by parents in giving children a right start in music."[32]

As noted above, Francis and Harold Card were classmates at the Academy. Their exact class size is unknown but estimated to be about ten. There were two literary societies that Academy boys could join— the Adelphians and the Amphictyons. (There were also two literary societies available to female Academy students. These were the Athenians and the Clionians.) The all-male societies each had debating teams and athletic teams that competed against each other. They also engaged in weekly programs and "various social gatherings of the brother and sister societies." No records have been found to indicate whether Francis joined one of these groups. But given his propensity to engage in outside school activities and his love of the spoken word, it is likely that he did. In any event, during and after his college days at Dakota Wesleyan, Francis would become very involved with the Academy.[33]

That October, Herbert and four-year-old Esther visited the elder Cases in Clear Lake for three days. During their stay, Mary A. told her diary that she "want[ed] to live by our Herbert." And when her son and granddaughter left on the train to return to Mitchell, she remarked: "I am so lonesome now. Have to live it all over every time with grief heart ache." Herbert was able to join his family in Mitchell for Thanksgiving, and he also was on hand for Esther's fifth birthday the next month. On Christmas day, he officiated the wedding between Myrtle Bovee and George Vodden at Sturgis. Joyce also attended the marriage ceremony of her good friend.[34]

Joyce graduated from the Academy on May 31, 1913. By mid-summer of that year, Herbert had dedicated at least four churches and held revivals at Philip and Newell. He had also visited Bishop Naphtali

Luccock at Helena, Montana, who supervised the Black Hills Mission and conferences in Montana and North Dakota. In early August, Herbert attended the Annual Conference of the Black Hills Mission held at Lead. His report to the Mission stated, among other things, that "great financial depression has sapped the life out of Church activities as well as out of Business enterprises." He emerged from the conference with a new assignment. His superintendent position was abolished when the Cheyenne River District merged with the Dakota Conference of the Methodist Church. He then accepted a call to become the Methodist minister at Hot Springs.[35]

HOT SPRINGS IS LOCATED IN THE Minnekahta Valley at the southern edge of the Black Hills. Its 1910 population was 2,140. In contrast to other towns in the Hills that began as mining or ranching centers, "Hot Springs was created to dispense health" through its abundant, naturally-warm mineral springs. In his guidebook, originally published in 1949, Leland made these observations about the town's origins:

> Hot Springs was settled by people who, although ambitious for their new town, were determined that it should have a moral tone of a level much higher than was found in the mining camps. Churches were established early and although saloons abounded, there were no dance halls.
>
> * * *
>
> But to assume that Hot Springs of early day was goody is to obscure the fact that it was "town" to the cowboys of the ranching country to the south... [who enjoyed] boisterous goings on[.]

And he described its main street as "wind[ing] along one side of Fall River, facing a pine-spotted cliff of conglomerate stone—gravel in a natural pink-brown cement." The State Soldiers' Home was established in Hot Springs in 1889, and "a national hospital for veterans called Battle Mountain Sanitarium opened in 1907."³⁶

HERBERT ASSUMED HIS DUTIES AS pastor of the Methodist Episcopal (ME) Church in August. In conjunction with that assignment, he "'kept the [horse] team I took with me to the Hills. In doing pastoral calling over Hot Springs' many winding streets, rode the half-blood Belgian, tying her to be ready and lope her back home when needed.'" He moved his family to Hot Springs in early September. His church was in an area called Lower Town, and the family moved into the nearby parsonage. Joyce remained behind in Mitchell to attend Dakota Wesleyan as a freshman. The remaining Case children enrolled in school soon after they arrived in their new town. Esther, Carol, and Leland attended the grade school. Francis began his senior year at the high school.³⁷

The five-member high school faculty was led by superintendent Thomas O. Tacy and principal Mrs. W. E. Proffitt. The remaining three teachers were two women and one man. All five divided teaching duties among the school's available subjects, which included mathematics, physics, commercial law, German, Latin, algebra, history, English, civics, natural science, and music. The high school academic year consisted of three terms—each lasting nine weeks.³⁸

Francis had 18 classmates. Ten of them were girls and eight were boys. He, and possibly one other student, were the only class members who had not "started the four-year course together." Despite being an "outsider," he quickly got involved in the school's extracurricular activities. A few weeks after school began, the superintendent founded the Milton Literary Society, and Francis became one of its nearly 50 charter members. The society met on "each Monday night throughout the year." At these meetings, "numerous essays, orations, debates, impromptu talks and discussions, mock trials and original local newspapers" were presented. Francis was elected society president for the school's second term and sergeant-at-arms for its third term. He later joined the high school "Annual Staff," and was put in charge of describing the Literary Department and Milton Literary Society in the school yearbook.[39]

Francis also tried out for the football team that fall and became its right end. That 1913 team was the school's "first form of organized athletics." It played Rapid City and Lead twice (once at home and once away). It also played Sturgis at home, and it ended its season with a "Thanksgiving Game" against the town team. The Hot Springs gridders lost both games to Rapid City (by 21-0 and 42-7), and the second game's description mentioned Rapid City's "vicious" American Indians who "strongly reinforced" their team. On the positive side, Sturgis was "outplayed throughout the game," and Hot Springs won 44-0. Francis undoubtedly went up against some of his former Sturgis schoolmates in that contest. The game at Lead was played in an "abandoned rock quarry a mile above the sea" with an October snow covering the ground. Hot Springs was behind 6-0 for most of the game. Late in the last quarter, it "carried the ball over Lead's goal line." But the touchdown was nullified when the referee "penalized Hot Springs for the alleged hurdling" of its right halfback, and Lead won the game 6-0. Hot Springs got its revenge in the rematch when Lead came to town on a day that was "ideal... for football." Lead's line "was battered into fragments" by Hot Springs's "plunging backs," and the home team won 37-10. In the final game of the season, the high school beat the Town Team 7-0. Thus, Hot Springs finished its 1913 football season with a 3-win, 3-loss record.[40]

When the season was over, Lead admitted that the "Rapid Indians" were eligible to play but contended that they should be banned from playing "inasmuch as their physical power is so much in excess of that of the ordinary high school player." After its own challenge to the American Indians' player-eligibility was unsuccessful, the Hot Springs team came to the opposite conclusion. It "failed to see justice" in Lead's position and said the "Indian boys" should be allowed to play. Its closing remarks on this subject summed up where it stood on the matter: "We will fight them as hard as we can if they try to cross our goal: but it would be unjust to the boys to bar them for racial reasons if they are otherwise eligible."[41]

IN THE FALL OF 1913, Frank and Mary A. decided to fulfill the latter's wish "to live by our Herbert" and move to Hot Springs. They were both 76 years old. On October 2, they sold their house. Shortly thereafter, Herbert arrived and stayed for three days to help them pack and get ready for the move. After Herbert returned to Hot Springs, Mary A. and Frank spent the next week completing their packing, saying goodbye to friends, and loading a box car with their household goods. Accompanied by their daughter Hattie, they started their long train journey at 2:00 p.m. on October 16. Two days later, they arrived in Hot Springs and had "three meals at Herbert's house." Mary A. told her diary that "it seems so good to see the children [Herbert and Hattie] again together."[42]

Herbert had purchased a house for his parents in Hot Springs. It was located on the edge of College Hill (so named for Black Hills College, which was built by Methodists in 1889-90 and situated on the hill overlooking Lower Town). To obtain the money necessary to buy this home, Herbert and Mary E. sold their claim near Bear Butte.[43]

On Sunday, October 26, Mary A. and Frank "were taken into [the] ME Church... by Herbert Case." They spent the next few days—with the help of Hattie, Herbert, and Mary E.—"cleaning and papering" their new house. The railroad car containing their household goods arrived on Halloween. They unloaded it and moved into their Hot Springs home the next day. Herbert later remarked that "'at the house I purchased for them, I kept a rubber tired buggy (phaeton) and Mother and Dad could drive down to hear me preach.'" The following Sunday, Herbert preached three times. That afternoon, his entire family (except for Joyce, who was at college) visited the elder Case home. Mary A. remarked that she was "so glad to see my things again."⁴⁴

Hattie returned to Mason City on November 24. Herbert accompanied her on the train from Hot Springs to Rapid City, and she made the rest of the journey alone. Mary A. was "sorry she had to go." Three days later, she and Frank celebrated Thanksgiving by having a chicken dinner at Herbert's house. On the first Sunday in December, they attended Herbert's evening service. It had been a "cold but pleasant" day, so they decided to "walk up the hill" to their house when the service concluded. Francis visited them several times that month. He would often "call" alone but sometimes with a family member. Sometimes he would come to see them just to chat, sometimes to eat breakfast, dinner, or supper, and sometimes to help Frank gather a load of wood.⁴⁵

On Christmas eve, Mary A., Frank, Francis and probably the other Case family members went to a Christmas program at the ME Church. The Methodist Sunday school presented the program. In it, "the enunciation to the shepherds and the visit of the shepherds and the wise men was pictured out by recitation and song in cantata style." Responding to invitations, the program was repeated at the State Soldiers' Home on Christmas night and at the Battle Mountain Sanitarium on the following Sunday evening. It held a special memory for Francis because it was his "first recollection of Charles Badger Clark," who, with two other "young men, gowned and bearded, sang 'We Three Kings of Orient Are.'" Francis and "Badger" Clark (as he preferred to be called) would become good friends and associates who greatly admired and respected one another.⁴⁶

On Christmas morning, Francis picked up Mary A. and Frank at their home and took them down to the parsonage. Joyce had returned from Dakota Wesleyan a few days earlier, so the whole family was able to enjoy a four-chicken Christmas dinner together. Afterwards they gathered around the Christmas tree and exchanged presents. The next day, Francis and Joyce ate supper at their grandparents' house. As the year ended, Francis again helped his grandfather haul wood.[47]

Once they became settled in Hot Springs, Frank resumed a veterinary practice to a limited extent. In mid-December, he "dressed horse teeth" and was paid four dollars for doing so. A few weeks later he and Francis went "out in the country to see [a] sick horse." They ended up staying all night with the animal, which unfortunately died the next morning. To supplement his veterinarian work, Frank also sold eggs and bibles.[48]

During the winter and spring months in 1914, Francis continued his practice of seeing Mary A. and Frank on a frequent basis. After coming to their home, he read to them, put on a magic show for them, ate meals with them, and sometimes stayed overnight. He was often accompanied by one or more Case family members, and in early April his friend Earl Bovee joined him for two visits.[49]

THE LAST HALF OF MAY WAS dominated by activities related to the senior class's graduation from high school. Those activities began on May 13 when superintendent Tacy and his wife entertained the class at the Tacy home on College Hill. Their house was "appropriately decorated" with the class colors (red and white). Most of the evening was spent in "games and seances," followed by "delicious refreshments" served near midnight. The following Saturday afternoon, the class took an auto trip to Cascade Springs, where a series of warm artesian springs fed water into Cascade Creek. The class members, the Tacys, chauffeurs, and others piled into four large automobiles and made the eight-mile trip to their destination, where they spent a couple of hours "in good old picnic fashion." After finishing their supper and "elaborate refreshments," the group came back to town and attended a concert given by the Battle Mountain Sanitarium Band.

When it was completed, they drove "thru the city" and were taken to their homes.⁵⁰

Events during the next week occurred on three successive days. On Tuesday evening the class enjoyed a swim at a "Plunge Party," which was followed by a trip to a classmate's home to enjoy music, storytelling, and refreshments. The next night, two seniors entertained their classmates and faculty at the high school treasurer's home. Many "novel and interesting games and contests" kept the group occupied until midnight, when a banquet was served. And on Thursday evening, the literary banquet was held in the downtown Minnekahta Block building.⁵¹

The next week's graduation activities began with the baccalaureate sermon on Sunday. It was presented by Reverend Edward J. d'Argent at St.Luke's Episcopal Church. The McRoberts Oratorial Contest was held two days later. Dr. W. J. Roberts established this annual event in 1909. Its purpose was to foster "the development of those powers of self-expression and the practice of those principles of correct English taught in the classroom." Cash prizes were awarded to the top three orations: $20 for first place, $10 for second, and $5 for third. The 1914 contest had four contestants, including Francis. All four were boys in the senior class.⁵²

The oratorical contest "drew a large crowd" at the downtown Morris Grand Theater on Tuesday evening. Francis was the third speaker on the program. His presentation was titled "The Blazed Trail." Its overall theme was that America had made significant progress in many endeavors over the past fifty years, and future leaders and innovators must continue to "blaze the trail" to ensure progress for the next half century. The oration gave several examples of American men and women "pioneers" in our nation's history who "lead civilization onward and upward." It then broadened the discussion by citing many political and religious leaders throughout history—described as "tradition destroyers" and "precedent breakers"—who have advanced civilization by making unique contributions to it. Toward the end of his speech, Francis made this plea to his audience: "Let us not rest upon our heritage of noble deeds, but rather let us provide a still greater heritage for the next generation. Until that shall become the aim of every true patriot, the trend of progress in this nation will not be measured and uniform."[53]

The local newspaper had this to say about Francis's oration: "From the moment of his appearance on the stage until the close of his oration he held his hearers spellbound. 'The Blazed Trail' was the subject and the masterly manner in which it was handled has caused numerous comments since as to the young man's exceptional ability as a speaker." It then summed up the four orations as "perhaps among the best ever given at any of these contests and were a treat to the large crowd present." After they were all completed, the three-judge panel retired to the theater's ante room "where each oration was marked as to thought and composition and the young men were given ratings as to delivery." Francis was awarded first place and received his prize of $20.[54]

The junior-senior banquet took place at the Hot Springs Hotel on the following evening, and the next day was "Commencement Day." It began with a breakfast given to the class and faculty by two senior girls at one of their houses. After breakfast, a faculty member and several class members "hastened to school to finish examinations." Those were all completed, leaving the examinees "tired but happy." That evening, the seniors returned to the Morris Grand Theater for commencement exercises, which "passed off very nicely." Dr. Osborne from the University of Colorado delivered the commencement address, Superintendent Tacy gave the offertory speech, and Charles Eastman, president of the Hot Springs Board of Education, made the presentation speech. Nineteen diplomas were then handed out to the seniors, making this the largest class ever to graduate from the high school up to that time. The class was also "unusual" because of "the large percentage of boys, nine in number." After the ceremony was completed, flowers and presents were distributed. Then, at Francis's invitation, the class "proceeded to 'cool off' at Highley's ice cream parlor"—thus marking the "first official gathering of the alumni of the class of '14."[55]

THE SUMMER OF 1914 WENT by quickly for the Cases. Francis continued to visit his grandparents on a regular basis. In early June, he gave his Blazed Trail oration to Mary A., who found it to be "fine." On June 29, he began working at Wind Cave National Park, which was located ten miles north of Hot Springs. His duties included helping build a fence to keep the buffalo and elk herds in the park, and perhaps working with crews that were building park roads or repairing buildings near the entrance to the Wind Cave.[56]

Mary E.'s parents—Armenia and Samuel Grannis—arrived in Hot Springs in early July. On the 13th they, along with Frank, Herbert, Mary E., and Joyce, "all went out to Wind Cave." Francis was kept quite busy with his summer job, but he still managed to have supper at Mary A. and Frank's house on every Sunday from July 5 through August 2. And he ate dinner (what we now call lunch) there on the next two Sundays. The Grannises returned to Mankato on August 8 after spending more than a month in Hot Springs. Frank continued to sell bibles at a downtown "Bible Stand" in August. And he still performed limited veterinary work, as he and Leland "went out [to] see [a] horse that broke its leg" on the 24th. That same day, Herbert traded a farm he owned in Nebraska for a 300-acre farm located one-half mile out of town. A week later, Joyce started out for school at Mankato Commercial College—having transferred from Dakota Wesleyan after completing her freshman year there. On September 11, Francis stayed all night at the elder Cases, ate breakfast there the following morning, and spent the rest of the day at the recently-acquired Case farm. The next day he returned to his grandparents' home to say good bye before heading off to college. After he left, Mary A. predicted that "in a few years [he] will be in business of his own"; and she was amazed at "how the time is rolling by us."[57]

CHAPTER 3

COLLEGE CAREER AT DAKOTA WESLEYAN BEFORE AMERICA ENTERED THE WORLD WAR

We are witnessing the greatest paradox of all history. Five years ago war was declared impossible—today the greatest nations of the globe are in arms.

—Francis Case

When Francis enrolled as a freshman at Dakota Wesleyan University, it "was one of the largest independent colleges in the state and a leading innovator in curriculum." The college faculty were mostly graduates from private schools in the eastern part of the country. They had often received their degrees from "Methodist universities such as Boston and De Pauw." By the time Francis arrived in the fall of 1914, the college curriculum had been grouped into four general areas: "English, ancient and modern languages, science and mathematics, and history and social sciences." Each student was required "to select one major subject for specialization and two minor subjects, chosen from at least two different groups." Consistent with these requirements, Francis decided to major in history and minor in English and public speaking.[1]

Although the women students were able to stay in the college dormitory, no such facility was available for the men. That turned out to be no problem for Francis. Harold Card, his former schoolmate at the Academy, was also a freshman at Dakota Wesleyan in the fall of 1914. Harold was living with his parents at their home on South Edmond Street, and Francis became his roommate. The Card home was only two blocks from the house the Case family occupied when they lived in Mitchell during 1912 and 1913. Francis was back in familiar territory.[2]

The Dakota Wesleyan literary societies provided the center for social life on campus. By 1914, there were six such societies in the college department—three for women and three for men. Each men's society was paired with a "sister society," for which it had "a strong affinity." The societies combined "literary work... with social good times." Competition among them was "intense in all lines of activity" and was a "vitalizing factor" in college life. Although social fraternities and sororities were not allowed at Wesleyan, the literary societies functioned like the social societies did. Thus, the literary societies "rushed" new students for membership, selected them as "pledges," and elected their own leaders. According to the school's newspaper, "It is the ambition of every student to become a member of one of these societies."[3]

The societies played an important role in the school's forensics program. They held intersociety debate and oratorical contests, whose winners went on to represent Dakota Wesleyan in intercollegiate competitions. During Francis's freshman year, "Dakota Wesleyan, Huron College, and Yankton College organized the South Dakota Intercollegiate Debating League" in the fall, and Wesleyan won the league championship in March. That year also featured "three major oratorical contests: the 'old line,' peace and the prohibition." Each held "local, state, regional, and national meets," and Wesleyan achieved second place finishes at the state level in all three.[4]

On Saturday evening, February 20, 1915, Francis and five other students were formally initiated into the Daedalian Literary Society. The initiation ceremony took place in the Daedalian hall and lasted an hour and a half. After it was concluded, the group went to a banquet served in the Methodist Church basement. Present and former Daedalians gave several toasts, and "Mr. Louis Lovinger sang two solos."[5]

The Daedalian Literary Society was founded at Dakota Wesleyan in 1903. Its purpose and goals are aptly described in the *1913 Tumbleweed* yearbook:

> The aim of this society is to prepare the college student for bigger things; to secure for him a training that cannot be obtained elsewhere. It aims to develop his ability to mix with other men, to make him a leader among his fellows, to give him a social culture that will train his personality and make him a live and helpful influence for good. Each member is given an opportunity to prove his worth, and to develop every talent he may possess. Extemporaneous speaking is encouraged, and every phase of literary work is emphasized.

The society's patron saint was Daedalus, "the old Greek hero" who "did things... and left something to posterity." The Daedalians strived to be "men of the same type" as their hero. They saw themselves as "men who see things... who are on the spot... [and] who build, and will continue to build throughout life, brain, brawn and character."[6]

The Daedalians' "sister society" was the Thalians. A week after the Daedalians initiated their new members, the Thalians did the same thing. The two societies then held their annual banquet at the Methodist Church. In addition to their old and newly-minted members, several alumni "of their persuasion" and two faculty members—accompanied by their wives—attended the banquet. The "feast" was followed by a toast to each society given by a member of the "paired" one, and Mr. Lovinger again "entertained with two vocal solos." Next came a Thalian piano duet that, upon demand, provided an encore. A 1909 alumnus and current city editor of a local newspaper closed the program with a discussion of "'Memories.'"[7]

On May 18, Dakota Wesleyan held its annual spring festival on campus. This celebration featured a May Day pageant in which students impersonating "'King Sun'" and his "'Sunbeams'" drove away "'Jack Frost'" and "ushered in 'Spring.'" In addition, "over 100 college girls elaborately costumed represented meadow larks frost fairies and May flowers." They performed several rhythmic dances, "which included the winding of the May pole." The pageant concluded with "a song of praise to the queen of May." Beginning at seven o'clock in the evening, the college orchestra, the young ladies' choral club, and the boy's glee club gave a musical program in the college chapel. Following this concert, "the large crowd assembled on the campus where the play, 'The Glory of the Morning,' was presented." This play portrayed the struggle of a Winnebago Indian whose French husband was recalled to his home country and took the couple's little girl with him. Francis was a member of the play's five-member cast, and their acting was described as "very good."[8]

Two days after appearing in the play, Francis arrived at home in Hot Springs. He had not been there since leaving for college the previous fall. The next night, he had supper at his grandparents' house, and that Sunday he and Leland ate dinner there. Toward evening, Francis "started for Yellowstone Park," where he had lined up a summer job. It is not known what his exact job duties were, but they most likely involved work at one or more of the park's existing buildings or on its roadways.[9]

AFTER HIS SUMMER JOB ENDED, Francis returned to Hot Springs on September 18. Herbert and he ate supper at the elder Cases' house that evening. The next day Joyce and he took the train to Rapid City. From there she would travel to Brookings and he to

Mitchell "for school work." It would be a busy sophomore year for Francis. Sometime the previous spring, he had been elected president of his class, which included 27 women and 20 men by the second semester. He was also chosen to be assistant manager of the school's newspaper—*The Phreno Cosmian*. And he decided to take an active role in the college's forensic programs.[10]

To kick off the fall social season, the sophomores scheduled their class hike for Wednesday, October 6. This turned out to be "the coldest, windiest day of a cold and blustery week." A "drizzling rain" began in the mid-afternoon, forcing the participants to go into a tent and try to eat there. But the tent was not big enough to accommodate everyone, so professor Hilton Jones (chemistry professor, acting physics professor, and sophomore class advisor) "came to the rescue by inviting the class to his residence." There the would-be hikers jumped rope (with the professor participating), then had supper, and then played card games. The "jolly and satisfied" crowd departed about seven-thirty, declaring that professor Jones and his wife were the "most royal entertainers." Three and a half weeks later, a "splendid proportion" of the sophomore class attended a Halloween party at University President William Seaman's home. One of the activities had professor Jones draw silhouettes of each student, post the drawings up on the wall, and then ask the group to "name the various faces." Francis and Lila Kehm named the most, and they "were each awarded a Wesleyan Pennant" for doing so.[11]

The annual literary society debates were held on Monday, December 13. They had two purposes: to determine the school's debate champion and to select those men who would represent Dakota Wesleyan in the intercollegiate debates scheduled for next March. The present debates had teams from two societies—the Daedalians and the Delta Rhos. Two separate debates occurred between them. Both teams had three members in each debate, so 12 students participated in this contest. The topic discussed (in both debates) was "It being Resolved:

'That socialistic control of the means of production and exchange is preferable to the present capitalistic system.'"[12]

The first debate pitted the Delta Rho affirmative team against the Daedalian negative team, which included Francis, Harold Card, and Myron Brink. After it was finished the three judges issued a unanimous decision in favor of the negative. In the second contest, the roles were reversed, with the Delta Rhos arguing the negative position and the Daedalians the affirmative. The three judges for this debate scored it as two to one for the negative. Since the Daedalians won four out of the six judges' decisions, they were declared the winners and awarded the "silver loving cup." (Professor Elmer Wilds, who taught Ancient Languages and Public Speaking and coached the school's forensic programs, had procured the trophy in the spring for this debate's winner.) After both debates were concluded, a three-member committee, which included Professor Wilds, chose eight men for the upcoming intercollegiate debates with Huron and Yankton colleges. All six members on the two Daedalian teams were chosen, and Delta Rho debaters were selected for the two remaining spots.[13]

The "formal presentation" of the Wilds loving cup was made on Saturday morning in the college chapel. In a short speech, President Seaman "congratulated the winning society" and "reviewed the value of public speaking and debating." Donald Hoffman, president of the Daedalians, accepted the cup on their behalf. He then thanked Professor Wilds "for making it possible to win such a cup," and for his "innovations which ... [he] had instituted in debating circles at Wesleyan."[14]

Francis and Joyce both made it back to Hot Springs for their Christmas vacations. On Christmas Day, Francis and Leland had a chicken dinner with their grandparents at the latter's house. Mary A. and Frank later joined the entire Herbert Case family for a turkey supper at the parsonage. Sometime during the holidays, Herbert, Mary E. and their five children were photographed standing outside the

Methodist Church. All were attired in dark, formal-looking clothing that would be appropriate for attending a church service. Joyce, Esther, Mary E. and Carol all wore dresses. Francis and Herbert had on suits, white shirts, and bow ties. Leland was dressed the same, except he wore a long tie. Downtown Hot Springs buildings, and the grade school on its hill, can be seen in the upper right portion of the photo. It was later made into picture postcards, and Mary used them to write post-holiday messages and thank you notes.[15]

On New Year's Eve, Francis, Leland and Herbert called on Mary A. and Frank for "a chat" with them. Their son and grandsons then left to attend an oyster supper and Watch Night service at the parsonage. Francis and Leland revisited their grandparents the next day "to wish us Happy New Year and many returns." Three days later, Joyce and Francis "went back to their school work again." Mary E. was very happy that they were there for the holidays. She wrote to one of her sisters that "our Xmas was lovely this year" and although "it cost considerable to have . . . [Joyce and Francis] home . . . we felt we must."[16]

FRANCIS ARRIVED BACK AT DAKOTA WESLEYAN in early January. He spent most of the next three weeks preparing for and taking final exams. But January was not entirely devoted to academic pursuits. He also found time to entertain the Thalians "in the dining parlors of the Widmann hotel," where he and other Daedalians presented orations in a mock contest. Two days later, the annual Thalian-Daedalian banquet was held, and presumably he attended it. The first semester ended on Friday, January 28, and second-semester classes opened on the following Thursday.[17]

The annual peace oratorical contest was held in the college chapel on February 7. Francis was among the five contestants. He had "worked hard" on his oration and had "contacted various members of the Dakota Wesleyan faculty to get their ideas and put them through with his own convictions." In his speech, titled "Man to Man," he "proposed public opinion as a solution for war," and asked "'Is it not as noble to live for one's country as to die for it?'" The *Phreno Cosmian* described his presentation as "masterful." It further wrote that "the thot in his oration was exceptional and his delivery was smooth and pleasing." Francis was awarded first place—receiving two first place votes and one second place vote from the three judges. He also was given $25 for winning the contest. More importantly, his victory meant that he would represent his school in the state-wide peace contest to be held at Dakota Wesleyan in March.[18]

After presenting his winning oration, Francis began "burning the midnight oil" with his teammates in preparation for the upcoming intercollegiate debates. The question for discussion (positing that socialism should be preferred to capitalism) was the identical one utilized in the intersociety debates held in December. Francis, Elmer Lushbaugh, and Myron Brink were assigned to the affirmative team, with Bennett Grotta as alternate. They were tasked with arguing that socialist control is preferrable to capitalism. This team was scheduled to meet Huron College's negative team at Huron. The Wesleyan negative team, which would argue in favor of the capitalistic system, consisted of Harold Card, Frank Petrie and Frank Leffert, with Walter Ludeman as alternate. It was to appear against Yankton College's affirmative team "on the home platform."[19]

The Wesleyan debate teams spent the remainder of February researching the issues involved and honing their arguments for their respective positions. During that month, Harold Card also found time to enter and win the annual prohibition oratorical contest. His oration, titled "Post Bellum Dies," was "well prepared ... and was delivered in a pleasing and confident manner." It was judged to be the best of the six presentations and allowed Harold to represent Wesleyan "in the state contest to be held later in the year."[20]

The triangular intercollegiate debates among Wesleyan, Huron, and Yankton occurred in the evening on Friday, March 3. Wesleyan's affirmative team (arguing for socialism) met the Huron College team at Huron, and Wesleyan's negative team (arguing for capitalism) hosted Yankton College's team in the home team's college chapel. Finally, Huron's affirmative team opposed Yankton's negative team at Yankton. The *Phreno Cosmian* summarized each debater's arguments and evaluated his performance. With respect to Francis, it noted that "Case wound up the arguments for the affirmative. He argued that socialistic control is the only method whereby the inequitability of wealth can be remedied." It added that "Case was probably the most convincing speaker of the evening." And in the final rebuttal of the debate, "Case excelled. He penetrated the very core of his opponent's arguments; then exposed their faults. The clean-cut thinking and the whirlwind delivery of Wesleyan's leader, closed a very interesting debate."[21]

The three judges scored this debate 2 to 1 in Huron's favor, but the Wesleyan team was "congratulated as being the only affirmative team in the state to get one vote." And that turned out to be crucial when the final vote tally was made. Wesleyan's negative team was awarded a unanimous 3-0 decision over Yankton, thereby giving Wesleyan 4 out of 6 possible votes. Since Yankton won the Yankton-Huron debate in a unanimous decision, it received 3 votes. Huron's only 2 votes came from its 2-1 decision over Wesleyan. So, Wesleyan won the state championship for the second year in a row. Its two teams celebrated their victory the following Sunday with a dinner party at Harold Card's home. At this gathering, "peace was declared forever between the Capitalists and the Socialists."[22]

Representing his school in the state peace oratorical contest was Francis's next forensic event. It occurred in Wesleyan's college chapel on a Friday evening—the last day of March. Three other schools—Yankton College, State College at Brookings, and Huron College—also sent contestants. Francis again gave his "Man to Man" speech—this time to a "rather small audience." After all the presentations were made, he was awarded first place. The Wesleyan school paper maintained that "at no time during the entire contest was Case's rank for first place in danger" and "the entire audience was of the same opinion as ... the judges." By winning this contest, he received $50 and was "entitled to represent the state in the interstate contest to be held at Omaha on the 28th of April."[23]

The South Dakota International Prohibition Association held its Eighth Annual Convention and Oratorical Contest at Augustana College in Canton on April 14 and 15. The proceedings opened on Friday afternoon in the college chapel, where delegates were welcomed and different committees were appointed. The convention's "big feature" was the oratorical contest held in the Kennedy opera house that evening. A crowd of over 400 greeted the contestants. Six were entered, including Harold Card. The other five came from Lutheran Normal, Huron College, Sioux Falls University, State College, and Augustana. Three judges had graded the speakers on "thought and composition" prior to their oral presentations. Three different judges "would rank the orations on their delivery." Harold's oration was titled "Reconstruction." In it, he "advanced the plan of a rebuilt social order in which the saloon will be conspicuous by its absence." He was awarded second place. The more experienced Mr. Husted, representing Sioux Falls, finished first. During the convention's business session held Saturday morning, Harold was named "leader of the South Dakota delegation to the National convention," which was scheduled to meet in Minneapolis in the early summer.[24]

On Friday evening, May 5, the interstate peace oratorical contest was held "under the auspices of the University of Omaha." Five schools, representing five states grouped in the contest's Western division, each had an entrant. Francis appeared for Dakota Wesleyan and represented South Dakota. Students from the University of Kansas (representing Kansas), Creighton University (representing Nebraska), Simpson College (representing Iowa), and William Jewell College (representing Missouri) also competed. At this competition, Francis changed the title of his presentation to "The Modern Paradox." Its substance remained the same as it had been in the two previous peace contests. He was the last speaker to address the audience and the five judges. After he finished, the judges declared him to be the winner. Two of them gave him first place votes, and the remaining three put him in second place. The "general uniformity" of these scores showed "that there was no doubt as to who was entitled to the contest." He was awarded $100 for receiving the top prize. His victory also meant that he would represent the Western division at the national peace contest to be held in Mohonk, New York, later in the month. This win was a significant honor for both Francis and Wesleyan. It marked "the first time that a representative from any South Dakota school has won his way to the highest contest in collegiate circles, the National Contest."[25]

Less than a week later, Francis and seven other students—including Harold Card—were initiated into Wesleyan's chapter of a national forensic society named Pi Kappa Delta. The dean of the college was also admitted as an honorary member. An evening banquet and the formal initiation were held at the Widmann Hotel. Because he won the interstate peace oratorical contest, Francis now held "the highest honor of any of the members" and the "highest distinction possible in the order." Those designations entitled him "to wear a diamond in his fraternity key"—the society's "official emblem."[26]

ON OR ABOUT MAY 12, FRANCIS left Mitchell on the Milwaukee evening train bound for New York. His ultimate destination was the Mohonk Mountain House, where the national peace oratorical contest was to be held on the 18th. Before arriving there, he stopped at Niagara Falls in western New York to view "one of the most spectacular natural wonders of North America." After doing so, he made his way to the national-oratorical-contest site. It has been described as a "majestic, castle-like compound nestled in the peaceful grandeur of the Catskill Mountains." Originally opened as a renovated and expanded inn in 1870, this large Victorian resort is situated 90 miles north of New York City. It is near Lake Mohonk and overlooks "the quaint college town of New Paltz."[27]

In 1895, the Lake Mohonk Conference on International Arbitration was founded "for the purpose of creating and directing public sentiment in favor of international arbitration, arbitration treaties, and an international court." It held its annual conference at the Mohonk Mountain House from 1895 to 1916. The first conference included fifty "eminent American men," but attendance soon grew to "300 leaders of government, business, religion, the press, and education." Among the prominent "leaders of government" who attended the 1916 conference were William Howard Taft—former president of the United States and future chief justice of the United States Supreme Court; and William Jennings Bryan—three-time unsuccessful Democratic candidate for the United States presidency and former Secretary of State in president Woodrow Wilson's administration.[28]

The Intercollegiate Peace Association (IPA) was founded in 1905 "to promote peace-oriented activities among faculty and students." That same year the IPA began conducting college peace oratorical contests throughout the country. By 1912, that competition involved "'at least 300 undergraduates from 80 colleges in some 16 states.'" It culminated in the national peace contest, which was held at Mohonk during the Conference on International Arbitration's annual meeting.[29]

After Francis arrived at Mohonk, he reviewed and rehearsed his "Modern Paradox" oration and "added some little phrases ... to make it adaptable to the beautiful Lake on which the contest was held." For example, early in his presentation, he referred to "hills and valleys, once as peaceful as these Catskills," and "nations once as placid as

Lake Mohonk." When contest day arrived on May 18, he was ready to give it his best effort.[30]

The eleventh annual national peace oratorical contest was held in the afternoon. William Jennings Bryan—who inspired Francis with his oratory when Francis was a young boy—presided over the program. There were five contestants from five separate geographical "groups" spread throughout the country. Each entrant had previously won the interstate contest in his respective group. (A sixth entrant from the University of Utah, who represented the Pacific Coast Group, did not participate in the final contest for unknown reasons.)[31]

Francis was the second speaker on the program. He opened with a straightforward statement: "We are witnessing the greatest paradox of all history. Five years ago war was declared impossible—today the greatest nations of the globe are in arms." He went on to give several illustrations of the "modern paradox," including "that if you and I were asked to state our position on war this evening, we would record ourselves as opposed to it and yet if tomorrow a call should be issued for volunteers to defend the nation's honor in Mexico, we might be found among the first to enlist"; and "War... is despised and condemned by individuals, yet upheld and sustained by nations." Then he discussed how wars originate, how our nation's schools have glorified war "from our earliest childhood," and how "we have been taught to honor the man who invents some new death-dealing device, while we pass by the man who invents for the happiness of mankind." Next he posed a series of piercing questions, such as "Are we so destitute of reason that he represents the highest degree of patriotism whose body is mangled by shell or shattered by shrapnel? Is it a greater measure of devotion to die for one's country than to live for it?" And more generally, "Will world peace ever triumph?" He then predicted that "just as long as military devotion to one's country is the criterion of patriotism, just so long must international peace be delayed" because "real patriotism must come to mean more than mutilation of human beings," and "real national honor must be based upon justice and not power."³²

Regarding the solution to the paradox, he offered that "it is public opinion drugged and illusioned which retains war; and it shall be public opinion, freed and enlightened which shall abolish war." Toward the end of his speech, he suggested ways that public opinion could be "enlightened." These included "Unmask War! Abolish this false standard of honor! . . . Do not reiterate the glories of war in times of peace and expect the people to refrain from it in times of crises. . . . Tell the whole tale. Let war be known for the farce that it really is. . . . Strip it of sentiment." His final plea summarized how the paradox can be solved: "Dethrone the god of war, enthrone the Prince of Peace."³³

Francis "was continually interrupted by applause from the audience while the oration was being delivered." After the three remaining presentations were given, the judges awarded him first place. William Bryan presented him with the $100 prize and "took him aside, analyzing his talk and telling him why he won." The contestants' order of finish, name, school, and group represented were as follows: first place, Francis H. Case, Dakota Wesleyan, Western Group; second place, Lester H. Jayne, Cornell University, North Atlantic Group; third place, Harry D. Hubbard, Michigan State Normal College, Central Group; fourth place, Roy L. Aterbury, Vanderbilt University, Southwestern Group; and fifth place, J. J. Brayer, University of Kentucky, South Atlantic Group. According to the *Phreno Cosmian*, "in the contests leading up to . . . [the national] one, there were over one hundred and fifty colleges represented by approximately five hundred and fifty speakers." And with respect to Francis's victory, the school paper concluded that "too much honor cannot be accorded the man who has put Wesleyan in oratorical standing upon the same basis with the largest and strongest universities of the country."³⁴

At some point during the competition, Francis joined 135 other Mohonk Conference attendees for a large group picture taken outside of the Mohonk Mountain House resort. He stood in front of the building's main entrance in the second row next to an unidentified woman. Former President Taft and former Secretary of State Bryan were also among those photographed. Taft was seated in the first row near the center of the group with his hat in his left hand. Bryan was also in the first row—holding a hat with both hands. He was seated to Taft's left, with eight people in between them. The entire group was well-attired: the women in long dresses, and the men in coats and ties.[35]

THE NEXT DAY, FRANCIS LEFT Mohonk for Washington, D. C. While there he visited some congressional pages in the House of Representatives who were from South Dakota and "had been in his father's Sunday school class." When he left the city, it was "with the ambition to be a representative some day." From Washington, he passed through Chicago and finally arrived in Mitchell on May 25. It was "raining hard" when his train pulled into town that evening. But despite the rain, about 125 faculty members and students "marched to the train to meet the winning orator."[36]

The student body gathered in the college chapel the following afternoon to elect Students' Association officers and *Phreno Cosmian* managers for the following year. In the *Phreno* elections, Herbert Allen was chosen as editor-in-chief by two votes, and Francis was an "easy winner in the race for business manager." That night, a large crowd gathered in the city hall to hear his winning oration and honor that achievement. Before "the big event of the evening," Wesleyan students gave "rousing" yells, cheers, and songs. Then Miss Violet Jones, president of the Wesleyan Students' Association, introduced Francis, who gave his *Modern Paradox* speech. The *Mitchell Capital* described his presentation as a "masterful handling of the thought and language," which was enhanced by "entirely appropriate and forceful gestures." This combination "made the oration grip the heart of every inspector and hold him almost breathless with the intensity of the plea." The

Phreno Cosmian also recorded a positive reaction to the speech, noting "the audience was entirely satisfied that Mr. Case was deserving of the high honor he had won." After the oration was completed, the vice president of the Mitchell Commercial Club expressed appreciation to Francis for the honor he had brought to the college, to the city of Mitchell, and to the state. He then presented the guest of honor with a Hamilton gold watch. Its engraved inside cover read "'Francis Case, Mitchell, S. D., National Peace Contest, 1916.'" Francis acknowledged the gift "with a few well chosen words," and with that the program came to a close.[37]

AFTER THE 1916 SPRING SEMESTER came to an end, Francis and Harold Card became "summer salesmen" near Corsica—a small town in Douglas County situated about 28 miles south and west of Mitchell. Their product was Harper's Brushes, which they bought for $1.75 a set. It was actually "a brush combination, sweeper and window cleaning brush," and it had some "gadgets that went with it." But instead of selling this product directly to Douglas County farmers, they traded the brushes for chickens (which they then presumably sold in Corsica or perhaps Mitchell). As Harold remembered, "we would go out in the season of the year when the old hens were clucking, as we used to say, and we would trade... the brushes for the setting hens." They divided Douglas County into halves, with Francis taking the west half and Harold the east. Each salesman "worked for himself," and each had his own horse and buggy with a chicken coop built on it. For accommodations, they "rented a vacant house and slept on the floor and did a good deal of our own cooking." Harold regarded this brushes-for-chickens-for-money venture as "an interesting experience." Although he didn't recall "how much we made," his general assessment was that "we did pretty well."[38]

The Case-Card business venture turned out to be of short duration. Harold and Francis had been elected officers in Wesleyan's chapter of the Young Men's Christian Association (YMCA) during the previous spring—Harold as president, Francis as recorder. In late June, they were among the "900 delegates gathered from the colleges of the north Mississippi Valley" for the YMCA Conference at Lake Geneva, Wisconsin. During that meeting, the group "pledged $10,000 to inaugurate the Four Year campaign," which sought "to line up the real leaders of the next generation, and inculcate into them the highest ideals of service to fellowmen." The 1916 Geneva Conference also adopted a resolution, wherein the delegates pledged support for eradicating "gambling, profanity, dishonesty, immodest dancing and other social excesses" (which included using liquor and tobacco) from student life at their respective colleges and universities.[39]

The YMCA Conference adjourned in early July, and Frances and Harold arrived back in Mitchell on July 5. Herbert wrote a letter to Francis dated two days later. That letter stated "we are all agreed in wishing you would come home and spend the rest of your vacation and see if there isn't something here that you can do." Francis did decide to go back home to Hot Springs. He arrived on a Saturday morning and made almost daily visits to his grandparents' house during the following week. On July 15, Earl Bovee and he drove up to Mary A. and Frank's house, and Earl took them for a ride in the new "Bovee auto." The next evening, their mode of transportation switched back to horse and buggy. Herbert picked them up "with his team" and took them to hear Francis's "little piece" (presumably his *Modern Paradox* oration). His presentation was given to a "full house," and Mary A. declared that it was a "fine lecture."[40]

After the lecture, Francis, Earl and Leland "stayed all night" at the elder Cases' home. The next day, Earl and Francis "went to Sturgis... to see his horse." Apparently, Francis spent the rest of the summer working at the Bovee ranch and taking care of his colt named Madge who was quartered there. By September 2, he had returned to Hot Springs. That day, he and Esther ate dinner at their grandparents' house. And the next day, he and Carol were there for supper. On the following Friday, Francis returned "back to school again." Mary A. sent him off with a pair of "sock elastics," a "kerchief," and a "button hook." She and Frank "saw him go" and "waved at him" as his passenger car left the train station.[41]

WHEN FRANCIS ARRIVED IN MITCHELL, he immediately became involved in YMCA activities. On the Sunday before school opened, he, Harold Card, and other YMCA officers met "to arrange for the meeting of students at trains, and for locating them in rooming and boarding places, and for finding them places to work." In addition, "plans were... made for the social gatherings of the week," and these "were well carried out." Francis had other duties that required his attention when he returned to Wesleyan. He was now the business manager of the *Phreno Cosmian*, and its first issue was due to come out soon after school started.[42]

The new school year officially began on September 13. Dr. Seaman had resigned as college president during the summer, and Dr. C. V. Gilliland had been named as acting president. He "gave a few well selected words of greeting" to students and visitors who had gathered in the auditorium for the school's "thirty-second formal opening." He then introduced distinguished guests and new faculty members to the audience. Those introductions were followed by the "main address of the day." It was presented by Dr. Eugene Allen, pastor of the First Methodist Church in Sioux Falls. His topic was "Provincialism"—which he defined as "narrowness and egotism"—and he argued that it was the "foe of progress." The *Phreno Cosmian* described Dr. Allen's address as "scholarly and refined."[43]

ON SEPTEMBER 25, HERBERT TOOK the train to Watertown, South Dakota, to attend the Methodist Episcopal Church's annual conference. At that meeting, the group "adopted resolutions urging statewide and national prohibition and active cooperation with the Anti-saloon league." In addition, several pastors were reassigned to various churches "over the state." Herbert was among those pastors. He was made "district Evangelist at a salary of $1,500" and assigned to the Methodist Church in Spearfish—a town located in the northern Black Hills about 75 miles north of Hot Springs. Its population, according to the 1910 U.S. census, was 1,130.[44]

After the conference had concluded, Herbert returned to Hot Springs. Then he travelled to preach at his new church on October 8 and came back home the next day to attend a reception in his honor. During the days that followed, the Case family packed their things, moved out of the parsonage, and stayed at the elder Case house. Frank helped Herbert pack the heavy items, and Mary A. prepared meals for all of her temporary boarders. Finally, on October 13, the Cases moved to Spearfish. "The family went with the team and Herbert went on [a train] car with goods & cow... to do the Master's work." The next evening, Mary A. told her diary that "I miss Herbert tonight not coming in one minute."[45]

THE 1915 WESLEYAN FOOTBALL TEAM, under first-year coach Chester Dillon, had been outstanding. It completely shut out five teams on its way to a final record of seven wins and two losses, and it outscored its opponents 188 to 45. In the second game of that year, sophomore Mark Payne, "a 160-pound halfback from Lake Andes," drop-kicked a 63-yard field goal. That kick broke by one yard the 1898 world record set by a player from the University of Wisconsin. The 1915 Wesleyan football team would be a tough act to follow.[46]

Now it was 1916, and the football season began with a different coach and high hopes. Over the summer, coach Dillon had moved on to Simpson College in Indianola, Iowa. He was replaced by James C. Loman—a four-year star fullback for Hobart College at Geneva, New

York. Although several men from the 1915 team had either graduated or left school—including star kicker/punter Mark Payne—the outlook for a successful season became "brighter daily with the influx of new men and the return of two or three veterans that were hardly expected to appear on the Wesleyan field this year."[47]

The first game of the season was played at Mitchell on September 29. Wesleyan (also known as the Blue and White—its school colors) beat Madison Normal 14 to 6. The *Phreno Cosmian* described the contest as a "ragged game" that was "marked throughout by lack of form and material." Clifford Knox, the Blue and White's team captain and starting left end, was praised for stopping a 45-yard run and preventing a touchdown. Roberts (first name unknown) played the entire game at quarterback. He punted the ball for Wesleyan, scored a touchdown on a 45-yard running play, and kicked two extra points. During the next week, Captain Knox and Roberts left the team for unknown reasons. Floyd Wilder was appointed its "temporary captain," although he would remain captain for the rest of the year. In addition, Francis joined the team in time to suit up for its Friday home game against Nebraska Wesleyan. It was a pretty even match until the third quarter, when the Nebraska team scored three touchdowns and converted one extra point. Those points, plus a safety scored in the first half, accounted for the final score: 21-0 in favor of the visitors. Coach Loman gave this assessment: "They showed the fight, anyway, and that is what counts. Had we changed our punter earlier in the game we would have won." Francis got in the game as a substitute for Elliott Hathaway at the end position, and Harold Card substituted for Herbert Wolcott at left guard.[48]

The remaining two games played in October were blowouts in favor of the opposition. On October 14, Wesleyan lost to the University of South Dakota Coyotes at Vermillion 55-0. Two weeks later, the Blue and White travelled to Sioux City, Iowa, where the Morningside Maroons beat them "with the annihilating score of 112 to 0." Francis substituted at left end in the USD game and at right end during the Morningside game. Card started at center against the Maroons, and he "put up a desperate battle against odds that would be a credit to any Wesleyan man time past or present."[49]

The second half of Wesleyan's season began with Wesleyan hosting Sioux Falls College on November 4. Francis reported on this game in a letter to his "Homefolks" who were now living in Spearfish. Wesleyan lost 12 to 0, but it "was a good game, and they really didn't have so very much on us." He started the game at end "for the first time" and played the entire first half, but his substitute was in for the second half. He added that there were "three games left all away from here." They were with "schools more of our own class than the teams we met at Vermillion and Soo City," so he would not "be playing against men weighing anywhere from forty to sixty lbs more than I do[.]" Finally, he told the homefolks not to "fret about my getting hurt" and let them know he was wrapping his ankles to avoid spraining them.[50]

On November 18, the Blue and White battled against Huron College on the latter's home turf. The *Phreno Cosmian* reported that this game was "ragged, erratic," and "full of fumbling and crude football." Wesleyan once again came up short—losing 20 to 0. Francis started at left end and played the entire contest. His overall performance was summarized as follows: "Case practically a new man in college football, played a fast gritty game at left end, frequently downing his man for losses." And the quarter-by-quarter account noted that "Case downs Broughton for 5 yard loss" in the second quarter; and he "downs Whaley for a 5 yard loss" and "returns [Huron's kickoff] 15 yards" in the fourth.[51]

Six days later, the Wesleyanites went to Madison for a rematch with their first opponent of the season—Madison Normal. The latter team got their revenge and then some—winning the game 58-0. Francis played the whole game at right end. It "was characterized by considerable off color football; slugging, kicking, holding and tripping being the tactics of the Normal men. Madison was fortunate in having her own choice of a referee." Wesleyan's final game was played on Thanksgiving Day at Yankton. Following a too-familiar pattern, the Blue and White failed to score and lost 42-0. Both teams completed four passes, and two of Yankton's completions resulted in touchdowns. Francis once again played the entire game at right end.[52]

Wesleyan's long and disappointing season had finally come to an ignominious end. The team won only its first game, did not score in the remaining seven games, and was outscored by its opponents 326 to 14. A *Phreno Cosmian* editorial did not pull any punches in describing these results: "The sorry season of 1916 is done and our braves come marching home again—out of step. Silence reigns on the hill, for we have no long and tiresome alibi to salve over our lacerated record. Whatever may have been this past record we are not going to practice the inanity of excusing our failures with eulogistic post-mortems. A team . . . can make its best excuse for defeat by respecting the evidence of the score sheet and keeping a closed mouth."[53]

After the season ended, Yankton's Coach Montgomery named two "All Conference Denominational Teams." They included players from the four church-affiliated schools in the state: Huron College (Presbyterian), Sioux Falls College (Baptist), Yankton College (Congregationalist), and Dakota Wesleyan (Methodist). Three players were named from Wesleyan. They included Francis and Arthur Shepard on the first team, and Floyd Wilder on the second team. The *Phreno Cosmian* derided these mythical teams and sarcastically remarked: "We would like to see the 'Denominational Stars' take on the champion high school team of South Dakota. It might be a good game." But despite its unvarnished assessment of the 1916 football season, the *Phreno* editorial argued that those on the team who met the requirements for receiving the "W" monogram letter "should be rewarded accordingly," and it ended with a note of optimism: "And also there is another year coming. For, no more than one swallow makes a summer does one slump decree a football failure."[54]

Twenty players from the team met the requirements and were awarded the monogram letter. Seventeen of them, including Francis and Harold, were "first year men" and received "a white 'V' neck jersey with a large blue 'W'." The remaining three—Captain Wilder, Elliot Hathaway, and Arthur Shepard—had played for two years, so they received "sweater coats with the monogram." The annual football banquet was held in the parlors of the Methodist Church in the evening on December 5. Shortly before it occurred, Floyd Wilder had been unanimously elected as captain for next year. The football team, several students, and those participating in the after-dinner program attended the banquet. After a two-course dinner prepared by the Ladies' Aid Society, Dr. Gilliland acted as toastmaster for a "splendid program." It featured musical selections by the University quartet and speeches by "several faculty members, alumni, guests, and members of the team." Coach Loman "eulogized the team for its perseverance in the face of defeat after defeat." He also "expressed the hope that the men held no hard feelings toward him for his impulsive outbreaks and assured them that there was no hard feeling behind it." In his toast to the future, Floyd Wilder "expressed an optimistic view for the coming season and reiterated the 'never-say-die' spirit of Wesleyan."[55]

FRANCIS HAD A BUSY FALL semester away from the football field. In addition to maintaining a full schedule of classes, he became the Public Speaking teacher and coach for the Wesleyan Academy debate teams. After less than two months on the job, he reported that he was "getting along alright I guess. Don't know where the real test will come. Suppose will be judged more or less on ability to turn out winning interacademy teams. Would like to hold job for next year, for it would be so much easier then, and it really doesn't bother me very much."[56]

The annual intersociety debates among the Kappa Pi Phi, Delta Rho, and Daedalian literary societies were held on December 16. That year's question for debate was "Resolved; That the United States Government should own and operate all railroads engaged in interstate commerce, Constitutionally granted." In the morning debate, the Kappas—arguing for the affirmative—prevailed over the Delta Rhos in a split decision. For the afternoon contest—described as "the most interesting debate of all"—Francis, Harold Card, and Bernie Brereton argued for the Daedalian affirmative team. They won a unanimous decision over their rivals from Delta Rho. Finally, the Kappa affirmative team lost to the Daedalian negative team by a unanimous decision in the evening session. Since the Daedalians won both of their contests, they were declared intersociety-debate champions. From this group of eighteen participants, nine debaters and three alternates were ranked and selected to represent Wesleyan at the intercollegiate events to be held in the spring. Francis was ranked number one, and his debate partners Card and Brereton tied for second and third place.[57]

Francis spent the 1916 Christmas vacation in Mitchell. He likely attended Dr. Gilliland's evening party given for "a group of vacation 'leftovers'" at the latter's home on December 28. The next day, Francis and four other Wesleyan students—including Harold Card and Floyd Wilder—travelled ten miles east to Fulton. These Wesleyanites made up one of two "Gospel Teams"—also known as "Deputation Teams"—that represented Wesleyan's YMCA organization. Their mission was "to aid the strengthening of the moral, social, and religious forces among the boy life of this section of the state." At Fulton, the team "organized various social affairs, took a long hike on Saturday with the Fulton boys and generally made themselves agreeable to the youngsters." They also held an evening meeting there on Sunday before returning to Mitchell.[58]

In mid-December, the Wesleyan Board of Directors chose Dr. William D. Schermerhorn as the college's next president. He was described as "a man in the prime of life, about forty years of age, of strong physique, winning personality and fine Christian spirit." He had done graduate work at the Garrett Bible Institute—the "theological division of Northwestern University at Chicago"—and was currently teaching there when the selection was made. After making a "visit of inspection" to Wesleyan in early 1917, Dr. Schermerhorn formally accepted the position on January 6. That spring, he made further visits to Wesleyan and performed other duties for the college as president-elect. On June 1, he officially became Wesleyan's president.[59]

On Friday evening, January 12, the two Wesleyan Academy debate teams won the championship of the Huron-Wesleyan-Yankton triangular contest. They did so by beating the Yankton affirmative team in Wesleyan's Science Hall and by defeating the Huron negative team at Huron. The question argued "concerned the compulsion of military training for minors in the schools of the United States." Huron College's debate coach Hunt judged the Yankton-Wesleyan match, awarded it to the Wesleyan negative team, and "predicted great development for the six men." At Huron, the Wesleyan affirmative team won "under a tremendous handicap," since its team leader was barred from participation "at the last minute" due to a technicality. Nevertheless, the two remaining Wesleyan debaters were awarded the victory over Huron's three-man team by Yankton's coach and judge Fifield. Francis judged the third debate of the "triangle." Held at Yankton, it featured the Yankton negative team versus the Huron affirmative team. Francis ruled that Yankton won. After summarizing these debates, the *Phreno Cosmian* remarked that "[t]he excellent showing of the two Wesleyan teams demonstrated hard work and good training, due to the efforts of the academy debate coach, Mr. Francis Case."[60]

By late January, Francis's final exams were "all over," and his term papers completed. He had not received all his final grades yet, but those that had arrived were "highly satisfactory." The spring semester was set to begin in early February, and he expected to be "in it strong again in a few days." Three weeks later, he wrote to his mother that he had just completed "a mighty busy week," was "way behind" on his debate speech, had been "working debate until late" for the past few nights to catch up, and had much work to do on the school paper. He added that "it seems... my Sundays are as full as any other day, although I do try to let up." His Sunday commitments included "Bible study... at 9.30, Church at 10.30, YMCA Cabinet meeting at 12.30... [and] church at night." Apart from his hectic schedule, Francis had recently been thinking about his "future life work." He was considering the ministry, and he had talked "with several ministers and other friends" about it.[61]

FORENSIC ACTIVITIES WERE A DOMINANT activity in Francis's life during March. On the first day of the month, the Wesleyan debate team—consisting of Francis, Frank Petrie, and Elmer Lushbaugh—met the Nebraska Wesleyan team at 7:30 p.m. in Wesleyan's Science Hall. The question argued was the same one used in the intersociety debates—whether the U.S. Government should own and operate railroads engaged in interstate commerce. The home team "supported the negative." Dr. Gilliland presided over the contest. The *Phreno Cosmian* was quite effusive in describing the Wesleyan debaters' performances. That was especially true for Francis. It said that "Mr. Case, first and last for the home trio was by all odds the best man on the floor when clear and decisive argument and keen thinking accompanied by forceful delivery is considered." It added that "his work had a rare quality unusual in the average debate—easy for the average listener to follow. Excellent construction and emphasis of salient points at issue brand Case the premier debater of the year." Finally, it concluded that "his insistence on the one wavering point at issue without doubt was the element that swung the decision to Wesleyan." The three-judge panel unanimously declared Wesleyan the winner.[62]

Three weeks later, the same Wesleyan debate team was at it again—this time participating in the All-State Forensic Quadrangular meet. Earlier that year, Sioux Falls College had been added to the previously-existing Huron-Wesleyan-Yankton triangle, so there would be four debates in all. The government-ownership-of-railroads question was again the topic for dispute. All four schools had two teams in the competition. In addition to its negative team that had beaten Nebraska Wesleyan, Dakota Wesleyan's affirmative team—consisting of Harold Card, Walter Ludeman and Lloyd Thompson—was selected to represent its school. (Bernie Brereton, who had been named to the intercollegiate debate team the previous December, had since left Wesleyan and enrolled at the University of Minnesota.) On March 22, the Wesleyan negative team went against the Yankton affirmative team at Yankton, and the Wesleyan affirmative team faced Huron in Wesleyan's college chapel. Instead of employing three judges, "[t]his year each of the four contests was judged by the debate coach of one of the disinterested colleges." When the dust settled, Wesleyan won both of its debates, Yankton and Sioux Falls each won one and lost one, and Huron lost both. This meant that for the third consecutive year, Wesleyan had won "state debating honors."[63]

Francis established an Academy oratorical contest in the spring of 1917. Its aim "was to stimulate academy forensics and provide a reliable source of forensic material for college activities." Any Academy student was eligible to enter the contest, and each was allowed to choose his or her own subject. To help stimulate interest and encourage participation, Francis offered a gold medal to the first-place winner if three persons entered the contest, and a silver medal for second place if the number of entries were five or more. The medals were inscribed with the words "Oratory—DWA—Case Trophy" and the year when the contest occurred.[64]

The first annual Academy oratorical contest (also known as the Prep Oratorical) was held on March 23 in Science Hall. There were six entrants and three judges. After all the presentations were made, Louis Todnem was awarded the gold medal for his oration "The Sacrifice of Verdun." Laren Spear—whose speech was titled "Thomas Mott Osborne"—received the silver medal for finishing in second place.[65]

FRANCIS'S INVOLVEMENT WITH THE YMCA also continued in the spring of 1917. He and Charles Bintliff were nominated for president for the next term. The election for that position and other officers was held on March 22, and Bintliff won. On April 1, Harold Card's term as president—and Francis's term as recorder—expired, and the newly-elected slate of officers was installed. Harold and Francis were both assigned to positions in the YMCA's cabinet. Harold was put in charge of the Social Service Department, and Francis became the Religious Meetings Chairman. The next weekend (which marked the start of Wesleyan's spring break and included Easter Sunday), both men resumed their gospel work with younger boys in nearby Spencer and Canistota. They were members of two separate teams, and presumably each team went to one of these two towns. Francis also became the third YMCA member to teach a Sunday school class.[66]

CHAPTER 4

DAKOTA WESLEYAN AFTER WAR DECLARED

I will go if they call me.
—Francis Case

Just when Wesleyan was about to begin its 1917 spring vacation, the United States declared war on Germany on April 6. When the students returned to campus in mid-April, the men were met with immediate advice regarding how they should respond. President-elect Schermerhorn, in a letter to Dr. Gilliland, told the male students to "'stick to their work'" for the present rather than enlist "'as privates'" and "'to hold steady, at least until commencement.'" He also recommended that a class in military drill and tactics be organized and offered as an elective. The Students' Association agreed with this proposal and quickly organized a Military Drill class. It was not compulsory, but those who regularly attended it for the rest of the year were given a one-hour credit. By early May, "every man on the campus" had enrolled in this military training.[1]

When the country joined the World War, the War Department's Commission on Training Camp Activities chose the YMCA to be its first "religiously affiliated civilian partner." To carry out its war-related activities, the "YM" established a National War Work Council (NWWC). The Council operated "huts" in both United States and

European military camps. Those huts consisted of "anything from simple wooden structures in training camps to pre-existing buildings in leave areas to makeshift dugouts in the trenches," and were "designed to uphold morale and morality among American and allied soldiers." The activities and services in the huts varied, but typically they "included recreation (sports, films, concerts, and singing), library services, religious services, and the sale of refreshments, cigarettes, and other personal items." To manage and operate the huts, the NWWC sought "the services of 1,000 experienced secretaries who can win the confidence of the boys, [and] give them encouragement and advice when inevitable spells [of] lonesomeness and homesickness come upon them."[2]

Six Wesleyan students—including Francis—applied to the NWWC for a war-work-secretary position. As of mid-May, he "hadn't heard a word" about his application. He added that "Prof. Wilds [the forensic coach] is quite determined that I shall come back here next year. Thinks he'll write in and try to have them put me on reserve for a year. But I will go if they call me. Think the year's training would be quite valuable." Two weeks later, the Council notified Francis that his application had been considered, a "decision favorable to your engagement has been reached," and his name had been put on the Approved List. The letter also requested that he hold himself "open to engagement" pending word of a definite assignment from the NWWC's Executive Committee.[3]

Apart from his response to the war, Francis kept involved with journalistic endeavors after spring break. The Students' Association met on Friday, April 20 to nominate students for various offices next year. Both the inter-society committee and the senior committee nominated Francis for editor of the *Phreno Cosmian*. The annual election was held a week later in the chapel auditorium. Francis was elected editor without opposition. The Student Association also combined with the *Phreno* board to host the initial annual meeting of the

South Dakota College Press Association. The purpose of this Association, and the annual convention, was "to create a better acquaintance among the college papers of the state so that each may profit by the suggestions of the others." Representatives from Sioux Falls College, the University of South Dakota, Huron College, Yankton College, Northern Normal and Industrial School, and Wesleyan attended the two-day meeting on May 11 and 12 on Wesleyan's campus. After forming committees, holding several discussion groups, and listening to speakers from prominent newspaper editors and journalists, the newly-formed organization elected student officers for the oncoming year. Francis was chosen as president, Miss Brookman (University of South Dakota) as vice-president, and Mr. Nelson (Sioux Falls College) as secretary-treasurer. Plans were also made for "an inter-collegiate news service."[4]

Francis attended one more forensics event before the 1917 term ended. The Pi Kappa Delta forensic fraternity held its second annual banquet at the First Methodist Church on Wednesday evening, May 23. A six-course dinner was served and "war time economy in wall and table ornament dominated." Thirteen new members were initiated. Six of them were women debaters—making the chapter "'co-ed'" for the first time. The outgoing officers conducted the initiation ceremony, and Professor Wilds "installed the newly elected officers for the coming year." They were Francis Case, Cancellarius (president); Matilda Tarleton, Vice-Cancellarius; Harold Card, Malletorius (secretary); and L. E. Lushbaugh, Triangularius (treasurer).[5]

ON HIS WAY BACK TO his family's home in Spearfish, Francis decided to go through Hot Springs to visit and stay with his grandparents. He arrived there on the 11:00 a.m. train on June 1. For the next few days, he frequently read the Bible and prayed with Mary A. and Frank. He also ate all his meals at their house and helped Frank work in his garden. During that visit, Mary A. complained that she was "not breathing good," had a "bad spell," and "had a poor spell this morning." On June 4, after having breakfast and reading the Bible one more time, Francis "took [the] train for Spearfish."[6]

After arriving in Spearfish, Francis stayed in touch with the NWWC to determine whether he would be sent for training sometime during the summer. In mid-June, a letter from one of the Council's secretaries suggested he should "train this summer." Later that month, he received another letter—written prior to the first one by a different NWWC secretary—that informed him it was "not necessary to leave college." Francis sought clarification of his situation by sending a June 30 telegram to the Council's Director. In that message, he also asked if he could "take training and go on reserve until complete college next spring." The NWWC quickly responded to this inquiry. Its July 3 letter told Francis that it was "inadvisable" for him to undertake training at "the present time" because he would have to complete his college course "before taking up the War Work" and because he was only 20 years old and subject to unspecified "rigid restrictions" applicable to men under age 21. The letter concluded by stating: "When you are nearer the time of readiness for actual service next spring, we can open the case with you anew. In the meantime, you will continue to be upon our approved list for War Work, reserved for later placement."[7]

The Council's July 3 letter made clear that Francis would not be training anywhere for War Work that summer. After receiving it, he apparently spent the rest of July and August attending summer school at Spearfish Normal, taking care of Herbert's horse and cow, fishing for trout in Spearfish Canyon, and recruiting new students to attend Dakota Wesleyan in the fall.[8]

Mary A.'s health continued a steady decline throughout the summer of 1917. In June, she became "to[o] sick to go to church anymore," felt "bad all the time," and was "real miserable." In July she experienced "a sick night and the worst spell for me I ever had." That was followed by "the worst night yet... so faint." Her last daily diary entry occurred on July 27 and consisted of two words: "Inez birthday." Herbert made several trips to Hot Springs throughout the summer to assist Frank in taking care of her and to pray with her. In August, he came for yet another visit, and Frank "was constantly by her bedside" during his wife's "last illness." She died on Saturday, August 25, at 3:30 in the afternoon. A funeral service was held the next day at the Methodist Episcopal Church. That evening, her body was taken to Mason City, Iowa, by train "to be laid to rest by the side of James Francis and Duwane Davidson, the little sons who died so many years ago." One year later, Francis wrote to his dad that "I remember as clearly as anything the morning I got your letter at Mitchell telling of grandma's death."[9]

FRANCIS'S SENIOR YEAR IN COLLEGE officially began on Wednesday, September 12, with services held in the University chapel. Dr. Schermerhorn, who had assumed his duties as college president the previous June, was in charge of the occasion. A "large audience of students and townspeople" attended. Dr. Gay Charles White—from Watertown, South Dakota—gave the formal address titled "Education, a Search for Truth." His remarks were well received. Next, President Schermerhorn presented both new and veteran faculty members and the YMCA's General Secretary, Carroll West. Professor David H. Munson was among the new faculty members introduced. He was brought in to head the English Department and to coach forensics. Professor Elmer Wilds—the forensics coach for the previous three years—had left Wesleyan and taken a job with the Wisconsin State Normal School at Platteville. After new athletic coach Ray McLean was presented, "several college yells were given," and football-team captain Floyd Wilder announced that the first practice would begin at 3:30 that afternoon. Chaplain A. B. Hart then closed the proceedings with the benediction.[10]

Shortly after he was introduced to the audience at Wesleyan's official opening ceremony, Carroll (Cal) West was granted a leave of absence so he could go into YMCA War Secretarial Work at Battle Creek, Michigan. For the past year, Cal had served as the YM's general secretary at Wesleyan. During his tenure, he "worked himself into the college life to a remarkable degree" and made the YMCA "the most vital student organization on the campus." Harold Card was elected to take over West's position while the latter was on leave. To prepare himself for this work, Card attended a secretary training conference in Niagara Falls, New York. Selected as chairman of the Religious Meetings committee the previous spring, Francis would be filling that role for the YM during his senior year.[11]

The *Phreno Cosmian*'s first issue for the fall semester came out on September 20. As its new editor, Francis wrote a column titled "Your Paper." In it, he stated it was his intent "to make the Phreno strictly an 'all-college' paper" and reminded the Wesleyan "faculty, alumni and students" that it was their paper. He also encouraged them to "register your kicks where they should be registered," but encouraged them not "to knock merely for the sake of knocking" because "honest constructive criticism in the right spirit and delivered in the right place is what every organ and organization properly expects and desires." In a second column—"Getting Acquainted"—he advised the new and old students to quickly "get together," praised the *Phreno* staff, and noted that "the Intercollegiate Press Service [created by the College Press Association the previous spring] looks to be of real value."[12]

During his first three years of college, Francis had roomed with Harold Card at Harold's folks' house. For his senior year, he decided to live in and co-manage the X.L.N.T. Boarding Club. Harold described this "club" as "a combined boarding house and rooming house for male students." It was situated in a large, multi-story home at 717 South Sanborn Street. As one of the managers, Francis's main job was to buy "the food that was purchased for these college students." In return, he was given a room and his meals for free. Richard Bunt—a junior and football teammate—was the other co-manager. There were 25 members of the "X.L.N.T.," and they included Francis's fellow Daedalians, debate partners, and football teammates.[13]

As noted above, football practice began on the first day of school. By the end of that week, ten "old" men who had lettered last year had reported for practice, as well as ten "new" men. Additional recruits joined the team during the following week, so there were more than enough players to form two teams. The men went "into their work with a spirit determined to avenge the disastrous season of last year." A month or two after that season ended, coach Loman resigned and went to work at a Detroit high school. Loman was replaced by Ray L. McLean from Mount Union College in Alliance, Ohio, where he was known as "the best football man they have had during the past six years" with "a reputation for clean and fair playing."[14]

The South Dakota College Conference included six teams—Huron, Yankton, Sioux Falls, Northern Normal, South Dakota School of Mines, and Wesleyan. Wesleyan was scheduled to play all five of their conference opponents, plus three non-conference foes. When the 1917 campaign was about to begin, coach McLean had "the confidence of the squad and the entire school," and he counted on "the memory of last year's season to develop more than the usual amount of ginger." To encourage school spirit, the *Phreno Cosmian* printed the words to all of Wesleyan's "songs and yells" in its paper. Then the students held a well-attended "pep meeting" before the first game.[15]

Wesleyan's confidence in its new coach was bolstered by the outcome of that contest. In what was referred to as a "practice game," the Blue and White defeated overmatched Augustana College 91-0 on a windy day in Mitchell. Wesleyan scored 13 touchdowns, 11 goals on touchdowns (now referred to as extra points), and 1 safety. Francis started at right end and played the entire game. He made some significant contributions, including returning a kick for 25 yards, scoring a touchdown after catching a pass, and recovering Augustana's fumble on the ensuing kickoff.[16]

The next Saturday, the Wesleyanites travelled to Mizzou Park in Sioux City, Iowa, to play Trinity College. Before that trip, the Wesleyan players' weights were recorded. Francis weighed in at 145 and Harold Card at 170. The entire team averaged "153 pounds per man." They were greeted by a small crowd and a team "about equal in weight." Although Wesleyan gained more yards than Trinity, the Dakotans were down 9-0 until late in the third quarter. Then Wesleyan came back by scoring a touchdown but missing the point-after kick as the quarter ended. It was a back-and-forth game for most of the final period until Wesleyan's Johnnie Reierson kicked "a perfect field goal" to tie the score with two minutes left on the clock. Neither team threatened the other's goal after that, resulting in a 9 to 9 final score. Francis played every down at right end, and Harold substituted at both right and left tackle.[17]

Wesleyan's first conference game was played the next Saturday, October 20, against Northern Normal and Industrial School at Johnson Field in Aberdeen. Although making 21 first downs to Normal's 11 and completing 13 passes to Normal's two, Wesleyan "failed at critical moments" and lost the game 13 to 0. Two minutes before the end of the second quarter, Francis was involved in a controversial play—at least from the *Phreno* sports reporter's viewpoint. He described the action as follows:

> Case received a pass from Wilder for 20 yards, and started for the goal line 15 yards away. A Normal tackler hit Case, throwing him to his knees, but failed to stop him, and he crossed the goal line, but the referee called the ball back to the 15 yard line, having blown the whistle when the attempt at tackle was made.

Apart from whether the referee made the right call on that play, Francis had a big day in the pass-receiving department. He caught five passes for a total of 83 yards, which accounted for almost half of Wesleyan's yardage gained through the air. As an example of "failing at a critical moment," Wesleyan ran the ball down to Normal's one yard line in the fourth quarter, but its next two attempts at scoring a touchdown were unsuccessful. Harold once again substituted at right tackle, and Francis stayed in the game from start to finish.[18]

Four days after the Normal game, Francis broke his collarbone in a practice scrimmage. The injury was serious enough for the *Phreno*'s assistant editor to predict that he "will be unable to play in any of the remaining games this year." It thus appeared that his college football career was over after playing in only three matches during his senior season.[19]

THE METHODIST EPISCOPAL CHURCH'S ANNUAL Conference met in Pierre, South Dakota, from October 10 through 14. Over 200 ministers—presumably including Herbert Case—attended. Miss Wade—superintendent of the Methodist Deaconess Hospital in Rapid City—was also present. The hospital was only five years old and had experienced "steady growth" since its founding. Its current field secretary, Reverend Hartung, had decided to resign his position. At the Annual Conference, he was assigned to the Methodist Church in Tripp, South Dakota. After serving in the ministry for 28 years, Herbert was ready for a "different kind of work." He was offered the hospital field secretary position, and he accepted it.[20]

The Case family moved from Spearfish to Rapid City sometime in late October or early November. They found a house located at 909 West Boulevard. In his new position, Herbert's principal duty was to raise money for the hospital. To make it easier to solicit potential patrons located in Rapid City and its surrounding area, he learned to drive the hospital's old Model T Ford. He also became a member of the hospital's board of trustees, which met once a year to analyze reports on the institution's past performance and make decisions regarding its future development.²¹

At about the same time the Cases relocated from Spearfish to Rapid City, the Mitchell community showed its support for the war effort. On October 24, more than 10,000 people marched down the city's main street to encourage the public to buy Liberty Bonds. The parade—composed of nearly 50 separate units—was a mile and a half long. It was led by the Mitchell Municipal Band. The other units included local businesses and banks, school children, the Red Cross, the Women's Relief Corps, Dakota Wesleyan, and many other groups. Wesleyan's unit—composed of students and faculty—"marched in classes each representing some phase or side of the great World War." After the parade broke up, the crowds "went to the Methodist Church and Metropolitan theatre where they listened to addresses by the speakers of the day." During the ensuing bond drive, several Wesleyan students purchased bonds. They included Francis, who bought one for $50.²²

THE WESLEYAN FOOTBALL SEASON CONTINUED with Francis relegated to the sidelines. On October 27, the Morningside College Maroons arrived in Mitchell, played the game before a small crowd, and defeated the host team 33-0. The Wesleyanites were "outweighed 20 pounds to the man." They were subject to "much unnecessary roughness" and "piling up" by their opponent. These tactics were imposed upon Richard Bunt (co-manager of the X.L.N.T. Boarding Club), who "was tackled by a Maroon player and immediately assisted by two others in such a way that his right leg was broken in five places." Herbert Fox took Francis's place at right end. Harold Card had been moved up to starting right tackle, and he played the entire game. His "work on backing up the line [on defense] brot repeated comment on the sidelines." The following Friday, the Blue and White met the Sioux Falls College eleven at Sioux Falls. Both teams "played a sluggish game" and neither was able to score until there were only 23 seconds left on the clock. At that point, "with the ball on the 15 yard line, . . . [Wesleyan's] Rierson/sic/ kicks a perfect drop-kick for the only score of the game."[23]

Eight days later, the Mitchell team faced the South Dakota School of Mines team on its home field in Rapid City. Wesleyan was forced to make lineup changes, as Ward Steiber had broken his leg in a scrimmage earlier that week, and Herbert Fox left school to train for the Ordnance Corps. Card was shifted to right end on offense and to "full" on defense. Captain Floyd Wilder "took pass after pass for good gains," Kenneth Harkness "played his strongest game of the season," Henry Hoagland "made some brilliant end runs," and Wesleyan won the game 13-6. Francis did not make the train trip to Rapid City with the team. But he, along with Percy Wiseman (Wesleyan junior from Mount Vernon), Margaret Card (Wesleyan senior and Harold's sister), and Irma Graves (Wesleyan junior from Mitchell) drove to nearby Mount Vernon on a Sunday afternoon and returned "on the evening train from the west with the football team."[24]

The Wesleyan gridders were back on their home field against Huron College on November 17. A "good-sized crowd witnessed the game," which ended in a scoreless 0-0 tie. Neither team got within ten yards of the other's goal line, and neither made its attempted field goals. Harold played every down—starting the game at right end and shifting to right tackle in the fourth quarter. Although he had sustained a broken bone only three-and-a-half weeks earlier, Francis "refused to be laid up," "donned his togs," and got in the game "for a short time."[25]

Wesleyan's final game for the 1917 season was against Yankton College. It was played at Mitchell on Thanksgiving Day. The weather conditions were ideal. More than 2,000 spectators were on hand, and the Mitchell Municipal Band played rousing music "throughout the contest." Yankton ended up winning 19 to 13 in a "doggedly fought" battle. Wesleyan's Kenneth Harkness was the "brilliant player of the game," scoring both Blue and White touchdowns and playing strong defense. Francis, who was "still handicapped with a broken clavicle sustained in a scrimmage about a month ago ... appeared at his old position at right end and played the entire game." He made some important plays on both offense and defense, including receiving a pass "for a gain of 40 yards," recovering a fumble by Yankton's quarterback, and combining with Harkness to throw Yankton's fullback for a four-yard loss. Senior Ward Steiber, who suffered a broken leg earlier in the year, entered the game in the third quarter and showed "more fight than any other man on the team." After the game, Francis sent a telegram to his mother. Its message read, "We lost game played out absolutely all right. Love, Francis Case."[26]

So, the 1917 football season ended with three wins, three losses, and two ties. Wesleyan had outscored its opponents 129 to 80. The team celebrated its "worth while season" at the annual football banquet—held on the Tuesday evening after the Yankton game. Shortly before it began, the team met and elected Kenneth Harkness as its captain for the next year. The banquet itself was well-attended, with "over a hundred plates" sold. Following the four-course dinner, President Schermerhorn served as toastmaster for the program. It included a speech by Coach McLean and toasts by players Bunt, Wilder, and Card. Coach McLean's talk "was particularly well received," as he pointed out the positive aspects of the 1917 season. Harold gave the final toast of the evening. He ended it by suggesting "the slogan for next year, 'Over the Top.'"[27]

On December 8, Coach McLean announced his mythical all-conference team. It included five players from the conference-champion Yankton team, three players from Wesleyan, two from Northern Normal, and one from Huron. The Wesleyan players included Case at right end, Harkness at left half, and Wilder at right half. Francis was "somewhat surprised" at his selection, because he thought that "being out of the game so much" would deprive him "of any claim to such a position." But he added: "Coach says he talked it over with some football authorities, and they agreed that it was perfectly proper, especially since I played the Thanksgiving game." In explaining his choices to the press, McLean stated that "Case, though kept out of the game for a month by a broken clavicle, played enough to place him among the best. His work against Aberdeen, in taking passes and turning in runs, was exceptionally good." Regarding his selections of Harkness and Wilder, the Wesleyan coach noted "Harkness . . . as a linebacker is almost without a superior" and "takes passes well." Although Wilder played quarterback for Wesleyan, he was chosen as right halfback because of his "brilliant broken field running and hammerlike jabs at the line combined with deadly tackling on defense[.]" McLean also named two Wesleyan players deserving "honorable mention." They were Estell Deller at center and Laren Spear at guard. Yankton's coach Montgomery chose a first and second all-conference team. He put Wesleyan's Johnnie Riereson on his first team at fullback. His second team included three Wesleyanites. They were Francis at right end, Louis Todnem at left guard, and Henry Hoagland at left halfback.[28]

DECEMBER 9 WAS FRANCIS'S 21st birthday. He "became of age" that day and wrote a long, soul-bearing letter to his father. The letter discussed several topics, including his "war plans," his thoughts on future "life-work," and his "birthright." Regarding war plans, he stated:

> I discovered yesterday that enlistment is not closed to me although I am 21, inasmuch as I was not 21 when registration occurred. So it would seem that it is safe for me to go ahead and finish school, at least until there is a prospect of a new registration for those who have become 21 since the first registration.

* * *

> If it comes down to it, I think I would enlist rather than be drafted and sent anywhere. The thing I don't like about the association secretary work is that it doesn't protect one from the draft. In fact the Bureau of Personnel is giving very few appointments to men who are within the draft age limits.

With respect to his future life-work, Francis noted:

> I like this journalistic game, on the whole. I don't know that there is much money in it, but I do think that it affords one an opportunity to be in the heart of the fight. It gives one a chance to be in the world's work. But most of all it seems to me that it gives one a real chance to make this world a better place to live in. The editor of a semi-metropolitan newspaper today, fashions the lives and thots of more people than the minister of a great church.

He also made clear his reservations about ever becoming a minister.

> The idea of being a minister is not repugnant to me in most of its phases, but there are some things which I do not feel capable of doing. There are also some things which I could hardly do conscientiously, or ask others to do. I would hesitate to preach a funeral sermon. I could not administer the sacrament nor could I urge whole-heartedly others to partake of it. Neither could I baptize anyone. The matter of preaching wouldn't be so hard, for a while, if I didn't run out after a period of time.

* * *

> So much, so very much of what is preached in the average pulpit simply doesn't register with me that I doubt if I could pass an orthodox examination. Or if I could, I wonder if I could hold a congregation.

After stating these concerns. He concluded this point by observing

> I do know that it would have not displeased you had I by this time determined that I should be a minister. I have written the

foregoing simply to explain, if I could, why I could never be the minister you would want me to be....

On the other hand, I can go into Journalism and work for the highest good as I see it, with no pangs of conscience that I am parading under false colors.

Lastly, he claimed to have "one of the best birthrights ever a boy had on attaining his majority," which he described as "the training, the good health, the pure blood, the wide experience, the excellent educational opportunities, and the optimistic outlook on life which you and mamma have given me."[29]

THE ANNUAL INTER-SOCIETY DEBATES were held on December 15. The question for those contests was "Resolved, that in time of war the administration be granted absolute censorship of the press." In the first debate—held in the morning—the Daedalian affirmative team lost to the Kappa Pi Phi negative team in a 2 to 1 decision. The Kappa affirmatives scored a unanimous decision over the Delta Rho negatives in the afternoon contest. The third and final debate, which took place in the evening, was described as "the most interesting and closely contested of the series." Delta Rho's affirmative squad, led by Walter Ludeman, defeated the Francis-led Daedalian negative team by a 2 to 1 judges vote. So, the Kappas won the Elmer H. Wilds Trophy, the Delta Rhos finished in second place, and the Daedalians in third. After the debates concluded, twelve men were chosen to represent Wesleyan in the upcoming inter-collegiate debates. Five Daedalians (including Francis and Harold Card), four Delta Rhos, and three Kappas were selected. Harold was not on either of the three-member Daedalian teams that debated on December 15. But he won a place on the inter-collegiate squad in an open tryout held immediately before the evening debate. The three professors who chose the inter-collegiate team ranked their selections. They put Francis at number one and Ludeman at number two.[30]

WESLEYAN'S SPRING TERM BEGAN SOMETIME in January, 1918. As an "all-college contribution to the war program," the school had decided to adopt a "'speeding up'" process for the semester by holding classes six days a week. Doing so would shorten the school year "by approximately five weeks" and put "commencement in the first week of May." Francis already had enough hours to graduate—having been given full credit for the courses he took at summer school in Spearfish. He therefore registered for only two regular college courses—one in history and one in physics. The latter course concentrated on electricity and was "devoted mainly to wireless work." He also enrolled in a course in telegraphy. It was taught by professors from Wesleyan's Commercial Department and met downtown three nights a week. Under this program, he hoped to pass the telegraphy exam as soon as he could and then enlist in either the Army or Navy as a telegraph operator.[31]

Aside from his limited academic schedule, Francis had plenty of other things to keep him busy. They included teaching public speaking and coaching forensics at the Academy, acting in the senior play (which scheduled rehearsals three times a week), editing the *Phreno*, taking an active role in the Daedalian Society, co-managing the boarding club, and volunteering for the Home Guards. He originally "was not counting on going into debate," but that decision changed during the semester.[32]

In early January, President Schermerhorn announced that "the down-town people" were seeking new recruits for the Home Guards. They were troops charged with protecting local and state governments from civil disturbances, sabotage, insurrection, and disasters. In Mitchell, the local unit was primarily concerned about sabotage, and its guards "patrolled the railroads and other sensitive areas" in the city. The college responded immediately to Dr. Schermerhorn's announcement. Twelve faculty members and 16 students volunteered to become Home Guards. Dr. Schermerhorn, Dr. Gilliland, and Professor

Munson (new forensics coach) were among the faculty volunteers. Francis and his boarding-house roommate and fellow Daedalian—freshman Kenneth West—were included in the group of students who agreed to serve.[33]

Francis was on guard duty for the first shift on Friday night, January 27. Two nights later, Kenneth West and two others had taken that shift and had been relieved of duty at about 1:00 a.m. Monday morning. On their way back to campus, they came up behind two other Home Guards—Donald McPherson and Stanley Flocker—who were checking out a wagon shed with their flashlights. West reached down, grabbed a handful of snow, and was about to throw it at his good friend McPherson. When McPherson heard a noise, he turned around to find West about five feet away from him with his arm upraised. Not recognizing West in the dark and thinking it was "'my life or his,'" McPherson drew his revolver and fired a single shot at his assumed assailant. The bullet hit West in the chest, and "death was practically instantaneous." A coroner's inquest ruled that the death was an accident and "completely exonerated McPherson."[34]

Dr. Gilliland had the somber task of informing West's parents what had happened. Upon receiving this terrible news, Mr. West requested that Francis make the plans necessary to take his son's body to Presho—the Wests' hometown located in west-central Dakota. On Monday afternoon, President Schermerhorn conducted a service for West at the Noble Undertaking Parlors. Despite the short notice, the rooms were filled to capacity, and "scores of people were unable to gain admittance." The Methodist Church minister offered a prayer, and hymns were sung. Dr. Gilliland, Harold Card and Francis all made brief remarks. Early the next morning, the body was taken by train to Presho. It was accompanied by Dr. Gilliland, Francis, Mildred Prisch, and Alice Redfield. They all attended a service there and returned to Mitchell a day later. On the editorial page of that week's *Phreno*, Francis wrote a heartfelt tribute to West. It stated in part:

"Kenneth West, fellow student, friend, society brother, and to me room-mate is gone. But as an influence in the lives of those who knew him, he will be ever present." Francis also penned a short column that recognized McPherson was "making a fight as few men are ever called upon to do," and it encouraged all of West's friends and McPherson's friends to aid and support his efforts "to be all he is striving to be."[35]

FRANCIS PARTICIPATED IN ONE forensic event and coached another during January. On the 10th, he entered the local old line oratorical contest against two other contestants—Lloyd Rising and Leslie Fislar. Rising was a fellow senior, Daedalian society member, and resident at the X.L.N.T. Boarding Club. He had entered the local old line contest every year since he was a freshman. As a junior, he won the local contest, represented Wesleyan at the state contest, and lost first place there "by a slight margin." Fislar was a sophomore who had won the local prohibition contest and placed second at the state round the previous year. His oration—"America for Americans"— was presented first. Next, Rising gave his speech titled "The Renaissance from War." Francis ended the competition with his oration—"Democracy in Action." In a decision described as "exceedingly close," the three judges awarded Rising first place.[36]

Francis took second. He had not lost an oratorical contest since finishing in second place at the Black Hills regional declamatory contest when he was a sophomore at Sturgis High School, and he probably expected to win this one. Nevertheless, he did not react as a "sore loser" when the results were announced. Responding to his parents' inquiry about the "much discussed oratorical," he wrote that "Rising and I belong to the same society," we "feel alright about it," and "in fact are as friendly as ever." And the *Phreno* editorial page encouraged Rising to do well in the next round of competition: "Rising will battle for Wesleyan in the State Old Line at Huron a week from today. Let's everyone [get] behind him. It's time we copped another State Old Line."³⁷

The Wesleyan inter-academy debaters for the 1918 season were divided into two, three-member teams. Francis had to teach them basic debate skills and procedures, since none had any "previous inter-academy experience." On January 18, the two teams met their counterparts from the Yankton Academy. Wesleyan's affirmative team debated the Yankton negatives on Wesleyan's home floor, and those arguing the negative position for Wesleyan travelled to Yankton to face its affirmative team. The question at issue was "Resolved, That South Dakota should adopt the Unicameral System of Legislature." Both Wesleyan teams won unanimous decisions. The *Phreno* attributed that result to the two teams' "careful study on the question and consistent coaching on the part of the Academy coach."³⁸

FRANCIS WROTE AN EDITORIAL TITLED "Dominant Reform" that appeared in the *Phreno*'s February 7, 1918 edition. In it, he argued that

> Final examinations for the second semester constitute an unjustified expenditure of time and energy. They require a week to conduct. They encourage students to "slide" in the hopes of pulling grade in the final. They indict the ability of the teacher to determine a grade from daily work. In brief, they are not efficient.

The remainder of the editorial expanded on the thesis quoted above. It contended, among other things, that eliminating final exams would enhance the speeding-up-the-semester program (already adopted) by ending the term a full week earlier, would provide students with an incentive to increase their academic efforts during the shortened term, and would save both students and faculty from engaging in "unnecessary efforts" that, for the present semester, were "not justified." Two weeks after the editorial appeared, the *Phreno* noted that "a great majority of students are in favor of eliminating final exams as a 'war measure.'"[39]

On February 22, Wesleyan held its sixth annual celebration of George Washington's birthday. All classes were dismissed for the day. The ceremony began in the college chapel, where Wesleyan's "great service flag"—containing 126 stars—was formally dedicated. This flag was adorned with blue and gold stars. Each star represented a faculty member or student who had been affiliated with Wesleyan in the past and had recently joined the armed forces. The blue stars represented Wesleyanites who had served or were presently serving, and the gold stars represented those who had lost their lives. An "Honor Roll" accompanied the flag. It listed the men's names, ranks, branches of service and addresses (if known).[40]

The current flag contained two gold stars—one for Kenneth West and one for John Berry. Berry had graduated from Wesleyan in 1916 and subsequently joined the Ambulance Corps. He had just recently died in an explosion at a munitions plant at Cliffside, New Jersey. As the service flag was unveiled, Dr. Gilliland read the names of the men who were represented by the stars upon it. Following the flag dedication ceremony, "the entire student body, headed by the Kappa Society of which John Berry was a member, marched to the Catholic Church to attend the funeral of the second Wesleyan man who has lost his life because of the war."[41]

The Washington Birthday celebration concluded with an all-college banquet held at the Methodist Church that evening. More than 250 people attended, including "prominent alumni," students from the college and Academy, and faculty. During the after-dinner program, several students and a faculty member gave "clever toasts." Then, "a word from Dr. Gilliland brought the day's events to a close."[42]

Since the latter part of January, Francis and his fellow senior-class actors had been rehearsing for the class play. They chose "All of a Sudden Peggy" by Ernest Denny. Mrs. William North was selected as their coach. She was a Mitchell resident who had previously taught dramatics and had coached this play at Springfield High School in Springfield, Missouri. After several weeks of rehearsal, the play was presented to a full house at Mitchell's Metropolitan Theatre on March 12. Described as a "delightfully clever comedy," the *Phreno* noted that Anna McKay "very cleverly acted the part of 'Peggy' and was well supported by other members of the class." They included Francis—"who ultimately understood and won Peggy"—Harold Card, Lloyd Rising, Elmer Lushbaugh, and Walter Ludeman. The women supporting actors were Mildred Prisch, Mildred Test, Matilda Tarleton, and Kathleen Swartz. Proceeds from the play were used to buy a master electric clock for the college. It would serve as the class memorial.[43]

WESLEYAN REPEATED ITS SUCCESS ON the debate floor in March. Since last year, State College of Brookings had been added to the four-member South Dakota Debating League (which included Huron, Sioux Falls, Wesleyan, and Yankton). So now the previous quadrangular college contest had become a pentangular arrangement to determine the state champion in 1918. The question for that year's debate was "Resolved that the Administration be granted Absolute Censorship of the press in time of war, constitutionally granted and Congressional action waived." On March 14, Wesleyan's affirmative team—consisting of Walter Ludeman (captain), Ralph Dunbar, and Leslie Fislar—won "an easy victory" over Yankton on Wesleyan's home platform. Her negative team, which included Elmer Lushbaugh (captain), Lee Seymour, and Laren Spear, was scheduled to debate Sioux Falls College at Sioux Falls, but the latter team forfeited. When all the debates among the five colleges were completed, Wesleyan emerged as the "only school with two undefeated teams," making her state debate champion for the fourth consecutive year in a row.[44]

Eight days later, two different Wesleyan teams met their counterparts from Morningside College for a dual debate. Harold Card was captain of Wesleyan's affirmative team that hosted Morningside, and Francis headed the negative team that travelled to Sioux City. A group of "rooters"—including Drs. Schermerhorn and Harkness, students Ward Stieber and Percy Wisemen, and "Rev. H. L. Case of Rapid City"—also made the trip to support the Wesleyan team. Neither Harold's teammates (Henry Hoagland and Louis Richardson) nor Francis's (Louis Todnem and Kenneth Harkness) had ever competed in an inter-collegiate debate before. The question (involving absolute censorship in wartime) was the same one used in the pentangular debates described above.[45]

Both contests were decided by a single judge. Both Wesleyan teams won. And for both Harold and Francis, it was the last debate of their college careers. Describing their respective performances, the *Phreno* noted that Card was "strongest on his logic and sound reasoning," and "his remarks had more weight than any other speaker of the evening." And it had this to say about Francis: "At Morningside Case was by far the best man on the platform.... He is largely responsible for the success of the team, more than [that] he is the best debater that Wesleyan has produced in the last four years and easily among the best that she has ever produced."[46]

The second annual Academy Oratorical for the Case Trophies was held in the college chapel on March 27. Five speakers entered the contest. Cecil Monroe won first place with his oration titled "The New Russia." Floyd Brominghim, speaking on "The United States and the War of Democracy," took second. Francis presented these winners with their gold and silver medals. The *Phreno* observed that offering "medals for first and second places in the Prep oratorical contest... has been one of the greatest promoters of that event."[47]

In addition to his activities on the play stage and debate floor, Francis became Publicity Secretary for Wesleyan's Educational Jubilee Campaign in late March. The campaign's goal was to raise $400,000 for the college. Those funds were sought so Wesleyan could complete the new gymnasium on campus, offer new college courses, increase teachers' salaries, enlarge courses "in military training, Red Cross Aid, [and] surgical dressings," and generally "ensure a productive endowment adequate to meet the demands of a high standard of school efficiency." Francis's main duty as publicity secretary was to prepare, coordinate, and send out information about the campaign to prospective subscribers. By early April, he had "dropped regular college work" to devote more time to this job.[48]

In mid-April, Francis's term as president of the South Dakota College Press Association came to an end. The organization met in Sioux Falls on the 15th and 16th for its annual convention, and a new slate of officers was elected for the oncoming year. While this gathering was taking place, Wesleyanites met in their chapel "to express the respect and love" they felt for Coach McLean. He had decided to enter the Army, and the college opted to give him a proper send off. After a short speech of "sincere appreciation," Dr. Schermerhorn presented McLean with a camera from the faculty. On behalf of the male students, Harold Card gave him a wrist watch.[49]

The next Monday, the Pi Kappa Delta fraternity held its third annual banquet and initiation ceremony at the Methodist Church. Sixty people attended. After a four-course dinner, "Cancellarius Francis Case" directed the formal initiation. Several new members were admitted. Following the ceremony, officers were elected for the next year, and "the history of Pi Kappa Delta for this year was read by Malletorius Harold Card."[50]

The 1918 spring term came to its "speeded-up" end in early May. Following up on Francis's February editorial that argued final exams should be eliminated, the Student Senate submitted a petition to the faculty requesting that this action be taken. The faculty voted in favor of the petition with the express conditions that "it was granted for this year only as a war measure," that it did not apply "to the requirement of special examinations for exceeding the prescribed number of class cuts," and that "unexcused absences during the last week condition the work of the entire course." Both students and faculty greeted this measure "with marked approval."[51]

The *Phreno*'s last issue for the semester was published on May 2. On its editorial page, Francis said goodbye to its readers, thanked all the staff members for their assistance and cooperation, and encouraged the students to support Wesleyan's endowment campaign over the summer. On the following Sunday, Wesleyan formally launched that campaign under the slogan "'A Greater Wesleyan for a New World.'" The launch was accompanied by "an educational sermon" that explained the campaign's purpose, its progress to date, and its intention to raise $400,000 by the campaign's June 26 closing date.[52]

Wesleyan's commencement week also began on Sunday, May 5. Dr. Schermerhorn gave the baccalaureate sermon at the Methodist Church that morning. It was followed by the traditional on-campus vesper service at 6:30 that evening. The graduates then returned to the Methodist Church, where Dr. John Jenkins—the university's vice-president—presented the university sermon. Commencement activities continued Monday through Wednesday. Monday had the seniors attend their final chapel service in the morning and a recital by the school of music in the evening. On Tuesday, the festivities included unveiling the class gift to the college (a master electric clock with secondary clocks installed in three campus buildings), a university luncheon, an alumni banquet, the traditional May Day pageant, and society reunions scheduled from 11:00 p.m. until midnight. The next day, breakfast was served in Graham Hall, and formal commencement exercises were held in the chapel auditorium later in the morning. Bishop Charles Bayard Mitchell (from the St. Paul episcopal area) delivered the address, and President Schermerhorn conferred the degrees upon Wesleyan's 21 college graduates.[53]

After commencement was completed, Francis stayed in Mitchell and continued his work on the Jubilee endowment campaign. He agreed to stay on as Publicity Secretary until his replacement arrived. That person, from San Jose, California, did not get to town until May 26. Francis left for Rapid City the next day—armed with his newly-minted college degree and his determination to enlist in the armed forces "as soon as possible."[54]

CHAPTER 5

BECOMING A MARINE

It's U.S. Marines for me.
—Francis Case

In a letter to his "Homefolks" written four months earlier, Francis explained why he decided to actively serve in the war effort. He first related what he said to Dr. Schermerhorn when the two met to discuss the subject: "Someone has to go," and "there is a subconscious feeling that can make no plans, that anything I might plan to do is minor so long as big thing of age is on, and I am not in it." He then expanded on his "state of mind" with these additional comments:

> You see I don't want to slack. I want to do my part. And somehow I cannot make myself feel that I am doing bit unless get directly into it. There are many other things which must be done. But we must win the war. We must have trained men.
>
> Then too, in later years I want a clean record. Don't want anyone coming to me and saying that I took easiest way out because looked safest for my skin. . . .

* * *

> Now, of course, one could look at casualty list every day, and get into a state of cowardice. But that isn't the question at all. The question is one of doing duty, of holding self-respect. I don't

expect to wade right in and throw my life away. Not by a long shot. But I do want to do what I should, cost what it may. I believe this war has got to be won. The sooner the better.[1]

FRANCIS ARRIVED IN RAPID CITY on May 27. He stayed at his parents' house for a few days and spent one day in Hot Springs. He had decided to enlist in the Marine Corps, and the nearest recruiting station was in Denver. It was necessary to get there by train in early June so he could enlist "before voluntary enlistment stopped and the draft began." His mother suggested that Leland accompany his brother to Hermosa—a town located 16 miles south of Rapid City—to catch the train headed for Denver. So, Leland and Francis took off in the family Ford—which Leland had named "Wounded Knee" because "we were always having trouble with it"—on Sunday night, June 2.[2]

After Francis had driven a while on a road composed of "blue gumbo" that was wet and sticky from the last rain, Leland took the wheel. In a 1972 interview, he told what happened next:

> Going over a hill I saw ahead, two streaks of water and in between, and on the sides was the gumbo. Well, I made a quick decision, thinking I better stay on what looked like solid land, than to splash through the water. But it was a bum decision. As we got halfway through, the car stopped. It was one of the worst moments in my life. I was responsible you see. I was driving and here was my brother going off to war. If I didn't get him over there, to Hermosa in time, he would miss that train and then would be drafted and that would be ignominy without end for the family.... I got out and yanked out a fence post, I remember, and I used gunny sacks and rocks and everything I could find to give the car traction.... Along after midnight, we pulled out of the mess and rolled along toward this little town of Hermosa. When we were out about two miles "Wounded Knee" didn't make it up the hill. We tried and tried and tried. Finally, there was nothing

to do but to leave the car by the side of the road and go in and try to get a little sleep at a hotel.³

The next morning, Leland said goodbye to Francis and trudged back out to the car. He adjusted the carburetor to get it started, then "steamed up that hill" and "stalled again." After backing down the hill and making another unsuccessful run at it, "an idea began to glimmer." The gas tank was under the car's seat. Since gasoline flowed from it by gravity only, he needed to ensure that the reduced amount in the tank made it into the engine. So, he "turned Wounded Knee around and backed up the hill like a sky rocket!" After filling up the car with gas in Hermosa, he "finally got home." Because he "had rolled in that mud so much" on the previous day, his "dried out trousers would stand by themselves in the corner."⁴

Francis did catch the train for Denver on June 3. After a three-hour wait that night in Edgemont—a small town in southwestern South Dakota near the Wyoming border—he arrived in Denver and went to the Marine recruiting station the next morning. He was a bit nervous about the physical examination given to all potential enlistees, because out of the 11 candidates examined ahead of him, only three passed. But Francis passed his physical "without a condition." The "Acting Assistant Surgeon" described him as having gray eyes, light brown hair, and a ruddy complexion. His height was recorded as 67 inches and weight at 152 pounds. The examiner also certified that "in my opinion he is free from all bodily defects and mental infirmities which would in any way disqualify him from performing the duties of a marine[.]" After the exam, the recruit signed some forms and was ordered to report to the Marine recruit training facility at Mare Island, California. Upon leaving the Denver recruiting station, he noted: "Believe me a fellow in the Marines will have to keep on the jump. The bunch they sent out this a.m. were a mighty clean looking set of fellows." And he added that he was "anxious to hear how Leland made out after I left."[5]

Mare Island is in Vallejo, California. The island is separated from the main part of that city by the Napa River. Vallejo is located 30 miles north of San Francisco. In 1911, the Marine Corps establish a training facility on Mare Island, and "from 1917 to 1922, the Marine Barracks was the boot camp for all recruits who enlisted west of the Mississippi." Their training typically lasted for two months and included close order drill, physical training, marksmanship instruction with the M1903 Springfield rifle, and training for personal combat.[6]

The day after he was "accepted for enlistment" at Denver, Francis took the afternoon train to Mare Island. Upon arriving there, he checked into the Marine Barracks. On June 13, he was given another physical exam and was fingerprinted. The next day, he formally became an enlisted Marine by repeating and signing the oath required by Marine Corps regulations. In that oath, he acknowledged "to have voluntarily enlisted as a PRIVATE in the UNITED STATES MARINE CORPS, for duration of war, unless sooner discharged by proper authority." He also swore, among other things, to bear allegiance to the United States, to serve "them honestly and faithfully against all their enemies whomsoever," and to obey the orders of the United States President and "of the officers appointed over me[.]" After the "swearing in" process was completed, the new enlistee was issued a toilet kit and a rifle.[7]

The *Rapid City Daily Journal* reported on a letter that Francis wrote home in either late June or early July. According to the *Journal*'s summary of that letter, Francis was "nicely located as a Marine at Mare Island," and the "boys expected to spend the 4th [of July] in San Francisco," where they "will take part in the celebration program there." The next thing known about Francis's "boot camp" experience is that in late July, he broke his right arm and sprained that wrist during "wall scaling practice." His arm was put in a cast, he was put on "sick report," and he was assigned to restricted duties. On August 19, the cast was removed.[8]

One day later, Francis wrote a letter to his mother. Despite still being on sick report and performing limited duty due to his arm/wrist injury, he assured her that he was not "in dire straits" or "bad off." To illustrate this point, he noted that the "Post Exchange has a library" where he had access to "magazines, novels or even encyclopedias." The PX also showed free movies "four nights out of the week." Since his cast was taken off the previous morning, he noticed that his arm was "not as strong as it was before." He reluctantly decided not to report for football tryouts that day, concluding that his "wrist wouldn't be strong enuf to play as they will play here."[9]

His wrist injury also prevented him from joining a detail that recently left for the Marine installation in Quantico, Virginia. Harold Card and one-time debate partner Bernie Brereton were based at Quantico. Francis wanted to go on that detail "in the worst way but this wrist held me off." Instead, his superiors decided he was to be "Held for Instruction," and he was formerly detailed as a Drill Instructor on August 20. Francis had some misgivings about this assignment:

> This instructor business... isn't the choicest detail for it is miserably the same thing day in and out, its not actual service, and unless you pull a bonehead it is almost impossible to get away from for actual service.... Then too promotion is very slow in a recruit camp for Marines. More active service means faster promotion and more opportunity. However one must do what he is told here—so all one can do is to obey orders and hope for the best.[10]

By the end of August, Francis was much more upbeat. He wrote to his dad that "the past ten days have passed rapidly enuf. The recruits got their rifles in the forepart of the week and have been doing very well with them." He also mentioned that he had "just mailed mother a picture of the section and the 4 instructors. We don't look very spick and span for had just come in from drill and they lined us up to be 'shot.'" And he added that "the first Seg't of the Co told me yesterday he had turned in my name for First Class Private. That will mean $3 a month more if the Major approves it." The photo mentioned in Francis's letter shows 51 Marines who are members of Section 5, Company D. They are lined up on the Marine Barracks steps and facing the camera. Two of the drill instructors—who appear to be older men—are standing in front of lampposts at the bottom of the steps. Francis, the fourth drill instructor, and seven other Marines are in the first row. There are five rows behind them, and each of those rows contains eight men.[11]

CAMP FUNSTON WAS AN ARMY BASE located in central Kansas. It "grew up practically overnight and consisted of hastily built wooden barracks, mess halls, headquarters, community buildings, and latrines." On March 4, 1918, Private Albert Getchall went to the post hospital and complained that he had "the flu." His symptoms included fever, headache, sore throat, bad cough, and muscle pain. Getchall thus became the first reported case in the United States of an influenza virus that would become known as the "Spanish flu." It soon developed into a pandemic, which "occurs when an entirely new and virulent influenza virus, which the immune system has not previously seen, enters the population and spreads worldwide." This virus infected cells in both the upper respiratory tract and the lungs of its victims. It damaged deep-lung tissue and often led to viral or bacterial pneumonia.[12]

The 1918 pandemic lasted about 15 months, and it became the "deadliest disease outbreak in human history." It infected an estimated 500 million men, women and children throughout the world, which was about one-third of the earth's population. And according to a widely-accepted analysis, it killed somewhere between 50 and 100 million people. For those who survived, the disease typically followed this pattern: "At the onset, body temperature increased rapidly, the face became red, body aches commenced, and the patient endured a throbbing headache. Symptoms continued for about a week and suddenly subsided after considerable perspiration. In the aftermath, the patient remained weak for about two weeks before making a full recovery." And for those who succumbed to the disease, an Army physician wrote a graphic description of that process in 1918:

> 'These men start with what appears to be an ordinary attack of LaGrippe or Influenza, and when brought to the Hosp. they very rapidly develop the most vicious type of Pneumonia that has ever been seen. Two hours after admission they have the Mahogany spots over the cheek bones, and a few hours later you can begin to see the Cyanosis'—the term refers to a person turning blue from lack of oxygen—'extending from their ears and spreading all over the face.... It is only a matter of a few hours then until death comes... It is horrible[.]'

The final hours of life could also display additional "horrific symptoms," such as "a foamy blood coughed up from the lungs, and bleeding from the nose, ears, and even eyes."[13]

Normally influenza epidemics kill a disproportionate number of the elderly and the very young. But in the 1918 pandemic, young adults—between the ages of 18 and 40—were "killed in the highest numbers." One possible explanation for this fact is that "young adults have the strongest immune systems," and these systems "attacked the virus with every weapon possible—including chemicals called cytokines and other microbe-fighting toxins[.]" This attack occurred in the lungs and created so-called "'cytokine storms,'" which further damaged the lung tissue and often led to death.[14]

No one is certain as to where the pandemic originated. Some researchers believe it began in China in 1917, others contend that it emerged from a large British Army Hospital in France in 1916, and historian John M. Barry argues that its source can be traced to Camp Funston, Kansas, where crowded conditions made it a "great incubator for the disease" in early 1918. Regardless of its origin, there appears to be general agreement that the pandemic hit the world in three separate waves. Although the dates are not exact, the first wave lasted from roughly March to July, 1918, the second from August to November of that year, and the third from January to April, 1919.[15]

As noted above, the first reported case of the "new" influenza in the United States occurred on March 4 at Camp Funston. Within three weeks, 1,100 soldiers at that camp were hospitalized, roughly 20 percent developed pneumonia, but only 38 died. This relatively low death toll was attributed to strict quarantine measures implemented after the first reported case, and the deaths "did not cause undue attention either on the post or with the authorities at the War Department." During that initial wave, the flu spread from numerous American military camps to the civilian population located mostly in the eastern states. And while dozens of these training camps reported the flu, "infected soldiers were still being transported overseas in significant numbers."[16]

Among the French soldiers, the first flu case was reported on April 10, and the disease soon made its way to the battlefront. By early May, "influenza was firmly established in Europe." In June, it peaked in Great Britain and had begun to appear in Japan and China. It had also spread to the Allied troops on the Western Front. While "extraordinarily contagious," the disease was described as "a mild strain that did not seriously affect the activities of the American Expeditionary Forces (AEF) in France." Wartime censorship limited public awareness of the disease among the Allied countries. That situation changed in the early summer. By then, the virus had "jumped the Pyrenees Mountains and sickened a large segment of the Spanish population," including Spain's King Alfonso XIII and his cabinet. The Spanish press—not subject to censorship since its country was not at war—"reported its health problems to the world." That is how the 1918 pandemic became known as the "Spanish influenza" or, in shortened form, the "Spanish flu."[17]

By July 1918, there were reports indicating that the flu epidemic had ended. During this respite, which lasted about a month, the virus mutated and became much more deadly. In early August, it resurfaced in Switzerland, thus marking the beginning of the second wave. This "new and more lethal strain" arrived in the United States soon thereafter. Camp Devens—an Army training base 35 miles from Boston—and the Boston-area civilian population were the first places to be hit. By September, the virus "had rapidly spread through naval training facilities in Boston, Philadelphia, Quantico, and the nation's largest naval training base at Great Lakes in Illinois." With respect to Army camps, "the epidemic travelled from the northeast to west and south." It struck at Camp Dix, New Jersey, Camps Wheeler and Greenleaf, Georgia, Camp Dodge, Iowa and Camp Kearney, California. Among both Army and Navy facilities in the United States, the influenza rates "exhibited extraordinary variability," and at least one study of Army camps provided evidence that infection rates "were related to camp conditions."[18]

One of many examples illustrates the disease's devasting impact on the United States' civilian population during the flu's second wave. A Navy ship from Boston carried the virus to the Navy shipyard in Philadelphia in early September. Sailors got sick and began dying in increasing numbers. Despite these circumstances, Wilmer Krusen, the city's public health director, assured Philadelphians he would "'nip the epidemic in the bud.'" Doctors urged Krusen to cancel a large Liberty Loan parade scheduled for September 28. He refused to do so. Doctors also convinced news reporters to write stories about the danger. But editors refused to run those stories, and they would not print cautionary letters from doctors. The parade proceeded on schedule. A widespread epidemic followed. Krusen "finally and belatedly ordered all schools closed and banned all public gatherings." But it was too late. The Philadelphia epidemic had taken hold. On its worst day, 759 people died. When it had finally run its course, more than 12,000 Philadelphians had lost their lives to the virus. Nearly all of them had died in six weeks.[19]

During the first week in October, the U.S. Public Health Service "reported that influenza was prevalent in forty-three states and the District of Columbia." A similar situation occurred with respect to American soldiers fighting in Europe. General John J. Pershing—who commanded the AEF in France—observed that incidents of the flu among his troops had "reached significant proportions" in the fall. During October's first week, over 16,000 new cases were reported. And by the time the war ended on November 11, "nearly 70,000 American soldiers were treated for the disease." Then in the late fall of 1918, the influenza "seemed to disappear" again.[20]

A third flu wave returned in January 1919. It "was lethal by any standard except the second wave." After it ended in the spring "by running its course without significant human intervention," the virus "did not go away." Instead, it lost "its extraordinary lethality, partly because many human immune systems now recognized it and partly because it lost the ability to easily invade the lungs. No longer a bloodthirsty murderer, it evolved into a seasonal influenza."[21]

The statistics regarding this disease starkly confirm its horrible impact on the United States. In 1918, the country's population was 103.2 million. A total of 25.8 million Americans contracted the disease, and between 670,000 and 675,000 died from it. Twenty percent of those deaths occurred in children age five or under. Life expectancy dropped by 12 years. With respect to military deaths, "more American soldiers, sailors, and Marines would succumb to influenza and pneumonia than would die on the industrialized battlefields of the Great War." One study calculated that of the 115,660 servicemen who died in World War I, 57,460 died of the flu, 50,280 died in battle, and 7,920 died from other causes.[22]

THE MARINE BARRACKS AT MARE ISLAND reacted to the flu outbreak by imposing a quarantine in late September, 1918. Francis assured his mother that "every precaution" was being taken while his unit was "deprived of all shore liberty & confined to the Island." As examples of these "precautions," he noted that the bunks had been moved apart, hats were required to be on at all times—"even when marching to mess hall"—and no indoor gatherings "of any sort" were allowed. On a personal level, he claimed to have "more pep last week than for quite a while—and 'pep' is an anti-symptom to the depression of grippe or similar diseases." He was surprised to learn from his dad that the School of Mines in Rapid City had reported 85 cases out of 125 students, and he expressed the hope that "the Spanish flu doesn't hit D.W.U." And although the flu "hasn't been very startling" among the Marines, the base had become "a sort of mad house of restlessness," because "pay day & no liberty of any sort makes a bunch of men nervous!"[23]

After finishing "chow" on the evening of October 6, Francis and his training section marched five miles out to the rifle range. They carried their fully-loaded packs with them and expected to be there from two to four weeks. Two days later, Francis wrote home and described his initial experiences. He had spent the first day on the firing line—lying down in the dirt and "shooting... 500 range slow fire." He reported doing "only moderately well." On the second day, he and other members of his section were "in the butts—marking targets." This duty was "pretty soft." Francis "had general charge over 4 targets—with 2 men to each one—so it was sit down most of the time[.]" Being on the range was "much like camping out—eat in open air with our mess kits—not a modern Hotel system—but eats are good and plenty of them." By the end of the second day, Francis was so "dirty enuf &

needing a shave enuf" that he decided to walk back to the barracks. There he would "indulge in a shower bath—a good shave & some clean clothes" and would mail "some letters for several of the fellows." He returned to the range for the next several days, and on October 17, he qualified as a marksman with the M1903 Springfield rifle.[24]

Meanwhile, by mid-October, the flu had hit "hard" at the Rapid City Deaconess Hospital where Herbert worked. In a letter to one of the hospital's subscribers, he noted that "all the Force in the Kitchen and Laundry have been down with it and all of the Nurses but Two besides Miss Wade." To fill in for these sick staff workers, Mary worked in the kitchen, and Herbert "helped wash dishes and scrubb/sic/ floors." The letter asked the subscriber to pay the balance of her subscription as soon as she could, noting that "having this 'Flu'" had caused the hospital's expenses "to run up very heavy while our income from all sources is very slight."[25]

The Spanish flu was also a prominent topic in Francis's November 1 letter to his sister Esther. He wrote that

> We are under quarantine and have been for a month. That makes us all pretty tired of this island and we should all like a change of scenery.
>
> * * *
>
> Here there have been no Marines died of the Flu although there have been several who have had it. Quite a few sailors have died. You would laugh tho to see us all wearing masks. We have all had three vaccine shots in our arms, and get our throats sprayed twice a day. So, we really shouldn't get sick.[26]

Francis also admitted to Esther that he was "feeling some blue" about not getting promoted. He explained:

> I was the last instructor appointed in this company so was naturally the last one up for promotion. Today,--or rather a couple

of days ago the entire list of instructors in the company (that is those who had made good) had their names turned in for promotion. My name was clear at the bottom. The company is allowed only so many men as actual corporals,--that is with chevrons. The quota was filled two from the bottom so there were two of us who did not get a chance at the examination to be given for actual promotion.

So here I am after five months here—with nothing to show for it seemingly. Of course I haven't had things so awfully bad since I have been instructor,—for I have gotten out of all the dirty work, and then also I get a chance to run a bunch of men around. But actually I don't get the extra pay I should.

And he made it plain to her that he still wanted to get into the fight: "I am trying hard to get off on the next detail for the east coast. It looks as tho the war would be over before long and if I don't get to France soon,--I never will. So I am hoping to leave if possible with the next bunch." Francis was correct that the "war would be over before long." It ended ten days later.[27]

THE QUARANTINE WAS FINALLY LIFTED at Mare Island in mid-November. Francis celebrated by leaving the island, going to a movie, and having "a taste of some home cooking at the Vallejo 'Y' grill." He reported receiving a letter from Harold Card that was written in France on October 22, and he admitted feeling "envious" that Harold had engaged in "actual fighting" and he had not. In the first few weeks after the war ended, Francis was uncertain about his future. Since he was "what is known as a 'Duration of the War' man," the Marines could keep him in the service "for at least 6 months from declaration of peace." But if he were released before February 1, 1919, he expressed an interest in going to graduate school at Stanford for the second semester. As things developed, those plans changed.[28]

Francis spent Thanksgiving Day in San Francisco. He had been "invited to dinner thru the Defender's Club [for enlisted men, located in Vallejo] to a home where a boy had gone to the service." He enjoyed a good meal and visit, but again expressed concern about his future: "One surely wonders what is going to happen—But guess he can only eat, sleep, and wait."[29]

Sometime between Thanksgiving and December 8, the flu quarantine had been reimposed on Mare Island. On the 8th, "the entire company was marched down to the hospital for the taking of our second throat cultures. We've had one—3 'negatives' release from the quarantine. But even if no 'positives' show up it will be a week to ten days yet." Commenting further about the flu, Francis noted that "it seems to be coming back pretty strong in many places—Frisco is wearing masks once more—... Nelson, my side kick here, whose mother & sister are alone in Denver—both have it now in its reappearance there." And he added that he had not "heard any definitive word as to discharges yet."[30]

On December 15, Francis was reassigned as Company Clerk. That position was available because the head clerk became acting first sergeant and the other clerk decided to go to officers' training school. Francis volunteered to take this job because "there wasn't any immediate prospect of there being more in my section (the 5th) to drill," and the position offered "more work and responsibility right now than there would be just bumming the time away as mail orderly or something like that." A board of officers had recommended him for the Officers' Training Corps, but Francis "didn't push the matter for I had in my application for discharge and think it preferable to going into the service for from 2 years to a lifetime just for the sake of a commission." If the war had still been on, he would "like nothing better than the chance to try for a commission but it's different now. There were several other fellows who had a chance to be appointed and turned it down also." As of December 22, he still had heard "nothing official regarding discharges[.]"³¹

Francis most likely spent Christmas Day in San Jose with his friend Lawrence Nelson and Nelson's relatives. He missed not being back in South Dakota for the holidays and knew he would not "feel the atmosphere of it like I did for so many years at home—or with anticipation which I did when at college." Given "that Uncle Sam's pocketbook isn't big enuf to pay us enuf to properly fill ours for buying gifts," he was only able to afford "merely a souvenir" gift for the family. But "in spite of the lack of many costly presents this year, I think it is to be the gladdest holiday season the world has known in centuries. True many homes will feel a burden they didn't a year ago,--but more will feel the shadow lifted."³²

On December 30, 1918, the Major General Commandant of the Marine Corps ordered that 53 Marines stationed at Mare Island—including Francis Case and Lawrence Nelson—be discharged "for convenience of Government." Company D's Commanding Officer, Second Lieutenant W. R. Affleck, carried out this command, and Francis was honorably discharged on January 15, 1919. Despite his regrets at never seeing combat, he achieved a very respectable military record. After being on active duty for only two months, he became a drill instructor in August and volunteered to be Company Clerk in December. His manner of performing both of these "details" was rated as "Excellent." His professionalism and conduct—assessed on December 31, 1918, and again on January 15, 1919—were given a "5" rating in all three of the categories graded: Military Efficiency, Obedience, and Sobriety. (A rating from 4.5 to 5 was considered to be "Excellent.") His record noted that he committed "No Offence" while serving with Company D. Finally, his Honorable Discharge stated that his character was "Excellent." Two years to the day after he was discharged, Francis was awarded the Good Conduct Medal. Its accompanying certificate proclaimed that his enlistment in the Marines was "distinguished for

OBEDIENCE, SOBRIETY, INDUSTRY, COURAGE, CLEANLINESS, and PROFICIENCY."[33]

Shortly after his discharge, Francis returned to Rapid City. He came "direct from Mare Island, Cal." and arrived in the evening on January 20. Soon thereafter, he left for Mitchell to join the Wesleyan faculty there. And several years later, he would rejoin the Marines as a commissioned officer in the Marine Corps Reserve.[34]

CHAPTER 6

RETURN TO ALMA MATER

Prof. Case... briefly reviewed a few of the main points to be observed in working up a debate speech and gave the girls as nearly as possible a general idea of the mode of procedure.

—*The Phreno Cosmian*

Ten days after returning from his "blue gumbo" car trip that sent Francis to the Marines, Leland graduated from Rapid City High School. His class was "composed of 18 young men and 21 young women." The commencement program was held in the high school auditorium on June 13. Dr. Harry Gage, president of Huron College, gave the commencement address titled "Present Day Leadership." School superintendent R. B. Irons handed out the diplomas, and "Rev. H. L. Case" gave the benediction. Leland had decided to follow his brother's footsteps and attend Dakota Wesleyan. After graduation, he lived at home that summer and worked for the university as a member of its Student Campaign for New Students.[1]

Leland had also opted to enlist in the U.S. Students' Army Training Corps (SATC) when he began college. Francis had urged him to join and "to try for a commission—preferably in the Engineer Corps." The SATC was a program established by the War Department sometime during the summer of 1918. Its stated purpose, according to a government pamphlet, was

> 'to provide for the very important needs of the army for highly trained men as officers, engineers, doctors, chemists and administrators of every kind. The importance of this need cannot be too strongly emphasized. The plan is an attempt to mobilize and develop the brain power of the young men of the country for those services which demand special training. Its object is to prevent the premature enlistment for active service of these men who could by extending the period of their college training multiply manifold their value to their country.'[2]

Dakota Wesleyan had originally planned to start its fall quarter on September 9. (The school had previously decided to switch from a semester system to a quarter system, and thereby became the first college in South Dakota to adopt what Wesleyan claimed to be "the latest and most approved method of division of the college year.") At the end of August, President Schermerhorn announced that rather than starting school on September 9, it would begin on the 18th instead. His stated reasons for choosing the latter date were that it would be "more satisfactory on account of the labor conditions brought about by the war," and "it will allow greater opportunity for giving publicity to the advantages that the Student Army Training Corps will afford for young men students."[3]

An example of "publicity" favorable to the SATC appeared in the *Rapid City Daily Journal* a week later. An article titled "Free College Training at Dakota Wesleyan U." began by stating "Young men college students, 18 and over, will receive free board, lodging, tuition, uniforms, and equipment besides getting a regular private's pay at Dakota Wesleyan University, due to the organization of the Students Army Training Corps." It went on to inform the reader that "members of the Corps are in active service of the U.S. Army and will receive collegiate and special military training to fit them for an officers' training camp. Male students 18 and over in the preparatory department also receive especial advantages." The article concluded by noting that the SATC program provided "wonderful opportunities for young men" and that Dr. W. D. Schermerhorn could be contacted at Mitchell for further information.[4]

WESLEYAN'S DATE FOR ITS SCHOOL opening was postponed a second time and moved to October 1. This change was made to accommodate the federal government, which had decided to designate that day for a simultaneous nationwide observance and SATC-induction ceremony. These exercises would involve "more than 500 colleges and universities throughout the United States" and would result in 150,000 student volunteers joining the SATC. So at 11:00 a.m. on that date, 85 SATC recruits at Wesleyan—including Leland—"stood in formation in front of Science Hall and saluted the flag while the Mitchell Municipal Band played the Star-Spangled Banner." Then the recruits pledged "their manhood and their lives in honor and defense of their country" and became soldiers on active duty. Patriotic messages from President Wilson and military officers were also read during the ceremony. The Science Hall's basement was converted into the SATC's barracks. Later, when men from the Academy who were at least 18 years old were allowed to join, additional living quarters—known as "Barracks II"—were added.[5]

As previously noted, one of Francis's letters written to Mary while he was in the Marines expressed his "hope [that] the Spanish flu doesn't hit D.W.U." Unfortunately, it did. By October 15, Mitchell reported 47 cases of influenza. Seventeen of those cases were SATC students, and 11 were women who lived in Graham Hall. The school suspended classes and imposed a quarantine on that day, and Mitchell's motion-picture theaters were shut down. A few days later, churches were forbidden from holding services. As of October 18, approximately

200 cases existed in Mitchell, but the rate of new ones appeared to be slowing down. On the 22nd, Harold Gage—a sophomore SATC student and captain of the football team—died of flu-related pneumonia. Despite his death, local health officials asked the SATC to resume training—based on the belief that exercise in the open air might be more healthful than staying indoors. No new cases were reported in Mitchell on November 1, and most patients were getting better. The worst of the pandemic appeared to have passed.[6]

Ten days later, the armistice was signed, and the World War was over. People in Mitchell "flooded the streets of the city in the early morning hours of Nov. 11 to celebrate," and they "repeated the festivities the next day." On November 18, the college lifted its quarantine and resumed normal activities. Local high schools, movie theaters, and churches were also reopened.[7]

The fall festivities had obviously been disrupted by Wesleyan's 34-day suspension. Before the pandemic, the football team had anticipated a busy and successful season. The "largest and best schools of South Dakota" were on the schedule, including "the University of South Dakota, Brookings, Huron, and Yankton." Kenneth Harkness, who had previously been named captain-elect for the 1918 season, was serving as a lieutenant in the SATC program at the School of Mines in Rapid City and was no longer with the team. Sophomore Harold Gage, who had played on the team as a freshman, had been selected as captain to replace Harkness. But as noted above, Gage died on October 22. And many others on the team were "taken sick." Nevertheless, when the college reopened on November 18, the coach announced that the team would play the University of South Dakota at Vermillion on Saturday, the 23rd. After a sluggish start by both teams "on a wet slippery field," the Coyotes made steady gains in the second half and ended up winning 33-0. It was the only game Wesleyan would play during the 1918 season.[8]

The day after the football game, a memorial service was held in the college chapel to dedicate Wesleyan's second service flag. As previously mentioned, the first service flag was dedicated during Washington's Birthday celebration in February. The two flags combined now contained 333 stars, and 11 of them were gold. A SATC bugler opened the proceedings by playing the Army assembly call. The congregation sang a hymn, and Dr. Schermerhorn gave a scripture reading and prayer. Then students unfurled the new flag and "read the names of all the new stars." After an address given by the pastor of Mitchell's Baptist Church, Dr. Gilliland read the names of each gold star and "spoke a few words in memor[y] of each man." Tributes to Corporal Harold Gage and Sergeant Carroll West were included in that speech. West had come to Wesleyan as YMCA general secretary in the fall of 1916. About a year later, he left the college to do YMCA war secretarial work. He subsequently enlisted in the Army and became a member of a machine gun battalion. Sergeant West died of his wounds in France on October 2, 1918. After Dr. Gilliland made his remarks, sophomore Irene Knott read her class's resolutions that honored Harold Gage. Following that reading, the congregation sang a second hymn. Dr. Schermerhorn closed the meeting with the benediction.[9]

AFTER THE ARMISTICE WAS SIGNED, the War Department decided it was necessary to "immediately discontinue all military preparations not clearly needed." Consequently, on November 26, the federal government announced that the SATC would be demobilized. When word of the impending demobilization reached the Wesleyan SATC company, most of the men were "ready to leave." As of late November, none had been paid, no rifles had been received, and many had never gotten a uniform (although Leland did). After the war ended, the unit's morale steadily declined, and by early December over half the men had stopped attending classes. The federal government ultimately ordered that Wesleyan's unit be formally disbanded on December 21.

That order spawned a new meaning to the letters SATC among the school's student-soldiers: "Stick Around Till Christmas."[10]

The *Phreno Cosmian* was another Wesleyan institution disrupted by the flu pandemic. No issues were published during October or November. The first issue did not emerge until December 12. The lead editorial in that paper declared that "the most trying time that has ever come to Wesleyan is the present year." It went on to observe that "many of the upper-class men have been taken away to the army," and "those who are left, and were eligible joined the S.A.T.C. which allowed no time for outside activities." As a result, Wesleyan was "practically destitute of men who can engage in extra-curricular work, and all the responsibility that has been carried by many in the past years has fallen upon a few." Due to these circumstances, the editorial asked its readers to be patient for the next few weeks, and "if the Phreno Cosmian does not come up to your highest expectations, remember the situation, and give us, the editors, time to get settled."[11]

Leland—no doubt—had little time for "outside activities" that fall. But he did find time to become a new pledge in the Daedalian Literary Society. And shortly before the quarter ended, the freshman class elected him as its representative on the school's Forensic Board.[12]

The fall term came to an end during the third week in December. At the same time, the college's SATC unit was demobilized. The "formal demobilization of Wesleyan's soldier boys" occurred on Saturday, December 21. At the request of Mitchell's Chamber of Commerce, the unit "marched in a final parade down Sanborn Avenue and the main street of the city," and it "presented a splendid appearance." This was the first time that the "boys had been able to appear in their total strength, due largely to the influenza epidemic which so fiercely invaded their camp." Mr. W. R. Arnold—editor of the *Mitchell Republican*—addressed the group after the parade was over. His speech "expressed the appreciation of the people of Mitchell for the members of the corps." Following his remarks, "the men were guests of Manager Wm. Fraser at the Gale Theater."[13]

REGISTRATION FOR WESLEYAN'S SECOND QUARTER took place on Monday morning, December 30, and regular classes began that afternoon. Leland signed up for three courses: English, European history, and chemistry. Under the quarter system, each course was "concentrated" and "had five recitations a week." For living arrangements, he and his former SATC roommate Charles Spear decided to move into the newly-designated boys' dormitory—now known as Phillips Hall. This dorm, which had recently been given to Wesleyan by the late Rev. O.A. Phillips, was originally built as a rooming house, and it was located near the campus. When the SATC was at Wesleyan, the house was known as Barracks II, and over 30 student-soldiers lived there. Leland and Spear took a room in the basement. In return for "cleaning the place up" and "tending to the furnace," they were each paid about $5 a month and allowed to stay in the room for free. [14]

Leland also became a reporter for *The Mitchell Gazette*—a local weekly published in Mitchell. He covered "activities of the college campus" for the paper. During the month of January 1919, he made about $13 as a *Gazette* reporter. And he agreed to join the *Phreno* editorial staff during the winter quarter, where he provided stories as one of three "Campus Gossips" and later reported on the YMCA's activities.[15]

When the year 1919 arrived, Wesleyan took immediate steps to put the "irregularities and uncertainties and sickness" of 1918 behind it and return to normal college life. On January 3, Dr. J. Charles Hazzard—now head of Wesleyan's forensic department—called a meeting of the forensic board to determine whether the school should engage in public-speaking activities with other colleges during the winter quarter. At that meeting, "it was unanimously decided to have intercollegiate debate and oratory at Wesleyan this year if 'the powers that be' will only permit." Dr. Hazzard promised "to devote every moment of his time to put out a winning team[.]" He also stated that "the Academy teams... will commence their work immediately preparatory to at least a triangular and possibly a quadrangle debate with other schools in their class within the state."[16]

One day later, Leland, his roommate Charles, and seven other students were formally initiated into the Daedalian Literary Society. The Thalians witnessed the ceremony and "added their welcome to the new men in the society." After the evening program, the two groups played games and listened to music until 10:30 p.m., when they "started home feeling that we knew each other better." The students also got welcome news early in January when they learned it "was altogether possible" that Coach Ray McLean "would return to us as soon as he is released from the service." His wife wrote a short letter to Dr. Schermerhorn that stated her husband "'expected to march on to Germany after Thanksgiving,'" and she was sure he "'will be glad to return to Dakota Wesleyan if he can only get back in time.'"[17]

Two weeks after Wesleyan decided to take part in intercollegiate debates and oratorical contests, a meeting among the participating colleges was held in Mitchell to discuss and decide how these events would be structured in 1919. Representatives from Huron, Sioux Falls, State University, Yankton, and Wesleyan all attended. The first order of business was to select officers for the State Oratory and Debate League for 1919-20. Dr. Hazzard was elected president, Professor Lyons from State University became vice-president, and Yankton's coach Montgomery was chosen as secretary-treasurer. Since some colleges believed it would not be possible for them to field two men's teams, a proposal was made to allow "mixed teams" of men and women. That idea was voted down, and two alternative schedules were set—depending on whether certain schools could produce two "unmixed teams." The group also agreed to revive intercollegiate debates "among the girls of various colleges," and different debate questions for the men's and women's debates were adopted. With respect to Academy debates, a tentative schedule and separate debate question were agreed upon. Finally, it was decided to drop intercollegiate oratory entirely for the year. The committee concluded that due to the "scarcity of men in college," it would be "almost impossible" for some of the contending schools to produce an orator plus two debate teams.[18]

On January 27, Dr. Schermerhorn returned to the campus after addressing the students at Simpson College in Iowa. The Wesleyan students "were overjoyed" when he officially announced that Francis would be there soon to "take up the work of debate coach." He was also hired to assist in the student campaign to recruit new Wesleyanites. Four nights later, he arrived in Mitchell on the evening train. On the previous day, Wesleyan's forensic board had decided there would be no intersociety debates for the college men that year. In the past, those debates were used to select the two intercollegiate teams. But for the 1919 season, those teams would be selected by tryouts, which were scheduled for Saturday, March 1. The new debate coach would therefore have the month of February to work with those students who wanted to be on one of Wesleyan's intercollegiate debate teams.[19]

When Francis had been back at Wesleyan for a week, he assumed a duty that had nothing to do with coaching debate. Instead, he served as chaperon for a sleigh ride with 51 members of the Thalian and Daedalian societies. The *Phreno Cosmian* provided a colorful account of that event. It began when four "well-packed bobs left College Hall for the fairer and more distant climes." As the "merry bunch . . . glided through the falling snow," they filled the air with "joyous shouts," "college yells and songs," and "society yells." Francis acted as chaperon, and "a worthy chap he was. He not only kept the pep moving, but also kept an eagle eye out for any casual violations of social order. The party would have lost its significance had not the chaperon been there to perform his nice duties." At 10:00 p.m., "the party retired to the Widmann where everyone enjoyed a good oyster stew." After "the feed" was finished, the "company... broke up into its constituent parts and departed for home[.]"[20]

FRANCIS CONTINUED TO ENGAGE IN non-debate activities during the following week. For instance, on Wednesday, he filled in as coach and faculty representative for the Academy basketball team in its game at Fulton (outcome of game unknown). The next day he gave a toast at the Father and Son's Banquet, and that night he kept the score for Wesleyan's college basketball game against Yankton (which Wesleyan won 28 to 10). He gave a speech in the college chapel on Friday and taught a Sunday School class two days later. He also spent some time that week trying to get his "student campaign list lined up" but did not get "very far along" with that project. Despite these "interruptions," Francis made it a point to see Leland when he could and "hike around with him sometimes." He wrote to the Case family that Leland "is very well liked here and is considered a worth while personage in many things. He is creating a distinct place for himself and works to fill it." And the city editor for *The Mitchell Gazette* told Francis that Leland "'rings the bell everyday.'"[21]

Francis's first debate-related work occurred on Saturday, February 15. On that day, the two Academy literary societies—the Adelphians and the Amphictyons—held their annual inter-society debates. The question at issue was "Resolved: That all corporations engaged in interstate business be compelled to operate under a federal charter, constitutionally granted." The Adelphian team defended the negative position in the afternoon debate, and its other team argued for the affirmative in the evening contest. The Adelphians won both debates. Thereafter, the "committee of ranking judges"—composed of Francis, Dr. Hazzard, and two others—chose six men and two alternates to be inter-academy debaters. Five days later, Francis went to nearby Mt. Vernon to judge a debate between high school teams from Mt. Vernon and Fulton. Both were coached by his college classmates—Mildred

Test (for Mt. Vernon) and Walter Ludeman (for Fulton). Because Francis was the only judge, he "did some mighty close work." He did not know "how satisfactory it was," but since he awarded the decision to the home team, "everyone felt alright over there."[22]

The *Phreno Cosmian* issued its second "Special Patriotic Number" on February 27. (The first was published on February 21, 1918.) The February 27 version featured an editorial thanking Wesleyanites for their service, a poem about the service flag, photographs and an article about "Wesleyan's Gold Star Men," a photograph of Wesleyan's SATC unit, and a list titled "Wesleyan Men Who Entered the Service." That list now contained 395 men with a connection to the college. It included 12 who had lost their lives. These "gold star men" were listed at the top in alphabetical order. They were Daniel W. Bannister, John C. Berry, William Bradshaw, Capt. Peter Brethorst, Capt. Harvey W. Coacher, Segt. Harold Gage, William Jordan, Major Emil Laurson (later corrected to Lieut. Colonel Emil Laurson), Lieut. Roy McNaught, Arthur E. Shale (whose name had been added after Wesleyan dedicated its second service flag on November 24, 1918), R. Carroll Thompson, and Segt. Carroll B. West. Next came the names of the 383 "blue star men." Harold Card, Francis, and Leland, together with their respective units, appeared as follows: "Harold W. Card, 78th Co., 2nd Bat., 6th Reg., 2nd Div., U. S, Marine Corps, Germany; Francis H. Case, Co. D., U.S. Marine Corps, Marine Barracks, Mare Island, Calif.—Discharged; Leland D. Case, S.A.T.C. Dakota Wesleyan Univ.—Discharged."[23]

The men's tryouts for the intercollegiate debate teams were held as scheduled on Saturday, March 1, in the college auditorium. Thirteen students entered the contest, which was held in two separate sessions. Seven speakers presented their arguments in the afternoon, and the remaining six spoke in the evening. Francis presided over the afternoon contest, while Dr. Hazzard was the timekeeper. The two men reversed roles for the night session. After all the presentations were made, a three-man "committee of ranking judges" selected and ranked eight men (with two designated as alternates) for the squad. Leland, who gave his speech in the afternoon, was ranked third. The *Phreno* noted that he "displayed good possibilities" and "has a rich voice which adds much to his careful study of a subject."[24]

Francis also found time that afternoon to meet with "all girls who intended to try out for the intercollegiate teams." These women—about 30 in number—came from Wesleyan's freshmen, sophomore, junior and senior classes. At the meeting, "Prof. Case... briefly reviewed a few of the main points to be observed in working up a debate speech and gave the girls as nearly as possible a general idea of the mode of procedure." It was also officially decided that inter-class debates would be held. The sophomores had their class try-out debates on March 10. Eleven women spoke that evening, and eight were selected (including two alternates) to go against the freshmen teams. Two days later, the freshmen competed in the college chapel for spots on their teams. Nine women—many "who had never heard a debate before"—participated in the competition. After all presentations were made, it was decided that these nine debaters would be split into three freshmen teams, the sophomores would be allowed to assemble a third team, and the freshmen-sophomore debates would occur "sometime during the week after vacation." Francis was one of two judges for each of those tryout sessions. There were no team tryouts for juniors or seniors, presumably because not enough women in those classes chose to participate.[25]

In mid-March, Francis "changed rooming places" and was "now back at the old Club house which has been fixed up, redecorated and painted." He occupied a "little northwest room" upstairs, which was "quite cozy." This arrangement was "really more satisfactory than the other place and .75 cheaper a week."[26]

The *Phreno* published its last paper for the winter quarter on March 20. It was prepared by freshmen class members and titled "Freshman

Souvenir Edition." That edition contained several articles emphasizing the freshmen's participation in, and contributions to, college life. But it also included stories about events and activities that involved all the university's classes and select members of its faculty. Leland's name appeared at the top of three editors listed under "Freshman Staff," and he apparently had major input into the paper's production. His older brother, who spent three years on the *Phreno* staff during his Wesleyan student days, noted that "Leland edited the best class Phreno, I have ever seen published."[27]

DR. SCHERMERHORN RECEIVED TERRIBLE NEWS on March 27, when a message informed him that coach Ray McLean had died "at Coblenz, Germany, after an attack of bronchial pneumonia." The message came from McLean's wife, whom he married immediately after leaving Wesleyan in May, 1918. Soon after his marriage, he enlisted in the field artillery corps and was sent to France. He fought in the Battle of Argonne but "escaped without a wound." After the armistice was signed, he was sent to Germany with the army of occupation. He had hoped to be discharged from there and returned to the United States by summer. A resolution of sympathy to his relatives—signed by Dr. Schermerhorn and Student Association President Marion Walrath—was unanimously passed at the regular college chapel service on Thursday morning. After setting forth four "whereas clauses" that acknowledged McLean's death and praised his life, the resolution concluded by declaring: "Be it Resolved by the Faculty and Students of Dakota Wesleyan University, that we express this appreciation of the friendship of such a man and extend to his bereaved relatives our most sincere sympathy in this, our time of mutual sorrow."[28]

Wesleyan's winter quarter ended, and after a four-day vacation, the spring quarter started either on Monday, March 31, or shortly thereafter. Francis was involved in two debate contests at the beginning of the spring term. The first event was the inter-academy debates against

Yankton and Huron. On the Friday night before they occurred, Francis worked over his teams' "debate speeches until nearly four in the morning." Both debates were held on April 1 in the evening. The question at issue, as previously noted, concerned whether there should be federal control over corporations who engaged in interstate business. Wesleyan's affirmative team met Yankton's negative team on the former's home floor, and the single judge awarded the victory to Wesleyan. Its negative team—accompanied by Dr. Hazzard—travelled to Huron. The opposing Huron team—consisting of two women and one man—upheld the affirmative and won the debate. On the following Monday, Dr. Hazzard was informed "that one of the Huron trio had been found ineligible to debate, and the contest was therefore forfeited to Wesleyan." Dr. Hazzard offered to debate the question again, but Huron declined the offer. Its forfeit therefore stayed in place, and the Wesleyan Academy won its third consecutive Inter-Academy Championship.[29]

The second "debate event" occurred two days after the Academy's victory. These debates were between Wesleyan women in the freshmen and sophomore classes. Their purpose was to determine who would represent the college in the upcoming intercollegiate debates against Huron and Yankton. Both classes fielded three squads, with three members on each team. The question at issue was "Resolved that for a period of five years following the signing of the peace such restrictions should be placed on all immigration as are now placed upon the citizens of China." The first debate began at 8:30 a.m. in the college chapel. Defending the negative, the freshman team won that contest in a two-to-one decision. In the afternoon, the sophomore debaters again argued the affirmative position. They won all three votes from the judges. Finally, the third freshman team, upholding the affirmative, again won a split decision in the evening contest. After the three debates were concluded, Dr. Hazzard and Francis chose six debaters and two alternates to be on the Wesleyan women's intercollegiate team. The six-member squad included four freshmen and two sophomores. One of the alternates was also a freshman, and the other was a junior "who tried out individually for the team."[30]

Francis was "very, very busy" during the following week. He turned down various requests "all the time," including those from nearby high schools that had asked him to work on improving their students' oration skills. On one of those days, he intended to meet with Leland but was not even able to "sit down and talk to him for 10 minutes." This made Leland "sort of sore" at him. Carol's 16th birthday was on Saturday, April 12. At 11:30 p.m., Francis finally found the time to write her "before the day is over." In that letter, he asked Carol to thank Esther for her "exceptionally good" box of homemade candy. He also described the birthday present he would be sending—"a gold lavalier and chain—the lavalier being the Marine Corps Emblem with a pearl pendant below." The letter ended with words of praise and support: "Here's a host of love to you from your proud brother—I know you are a really good girl who is living a happy helpful life.—and just remember that one person you can always count on to back you to the limit is your big brother."[31]

Perhaps inspired by her younger sister, Carol sent both brothers her version of homemade candy the following week. They each thanked her in separate letters written on Easter Sunday. Francis described it as "mighty fine." He shared it with the women's debate teams, which "pronounced it very good." Leland's response to her gift resorted to alliteration: "That candy was simply spiffyspif splendid." He also "passed it around" to his fellow students in Phillips Hall, and they said "she must be some candy maker, which of course wasn't news to me."[32]

EARLIER IN THE SPRING, WESLEYAN had challenged Morningside College to a men's single or double debate. Morningside accepted the challenge, and it was agreed that a dual debate would take place sometime during the first half of April. That timeframe was later extended, and the date was finally set for Saturday, April 26. The question at issue was the same one chosen for the South Dakota intercollegiate debates at the meeting held in Mitchell on January 17: "Resolved: That the Federal Government should require every able bodied man between the ages of 16 and 21 to take at least one year of military training. Constitutionally granted, Congressional action waived." Both debates would be held in the evening, with Wesleyan's negative team travelling to Sioux City and its affirmative team meeting Sioux City on Wesleyan's home floor.[33]

Wesleyan's negative team—composed of Leland, sophomore Virgil Garrett, and sophomore Louis Todnem—took the morning train to Sioux City on the day before the debate. Francis arrived on the evening train and joined the team at the Hotel Martin. A few hours before the debate commenced, Francis wrote a letter to his "Homefolks" while the debaters were taking a "cat nap." He began by noting that the team was "enjoying the trip," and it was the first one "for Leland to a city any larger than Mankato." Then he provided an assessment of the team and its prospects for victory: "Just now I think our chances of winning are alrite. If the fellows are beaten it will simply be lack of experience that does it. They have their constructive speeches in good shape and should do good work in rebuttal." On an entirely different subject, he stated he had "received notice of election to a fellowship at Northwestern for next year carrying $300.00. If I accept it I will take part of my work in Garrett & part in the History Department." In addition, he "turned down the tuition scholarship at Chicago—didn't feel keen about going there for various reasons," and he had not "heard from the Leland Stanford application as yet." The letter concluded on an optimistic note: "Close for now—this is before the debates. I expect we'll win both—wait and see!"[34]

As the debates unfolded, Wesleyan did not achieve the success it was used to achieving. At Morningside, "the debate was very close," but the home affirmative team "won the decision through a greater ability as a team to talk more fluently and easily." After the contest was over, the single judge (from the University of South Dakota) made a positive remark about Leland's performance, declaring that he "open[ed] the debate in a better fashion than that of the affirmative." And the *Phreno* reporter who covered the story had this to say about Leland's argument in rebuttal: "Altho it was his first time in a college debate, Case did some splendid extemporaneous work and gives promise of being one of the best debaters Wesleyan has had." At Wesleyan, the home affirmative team lost to the visitors' negative squad. The judge for that debate (Dean of the University of South Dakota Law College) awarded the decision to Morningside "on the grounds that the affirmative had not shown that their plan alone would meet the existing conditions, and therefore had not established the burden of proof."[35]

Three nights later, the Wesleyan debate teams were competing again—this time in the South Dakota men's intercollegiate triangular debates with Yankton and Huron. The question at issue (advocating compulsory military-training) was the same one used in the Morningside debates. Wesleyan's negative team—now consisting of Case, sophomore Frank Dobrovolny (instead of Virgil Garrett, who had debated at Morningside), and Todnem—travelled to Yankton. Its performance was reported to be "clearly superior in argument and delivery," and the judges awarded Wesleyan a two-to-one decision. The tables were turned on Wesleyan's home floor, when its affirmative team lost to Huron's negatives—also in a split decision. Finally, in the third debate between Yankton and Huron at Huron, the Yankton negative team was awarded yet another two-to-one decision. Since each of the three teams scored one victory by the same two-to-one margin, the 1919 South Dakota men's collegiate debate championship ended in a three-way tie with no outright winner.[36]

Dakota Wesleyan's faculty decided that May 1—also known as Arbor Day—would be observed as a holiday at the college, and no classes would be held. Francis was a member of a five-person committee that planned the events for the day, which was dedicated "to the memory of the men who have fought and died for the principles of Americanism." In the morning, men from the Academy, each college class, and the faculty planted 72 donated honey locust trees in holes that were previously dug in a pre-arranged pattern. They were placed in two rows on either side of the u-shaped memorial drive between College Hall and the new Morrow Gymnasium. At 2:30 p.m., Wesleyanites gathered in the college chapel. There, several classes read short memorial papers, and Mitchell's Dr. G. T. Norton gave the Arbor Day address. Following these presentations, the Wesleyan baseball team played its first game of the season. It was against Northern Normal of Aberdeen. Wesleyan won by "a one sided score of 15 to 2."[37]

On the following evening, the last college debate for the season was held in Wesleyan's Science Hall chapel. It featured the women's teams from Wesleyan and Yankton. When the six Wesleyan women were chosen for two intercollegiate teams back in early April, the forensic council had planned to have a triangular contest among Huron, Yankton, and Wesleyan. But shortly before the debates were to occur, Huron announced that it was unable to "put two teams in the triangle" and pulled out of the competition. So, it was ultimately decided to have only a single contest between Wesleyan and Yankton. That meant that three of the six students selected for the Wesleyan intercollegiate squad were not able to participate in an intercollegiate debate that year. The Wesleyan team chosen to compete against Yankton included one sophomore and two freshmen. It was the first intercollegiate debate for all three. They upheld the affirmative position on the restricted-immigration question previously used in the women's tryouts. A single judge awarded the decision to Yankton. As recounted in the *Phreno*, "the debate... was extremely close and in the opinion of the judge was not decided until the last rebuttal speeches had been given."[38]

With the debate season over, Francis was now able to devote more time to coaching and conducting rehearsals for the Academy's senior class play. Ruth Goodrich—his college classmate and current English teacher at the Academy—assisted him in these efforts. The play was a three-act comedy titled "What Would a Gentleman Do?" A few weeks before it was to be performed, the senior class unanimously decided to use the play's proceeds for a memorial gift to Wesleyan. That class would become the first one from the Academy to make such a gesture to the college.[39]

The play was presented at Mitchell's City Hall on May 14 at 8:15 p.m. The *Phreno* reported that it was "well attended" and "each player showed skill in acting his part, owing to the careful training of Mr. Case and Miss Goodrich." The performance also garnered praise from the town's newspapers. Mitchell's *Daily Republic* said, "'it was one of the most credited amateur productions which have been seen in Mitchell this season.'" And *The Mitchell Gazette* described the play as "a pleasing departure from the usual amateur efforts." For its gift to the university, the class wanted to provide "something useful as well as ornamental." With these goals in mind, it was decided that a "concrete walk" that connected the president's home to the nearby "main walk" would be constructed. This new walk would divide 16 feet before it reached the main one and thereby form an "equilateral triangle." A flower vase, and an engraving that included the names of the 23 seniors and their advisor, would be placed inside the triangle. When it announced this memorial, the 1919 Academy class expressed its hope that future senior classes would "leave behind them some gift to the college."[40]

The final forensic event during the spring term was the Academy Oratorical Contest. This was the third year in a row that it was held. In late February, Francis "officially announced" that he intended "to make the 'Case Trophy' Academy Oratorical a permanent feature at Dakota Wesleyan." This year's contest—which took place in the chapel during the evening on June 5—had three participants. Charles Andreason, whose oration was titled "The American Mission," finished in first place. Second place went to Harry Wolcott, who spoke about "The Cataclysm of Imperialistic Culture." Francis presented the gold medal "trophy" to Andreason. But since only three students entered the competition, the contest's regulations specified that no silver medal be awarded.[41]

During late May and early June, several Wesleyan faculty members gave commencement speeches at graduation ceremonies held in the state. President Schermerhorn was the "most in demand." He delivered addresses at two colleges and eight high schools that spring. Francis "filled engagements" at seven high schools, including "Belvidere, Pleasant Lake Consolidated, Tripp, Ravinia, Plain Center Consolidated, Philip and Viborg." His experience at Viborg—a small community located 60 miles southeast of Mitchell—was described in a letter he wrote to "Mother, Esther, Carol and Grandpa." He presented his address on June 12, and it was the last one he gave in his commencement "series." Although he "thot I did not do as well as at some places," the "sup't seemed pleased & said I had retrieved a commencement address for them since it had come into ill repute thru dry speeches[.]" To illustrate his point, the superintendent related that one of the recent speakers "had read a 2 hr. speech." During his presentation, Francis "thot the audience restless." But the superintendent "seemed to think that when some of the folks stood up in rear thruout without leaving that I had scored a triumph." It was "tremendously hot" the entire time, and Francis was "wringing wet when [he] sat down." Overall, he had "a good time" at Viborg but "was glad the series was over."[42]

Wesleyan's own "commencement week" took place from June 15 to June 18. It included all the usual activities—beginning with a baccalaureate service on Sunday and culminating with 75 graduates receiving their degrees or diplomas on Wednesday. The *Phreno* released its final edition for the spring term on the next day. That issue completed Volume XXX of the paper, which was "published under the most abnormal conditions in the history of the school." The 1918-19 school year had indeed forced Wesleyan to deal with "abnormal conditions" and suffer loss created by the war and the Spanish flu pandemic. By mid-June, the service flag now contained over 400 stars. Two of those were gold—one for Coach Ray McLean and another for former Wesleyan student Olin V. Dunn. Dunn died in France from pulmonary "trouble" and "an infection in the left eye—probably from mustard gas." And in addition to losing their football team captain, two women with Wesleyan connections died from the flu. They were sophomore Ada Ferguson, who succumbed on December 10, 1918, "after several days' illness," and Winnette Lindamood Wood, a former member of the class of '20 who "was taken ill . . . early in the fall" and passed away in mid-April, 1919.[43]

Despite the hardships and disruptions, Wesleyan could point to several positive developments achieved in the 1918-19 school year. Total enrollment for the year was 717. That was a 57 per cent increase over the previous year, and the increase was "found in all departments." The year 1919 marked the first time Wesleyan participated in intercollegiate basketball. The team finished with a seven-win-two-loss record and won the South Dakota Conference Collegiate Championship. The varsity baseball team, assembled in the spring, compiled a 4-1 record against two other colleges and two town teams. And although the college men's and women's debate teams managed only one victory between them, the Academy teams won their third consecutive championship.[44]

Sometime after receiving the offer for a graduate fellowship at Northwestern University, Francis "was also offered the Seabury Fellowship in World Politics at Leland Stanford." By mid-June, he had decided to accept the fellowship at Northwestern. He remained in Mitchell during the summer and continued to work on the Wesleyan student recruitment campaign. The job required frequent trips out of town to meet with potential "prospects," and he "generally hit 2 towns a day." By September, he was ready to move to Chicago and become a student again.[45]

CHAPTER 7

GRADUATE SCHOOL AND TRADE PAPER JOB IN THE WINDY CITY

It may seem that I am ambitious.... Yet I hope it is an ambition for greater usefulness. My only defense can be that ... if a man of 23 is content to do nothing better than he has already done, he isn't fit for any job. If at 23 he has quit dreaming he has failed to live up to the trust and responsibility which the race imposes upon youth. The farther we push back the age limit on vision, the more rapidly will civilization advance. To attain the complete virtues of age, the world must exhaust the ambitions of youth. If at 23 men were to become indifferent, this world would soon be a static, inert affair.

—Francis Case

Francis arrived in Chicago in mid-September. Soon thereafter, he was assigned to "a splendid room facing the lake" in a dormitory known as Shaffer Hall or Garrett Dorm "D." This dorm was in Evanston, Illinois, on the Northwestern University campus. (Evanston is situated on the north shore of Lake Michigan—12 miles north of downtown Chicago.) Francis registered for 20 hours of classes for the fall semester. Most of those were in Northwestern's Graduate School of History—with his "major work" concentrating on courses in Latin

American history. He also signed up for a class titled Principles of Religious Education.¹

THE EPWORTH LEAGUE WAS FOUNDED in 1889 as "a young people's service organization within the Methodist Episcopal Church." The name came from the town of Epworth, England, where Charles and John Wesley were born. Charles became the author of six thousand hymns—many of which are familiar to all Christians. John organized and led people who became known as Methodists. Upon its founding, the League adopted a constitution and the motto "Look Up, Lift Up." It was established "with two great purposes in mind: to get young Methodists involved in good works, and to train Christian soldiers for the ministry." Within ten years, "it claimed over 1.75 million members in 19,500 chapters internationally." In the United States, the Epworthians were organized into Junior League chapters and Senior League chapters. The junior members were girls and boys aged from 12 to 16. Their league was described as "a workshop for Christian character; a Junior training school for leaders in the Church so that the great to-morrow and its needs will be met by trained Christian men and women." According to the League constitution, the Senior chapters were "'as far as practicable... confined to persons between the ages of sixteen and thirty-five.'" Consistent with their goals of doing good works and training future ministers, the Senior chapters organized fellowship gatherings, literary events, lectures series and day camps for children. They also raised funds for, and became directly involved in, both local and foreign mission work. By 1920, there were 8,340 junior chapters (containing 202,426 members) and 14,814 senior chapters (that included 503,879 members) spread throughout the country.²

The *Epworth Herald* began in 1890. In its early days, it was known as "the official newspaper of the Epworth League in the northeastern United States." Published in Chicago, the paper was "intended for young Christians, who like fun and fellowship, but who like that the more because it is all a part of their religion." Its "one central business" was "to say a good word for Jesus Christ, and to encourage everybody to fall in love with him and his desires for our life and the world's life." By 1914, the paper had about 100,000 subscribers. Dan Brummitt, who had become the *Herald's* editor by that time, described his publication as follows: "first of all, and last of all, it is the trade paper of the Epworth League."[3]

In 1920, the paper's subscription price was "$1.50 a year in advance." The *Herald* was published each Saturday and contained 24 pages. Dan Brummitt continued to be its editor. Its regular features included a cover page that often displayed a large photograph; a column of jokes titled "A Little Jest and Jollity"; articles of current interest by the editor and stories by guest contributors; a column labelled "The Editor's Isle of Safety" that contained Brummitt's editorials; a devotional meetings page; a section titled "The Department Round Table" that reproduced articles supplied by the paper's readers; a section that described "What the League is Doing" in the northeast, Midwest, and western "areas" of the country; a section titled the "Junior Herald" featuring stories and advice for Junior League members; and lastly, a column designated as the "Post Card Confessional," which reprinted poems and amusing messages sent to the editor on postcards.[4]

On September 22, Francis began a part-time job at the *Herald* in its downtown Chicago office at 740 Rush Street. His main task was "working on the Subscription & Circulation." He worked on Tuesday and Thursday mornings and all day on Saturday, and he was paid $16 a week. His co-worker was a "Garrett man" with the last name of Browns, and "Brummitt is the boss." Brummitt generally used Francis's suggestions regarding advertising policy, so the latter felt "he must be earning a part of my salary anyway." After he had been with the *Herald* for about seven weeks, Francis and 14 others "acted as jurors or reviewers of the books which have been sent the Herald for review this fall." The review was held in the *Herald*'s office on November 8. Francis was quite impressed with the group, which included "a literary writer from a daily," "a society woman," a "man from 'Printer's Ink,'" Brummitt, and Dr. Charles E. Guthrie (General Secretary of the Epworth League). After the book selections were made, the reviewers adjourned to a "spiffy hotel" for a "big dinner party" that included "Oysters on half shell, etc.—etc."[5]

SOMETIME IN EARLY TO MID-NOVEMBER, Francis informed the Dean of Northwestern's Graduate School that he was interested in "the possibility of going into some phase of legal study." Dean J. A. James followed up by writing a letter that introduced Francis to J. H. Wigmore—Dean of the Northwestern University Law School. Francis then obtained the law school's "time schedule for the second quarter" of certain law courses, although he had previously written to a federal government employee that he "will probably get a master's degree" and planned on "going to law school next summer." In mid-December, a good friend wrote that he "was surprised" to learn that Francis had "law aspirations." Francis replied by stating: "I do not understand why you should be particularly surprised at my liking for the law. I sort of thot that followed from a love for debating, a love for history, political science, sociology and kindred subjects." He added that "I crave excitement, intellectual combat, and public speaking. Newspaper work would suit me fine were it not that one is not given opportunity for public speaking. Yet, as I may have written, I should try in time to secure an interest on a good paper."[6]

On December 20, Francis and his co-worker Browns were moved into a new office. A suite of offices had recently become available in the building, and the *Herald* "claimed one for its circulation department." It turned out to be the largest one in the suite, and Francis relished describing it to his family. He noted that the rooms were collectively labelled "'General Publishing Agents'" and featured several entrance doors. His new office was the first door on the right, which had a "full length panel of frosted glass" and was labelled "'Private.'" The office itself had "heavy oak chairs... with large oak tables, three mammoth windows, finely rugged floors, and... a giant totter chair, leather upholstered." He added that "when our hands become grimy with Chicago soot, we step over to the private wash closet in a corner of the room—where there is both cold and hot water." Francis was uncertain about "how long we shall reign in this majesty," and he predicted that "we might be back in the perfectly fine Epworth Herald editorial rooms, before long."[7]

As Christmas approached, he admitted that he was "terribly homesick," and as his family celebrated the holidays, he asked them to "realize just how much I'd like to be with you all." As things turned out, he celebrated Christmas at three different events. The first was a dinner party held on the 21st at the home of Professor Cox—described as "the man under whom I am taking my major work." Francis assumed it would be a "regular Sunday dinner" and was delighted to "find that it was their Christmas dinner," since the professor and his children would be gone "for most of the holidays." Three other guests attended, a five-course turkey dinner was served, and Francis felt "quite at home." He helped do the dishes when dinner was finished, and the group then went into the living room and "sat in a semi-circle before the fire place." Mrs. Cox played Christmas carols and "old tunes" on the piano, and the guests sang along as she did so. Francis left the gathering shortly after six, and "Mrs. Cox seemed very pleased when I told her I'd surely write my mother and tell her of the fine time I had had."[8]

The second and third holiday celebrations took place on Christmas day. One was held at the home of Dr. Ernest Burch, and the other at Professor Ernest Hahne's house. Burch and Hahne were on the faculty at Wesleyan while Francis was a student there. Both now taught at Evanston—Burch in the Garrett Biblical Institute and Hahne at the

School of Commerce in Northwestern's College of Liberal Arts. Francis described these events as "Wesleyan gatherings in both instances," and they contributed to his "very pleasant Christmas."⁹

His expectation that he would not be allowed to stay in his new *Herald* office turned out to be true. The "powers that be decided a great large office ... was entirely too great an outlay for young fellows who are down there but two days a week." Consequently, on December 30, "he was in for a moving job." With the assistance of two other men, "We carted our papers, etc. and desks, into the main accounting room," where he and Browns "were assigned a very nice, well lighted, section of the circulation office proper." Francis regarded this development as having "some advantages." It meant that he would "have a very important looking place in the main office with the main force." He also concluded that being in the main office would allow him to "learn more of the general office organization" as well as "cultivate a better office disposition and attitude toward the work." And as 1919 ended, Francis had this to say about Mr. Brummitt (whom he later nicknamed "the Chief"): "He is a real gentleman, and it is a pleasure to be working with a proposition that he directs. He is absolutely the most generous and most courteous man one can find.... Yet he is certainly fearless for himself as his editorials in the Herald will show."¹⁰

AS NOTED IN CHAPTER 2, Joyce decided to follow in her mother's footsteps and attend Mankato Commercial College in the fall of 1914. She took the Shorthand and Typing course, "made a very fine record as a student," and won a gold medal in a short hand contest. After completing the program in March 1915, she returned to Hot Springs and spent the summer with her parents. The next fall, she enrolled in the South Dakota State College at Brookings. Anticipating that she might spend only one year there, she decided to concentrate her studies mostly on Home Economics. That decision led her to take all four of the school's cooking courses, plus sewing and nursing classes. Her studies also included courses in Spanish, English, and history. In addition to her school work, she "tended door bells at the Dorm for $10 a month, waited on the teacher's table for half my board, [and] took care of the kitchen and dining room in the Domestic Science Dept." After finishing the academic year in the spring, she again returned to Hot Springs for the summer and early fall.¹¹

In the late fall of 1916, Joyce "accepted a position in an office" and returned to Mankato. She stayed on that job until early 1918, when she was appointed as instructor of stenography and typewriting at Mankato Commercial College. In that position, she had "charge of 275 students" and was paid $75 a month. She taught there for a little over a year. Then, in the spring of 1919, George Nettleton, who had been half owner of the college for the past 20 years, decided to leave Mankato and start his own business college in Sioux Falls. After moving there, he secured "the third floor over the Minnehaha National Bank" and opened the Nettleton Commercial College on June 1. Joyce joined him on the faculty and became head of the shorthand department. She taught at the new school for that summer session and during the fall term, which began on September 1.¹²

At some point after the Case family moved to Hot Springs in 1913, Joyce and Clifford Wilson met each other while attending the Methodist Church. When he was just under three years old, Wilson moved to Hot Springs from Iowa with his parents—Lucy and Stephen. Clifford graduated from Hot Springs High School in 1901. He then went to the Lincoln Business College at Lincoln, Nebraska. After Lincoln, he became a land surveyor and later secretary at the Battle Mountain Sanitarium in Hot Springs. Then after a few years, he decided to study law, attended law school at the University of Colorado, and graduated in 1911. He joined the South Dakota Bar in 1912 and entered a law partnership with his father. The firm became known as Wilson & Wilson. In early 1918, he temporarily left the law to become a secretary with the Navy Branch of the YMCA. After service at Valparaiso, Indiana, and the Great Lakes Naval Training Station in Illinois, he was sent to France in January 1919 and stayed there for six months. Shortly after he returned to Hot Springs and resumed his law practice, Joyce and he announced that they were engaged to be married.[13]

The wedding was originally scheduled for September but later reset for the following January. Earlier that month, Francis ordered 200 wedding announcements and "enclosure cards" from a Chicago stationery company. The announcement declared the wedding would occur on January 21, 1920, in Rapid City, and the enclosure card stated the couple would be at home in Hot Springs after March 1. At 4:00 in the afternoon on the 21st, the wedding was held at Herbert and Mary's home. Herbert performed the ceremony, "using the beautiful ring service of the Methodist Church." Relatives and "a few close friends of both families" were the invited guests. In addition to the bride's parents, the relatives included her grandfather Frank and the groom's father, Stephen. At 5:00 p.m., a "bountiful four course wedding dinner" was served. Carol acted as "head waitress," and Esther assisted her. After the wedding was complete, the newlyweds left for an extended honeymoon trip to "Denver and other western points." Since Francis and Leland "could not be home," their mother typed a two-page account of the whole affair and sent a copy to both.[14]

ON JANUARY 31, FRANCIS FINISHED his last exam for the preceding semester. For one of his answers, he "wrote three hours and a quarter spilling ink thru two complete books." Two weeks later, he learned that he received As in his three history courses and a B+ in his Religious Education class. (These results did not include all his lecture courses taken during his first semester; nor did they include grades in his seminar courses.) The B+ may have later been converted to an A. Dr. Richardson, the professor who reported that grade, was new to Northwestern and "understood that B plus was between 90 and

95 [percent] and A over 95." Francis, whose "percentage average was about 93" in the course, was "quite sure A is supposed to be anything over 90." In any event, he concluded that whether that final grade was a B+ or an A "makes little difference."[15]

With respect to his work at the *Herald*, Francis was presented with an opportunity for advancement in late March. The current assistant editor had decided to resign from his job and leave the paper on March 31. Brummitt asked Francis "to take up the work," and Francis "consented to do it temporarily." When he accepted the offer, he did not know what he would be paid, although "Dr. B said it would mean a considerable raise." The main reason that Francis agreed to accept the job on "a temporary basis" was because his Latin-American history professor had recently shown him "a letter from someone in the State Department" that asked the professor "to recommend some young fellow interested in Latin America for a position at Washington." The professor indicated that he would recommend Francis. This opening was appealing because the "pay would be 3000," "there would be opportunity to attend George Washington law school in the evenings," and the job would give Francis a chance to realize his "dream of working to better Latin-American relations." After explaining this potential opportunity to Brummitt, the latter agreed that Francis could become "temporary" assistant editor at the *Herald*.[16]

Dr. Brummitt obviously had faith in his new assistant. Francis officially took over the job on April 1 and was assigned to a "cozy little office." Two days later, Brummitt left the *Herald* "to be gone 2 weeks," and it was Francis's responsibly "to see that the paper gets out O.K." The *Herald*'s April 3 and April 10 issues were printed and distributed without incident. And in the future, Francis would be put in charge of getting the paper out for longer and longer periods of time.[17]

On April 25, Francis wrote that he was "completing a thesis and the work for a Master's degree." Over the next three weeks, he was "busily engaged in the final details" of his Master's thesis, titled "'The

Motives underlying the Revolt of the Thirteen Colonies compared with those which brought to an end Spanish Rule in Latin America.'" In a moment of mock reflection, he suggested that "with so long a title, a thesis should hardly have been needed." He submitted the finalized document in mid-May and defended it at his oral examination held on the 17th. A week later, Wesleyan's President Schermerhorn congratulated him "upon your completion of your year at Northwestern, and upon your attainment to the measure of a full-fledged M. A.!"[18]

DURING THE LAST WEEK IN MAY, Francis left the Windy City for a much-anticipated trip to South Dakota. He saw many of his "old friends" in Mitchell and then continued west on to Rapid City. There, he spent ten days visiting his parents, his younger sisters, and presumably Joyce and new husband Cliff. He returned to Chicago on June 6. For the next two days, he was in Indianapolis and "present at all sessions" held by the Church Departmental of the Associated Advertising Clubs of the World (AACW) during its 16th annual convention. Dr. Norman Richardson, who had given Francis the unclear final grade in his Religious Education course, had arranged that his student attend the convention. It featured several speakers who discussed church advertising. Francis previously agreed to write a book on that subject under Professor Richardson's supervision, and the book was to be based largely on the "material presented" at the convention.[19]

Francis enrolled in summer school at the Garrett Bible Institute in 1920. There he took courses that would provide credits toward a PhD in Religion. The subject in one of his classes was Ephesians (the tenth book of the New Testament). The professor required that the students memorize a great amount of material, and repeating it made Francis feel he was "talking like a parrot." Dr. Schermerhorn admitted that he could not see any "pedagogical value" in that requirement, although he assured Francis that "it will do you good."[20]

In addition to his summer academic work, he got a good start on producing his book. It was to be titled *Handbook of Church Advertising* and to be published by the Abingdon Press in New York City. That publisher was "the non-denominational name for the Methodist Book Concern." The Methodist Book Concern was a publishing house founded in 1789. It published many Methodist-related materials, including *The Epworth Herald*. During June and early July, Francis read books on advertising in general and church advertising in particular to gain a general knowledge of the subject. He also took steps necessary to obtain copies of the speeches given and the materials presented at the convention on church advertising in Indianapolis. After receiving and digesting these materials, he began preparing the book's manuscript and sending draft chapters to Dr. Richardson for his review and comment. By the end of August, all 12 of the book's chapters had been sent to Richardson, and Francis had received "numerous inquiries concerning the date of publication and the price of the book."[21]

Apart from attending school and researching, organizing, and writing his *Handbook of Church Advertising*, Francis continued his work at the *Herald* during the summer of 1920. As of June 15, his salary as Acting Assistant Editor became $1,800 a year. For the next two months, he struggled with deciding whether to stay on at the *Herald* or to pursue a teaching position, a job "in the newspaper field," or an "opening in the Latin-American work of the State Department as there was last spring." The latter possibility had an additional attraction, for it would allow him to "study international law on the side with a view to the enlarging field as international law replaces force." Nevertheless, after much soul-searching and several frank conversations with Dr. Brummitt, Francis opted to continue as the *Herald*'s Assistant Editor. When he reached this decision, his boss was out of the city. Francis therefore wrote Brummitt a letter that stated in part: "I am decided that if you still desire me to continue on the Epworth Herald, I shall be happy to do so and shall pray [to] God that through you I may be used for the largest services of which I am capable." On the day he received that letter, Brummitt responded by noting "it was a joy to get your final decision to stay with the job" and "I am praying today that the relationship which is now assured may be worth as much to you as it is going to be to The Herald."[22]

In its September 18 issue, the *Herald* noted that Francis had become its Assistant Editor. The article containing this announcement stated that "Mr. Case has been in the office for several months, but not until recently were we sure he could be induced to stay." After reviewing his background and credentials, the story concluded that Francis was "remarkably well prepared for his work with THE HERALD"; and it told its readers that "we expect him to have a good deal to do with future improvements in the paper, as he has had with those presented this week." Given his expanded role at the *Herald* and his continued involvement in finishing his book for publication, he decided to take only two graduate-school courses for the fall term. One was a writer's seminar and the other a sociology seminar.[23]

About the same time Francis was settling into his now-official role at the *Herald*, Mary and Herbert decided to move the family from Rapid City to Mankato to help Mary's father close his S. H. Grannis Coal Company business. Grandpa Frank Case, who had lived with the family for the past three years, moved with them as well. Once they were situated there, Herbert sold life insurance policies, and Frank sold bottles of liniment, which now became known as "Out-O-Sight" Liniment. He unsuccessfully sought to obtain a patent on the product the next year, but he did secure a registered trademark for it. Herbert later described the father-and-son sales efforts as follows: "My father still rides in the back seat of the car nearly everywhere I go and often gets in more money from his liniment than I do from insurance."[24]

Shortly after the family arrived in Mankato, Leland enrolled at Macalester College in St. Paul. After spending two years at Dakota Wesleyan, he "felt that he was in the shadow of his brother" and "found his brother's reputation a bit heavy to carry." Many years later, Leland explained that he decided to change colleges for "two reasons: One was, I found that I was getting a lot of things on Francis' residual reputation, which I didn't appreciate; the other was that my folks moved over there—to Mankato."²⁵

In the late fall, Francis was elected president of the Graduate Club at Northwestern. That group was organized soon after the graduate school was founded in 1910. Now—ten years later—it had about 200 members who represented 27 states and 11 foreign countries. The club met once a month. Prominent faculty and community members addressed it at these meetings, which also included a social hour with refreshments. Francis's main duties as president were arranging for speakers to appear and recruiting present and future graduate students to join the club.²⁶

He spent the Christmas holidays with his family—only the fourth time he was able to do so since 1912. Because "the folks" now lived in Mankato, it was a much easier trip going there than travelling to western South Dakota. He arrived a few days before the 25th and celebrated the day with his grandparents, parents, younger siblings, and relatives from one of Mary's sister's families (the Esther and Harrison L. Schmitts). By December 30, he had returned to Chicago and answered yet another letter regarding the status of his book project.²⁷

FRANCIS WROTE TO HIS SISTER Carol on January 24, 1921. In that letter, he discussed several subjects, including the traits he admired in young women. On this topic, he stated:

> Now I like a girl with a pretty face, but I don't like her very much if that is all she has. I want to think that she isn't entirely ignorant when current events are being discussed, that she isn't going to say "I can't" when someone is needed to play at Sunday school or at a pep fest, that when some idea for entertainment is needed she is able to think of something besides a dance or the movies, and that

if the call is for a little physical exertion on a hike or something of this sort, she must ride in a bus.²⁸

Within the next few weeks, Francis informed his mother that he was "in love with a Girl," and he apparently discussed marrying her. Upon hearing the news, Carol wrote him that "there is one [girlfriend] in particular that I would like to know for I heard a rumor that—someday I am going to have a new sister, who is just a little bit older than I." Herbert, Leland, Carol, and Esther all sent their congratulations to Francis, and the latter three all asked him to send a picture of his newfound love. The "Girl" was named Louise Wood. She was born and grew up in Sheldon, Illinois—a small village located about 75 miles south of Chicago. As a sophomore at Northwestern in the spring of 1921, she actively participated in college life. Louise was a member of the Alpha Gamma Delta sorority and was treasurer of the all-female Ro Ku Va—a literary organization. She also belonged to a women's literary society named Calethia, where she served as sergeant-at-arms for the first semester of the 1920-21 school year.²⁹

In mid-March, Francis let Carol know that "Louise & I won't be married for at least 2 & possibly 3 years yet." He also sent pictures of Louise to Carol, Esther, and Leland. When Mary learned of the delayed wedding plans, she approved of the decision and wrote to Francis that "neither of you are old yet so would advise to take time to do the things you want to. It may seem a long time to wait till Louise is thru College—But it may be worth while... How we wish we knew Louise!"³⁰

While Francis was falling for Louise, he was also busy putting the finishing touches on his *Handbook of Church Advertising*. At the Methodist Book Concern's request, he revised the book's author's preface section. He also sent a complete set of page proofs to the publishers and made plans to have complimentary copies sent to "each of the men whose Indianapolis address was incorporated in the book." A few weeks later, Francis received six advance copies to which he was "entitled as author." He promptly sent one of those to his father for the latter's 50th birthday present.[31]

The *Handbook* was published on March 3. It included an editor's introduction by Norman E. Richardson, the author's preface, and 12 chapters. It was 186 pages long, contained several illustrations, charts, and diagrams, and sold for $1.25 per copy. Two weeks after its publication, the book's first review appeared in the *Christian Advocate*. The *Advocate* was a weekly newspaper that served as the organ of the Methodist Episcopal Church, South. Its review stated, in part, that the book "is meant to be a handbook for the busy pastor or whoever has charge of Church advertising. Reasons for advertising the Church are given; channels through which it can be done are discussed; what to advertise, when to advertise, seasonal advertising—are all presented in a practical way."[32]

Additional positive reviews soon followed in several Methodist publications. Francis quoted them in a May 26 letter he sent to the Methodist Book Concern's Business Manager. These reviews stated, among other things, that the *Handbook* "is one of the best books of its kind ever written and no pastor who desires to reach the last man in his community can afford to do without it"; that "for church leaders who do not desire to be imitators and who are anxious to learn invaluable principles of advertising, nothing better than this volume has yet appeared"; and that the book "has the warm endorsation of religious leaders." One review also suggested that "every church should have an Advertising, or Publicity, Committee," and this committee, along "with the pastor, [should] devote the study period of the Sunday School hour to the study of this book, whose author has had always in mind its adaptability as a text-book." And a later review in the June 22 edition of the *Pacific Christian Advocate* (Methodist newspaper published in Portland, Oregon) noted that "the author . . . manifests a good degree of knowledge" about church advertising, and the book "is undoubtedly the best brief treatment of the subject."³³

ON APRIL 11, PRESIDENT SCHERMERHORN invited Francis to give the evening university address at Dakota Wesleyan on baccalaureate Sunday, June 5. He promptly accepted, stating that "I'll be very glad to stand on the old Wesleyan Chapel platform once more." When Harold Card read about this arrangement in a newspaper, he "heartily congratulate[d]" Francis for the honor and assured him that "I shall be an appreciative listener." As the event drew nearer, Francis decided to go to Mankato in late May and spend time with his family before travelling on to Mitchell to give his address. But on May 22, he received a letter from Joyce that made him change his plans. Joyce gave birth to a son—Allen Grannis Wilson—on May 6. Eleven days later, she wrote that her new baby was "so plump and fat and terribly good looking." She then added that "you certainly must come here while you are in S. D. I'm sure you want to see our home as well as your one and only nephew. . . . It might be a long time before you have another good chance to come. Please plan on coming!"³⁴

The day after receiving Joyce's letter, Francis wrote to his "Homefolks" that he had decided "to include Hot Springs, Allen, and the Wilsons in my itinerary." This meant that instead of coming to Mankato in late May, he would not start his journey until June 1, and either go to Mankato first, then Mitchell, and then Hot Springs, or "go the other way, taking Hot Springs first." Delaying this trip until the 1st would have several advantages. It would allow him to get a "summer excursion rate" for a round trip train ticket, and it would enable him to finish some class work, an article on "advertising the Sunday School," and preparation for his "talk for D.W.U." It would also permit him "to see and meet Louise's folks either by a run down there or when they come here for the Music Festival next Monday."³⁵

Francis ultimately decided to go to Hot Springs on the first leg of his journey. On June 1, he left Chicago on a 12:15 a.m. train, and he arrived in Hot Springs at 10:15 a.m. on June 3. It was a short but enjoyable visit. He stayed at Joyce and Cliff's house and met his new nephew, who aptly demonstrated that he "can make himself heard." While in town, he also called on Reverend Charles B. Clark (Badger Clark's father), who had been the chaplain at the Battle Mountain Sanitarium for Veterans for many years. Francis left the next day for Rapid City, took the evening train to Mitchell, and arrived there on Sunday morning. That night he presented the university address in the Wesleyan chapel. Titled "In Defense of the Younger Generation," the main points made in his speech were that the younger generation was presently under unjustified attack; that "America... must seek out new horizons for its youth"; that it was the opportunity and responsibility of the young to help vanquish the "new frontier," (which included "the conquering of poverty, disease, crime, illiteracy, physical hunger and spiritual starvation"); and that "there is no antagonism, no cross purpose between youth and old age as we contemplate the new frontier."[36]

Francis opted to stay in Mitchell and attend the remaining commencement exercises. He later described his four days there as "among the happiest memories I have ever registered." He took "personal pleasure" in seeing his former fellow debaters graduate and remarked that "[t]heir commencement meant more to me so far as immediate appreciation is concerned than my own did." He left Mitchell for Mankato on Wednesday evening, arrived there at 5:45 a.m. on Thursday, and spent the next four days visiting his family. Finally, he concluded the last leg of his marathon trip by leaving Mankato on the Sunday evening train and arriving in Chicago the next morning.[37]

FROM MID-JUNE UNTIL THE end of July, Dr. Brummitt was in the *Herald* office for about four days. During his absences, he fulfilled several Epworth-League-related engagements. His schedule meant that Francis was largely responsible for ensuring that the *Herald* was produced on a weekly basis throughout the early-to-mid summer. In addition to this responsibility and "more ambitious work" at the trade paper, Francis devoted time to completing a writer's seminar in Religious Education that he began in the spring semester. He also was put in charge of leading the Recreation program at the Bethany Park Epworth League Institute near Indianapolis during the last week in July. Finally, he found time to make a weekend visit to Louise at her "little town." Given these commitments and activities, he decided not to enroll in summer school.[38]

In early August, Dr. Brummitt left the country for an extended trip to Europe. He expected to be gone for three months. Before he left, he wrote a letter to the Epworth League's General Secretary (Dr. Charles Guthrie) that stated "in all matters other than the General Secretary's message Mr. Case will have the widest discretion to act exactly as he thinks I would act if I were here. Of course, the final responsibility is mine, but Case will take care of that." He added that "Mr. Case has been getting more and more into the active Epworth League work, and if occasion should arise I know he will be glad to respond to calls for Conventions and other League activities, so far as these do not interfere with his office work." In a separate letter to Mr. Allen at the Methodist Book Concern office in Chicago, Brummitt explained that "Mr. Case . . . is in full charge of the office while I am away. He is authorized to sign checks, to make arrangements for office routine, and to adjust it where necessary to the work of the other departments, and in general to be my other self."[39]

In mid-August, the Methodist Book Concern's New York office sent to Professor Richardson a "page from the August 20 issue of the Literary Digest which we believe will be of interest to you as it relates to 'Handbook of Church Advertising', Case." Richardson forwarded this letter and its enclosure to Francis accompanied with a handwritten note: "Thought you'd like to see this—Richardson." Francis replied that he "was intensely interested in that page which you sent me from the Literary Digest." After receiving it, he "secured a regular number and found that an additional quarter page was also given to exploiting the 'Handbook of Church Advertising.'" He added that "nothing better could have been done to promote the standing and sales of the book," that "Literary Digest Advertising is rated as high as any in the country and on this particular subject it is probably the best to be had," and that "I am sure this will be a big boost for the book."[40]

Regarding the review's content, Francis remarked the "one thing is very good. Most of the material which the Digest quoted was that which is designed to sell the idea of Church Advertising to those who have had a wrong conception of it." Examples that illustrated this point included the following passages in the review that quote directly from the book: advertising the church's message "'is like advertising a general commodity, such as bread. Every one ... needs it'"; "'The goal of church advertising is identical with the goal of the Church. All advertising must stand this supreme test'"; "'Church advertising is an aid to, not a substitute for, religion'"; and church advertising "'is not the method of shameless self-exaltation or of wanton intrusion into the shop and market-place. It is, rather, the method of the one in the parable of our Lord who went out into the highways and hedges and compelled others to come in.'"[41]

In addition to appearing before its national readership, the *Digest* review became a story in the local Evanston newspaper—*The Evanston News-Index*. Its September 6 issue included an article titled "Francis H. Case's Book on Church Publicity Praised by Famous Periodical." The story began by stating "The Literary Digest ... contains a very remarkable article on 'Church Publicity' which occupies a page and a quarter. This article makes special reference to a book edited by an Evanstonian, Francis H. Case[.]" It went on to describe the book, its author, and how the book was prepared. It also predicted that "this extraordinary volume promises to be a textbook on Church Publicity." That prediction proved to be accurate in at least one instance, as Francis was later informed that the AACW's Church Advertising Department had decided "to use your book as the Text Book of the training classes."[42]

THE ACACIA FRATERNITY WAS FOUNDED at the University of Michigan in 1904. It came into being to replace that school's Masonic Club, which had folded the previous year. One of Acacia's founders stated that "'we've got to organize on a fraternity basis'" and "'will take only those who are interested and will work, rather than keep it open to all Masons of the university.'" In 1909, an Acacia chapter was established at Northwestern University. But for an unknown reason, the fraternity had lost its charter sometime prior to 1921. In the spring of that year, Francis led an effort to "recharter" (i.e. reinstate) the group at his university. That effort was successful, and on May 12 the chapter at Northwestern became the "first Acacia chapter to be rechartered" in the fraternity's short history.[43]

The rechartered Northwestern chapter's 1921 membership included four facility members, four graduate students, four medical students, and twenty-seven undergraduates. One of those undergraduate students—a junior from Toledo, Ohio, was named Art Brown. Francis described him as "one of the hardest workers I have ever known," a man who "makes anything go he touches," and one who "has highest of ideals and ... plenty of punch." Brown would become Francis's roommate, one of his best friends, and a future business associate.[44]

During that summer, Francis arranged for the fraternity to purchase a home in Evanston. By early September, the house had been "fumigated," the roof repaired, two parlors redecorated, the kitchen repainted, and a doorplate installed. Before all of that work had been completed, several Acacia members, including Francis, had already moved in, and the latter had made his room "into a real study den."[45]

Francis continued to be "particularly busy" with his work at the *Herald* during September and October while his boss remained in Europe. In addition, he took on several "speaking engagements," which kept him going "rather strenuously to keep up with them." Consequently, he opted for "a very light enrollment" during the fall school semester—apparently taking only one class. Dr. Brummitt continued to be satisfied with Francis's work while the former was out of the country. From London in late September, he remarked that "'I never left the office for an extended trip feeling so confident that everything would be so well handled in my absence and in good shape upon my return, as this time.'" And on October 10, he wrote to Francis "God bless you for your patience and pluck; if anybody has cause to be thankful for a true associate, I'm that man."[46]

Five days later, Brummitt and his wife embarked on the SS "Aquitania" and sailed for home. They arrived in New York on Saturday, October 22, and the "Chief" was back in the *Herald* office on the following Monday. Francis felt "muchly relieved" when his boss returned; and he noted that "while he was away I didn't realize quite that the work was so burdening as I now see it to have been."[47]

After his weekend visit to Louise during the summer, Francis wrote her letters telling her "how anxious ... [he] was for her to return" and "how busy" he was. On Saturday, September 17, she arrived in Chicago to begin the fall semester of her junior year. That evening, she joined a "little theater party" that Francis had previously arranged with one of his friends from high school who happened to be visiting the city. Francis continued to see Louise when he could during the fall. But by late November, it became apparent that she was no longer the sole object of his affections. Responding to one of his recent letters, his mother wrote that she was "glad you are having such a good time, yes we are if it was three different girls. Don't settle down to so steady Business that you grow old too fast."[48]

On December 22, Francis took an evening train to Mankato, where he spent the second Christmas in a row with his family. Christmas dinner was held at the "old house" where Mary and Herbert had been married in 1894 and had bought after they moved to Mankato the previous year. The next day, Francis received his first royalty check for sales of *Handbook of Church Advertising*. The accompanying Copyright and Royalty Memorandum indicated that from its publication on March 3 through July 31, 1921, 504 books were sold. Since he received a $.10 royalty per book, his check amounted to $50.40. Francis wrote to the Methodist Book Concern's executive manager that receiving the check on the morning after Christmas made for "a nice happy greeting," especially since he had not expected it "until six months after the December inventory."[49]

While he was home for the holidays, Francis and his mother talked about the "three different girls" he referred to in a previous letter. (It is not known whether Louise was one of the three.) After these discussions, Mary wrote to her son that she was "sure you will be so surely drawn to the one God has for you, to be your life partner[.]" She then summarized the "many good, excellent qualities" of the three women. One was "modest, quiet but a homemaker" who "would be a devoted admirer of her husband and intensely interested in all his work but not take perhaps an actual a part as some might in it." The second "thinks more of public life, dress and social activities—some perhaps you would not care... to engage in." The third "likes public life, probably is not the house keeper that the first, does not care for dress as much as the second—But is a good whole souled girl." She concluded that "any of these would be a prize for any young man to win," and added "may God bless our boy in this most important time of his whole life, next to being a Christian."[50]

The Epworth Herald ended 1921 on a positive note. Its list of subscribers that year "was the best since before the war." When compared to a similar reporting period for the previous year, 1921 showed "a

25% increase in new subscriptions and an 80% increase in renewals." In addition, the paper introduced "some economies and readjustments" in the fall, including hiring an additional staff member. These moves "produced a weekly reduction in manufacturing costs of $34.43, the average over a fifteen week period up to Dec. 31." The cost savings "more than paid" for the new hire's salary. And according to Francis, the reduced costs also "enabled better attention to all work, permitted us to do some long neglected things, saved my life and time, and otherwise [have] been a blessing."[51]

FRANCIS RETURNED TO CHICAGO in early January. He enjoyed being in Mankato for the holidays. It was the "longest visit at home that ... he had since the summer of 1917." Upon arriving back at the Acacia House in Evanston, he discovered that "a spark caught in the shingles of our house on New Year's Day and blazed right merrily before some passerby informed the boys who were here that the house was on fire." The roof, attic, and plaster on the walls (which became soaked when water used to extinguish the fire ran down between the partitions) received the most damage. Although the fire burned through the ceiling in Francis's third-story room, it did not damage his books or personal belongings. It "cost $2,000 to roof and redecorate" the house; and fortunately, the loss was covered by insurance. Nine days after the event, Francis still had "stray pieces of soot and bits of plaster dust" in his room, but the house repairs were completed soon thereafter.[52]

Due to Francis's suggestion and "general agitation," by late January the *Herald* had determined to make "another readjustment" at its office. In consultation with the Epworth League, it was decided that a woman who worked in the League's Central Office would become "a liaison officer ... on the staffs of both the League and Herald." She would "have charge of certain departments in the paper and ought to bring to the Herald, news and methods articles that we need." Francis predicted that this arrangement would "usher in a new day for both the offices." And he continued to enjoy a positive relationship with the chief: "Dr. Brummitt and I get on together like the wind and leaves in autumn. He seems content to have me make my mistakes and learn by them so I have no reason for complaint if things are not perfect."[53]

For the 1922 spring semester, Francis decided to enroll in three courses for eight hours of credit. Each course was taught "by the head of a department." He started the semester on February 9 by attending a class titled "Magazine and Periodical Writing." It met once a week on Thursday evening from 5:15 to 7:00 at Northwestern's "downtown school." Professor H. F. Harrington, director of the Joseph Medill School of Journalism, taught this two-hour course. The other classes—"Recreational Leadership" taught by his *Handbook of Church Advertising* advisor N. E. Richardson, and "Living Religions" taught by Professor E. D. Soper—each awarded three credit hours. They both met on Monday, Wednesday, and Friday afternoon at the Evanston campus. This meant that Francis had to leave the *Herald* office "at one o'clock on three days out of the week." He believed that this schedule would force him "to get back into the fighting swing of more regular hours all around." He admitted that "studies worry me so much more than they did once upon a time," but noted that "when the semester is over, if I have survived, I will have credits totalling the equivalent of two years of regular residence work[.]" And if the two-year-residence-work goal were achieved, that would mean that he "could complete the Ph. D. requirements even if I were living elsewhere."[54]

On the evening of March 25, Herbert sent a telegram to Francis addressed to "Acacia House Evanston Ill." The message read: "Grandma Grannis and mama were at Bretts Store this afternoon when grandma was taken sick She was conscious when she got home but grandma passed away at 915 Waiting to hear from the girls before arranging services." Francis responded with a "comforting and beautiful message" to his mother that she received the next day. He then wrote a letter to his grandfather, which the latter "showed to everyone who came in" and said he would keep "'always.'" The funeral was originally scheduled for Tuesday, the 28th. But since the Grannis's second youngest daughter (Estelle Adeline Monkman) decided to attend the service, and her train from California would not arrive until the morning on March 30, the funeral was postponed until that afternoon (or Friday if "she misses connection"). Both Francis and Joyce said they could attend. But their parents persuaded them to come to Mankato in June instead, so they could spend more time there when Mary and Herbert "will need cheering up." Grandpa Grannis was understandably "crushed" by his wife's death (at age 71), which "came so sudden and unexpectedly." And daughter Mary wrote: "Oh how I shall miss her coming over and I going over there. Watching her sit by the window and so many many things she has done for me."[55]

IN THE EARLY SPRING OF 1922, Francis became interested in the possibility of combining with others "to go in on a newspaper proposition." By mid-February, while serving on an Epworth League committee with a young lawyer from Montana (who was also a state senator and Epworth League state president), he learned of a "good opening for a Republican newspaper" in Great Falls. Francis, who had "always hankered to go west again," decided to investigate this opportunity. Over the next month, he researched the city of Great Falls and its existing newspapers; and he contacted Wesleyan friends, an experienced South Dakota newspaperman, and others to determine whether they would be interested in joining him in the venture as either active investor-participants or just willing investors. Out of this group, Harold Card expressed the most interest. Like his good friend, he had "always had a desire to go west" and thought the two of them "could make a success of a newspaper."[56]

Francis also informed his parents about the Great Falls proposal. Neither was enthusiastic about it. His father wrote that "Montana is not Dakota," he did not "believe the conditions would favor the building up of a great daily there like they would some other places," and he did not want "to see you lose a mighty good job till you have a sure thing Better." Mary's reaction was lukewarm as well: "I do not know what to say about the 'Daily' proposition. It seems as tho it was a big undertaking for you—Especially since you must borrow so much to start with.... If you want a Daily why not work for Rapid."[57]

Despite his parents' misgivings, Francis continued to actively explore the Montana idea. By the end of April, he had "talked things over with the Chief and although he isn't anxious to have me leave, yet he will interpose no objection if I don't leave him in the lurch." Francis and Harold had also decided that they needed to make a trip to Great Falls. Both spent the next month continuing to seek out others to join them in the project and/or provide much-needed capital for it. They also firmed up their plans for a personal visit to Montana in early June, and Harold suggested that they check out the newspapers in Rapid City and Lead while on their way back. Finally, Francis reassured his dad that "Card and I won't tackle ... [the Great Falls undertaking] unless we get an older experienced newspaperman to go in with us."[58]

In late May, the president of the Dakota Wesleyan Alumni Association requested that Francis attend the inauguration of Dr. E.D. Kohlstedt as the seventh president of the university. Two months earlier, Dr. Schermerhorn publicly announced that he had resigned the Wesleyan presidency to become chair of the Biblical History and Literature Department at the Garrett Biblical Institute. Kohlstedt, who was serving as director of field activities for a Methodist Episcopal Church committee at the time, was subsequently chosen to become Schermerhorn's successor. A former fellow Wesleyanite also asked Francis to attend alumni meetings scheduled to occur earlier on inauguration day so he could assist in the effort to adopt a new association constitution. He agreed to attend the meetings and speak at the inauguration ceremony.⁵⁹

By early June, Francis had finished his three graduate classes at Northwestern and was ready to head west. He boarded an evening train in Chicago and arrived in Mitchell on the 7th. It was a busy day at his alma mater. In the afternoon, he attended alumni meetings and "help[ed] to put across that constitution." Among other things, it expanded the association's membership to include both graduates *and* former students; and it provided for an executive committee with significant powers. By adopting this document, the newly-formed "Alumnal Association" in effect replaced the old Alumni Association. Francis was then elected as Alumnal Association president. Next, he and several other Wesleyanites attended the alumni banquet at the church. At eight o'clock that evening, the new president's inaugural ceremony was held in the college chapel. During those proceedings, Francis gave a brief speech about "Dr. Kohlstedt and his past work." Harold and Francis then left Mitchell on the midnight train, and they arrived in Great Falls on Friday afternoon, June 9.⁶⁰

The two spent the rest of Friday and the next three days investigating the Montana newspaper situation. Although the details of their investigation are not known, it presumably included an inspection of the newspaper plant they were interested in buying, discussions with that paper's current owners about a potential deal, and meetings with Great Falls businessmen to assess their willingness to advertise in the sought-after paper if it changed ownership. It is also likely that they toured the city to confirm it was a place they would like to live.⁶¹

On June 13, Francis left Great Falls by train. He arrived in Mankato a few days later. While there, he attended and spoke at the Epworth League Convention in nearby St. Peter, enjoyed a reunion with Joyce, Cliff, and their one-year-old son Allen, and "had great sport playing golf with Leland, Dad and my brother-in-law." On the 19th, he returned to Chicago. Harold also left Great Falls on the 13th. His return trip to South Dakota included a four-day visit to the Black Hills, where he took in several tourist attractions, met with old friends, "went through the [Rapid City] Journal plant, and "investigate[d] the paper some" in Lead. He arrived back at his parents' home in Mitchell on June 20.[62]

Francis's first few days back in Chicago were consumed by activity at the *Herald* office and a difficult end to a personal relationship. He spent Tuesday and Wednesday working on the paper and getting "caught up on other matters" while "the Chief was busy in committee meetings." Dr. Brummitt left for his trip to the west coast the following evening. That same night, Francis broke up with an unnamed "young lady." He described their relationship as "another case of honest attraction for each other but where was a real difference in ideals and interests which would cause much sorrow in the long run." The breakup, which came "at the end of a good evening," was "hard," and he "wish[ed] we could have gotten thru without causing either any pain." But he added that "we have both survived thus far and things will go all right now."[63]

Regarding his search for a newspaper deal, Francis wrote to Harold that "if the G. F. deal does not open up, I think I would be willing to put my stake on the [Rapid City Daily] Journal[.]" After hearing from Harold that the "Rapid City proposition is much better than the one in Lead" and that a "fellow ... has bought some [Journal] stock and is almost completely in charge," Francis wrote to Joseph Gossage—the paper's founder and current publisher. In that letter (dated June 30), Francis introduced himself and inquired whether there would be a possible opening for him at the *Journal*. During July, he exchanged correspondence with F. W. Meyers, the man who had recently become the paper's business manager, and Mrs. Alice Gossage, who was effectively in charge of the *Journal* due to her husband's illness. That correspondence indicated that Meyers believed the Gossages were "greatly esteemed by all" but were "impracticable and unbusinesslike," and their paper's "business management has been poor and without system"; that the Gossages recognized Meyers as a "live wire" but were not happy with his management style and attempts to dictate how the paper should be run; and that both Meyers and Mrs. Gossage encouraged Francis to come to Rapid City and explore the possibility of joining the operation.[64]

During the second week of August, Francis visited Rapid City and met with Meyers and the Gossages. The group discussed several issues related to the paper's future operation, the role Francis would be expected to play in its development, and the financial contribution he would be required to make in order to become a part-owner. The meetings went well, and Francis decided to commit to investing in, and working for, the *Journal*. After returning to Chicago, he sent a letter to the "Journal People" that followed up on their discussions and sought clarification of the proposed written contract among the parties. In response, Mrs. Gossage wrote that "I am sure things will be adjusted all right—as far as you and the Journal are concerned, but as for Mr. Meyers I think you and 'us' will have to buy him out some day and let him try his . . . tactics where they will be more appreciated."[65]

Francis spent the last few days in August wrapping up his affairs in Chicago and Evanston. He resigned his position at the *Herald*, packed up his things at the Acacia House, wrote some last-minute letters, and said his goodbyes to several people. On August 29, just two days before he was scheduled to leave Chicago on a train bound for Mankato and then Rapid City, he received a telegram from Dr. Hahne, who had promised to arrange a loan for this newspaper venture. That message read: "Phoned bank can not get loan my funds in Lincoln tied up try elsewhere delay action letter follows."[66]

In response to this surprising and unwelcome news, Francis wrote a letter to a fraternity brother and asked him if he could "arrange a ninety day loan for three thousand." He also went ahead with his preplanned trip to Rapid City on the 31st—making a two-day stop at his parents' home on the way. After arriving in Rapid on September 5, without any funds to invest in the *Journal*, he learned that the Gossages and Meyers had come to a "disagreement" and Meyers had been "discharged" from the paper. He also received a telegram from Great Falls. It informed him that the paper he and Card had wanted to buy had dropped its selling price from $40,000 to $25,000. Despite these unpredicted and unsettling developments, Francis reported for work at the *Journal* on September 7. But given the turmoil caused by the Meyers-Gossages split, his uncertain financial situation, and the Montana proposition suddenly becoming more feasible, he commented that "how long I will or can stay [at the *Journal*], I do not know."[67]

CHAPTER 8

RAPID CITY NEWSPAPERMAN AND INVOLVED CITIZEN

No doubt Rapid City has a brilliant future as such towns out in the west have.

—Ernest Hahne

After he had been working at the *Journal* for a week, Francis reported to Dr. Hahne as follows: "I have been catapulted into a whirl of long hours (16 and 18 every day since I started)." He spent those workdays "trying to get in touch with the men who could give good leads on news"; handling "the telegraph"; giving "some attention to straightening out the difficult and delicate situation with Meyers"; and "personally setting headlines and putting the type in the forms myself until three and four in the morning." But, he predicted, "we will win, if I can get any help at all." Francis also asked Hahne for a $1,000 loan, which would allow the newly-hired newspaperman to "stay and have more time to see what can be done about buying Meyers out." Finally, he noted that although he had not given up on the potential Montana deal, he was "beginning to believe" that Rapid City "is a better field than Great Falls," even though the selling price for the latter's newspaper had been dropped to $25,000.[1]

Ten days later, Francis's typical day at the office had not changed: "I generally get to bed about five a.m. and sleep until eleven and get to the office at twelve, noon, and from then on, my time is not my own." And in mid-September, Meyers filed a lawsuit that sought to force the Gossages to return him to his former position at the *Journal*. Nevertheless, Francis felt that things were generally heading in the right direction. Dr. Hahne did come through with a $1,000 loan, which Francis profusely thanked him for providing. He immediately put the money in a bank until he could determine "just what I want to do with it." Unlike Meyers, Francis had a good working relationship with the Gossages. With respect to Joe Gossage, "the Old Man and I have disagreed on policy... and I must admit that later events have proved him right quite as often as otherwise. Surely I can learn some things from a man who has been running newspapers for fifty years, and this one for nearly forty-five." And Alice Gossage "does her share and more," agreed with Francis's assessment of how the operation could be improved, and agreed he could recruit his friend Art Brown to assist in that effort. In addition, Harold Card "said he is willing to go half when the time comes to buy Meyers' holdings." Despite these positive developments, Francis still had concerns that the "paper is not shaping for progress as I think it should." He therefore continued to keep "a line out at Great Falls" by writing a letter to the man who had offered to sell his paper to Harold and Francis. That letter stated in part: "I'm likely to make a permanent arrangement here any time," but "if you still want to deal, let me know." No response to this letter has been located.[2]

On October 5, a hearing was held on Meyers's motion for an injunction, wherein he sought to "put the Gossages out and install him with free hand for the remainder of the year." Through sworn affidavits, both sides presented their version of events that led up to Meyers's dismissal, and the parties' attorneys made arguments based on that evidence. The court subsequently denied Meyers's motion. Later that month, Art Brown decided to leave his position as an instructor at Northwestern's Medill School of Journalism and accept Francis's plea to join him on the *Journal* staff. After saying goodbye to his friends in his home town of Toledo, Ohio, Art returned to Evanston to tie up some loose ends. He then boarded the night train for Rapid City on October 29.[3]

THE RAPID CITY DAILY GUIDE MADE its initial appearance on November 8, when local newsboys distributed complimentary copies on the city's streets. The paper's creator and editor—Theodore B. Werner—stated in his introductory editorial that the *Daily Guide* "'will give local news ... first importance'"; that "'news will be supplied without favoritism or prejudice, and without distinction as to class, creed or ... politics'"; and that "'the personal element will be excluded from its news columns and in these it will have neither friends nor foes, but will be an honest, fair-minded chronicler[.]'" Speaking to a "Journal man" that evening, Werner added that "'The Daily Guide ... is here to stay. In politics, it will be independent, and in news scope, it will cover the field.'" Now that the *Daily Guide* had come into existence, the *Journal* was no longer the only daily newspaper in Rapid City.[4]

Art began working at the *Journal* in early November. On the 11th, he and Francis attended their first meeting of the Black Hills Press Association. The meeting was held in Rapid City. Association members representing newspapers in Lead, Belle Fourche, Spearfish, Deadwood, Newell, Rapid City (including Theodore Werner, editor of the newly-formed *Guide*), and Hot Springs were there to consider "matters of development, policy and co-operation." Francis and Art were introduced to the group at that meeting.[5]

The two spent Thanksgiving Day and the next day in Sturgis. On Thursday evening the "annual union Thanksgiving services" were conducted at the Sturgis Presbyterian Church "with an audience that filled all the pews." During the service, the choir performed musical numbers, proclamations from the president and governor were read, and Francis "gave the oration, an earnest appeal for Thanks-living for the spirit of sacrifice and public service." While they were in Sturgis, Art and Francis also visited with Francis's friends. Earl Bovee was most likely one of them, as he had previously written a letter in October that asked Francis to "come up and make a visit."[6]

On December 7, Joseph B. Gossage, Alice R. Gossage, and The Rapid City Journal Company (Company) entered a signed, written agreement with Harold W. Card and Francis H. Case. (Francis signed the agreement for himself and for Harold as "his duly authorized agent.") The agreement provided that Harold and Francis would purchase Meyers's capital stock that represented one-quarter ownership in the Company in exchange for Meyers's full release of all claims he held against the Gossages and the Company. The parties also agreed that Harold and Francis would each receive capital stock from the company's treasury with a face value of $500, and that Francis would receive additional capital stock from Joe Gossage with a $500 face value.[7]

The agreement also spelled out that Joe Gossage would continue as publisher of the company, Alice would serve as its managing editor, Francis would be retained as assistant publisher and editor, and as soon as Harold reported for work, he would be assigned such duties as would be in "the best interest of the Company." Finally, the agreement attached a document titled "Statement of Agreed Policies," which was explicitly made part of the main agreement. Among other things, the attached document set forth the *Journal*'s general policies regarding editorials, news, and advertising, its commitment to "building the Journal as The Newspaper of Western South Dakota" and organizing the company's activities into defined departments, and a statement that the agreement's employment provisions referred to above were intended to continue for three years.[8]

Five days after the agreement was signed, the *Journal* announced that "Francis H. Case, of this city, and Harold W. Card, of Tyndall, have purchased an interest in the Rapid City Journal Company, including the block of stock formerly held by F. W. Meyers[.]" After providing brief backgrounds on Francis and Harold (including the fact that Harold presently managed the *Tyndall Tribune* in Tyndall, South Dakota), the announcement added that W. B. Andrus would continue as a *Journal* reporter, and "Art Brown... who joined the Journal force last month will assist in handling the news." The article concluded by noting that "the purchase of... [Meyers's] stock at this time completes the severance of his relations to the Journal." On December 17 and 18, Harold came to Rapid City to meet with friends and discuss "final details" of his new arrangement with the paper. Although it was reported that he would return to the city "within a few months" to take up his duties with the *Journal*, Harold did not begin work there until late June 1923.[9]

Signing the agreement made Francis "anxious to work harder than ever." But he did manage to send Christmas cards to several of his friends and former professors. And he celebrated Christmas Day with "Allen and his parents" in Hot Springs. While there, he admired a wagon that Grandpa Grannis had recently made for Allen. On New Year's Eve at 11:00 p.m., he wrote his mother to wish her a Happy New Year and report on his recent activities. They included the fact that he and Art recently moved in at the Breretons. (Bernie Brereton, a fellow Wesleyan debater, had relocated to Rapid City with his mother and brother earlier in the year.) With respect to his job at the *Journal*, he noted that "fortunately we are working with kindly people and they are pleased with good intentions... I do believe that in time we'll be where we want to be. Art Brown is sure a great help and real stimulant. He is wide awake, all the time." Turning to the subject of women, Francis stated that he had received several good, cheery letters in the autumn and winter from a fellow Wesleyanite who was "a real friend." Joyce introduced him to one of her friends a few weeks ago, who was "a very nice girl and one of the most striking faces I have ever seen." He also had gone out with a woman at Sturgis a couple of times, whom he described as "a real girl, capable, good-looking, athletic, etc." Nevertheless, he concluded that "I'm not thinking of marrying anyone for some time, now. . . . So don't worry about wedding presents for me for many moons."[10]

DUE TO ART'S ABLE ASSISTANCE at the *Journal*, Francis was no longer required to spend 16-to-18-hour days at the office. That meant he was able to engage with the community in early 1923. On Sunday, January 7, he gave an address during the morning service at the Methodist Church. Both he and Art joined Rapid City's American Legion Post No. 22, where Art became chairman of the Public Relations Committee. (He served in the U.S. Navy during the World War.) Later that month, Francis was elected as an active member of the Black Hills Press Association. In March, he joined the Lions Club, and he paid his dues to the Masonic Lodge in Mitchell so he could continue as "a Master Mason in good standing" there.[11]

Francis also found time to act in a play sponsored by the Ladies Auxiliary of the Methodist Church. Titled "Turning the Trick," the production was described as "a three act dramatic comedy" that had an interesting plot, and its carefully placed "spots of humor keep the audience in good nature." Its storyline centered around a rich, old, retired Irish contractor whose family try to remake him so "they can climb the social ladder." Despite their efforts, the old contractor "brings them all to earth" by turning the trick in an interesting and humorous way. Tryouts for the cast were held in late March. Frank Gormley was chosen for the role of the retired contractor, and Francis was selected to play his son. The eleven-member cast conducted rehearsals during the rest of that month. On Monday evening, April

2, the play was performed at the Elks Theater. For the ticket price of fifty cents, the public was entertained by this "excellent production."[12]

Memorial Day in 1923 was observed on May 30. On that day, "Rapid Cityans laid aside their regular activities," placed "flowers upon the graves of those who laid down their lives for their country," and held "appropriate patriotic services in the morning and afternoon." Several "patriotic orders," including "the G.A.R. Post [for Civil War Veterans], Women's Relief Corp., Spanish War Veterans, American Legion and Women's Auxiliary," participated in the grave-decorating ceremony held at Mountain View Cemetery in the forenoon. At three o'clock, the afternoon exercises began in the Methodist Church. During that program, patriotic songs were sung, a "sturdy" civil war veteran read the General Order that instituted Memorial Day, and a local judge read Lincoln's Gettysburg Address. Francis gave the Memorial Day Address. At the request "from many who expressed a desire to have the address in full," the *Journal* published its complete text in its May 31 issue.[13]

Francis began his speech by saying, "We are here today to quicken our love for our country by recalling what it has cost and how it came about." After quoting from the Declaration of Independence, he traced America's involvement in armed conflicts from the colonists who "proved invincible" in the Revolutionary War to the boys from Rapid City who fought in the World War. He then explained how that critical document and those events shaped the concept of patriotism in America. Next, he reminded the audience that "each one in whose heart there surges a wild, exultant passion when he sees fluttering the stars and stripes, in whose throat there comes that choking sensation, may know that he has a real part to perform in achieving the true greatness of the American nation." Toward the end of his talk, he recited a poem titled "In Flanders Fields." John McCrae—a Canadian soldier, physician, and poet—wrote the poem during the World War to memorialize those who died in a 1915 battle fought in Belgium.

The last stanza called on the next generation's responsibility to "take up our quarrel with the foe." In response to that challenge, Francis closed his address by stating, "Rest ye in peace, ye Flanders dead. The fight that ye so bravely led, We've taken up and we will keep true faith... Fear not that ye have died for nought... We've learned the lesson that ye taught/In Flanders Fields."[14]

HAROLD CARD MARRIED IRENE LYSEN on June 6. The former Miss Lysen, from Lowry, Minnesota, graduated from that state's university with a bachelor's degree in home economics in 1922. She taught that subject during the 1922-23 school year at Tyndall High School. There she met Harold, who coached football and debate and taught part-time at the school. Four days after the couple held their wedding at the Lutheran Church in Lowry, the *Journal* announced "two changes in its staff for the summer." W. B. Andrus, who had worked on the paper's local news staff for three years, resigned from that job to manage a canteen at a tourist park, and Art Brown decided to take a leave of absence so he could return to the Medill School of Journalism to teach summer school. These departures would be replaced by Harold Card, who was expected to move to Rapid City "during the latter part of the month"; and Leland Case, who had been city editor at the *Journal* during August 1919 and was hired for the present summer "during the absence of Mr. Brown."[15]

After a short honeymoon "among the Minnesota lakes" and a stop at the groom's parental home in Mitchell, Mr. and Mrs. Harold Card arrived by car in Rapid City on June 21 "to take up their residence." Harold began work on the *Journal* staff a few days later. One of his first projects was to create a page titled "'The Journal's Weekly Forum for Thrifty Housewives.'" This page contained "special announcements and bargains of local grocerymen and meat marke[t] men," and Harold proposed to make it "occupy an important place in the minds of all thrifty Rapid City buyers."[16]

ART BROWN TOOK THE EVENING train for Evanston, Illinois, on June 13, and Leland joined the *Journal* staff to temporarily take his place. Many years later, Leland recalled working for the paper that summer. He remembered Alice Gossage "was a very devout member of the Congregational church and was always doing something for people in trouble, unwed mothers, Indians, people who had hard luck." She wrote articles and editorials that usually dealt with "something local and having to do with Indians on the other side of the track or something like that," and she was glad to turn over editorial writing on other subjects to the "boys" on the *Journal* staff. Leland also recollected working with L. W. Chandler, whom he described as "a writer of the old school, I mean the high flown rhetoric school" with "a quiet little sense of humor[.]" After he "had beaten his way around the country working as an editorial writer for various papers," the *Journal* hired him as an editorial writer in the spring of 1922. During the summer of 1923, he was "a good guy to have around because if Francis wanted to go fishing or something, Mr. Chandler would fill in."[17]

Mr. Chandler most likely "filled in" in mid-July, when Wesleyan's Alumnal Association held an executive committee meeting in Mitchell. Francis presided at the meeting, where the association decided to increase its activities "by the publication of a quarterly magazine, the organization of Wesleyan Clubs throughout the state and the employment of an executive secretary." He stated that by taking these measures, his alma mater hoped to extend "'the spirit of the school into community life where its former students now live.'"[18]

Shortly after he returned to Evanston to teach and serve as editor for the school newspaper's summer edition, Art met and began dating a woman from Mitchell named Della Kjelmyr. He wrote to Francis that "I'm spending most of my spare time with Della. And I'm serious. . . . I like her better than any girl I ever knew," and "I think she's just the right sort of girl for me." And at the end of July, he wrote that "during the first twenty-nine days I knew her, I had pretty near twenty-nine dates with her[.]" On August 2, Art "finished his last class in the School of Journalism" and began "to realize how quickly the summer has sped by." He noted that "Della is enthusiastic about Rapid City," although "she hasn't told me yet that she wants to go out there and help us." Two days later, Art informed Francis by letter that he "asked Della to marry me . . . and I think she will all right, but I don't want her to say so until she is sure about this guy in Mitchell." He added that he planned to return to "the Black Hills about the first of September" and would "like Della out there before Christmas."[19]

In mid-August, Joe Gossage made a trip east that included stops in Ottumwa and Red Oak, Iowa, Pekin, Illinois, Chicago, and Omaha. While in Chicago, he "looked up Art Brown and found him busy as a bee but looking forward to coming back to Rapid City." During that visit, Art reported that he and Joe "walked a great deal, rode cars and climbed stairs getting to the various places he had on his schedule, but he never faltered a moment. I never did see him so spry as he was down there among the traffic. He liked it. He was right in his element." Joe also told Art "a lot of things," including that Card "'is a damn good man'" who is "'making a great number of friends in Rapid City'"; that Leland had so "'many girls it was impossible to even try to keep track of them'"; and that Francis "'doesn't know who he wants to go with. One day it's one girl, and the next, it's someone else!'" Della met Joe and Art at the LaSalle Hotel, and the three of them "went out to lunch together." Della and Joe "found plenty to talk about," and Joe "was pleased when Della told him that she had heard of Joe Gossage long before she ever knew an Art Brown existed." Overall, Joe was "mightily pleased" with his trip to the Windy City, despite finding the weather "almost unbearable."[20]

On August 16, Della left Chicago for Mitchell aboard a 9:20 p.m. train. Art stayed in Evanston for another week or so to "clean up on the odds and ends" and collect and pay bills for Northwestern's student newspaper. While still there, he learned that F. W. Meyers would be returning to Rapid City to work with Werner on the *Daily Guide*. Just before leaving, Art summed up the past three months in Evanston as follows: "All in all, I had a humdoozer of a summer.... My being away has been a good thing for me, I know, and I think it has been a good thing for the Journal. I am mighty glad Leland had a chance to get out there." After "chas[ing] down to Toledo" to see his parents, Art headed west to Rapid City. He stopped at Mitchell along the way to visit Della, and he arrived in Rapid on September 4.[21]

SOON AFTER ART RETURNED TO the *Journal*, the "division of work" was clarified with respect to Case, Card, and Brown. In addition to their other duties, Francis was put in charge of editorial policy, Harold handled the paper's "business end," and Art worked mainly on advertising and circulation. Since February 25, 1923, the *Journal* had listed Joseph B. Gossage as Publisher, A. R. Gossage as Managing Editor, Francis Case as Asst. Publisher, and L. W. Chandler as Editor. Beginning with its September 11 issue, the paper continued to list the four names and positions mentioned above, but it added "Harold Card... City Editor," and "Art Brown... Advertising" to the list.[22]

After Art resumed his job at the *Journal*, Leland became city editor of the *Lead Daily Call*. While he worked there, the *Call* had two staff members: a woman who operated the linotype and wrote social columns, and Leland, who, in addition to the usual duties as editor, "did most of the reporting." He moved into a rooming house, where he "took a couple of rooms and a small bathroom on the first floor." Leland would keep that job for nearly two years.[23]

In October, Francis described the Rapid City newspaper scene in a letter to his grandfather Grannis. Francis had now been at the *Journal* for a little over a year, and he was able to say that "our situation, prestige, product and general internal feeling is much better—immeasurably better than it was a year ago." With respect to the *Daily Guide*—referred to as the *Journal*'s "rival newspaper"—he noted that it was "in a bad way according to all reports." Those reports indicated that the paper's "debts are more than the total value of their plant," and the *Daily Guide* had "given chattel mortgages and everything else to keep alive." Despite Werner's first editorial in November 1922 that promised the *Daily Guide* would exclude the "personal element" from its news columns, Francis stated that he had been "lampooned and ignored, called names and what not by the other paper and its publisher." On this point, Francis further remarked that "because I came first, I seem to get the brunt of the slams aside from what Mr. Gossage gets. Brown and Card are almost jealous when I get some new unfavorable mention."[24]

The Case-Card-Brown trio all pursued outside interests that fall. Francis drove to Mitchell with Miss Myrle Graves and Miss Florence Johnson—both teachers at Rapid City High School—to attend the Dakota Wesleyan homecoming festivities. While in Mitchell, the two young women also visited their parents and other relatives who lived there. Harold had become assistant coach for the School of Mines football team and was called upon to present a talk at the post-season banquet given by the Lions Club. And Art was appointed as chairman of an American Legion committee that presented "The Girl in the Glass"—a musical comedy that ran for three consecutive nights at the Elks Theater.[25]

On December 25, Francis and Leland "motored to Hot Springs... to enjoy Christmas dinner at the home of... Mrs. C. A. Wilson." That same day, Art and Della were married in Mitchell. A few days later, the *Journal* recognized the marriage in an article that began by declaring "the Journal is becoming a matrimonial center." It went on to exclaim that "during the past year four weddings in which the Journal force furnished principles to the contracts have occurred," and "the latest benedict of our force is Art Brown, the advertising wizzard /sic/, who is not only a hypnotizer in propagating business success, but thoroughly believes in making two blades of grass grow where only one before has been cultivated."[26]

IN MID-JANUARY 1924, FRANCIS again wrote to his grandfather about the current status of the Rapid City newspaper business. He stated that his most recent *Journal* assignments were to "get some work on the books" and "trying to find out where we can reduce expenses and make more money." As to the *Daily Guide*, he noted that it was now "running only 4 pages a day and carrying hardly enuf advertising for that." Werner had previously said that "his young business men friends in town would never desert him." Yet his closest friend, a bank president and president of the Rapid City Commercial Club, had "left town—his bank broke, and himself under $3,000 bond to answer an indictment by the federal grand jury for car stealing." Other Werner associates had either left Rapid, "gone to the wall," or had "become the Journal's best friends." Francis stated that these developments were "negative progress, in a way, and I wish none of these people ill-luck." He concluded that Werner's approach "does show that there is a difference between building friendship and business on bombast, hot air and hootch and on real service." And he predicted that "unless the other paper gets some unlikely financial help, it will certainly be forced to quit before long."[27]

Less than a month later, Francis's prediction that the *Daily Guide* would be "forced to quit" turned out to be accurate. On February 11, that paper suspended publication. When he announced the decision, Werner said that the *Daily Guide* "will suspend publication temporarily until such time as the business conditions improve sufficiently to warrant the continuation of the daily paper. This decision was reached after thoughtful and careful study of the situation, and this announcement is made with much regret on our part." He added that "many of the Evening Guide's closest friends and most loyal supporters were consulted and they have advised that in these times it was useless to burn energy with worry and fret." A few weeks later, the *Murdo Coyote* (a weekly newspaper published in Murdo, South Dakota) observed that the suspension left "Rapid City with but one daily, The Journal, (morning and evening) which is perfectly capable of covering the field and giving the news to the people of the territory." And although Werner indicated the suspension was temporary, the *Guide* never re-emerged as a daily paper.[28]

About the same time the *Guide* stopped daily publication, L. W. Chandler "severed his connections" with the *Journal*. He was in poor health and opted to "relax from the strenous /sic/ grind of daily editorial writing." Rather than put down his writing pen for good, he decided to assist his old friend Elmer George at the *Hill City News* "for several weeks." (The *News* was a weekly published in Hill City, South Dakota.) When it announced Chandler's decision, the *Journal* had this to say about its departed colleague: "He did yeoman service on the Journal, bringing the fruitage of many years experience both in writing and thinking on editorial topics. The Journal expresses the thoughts of hundreds of readers in wishing for him better health, congenial surroundings and plenty of copy paper."[29]

In early 1924, Francis began writing one article a month for *The Epworth Herald*. "My Citizenship" was the subject of these articles. He also became the oratory and debate coach at the School of Mines. On January 11, a senior at the Mines named Homer Surbeck won an oratorical contest over two other entrants. Winning meant that he gained the "right to represent his school at the South Dakota intercollegiate contest." Harold Card was one of the two judges that decided to award Surbeck first place. And he won second place at the state contest held in February at Aberdeen.[30]

The Mines debate teams entered four contests in March. The question for discussion was "'Resolved, that the United States should enter the permanent court of international relations as proposed by the late President Harding.'" The first two debates, held in Rapid City on March 17 and 21, pitted the Miners' negative team against affirmative teams from Huron College and Aberdeen Normal. The home team lost both of those debates by two-to-one votes from the three judges. Francis then accompanied the affirmative team to Sioux Falls for a debate against Columbus College on March 22. Columbus won that debate—also in a split decision. Two days later, the Mines team and its coach were in Mitchell, where Francis attended the Wesleyan Reunion Alumnal Dinner at noon, and his debaters faced off against a Wesleyan team that evening. The Miners lost in yet another two-to-one decision. That debate "was hard fought throughout," and, like the judges, the "audience was divided on the decision, many claiming it was a Miners' victory."[31]

DURING THE LATTER HALF OF MAY, Harold and Francis gave commencement addresses at graduation exercises in area high schools. Harold spoke to the graduating class at Scenic High School on May 23. (Scenic High was located about 40 miles southeast of Rapid City.) In his speech, he "pointed out the various [duties one] must perform in order to fulfill his obligations to his country for the benefits she has conferred upon him[.]" One week later, Francis addressed 28 graduating boys and girls at the Rapid City Indian School. It was the largest class of graduates in the school's history, and "many people from the city attended the program[.]" During Francis's talk, titled "The Prisoner," he stated that "'your people love America and you as the trained boys and girls of your race must join hands with the trained boys and girls of my race to solve our common problems.'" He also said that "'an uneducated race is an imprisoned race and some of you must free your people from ignorance.'"[32]

Francis was elected as president of the Rapid City Lions Club on May 20. A few weeks later, the local club appointed him as one of two delegates to attend the Eighth Annual Lions International Convention in Omaha, Nebraska. It was scheduled for June 23-26. Francis left for Omaha by car on the 21st. He was accompanied by two other Rapid City Lions, a delegate from the Mitchell Lions Club, and Joe Gossage, who decided to go to the convention as a guest.[33]

At least 2,000 Lions from "all over the United States and Canada" came to the yearly Lions' get-together. Over four days, the delegates elected a president and directors of the International Association of Lions Clubs and heard speeches from prominent Lions. In addition, the delegates, other Lions, and convention guests attended receptions, dances, and a cabaret, where they were entertained by "nationally prominent musicians." The Omaha gathering also marked the first time that an International Convention Parade was held. On the convention's second day, the Lions "marched down the streets of Omaha" in a "celebratory procession." And the event "became even livelier when Lions from Colorado began a snowball fight at the end of the parade. The Colorado delegates had brought in loads of snow by railway car from the mountains back home and couldn't resist sharing a mid-summer surprise—a first for Omaha in June."[34]

In the summer of 1924, Francis also began working on a follow-up volume to his 1921 book: *Handbook of Church Advertising*. As noted above, the *Handbook* was based on speeches given at the 1920 AACW Convention held in Indianapolis. The second book—titled *Advertising the Church: Suggestions by Church Advertisers*—utilized source material from "the church department of the Associated Advertising Clubs of the World with its departmental sessions at the annual conventions, at Atlantic City in 1923 and at Wembley, England, in 1924." Like its predecessor, *Advertising the Church* consisted of 12 chapters, and except for chapter two, all chapter heads in both books were identical. Each book sold for $1.25 per copy.[35]

The Abingdon Press published *Advertising the Church* in 1925. In a section titled "The Source and Scope of the Book," Francis acknowledged those who assisted him in preparing it. There he wrote the following about his brother: "Leland D. Case has collaborated with the author in handling this material, bringing to the work the zeal of an enthusiastic promoter of laymen's activities as well as the skill and point of view of a brilliant news writer." A brochure that promoted the book stated "in this volume, the churchman will find many useful, practical suggestions that will aid him in bringing his church to the attention of his local community." That brochure also included favorable comments about the book excerpted from nine different newspapers. Many years later, the following note appeared in a copy of *Advertising the Church* that Leland gave to then-Senator Case: "To Francis This book cost 39 cents, 1962 AD—which is a reminder that many things have happened since 1925! —From Leland 4/12/62."[36]

ON THE MORNING OF SEPTEMBER 9, Frank Case suddenly died of a brain hemorrhage at Herbert's home in Mankato. The day before "he had been unusually well and active," and death came after he had been sick for only an hour and a half. Herbert took his father's body to Mason City for the funeral and internment in the family plot at the city's cemetery. Soon after he heard the news, Francis wrote to Carol that "Grandpa lived a useful and honorable life and that's what counts. He hasn't handicapped us with a single regret, - and he has left us many things to be thankful for." And he added: "I hope that when my time to go, comes, that it can be said of me he was 'well, happy and active' up to the last night."[37]

NINETEEN TWENTY-FOUR WAS A presidential election year. Back in February, Francis was selected as president of the Rapid City Coolidge Club's 25-member executive committee. That group was organized to support Republican Calvin Coolidge's bid to retain the presidency. (Coolidge—elected as Warren Harding's vice-president in 1920—became president one day after Harding died in office on August 2, 1923; and the incumbent wanted to stay in office.) The executive committee, which included Harold Card, was also charged with recruiting other members to join the club. When Rapid City's Coolidge Club came into being in February, similar clubs had already been organized in several Black-Hills-area towns, including Deadwood, Lead, Custer, Edgemont, Hot Springs, and Belle Fourche.[38]

On September 18, Francis took on an additional role in the 1924 election. He became chairman of the South Dakota Republican State Committee's Western Division, whose headquarters were in Rapid City. The "Western Division" consisted of 23 counties. All of them were located west of the Missouri River and included in the state's third congressional district. When Francis took this job, Della Brown agreed "to help with the newspaper work" while he was in the Western Division offices.[39]

Ten days after Francis became chairman of the GOP's western headquarters, the *Journal* reported the October dates and locations in the "west river country" where the Republican candidate for governor (Carl Gunderson) and for third district congressman (William Williamson), as well as a Republican activist, would be speaking. It also noted that W. H. McMaster (the current governor and now U.S. Senate candidate) had already begun his west river campaign and was "expected in the central west river section after the middle of October." With respect to the presidential contest, the *Journal* cited evidence presented by Chairman Case that demonstrated Coolidge and his vice-presidential running mate Charles Dawes were "gaining votes" throughout western South Dakota in areas that were earlier reported to be in favor of Robert LaFollette—the Progressive party's candidate for president.[40]

On October 23, Francis wrote to Wesleyan's treasurer—John F. Way—that "we are so busy in the campaign," and "I see so much of it that I hardly know what to say as to how it is coming. I do believe that the Third District is going to go for a straight Republican ticket, but by how big a majority I will not venture to predict." One week later, Francis and three others (including Joe Gossage) left Rapid City by car to visit several county seats, where they planned to campaign for the Republican party. One of the group's members gave several speeches in Jackson County, while the remaining three (including Francis) went to six towns in South Dakota's northwestern counties. During those stops, Francis made "a number of political addresses." The group then returned to Rapid. Joyce and Cliff were in town after attending a meeting on Saturday night. Joyce saw Francis for "a few minutes" the next morning, and she wrote to their mother that "he will surely be glad when the election is over."[41]

On the night before the November 4 election, Francis stated that he was "confident that the west river section will go for the Republicans in both the state and national tickets." The voters went to the polls the next day. After they did so and the returns began to come in, it became apparent that Francis's optimism about the election outcome was justified. Joyce called him about midnight and reported he was "quite jubilant that the Republicans were carrying the State by a good majority." Indeed they did. On a statewide basis, McMaster was elected U.S. Senator in an eight-candidate field, all three Republican candidates easily won seats in the U.S. Congress, and Gunderson was elected governor by more than a two to one margin over his Democratic opponent. And at the national level, Calvin Coolidge won 50 percent of the popular vote in South Dakota, whereas Robert LaFollette received 37 percent and Democrat John Davis the remaining 13 percent. Six days after the election, Francis wrote again to Wesleyan's treasurer. Among other things, he said that he was "rather busy getting into the swing on the paper again for I put in most of my time on the campaign during the last few weeks. There is some satisfaction that efforts there were not in vain—so am feeling good."[42]

FRANCIS AGAIN TURNED TO POLITICS in early 1925, when he attended the governor's inaugural and reception at the state capitol in Pierre. At noon on January 6, newly-elected Carl Gunderson took the oath of office as governor in the house chamber. Then outgoing governor W. H. McMaster (who was elected to the U.S. Senate two months earlier) read a message to the "assembled legislators and to people of the state who crowded the galleries[.]" It was described as "his report of the stewardship that has been his for the last four years." Governor Gunderson followed with his inaugural address. It emphasized, among other things, the need for "tax revision to relieve the burden upon agricultural lands," "a thorough investigation of every state department for the punishment of any guilt and vindication of all others," and "consolidation of two dozen departments and boards under two departments, one of agriculture and the other of finance[.]" Francis described the two speeches as sounding "like a debate—only the rebuttal has been given by the friends of each in lobbies and over the tables since."[43]

The inaugural reception was held in the capitol rotunda from eight to ten o'clock that evening. There governor Gunderson and "other new state officials" greeted "the people of the state." No inaugural ball was held, but there was a grand march. Francis gave an unvarnished description of this event in a letter to Myrle Graves that was written after he returned to his room at the St. Charles Hotel: "Tonight was the grand soiree. No ball, but a receiving line which received for hours while farmers wives wore evening gowns, and mechanical smiles and bows could be found on all sides." He added that "the dames and their awkward husbands grand marched. The governor's daughter sang and the lady whose husband was bitterly attacked by the outgoing governor led a ladies' chorus in several songs. More bowing. More scraping." Toward the end of the evening, "farewells [were] said over and over—for the person you saw on the second floor and thot you'd not see again, you met on the first, he as aimless and vacillating in his resolve to go to the hotel, as you."[44]

Francis's general comment about the reception revealed his dislike for the social side of politics: "This is the sham-iest sort of life I've ever met. Half the people are not sincere. They pretend to know, to be glad, to be angry—or what not and I am not ready now to believe much at all." But despite these negative comments, he felt that he had "learned some things, chiefly this—to talk less, listen more and care only for my own business.—Oh, I haven't learned that fully, yet. I'll make mistakes on those points. But I am learning." And he confessed to Myrle that "for a day—or so—I'd like to be in the heart of it all with you.—just for the thrill of it, to stand in the receiving line.—only you're so much better looking than most of these dowagers,—they might want to rule you out."[45]

Apart from its frank comments about the governor's inaugural and reception, Francis's January 6 letter confirmed that he regarded Myrle Graves as much more than simply one of the passengers whom he drove to and from the Wesleyan homecoming activities in November 1923. He apparently began dating her sometime in 1923 or 1924, and in September 1924, he wrote to Carol that "Myrle is here, again, and it's a constant temptation to want to see her more often than is good for my work.... She rooms at McMahon's on Kansas City in a delightful home. She is, as you said, as winsome as ever in spite of her bobbed hair which she dislikes very much." The final paragraph in his January 6 letter described an imagined image of her that he wanted to connect with: "And always, I've been reaching, reaching, trying to touch your hand, to stroke it, to tell you I care, I care for you Myrle as for nothing else on earth."[46]

IN FEBRUARY, FRANCIS JOINED AN "all-star home-talent cast" in a four-act comedy titled "The Famous Mrs. Fair." The play—given "under the auspices of the Rapid City Young People's Union" and directed by Miss S. Edna Hesketh—was based "on the aftermath" of the World War. Its plot centered around an American woman who "won great honors as a war zone worker" in France and decided to join a lecture tour when she returned home, despite the strong objections of her husband. The unfolding drama dealt "with the conflict of home and career in the heart of a woman; with misunderstanding, jealousy and love, all intermingled, in the heart of her husband; with not uncommon problems that arise in the lives of their children." "The Famous Mrs. Fair" previously "had long runs in New York and Chicago" and was "generally regarded as one of the three or four best American plays of the last six years." In the Rapid City production, Miss Florence Johnson and Francis played the leading roles—Johnson as the famous Mrs. Fair and Francis as her husband Jeffrey. Miss Johnson's character was described as "'a vividly arresting figure,'" and Francis's as a 50-year-old "American man of affairs" who recognized that his wife was "extraordinary" but believed she should "resume her place in the home" after returning from Europe.[47]

The play was presented on two consecutive nights (February 26 and 27) at the Rapid City High School Auditorium. After the first performance, the *Journal* commented that "the presentation last evening was not faultless, yet it was well-done. All members of the cast took their parts in a capable manner and the audience left the high school auditorium, convinced that it had seen a worth-while play far above the usual standard." The paper's review after the second night was more enthusiastic. It described the play as "one of the best amateur productions ever staged here" and stated that "great credit is due every member of the cast for its splendid presentation." That article praised Miss Johnson's performance as showing "splendid stage presence and fine dramatic ability." It added that "Francis Case, as Mr. Fair, had one of the difficult parts in the play and carried it remarkably well." After commenting favorably on the performances by the ten other cast members, the review ended by noting that "a good audience saw the play the first evening, and an even larger crowd was present last evening"; and "the DeMolay orchestra furnished such good music before and between acts that they are sure to have many calls from hearers for future engagements."[48]

ON APRIL 28, FRANCIS AND HAROLD gave local attorney George Flavin an option to purchase the Case-Card holdings in the *Rapid City Journal*. Five days later, the *Journal* announced that Art Brown had "accepted a position on the editorial staff of the Nation's Business, official paper of the Chamber of Commerce of the United States, at Washington, D.C." Brown had gone to Washington two weeks earlier "to look over the position," and he wired the *Journal* on May 2 that he had decided to take it. Brown's wife Della, who had made weekly contributions to the *Journal*'s "Books and Things" column, was reported to be leaving for Washington in early May after she disposed of the couple's household furniture. The *Journal* announcement lauded Art's career at its paper and the contributions the Browns made to the local community. It also noted that "on the Nation's Business, his work will be that of layout man in the editorial department," and it described his new job as "a remunerative position with so great a future so that his friends could hardly advise him not to accept it."[49]

Francis informed Carol of these developments in a May 11 letter. He wrote that Art and Della's departure made him "lonesome and busy for so far I have been taking care of both his work and mine for three weeks." Apparently referring to the Flavin option-to-purchase agreement referred to above, he also mentioned that "we have a deal up on the Journal, and in another month I'll be either out or in more than ever."[50]

It actually took Harold and Francis less than a month to decide to sell their ownership interests in the *Journal*. On May 29, the paper reported that "Harold Card and Francis Case . . . yesterday disposed of their holdings in the Rapid City Journal Company to eastern newspaper parties and are severing their connections with the paper." The unidentified "eastern newspaper parties" referred to above were owners of the Lusk-Mitchell Corporation, which included W. C. Lusk from Yankton, Charles H. J. Mitchell from Sioux Falls, and others. The article went on to note that Harold was asked to continue with the *Journal* "'for a few weeks during the period of readjustment,'" and Francis expected "to be in Rapid City off and on during the forepart of the summer." It concluded by stating that the "amount of... consideration and... extent of the holdings involved in the complete transaction is not announced. George Flavin attorney who handled the negotiations said that the sale of the Card-Case holdings was arranged for in a 30-day option which the parties gave him the last of April."[51]

During the third week in June, the Gossages "sold everything but a small amount of stock" to the Lusk-Mitchell Corporation. The sellers decided to retain a minimal interest in the *Journal* "so that Mr. Gossage would not be entirely out of the paper he had founded nearly fifty years before." In conjunction with the sale, a new Journal Publishing Company was formed. Its officers included Charles H. J. Mitchell (President and Treasurer), G. F. McCannon (Vice-President), and E. F. ("Ted") Lusk (Secretary). These three men, plus Walter Travis, took "charge of the Journal" in mid-June. Although it was originally anticipated that Harold Card would stay on for only "a few weeks" after the change in ownership, he remained on the paper's staff as managing editor until 1928, when he left to "go into the newspaper business for himself in Webster, S. D."[52]

ON JUNE 5, FRANCIS ENTERED into an Agreement with R. L. Bronson, secretary of the Tri-State Roundup Association. By that contract, Bronson agreed to secure for Francis the "full concession rights" and "exclusive sale" rights of a souvenir program at the eighth annual Tri-State Roundup to be held at Belle Fourche on July 2, 3, and 4. That "roundup" featured three days of rodeo events, including a Tri-State Champion bucking contest, wild steer riding, bareback wild horse riding, trick and fancy roping, ladies' bucking exhibition, steer roping exhibition and contest, cowboys' and cowgirls' relay races, bulldogging, cowgirls' and cowboys' cow horse races, clowning, and wild horse races. For his part, Francis agreed to publish and sell the souvenir program, which would contain at least 24 pages, would give approximately equal space to advertising and "reading or illustrative material pertaining to the roundup and the Black Hills," would contain a "daily entry program," and would sell for 25 cents per copy. The parties also agreed that Bronson would provide admission passes to all program salesmen, and the net profits from advertising fees and program sales would be divided 25 percent to Bronson and 75 percent to Francis.[53]

In conjunction with the roundup, the interstate "konclave" of the Knights of the Ku Klux Klan was scheduled to begin at the fairgrounds after the roundup program concluded on July 4. It was anticipated that "Klansmen from all over the country... but particularly from the Dakotas, Nebraska, Iowa, Minnesota, Wyoming, Montana, Colorado, Illinois, Indiana, Ohio and Wisconsin" would participate. Between 75,000 and 85,000 were expected to attend the konklave. Its parade that night was to feature 10,000 robed and hooded Klansmen, with 500 of them mounted on robed and hooded horses. With respect to this plan, the *Journal* commented that "just what will happen when a robed and hooded man mounts a horse is a subject of considerable speculation." It was also predicted that "thirty or more crosses will be burned the evening of the celebration."[54]

Francis had assembled a large group to sell the souvenir programs during each day of the three-day roundup. Counting himself, he had a 16-person sales force, which included Leland and Bernie Brereton. Myrle Graves and her sister Bessie also helped him "at the stands." In addition, ten Camp-fire girls from Belle Fourche sold the programs. Revenue generated from these efforts increased on each of the three days, and on the third day, Francis sold "over 40 books in half an hour at the two-bit price." Still, he "did not make the money... [he] had hoped to make," which he attributed to "the crowds being so much smaller than we had expected." He summed up the venture by stating that "during June, when I worked at all, I worked on a souvenir program for sale at the Round up at Belle Fourche. Made some money at it, much better than a Journal salary, but not a fortune."⁵⁵

The reports on how many people attended the Tri-State Roundup varied widely. According to an article by the Associated Press that appeared in the *Daily Argus-Leader*, "no accurate estimate is available of the number in attendance [at the three-day event,] but it is conservatively placed by officials at 20,000." One day later, another *Argus* story claimed that the "crowd[s] at the grounds and in town the last day of the Belle Fourche roundup were estimated at 75,000." Both articles did agree that 36 states were represented, and the second article noted that visitors also came from Alaska, Canada, Honolulu, and Mexico. The first article added that the "round-up passed without a single reported accident either in the events on the program or among the spectators."⁵⁶

After the roundup program closed on July 4, "the grounds were turned over to the Ku Klux Klan organization." From the grandstand, bleachers, high bluffs to the south and east, and gradual incline to the west, thousands of spectators "looked down on the grounds with burning crosses and white robed figures." Klan officials from South and North Dakota led the parade. Its robed Klansmen marched four abreast. Most were on foot but some were on horseback. They were accompanied by "beautiful floats," a large "flag display," and some women participants. Although it was predicted that 10,000 Klansmen would take part in the parade, only about 1,000 did so. Another 480 arrived too late to participate. ⁵⁷

Those who watched the procession from elevated positions described it as "resembling a snowy white electric serpent over a half mile in length winding gracefully about, from the grounds over to town, back to the grounds and around the track, torches lighted on arena posts ahead of its progress." After the parade, a representative of the Klan's imperial wizard gave a speech to "much applause." At some point in the proceedings "about 100 new members were initiated" into the Klan. Its program closed with "a large fireworks display." Overall, "good order prevailed throughout the roundup and Klan demonstration." No "trouble of any kind" occurred, and officers reported "there was very little moonshine."[58]

CAROL CASE GRADUATED FROM MANKATO High School on January 20, 1922. Her graduating class had 14 members. Soon thereafter, she followed her mother's and older sister's educational path and attended Mankato Commercial College. She enjoyed the "practice and memory work" there, and she finished her course in July or August. That fall she became a freshman at Hamline University in St. Paul. After completing one semester, she returned to Mankato. In early April, 1923, she travelled to western South Dakota, visited Francis and her Rapid City friends for a few days, and then went to Hot Springs to live and work with Joyce and Cliff for the summer. The next month, the Wilsons' second child—Lois Arlene—was born.[59]

Over the summer, Carol decided she wanted to continue her college education but did not want to return to Hamline. After consulting with her parents and requesting information from other colleges in South Dakota, she chose to go to Dakota Wesleyan, and she enrolled there in the fall. In addition to taking classes, she also got a job working for the college. During her first term, she met an upperclassman named Ralph Himmelhoch. Born and raised in Milwaukee, Himmelhoch worked as a brakeman for the Chicago, Milwaukee & St. Paul Railway Company in 1923. The railroad granted him a furlough so he was able to attend Wesleyan in the fall. Carol and Ralph entered a romantic relationship, and by the spring of 1924, it had become serious enough for her father to write that she and Ralph "both want to get your educations before you allow thots of affection to grasp you too deeply," and "we want you to move so slowly you'd never make a choice that you ever would have occasion to regret."[60]

Carol returned to Hot Springs for the summer of 1924 to live with Joyce and Cliff and work in Cliff's law office on a part-time basis. That fall, she decided to enroll in the School of Speech at Northwestern University. It allowed her "27 1/3 semester hours of credit" for the work she had done at Hamline and Wesleyan. It also advised her on the courses she needed to take for a Bachelor of Letters degree. Francis was "rightly glad" that she opted to attend his graduate alma mater, and he and Leland agreed to loan her money so she could afford to go there. Ralph attended the University of Chicago that fall, and he and Carol rekindled their relationship after being apart for the summer.[61]

When it became clear that Carol was going to Northwestern, Francis advised her to "not let boys take up too much of your time." In a letter dated March 15, 1925, Leland asked "How are you, and all of the Windy City's young men, Carol? Are you still keeping them guessing?" Three days later, Carol and Ralph were married at Blue Earth, Minnesota. The couple then moved back to Ralph's home town—Milwaukee, Wisconsin. Leland wrote to her on April 24 that "sometime, I suppose, I'm going to realize my Carol is married—but I don't know when." A few weeks later, Francis shipped a box of dishes (containing chinaware and "some specials in water sets, punch glasses, etc.") to the family home in Mankato, with the understanding that Carol would be there at the end of May for Esther's high school graduation. The dishes were a wedding present from Joyce, Francis, and Leland (and partly a belated birthday greeting for Carol).[62]

AFTER THE ROUNDUP WAS COMPLETED, Myrle, Bessie, Leland, and Francis spent the next day in the northern Black Hills. On July 6, Francis took the two women to "the Lake" and Wind Cave. His folks, Esther, and a woman named Meredith arrived later that day, and he was "delighted to see them." The group then went to Hot Springs, and Francis later wrote to Carol about their niece and nephew: "Wish you could see Lois and Allen now. Lois likes me better than any girl

I know. She follows me around generally and cries if I go anywhere in the car and leave her. I came off while she was asleep Friday." One week after he returned to Rapid City, Francis and Carol became uncle and aunt to another niece when the Wilsons' third and final child was born. They named her Dorothy Joyce.⁶³

Toward the end of July, Francis made a two-week auto trip to Minneapolis, Detroit, and Chicago. While in Minneapolis, he had a job interview with Dr. Kerfoot from Hamline University. During their meeting, Kerfoot offered him a position at Hamline that would involve doing publicity work for the college and possibly teaching one class in advertising. The job would begin on September 10, pay $2,500, and require a commitment for 11 months. On his way back to South Dakota, Francis stopped in Mitchell. Carol and Ralph were there at the time, and the three of them drove back to Camp Galena in the Black Hills, where "Mrs. Himmelhoch's parents and other relatives were camping." After catching up with some correspondence and finalizing his commitments to R. L. Bronson under their Tri-State Roundup souvenir-program Agreement, Francis joined the Camp Galena campers for supper on August 8.⁶⁴

Francis did not accept the offer at Hamline. Instead, in early September the *Journal* announced that he and Leland "just purchased the '*Times-Herald*' ... from Mrs. Virginia Harrison and her sister, Miss Lena Wilcox." Articles of incorporation "for the Times-Herald Publishing Company of Hot Springs" were filed with the secretary of state. The incorporators were Francis, Leland, Herbert, and Joyce and Clifford Wilson. Under the new organization, Joyce was to serve as corporate treasurer, Mr. F. Osgood—former foreman of the *Journal's* makeup department—was to manage the paper, and Lena Wilcox would continue as its city editor. The *Journal's* September 5 announcement concluded by adding that "neither Francis... nor Leland... will be actively associated with the Times-Herald this winter as Francis will study law at Chicago and Leland will take graduate work at Northwestern University, Evanston." That concluding statement turned out to be accurate regarding Leland but not with respect to Francis.[65]

CHAPTER 9

HOT SPRINGS NEWSPAPERMAN AND BLACK HILLS PROMOTER—THE EARLY YEARS

The Black Hills are like no other land in Christendom. Western South Dakota is peopled by pioneers whose spirit cannot be excelled anywhere.
—Francis Case

A few weeks after the Case brothers purchased the *Times-Herald*, the owners of the *Hot Springs Star*—the town's other weekly newspaper—raised the "possibility of joining forces" by selling a majority interest in their paper to Francis and Leland. Negotiations concerning this proposal began during the third week in September, and a deal was worked out whereby the *Star* became property of the newly-formed Star Publishing Company, the *Star*'s former owners (A. T. Johnson and his wife Cora B. Johnson) obtained minority ownership interests in the new company and the Times-Herald Publishing Company, and the Johnsons were given a two-year employment contract by the Star Publishing Company. Francis and Leland assumed "the controlling interest by a wide margin in the latter company, which in turn would come to own practically all of the stock of the Times-Herald Company." And Francis became the Star Publishing Company's president and manager.[1]

Given that the "Star deal" went through, Francis changed his mind about going to Chicago to study law that winter. Instead, he decided to stay in Hot Springs and run the expanded newspaper operation. He also opted to register "with Cliff [Wilson] for reading law" in the latter's office, and he enrolled in a home-study law course given by the Blackstone Institute in Chicago. Regarding this decision, Francis noted that after the two papers were up and running, he expected to "spend my evenings diligently, at law." He added that he had "been doing some reading in contracts and corporation law to get these deals worked out. So Cliff says I've started already." On the other hand, Leland went ahead with his plan to do graduate work at Northwestern's School of Journalism. He left for Evanston in mid-September and was "quite elated" when he learned that the *Times-Herald/Star* consolidation was finalized.[2]

On October 1, the *Star* announced that it and the *Times-Herald* were now united "under one Management, the Star Publishing Company." It further explained that "publication of both papers will continue, but the days of publication will be spread apart, the Star to be printed on Tuesday afternoon and the Times-Herald on Friday morning. This will give Hot Springs semi-weekly news service. The city is growing and deserves that[.]" The article maintained that "combining plant equipment of Star and Times-Herald at the Star office gives Hot Springs one of the best printeries in the state while pooling talents gives a staff of unusual versatility." It also expressed the desire "to give Hot Springs this semi-weekly news service at less cost rather than more." Toward that end, readers were told they "may subscribe to either the Star or the Times-Herald at their regular rates, $2.50 and 2.00 a year, respectively, but if you subscribe to them jointly, a combination price will be made of $3.50 a year," and "you will want both papers."[3]

The announcement (written by Francis) also noted that "editorially, the Star and the Times-Herald will have this creed: 'Hot Springs,

Fall River county, the Black Hills, South Dakota, the United States.'" In further explanation of editorial policy, Francis stated that "although Hot Springs papers, they will feel free to boost for the Rushmore statues or for the Pactola reservoir or the Tri-State Roundup though they be nearer Rapid City or Belle Fouche," because "we cannot help any section of the Black Hills without helping ourselves."⁴

The Johnsons wrote an editorial appearing in the same *Star* edition. There they said, among other things, that "the change that is being made in the newspaper business of Hot Springs is all for the greatest good of that business and of the people of this locality"; and they wished for the "young men who have joined forces with those of the Star ... nothing better than the friendship and cordiality which have been given us for the past seven years by the people of Fall River County."⁵

ON THE SAME DAY THE *Star* explained the new situation regarding the town's two newspapers, Francis attended what the *Rapid City Daily Journal* described as "the greatest historical event which has ever happened in the state." This "event" was the dedication of Rushmore Mountain "to the colossal statue of Washington, Lincoln, Jefferson and Roosevelt that Gutzon Borglum hopes to carve on its face." The proposed statue would probably cost "more than a million dollars." It would be the largest monument in the world, featuring figures whose "busts alone ... would measure 200 feet high and 80 feet at the shoulders."⁶

For the designated "Dedication Day," Fort Meade had "agreed to send a troop of cavalry and a band to take part in the ceremony." The Rapid City National Guard was assigned to control "the traffic and crowds both at the mountain and enroute to it." The *Journal* and the *Argus-Leader* both ran front-page articles that publicized the event the day before it occurred. And community officials throughout the Hills dismissed schools for the day so their pupils could attend.⁷

Rushmore Mountain is in the Black Hills—three miles west of a small town named Keystone and 18 miles south and west of Rapid City. The dedication site itself was "on the side of a ridge a quarter of a mile southeast of the Rushmore cliff and separated from it by a shallow canyon." A "rough pine" speakers' platform was located there, and a crowd that numbered about 3,000 had gathered in the area by the time the program began. After a chilly and overcast start, it turned out to be "a perfect day for the exercises, warm in the sun but a little 'nippy' in the shade."[8]

The ceremony began at 1:00 p.m. when the Fort Meade band played a "thundering" overture. Then a group of Sioux Indians performed dances, and several attending dignitaries gave speeches. Wright E. Campbell, justice on the South Dakota Supreme Court, represented the governor and the state. He gave "a dedicatory address of unusual effectiveness." In it, he "paid tribute to Senator Peter Norbeck and to Doane Robinson, state historian," who were identified as "sponsors of the memorial project." He also praised the "citizens of the West River and Mr. Borglum." While waiting for Norbeck and Borglum to arrive, Robinson "outlined the historical setting" of the project and explained that flags "hoisted on Rushmore" represented "the various periods through which the territory surrounding Rushmore passed on national ownership."[9]

Peter Norbeck served two terms as Republican governor of South Dakota from 1917 to 1921, was elected as U.S. Senator in 1920, and endorsed the Rushmore project. After he arrived at the dedication, he spoke about "the act of congress authorizing the memorial." C. D. Erskine, a state senator from Sturgis, "explained the action of the last legislature approving the memorial plan"; and Ewert W. Martin, former U.S. Congressman and now practicing attorney in Hot Springs, appeared as a representative of the "President and the people at large." He "accepted Rushmore from the state." Borglum, who had been described as "one of the best-known American sculptors" and "a dramatist and a romantic" by nature, also gave an address. During his talk, he declared that "'The hand of Providence has decreed that this monument be built! ... The statue of Washington will be completed within a twelvemonth! Meet me here a year from today and we will dedicate it!'"[10]

After the speeches were delivered, the program announced an intermission, during which Borglum and others climbed Rushmore Mountain. When the group reached the top of the cliff, Borglum signaled the band to play a fanfare, and a Sioux Indian chief named Black Horse appeared as a representative of the area's original owners. To the people assembled 600 feet below, the chief stood as a "distance-dwarfed figure." He stayed there, "regal and unmoving, throughout the rest of the ceremony." Meanwhile, on the top of the mountain, huge flags representing "the territory's other claimants—Great Britain, Spain, France, and the colonial United States—were successively raised and then lowered by a group of men dressed as early-day explorers." The "climax of the dedication" occurred when the "Stars and Stripes" was raised as "the band and audience joined in singing "The Star-Spangled Banner." But unlike the previous flags, this one was not brought down. Instead, it remained in place while Reverend Carl Loocke gave a benediction, the crowd slowly dispersed, and the sun began to set.[11]

FRANCIS SPENT THE REMAINDER of 1925 getting his newspaper operation up to speed. During November, he was "very busy moving presses and rearranging office equipment." By the end of that month, he reported having "a very well-equipped plant and the finest staff of folks to work with ... [who are] loyal to the core." As the year drew to an end, he wrote a long letter to Leland that included several newspaper-related subjects. Among the topics discussed was the prospect of publishing a daily paper. Francis believed that "to put on a daily," he would need "another machine; another operator, another floor man and a full time advertising man." Moreover, "talk of a daily would be conditional on the Commercial Club and business men going through the idea they talked the other day, possibly guaranteeing not less than $1,250.00 of local advertising a month."[12]

On January 22, 1926, the Hot Springs Commercial Club elected its officers for the oncoming year. Francis was chosen as secretary. During the previous year, the club had succeeded in securing a new veterans' bureau hospital in town, and it looked forward to pursuing projects and activities that would benefit Hot Springs and the Black Hills in 1926.[13]

With respect to the newspaper enterprise, Francis continued to adopt new innovations designed to improve the product and the papers' circulation. While he did so, the Johnsons left for an extended trip to California, due to A. T. Johnson's poor health. In the *Star*'s February 2 issue, it was announced that it and the *Times-Herald* would both "enlarge from six to seven columns per page; and doing so would "permit more news to be printed... [and] regular use of a current cartoon, a comic strip, short stories, and within a few weeks, a serial story." Answering inquiries about whether a daily could be published, the article stated that although it was aware of "only one town in the world" the size of Hot Springs that provided that service, "when Hot Springs is ready for a daily paper, we are here to publish it." Finally, the announcement offered a "special combination subscription price of $2.50... during February" to those who chose to take both papers for a year. That was $1.00 less than the prior combination rate, and it equaled the current price for a year's subscription to the *Star* alone. Three weeks after these innovations were implemented, Francis reported to Leland that advertising had increased in both papers, the company was having "a very good month for collections" and taking "in a good deal of money on the special subscription offer," and Badger Clark was "helping us some but on a 'string' basis."[14]

IN ADDITION TO EXPANDING THE newspapers and offering a new combination subscription rate, the *Star* published two articles in February that produced unintended consequences. Before getting to the articles themselves, a little background information is necessary. Colonel M. L. Shade "had been active in South Dakota public life for many years." He enlisted in the World War and "was given many important commands." After the war he returned to South Dakota and was appointed to the State Highway Commission. That job continued until February 1923, when Governor McMaster removed him while the legislature was in session. Shortly after Governor Gunderson took office in January 1925, he reappointed Shade to the highway commission—"an act which aroused considerable comment." Four months later, the *Rapid City Journal* confirmed that Shade would leave the commission and become superintendent of Custer State Park on July 1.[15]

On February 12, 1926, Adolf W. Ewert—former treasurer of the South Dakota rural credit board—was convicted "on charges of embezzling more than $211,000 of rural credit funds[.]" According to the *Argus-Leader*, the jury verdict "terminated the most notable trial in the history of South Dakota." That trial included "charges and counter charges of 'politics' involving high state officials and particularly Governor Carl Gunderson, who demanded and obtained Ewert's removal from office" shortly after Gunderson became governor.[16]

Four days after the Ewert verdict was announced, the *Star*'s February 16 issue included two articles that referred to Ewert, Gunderson, Norbeck, and Shade. The first article appeared on the paper's editorial page. It stated, in part, that "the conviction of Ewert is a triumph for Governor Gunderson"; that "Senator Norbeck [who championed the rural credit program] has not attempted to shield Ewert; rather he has said that if guilty Ewert should be punished. Yet some Gunderson partisans would like to have the public feel that Norbeck, not Ewert, was on trial"; and that "On the other hand, strong Norbeck sympathizers ask why Gunderson does not prosecute Shade, also tarred by a legislative investigation, and answer their own question by pointing out that the governor is a close friend of Mr. Shade and has given him an easy berth in the state park."[17]

On page eight of the same issue, under a new column titled "South Dakota Politics," the *Star* discussed various comments on the Ewert trial to demonstrate how "different minds react to the same set of facts." That discussion included the following two paragraphs:

> Another man, not a candidate, wants to know "if the governor will now prosecute Shade" since "he and Ewert were the two men charged by the last legislature with misuse of public funds."
>
> This man does not think Governor Gunderson will push the charges made by two legislative investigating committees against Mr. Shade because "he is a personal friend of the governor's."[18]

Two weeks after the February 16 articles were published, the *Star* revisited the quoted remarks concerning Shade that appeared in the "South Dakota Politics" column. Now, it explained that "the Star does not intend or knowingly permit publication of inaccuracies in any department and regrets any injustice done Mr. Shade by printing overstatement or misstatement of legislative criticisms. His case was not comparable to that of Mr. Ewert. Criminal charges were not made by the legislature." But it added that "the Star believes that Mr. Shade should not hold public office in South Dakota." And in that same March 2 issue, the "South Dakota Politics" column stated that "Governor Gunderson will not institute proceedings against Col. M. L. Shade as 'wondered' by one whose remarks were quoted in this column[.]" Based on its review of the legislative committee report that investigated the highway commission, the *Star* concluded that the committee did object to certain "transactions" conducted at the Supply Depot when Shade was in charge of it, and it criticized "other practices" that involved Shade and his brother. But "the last legislature did not charge Mr. Shade with misuse of public funds. Nor did the previous legislature so far as the Star is now informed. In justice to Mr. Shade and to Governor Gunderson, this correction is published."[19]

Despite the "explanations" and "correction" summarized above, Shade filed suit against the Star Publishing Company and its four owners on March 8. (Service of process was obtained only on the company and Francis, as Leland and the Johnsons were out-of-state when the lawsuit was brought. The latter three were subsequently dropped as individual defendants, and the action proceeded only against the Star Publishing Company and Francis.) Shade's complaint alleged that the February 16 articles were "libelous and defamatory" of his character, and he sought $15,000 in damages. When a reporter asked him why he filed suit, Shade responded by saying, "'They put me in a class with Ewert.'" Three weeks later, Francis wrote to his dad that "Cliff and I expect to go east this week to Pierre to get data for defense in the libel suit. For the life of me, I don't know what the man expects to get by suing—except more unfavorable publicity. Several papers around the state have ridden him already." He added that "you can be sure we will give him, in good conscience, all we can to prove our case."[20]

ABOUT THE SAME TIME FRANCIS wrote his dad about the Shade lawsuit, he noticed a front-page article in the *Sioux Falls Press* that said President Coolidge announced his intention to spend his summer "somewhere in the mountains." The article also indicated that an attorney from Omaha had offered the president "several small cottages at Lake Okoboji, Iowa"—a lake on top of that state's "highest mountain." On March 30, Francis reacted to this information by sending a telegram to Congressman Williamson. It read:

> "Press dispatches say President Coolidge will not return Swampscott this summer desiring mountains. Please present superior

climate, temperate altitude, accessibility and communication facilities of Black Hills particularly State Park and learn exact requirements. Confident Associated Commercial Clubs and Park Board will provide whatever necessary to establish summer White House in Black Hills. Western summer home means much for entire country."

Francis also attended a Kiwanis Club luncheon that day. There he urged the club to send telegrams to "Senators Norbeck and McMaster and Governor Carl Gunderson" that asked for their assistance with the summer-White-House idea. The club's secretary immediately did so. The message to Norbeck (other two not found but assumed to be the same or similar) was brief and to the point: "Reported President Coolidge wants mountain summer home Hot Springs Star has wired Williamson urge summer white House in State Park Will appreciate all assistance"[21]

Gunderson responded the next day. He sent a wire directly to the president that extended "an urgent invitation to establish summer White House in the Black Hills." Coolidge answered with a letter that expressed "cordial thanks" for Gunderson's "kind message" and added "I have made no plans for the summer." On April 1, Williamson wrote a letter to the president that invited him "to spend his summer vacation in the Black Hills." The letter described the area in glowing terms: "'These mountains rise to a height of more than 7,000 feet, are well wooded, have many clear mountain trout streams and abound in wild life such as deer, antelope, buffalo and elk.'" It also praised the climate, scenery and "'splendid roads [that] make motoring safe and a real pleasure.'" The letter concluded by noting "'the associated commercial clubs will arrange for a "summer white house" if given an opportunity'"; and it enclosed two pamphlets that showed the scenery and included a photo of the proposed "summer white house."[22]

Within a week, the president's secretary—Mr. Everett Sanders—responded to Williamson's letter by stating "the invitation will be taken into consideration when the time comes for making summer plans." Armed with this information, Williamson wrote to Francis that "'While the president is not in position at this time to say whether or not he will make a visit to the Black Hills, I think that the Associated Commercial clubs of the Black Hills should take steps to lease some property which would be suitable for a "summer white house"; and "'to my idea, the state lodge is the only suitable place that we have in the Hills.'" He then asked Francis to "'confer with the officers of the associated commercial clubs with a view to seeing whether the lodge can be made available at whatever time the president might see fit to occupy it.'"[23]

Work on the summer-White-House project continued over the next few days. R. L. Bronson, president of the Associated Commercial Clubs of the Black Hills, had previously wired George W. Wright, state Republican chairman who was in New York at the time, and asked him to personally confer with the president about the Black Hills proposal. Wright met with President Coolidge on April 9 and reported that during their meeting, the president indicated that "definite plans have not yet been made." That same day, John A. Stanley, a member of the Custer State Park board, assured Francis that the state game lodge would be available to the president. Francis passed this information on to Bronson, who called for a special meeting of the associated commercial clubs to take place in Rapid City on April 10. At that gathering, the clubs passed a resolution pledging to "do all in their power to bring Coolidge to the Black Hills for the summer and to attempt to secure the Game Lodge for a summer White House." They also appointed a three-member "Black Hills Committee" consisting of Francis, L. M. Simons of Belle Fourche, and J. A. Boland of Rapid City. That committee was given the "full power to act" on the associated commercial clubs' behalf with respect to the summer White House proposal.²⁴

On April 19, the South Dakota congressional delegation (consisting of Senators Norbeck and William McMaster and Representatives Charles Christopherson, Royal Johnson, and Williamson—all Republicans), plus U.S. Commissioner of Indian Affairs Charles Burke, met with President Coolidge and invited him to establish "a summer White House at the Game Lodge in Custer State Park." After that meeting, Williamson wired Francis that "While it will be extremely difficult to get the president so far from the executive headquarters, yet we feel justified in putting forth our best efforts." One week later, Williamson wrote to Francis that "since we called at the White House, the Secretary to the President has indicated that it is unlikely that the President will establish a 'Summer White House' at a point so far away from the National Capital as South Dakota"; and "it seems improbable, at this date, that the President will spend his vacation in the State."²⁵

In response, Francis wrote to Williamson: "Your letter of April 26 seems to close the matter of the President so far as any activity on our part is concerned but I want to assure that we will be ready to jump on an instant's notice in case something more develops." He added that "I want to thank you for myself and for the committee of Associated Commercial Clubs on the interest you have taken on this whole matter"; and "everybody has been enthusiastic on the proposition and your activity on it has been entirely to your credit throughout the district and the state." As things turned out, President Coolidge chose to spend his 1926 summer vacation at the White Pine Camp in New York's Adirondack Mountains. But South Dakotans did not give up on the idea of hosting a summer White House in the Black Hills.²⁶

AT THE SAME TIME EFFORTS were being made to convince President Coolidge to come to the Black Hills, it became apparent that Colonel Shade's continued tenure as Custer State Park superintendent was in jeopardy. In early April, rumors circulated in Pierre that Governor Gunderson had requested Shade's resignation. But "the governor's office was silent on the subject," and Shade stated he had "'not tendered my resignation to the governor.'" Nevertheless, the rumors persisted. On April 13, the *Star* reprinted an article from the *Evening Huronite* (a daily newspaper published in Huron, South Dakota) that stated, among other things, "it seems that the pressure has become sufficient to convince the governor that he should remove Col. Shade.... The general impression is that Governor Gunderson would like to see the colonel's resignation on his desk."[27]

Five and a half weeks later, Pierre's *Daily Capital Journal* ran this front-page headline: "Shade Will Resign Job in State Park." The article began by noting that "B. F. Meyers, secretary of agriculture, has won out in his objections to Col. M. L. Shade as superintendent of the Custer State Park." It went on to state that the resignation would be effective on July 1, and "J. A. Stanley, secretary of the park board, declared that '"Colonel Shade's resignation will be accepted.'" The next day, Shade told the *Rapid City Journal* that "'Announcement that my resignation will be effective July 1 is news to me.'" He added that he "had no difficulty with Governor Gunderson" but "Secretary Myers has been trying to get him ousted for some time."[28]

The *Star* covered Shade's resignation in its May 25 issue. Its news story mentioned the main points discussed in the Pierre and Rapid City newspaper reports, and it added that "Both the governor and the secretary [of agriculture] are in favor of greater centralization of authority in the park but Mr. Meyers refused to sanction placing that authority in the hands of Col. Shade." On the May 25 editorial page, the resignation was summed up as follows: "Col Shade did not have the confidence of the several state departments which have responsibilities in the park. That is all that needs to be said. His resignation leaves the way open to real team work and progress."[29]

Apart from keeping track of the Shade matter, Francis's other endeavors kept him quite busy that spring. He was shorthanded at the newspapers, since the Johnsons were still in California and would not return to work until late June—with Mr. Johnson's health much improved. In addition, Francis's "part-time help on the news" left in mid-May. Despite the lack of a full work force, he started a new paper—*Tourist News*—on May 21. Consisting of four pages, it was "furnished free to tourists" and included as a separate, stand-alone section in the *Times-Herald*. In a column titled "To the Tourist," its first issue stated: "The mission of this publication is to acquaint the visitor with western South Dakota and the Black Hills. When you are seeking some place to go; something to do; something to see consult the pages of Tourist News." That issue also contained a map of the Black Hills, short articles on the area's attractions, and several advertisements aimed at Hills visitors. Regarding those ads, the to-the-tourist column proclaimed: "We can conscientiously recommend our advertisers to our readers. Their services are reliable and courteous."[30]

Francis's secretarial work for the Hot Springs Commercial Club also "got heavier" as the tourist season began. In a May 24 club meeting, he reported that the Associated Commercial Clubs of the Black Hills had produced 174,000 Black Hills folders for use in 1926 (as compared to 50,000 the year before), that the local club had contributed $400 for their cost, and that Francis's office had already distributed 3,600 of them. In addition, since February 1, that office had "answered 315 inquiries for information about Hot Springs and the Black Hills"—either by sending literature only or literature accompanied by a personal letter. The local club was "now publishing a folder of Hot Springs, 10,000 of which will be struck off." Finally, its membership currently stood at 108, and the club hoped that number would be "raised to 150 inside of 30 days." Four days after the meeting, the club's directors allowed Francis "to draw $20 more a month," and he decided to "use it for stenographic help."[31]

As a final example that showed he "probably... [took] on too much" during May, Francis wrote to his dad that "I am trying to find a few minutes to get a speech for Memorial Day. Am to speak here... at the B. M. S. [Battle Mountain Sanitarium] at 10 o'clock a.m., and get away by 11 at least to get to Sturgis for another at 2 or a little after."[32]

On July 2, the *Times-Herald* announced that J. C. Dennison of Vermillion had been appointed to replace Shade as superintendent of Custer State Park. Although the transfer of power was supposed to take place on July 1, it occurred on the morning of July 4 when Shade and his family left the park by car for California. The *Star*, relying on an interview Shade gave to the Custer newspaper, related that "Mrs. Shade, whose health is not good, and their son will take up residence in California for the winter," and "Col. Shade states that he will retain his residence in South Dakota and when Mrs. Shade has regained her health will again make a home in the state."[33]

IN THE MARCH 29 LETTER to his dad that discussed the Shade lawsuit, Francis also made these comments regarding his relationships with women: "You persist in over-rating and misinterpreting any remarks I... make about girls. There is positively no chance of my making any plans for any serious event. If such a thing ever happens, which I seriously doubt, it will be done suddenly and without previous notice even to myself." Almost five months later—on August 18—he wrote to Carol and Ralph while on a train. That letter's first paragraph stated: "I'm on the train enroute to Mitchell—then Omaha where I'm to get a new car—Studebaker coupe, to drive home. What I'm going by way of Mitchell for, you can surmise—if you can read this. The train rocks badly." Later on in the letter, he added: "Am thinking of coming back by way of Denver to see if I can line up some work in case I can leave the paper this winter & get away to school." Although this letter accurately described what would later become a honeymoon trip, it did not mention any wedding plans.[34]

Francis married Myrle Graves the next day. Their wedding announcement suggested, and newspaper reports specifically stated, that the marriage took place in Mitchell. But a South Dakota State Board of Health's "Record of Marriage" indicates the wedding was "solemnized" at Plankinton, a small town 23 miles due west of Mitchell; and Thomas Taubman, a justice of the peace, performed the ceremony. On the morning he received the announcement, Jim Dolliver—an old family friend—wrote that "the event must have been consummated rather suddenly, as when I was in Hot Springs the first week of August, I had no inkling of the wedding." Apparently, Francis's late-March prediction to his father came true, as a "serious event" involving a woman was "done suddenly" and "without previous notice."[35]

Their honeymoon trip began with a train ride to Omaha, where Francis picked up his new Studebaker coupe. From there the couple drove west across Nebraska. They stayed overnight at the Keystone Hotel in McCook—a small town located in the south-central part of the state near the Kansas border. Leaving McCook, they motored on to Denver and arrived on August 23. For that night and the next two, "Case Francis & Wife" stayed in Room 420 at The Cosmopolitan Hotel. Their hotel bill was $18.10: $6.00 per night for the room and $.10 for two telephone calls. While in Denver, the newlyweds presumably did some sightseeing and other tourist-related activities. Francis also met with University of Denver personnel to discuss whether he would be able to teach some courses "in journalism while attending law school." As a result of that conference, it was decided that since he could not come to the school "until the second semester, if at all," he should write the Vice-Chancellor after the fall semester began about what courses he "would be willing to handle."[36]

Before coming home, Myrle and Francis spent a few days at Grand Lake, Colorado. Located 57 miles northwest of Denver, Grand Lake is "adjacent to Rocky Mountain National Park and Arapaho National Forest." The town was named after the lake upon which it is situated.

That lake is "Colorado's largest natural body of water" and sits at 8,369 feet above sea level. The Cases probably stayed at a cottage near the Corner Cupboard Tearoom. It also appears they visited the Gold Crest Art Shop before returning to Hot Springs in early September.[37]

The newlyweds received a telegram, a poem, and over 20 letters that congratulated them on their wedding. Art and Della Brown wrote the first letter on August 23—four days after the marriage. They both learned of the event independently—Art by a letter from Francis written while the couple was in Nebraska, and Della by reading the wedding announcement in the *Rapid City Daily Journal*. Over the next seven weeks, missives were received from relatives, friends, former professors, the *Epworth Herald's* current editor, college deans at Wesleyan and Oklahoma Agricultural and Mechanical College, the Hot Springs Publishing Company staff, and the corresponding secretary for the Methodist Episcopal Church's Board of Education. Leland, who by now had received his master's degree from Northwestern, had helped conduct a Northwestern student-faculty tour group that visited ten countries in Europe, and had taken a job with the Paris edition of *The New York Herald*, wrote in late September that "you're congratulated! Take it from me, kid, I'm proud of you. Durn but I wish I were there to tell you so."[38]

THE 1926 GENERAL ELECTION WAS held on November 2. Peter Norbeck was reelected to his second term in the U.S. Senate by a wide margin. All three Republican House members retained their seats, although Williamson won by only 2,030 votes. Carl Gunderson lost his reelection bid to William Bulow, a Democrat whom Gunderson easily defeated in 1924. Four days after the 1926 election, Senator Norbeck wrote a "Personal" letter to Francis. It stated in part: "Permit me to thank you and other friends in Fall River County for the interest taken in my campaign for reelection. My majority is very gratifying, and I appreciate your efforts in my behalf."[39]

WHEN COLONEL SHADE MOVED TO California in July, his leaving the state "was generally interpreted to mean that he had taken up residence there and would not go further" with his libel action against Francis and The Star Publishing Company. But Shade returned to South Dakota in the fall to prosecute his lawsuit, the parties prepared their claims and defenses, and trial began on Friday, November 19. The judge previously in charge of the case had recently been appointed as supreme court commissioner, so Judge R. C. Bakewell of Plankinton was assigned to preside over the trial. Attorneys Harold Hawley of Custer and Lauritz Miller of Mitchell represented plaintiff Shade. The lawyers representing defendants Francis and The Star Publishing Company were Clifford Wilson and E. B. Adams—both of Hot Springs. Twelve men were selected to be on the jury. A majority of them lived on ranches outside of Hot Springs, only one regularly subscribed to the *Star*, and none recalled reading the February 16 *Star* articles that allegedly libeled Shade.[40]

Before testimony was presented, the judge granted Shade's "motion to strike four paragraphs from the defendants' amended answer." These paragraphs—which pleaded "the substantial truth of the matter complained of, justification and privilege"—contained "the heart of the positive defense." Striking them meant that throughout the trial, defendants would mostly be "forced to confine their evidence to rebuttal of plaintiff's testimony" and would not be able to present a substantial portion of the evidence they had gathered before trial.[41]

Plaintiff's attorneys called Colonel Shade to the stand as their first witness. As "background" information before the alleged libel occurred, Shade stated that he attended an informal dinner held by the highway commission at Rapid City in January 1925, and at that dinner, Francis (a *Journal* staff member at the time) asked him for news. When Shade responded that he had no news to give, Francis allegedly "'shook his finger under my nose and told me he'd make me 'pay dearly' for keeping the news from him.'" With respect to his libel claim, Shade declared that the February 16 *Star* articles "had injured his reputation, brought reproach to his family and affected his wife's health adversely"; that "people who had formerly been friendly shunned and avoided" him; and "that his dismissal as superintendent of the state park had come about as a result of the publications." When asked on cross-examination to name those who had shunned him, Shade mentioned "four or five people." But none of those people subscribed to the *Star*, and none appeared at trial to corroborate Shade's testimony.[42]

Shade's trial team then called Francis as an adverse witness. He was primarily questioned about the alleged encounter with Shade at the highway commission dinner in 1925. While admitting he may have interviewed Shade on that occasion, Francis "flatly denied ever having shaken his finger or fist under Col. Shade's nose" or making the statements Shade attributed to him.[43]

Shade's attorneys called no further witnesses and rested their case. After the judge denied their motion for a directed verdict, it was the defendants' turn to present evidence. John A. Stanley, their first witness, testified that "Shade's dismissal as superintendent of the park, resulted from friction between Mr. Shade and certain departments, mainly the division of fish and game," and that when he (Stanley) "met with Governor Gunderson to consider Mr. Shade's dismissal, he had not read the articles in the Star[.]" Next, C.C. Gideon, former gamekeeper in Custer State Park who now leased the park's Game Lodge from the state, testified about the friction between Shade and B. F. Meyers. Francis then took the stand. He testified that "he had written the principal article under discussion and declared that it had been based on his reading of sections of the legislative journals, on articles in the papers and on conversation with members of the committee which probed the highway department." Thereafter, the defense called four additional witnesses to support its case.[44]

After the testimony was concluded about 10:00 a.m. on Wednesday, November 24, Judge Bakewell denied plaintiff's motion for a directed verdict and gave his instructions to the jury. At about noon, each side was allotted one hour and a half to make its closing argument. During their presentation, Shade's attorneys "scored the defendants as 'wreckers of character,' reviewed Col. Shade's war record, lauded his public service, [and] pleaded his misfortunes as damages." Responding to the plaintiff's presentation, the defense attorneys "ridiculed the matter of damage 'for two lines on the back page of a weekly paper' as compared with the publicity which attended Shade's first removal from the highway commission, the investigation during the second term, the transfer to the Park and the friction there." One of the defendants' lawyers summed up the argument with these final words to the jury: "Gentlemen, you must not muzzle the free press of South Dakota. A verdict for the plaintiff will do that. A verdict for the defendants will bring thanksgiving to those who believe that a public position is a public trust and that the newspapers are guardians of that trust."[45]

The case was submitted to the jury "shortly after 4 o'clock." They deliberated until suppertime, ate their meal, and then "returned a verdict 'for defendants on all the issues.'" The verdict was unanimous, and it was decided on the first ballot.[46]

In the days and weeks following the verdict, Francis received several letters that congratulated him on the Shade-trial outcome. John Stanley wrote one of the first ones. After offering his "congratulations on the libel suit victory," Stanley noted that he

> happened to have the privilege of being the one to inform the Colonel of the decision, as I was on the street talking to him when I heard of it. He only grunted audibly. But don't quote me on it—I'm in bad enough with him I suppose. However, I was glad

to testify to the truth of the matter, and hope it had some bearing on the case.

And two days before Christmas, George Miller—member of the jury and teammate with Francis on the 1913 Hot Springs High School football team—wrote this to "Friend Francis": "In regard to the libel suit I will say that it was a pleasure to me to be able to be one of those who helped to render you this justice."[47]

The Shade trial had taken up much of Francis's time, energy, and money in November, and despite its favorable outcome, he was "not looking for any more libel suits." As the year 1926 came to an end, he and Myrle had moved into a house and "were busy getting settled."[48]

ON JANUARY 8, 1927, CONCURRENT RESOLUTIONS were adopted in the South Dakota Senate and House that extended a "'cordial and sincere invitation to His Excellency, Calvin Coolidge, president of the United States; his family, friends, and staff, to spend their vacation in the summer of 1927 in the Black Hills.'" Governor Bulow "promptly transmitted this resolution to the president." In the weeks and months that followed, Senator Norbeck and Congressman Williamson "began a soft campaign" to try to convince President Coolidge to accept the state legislature's invitation. For example, they took two pictures of the Black Hills that had been "enlarged, colored like oil paintings and artistically framed" and gifted them to First Lady Grace Coolidge. This gesture may have subtlety influenced her husband. After a meeting at the White House on another subject in mid-April, Coolidge asked Williamson several general questions about the Black Hills and "said he would send a man out to have a look."[49]

The man sent out to "have a look" was Colonel Edmund Starling—the president's "personal security officer" and chief of his secret service detail. Locations in five other states were also being considered as potential sites for the summer White House, and Starling left

Washington in early May to tour them all. He arrived in the Black Hills on May 12, toured Rapid City and Custer State Park, stayed overnight at the Game Lodge, made some preliminary arrangements, and "assured himself of the feasibility of the whole idea." After his potential-sites tour was completed, Starling returned to the White House a week later; and he recommended that the president stay in the Black Hills. Norbeck got word of this recommendation, and he "sprang into action" by "making daily visits to the White House throughout late May to answer questions and relay instructions back to South Dakota."[50]

During the afternoon of May 24, the *Star* received a telegram from W. H. King, secretary of the Mitchell chamber of commerce, who was in Washington, D. C. on business. The telegram read: "'Following daily visits by Senator Norbeck to the White House for the past three days, President Coolidge today practically announced acceptance of the South Dakota State Game Lodge as his summer home. I am certain he is going there.'" Shortly after that message arrived, the Hot Springs Commercial Club received one from Senator Norbeck. It stated in part: "'I consider it almost a certainty that the president is going to be in the State Park this summer. I don't know what town will be selected as official headquarters.... I gave assurance that accommodations would be provided at reasonable rates for the newspaper men ... [and] those officially connected[.]'"[51]

In response to these missives, Francis sent W. H. King a telegram on May 24 that stated: "Thanks for message and congratulations on aid you have given[.]" He also forwarded a telegram to President Coolidge and a night letter to Senator Norbeck. To the president, Francis wrote that "the Picture Town of Black Hills bid you hearty welcome and will do its part to make your vacation memorable[.]" His night letter to Norbeck stated, "Thanks for message and congratulations on effective part you have played in achieving this great victory for Black Hills and South Dakota ... Please call on us freely for assistance in working out accommodations promised We want realization to be even greater than anticipation[.]"⁵²

One week later, the president formally announced "that he has decided to go to the Black Hills for his summer vacation" and "would arrive in mid-June to take up residence at the State Game Lodge in Custer State Park." The next day, the Hot Springs Commercial Club passed a resolution that stated

> "Resolved that we most highly compliment and congratulate Francis H. Case, secretary of this club for having originated and given currency to the idea that the president might make the summer White House for 1927 in the Black Hills; and, we also appreciate the efforts of all persons who have assisted in bringing this idea to a successful fruition."

Several years later, Leland offered this comment regarding his brother's involvement in the summer-White-House effort: "People there laughed at the idea of having the President of the United States come out here and all that, but he persisted."⁵³

THE *STAR'S* JUNE 14 ISSUE included a poem by Badger Clark titled "Leave It to The Hills." Consisting of six stanzas, the poem advised its readers to let the Black Hills, as opposed to its residents, entertain the Coolidges during their visit. That visit began the next day, when the president's train arrived in Rapid City at 5:30 p.m. In addition to the first couple, a presidential party of approximately 80 people and three animals were among the train's passengers. That party included the "regular White House staff, office help, newspaper men, photographers, household employees, some negro servants and the White House pets, Rebecca, the racoon, and the two collies, Rob Roy and Prudence Prim." Upon their arrival, the president and First Lady were greeted by a welcoming committee that consisted of Senator Norbeck, Congressman Williamson, and local dignitaries. Francis was not able to join this group. Myrle and he were in Mitchell attending the burial of Myrle's mother Elizabeth, whose death was greatly mourned by the Graves family.[54]

After they disembarked from the train, the first couple boarded an open-air automobile and led a ten-vehicle caravan that paraded through Rapid City. A crowd estimated at between 7,000 and 10,000 pressed together on both sides of Main Street and cheered as the Coolidges passed by. Near the city's eastern edge, they transferred from their open-air car to an enclosed presidential limousine. The caravan then headed south toward the State Game Lodge—about 26 miles away. They arrived there at 7:30 p.m. Before retiring, the president sat by "one of the lodge's massive stone fireplaces" and read "some communications from Washington, D. C."[55]

The president went trout fishing during his first full day in the Black Hills. After that he fell into a regular routine. On weekday mornings, he travelled to his office at the Rapid City High School to conduct presidential business and meet visitors. He then returned to the Game Lodge for lunch with the First Lady—usually followed by a nap. On most afternoons, he either fished, went sightseeing, or engaged in other forms of recreation. And on Sundays, Grace and he attended services at the Hermosa Congregational Church, which was located about 12 miles northeast of the Game Lodge.[56]

On June 21, president Coolidge reviewed a national guard troop at a camp west of Rapid City. He also received a group of promoters from Belle Fourche. They invited him to attend the Tri-State Roundup to be held in early July and presented him with a ten-gallon cowboy hat. One reporter described the hat as having the "'size and shape that would make a movie actor or a cowboy justly envious . . . It pointed fully 10 inches into the air and its brim was so wide that he had to bend it slightly to get into his limousine without disturbing its contour.'"[57]

In the latter part of June, a mountain and a creek in Custer State Park had their names changed to honor the Coolidges. Sheep Mountain—situated about five miles west and a little south of the Game Lodge—is one of the highest peaks in the park. On June 22, the South Dakota legislature changed the peak's name to Mount Coolidge. Three days later, Senators Norbeck and McMaster, plus 200 members of the state legislature, visited the Coolidges and then went to the top of the newly-named mountain for a formal dedication ceremony. And on the last day of June, the state legislature changed the name of Squaw Creek—the stream that ran by the Game Lodge and contained planted trout for the president to catch—to Grace Coolidge Creek. Both name changes have remained in place since they were made in 1927.[58]

In addition to conducting the nation's business and meeting with state, national, and foreign officials at his Rapid City offices, the president's July schedule included a birthday party and visits to several towns in the Black Hills. After celebrating his fifty-fifth birthday at the Game Lodge on the Fourth, the Coolidge's attended the Tri-State Roundup rodeo in Belle Fourche, visited the Rapid City Indian School, and were guests at the annual Tri-State Farmers Picnic near Ardmore and the Gold Discovery Pageant at Custer. Then at noon on August 2, the president handed slips of paper to about three dozen reporters assembled in his classroom office at the Rapid City High School. Those slips of paper contained a note that read "I do not choose to run for President in nineteen twenty-eight." After the reporters read the message, the president refused to answer their questions and "watched them dash out the door" to spread the shocking news. It "stunned the country."[59]

Two days after his surprise I-do-not-choose-to-run-for-President announcement, the first couple attended the Days of '76 celebration in Deadwood. While there, a delegation of Sioux Indians made the president an honorary member of the Sioux Nation and named him

Wanbli Tokaka, which translated into English as Leading Eagle. During his adoption ceremony, a "war-bonnet headdress consisting of 180 large eagle feathers" was placed on the president's head.[60]

SOON AFTER THE COOLIDGES ARRIVED at the summer White House, Senator Norbeck, sculptor Borglum, and others lobbied the president to visit Mount Rushmore during his Black Hills vacation. Those efforts were ultimately successful, and Mr. Coolidge agreed to attend the "second dedication of the project" that occurred on August 10. (Although Borglum had boldly promised that Washington's statue would be completed "within a twelve month" after the first dedication held in October, 1925, no carving had yet commenced, largely due to lack of funds.) Between 1,000 and 1,700 people attended the second dedication ceremony—as compared to the 3,000 or so who showed up at the monument's "Dedication Day" two years earlier. President Coolidge was driven to Keystone by limousine. He completed the three-mile journey up to the dedication site on horseback. The ceremony began at 2:30 p.m., with Norbeck serving as emcee. When he introduced the president, the latter removed his now well-known ten-gallon hat, put on his reading glasses, and read his speech. In it, he explained the reasons why each of the four presidents would be included on the mountain and "showered praise on the proposed carving, its setting and the people trying to make it happen." Then, near the end of his talk, he suggested the possibility of federal financial aid to the project by saying in part: "'The people of South Dakota are taking the lead in the preparation of this memorial out of their meager resources.... Their effort and courage entitles them to the sympathy and support of private beneficence and the National Government.'"[61]

After his talk, Mr. Coolidge presented Borglum with six drill bits. Borglum then gave his own "bravado-filled speech." Next, he "turned to climb the 1,400-foot plank stairway that had recently been installed for workers to reach the top of the mountain." While he did so, a flag-raising pageant—similar to the one in 1925—was held near the edge of Rushmore's cliff. When Borglum reached the mountaintop, he was lowered by cable "over the face of the mountain in a bosun chair, ... [and] dramatically began the carving of Mount Rushmore by manhandling a heavy drill and using each of the six drill bits ... to drill six holes where the carving of Rushmore was to begin." Thereafter, Borglum returned to the speakers' platform and gave one drill bit each to the president, Senator Norbeck, and State Historian Doane Robinson. More speeches by other program participants followed. Rolf Lium—the young college student who had served as the minister at the Hermosa Congregational Church where the Coolidges worshipped all summer—then "pronounced the benediction, and the dedication of the mountain was done."[62]

On August 18, the Coolidges came to Hot Springs. They were accompanied by their son John, who had recently arrived in the Black Hills to spend time with them. A local planning committee—in consultation with the president's staff—had previously prepared a detailed schedule for "Coolidge Day." It included providing "waiting automobiles" to meet the president's special train when it arrived at Union Station in the late morning. The presidential party would then visit and tour the Battle Mountain Sanitarium—followed by a slow drive through the city so people "desiring to see the President and Mrs. Coolidge ... [would] have ample opportunity" to do so. Next on the agenda was a luncheon at the Country Club, to be hosted by "the mayor, the directors of the Country club and the Commercial club and their wives." The final event was a short visit to the South Dakota State Soldiers Home, after which the president's group would be returned to Union Station to "board the train for Hermosa and the Summer White House." Senators Norbeck and McMaster, and Representative Williamson, had all "accepted invitations to be present for the day."[63]

The president's visit to Hot Springs went largely as planned. But it did include two "unscheduled features." The first occurred after a tour of the Battle Mountain Sanitarium grounds, when the president's car swung back to the sanitarium's front door and he asked to see Hezron Day. Mr. Day, an 85-year-old Civil War veteran staying at the sanitarium, was from the president's hometown of Plymouth Notch, Vermont. According to Day, when the two met, they "just talked about old Plymouth folks. The President knew many people I knew but I was not an intimate acquaintance of his father as some of the stories have said. I met him at the Notch, once." The second unscheduled feature originated while the Coolidges were at the luncheon table at the Country Club. There, the president said he wanted to meet the author who wrote the poem "A Cowboy's Prayer." No one on the Coolidge Day planning committee had thought to include Badger Clark—the poem's author—in the group that would attend the president's Country Club luncheon and reception. Clark was "hurriedly sent for" and arrived in time to greet the president, who "spent a good part of the afternoon chatting with Badger." During their conversation, Clark did most of the talking, and the "taciturn" president mostly listened.[64]

Three days after their visit to Hot Springs, the Coolidges (including son John) took a train to Yellowstone National Park. They spent a week there. Six "colored people," who cared for the president's household as "cooks, servants, butlers, [and]maids" at the summer White House, did not accompany the presidential party to the nation's oldest national park. Instead, they stayed behind and were entertained by Steve Hurley, the manager of Camp Galena who had often seen and dealt with them throughout the summer. While the president was at Yellowstone, Hurley "put his own light truck at their disposal and gave them a trip through the park, to the Needles and Sylvan Lake." A month or so after the presidential party returned to Washington, the "colored people of the President's party" sent a note to Hurley that thanked him "for the friendly courtesies of the summer." They also sent him a "choice ebony cane" with his initials engraved on a sterling silver nameplate. In an editorial titled "An Unwritten Despatch," Francis thanked Hurley for his "thoughtfulness" in treating this six-member group as "guests of South Dakota."[65]

After the Coolidges returned to the Game Lodge in late August, they remained in the Black Hills for twelve more days. During that time, the president met with U.S. Senators from Washington and Connecticut, dedicated Camp Coolidge State Boy Scout Camp in Custer State Park (where the boys subsequently gave him the Scout Name of "Chief No Chatter"), and received the South Dakota Regents and a delegation from the American Society of Agricultural Engineers. Accompanied by the First Lady and their son John, he also travelled north of the Black Hills to inspect an irrigation district at Newell and then attend the Butte County Fair at Nisland. On September 7, the Coolidges celebrated John's 21st birthday at the Game Lodge. The next day, John toured the Badlands while his parents visited the South Dakota School of Mines Museum in Rapid City.[66]

In an editorial published shortly before the Coolidges departed, Francis discussed the positive impact their visit had on South Dakota, praised the president's family, highlighted the many activities the Coolidges engaged in and near the Black Hills, and thanked fellow South Dakotans and presidential staff members who made the summer sojourn a success. Although admitting "it is too early to measure what the Coolidge visit means," Francis concluded that "the stay of Coolidge has not solved all problems. . . . , but the summer White House came at a time when many hard-working people need a bit of encouragement. He gave it."[67]

The Coolidges' last day in the Hills was September 9. A "monster demonstration that brought out what seemed to be the whole town" assembled to say farewell at the Rapid City High School. Every city "shop, office, industrial plant, and mill had closed so that their employees could attend the demonstration." It included a short address by Rapid City Mayor Victor Jepsen—followed by the president's reply. He spoke for almost five minutes. During his remarks, he said in part: "I want to thank you, Mr. Mayor, and you, my fellow citizens, for coming out here in such generous numbers to express your farewell greeting to me and my family and my associates in public office.... The hospitality that has been extended to us has been nothing less than remarkable." After the "farewell party," President Coolidge spent the rest of the day "in last minute work at his desk" before his train departed for Washington that evening."[68]

IN 1912, THE FEDERAL GOVERNMENT transferred a rectangular-shaped piece of land to the state of South Dakota. That land, consisting of 61,440 acres, was located "in the heart of the Black Hills." One year later, the state legislature designated the area as a State Game Preserve. A fence was built around it, and soon it was stocked with elk and buffalo to accompany the native deer that were already there. Then in 1919, at the urging of then-governor Norbeck, the legislature redesignated the preserve as Custer State Park. That legislature also established a three-member Custer State Park Board, gave it "full authority to manage and control" the park, and authorized it to purchase—for "park purposes"—other state-or-privately-owned lands in or adjacent to the park's boundary lines.[69]

The next year, the state bought privately-owned Sylvan Lake (built during the winter of 1891-92 by "damming the head waters of Sunday gulch"), its hotel, and "approximately 200 acres of land connected therewith." After the U.S. Congress set aside more lands (commonly known as the Harney Peak District) for the state's use, the 1921 state legislature added those lands (plus the previously-purchased Sylvan Lake area) to the existing park. These lands were located north and west of the park's 1919 northern border. They included Harney Peak, Sylvan Lake, and vertical rock formations known as the Needles. Custer State Park's total area was now 107,000 acres.[70]

In addition to expanding the park, the 1921 legislature also adopted the following provision: "To encourage the erection of summer cottages, the Park Board is hereby authorized to make term leases of lots for this purpose, but no lease shall be made on the slopes of Sylvan Lake or within view of the Lake." By the mid-1920s, "a considerable number of cabins... [had] been erected" in the park. The cabin sites were "secured through the Park Board at the rental price of ten dollars per annum." And the site lessee was "protected in his renewal privilege." As long as he made "prompt payment of the rental fee," the site could "be held indefinitely."[71]

The park was enlarged once again in January 1925, when the federal government made an additional allotment of 15,000 acres to be included within the park's boundaries. That expansion occurred primarily "to the north and to the south of the original park lands." After it was implemented, the park included "approximately 122,440 acres," and its southwestern border now extended south to the northern border of Wind Cave National Park.[72]

In April 1926, the Hot Springs *Times-Herald* published an editorial titled "Growing Pains" that advocated giving the Park Board "full power" to run Custer State Park. The article pointed out that "theoretically the park is under the state park board," but "in reality, five different parties determine its diet." Those parties were the Fish and Game Department, which looked after the park's game; the Commissioner of Public and School lands, which looked after its forests, the Highway Commission, which had responsibility over the park's highways; the Park Superintendent (Colonel Shade at the time)—who "draws but does not earn a big salary because there is nothing for him to do"; and the Park Board, "which should have central jurisdiction over all park affairs but doesn't." After criticizing this arrangement for its lack of unified control, the editorial argued that "there should be a central jurisdiction with full power resting in the State Park Board. And the board should have ample funds to carry on a sane development program. Other states spend millions to create a pitiful pittance of the beauties God has given South Dakota."[73]

Other South Dakota newspapers, including those published in Newell and Huron, endorsed the ideas expressed in Francis's "Growing Pains" editorial and concluded "it is time that a more businesslike policy was adopted for government of the State Game Park." And in its August 3 edition, the *Star* addressed the issue. After summarizing the main points made in the "Growing Pains" piece, the *Star* noted that Colonel Shade, while "motoring to California," paused long enough to send an "unofficial report" about "his superintendency of the State Park." Shade's report joined the demand for "a centralized park administration," and the *Star* admired him for doing so. After quoting extensively from recent articles in the *Evening Huronite* and *Lead Daily Call* that advocated centralization of authority over the park, the August 3 editorial ended by stating "the Star sincerely hopes that the state at large will note all these who have had personal contact with the park situation... join in one conclusion: that the next legislature should end the division of authority and responsibility in the state park"; and "the park board should be given powers and funds commensurate with its importance."[74]

Less than a year later, when the Coolidges were visiting the Black Hills, a bill was introduced in a special session of the South Dakota legislature that incorporated the unified-administration-of-the-park concept. Peter Norbeck, now a U.S. Senator, authored the bill. It eventually passed both houses of the legislature and became law. Among other things, the new law perpetuated the park "as heretofore created, acquired, defined and established." It also gave the Park Board the "exclusive authority" and "duty to use, manage, and control" all state-owned property within the park and provide for its "care, maintenance, preservation and improvement." The park superintendent, under the Board's direction and control, was charged with caring for park property and managing park "enterprises and activities." His job included maintaining highways and trails, supervising other park employees, and "performing such other duties as the Board may require." With respect to cabin site leases, the 1927 legislation again authorized the Park Board "to make term permits or leases to encourage the erection of homes within the Park[.]" And it added a new requirement—that "leases shall be made only upon locations designated, surveyed and platted by the Board."[75]

In January 1927, Badger Clark "holed in" for the winter at one of the private cabins built in Custer State Park. That cabin, owned by one of Badger's friends, was located "on a hillside ... about eight miles east of Custer." It consisted of one room that measured 10 feet by 18 feet. Clark furnished it with a small table, two chairs, and a bed. Orange crates served as cupboards. The cabin had no electricity or running water. Despite its raw simplicity, this one-room structure was declared to be "the most ideal place in which to 'poetize' that [a] poet ever had." Badger, who did not know how long he would stay when he first moved in, ended up living there for ten years.[76]

Francis also decided he wanted to have a cabin in the park. During the summer of 1927, he "had it built ... and made a road to it[.]" His father-in-law—John Graves—assisted in the one-room cabin's construction. It was situated on the top of a small hill next to French Creek and located "about twenty-five miles" from Hot Springs. The exterior walls were covered with pine "shiplap" siding, and the bark was simply left on the outer side of the wood. The interior floor measured slightly over 19 feet by 19 feet. The cabin's contents included a "huge old rocking chair," an icebox, and apparently some beds, a table, and some chairs. Like the cabin Badger moved into about six months earlier, this one had no electricity or indoor plumbing. But it did have a cobblestone fireplace with a wood mantel and brick chimney. M. E. "Monty" Nystrom, who had done the extensive stonework at the Game Lodge and had his own cabin in the park, built the fireplace.

Francis named the cabin "Myrlin" and described it as "a quiet, peaceful place far away from the madding crowd."[77]

ESTHER CASE GRADUATED FROM MANKATO High School in late May, 1925, and she attended Mankato State Teachers College that fall. She spent her freshman year there and studied a variety of subjects, including history (American, Contemporary American, and Modern European), psychology, intermediate children's literature, English composition and reading, music, sociology, and public speaking. The next year she transferred to Gustavus Adolphus College in St. Peter, Minnesota. At Gustavus, she took courses in history of Bible Times, general animal biology, modern European history, advanced rhetoric, elementary French, and public speaking. In early August, 1927, she accompanied her parents to Hot Springs and went to work at the Star Publishing Company office, where she replaced a worker who had left in July. Francis enthusiastically welcomed her assistance, commenting that "if it had not been for Esther to help in the office, I do not know what we should have done.... She is helping us very materially now."[78]

THE STAR PUBLISHING COMPANY'S LAST two months in 1927 were dominated by two events—a "subscription contest" and construction of a new print shop and office. The subscription campaign was first announced in the *Times-Herald* on October 28. The *Star* followed up with its separate announcement in its November 1 issue. There it was explained that "the Star and Times-Herald campaign" would officially open on Wednesday, November 2, and run for six and one-half weeks. Those who chose to enter the contest became "candidates" who acquired "votes" based on the number of new and renewal subscriptions they obtained for either or both Hot Springs newspapers. The contest was broken down into three distinct periods. Each period ended on a Saturday, with the first concluding on November

26, the second on December 10, and the third on December 17—the contest's final day. The vote value for subscriptions declined as each period expired. Double votes for new subscribers were awarded during the first two periods, but not for the week-long third period. The campaign—officially known as "The Hot Springs Star and Times-Herald Community Club Christmas Prize Distribution"—announced at its onset that five prizes would be awarded to the candidates who received the most votes. The "First Grand Prize" was a Buick 4-Door Model 1928 Sedan priced at $1,595. Second prize was $300 in cash, third was an Atwater-Kent radio, fourth a diamond ring, and fifth was $50 in gold. In addition, those candidates who did not win a prize but remained active until the campaign finished would "be paid a twenty per cent commission on all subscriptions turned in to their credit."[79]

In the weeks that followed, the *Star* ran front-page stories about the contest, published the names and vote counts of the candidates, and constantly repeated the campaign's slogan: It Can Be Done. It also ran large advertisements with bold tag lines such as CANDIDATES! - - -THE RACE IS ON! - - -YOU CAN WIN BY TRYING! NEW SUBSCRIPTIONS COUNT MOST!; and TO THE VICTOR, THE SPOILS! The December 13 issue, which was the last one published before the contest ended, included photos and stories about the three leading candidates. Four days later, when the campaign ended and the judges tallied all the votes, that group ended up winning the top three prizes, although Alcesta Murphy went from third place to first—moving Ruth Kipp and Clarence Cowalski into second and third, respectively.[80]

The *Star* described the subscription campaign as an "unqualified success" and thanked all who participated in it. The "aggregate total vote" for all the candidates "reached enormous figures, representing over 900 new subscribers and additional hundreds of renewal subscriptions." Among other things, those results "made possible the changes and improvements that before the campaign were merely dreams—changes which will mean better newspapers for a better community." In a separate article, the *Star* and *Times-Herald* also publicly thanked C. N. Alleger, who worked for a weekly newspaper in Belle Fourche. Mr. Alleger "had charge of the big campaign," and he made it "as fair to everyone as it could be."[81]

Three days after the "big campaign" was first announced on October 28, the Star Publishing Company broke ground for construction of a new print shop and office for the company's two newspapers. The building would be constructed on a lot located in the center of downtown. The company decided to build it in order "to save rent and to provide a building designed particularly for a newspaper and job printing plant." The project was to be financed "partly by borrowing money from the Federal Building and Loan association and partly by the returns from long term subscriptions in the subscription campaign" described above. The plans called for a structure that was "simple in design, but fireproof." Its floor plan measured 25 by 55 feet. The front was to be trimmed with "smooth finished native Fall River stone," and "fired tile" would be used for its side walls and back. It would have a concrete floor "throughout," and the ceiling would be made of pressed metal.[82]

Construction got underway in early November. The cornerstone was laid on the 8th. By the middle of that month, despite some delays caused by snow and cold weather, the side walls were "up to the first story," and Francis had decided to add a second story that would include office rooms and two apartments. When November ended, the front trim had been installed, the building was "well into the second story," and it was anticipated the roof would be put on in early December. As Francis had originally hoped, the building was finished and connected to water, sewer, and electricity lines shortly before Christmas. On that holiday, the Star Publishing Company's "big newspaper press" was "torn down, moved and reset in the new building." Two days later, "job presses and type cases" arrived, and the company printed both the *Star* and the *Times-Herald* in the new building that day.⁸³

Thirty years later, Francis reflected on his decision to build a new building for the *Star* and *Times-Herald*, and the impact that decision had on the city's development. He said in part:

> We also tried to be a good citizen as a business enterprise in the community.... Hot Springs in 1925 definitely had Upper Town and Lower Town. We decided the Star should have its own building. We... built the building..., announced that the Star was now "On the Midway" and that henceforth there was to be no division of the town, business-wise or otherwise. I always liked to think that contributed to community unity.

As the year 1927 came to a close, Francis was encouraged and invigorated by the success achieved in the newspaper-subscription and the new-building campaigns.⁸⁴

CHAPTER 10

HOT SPRINGS NEWSPAPERMAN AND BLACK HILLS PROMOTER—THE LATER YEARS

To the many readers of the Star, to the many correspondents, business associates, and to the immediate members of the staff, we express our sincere appreciation for your helpfulness, confidence and cooperation.

—Francis Case

Francis spent the winter and early spring of 1928 running in the primary contest to become the Republican candidate for the U.S. Congress. He was unsuccessful in that effort. This topic, and his subsequent attempts to become the congressman from western South Dakota, are discussed in detail in Chapter 12. After his primary defeat, Francis turned his attention back to running the Star newspaper operation. He had spent $1,500 of his own money on the primary campaign and decided to "work my way out" of this debt by devoting "full time" to the Star Publishing business.[1]

During the summer, Francis took steps to realize his goal of starting a daily newspaper in Hot Springs. Toward that end, he had carpenters, plasterers, plumbers, and a painter put the finishing touches on the two apartments on the Star Building's second floor so they could be rented and contribute income to the newspaper business. He also installed "many new pieces of machinery" to handle the papers' anticipated increased production needs. Finally, he renewed his previous application for membership in the Associated Press—an independent news cooperative headquartered in New York City that provided state, national, and international news stories to its members.[2]

The Associated Press accepted Francis's membership application, and on September 15, it notified him that its "telegraph news service" would begin on September 17. Two days later, the first edition of the now-daily *Times-Herald* was published and distributed. And on the 21st, the *Times-Herald* was officially converted into a daily and renamed the *Hot Springs Evening Star*. The newly-named paper was published every day except Sunday, and it was formatted in "tabloid size, the same as the New York Daily News." In addition, the *Hot Springs Star* continued to be published every Tuesday afternoon, and it subsequently became known as the *Hot Springs Weekly Star*.[3]

Shortly after launching his new daily, Francis took a break from the newspaper business and entered the Hot Springs Country Club's Sixth Annual handicap golf tournament. The golfers were put into three classes—A, B, and C—"based on best average records proportionate to par." Francis was placed in Class C, and his first-round opponent was A. A. Cowling. Cliff Wilson was also put in Class C. He was matched against A. G. Allen for the initial game. The local golf course, which many called "the most beautiful in the Hills," presented a formidable challenge to all golfers. It consisted of 18 holes, measured 5,806 yards, and set par at 71. The par six, 640-yard hole was the longest. Hole number 17 was considered the most difficult. It had two nearby canyons classified as "water hazards," even though neither contained water. The first and eighteenth holes were surrounded by sand traps, and the first also featured man-made embankments as additional hazards. Holes two, six, nine, ten, and eleven all had "dog-legs," which forced the players to hit their tee shots at "a right angle [to the hole] because of hills, trees or other hazards[.]" The course had six par-three holes, eight par-fours, three par-fives, and the one par six. According to the city champion I. H. Alarie, "the rolling ground... adds to the sportiness because of the greater difficulty in judging distance."⁴

It is not known whether Francis or Cliff won any of their matches, but it is known that Paul Martin became the class C champion. Other winners were Ben Potts (Class A) and E. B. Adams (Class B). The final matches were played on Sunday morning, November 4, "in the first snow of the season." These conditions made play "'difficult, but not too difficult,' according... [to] the golfers."⁵

The *Evening Star* made "headway" during its early months of publication. To encourage more subscribers to that paper and the *Weekly Star*, the latter ran an advertisement in its December 4 issue. The ad made a "December Special Anniversary Offer" to celebrate "one year in our new home." The offer provided a one-year subscription to the *Weekly Star* for $2.00 (regularly $2.50), and the *Evening Star* could be obtained for a year for $3.00 (regularly $4.50). The ad also noted that the *Weekly Star* was "now bigger and better than ever—7 columns wide—from 8 to 16 pages," that it contained "local, state and world news," and that it had "live correspondents in 29 Southern Hills communities." As for the *Evening Star*, the advertisement emphasized that this paper included "Associated Press dispatches from all over the world," and that "a daily newspaper means a larger Hot Springs and development for all Southwestern South Dakota." Two weeks later, it was announced that "Badger Clark has joined the staff of the Star as a contributing editor. He will not accept the responsibility of a regular column, but he has agreed to supply an occasional verse or story."⁶

On December 20, Myrle and Francis drove up to Rapid City so Myrle could catch a train to Mitchell, where she would spend the Christmas holidays with her relatives. That same day, Francis wrote to D. Wayne George, the editor of the weekly *Sundance Times* in Sundance, Wyoming. This letter noted that because Francis still wanted to study law and then return to the Hills to practice, and Leland wanted "to follow some leads he has in Chicago," the two proposed selling a controlling interest in the Star Publishing Company to George under terms set forth in the letter. George responded in writing on January 4. He stated that although "there is no doubt but that your proposition is a good one and it is hard for me to give up the prospect of owning the Star some day," he had decided to pursue his interest in aviation and take a job involving "sales, company and club organization, and publicity work" at Rapid Airlines in Rapid City. It appears that Francis did not pursue the idea of selling an interest in the Star company to others—at least not during the next two years.[7]

THE RED CANYON OIL WELL was located "five miles northeast of Edgemont and about 23 miles southwest of Hot Springs." On January 10, 1929, at 7:30 in the morning, two men from Edgemont were "trying to blow out obstructions" in the well so they could pull out its casing. When the charge went off in the well, they "broke something loose" and "'black liquid gold,' oil, shot out to great heights[.]" Word of this event spread quickly. By 9:00 a.m. the next day, the *Evening Star* "became a morning star" by printing an "Extra" edition. In large, bold letters, its front-page headline proclaimed **"Big OIL Strike in Red Canyon Hole."** Underneath the headline, there were two "oil" stories. They were titled "Is First Flowing Well in State of South Dakota" and "Oil Found There in 1925 But Operations Held Up." A short article that described Red Canyon was also included. Over 1,000 copies of this edition, printed on green paper, "were flashing the big news throughout the Black Hills by 11 o'clock," and all copies were soon "exhausted." In addition, the Star office sent dispatches to the Associated Press, which "brought back long distance calls from Pierre, from Omaha Denver and Chicago for further details as rapidly as they could be supplied."[8]

By the afternoon, Associated Press newspapers were printing the Star's story "all over the country," and before sundown, Francis and two companions apparently joined "over 80 cars carrying from three to five people each who... visited the well and took away samples of the oil." That night, Chicago's WGN radio station included the oil-discovery story in its broadcast. Four days later, Cliff Wilson—Fall River County's representative in the state legislature—sent word to the Star that the oil strike was "the big subject around the state house today," and that "the special message announcing the state's first flowing oil well would be read before the legislature" that afternoon. And "local business men... agreed that the showing at Red Canyon should speed drilling of the other known structures throughout Fall River county."[9]

In the weeks and months ahead, interest in developing southwestern South Dakota's potential oil resources flourished. The Star Publishing Company was actively and enthusiastically involved in that effort. Nine days after the Red Canyon strike occurred, it released the first edition of *The Black Hills Oil and Mining Review*—a publication created to "give accurate and complete information on Black Hills oil and rare mineral developments[.]" The *Review* cost ten cents per copy and was published every two months. Soon the Star company obtained subscriptions "from out of town oil men." In addition to the *Review*, almost every issue of the *Weekly Star* carried multiple stories about oil developments throughout 1929. In early March, it reported that Governor Bulow signed a bill amending the state's Blue-Sky law to make it easier for "oil and mining companies to organize and sell stock." Subsequently, the paper told its readers about companies that had decided to explore and drill for oil in areas near Hot Springs, the progress those companies achieved and the problems they encountered, and geologists' optimistic reports about the potential for oil discovery. The *Weekly Star* also included editorials that endorsed the search for oil and advertisements that informed "OIL Men" they could obtain new county maps, oil lease blanks, stock certificates, corporate seals and filing covers at the Star office.[10]

Apart from the Star Company's extensive oil-exploration coverage, Case family members decided to take preliminary steps toward forming their own exploration concerns. In May, Francis, Leland and Cliff became directors for Associated Royalties company and for United Oil company—both of which filed articles of incorporation with the secretary of state. And in late November, the *Weekly Star* announced that Western Securities, Inc. was organized as "'a co-operative pool for oil and mining leases, royalties, stocks, industrial bonds and other securities[.]'" That company's five directors included Cliff and Leland. Cliff was also Western Securities' president and Leland its field secretary.[11]

Black Hills Petroleum Company (BHP) was one of the entities that searched for oil in 1929. It was financed by selling stock to the public. On May 15, the company announced that it was moving a recently-purchased big standard rig to the Barker structure—a potential oil field located 27 miles northwest of Hot Springs in Custer County. In late June, BHP began drilling Black Hills Petroleum Well No. 1 (soon referred to as Barker No. 1). That operation continued through the summer and fall. On December 5, two drillers at the site encountered the strong odor of gasoline in the well, and they immediately capped it. A short time later, the company's secretary asked Francis to "'take a ride to the well' with him." Their visit was brief. Francis reported that the "hissing of the gas could be heard as soon as one entered the [drill] shack. The odor, like the foul breath of some subterranean gasoline guzzler, was unmistakable."[12]

Twenty-five days after Francis's visit to "the gasser," a "commercial flow of oil estimated at between 15 and 25 barrels a day was struck at the Barker well." As with the Red Canyon strike in January, this news travelled fast. Several interested parties visited the site soon after the oil began flowing, and they celebrated by smearing their faces "with the real Black Hills Gold." Telegrams announcing the strike were promptly sent to Governor Bulow and out-of-staters who strongly backed the Barker operation. Francis was taking an Army training course at Fort Snelling, Minnesota, when he got the news. That night, he wrote a letter "To the Readers of The Evening Star." There he stated, among other things, that "Our Slogan, 'Let's Find Oil or Find Out' must now give way to '*All South Dakota Forward*'"; and "Black Hills Petroleum richly deserves gratitude for persistent pioneering in the face of mounting obstacles." So, the year 1929 ended as it began—with an oil strike that created great excitement and convinced many people that South Dakota could become a significant oil producer.[13]

The Barker well strike "ushered in" the new year in Hot Springs. During the celebration, two barrels of "thick, dark, and highly inflammable" Barker oil were "burned in front of the Evans hotel and oil was spread over the pavement on River avenue." In mid-January, a newly formed Hot Springs Oil Exchange opened for business in a room off the Evans' lobby. Western Securities, Inc. sponsored the exchange and stated its purpose "was to give better service to the people who have purchased stock in the local companies." An early advertisement emphasized that the exchange specialized in "South Dakota and Wyoming Oil issues." It also listed the price per share (ranging from $.10 to $20.00) of seven local companies, including Associated Royalties and Western Securities, Inc. The *Weekly Star* proclaimed that "with headquarters here for the oil exchange, Western Securities, Inc.... [and other companies], Hot Springs bids fair to become the 'Tulsa of the Northwest.'"[14]

General enthusiasm for oil exploration continued through the spring and summer of 1930. During its first three weeks in operation, the oil exchange received inquiries from Washington, Illinois, and Indiana, "as well as many letters from nearby states." Geologists conducted investigations and issued optimistic reports. New exploration efforts—sometimes backed by new companies—occurred in the area. For example, in late March, a well was "spudded in" (i.e. drilling began) in the Country Club structure—located just two-and-a-half miles west of Hot Springs. A Rapid City syndicate and a company from Denver jointly financed that venture. Two months later, BHP began drilling a second well named Rockford No. 1. It was located on the Barker structure—about three-eighths of a mile from Barker No. 1. The latter well was now pumping several barrels of oil into storage tanks on a daily basis. In July, Cliff was reelected as president of Western Securities, Inc., and Leland was chosen as vice-president. The company's officers reported "much progress" for its first year, and they indicated "several deals... for additional holdings" were underway.[15]

Meanwhile, the Red Canyon well, whose discovery in January 1929 spawned the oil-exploration boom, had not been in production for "over a year." A legal dispute over who had proper title to the land where oil was found had prevented any activity with respect to that well. The dispute was eventually resolved by a court decision, and The Morgan Holding Company in Minneapolis subsequently purchased the land's oil interests. In early August, Morgan announced that it planned to immediately "put this well on production" and drill "one and possibly two more wells this year." The Rockford No. 1 well also started producing oil that month, and BHP made plans "to get a third well underway."[16]

The positive oil development situation began to change in the fall of 1930. The two Barker-structure wells "were shut down when oil and business conditions throughout the country made it impossible to prosecute field development on a profitable scale." During October, two cuts were made in the price paid for Osage crude oil. (This oil was produced in northeastern Wyoming about 50 miles northwest of Hot Springs.) Further cuts occurred. In early November, drilling operations were also suspended at the Country Club structure. Notwithstanding these problems, the *Weekly Star* provided some encouraging news on the oil-development front in early 1931. It noted, among other things, that BHP was negotiating for "'a resumption of operations at the Barker field early in the spring'"; and it later announced that "arrangements have been made for completion of the so-called

Country Club well[.]" But by March 1931, the price for Osage crude oil had dropped from $1.65 to $.50 per barrel.[17]

Despite the headline grabbing oil strikes in 1929, the continued optimism, and the efforts expended toward making further discoveries in 1930 and early 1931, Hot Springs never became the "Tulsa of the Northwest." In his 1972 interview, Leland summarized the short-lived Hot Springs oil boom by saying "it looked for a while as though we were sitting on something really big" but it later became apparent that "there was just one big lack in this whole picture—that was oil! We were set right, for it—but it didn't come!"[18]

IN ADDITION TO PUBLICIZING THE oil strike in January 1929, Francis participated in gatherings that assessed recent local developments and sought ways to improve the state's future. The first was a meeting of the Hot Springs Chamber of Commerce held during the evening of January 21. (This organization, formerly known as the Commercial Club, had changed its name a month earlier to align itself with a modern trend taking place "all over the country.") The meeting was attended by "150 enthusiastic men and women" who assembled in the Evans Hotel dining room. After dinner, various speakers noted that the group had recently grown from 100 to 169 members, that an important stretch of road in Wind Cave National Park would be completed "early in the tourist season," that membership at the State Soldier's Home was expanding, and that the "Battle Mountain sanitarium brings in nearly a half million dollars into this community nearly every year." Francis, the Chamber's secretary, spoke last. After he reviewed "the year's activities and financial condition," he "was given a rising vote of thanks for his work during the past year."[19]

The second gathering was a much larger event. The state secretary of agriculture (Louis Crill) and his department had organized the first-ever Greater South Dakota Congress. Its purpose was to "'coordinate the state's activities,'" and Mr. Crill hoped "'that the result would lead toward marked advancement in South Dakota's development.'" This four-day event, held at Rapid City's Alex Johnson Hotel from January 22-25, featured 50 speakers who addressed "a dozen subjects relating to South Dakota's resources and their development." The speakers included Governor Bulow, other state officials, and "state organization heads and prominent persons from other states."[20]

Francis spoke during the program's first session, which dealt with the state's scenic and recreational resources. His talk was titled "How Permanent Summer Homes in the Black Hills Will Build for a Greater South Dakota." He began by asserting that "more summer homes in the Black Hills means more permanent homes everywhere in South Dakota." He then observed that impressive buildings in Deadwood, Hot Springs, Lead, Belle Fourche, and Rapid City, and many homes in every town, are evidence of growth that has "followed the exploitation of our recreational resources." Turning his attention to Custer State Park, he stated, "'there now are some 30 private summer homes, five tourist parks, and the American Legion Camp, Blue Bell Lodge, Camp Galena, Sylvan Lake hotel, the State Game Lodge and inn, providing summer homes for a good-sized city.'" Next, he proclaimed that, "'there is room for 5,000 private homes, allotting 20 acres to each. These yielding $10 a year in lease fees would create a $50,000 fund for further development. The time is coming when this will be. It can be speeded.'" He also told the audience that "'summer homes are not confined to the State park, of course, although the game preserve and the degree of protection given by Park officials give it an advantage.'" His presentation ended with this observation and suggestion: "'The Boy Scouts have dedicated a site there [in the park], and the Knights Templar have leased a site. These should have buildings on them, and that will lead to more of such organizations coming.'"[21]

Approximately 1,000 people attended the four-day congress. On its last day, a committee of representative delegates was appointed to formulate resolutions that would memorialize the proceedings and make recommendations for the future. One of those resolutions requested that the legislature provide a fund to the congress's "various boards and commissions" to use to discover and advertise the state's "great resources." Another extended appreciation to "the speakers who took part in the program" and other groups and entities. The *Rapid City Daily Journal* described the gathering in a brief editorial. It noted that the "Greater South Dakota congress... saw the chemist, the banker, the farmer, the publisher, the manufacturer and businessman, the educator, the poet, the official, the lawyer, and the out of state observer" who appeared "on the same platform," where they told "what they thought of the future of South Dakota," and made "suggestions to make that future brighter." "That," the *Journal* concluded, "was one big accomplishment of the session."[22]

DURING HIS MOUNT RUSHMORE DEDICATION address delivered in August 1927, president Coolidge had indicated that "the people of South Dakota" were entitled "to the sympathy and support of private beneficence and the National Government." No federal legislation incorporating this concept was passed in 1928. Meanwhile, the Rushmore project had run out of money, carving work was suspended, and the planned memorial "remained in limbo throughout that year." But in February 1929, both houses of Congress approved a bill that gave new life to the project. And on February 25, with only six days remaining in his term, President Coolidge signed the bill into law. Among other things, it created a 12-member Rushmore National Memorial Commission to be appointed by the president, and it empowered that group "to complete the carving" of the memorial. The new law also provided up to $250,000 in federal money "'to match the funds advanced from other sources.'"[23]

When he signed the bill, President Coolidge appointed ten of the twelve commissioners. Three of them were from South Dakota: John A. Boland, Rapid City businessman; Delos B. Gurney, Yankton businessman and owner of WNAX, the state's most powerful radio station; and Charles M. Day, Sioux Falls publisher of the *Daily Argus-Leader*. The remaining seven included five prominent businessmen, a social and civic leader, and a political leader. They were scattered throughout the country, and four (including the only woman appointee) were Gutzon Borglum's personal friends. Shortly after his inauguration on March 4, President Herbert Hoover appointed the last two commissioners—William Williamson and Royal Johnson. Both were U.S. congressmen who represented South Dakota. But before the project could receive any federal money, the president was required to call a meeting and formally organize the commission. That was finally accomplished on June 6. A few days later, the government committed to giving the commission "a check for $54,670.56 to match a like amount of private funds already spent" on the project. And on June 10, long-delayed carving work was resumed on the mountain.[24]

IN THE SPRING OF 1929, Francis considered ideas that would expand his newspaper operation. They included acquiring the *Daily Call* in Lead or the *Daily Pioneer-Times* in Deadwood—and perhaps starting a paper in Lemmon, South Dakota (located 132 miles north and east of Deadwood, very close to the North Dakota border). None of those propositions came to fruition. But later on, he did make a deal that, in his view, increased the Star Publishing Company's influence and value. In August 1928, a new paper—titled the *Hot Springs News*—appeared in town. W. E. Latham owned it, and George E. Lee became its editor and manager. Since the early 1920s, Latham had also owned and published the *Edgemont Express* in Edgemont.[25]

In May 1929, Francis reached an agreement with Latham. By its terms, the Star Publishing Company bought the subscription list and good will of the *Hot Springs News* and the *Edgemont Express* from Latham, and those two papers went out of business. For its part, the Star company agreed to transfer the rights on two of its publications:

the *Black Hills Oil and Mining Review* and the *Tourist News*. As previously stated, the former came into being shortly after oil was discovered in nearby Red Canyon in January. It had published three issues. The *Tourist News*, described in Chapter 9 above, was published each summer since its inception in 1926. The publication rights to those two papers were transferred to a new paper named the *Black Hills News*. The *Oil and Mining Review*'s subscription list was included in that transfer. Francis believed that by obtaining the *Hot Springs News* and *Edgemont Express* "block addition" of subscribers, the Star papers had gained "a coverage of Fall River, Custer and Shannon counties far beyond anything in mind before."[26]

In his speech at the Greater South Dakota Conference in January, Francis asserted that building more private homes in Custer State Park would lead to "more permanent houses everywhere in South Dakota." Five months later, the Sioux Falls *Daily Argus-Leader* gave a boost to this more-private-cabins-in-the-park idea. It did so in an article that appeared in the "Sunday Magazine and Feature Section" of the paper's May 18 issue. That story began by urging its readers to "build your summer nest in forests of the Black Hills. There is every reason why you should." Although the article focused most of its discussion on cabin sites in Black Hills National Forest lands, it specifically noted that similar sites with similar features were available in Custer State Park. It then pointed out that permits for these cabin sites—whether on federal or state park land—cost $10 per year. The sites were described as surveyed-and-platted lots being "about one-fifth of an acre in size" and typically located "at the bottom of gulches, or along creek bottoms." The lots were "grouped together for convenience in supervision, sanitation, and protection." The story also emphasized that the sites were "permanent," and "your summer nest can rest assured of its location, after once it is built." With regard to construction of a cabin, the article noted that some of the cabins already there "were built of logs and some of lumber." It advised that logs could be obtained for

$3.00 per lineal hundred feet, that "rough lumber' could be secured by paying $25 to $30 per thousand feet, and that skilled help was available in the Hills for those who did not choose to build their own cabins.[27]

Newspaper editors in the Black Hills took notice of the *Argus-Leader* cabins-in-the-Hills story. A slightly shorter version soon appeared in the *Custer Weekly Chronicle* under the heading "Cabin Sites Cost But $10 A Year in the Black Hills." That paper also ran an advertisement: **"BUILD a summer cabin."** There, a local lumber company proclaimed: "Now is the time and this is the place. We have the material ready to deliver to the job. Why not let us figure the cost? Let us measure your windows for screens. You will need them on soon. And don't forget screen doors. We have them." And the *Hot Springs Evening Star* summarized the *Argus* article in a story titled "Build Summer Nest in the Hills—Klock."[28]

Because it had "many inquiries" about the Black Hills summer homes described in the article above, the *Argus-Leader* published another story on the subject in its June 29 issue. Whereas the first article told how to secure a summer home site (also referred to as a "summer nest"), this "supplemental" one—employing flowery language throughout—gave advice regarding what to do and what to enjoy after the nest had been secured. It began by suggesting the cabin owners should "feather" (i.e., decorate) their nests with several items that were appropriate for the cabins' natural setting. These included "pieces of deer horn, bits of quartz, chunks of petrified wood... specimens of mineral ore, of all sizes and colors; and sometimes Indian relics." The article also suggested building a fireplace "made of curious rocks and highly colored stones," placing an old firearm over the mantle, and mounting a deer head on the wall. It then shifted its focus to the nest's location and its surroundings. It noted that the cabins would "likely be in a small group" and connected to the main highway by a side road that had been surveyed by "State park authorities." The nearby vales and hillsides would be decked with several different kinds of "beautiful flowers" featuring "all colors of the rainbow." Cabin owners could expect to see many animals near their site, including white-tail deer, elk, buffalo, an occasional antelope or big-horn mountain sheep, goats, ground hogs, ruffled grouse and sage hens. The cabin would be situated by a stream, which would include waterfalls, beaver dams, and deep holes. It would contain one or more species of trout: brook, lochlaven, rainbow or speckled. The article concluded by advising the cabin owners to end their day by sitting on their porches at dusk—listening to the wind "stealing" through the tall trees, the creek "murmuring" close by, and the "brisk fire of pine and pitch ... crackling on the fireplace just inside."[29]

Regardless of whether he read the articles in the *Argus*, *Chronicle*, or *Evening Star*, in 1929 Badger Clark decided he would build a much more substantial cabin in Custer State Park than the one he had lived in for the past two years. His new cabin would be located about two hundred feet from the current one, and it would take eight years to complete. In the fall of 1929, he began working on the cabin's foundation. Among other things, that task involved hauling buckets of sand and water by hand "from Galena Creek up the steep hillside to the cabin site" to mix with cement and form the concrete used to build a rock foundation. It took "many years" and an estimated 1,276 buckets filled with sand and water to finish the foundation work.[30]

FRANCIS EXPERIENCED A RELATIVELY RELAXED summer and fall in 1929, and he had only a few out-of-town speaking engagements and meetings during that time. From mid-July to mid-August, Myrle and he were hosts to Myrle's father John and her sister Bess. On July 29, the Methodist summer camp began its annual, weeklong conference in a scenic, isolated area near Pactola—a small mining town located about 20 miles west of Rapid City. Young people from "all parts of the state" attended this camp (sponsored by the Epworth

League), where they received "religious education, moral training and inspiration." Francis and Badger were among the outside speakers chosen to address this group during one of its evening programs. Two months later, Francis attended a meeting of "Republican vice chairwomen from all counties in the Black Hills district" held at Rapid City's Alex Johnson Hotel. During the afternoon program, he made a "presentation of the primary law as amended." A "general round table discussion" concerning that current primary law followed his talk. And in early November, he returned to Rapid City to participate in the Associated Commercial Clubs of the Black Hills' annual business session. There he was elected for a two-year term on the Association's newly-created, five-member board of directors.[31]

On December 24, Myrle and Francis passed through Rapid City on their way to Mitchell, where they spent Christmas day with Myrle's relatives. Shortly thereafter, Francis reported to Fort Snelling in St. Paul, Minnesota, to take a two-week Army training course—apparently with the 3rd Infantry Division. In 1925, he had applied for and received a commission as a second lieutenant in the U.S. Army Reserve. But the Fort Snelling training course was his first actual "tour of duty" as a reserve Army officer.[32]

AS PREVIOUSLY NOTED, ESTHER BEGAN working in the Star office in August 1927. It appears that she lived at Joyce and Cliff's house while doing so. By the spring of 1928, she had taken on several duties at the organization. Leland described her position as "head of the Accounting Department." In that role, she kept the books, answered telephone calls, occasionally wrote letters, prepared the weekly payroll, and billed local and foreign advertisers once a month. She also "read all the proof sheets" and corrected mistakes before the paper was printed, and she helped wrap the papers for mailing and distribution after they were printed. In June, she assisted Francis when he "worked out" the company's income tax report. Esther was paid $20 per week and liked her job. Her only complaint was that she frequently had to spend money to have her dresses (and, at least once, her coat) dry-cleaned, because she was "always getting into the [printers] ink, where I get it is a mystery but one thing is certain and that is that I get into it good and plenty."[33]

That fall, Mary and Herbert visited four of their five children in the Black Hills. (Carol was living in Chicago at the time.) After the elder Cases returned to Mankato, Mary wrote to Carol about the current situation in Hot Springs. With respect to the Star operation, she told Carol that Francis and Leland "sure are putting in long hours" and "so far the new daily is meeting with success." She also noted that "Esther is on the job too," has her own desk, "is busy every minute," and has decided she can't attend school this year. Mary further reported that the "steno" employed in the Wilson Law Office had gone to California for an indefinite period of time, so Joyce had taken over that job. Mary concluded that although Joyce "likes the office work," she "should not have the house, children & office work too."[34]

By February 1929, Esther had decided that she wanted to return to school. During that spring or early summer, she left Hot Springs and moved back to her parents' house in Mankato with the intention of attending the commercial college there. In June, she looked for a summer job and was hired as a saleswoman for the C. & D. Company. Headquartered in Grand Rapids, Michigan, that company manufactured "Beautiful Dresses, Scarfs and Lingerie. Hosiery and Underwear for Every Member of the Family." Its advertising slogan was "'Things to wear for those who care.'" In her first three days going from house to house, she received six orders. She also had garnered "promises... for at least four more sales, [of] dresses, slips, stockings, etc."[35]

Esther changed her mind about enrolling in Mankato Commercial College that fall. Instead, she went to work in the advertising department at the *Mankato Daily Free Press*. Her experience working for the Star papers "counted," and she was glad she learned "all I did at H.

S." Soon after joining the *Free Press*, she was putting in ten-hour days and keeping very busy. In addition to returning to newspaper work, Esther's life changed in a positive, permanent way that fall when she fell in love with Raymond Sunderman and accepted his marriage proposal. Sunderman lived and worked on a farm with his brother Willard. That farm—located near Le Sueur, Minnesota—was a 30-mile drive from Mankato. Esther described her future husband to Leland as being "a few hairs taller than Francis" and having "the same hat size" as their brother. Regarding her decision to marry Raymond, she wrote to Carol in November that "I know I am right and that as God joined us in meeting, he will join us—and I think it will be soon.... As for plans, I can't say what they are yet."[36]

By mid-January, Esther and Raymond had decided to get married on February 12. After informing their families of their plans, the couple went shopping on a Saturday afternoon. They bought a new brown suit for the groom-to-be and several items of furniture for the two-story farmhouse where they would live. Two nights later, after Esther put in a full day at the office, seven of her coworkers held a pre-wedding supper party for her at the *Free Press* bindery. It featured more than enough "eats" for everyone, including a "bride and groom on the cake." Each coworker gave Esther a tea towel with that coworker's initials sewn onto it. In addition, they collectively presented her with a Pyrex casserole dish, which she described as "a beauty." According to the honored guest, the party was "sure one surprise," and she didn't have "the least suspicion" that it had been planned.[37]

The wedding was held on Wednesday, February 12, at the Case family home in Mankato. Reverend Herbert performed the "beautiful ring ceremony." While he did so, Esther and Raymond stood in the same place Mary and Herbert did when they were married 35 years earlier. The event was described as "a quiet affair" with a "small group of relatives and intimate friends" in attendance. Out-of-town relatives included Raymond's mother, sister, and brother (with his wife and daughter); and Esther's great uncle and second cousin (with his wife) from the Grannis side of the family. "Three fine chickens" were the main course for the dinner, followed by "a most wonderful wedding cake." A few days after the wedding, the new bride's father commented: "Esther seems very happy as I trust they always will be."[38]

SOMETIME AFTER ESTHER LEFT THE Star Office, Francis concluded that the papers' printing plant had become too small for its present business volume and his plans for future expansion. So, he hired two local builders to construct a new addition that would double the Star building's present size. That work was basically completed by late January 1930. But finishing the basement, cleaning and painting the interior, moving equipment, and installing new machines—all while continuing to produce the Star papers—became a process that took about six months.[39]

In the *Weekly Star*'s February 4 issue, the Star Publishing Company announced that it had decided to install a modern, high-speed newspaper press that could print and fold 3,500 eight-page papers in an hour. To help finance that purchase, the Star also told its readers that it would soon be starting a circulation campaign that would reward "valuable prizes" to those who procured the most newspaper subscriptions; and it had hired an experienced circulation manager (Lyman H. Tucker) to assist the contest entrants. It summarized the subscription campaign's dual purpose as follows: "to acquaint many of our weekly readers with the spot news values of the Evening Star and also to win many entirely new readers for both papers—and at the same time, enable us to install the high speed newspaper press."[40]

The *Weekly Star*'s next issue formally announced the subscription campaign. Similar to the Star's previous contest held in late 1927, this one featured prizes to be "awarded on the basis of vote credits issued to contestants for soliciting and turning in subscriptions" for the two papers. It also printed a schedule that showed "the number of Vote

Credits awarded contestants for subscriptions secured" and a detailed set of rules explaining how the contest would be conducted. But in contrast to the first, this second contest featured more prizes, chances to win Special Cash Prizes while the contest was in progress, and a longer contest period. And instead of having the vote value for subscriptions decline as the contest progressed and awarding double votes for new subscribers, the 1930 contest employed a Bonus Vote Schedule that awarded extra vote credits to those who procured "subscription business" for either or both papers throughout the contest period. (Subscription business was defined as new subscriptions, renewal subscriptions, or collections on past due subscription accounts.) That Bonus Vote Schedule was structured so that as the contest went forward in time, the dollar amount of subscription business required to secure specified amounts of bonus votes steadily increased. The new contest also included a Special Bonus program that awarded extra votes to the top four contestants who turned in cash for subscription business on March 1, 8, 15, 22, and 29. The contest end-date, originally set for April 5, was later extended to April 12.[41]

The prizes to be awarded at the end of the contest, and their dollar values, were: first prize— Marquette, rim-Deluxe 4-door Sedan, Buick Built, $1,385; second prize—Chevrolet Coach, $732; third prize—Majestic Electric Radio, $167.50; fourth prize—choice of Westinghouse Electric Range, $147.50 or R.C.A. Radiola Battery Model 22 full cabinet size, $148; fifth prize—100 shares of Black Hills Petroleum Co. stock, valued by company at $250; and sixth prize—100 shares of Dillon Oil & Development Co. stock, valued by company at $50.[42]

After the contest had been officially open for a week, 51 potential contestants from 10 towns in southwestern South Dakota (and one in Wyoming) had either entered the contest themselves or had been suggested by their friends as possible entrants. Through the remainder of February, the *Weekly Star* continued to print articles and full-page advertisements that described the contest's particulars, touted its top prizes with photographs, and encouraged participants to work hard and become winners. By early March, the list of active contestants had been substantially and predictably reduced, and the Star Company began awarding special cash prizes to those who turned in the most total business, the most cash subscription business, the greatest number of new subscribers, and to those who met other stated requirements. Those prizes ranged from $25 to $5 and totaled $150. They were awarded on a weekly basis from March 1 through April 5.[43]

By April 1, there were nine contestants who were still active in the contest. It officially ended on Saturday, April 12, at 5:00 p.m. Three judges tabulated the results, which were announced later that night at the City Auditorium. The three top winners were Mrs. A. W. Fellows, Hot Springs, first prize plus $50 in special cash prizes; Miss Edna Christensen, Ardmore, second prize plus $40 in special cash prizes; and Mrs. Halle B. N. Lewis, Pringle, third prize plus $25 in special cash prizes and a $25 prize for turning in the most business from Custer County. The next three finishers were awarded the fourth, fifth, and sixth prizes, and $15, $5, and $5 in special cash prizes, respectively. The remaining three contestants received commission checks that totaled ten per cent on all the subscription money turned in and credited to their accounts. Two of these three also received a $5 special cash prize. The nine winners consisted of eight women and one man. The "only masculine representative" in this group was Reno J. Barnes from Pringle. He won the fifth prize and also received a $5 special cash prize during the race.[44]

Sometime during the subscription contest's first month, the Star Publishing Company purchased and had delivered the high-speed printing press referred to above. Between mid-March and mid-April, Star staff member Harry Brereton installed this Goss Comet Press in the half-story basement under the building's new addition. When the contest ended, the article that announced its results stated that "in spite of a local 'money tightness,' a satisfactory number of new subscriptions was added to both The Evening Star and the Weekly Star," and that since accounts on past-due subscriptions were collected during the contest, Star Publishing could now "present a very clean, paid-in-advance subscription list." One week later, the *Weekly Star* printed its first issue on the new press. Commenting on this event, the paper said that "naturally, there are some adjustments to make, but the speed, ease of operation and general eveness /sic/ of impression are an immense satisfaction."[45]

CITIZENS' MILITARY TRAINING CAMPS (often referred to by their initials CMTC) were authorized by the National Defense Act of 1920 "as an alternative to conscription." Through the CMTC, young men aged 17 to 31 received military and other training; and they were given the opportunity to become commissioned officers in the U.S. Army. But this program differed from Organized Reserve and National Guard training in one important respect: "young men attending the sessions were not obligated to be called for active duty." Starting in 1921, the CMTC were held each summer at roughly 50 Army bases scattered across the United States. The summer training session lasted for 30 days. According to a folder that described the program, its purpose was "to bring together young men... from all sections of the country on a common basis of equality and under the most favorable conditions of outdoor life; to stimulate and promote citizenship, patriotism and Americanism; and through expert physical direction, athletic coaching and military training, to benefit the young men individually."[46]

Francis endorsed the program and believed in its objectives. The *Weekly Star*'s March 12, 1929 issue included an article that announced the CMTC's dates and locations in the "Seven Corps Area" for the upcoming summer. That area included South Dakota, North Dakota, Minnesota, Iowa, Nebraska, Kansas, Missouri and Arkansas. The story noted, among other things, that those candidates who met the physical requirements will be sent to an assigned camp. Railroad fare and "all necessary expenses will be paid by the government," and "while at camp, food, uniforms, military and athletic equipment and medical and laundry service will be furnished without expense to the candidate." One month later, the paper included an editorial titled "Opportunity We Never Had." In it, Francis described the CMTC as a free "whole month's vacation." He conceded that the boys who enroll "will not loaf for they will be at camp." But he suggested "purposeful vacationing is better than idle wastreling," and the "discipline at these citizens training camps is more helpful than irksome." To support these points, the author stated that "one of the boys from the Star shop" recently spent August at camp, "came back fatter, browner, straighter, and far healthier," and "had learned a lot in the way of physical development, personal hygiene, first aid, orderliness of habits and self control." The editorial ended by inviting anyone interested in the program to come in to the Star office and ask for a free CMTC booklet.[47]

In the spring of 1930, promotional efforts were launched to recruit candidates for the CMTC to be held that summer. Lieutenant Colonel John True, director of training in South Dakota, and Charles McDonald, civilian aide for the state, oversaw that effort. The state was assigned an overall enrollment quota for the 1930 summer camps, and that number was divided among each county based on its population. Mr. McDonald appointed a chairman in each county "to assist in securing the county's quota." In early April, Colonel True announced that "'Lieutenant Francis Case is being named County Chairman for Fall River County and full particulars, application blanks and descriptive pamphlets may be obtained from him."[48]

Fall River County's quota was only four for the 1930 CMTC program. But other counties must not have met their quotas, because "seven Fall River county boys had a month's free vacation at one of the C. M. T. C. camps" that summer. Francis also served as CMTC

County Chairman in 1931. The county quota of four was exceeded again, and six boys went to camp at Fort Snelling that year. Commenting on South Dakota's overall participation in 1931, Colonel True expressed the opinion that the "progress made during the past year by the CMTC has been such that it can fairly be described as going forward by leaps and bounds[.]"[49]

ON JULY 4, 1930, MOUNT RUSHMORE held its third official dedication ceremony. The purpose of that gathering was to unveil George Washington's head—the "first complete piece" of the "world's largest memorial project." The head was 60 feet in height and "visible for miles around in the rugged Black Hills." A real-life demonstration of its enormity occurred during its construction, when "three workmen were missed during the noon hour, causing much anxiety as to their fate. After much frantic searching, they were finally found sitting in Washington's ear, calmly eating their lunch."[50]

On dedication day, weather conditions at the memorial "were perfect" with "a clear blue sky." An estimated 2,500 people assembled on Mount Robinson near Borglum's studio to view the ceremony. It began at noon when bands from Fort Meade and the Rapid City Legion Post provided music. A 21-gun salute, singing "America," and invocation by the American Legion chaplain followed. Next, Governor William Bulow welcomed the audience but left shortly thereafter to participate "in the Governor's day activities at the Black Hills roundup." Dr. C. C. O'Harra, president of the South Dakota School of Mines and eminent geologist, then traced the history of the Black Hills, noted that "this region is one of the oldest on the American continent," and predicted that the completed monument would endure for at least 100,000, and possibly 500,000 years. Dr. Doane Robinson—former state historian, current president of the Mount Rushmore society, and known as the "father of the memorial project," spoke next. He described the project's history from its inception in early 1924 up to the present time.

With respect to the mountain's now-completed portion, he said that "Rushmore is the latest, greatest, the crowning glory which America has or can bestow upon George Washington. Further the nation cannot go in expression of veneration."[51]

Gutzon Borglum followed Robinson on the speaker's podium. He made general remarks about the memorial's history and purpose, and he thanked several individuals by name who had assisted the project at the local, state, and national levels. Then the ceremony's actual unveiling took place. Up to this point, Washington's head had been draped with an American flag that measured 40 by 72 feet. Cables from winches on the mountaintop were attached to the flag's top. The unveiling began when Doane Robinson signaled his three-year-old grandson—Billy Doane Robinson—to press a button on the speaker's stand. That action sent a signal to the men in the winch-house on the mountain top, who slowly began reeling in the cables. As they did so, "the great flag began to slide upward and expose the features of Washington." While this occurred, "airplanes, volleys by a firing squad and bombs added to the celebration." After the head was fully exposed, the bishop from the Catholic diocese at Lead gave a benediction. The ceremony then ended with the audience singing "The Star-Spangled Banner."[52]

The ceremony received an "immense amount of publicity" for the Rushmore project. It was filmed by cameramen from "Fox, Pathe, Paramount, Universal Studios, and Kinogram"; and many newspapers, including *The New York Times*, gave it favorable coverage.[53]

FROM MID-SUMMER THROUGH THE late fall of 1930, the Cases experienced both disruptions caused by illnesses and joy when a new family member arrived. In early July, John Graves came to the Black Hills to visit and stay at the Case cabin in Custer State Park. Shortly after arriving, he became sick and received treatment at a local hospital. After being released, he went to the cabin and was soon joined by four of his five daughters. On July 25, Francis wrote that "Mr. Graves felt 200% better this morning than he was when he came out. I hope it lasts and he goes home in that much better strength." But about a month after Graves returned to his home, *The Rapid City Daily Journal* reported that "Mr. and Mrs. Francis Case were called to Mitchell Saturday by the serious illness of Mrs. Case's father J. H. Graves."[54]

Charles Leland Sunderman was born in the evening on October 28 at the Sunderman farm. A nurse and Mary Case assisted in the birth. Esther was described "as rugged and happy as could be all the way through," and Raymond was reported to be "walking on air." Herbert gave these descriptions in two letters written on the night his newest grandson was born. One—to his other four children—began by proclaiming, "Well the great event has just happened and we are Grandparents again." The other, written to Francis and Myrle, ended on a cheerful note: "Hurrah for Esther And Raymond and Charles Leland."[55]

Less than a month later, Joyce's family was quarantined for diphtheria. Cliff was out of town at the time, and he decided to stay with his sister Edith when he returned to avoid the quarantine. The doctor let "Joyce come down to the office in the evenings, so they are getting along in pretty good shape." The three Wilson children "all had shots," and although Dorothy "gave a positive diphtheria test," she "showed no signs of really being sick." The quarantine was lifted by early December, and Francis was able to spend Christmas Day with the Wilson family. Myrle was back in Mitchell caring for her father that day, and she did not return to Hot Springs until early January.[56]

Myrle went back to Mitchell again on January 18. Her sister Irma had been serving as John's caregiver, but she had to go to the hospital for an operation. She came home two weeks later, leading Myrle to write to Francis: "So now I have two patients. Two are better than one." In that same letter, she commented: "By now probably the paper is sold. If it is I hope it is what you really wanted to do."[57]

THE OPENING PARAGRAPH OF a story in the April 15 *Evening Star* stated:

> With this number of the Evening Star, control and management of the Star Publishing Company passes to Harry L. Hayden, formerly of Buchanan, Mich., who has purchased the interests of Leland D. Case, assistant editor of the Rotarian, Chicago, and Francis H. Case, editor of the Star, majority owners for the past five and a half years.

Six days later, Francis included an article titled "A Personal Word" in the *Weekly Star*. There he admitted that a "decision such as we have made with respect to the Star is not reached without some misgivings as to its wisdom and some regrets as to its meaning. But newspapers are greater than individuals. We will miss the Star more than it will miss us." He also thanked those who worked with him, praised Mr. Hayden's leadership abilities and newspaper experience, and listed the important topics the Star papers had covered since Leland and he became their owners. As to future plans, he indicated Myrle and he would continue to live in Hot Springs "at least for a considerable time to come," that he hoped "that now I can satisfy an old ambition and study law," and that Leland "expects to continue his work at the Rotarian" but would "occasionally" be in town. The personal-word article ended by expressing appreciation for "our successors on the Star" and looking forward to "continued association" with them "in the pursuit of our common goals for welfare and happiness in this community."[58]

Editorials from other South Dakota newspapers noted the Star's change of ownership and complimented the Case brothers on their work there. For instance, *The Daily Argus-Leader* said in part: "South Dakotans will regret the retirement of Francis Case and Leland D.

Case from the ownership of the Hot Springs Star. They have been vigorous workers for the benefit of their community and the State as a whole and have done much that has been worth while." And two newspapers—the *Deadwood Pioneer Times* and *Evening Huronite*—turned out to be prescient regarding Francis's future. The former wrote: "It is to be hoped that Mr. Case will become affiliated with another of the state's newspapers, for he has a loyal reader following in South Dakota." The latter opined: "Mr. Case is a comparatively young man of unusual ability. He writes with real force and is an excellent public speaker. He has had some political ambitions in times past and if he elects to follow a public career he is likely to go far."[59]

AFTER HE SOLD THE STAR, Francis remained active throughout the spring and summer of 1931. On the same day the Star-Publishing sale was announced, he joined about 30 people in a "testimonial dinner for Senator Peter Norbeck." It was held at the Alex Johnson Hotel in Rapid City. The program featured brief talks by Norbeck, Paul E. Bellamy and others. Norbeck thanked the chamber of commerce for the dinner, and he "touched briefly" on local highway matters and on "the establishment of the Bad Lands National Park." Two days later, the state chamber of commerce's president announced that Francis had been appointed to a 16-member committee "to promote aviation in South Dakota." The state chamber held its district meeting in Lead that afternoon, which Francis and a Hot Springs colleague attended.[60]

On Sunday, April 26, the Fairburn lodge of the Independent Order of Odd Fellows (a nonpolitical, nonsectarian fraternal organization), joined together with the Fairburn Rebekah lodge (the IOOF's female auxiliary) to "observe the anniversary of Odd Fellowship." After a "large crowd" was served dinner, Francis "delivered the address of the day at the afternoon meeting." His talk stressed the need to develop "the spirit of friendship, in local communities as well as in state and nations." The next evening, he, along with "over 200 members of American Legion posts," met at a farewell dinner for Roy Madera at the Evans Hotel in Hot Springs. Madera had recently resigned from his job at the Battle Mountain Sanitarium and decided to enter private business in California. Francis was one of many speakers on the after-dinner program. He "told of the war record of Madera, who worked up to sergeant-major of marines and secretary to General Smedley D. Butler."[61]

During the latter part of May, Myrle and Francis were finally able to take a long-postponed trip to Chicago. On the way there, Francis gave two high-school commencement speeches. The first was presented on May 21 in Kimball—a small town situated 47 miles west of Mitchell. The next day—22 miles north of Kimball—Francis "delivered an impressive commencement address before the graduating class of the Gann Valley High School." His message to the six graduates centered on the theme that "friendship, courage and loyalty ... [are] the three main gifts of education."[62]

The Cases then travelled on to Chicago, and got there sometime in the last week of the month. They stayed in the city, and Carol came downtown to help Myrle "see some things and find her way about in rather a strange place." Carol and Francis also enjoyed a lunch together, and Carol's husband Ralph took Francis on a tour of the former's law offices. On the return trip to Hot Springs, Myrle and Francis stopped in Mitchell, picked up Myrle's nephew Jack Breckenridge, and brought him home with them. Soon after arriving, the three went to the Case cabin, where they stayed "a couple of days doing some fishing and cleaning up."[63]

Governor Warren Green and his wife visited the Black Hills on June 20. They "spent Saturday night and part of Sunday at Blue Bell Lodge, resting and fishing." On that same weekend, Myrle, Francis, and nephew Jack were again staying at the Case cabin, which was near the lodge. It was reported that the "Governor, in company with Francis Case caught a nice string of trout, the largest one in his creel being

15 inches long." On Sunday afternoon, the Greens left for Pierre, and Myrle, Francis and Jack went to Mitchell. From there, Francis travelled on to Chicago to work on a project he had undertaken for the Mount Rushmore National Memorial Commission.[64]

IN THE SUMMER OF 1928, Leland was in Chicago, having recently returned from Europe. One night, a woman who was a faculty member at Northwestern University invited him to a dinner party. Seated on the opposite side of the table was a "small, vivacious young lady with a melodious voice" named Josephine Altman. She taught music appreciation at a high school in Evanston. Leland walked her home after the party, and thus began a life-long relationship between them.[65]

Leland came to Hot Springs in the spring of 1929 to help Francis "transform the weekly Hot Springs Star into a tabloid daily," and to help in getting "more mileage out of the oil-strike incident" in Red Canyon. He convinced Josephine to visit Hot Springs and greeted her when she "stepped off the train at Buffalo Gap." Miss Altman lived in town (with Joyce's family) for two weeks. The highlight of her stay occurred when she participated in a Sioux Indian dance on the Evans Hotel porch. During that event, an ancient chief "was charmed by her presence," "adopted her as his daughter," and "gave her the name 'Zitkaziwin,' or 'Yellow Singing Bird'."[66]

In July 1930, Leland was hired as a staff member at *The Rotarian* (the Rotary International's magazine) in Chicago. By October, he had become an assistant editor. Meanwhile, his relationship with Josephine (also known as Joan—pronounced "JoAnn") continued to blossom. On July 2, 1931, he wrote to his parents that the two had decided to marry. The elder Cases' reaction: "We have heard such very wonderful reports about Joan . . . and welcome her to the family with open hearts."[67]

The wedding was held on July 28 at Josephine's sister's home in Knoxville, Tennessee. The bride "wore her sister's wedding gown" and was given away by her widowed mother. Homer Shepherd (Josephine's sister's husband) was Leland's best man. The event was described as "a quiet wedding, with only family and intimate friends as witnesses." No Case family members were present. The groom's father wrote to Leland that "with your marriage it means all of our Birdlings have gone to homes of their own." For their honeymoon, the newlyweds "drove through New England' and "discovered in each other a love of things such as old stained glass." According to their wedding announcement, "Mr. and Mrs. Case will be at home in Evanston, Ill. after September 1."[68]

IN EARLY MAY, 1931, the Mount Rushmore National Memorial Commission hired Francis to edit a booklet that would contain, among other things, "a history of the project," a "recital of the accomplishments up to date," and articles by those who had knowledge of Mount Rushmore or involvement in the memorial work. This booklet, known as the "Jefferson Number," was the second publication of its kind. (The first, known as the "Washington Number," was published in 1930.) In addition to being its editor, Francis was also retained to secure advertising for the 1931 booklet.[69]

Francis worked on the project off and on for the next three months. During that time, he made at least three trips that generated travel expenses. Those trips most likely involved meeting with some of the booklet's potential advertisers and conferring with its printer in Chicago. On July 27, John Boland, chairman of the National Memorial Commission's Executive Committee, received 200 advance copies. Plans were made to ultimately print more than 25,000 copies. Of that number, about 15,000 would be distributed for sale at "the Mount Rushmore studio and in news agencies throughout the United States." The remaining copies would be distributed, free of charge, to "United

States senators, representatives, ambassadors, all foreign ambassadors in Washington, D. C., foreign correspondents, high officials of the army and navy and all newspapers in South Dakota and to others."[70]

The final product was described as "a handsome bit of printing art" that contained "a number of striking pictures and worthwhile articles." The 39-page booklet, done "in magazine form" and printed in sepia tones, included articles by Doane Robinson, Cleophas C. O'Harra, Lorine Jones Spoonts (national Mt. Rushmore commissioner), Gutzon Borglum, Congressman William Williamson, and Loyson G. Troth (South Dakota State Secretary of Agriculture). Interspersed among the articles were several "excellently reproduced photographs" that showed men working on the mountain and models for the Jefferson and Lincoln heads. Advertisements for Texaco Gasoline-Motor Oil, Northwest Bancorporation, Dupont Dynamite, Chicago & Northwestern Railway, Corpus Christi, Texas, and the Associated Commercial Clubs of the Black Hills were also included. After it described the Jefferson Number, the *Weekly Star* commented that the "booklet is an artistic production and should be a source of pride to Francis Case[.]"[71]

John Boland paid Francis his final project "expenses" bill in early August. As for his compensation, that was a matter to "be taken up with Mr. Borglum." It was ultimately decided to pay Francis a $300 salary for his work on the Jefferson Number. A check for that amount was entered in Boland's disbursement records on September 4—three days after Francis bought another newspaper.[72]

CHAPTER 11

BACK TO THE NEWSPAPER BUSINESS, AND PURSUIT OF OTHER INTERESTS

A newspaper, you know, is not a private enterprise. It is the product of its community—a picture of its life, of its ups and downs, of the goings and comings of people, of their joys and sorrows, their deaths and births, their trials and their triumphs. The Chronicle wants to be a good community paper.

—Francis Case

Founded in 1875, Custer is the oldest town in the Black Hills. It was named after General George Armstrong Custer, a civil war hero in the Union Army who, in 1874, led an expedition to the Hills. (The town name was chosen at a gold miners' meeting that included both Union and Confederate civil war veterans. The former Confederates wanted to name it Stonewall to honor their civil war hero—Stonewall Jackson. But they were outvoted by the Union veterans.) During General Custer's expedition, gold was discovered in French Creek near the location where the town was staked out a year later. Custer is located 27 miles north of Hot Springs. Its elevation is 5,301 feet above sea level, and its 1930 population was 1,203.[1]

On September 1, 1931, Francis bought the *Custer Weekly Chronicle* from C. W. Trent, its long-time owner and editor. Trent had experienced "ill-health the past year" and decided it was time "to place the paper in younger hands." When he sold the Star Publishing Company in April, Francis had not expected to go "into the newspaper business again, at least not for a couple of years." But as he explained to the *Chronicle*'s readers, "fall came on, the tang of Indian Summer in the Black Hills air, we heard that Charley Trent's health was such that he was going to sell the Chronicle—and here we are." The sale was announced on September 11, Francis "took active charge" of the paper on the 14th, and the first *Chronicle* produced under the new owner was issued on the 17th. The notation "Official Paper of Custer County, Custer City and Custer School District" appeared directly below its title on the first page.[2]

Two days later, Francis introduced Custer to the *Black Hills News*. It described itself as a "legal weekly newspaper consolidating the BLACK HILLS Oil & Mining Review, Est. 1929; Tourist News, Est. 1926; Hot Springs NEWS, Est. 1928; and the Edgemont Express, Est. 1889[.]" As previously noted, the *Black Hills News* was created when Francis sold his rights to the *Black Hills Oil and Mining Review* and *Tourist News* to W. E. Latham in May 1929. By the time he took over the *Chronicle*, Francis had also acquired publishing rights to the *Black Hills News*, so Custer would have two weekly papers.[3]

The September 19 issue of the *News* consisted of three pages with four columns per page. It measured 13 inches by 7 ½ inches. Subscriptions cost $1.00 per year. (In contrast, the September 17 *Chronicle* measured 21 ½ inches by 16 inches, had seven columns per page, and contained four pages. Its subscription price was $2.00 per year.) Almost all the main stories in the September 19 *News* were also in the September 17 *Chronicle*, and the latter paper included several additional articles, advertisements, obituaries, and local news that were not in the *News*. Both papers changed their formats for the next week's issues. The *Chronicle* became a six-page paper with six columns per page, and the *News* expanded to four pages, had four columns per page, and gained about two inches in length and width. These formats would remain the same until late 1931, although the *Chronicle* contained eight pages from early November until mid-December.⁴

Fellow South Dakota editors welcomed Francis's return to the newspaper fold. The *Rapid City Daily Journal* noted that "Francis Case is entering the newspaper game in the Black Hills again, buying the Custer Chronicle... He'll be welcomed back." The *Daily Argus-Leader* opined that the "work done by Mr. Case at Hot Springs indicates that he will maintain the excellent reputation of the Chronicle. He is young, energetic and enthusiastic. He has done much to keep the Black Hills in the limelight and will serve Custer and its community well." And the *Iroquois Chief* (weekly newspaper published in Iroquois, South Dakota) added that Francis "purchased the Custer Chronicle, a good paper in a good town, and as Case is a good newspaper man the combination should work out fine."⁵

THE SOUTH DAKOTA BOARD OF REGENTS (Board) "has constitutional responsibility for governing the unified system of public higher education" in the state. It "sets policy direction for the system, oversees management of its resources (personnel, facilities, and financial), and establishes and monitors its educational program." The Board "executes its authority" by adopting policies, approving programs, selecting and evaluating "institutional executives," setting "annual budgets, tuition and fees," and making budget requests to the state legislature. In 1931, the Board had five members and oversaw the administration of seven state-supported schools: Spearfish State Normal at Spearfish, South Dakota State School of Mines at Rapid City, South Dakota State University at Vermillion, Southern Normal at Springfield, Northern Normal and Industrial School at Aberdeen, South Dakota State College at Brookings, and Eastern Normal at Madison.⁶

Eleven days after Francis took charge at the *Chronicle*, Governor Green appointed him to the Board. He was chosen to fill a vacancy created when Mrs. E. P. Wanzer, a regent from Armour, died earlier that summer. Her six-year appointment was scheduled to expire on January 1, 1937. Upon accepting this position, Francis resigned his membership on the Dakota Wesleyan Board of Trustees, a position he had held since late 1924. Green's choice for the Board seat received favorable reactions in the South Dakota press. For instance, the *Argus-Leader* wrote that Francis "should be an excellent member of the South Dakota board of Regents of Education to which he has just been appointed by Governor Green. Case has been active in South Dakota for several years, is familiar with the educational institutions and their work and should render excellent service." One of the state capital's newspapers—the *Pierre Dakotan*—remarked that "Governor Green certainly has a warm spot in his heart for newspaper men. His latest appointment, that of Francis Case, to a membership of the board of regents elevates another newspaper man, and the appointment is a good one, too." And the *Evening Huronite* posited that Francis would bring "real ability, courage and constructiveness" to the Board.[7]

In mid-October, Board Chairman Alvin Waggoner announced the committees in charge of the seven state schools. Two regents formed each committee, and each was assigned to two or more designated schools. Waggoner, whose home town of Philip was located west of the Missouri River, assigned himself and Francis to Spearfish State Normal and the State School of Mines. During the latter half of November, Francis visited the two schools under his charge. He first went to Spearfish (where he attended summer school in 1917) and presumably conferred with its president Ethelburt Woodburn and others about the issues facing their institution. Then he met with Dr. C. C. O'Harra—president of the School of Mines—in Rapid City to discuss that school's interests and concerns.[8]

The Board met in Sioux Falls on February 19 and 20, 1932, to consider "the budget for the fiscal year beginning July 1" as well as "faculty lists and other matters affecting the same period." As a result of those meetings, faculties at the State School of Mines and Southern Normal were approved, the faculty at Spearfish Normal was given substantial, although "not conclusive" approval, and the faculty at Eastern Normal was considered and apparently approved. On March 31, the Board convened again at Huron "to elect faculties for the next year at the University of South Dakota, State college and Northern normal." In April, Francis explained in further detail the Board's decisions regarding school faculties and attempts to reduce the overall public-institution budget. He noted, among other things, that as a result of savings by salary reductions, elimination of some positions, and "other budget changes," between "$100,000 and $125,000 should revert to the state's general fund at the close of the 1932-33 fiscal year[.]"[9]

On November 18, the Board gathered in Rapid City for a regular two-day session. At some point prior to that meeting, a partial change in its officers occurred. W. S. Dolan (from Milbank) became president. He replaced Alvin Waggoner, who continued his service as Board member. Francis was chosen as vice-president. Guy Harvey—regent from Yankton—kept his role as Board secretary. At that fall meeting, the "most important item was the consideration and discussion of amounts of appropriations to be requested from the state legislature for administration of state schools."[10]

The 1931 legislature instructed the Board to investigate whether the state should adopt the so-called "Greater University of South Dakota" plan, whereby the seven higher-education schools would be consolidated under "general control of a chancellor." On January 5, 1933, the Board issued a written report that opposed this plan, concluding that it was "a relatively untried innovation which... would not assure improvements desired." Meanwhile, Democratic Governor Tom Berry, who defeated Warren Green in the 1932 gubernatorial election, had recommended closing two normal schools and eliminating "duplicated courses." Although the governor did not specify the two normal schools he would close, "most legislatures believe[d] he referred to Southern Normal at Springfield and Eastern Normal at Madison."[11]

Following up on its promise to present "its own economy plan" to the governor, the Board convened in Pierre on January 12. When their meeting concluded that night, the regents filed a report with the governor that included seven recommendations "for educational economy." Those recommendations included suspending one or possibly two unnamed normal schools; discontinuing State University's engineering department; discontinuing State College's four-year commerce course and "'limiting of such work to vocational training'"; discontinuing State University's home economics department; discontinuing State College's four-year-degree-course in music; withdrawing authority for summer school sessions at State College and School of Mines; and paying careful attention to "'the specific fields of each school to avoid overlapping and unnecessary duplication of courses.'" All five regents signed the report.[12]

Five days after the Board submitted its above-cited recommendations for economy and efficiency, Governor Berry appointed, and the senate confirmed, two Board members. Guy Harvey was reappointed for another six-year term. Will Wells, a Democrat and newspaperman from Webster, was "named to replace Francis Case of Custer for a term ending Jan.1, 1937." The Associated Press story from Pierre that reported this decision noted that "Case was serving under an interim appointment," and since that appointment "was never confirmed by the senate, it is contended he can be replaced before expiration of his term."[13]

IN THE SUMMER OF 1931, the Black Hills Mining and Industrial Association was formed at Keystone. Its stated purpose was "to promote mining and allied industries in the Black Hills." Francis became a member. During the same week he took over the *Chronicle*, he was appointed to the Association's Publicity Committee, along with Bert Bell from Deadwood and Theodore Werner from Rapid City. (Werner was the newspaperman who had "lampooned," "ignored," and called Francis names when the two had worked for different Rapid City daily papers in 1924. Their paths would cross again during the next few years.)[14]

The Association held an evening meeting at Newcastle, Wyoming, on October 2. About 80 members attended. They came from Lead, Deadwood, Keystone, Rapid City, Custer, and Hill City, as well as Newcastle and Osage, Wyoming. After dinner was completed, several speakers, including all three members of the Publicity Committee, addressed "topics concerning the development of natural resources of the Black Hills and nearby country." The group also passed three resolutions. They added "Wyoming" to the Black Hills scenic folder's name; agreed to include at least a full page in the folder that advertised "mineral resources of the region"; and demanded that a tariff be placed on crude oil and its by-products.[15]

During his first three-and-a-half months at the *Chronicle*, Francis took steps to improve its quality and increase its circulation. Beginning with the October 1 issue, the paper appeared in "a new type face, installed at considerable expense, to give *Chronicle* readers what printing experts and vision specialists say is the latest thing in readable types... developed and designed to give greater readability with less eye strain." In November, the paper offered a free ticket to any show at "Custer's famous Garlock Theatre" to those who paid $2.00 for a new or renewed one-year subscription. Later that month, the offer was expanded. Now, for $2.25, readers could get a one-year *Chronicle* subscription, a free Garlock Theatre ticket, and a year-long subscription to *The Pathfinder* (a "reliable family weekly" that contained "news from all over the world, the inside of Washington affairs—the truth about politics and business, science, discovery, personalities, pictures, stories—and no end of fun.").¹⁶

As the year ended, Francis decided to make changes to both of his newspapers. Beginning with its December 26 issue, the *Black Hills News* was renamed the *Black Hills Weekly Chronicle*. Its format was also changed. The paper now consisted of two pages—printed on both sides of a single sheet. It was full-size, measuring 21 ½ inches by 16 inches, and it had seven columns on each page. Starting with the last issue printed on December 31, 1931, the *Custer Weekly Chronicle* became the *Custer County Chronicle*. It continued to have six columns and six pages until March 1932, when a seventh column was added to its basic format.¹⁷

IN JANUARY 1932, FRANCIS AND MYRLE bought a home "in the west part of town." He described it as "a gray stucco house with green shutters, set on a hill-side smack against a wooded (pine) background." When summer arrived, another feature became apparent: "a yard and garden too big for anyone who doesn't have more time for them than I." To illustrate this point, Francis wrote to Carol in early July that "Today I spent a couple of hours cutting grass around the hedge and spruce trees, and could have put in the entire day at that and the garden."¹⁸

AN EDITORIAL IN THE *Custer Chronicle*'s March 24 issue began by declaring "AN INSULT to the Black Hills was delivered a few days ago that should not pass unheeded. It was the delivery of 25,000 posts from Michigan for building guard rails on a highway near Keystone." The piece went on to point out that "a million trees, suitable for posts" were on the "mountain sides by the highway," and men who had been "idle for months" were "in a dozen saw-mill camps within two hours' ride." Although speculating that the state Highway Commission may not be able to limit contractors to using South Dakota products, or perhaps Black Hills lumbermen do not produce "properly treated posts," the editorial nevertheless concluded that "it is ridiculous to say that posts can be cut in Michigan and hauled in a round-about way into Keystone at any economy or in good policy when men are idle and post fields are quiet in the mountains about Keystone." And it ended with this appraisal of the situation: "There is something rotten in this post pile! Maybe it's an opportunity for a new industry."[19]

Two weeks after the "post pile" editorial appeared, Governor Warren Green, while visiting Custer, raised the subject in a meeting with Black Hills woodsmen. He asked about the report that a contractor shipped in posts from Michigan and wondered aloud why local pine posts could not be used instead. It was explained to him that the local posts would "need to be impregnated with creosote to withstand action of water and prevent rotting"; and there was "no dipping or treating plant" in the Black Hills to apply the creosote to the posts. At the end of the meeting, Governor Green commented, "'I don't know how the other members of the Highway Commission will feel about it, but I can't see why we can't work out a solution of that some way. We use a lot of posts in this state.'"[20]

During the next week, the state Highway Commission and Governor Green held a hearing to discuss the possible use of Black Hills pine posts "in guard-rail, sign post and bridge construction on South Dakota highways." A delegation that included representatives from the Harney National Forest and the Black Hills National Forest—and two Custer men involved in the timber industry—also attended the hearing. During that proceeding, the commission announced that reports indicating 25,000 Michigan posts were used on the guardrails at Keystone were in error, as "the job was 25,000 yards long, and the posts required were about 2,000." The hearing also revealed that current specifications for federal-aid projects called for white cedar posts that came from Michigan. And it was reemphasized that there was no Black Hills treatment plant to apply the creosote to the guardrail posts. Despite these problems, the commissioners "were all in favor of using Black Hills timber whenever they could." They agreed to "seek a change in the federal aid specifications," to change their own specifications (which also required white cedar posts), and to immediately encourage using Black Hills pine wood for the sign posts that marked state highways. The *Custer Chronicle* lauded these developments. It editorialized that if the governor and the State Highway Commission "succeed in getting specifications on Federal Aid road guard rail[s] changed from Michigan white cedar to Black Hills white pine, they will have done a service for this section that we shall not soon forget." It added that "the Chronicle expects to see this achieved" because the governor "has told us 'That's the kind of thing I'll fight for.' And when the little farmer from Hamlin county gives his word, it stands."[21]

Over the summer, the Highway Commission apparently succeeded in getting the federal aid (and its own) specifications changed so Black Hills pine posts could be used in guardrail construction. In addition, a creosote-treatment plant was built about 12 miles south of Deadwood. These developments removed the impediments to using Black Hills timber on state road construction projects. And the *Custer Chronicle* again supported such use in an August 11 editorial, where it opined that "BLACK HILLS POSTS should be used on every guard rail project in the new emergency highway program. Black Hills planks should be used for the fencing. That is the logical way to get the maximum amount of local employment and South Dakota improvement that the law intends."[22]

In September, the State Highway Commission awarded several contracts for road construction projects in 28 South Dakota counties. Many of those projects included guardrail work, and Black Hills pine posts were used for that work.[23]

After the road construction season was over, an editorial appeared in the *Black Hills Weekly*—a newspaper published in Deadwood. It summarized how the use of local pine posts came to be and gave its assessment of that development. The editorial began by stating that "efforts a year ago by Francis Case, editor of the Custer Chronicle, and others, to have Black Hills pine specified for use in state road-building contracts, have been successful to the universal satisfaction of local people and the contractors[.]" It then noted that "Ponderosa pine posts have been used on all state projects during the year.... So far, fire killed posts, survivors of the fires of last summer and fall, have been used. They take the creosote treatment well and have proved satisfactory in every way." The article also observed that as soon as the use of outside timber was pointed out to "both the contractors and state officials," they decided to "give the posts a try." That trial was "successful," local labor was "used to cut down and prepare the posts," and they "have been cheaper than before, minus long distance transportation charges." The editorial ended with this succinct conclusion: "It looks like an occasion for congratulations all around."[24]

STARTING IN MID-MAY, 1932, Francis implemented further changes to the *Black Hills Weekly Chronicle*. He changed its name to *The Black Hills Chronicle* for the May 14 and 21 issues. No issues have been located for May 28 or June 4. Beginning with the June 11 issue, he shortened the name to simply *Black Hills Chronicle*. He also changed the format from a two-sided single sheet to a four-page, four-column, tabloid-sized (17 inches by 11 inches) publication. That format continued until October 1932.[25]

As was true when he lived in Rapid City and then in Hot Springs, Francis was asked to give the Memorial Day address at the Custer ceremonies held in 1932. The program began at 10:00 a.m. on May 30, when a parade formed at the court house and marched to the Community Hall building. Custer County's two remaining civil war veterans led the march. They were followed by veterans of the World War and Spanish War, American Legion auxiliary members and junior members, the high school band, and a firing squad. The exercises then began at Community Hall, "with every chair filled." After an invocation and songs sung by the Girls Glee Club and a soloist, Francis delivered his brief address. He said, among other things, that "Memorial Day is the sacred day among national holidays... The heroes we honor today, did not complain of the day in which they lived. They were proud to do their duty. This is our day to live. Our heritage is courage." Following his speech, the high school band played the national anthem and a benediction was given. The crowd then went out to the cemetery. There, services were held in which the firing squad participated, and "hundreds of people carried flowers and wreaths to the grave of some loved one."[26]

During June, Francis found time to do his "quota of fishing with varying luck." The trend was more positive toward the end of that month, when he reported catching "some nice Loch Loven." Although their exact size in not known, he "had to cut them to get them in the frying pan."[27]

ON SEPTEMBER 21, 1932, A GROUP known as the American Legion Lake Committee met at the *Chronicle*'s office and outlined plans for constructing a lake at the Legion's camp in Custer State Park. One day later, Dr. C. B. Lenker, the committee's chairman, announced that this work would "begin at once, as one of the relief projects to be undertaken in Custer county to relieve unemployment." The lake would be created by building a "20 feet long and 32 feet high" earthen dam and flooding a 7.4-acre area with water from Galena Creek—a small stream that ran "in front of the Legion park headquarters." Since the dam was to be constructed using mostly natural materials, labor would constitute "practically the entire cost" of the project. That cost would be funded by a loan that Governor Green and his relief committee obtained from the Reconstruction Finance Corporation (RFC)—a federal government agency created in 1932 that, among other things, provided "financing for state and local public works." And the

State Fish and Game commission agreed to pay for the "small amount of materials" needed to do the job "in return for fish pond nursery rights."[28]

Governor Green, accompanied by park superintendent Frank Fetzner, inspected the project in late November. At that point, the "heavy part of the work, putting the concrete core down to bedrock" was finished, and "straight dirt work" remained to be done. On February 18, 1933, "the last dirt was put on the dam site." The work still to be completed included cleaning the lake bed, installing rock facing on the dam's "water side," raising the road to create a lake shore drive, and moving the Legion's host house so it would be above the new lake's waterline. By the end of March, those remaining tasks were all done except for the last one. Water had begun to fill the lake. And the house was successfully moved during the first week in April, thereby completing the project. It was later reported that about $21,700 in RFC funds were spent to build the lake. Of that amount, "approximately $17,700 went to Custer county laborers and $4,000 to workers from Pennington county."[29]

A spirited campaign to name the lake began just as soon as it was finished. Francis began the process by suggesting "Lake Pershing" to honor the general who commanded the American Expeditionary Force in France during the World War. His suggestion drew a pointed response from Elizabeth Howe, editor of the *Black Hills Weekly*, who was "ardently indignant over the idea of 'Pershing Lake'" and wrote in an editorial that "somebody ought to think of a better name than that." She suggested names that were associated with Black Hills features or its historical characters, such as Granite Lake, Mica Lake, Lariat Lake (a cowboy term), or Calamity Lake (honoring Calamity Jane, who lived in Custer for a time). She also mentioned that Badger Clark "should be able to supply some suggestions."[30]

The day after Francis read Miss Howe's editorial, someone from the *Chronicle*—most likely its editor—ran into Clark on the street and told him he was "nominated to nominate a name for discussion." After he "floundered badly" and "admitted it was a problem," Clark "wound up by saying that perhaps 'Legion Lake' would be as good as anything." He said: "'It's a good, old name, you know... Goes back to Roman times. And it would tie in with the boys who built it and remain long after they are gone."[31]

In addition to Case, Howe and Clark, several newspapermen, *Chronicle* readers, and other interested parties offered potential names for the new lake and gave reasons for their suggestions. Francis published these suggestions in his papers. They included Leland's letter to the editor that disagreed with his brother's proposed Lake-Pershing idea and offered Wounded Knee as a possibility instead. That proposal prompted Francis to recall that Leland's old car had that name, and any reference to it "stirs his soul." In addition, Badger Clark—"perhaps spurred to a sense of duty" after his previous encounter with the Chronicle on this subject—suggested two more names: Lake Sans Arc—in honor of a Sioux Indian band, and Bear Track Lake—because the lake's basin was shaped like a bear's footprint.[32]

By mid-April, the Chronicle papers had received so many names that the *Custer Chronicle* listed them (27 in total) on a ballot printed in that paper's April 20 issue. One week later, that list had expanded to 41 names. Readers were invited to check the name of their choice (or suggest an additional one) and return the ballot to the Chronicle office. After the ballots were collected and tabulated, *The Black Hills Chronicle* published the results in its April 29 issue. One hundred sixteen ballots were counted. They included at least one vote for 36 out of the 41 names listed on the most recent ballot, plus at least one vote for five additional names that had been "suggested" on the ballot. The top four finishers—and number of votes received—were Crow Dog Lake-9; Legion Lake-8; Bear Track Lake-7; and McClelland Lake-5. The Case brothers' suggested names—Lake Pershing and Wounded Knee—each received two votes. Given the wide dispersal of votes among 41 different names, it was decided that further balloting "should be confined to those which have received at least four votes[.]"[33]

During the next week, "ballots came in from far and near" that overwhelmingly supported Legion Lake as the preferred name. In addition, at a district convention in Rapid City, the American Legion Auxiliary "endorsed the name 'Legion Lake' for the new lake in the State Park[.]" After the additional ballots were counted, the top four names—and votes received for each—were Legion Lake-58; Crow Dog Lake-10; McClelland Lake-8; and Bear Track Lake-7. *The Black Hills Chronicle* summarized the voting results and American Legion Auxiliary endorsement by stating: "'By popular demand' LEGION LAKE it seems destined to be."[34]

At some point, the Chronicle's name-the-new-lake voting results were provided to the American Legion's Camp Committee; and Ray Murphy, chairman of the Legion's national legislative committee, ultimately chose the name "Legion Lake." So, after all was said and done, Badger Clark's halting, original, default suggestion turned out to be the winning one.[35]

Legion Lake's "official dedication" took place on Sunday, June 11, in the afternoon. The ceremony began when the Army national guard's 109th Engineers' band from Rapid City played the opening number. Next came an invocation, which was followed by brief speeches from Senator Norbeck, former Governor Green, current state-government office holders, Legion officials, the president of the Legion's State Auxiliary, and an Army colonel. Then Dr. Lenker introduced Ray Murphy, who gave the main address. His talk "used the Lake as symbolic of the service efforts of the Legion in state and nation." Following Murphy's remarks, Battery "A"—a part of the national guard's 147th Field Artillery unit based in Aberdeen—fired four guns in a salute to former President Coolidge, who had died five months earlier. The salute "echoed and reechoed" and the "noise reverberated for minutes."

After it ended, taps were sounded, the 147th Field Artillery regimental band played the national anthem, a benediction was given, and the artillery band provided more music. As the program came to a close, an unidentified man swam across the lake. After the ceremony was over, the crowd gathered on the beach and watched as Fish and Game department officials stocked the lake with "25,000 baby brook trout." Senator Norbeck summed up the new lake's significance by describing it as "one more thing to put the Black Hills on the map and keep it there."[36]

FOR THE THIRD TIME IN his Black Hills newspaper career, Francis decided to hold a subscription drive to increase his papers' readership. The campaign was announced in the *Custer Chronicle's* September 29, 1932, issue and in the *Black Hills Chronicle* two days later. It was similar to the two he implemented for the Star papers in 1927 and again in 1930—although this one's basic structure most resembled the 1927 contest. As was done there, the campaign was divided into three "vote periods," and the vote value for subscriptions decreased as each period ended. But unlike the first contest, the Chronicle one did not award double votes for subscriptions. Instead, it awarded double votes to those contestants who sold both papers at "a combination rate of $3.00 a year" for one to five years. As with the previous two campaigns, prizes were awarded to the top vote getters, but this time the first-and-second-place finishers were given a choice of prizes to accept. The first grand prize winner could claim one of four prizes: a 1932 model Chevrolet Coach, 1932 Model Ford "V8" 2 Door Sedan, trip to Europe, or $500.00 in gold. The second grand prize winner could select either a trip to California or $200.00 in gold. The remaining list of awards were third prize: U.S. Radio valued at $107.50; fourth prize: R.C.A. Victor Radio valued at $59.50, and fifth prize: $25.00 in gold. And all non-prize winners who remained active in the contest to the end would be paid a ten percent cash commission on all subscriptions they collected.³⁷

The subscription drive continued for the next six weeks. During that period, the *Custer Chronicle* posted lists of candidates and their vote totals on a weekly basis, and the *Black Hills Chronicle* did so in at least two issues. The *Custer Chronicle* also ran articles and advertisements that encouraged people to enter the contest, explained its various procedures in detail, and reminded contestants of the prizes to be won. In mid-October, the *Black Hills Chronicle* went from tabloid size back to full size (the same size as the *Custer County Chronicle*) and changed its official name back to *The Black Hills Chronicle*. Now both papers had seven columns, the *Custer Chronicle* continued to contain six pages in most of its issues, and *The Black Hills Chronicle* had four pages.³⁸

The drive officially ended on Saturday, November 19, at 9:00 p.m. Three judges then counted the final votes, and the results were announced at the Chronicle office about an hour later. Mrs. Roy Brazell (from Pringle) won the first grand prize, Miss Frances Richardson (from Custer) won second prize, and Mrs. Mabel Carlson (also from Custer) took the third prize. It was not announced which prizes the first-and-second-place finishers chose. Of the eight candidates who competed in the contest until it closed, seven were women. The *Custer Chronicle* thanked all those who participated in the successful campaign. It noted that before the drive started, the two papers had "seen a 30 per cent increase in subscribers" over the past year, and now the Chronicle subscription list exceeded that "of 15 months ago by more than 50 per cent."³⁹

HERBERT CASE DECIDED TO ATTEND "Minister's Week" at the Chicago Theological Seminary to "brighten up myself and give better service to the Charge where I preach." He had retired as a Methodist minister several years ago. But since 1926, he had served as pastor for the Congregational Church at Pemberton, a small town located 15 miles southeast of Mankato. The "Minister's Week" Conference was held in Chicago from January 25 through 29, 1932. While attending it, Herbert spent some evenings with Leland and Joan in Evanston and others with Carol and Ralph in Chicago's Rogers Park area. After the conference concluded, he remained at Carol and Ralph's apartment for a few days and suspected that the couple were having "family troubles"—evidenced by Carol's "trembly voice" and the fact that Ralph came home "at late hours." Herbert's suspicions were confirmed when he and Carol went downtown to watch Ralph try a case. Carol "began to tremble" and pointed out a woman in the courtroom that Carol identified as "Ralph's woman." Carol later confronted Ralph about this incident. After their second encounter on the subject, Ralph did not come home that night.[40]

Throughout the spring and early summer, it became obvious that Carol's marriage to Ralph would come to an end. Limited correspondence during that period suggests that apart from Leland, Carol's siblings were not aware of the situation until August. In June, Leland saw Carol just before he left on an extended trip to western Canada, the west coast of the United States, and "Santa Fe Country." He wrote to his parents that the "most encouraging sign is that her mind is coming around to accept reality as reality without the loss of her own self respect. In fact, unless things crack somewhere, she'll before long be content to let him go his way, and she will her's. That is a lot—for her." In an August 12 letter, Herbert encouraged Carol to "let this Divorce proceeding be settled up at once and have it over with without seeing Ralph." And he praised her decision to come to Mankato: "Some how I believe a larger life will open to you as you come back to our home again . . . Dad and Mother Stand ready to help with Hearts full of Love."[41]

Carol did come to Mankato and stayed with her folks until early November. She then returned to Chicago to attend the Vogue School of Design and Institute of Art. Her divorce was apparently finalized by that time. Herbert wrote to Leland that "we believe time will heal her heart some of its soreness and that after a while she will see this was for the best." In early December, Herbert—on "behalf of Mrs. Case and myself"—thanked Carol's attorney "for befriending our daughter Carol when she was having her serious troubles, allowing her to stop in your home and then for your management of . . . her case in securing her divorce."[42]

THREE FAMILY DEATHS OCCURRED IN 1933. Myrle's sister—Mrs. Marie Smith from South Haven, Michigan—passed away in early January at age 42. Myrle went to Mitchell for the burial and remained there to take care of her ailing father. A short time later, Samuel Grannis—Francis's grandfather—died in a hospital in St. Cloud. He was 92 years old. His casket laid in state at a St. Cloud funeral home on Saturday, January 21, where a brief service was held. That night the American Legion formed "an honorary escort" that accompanied the body to the train station for the trip to Mankato, where the funeral and burial services were held the next day. It was a military funeral that included a flag-draped casket, a color guard, a gun salute from an assembled firing squad, and a bugler who sounded "Taps." A few weeks later, Herbert wrote a letter to the Mankato American Legion Commander "on behalf of the five Grannis daughters 'and the grand children and the great grandchildren.'" It stated in part: "The honors of a military funeral that you gave him . . . was in keeping with his wishes. We as a family are very grateful to all the members of the American Legion and the Veterans of Foreign Wars which made this honor possible. So from our hearts, we thank you."[43]

In February, Myrle reported that her father "has been subject to severe vomiting spells the past week," which was "one phase of the pernicious anemia from which he has been suffering[.]" His condition did not improve, and he died at home on May 22. John Graves was

82 years old when he passed on, and his anemia confined him "to his room most of the time for the past three years." Myrle took care of him during the last four months of his life. After his funeral was held in Mitchell, she returned home to Custer at the end of May.[44]

IN ITS MARCH 23, 1933 ISSUE, the *Custer Chronicle* listed a five-point program for Custer County:

1. Ten thousand summer homes in Custer State Park.
2. Better markets for the produce of east Custer county farms.
3. Establishment of modern mills in small units on 20 of the worthy gold prospects in the Harney Peak area.
4. Gravel on every main highway and county road.
5. Development of markets for timber products with cabin builders, mines, railroads and grain shippers.

Francis and his family had a personal connection to points one and three. As previously noted, he explained his reasons for supporting the first-listed point when he spoke to the Greater South Dakota Conference at Rapid City in late January, 1929, (although there he had argued for 5,000 private homes in the park—now he advocated 10,000). And he had built his own cabin in Custer State Park during the summer of 1927. Beginning in 1933, Carol (who had taken back her maiden name after her divorce), Francis, and eventually Herbert all took an active part in attempting to develop "worthy gold prospects" as mentioned in the third point, although their gold exploration did not occur near Harney Peak.[45]

AFTER GOLD WAS DISCOVERED DURING the General Custer expedition, it became apparent that the Black Hills contained an abundance of this precious mineral. In 1876, Moses Manuel, a mining prospector, located a claim at the boom town named Lead. A year later, Manuel and his partners sold the claim to George Hearst, a "prominent California mining capitalist." In November 1877, Hearst incorporated the Homestake Mining Company, and mining operations began there the next year. From 1878 to 1933, the Homestake Mine produced 11,400,000 ounces of gold that was valued at approximately $300,000,000. Homestake ultimately "became the largest gold mine in the western hemisphere."[46]

In the spring and summer of 1931, local newspapers emphasized a resurgence in Hills gold-mining activity by single prospectors and small mining companies. A few samples of the many headlines on the subject told the story: "Much Gold Being Mined in Custer County Streams"; "Great Strides Are Made in Mining in Black Hills Area"; "$2,000 In Gold Daily Taken from Hills by Placers." And in September, the *Argus-Leader* ran an article titled "Black Hills Reports Modern Gold Booms."[47]

Gold is found "in lodes or veins that are filled with mineral under the earth's surface." These lodes can be eroded and broken apart. When that happens, pieces of gold are carried "through waterways" and deposited "on the gravel or soil beds" at or near the ground's surface. Gold is mined by two primary methods: placer mining or lode mining (also referred to as hard rock mining or quartz mining). Placer mining is the process "used to find gold that has been eroded from the lode," and it generally occurs at or near the ground surface. The process involves separating the gold from gravel by a variety of methods, including "panning," using a "primitive rocker," and "sluicing." The first two methods can be performed by a single prospector; the third demands "the services of several men." All three methods require water. Large placer operations utilize specialized equipment to gather a substantial amount of earth and separate the gold from it. On the other hand, in lode mining, the gold is "extracted directly from the lode beneath the ground." This mining "requires the labour of many miners working together to extract the gold from tunnels or massive open pits in the ground."[48]

The federal and South Dakota mining location laws in effect when Case family members engaged in mining activities authorized "two main types of claims—lode and placer—depending on the character of the deposit." Lode claims were "staked on veins or lodes of quartz or other rock in place bearing gold... or other valuable deposits." Placer claims were staked "on all forms of deposit, excepting veins of quartz, or other rock in place." A lode claim could be located "on a plot of land not exceeding 1,500 feet in length along the lode or vein and 300 feet on each side of the middle of such vein at the surface." A placer claim could be "no larger than 20 acres for an individual." A "5-acre plot of nonmineral land" could "be staked as a mill site," and that land "need not be contiguous to the claim." The claimant was required to stake the claim's corners with markers so its boundaries could be readily determined. Wood posts were commonly used for that purpose. The claimant was also required to perform annual labor or improvements on the claim, known as "assessment work." This requirement could be suspended if the claimant filed a notice with the county Register of Deeds that stated the claimant's desire to suspend the work for a stated assessment year.[49]

After Francis took charge of the *Custer Weekly Chronicle* and the *Black Hills News*, those papers (and their successor publications) continued to run stories on gold-mining activities in the Black Hills. These articles typically mentioned the people or companies that were working their claims and the general area of their operations. Many of the mining projects were close to Custer. In 1933, Carol and Francis became personally involved in mining exploration efforts. On April 22, Carol "located" (meaning claimed) a placer claim and a lode claim. Both were situated about three miles southeast of Custer. Their notices provided legal descriptions of the areas to be explored. Both also claimed "all of the water, timber, and surface ground within the boundaries of this claim for the use, benefit and working thereof."[50]

Carol worked on her claims that summer and apparently built a cabin on her placer claim (named "Dusty"). In late July, the *Custer Chronicle* reported that "Miss Carol Case has been host to Allen, Lois and Dorothy Wilson, her nephew and nieces from Hot Springs, at her mining claim southeast of Custer, the past few days." Rex Morris, a friend who was between Allen and Lois in age, accompanied the group. On August 3, Carol signed a location notice for an additional lode claim situated about two miles southeast of Custer. One week later, she executed a notice for another lode claim in the same area. It was described as an "abandoned mining claim." On August 14, she left for Chicago to resume her studies at the Vogue School of Design and Institute of Art.[51]

Two weeks after Carol signed her April claim notices, the Acacia Mining Company filed incorporation papers in Pierre. Francis, M. W. Heumphreus (from Custer), and Charles H. Whiting (from Rapid City) were the incorporators, and Francis was president. On May 16, Francis Michaud and Palmer Hibbard, acting on behalf of Acacia Mining, located a lode claim situated about seven miles southwest of Custer. Ten days later, they located a second lode claim in the same area. Michaud and Hibbard continued to locate more claims in June. On the 9th, Michaud claimed four lode claims, and Hibbard claimed three. All were situated "about 6 miles southwest [of] Custer, S.D. on the north end of Twin Sisters Mountain" and were joined together. During that summer, Acacia Mining set up a camp on Lightning Creek—a stream that flowed past Twin Sisters Mountain and was near the claims located in June. In late September, a School of Mines graduate "came over Monday from Rapid City" to "do some work for the company" and stay at the camp. That work included "moving in parts for a mill."[52]

Francis did not confine his mining activities to the area near Custer in 1933. He also hired Ira Michaud (Francis Michaud's brother) to work on claims near Deadwood. Although no location notices for these claims have been found, contemporaneous correspondence suggests they were placer claims. Time records indicate that Michaud spent the latter half of June and early July working with "shovel and machine" and "staking claims and roadwork" on claims at or near Boulder Canyon, which is about eight miles east and a little north of Deadwood. Francis made at least two personal visits to the claims in 1933—one in mid-July and another on August 20. His main concern on both trips was the lack of sufficient water needed to properly work the claims.[53]

In 1934, Francis's gold-exploration efforts were hampered by a lack of money to finance Acacia's operations, a lack of water to conduct placer-mining activities near Deadwood, and a lack of time to devote to mining because he was running for Congress. Morris Wilcox—Francis's Acacia fraternity brother at Northwestern and now a Chicago businessman who had put up "some of the money" to work the Deadwood-area claims in the past—spent a day at those claims in late March. Francis visited them a week later. He then wrote to Wilcox that "although the moisture is improving, there is no running water of any consequence ahead. That does not look very encouraging."[54]

For the next few months, Francis's attempts to get financing for his mining activities were unsuccessful, and he continued to face time pressures while trying to run a newspaper and a political campaign at the same time. The newspaper-related pressures were greatly reduced in May when Myrle's sister Irma and her husband Laurence Weyler decided to move from Colony, Wyoming, to Custer and come to work for the *Chronicle*. They soon "became mainstays both in the shop and the work about town," and Myrle enjoyed having her sister and niece Bess nearby.[55]

Since mining-financing did not develop, Francis decided to file notices for the "suspension of assessment work" for six claims that were in his name. He also requested that Palmer Hibbard and Francis Michaud fill out forms necessary to suspend work on the nine claims they located in the previous year, because they agreed to turn over those claims to Acacia Mining. In a July 9 letter to Wilcox, Francis wrote that "my campaign and other interests now prevent me from giving the personal attention that the mining company needs to make a progress—plus the necessary finances"; so he was "just letting things coast, there hoping that when I get through with the campaign I will be in a better position to finance and from a better stand to get finances."[56]

In the same letter where Francis stated he was "just letting things coast" with respect to his mining business, he also noted that "my sister, Carol, is on her way out here with the folks. She is going to work on her claims." The elder Cases and their daughter arrived in the Hills a few days later. On July 12, Carol located a new lode claim that joined the two she had claimed the previous August. On that same day, she also located an additional placer claim. It was situated "about four miles east of Custer."[57]

In addition to working on her claims that summer, Carol also had guests visit her at her cabin. During the latter part of July, Mr. Sherman (from Rapid City) conducted a tour of the Hills for Frank Zipperer and his wife. Mr. Zipperer was superintendent of a sausage factory in Chicago, and Mrs. Zipperer was described as "quite a bicyclist and horsewoman." The tour reportedly included "every place of interest." Sherman and the Zipperers also "visited at the Dusty Claim . . . and were dinner guests of Miss Carol Case." And on August 30, the *Chronicle* reported that "Allen Wilson of Hot Springs, who has been visiting a few days with his aunt, Miss Carol Case, returned home with his grandfather, H. L. Case, today."[58]

It is not known whether Francis actively pursued any of his mining interests in 1935. On July 1, 1936, he filed two exemption claims with the Custer County Register of Deeds. The first listed six mining claims located in his name, and the second listed six claims located by Acacia Mining Company. Both exemption claims gave notice of the locaters' desire "to hold said mining claims during the assessment year 1935-1936 under the provisions of the Act of Congress entitled: 'An Act providing for the suspension of annual assessment work on mining claims held by location in the United States'."[59]

Carol and her parents returned to the Hills again during the summer of 1935. They came to visit Joyce's and Francis's families and "to do some work on their mineral claims east of Custer." Carol located two additional lode claims in July and another one in September. All three were situated in the same vicinity as her previously made claims. Herbert also took an active role in pursuing mining claims that summer. He signed as a witness to Carol's claim located on July 31 and to her amendment of that claim executed on August 17. In addition, he located his own placer claim in September. It was near Carol's Dusty Placer claim.[60]

It is not clear how successful any of the Cases were in finding gold through their mining efforts. Although Francis stated in 1934 that his Acacia Mining Company had "a reasonable showing" at its hardrock mill set up on Lightning Creek, author Richard Chenoweth has written that the company "operated for a few years on a limited basis but never very successfully." No evidence has been found to indicate whether Carol (or Herbert) ever made any significant discoveries, although it is known that she continued to locate mining claims in Custer County up until at least June 1945, and Herbert located at least one other claim there in July 1940. What can be said is that Francis, Carol, and Herbert (to a lesser degree) had an enthusiastic interest in exploring and mining for gold, and Francis would continue that interest—and expand it to other minerals and ores—after he became a congressman.[61]

FRANKLIN D. ROOSEVELT WAS ELECTED president in November 1932 on a platform that promised a "New Deal" to aid "the depression-ridden drought-stricken people of America." He was sworn into office on March 4, 1933. Five days later, he called Congress into an emergency session to hear about and authorize one of his New Deal proposals named the Emergency Conservation Work (ECW) program. It later came to be known as the Civilian Conservation Corps (CCC) program, under which the president "proposed to recruit thousands of unemployed young men, enroll them in a peacetime army, and send them into battle against destruction and erosion of our natural resources." Congress passed the ECW Act on March 31, and President Roosevelt signed it into law that day. The following week, he issued an executive order that authorized the CCC, appointed a national director, and established an Advisory Council whose members represented the federal government's departments of war, interior, agriculture, and labor. These four departments all helped to plan and implement CCC conservation projects. Shortly after the program was put in place, it was modified to extend "enlistment coverage to about 14,000 American Indians whose economic conditions were deplorable"; to authorize "the enrollment of about 25,000 locally employed men (LEM) . . . to train and protect the unskilled enrollees"; and to allow about 25,000 veterans of the Spanish American War and World War to join the CCC "with no age or marital restrictions."[62]

During the duration of the program, at least 45 CCC camps were established in South Dakota, and over 30,000 men served in them. Twenty-seven camps were in the Black Hills, and of this group, four were in Custer State Park. Each park camp was organized around a designated, numbered "company" unit that contained up to 200 men. An Army contingent provided "materials for housing, development, transportation, clothing, subsistence and medical attention" and "military officers ran the camps, enforcing the discipline and the laws." Later on, LEMs "were hired to assist in teaching job skills, and provide education where it was lacking in enrollees." Those who enlisted in the "CCC companies" at these camps were typically "men between the ages of 18 and 25 who would agree to send home $25 of their

$30-a-month pay and who would sign up for six-months periods of service." They were permitted to serve more than one six-month term, and most did so.[63]

In the spring of 1933, the National Park Service and the National Forest Service allotted two CCC camps to the park. Those camps' general mission was to undertake "a program of forest conservation by control of flood waters and soil erosion." Constructing lakes became the centerpiece of that program. After the CCC allotment was made, Senator Norbeck, as chairman of the State Park Board, met with Francis and others interested in getting a lake built near Custer. Norbeck informed the group that "the way was open to build the 120-acre lake in the Park" east of Custer if the state could acquire 19 privately owned acres "needed for the dam site and spillway." At Norbeck's request, Francis and five others from Custer (including two state legislators) created an "informal committee" to secure information about ownership of the 19 acres and to suggest how the state could acquire that land. Francis set forth the results of the committee's work in a detailed, five-page letter accompanied by supporting documents. The letter was dated June 8 and addressed to Governor Tom Berry's secretary. The next week, the Park Board "passed a formal resolution asking the Attorney General's office to proceed with acquisition of the dam site." Shortly thereafter, the governor's secretary and members of the attorney general's staff met with a Custer delegation in Pierre. That group "determined the procedure to permit immediate action on the camp and dam construction."[64]

Camp Doran (named after James Doran, the site's "homesteader of longest residence") was the CCC camp established to construct the lake and dam. The camp was located about three miles east of Custer and opened on or about June 17. Two-and-a-half weeks later, work began on clearing the dam site and lake bed. That operation was completed by August 1. Constructing the dam itself took nine months. On April 27, 1934, "water was turned into the lake" from French and

Bismarck Creeks, and the lake slowly started to fill. The dam was "56 feet high and 360 feet long and is rip-rapped the entire height of the back slope." The spillway was "50 feet wide." When the lake was full, the water would "cover 135 acres," be "about 50 feet" deep at its deepest spot, and create a shoreline that measured "about four and a half miles." The end result: a body of water that was "twice over the largest lake in the Black Hills." After the dam was completed, "a shoreline drive was built around the lake." In addition, a "1500 ft beach with log pier and parking facilities was constructed on the east side"; and "a picnic area and campground were developed" on the south side. As of early May, "five hundred Camp Doran men" had "worked on the project at different periods."[65]

As he had with Legion Lake, Francis took an interest in what this large, new lake near Custer should be named. But instead of recommending a name and then holding a naming contest as he did before, this time around he wrote an editorial that listed various proposed names and the rationale for each. He opined that the lake could easily be named "Lake Doran" or "Doran Lake" because "the CCC camp is Camp Doran," and "most of the lake will be on the Doran place." Or the lake could "readily be called 'Walsh Lake' as the dam is on the old Walsh place." He added that "Custer Lake" would be consistent with the lake site's first blueprints and would "have the advantage of identifying the location of the lake to visitors." Finally, he recognized that there was "a lot of sentiment" for choosing the name "'Stockade Lake' since the waters will back up to the shelter spot of the first white settlers, the Gordon Stockade." The editorial ended by suggesting that Park Superintendent (Ray Milliken) should name the lake.[66]

The lake-naming issue was not settled for 16 months following the Case editorial. Then, on October 19, 1935, the Park Board met in Pierre and officially adopted the name "Stockade Lake." In the meantime, the *Custer Chronicle* and other Black Hills newspapers had praised the lake, three men from Custer had built summer cabins near it, and Francis had written to Senator Norbeck in Washington, D.C.: "I certainly wish you could see the Lake east of town. It is perfect and the drive takes you to the points that give you some wonderful views."[67]

The second CCC camp established in 1933 was named Camp Pine Creek. It was located near the northern edge of the park in Pine Creek Canyon—one mile west and one mile north of Mount Rushmore. Shortly after the camp was assembled in June, work began on creating a lake by building a dam across Pine Creek. Sometime during the spring of 1934, the dam was completed, and an 18-acre lake with a one-mile shoreline was formed. It covered an area formerly known as Horse Thief Park—named after "a gang of rustlers who made this region their headquarters." The lake soon became known as "Horse Thief Lake," and the Park Board made that name official in the fall of 1935. After it was built, picnic units "were developed on the north and west sides," and a foot trail was added that went completely around the lake and connected the two picnic areas. Horse Thief Lake was colorfully described as being "like an aquamarine jewel in a setting of pines, spruce and granite cliffs in one of the most rugged and wildest sections of the entire forest."[68]

Two more CCC camps were allotted to Custer State Park in 1934. Camp Lodge was organized on July 11 and opened five days later. It was located on Grace Coolidge Creek about nine miles north of the Game Lodge and twelve miles northeast of Custer. The camp was built in a deer and elk pasture on a "nearly level, open grassy area surrounded by pine covered hills." The CCC men spent most of the summer building a permanent camp while they lived in tents. That fall, they began working on a dam one-and-a-half miles below the campsite. The dam would "bottle up Grace Coolidge Creek" and create a 26-acre lake. Colonel M. L. Shade (who had unsuccessfully sued Francis and the Star for libel in 1926) supervised the work. He predicted that the future lake would "be one of the most beautiful in the Black Hills region."[69]

In early April 1935, Shade reported that construction on the new dam "passed the one third mark." Camp Lodge enrollees continued to work on it that summer and fall. As with the other CCC-built lakes in the park, this one eventually included "adequate facilities to take care of the tourists who stop there." During the time it was built, the lake was known as "Lodge Lake." But at the same October meeting when the Park Board named "Stockade Lake" near Custer, it also decided to officially designate the lake on Grace Coolidge Creek as "Center Lake." That name was chosen because it was the "most centrally located in the Park."[70]

The second camp to be developed in 1934 was initially named after a historic outlaw camp called Robbers' Roost. Established on July 16, it was located 14 miles southeast of Custer and "built on the bank of French Creek surrounded by three heavily timbered hills." A sawmill had previously occupied this site, and the CCC enrollees' first task was to clean it up. Over the next several months, they undertook other projects to improve their camp and the park, including "construction of a water supply system to serve the camp, the superintendent's house and the new museum." In the spring of 1935, the camp's name was changed to Camp Narrows, which recognized "the closely spaced vertical granite formations bordering the creek." By April, the enrollees had built a few roads in the area with "a new type" of small wooden bridge. Francis was a direct beneficiary of that project. He thanked the camp's commanding officer of military personnel in a June letter: "Sunday, I was over the road and the bridge that the boys constructed going in to the cabins near Blue Bell. I thought they did a very five /sic/ piece of work and want to express my personal appreciation as one of the cabins serviced by that road is ours."[71]

The men at Camp Narrows went on to perform additional valuable work for the park. That work included constructing 30 miles of telephone lines, building more roads, completing three miles of fencing, excavating for a reservoir and pipeline, constructing a custodian house and barn, building four bridges with concrete and native stone, and reconstructing the Gordon Stockade replica on Stockade Lake.[72]

The four CCC camps discussed above closed at different times: Doran on April 8, 1937, Pine Creek on April 27, 1936, Lodge on July 30, 1942, and Narrows on October 1, 1941. Nationally, "though the CCC was never formally terminated, Congress had, by June 30, 1942, ended the program's funding and set aside money for its liquidation." Author Jessie Sundstrom observed that "World War II put an end to the CCC program because the men were needed for the war effort, either as enlistees in the military services or as semi-skilled and skilled workers in the defense industry." She has estimated that the CCC's work "put the Park ahead in projects and accomplishments by a decade, at least."[73]

IN MAY 1933, FRANCIS REPEATED an activity he started doing when he was a faculty member at Wesleyan after the war: speaking at commencement exercises. On May 19, he gave the address to the graduating class at Spearfish High School. Five days later he took part in what the *Rapid City Daily Journal* described as a "novelty of high school commencement exercises" at Hot Springs. He was the first alumnus of the school to give the commencement address; and Clifford Wilson, who was the first alumnus to receive his entire education at Hot Springs and now was president of the school board, handed out diplomas to the 39 graduates. Francis's speech told "a large audience" that the teacher is "the greatest thing in education." He also "stressed three points to the graduates: 'You are living in the most interesting era of the world's history; the part you play in that era is entirely up to you, and be true to yourselves, to your ideals and thus be worthy of your niche in life.'" Then on the 26th, he spoke at the Southern Normal school commencement in Springfield.[74]

After a summer of active involvement in gold-mining exploration and other activities, Francis returned to efforts to increase his paper's readership in the fall of 1933. But before doing so, he decided to consolidate his two newspapers into one. That development was announced in the *Custer Chronicle*'s August 31, 1933 issue, where it was noted that "with the Custer County Chronicle is now printed The Black Hills Chronicle." The "combined" issue contained six pages and maintained its $2-per-year subscription price. Although the title page remained "CUSTER COUNTY CHRONICLE," the running head at the top of pages two through six now identified the paper as "CUSTER COUNTY (AND BLACK HILLS) CHRONICLE." That practice continued until August 1, 1935, when the paper dropped the "(AND BLACK HILLS)" notation from its running head.[75]

The drive to attract additional readers appeared in the *Chronicle*'s September 21 issue. Unlike the splashy and time-consuming subscription contest held the previous year, this new approach was simple, direct, and easy to administer. It was revealed in an advertisement that offered to trade an 18-month subscription for either a 100-pound sack of potatoes or two 14 or 16-inch ricks of wood. The ad further stated that the "only restrictions on this offer are that the wood or potatoes must be home-grown and of good market quality," and the offer was good for one month.[76]

The offer garnered a favorable response—at least with respect to its subscription-for-potatoes option. Two weeks after the advertisement was published, the *Chronicle* remarked that its office "is taking something of the flavor of a potato cellar these days as many are taking advantage of the offer to pay for a subscription with home grown potatoes." It added that the potatoes were of "very fine quality" and mentioned the names of four people who brought them in on the previous Saturday. Two days before the offer expired, the *Chronicle* reaffirmed it in a second ad that stated in part: "Potatoes are cheaper but we'll stand by our offer to trade with you thru Saturday, October 21."[77]

AN AMERICAN INDIAN RESERVATION HAS been described as "a land base that a tribe reserved for itself when it relinquished its other land areas to the US through treaties." The 1868 Treaty of Fort Laramie created the Great Sioux Reservation. It comprised land in what was then Dakota Territory—land that would later span more than half of South Dakota and lay almost entirely in the portion of the state that was west of the Missouri River. The Great Sioux Reservation included the Black Hills, which were set aside "for exclusive use by the Sioux people." By the treaty's terms, the American Indians also retained hunting rights to a larger area west and south of the designated reservation boundaries. After General Custer discovered gold in the Black Hills in 1874, prospectors and settlers soon moved into the Hills and demanded that the U.S Army provide them with "protection"—all in violation of the Laramie Treaty. The Army was also "ordered to move against wandering bands of Sioux hunting on the range," even though the Sioux were allowed to hunt there "in accordance with their treaty rights." That order eventually led to Custer and his 7th Calvary detachment being "annihilated" by Sioux and Cheyenne Indians at the Battle of Little Big Horn in June 1876. Less than two months after Custer's defeat, the federal government took steps to enter another treaty with the Native Americans that "gave up the Black Hills and hunting rights in [modern-day] Montana and Wyoming." This second treaty—signed by American Indian chiefs "under military duress"—was ratified by Congress on February 28, 1877.[78]

On March 2, 1889, Congress passed an act known as the Sioux Agreement. It divided the Great Sioux Reservation into five smaller, separate reservations for "various Sioux tribes" that were located on land in the future state of South Dakota. Once that division occurred, the former Great Sioux Reservation lands were reduced to roughly half of their previous size. And on November 2, South Dakota became a state. In late December of the following year, the United States' 7th Calvary Regiment slaughtered between 150 and 300 Lakota Indians at Wounded Knee Creek on the Pine Ridge Reservation. That event, which became known as the Wounded Knee Massacre, "was the climax of the U.S. Army's late 19th-century efforts to repress the Plains Indians," and it "broke any organized resistance to reservation life and assimilation to white American culture[.]"[79]

The five reservations created in 1889 were Pine Ridge, Rosebud, Lower Brule, Cheyenne River, and Standing Rock. Between 1904 and 1913, the U.S. government "negotiated a series of agreements" with the Native Americans on those reservations, "whereby over half the reservation lands, a total of over four million acres, were made available for purchase by white settlers." As of 1934, the five reservations had eight of the thirteen "recognized tribes of the Sioux Nation... living in the largest numbers" within their borders. Numerous bands existed within each tribe. They were described as "firmly knit family groups who lived together in winter villages and had economic and social interdependence."[80]

The Pine Ridge Reservation was near the state's southwestern corner in Shannon, Washington, and Washabaugh Counties. It had the largest reservation population in South Dakota—over 8,000 members of the Oglala (meaning "To scatter one's own") tribe. The tribe was divided into 33 separate bands, and each had a tribal name. The Rosebud Reservation, situated in Todd County to the east of Pine Ridge, was one of two areas populated by the Sicangu (meaning "Burned thighs") tribe. The other area was at the Lower Brule Reservation. It sat on the western bank of the Missouri River, north and east of Rosebud, in Lyman and Stanley Counties. "Barely 600 Indians" resided there. Located in the north central part of the state, the Cheyenne River Reservation covered all of Armstrong and parts of Dewey and Ziebach Counties. At least four different tribes lived on this reservation in 1934: Itazipco (meaning "Without a bow"—also called Sansarc); Sihasapa (meaning "Blackfeet"); Miniconjou (meaning "Those who plant beside the stream"); and Oohenonpa (meaning

"Two Boilings"—also called Two Kettles). And finally, the Standing Rock Reservation was north of the Cheyenne Reservation. Standing Rock's boundaries encompassed most of the eastern half of Corson County in South Dakota, and the reservation extended into Sioux County, North Dakota. In addition to the Sihasapa, members of the Hunkpapa (meaning "End of the circle") and Upper Yanktonai of the Yanktonais (meaning "Little End Village") tribes lived there.[81]

Apart from the five "West River" reservations, three additional ones existed east of the Missouri River in 1934. All three were within South Dakota's future borders but were established well before the state was admitted into the Union. The oldest was the Yankton Reservation—founded in 1853. It was located near the Missouri River on land which later became Charles Mix County in the southeastern part of the state. The Yankton (meaning "End Village") tribe lived there. The Crow Creek Reservation was home to the Lower Yanktonai of the Yanktonais tribe. Established in 1862, it was situated in parts of Hughes, Hyde, and Buffalo Counties in central South Dakota, and the east bank of the Missouri River formed its western border. In the state's northeast corner lay the Sisseton Reservation. Its boundaries formed an inverted triangle, with the base extending slightly below and above the border between North and South Dakota, and the tip pointing south. Most of its land area was in Roberts County—with lesser amounts in Marshall, Day, Codington, and Grant Counties. The triangle's north "base line" also encompassed small portions of two counties in southeastern North Dakota. The Sisseton Reservation was founded in 1867 and populated by two tribes: the Wahpeton (meaning "Village among the leaves of deciduous trees") and the Sisiton (meaning "Marsh village").[82]

On July 28, 1934, Myrle and Francis attended evening "Indian ceremonies" at Little Eagle, a small village situated on the Grand River in east-central Corson County on the Standing Rock Reservation. During that event, Francis "became a member of the Standing

Rock Sioux." The ceremonies began when "great numbers of Red men, with painted faces and bedecked war costumes, together with women in costly beaded dresses, head pieces and ornaments filed into a large arena erected of poles and branches[.]" After numerous dances were held, six Sioux maidens unveiled a monument built "in honor of great Sioux chieftains and Indian World War dead[.]" Then one of the maidens—Miss Grace Brown—asked that Francis be called to the center of the arena, where she presented him with a "beaded head piece" and requested that he be named after her grandfather—Hehaka Hemaza (Iron Horn Elk). Next, Chief Grey Eagle "presided over rites which formed the adoption and the bestowal of chieftainship" upon Francis. When the adoption ceremonies ended, the new Chief Hehaka Hemaza briefly thanked the crowd for the honor, and he especially thanked Miss Brown "for the part she had taken in his adoption." He also "expressed desire that his public life would parallel that of the great man who bore that name before him."[83]

By 1936, Flandreau became the state's ninth American Indian reservation. It was placed in Moody County, whose eastern edge bordered on Minnesota and whose northern and southern borders were about halfway between South Dakota's northern and southern state lines. The reservation included about "2,500 acres of land along and near the Big Sioux River." It was the home of two Sioux tribes: the Mdewakanton (meaning "Mystery Lake Village") and the Wahpekute (meaning "Shooters among the leaves of deciduous trees"). Flandreau was the only South Dakota reservation formed since 1889, and it was the final reservation located in the state.[84]

THE FOLLOWING TWO-LINE ANNOUNCEMENT appeared in the *Chronicle*'s February 14, 1935 issue: "Born to Mr. and Mrs. Francis Case, February 10, a daughter, Jane Marie." The proud parents put out a subsequent one-page publication that provided more details. Cast in the format of a miniature newspaper and titled *Case*

Chronicles, it consisted of three columns with nine separate articles and was printed on "delicate pink paper" that measured five and three-eighths inches by seven inches. The lead story—"EXTRA! Population Up ½"—stated, among other things, that Jane Marie arrived at 4:30 p.m. on Sunday, February 10 "to make a 50 per cent increase in the family of Mr. and Mrs. Francis Case," she was born at Black Hills Methodist Hospital in Rapid City, she weighed six pounds and fourteen ounces and had black hair at birth, she made her first "public appearance" on February 22 when she "motored to Custer to make her permanent home," and "Auntie Irma Weyler and daughter 'Biji' are frequent visitors." An article titled "Life Begins at Two A.m." set out the family's daily schedule, starting with 2:00 a.m. Night Club and ending with 9:00 p.m. Lunch. Under "Neighborhood News," it was noted that the Case and Gates families lived two doors apart, and "within an hour of two weeks after Jane Case came, Janet Gates arrived." Janet reportedly weighed six pounds, two ounces and bore "considerable resemblance to her near twin." An article headlined "Animals" proclaimed that Woof Wigglesworth, the family's wire-haired terrier, had "asserted a proprietary interest in the new baby." And the "Mother's Page" column observed that "everybody asks about her and then proceeds to give the baby all the attention. (Editorial note: Father isn't even asked about.)." The remaining items' main, and sometimes only, points are quoted here: "Sports"—"Try-outs have begun for the weight events, using celluloid rattles"; Music"—"Critics are baffled by the sparing use of vocal ability"; "Markets"— "Plenty of bids. No quotations given"; and "Weather"—"Damp, with occasional showers."[85]

While she was in the hospital, Myrle received a telegram and several congratulatory cards and letters, including one from her sister Bess ("I am so glad the baby is a girl—now I have three nieces and three nephews.... We are eager to know what you name her."), and one from fellow Contract Study Club member Dorothy Cole ("Congratulations to you on the birth of your baby daughter. You know how excited we all were."). After the *Case Chronicles* was "published," more congratulations followed. Leland sent Francis his "sincerest congratulations and profoundest admiration on what you and Myrle have done to increase Custer's population.... We're anxiously awaiting snapshots.... Poor Woof. He must be leading a dog's life again." Dan Brummitt, now editor of *The Christian Advocate* (newspaper published weekly by the Methodist Episcopal Church), wrote that the "Case Chronicles reaches us on time, but this acknowledgement is a little bit late. You got a first-class announcement of a first-class event." *The Colome Times* (weekly newspaper published in Colome, South Dakota) ran an article that acknowledged receipt of the *Case Chronicles*, summarized its contents, and ended with this comment: "All that dad is supposed to be good for, brother Case, is to keep the feed bags full and the life insurance paid up." Finally, Art Brown congratulated "the Case family on the acquisition of Jane Marie" and offered his view that "life begins with the first child, as you no doubt have already discovered. It gives you something to think about!"[86]

IN A MEMORANDUM FROM THE War Department's Adjutant General's Office dated February 18, 1935, Francis was notified that his "commission in the Officer's Reserve Corps has terminated by reason of the expiration of the five-year period for which it was granted." Paragraph two of the memorandum stated the rationale for this decision: "In view of the fact that you served five years without eligibility for assignment, active duty or promotion, and no report was received that you had qualified for reappointment with full eligibility, which is a requirement under present regulations, you were not tendered reappointment." So, for unknown reasons, Francis apparently decided not to take steps necessary to ensure his reappointment, and his ten-year career as an Army reservist ended.[87]

Within two months after Jane was born, Myrle resumed being an active card player in the community. She rejoined the Contract Study

Club, which met periodically to play bridge, and she "entertained" the club at its April 10 session. One night later, the club members and their husbands met at Blue Bell Lodge for dinner and bridge. There, "Mr. and Mrs. Francis Case won high scores for the evening." And at the club's next meeting held on May 22, Myrle and Mrs. Glen Coe "were high score winners at their respective tables."[88]

During that summer, baby Jane was introduced to several family members. The Case grandparents and Carol met her for the first time when they came to the Hills in July. The next month, Jane was part of a family gathering that included her parents, three of her maternal aunts, and all her cousins from Myrle's side of the family. This group assembled on a Sunday afternoon and "enjoyed a picnic supper" at a cabin near Band Creek, Wyoming.[89]

In its May 30, 1935 issue, the *Chronicle* noted that "Mrs. Francis Case has purchased the north end of the bank lot, across from the Custer Cleaners." Francis decided that his paper needed a new facility, and he had a "brick and tile" building constructed at the bank-lot location over the next two-and-a-half months. The August 15 paper printed a front-page article titled "Chronicle's New Home." It stated in part: "Immediately after this Chronicle is off the press, we will start moving into the new building north of the Custer County Bank.... Facilities at the new home will help us to give you, we hope, the best Chronicles you have ever had."[90]

The excitement of moving into a new building was dampened by the news that the Weylers were leaving the *Chronicle* and moving away from Custer. After working for the paper "for the past 15 months," Irma and Laurence decided to purchase the *Daily Belle Fourche Post* and move to Belle Fourche with their daughter Bess. The *Chronicle* reported this development in its August 1 issue and remarked: "To say that they will be missed at the Chronicle is to put it mildly.... The opportunity to develop a newspaper of their own in ... Belle Fourche, however, came and they go to their new field with the good wishes of the Chronicle and the Custer County friends."[91]

IN THE EARLY MORNING HOURS on January 23, 1936, a fire started in the bakery at Hill City, and it quickly "spread across the alley" to the *Hill City News* building. Before it was brought under control, the fire completely destroyed the bakery, the newspaper's office, and its "valuable printing equipment." Shortly thereafter, Don Hare, the *News* editor and owner, contacted Francis and asked for his help. The latter agreed that Hare could print the *News* at the *Chronicle*'s facility until the Hill City plant was "re-established." Hare ultimately decided not to rebuild his plant. Instead, he announced in mid-April that due to "the condition of his health," he had sold the *Hill City News* to Francis and Frank Carrier (from Hill City). Subsequently, Francis took over sole ownership and control of the *News*, Carrier became an employee, and the paper continued to be published during the summer and fall.[92]

On the family front, Francis took delight in keeping his dad informed of Jane's development. In mid-January, he wrote that "today, she really mastered the technique of making her rocking horse go... She learned how to say 'get up' and make her body weight roll back and forth at the same time. That's the secret of most successes in this world, isn't it? To make action suit the word." And Francis sent Leland a photo, prompting this response: "That photo of Jane and Woof is a pipareeno. It was the occasion for popeyed admiration of everyone who came in my office the day it arrived."[93]

Myrle became an active member of the American Association of University Women (AAUW) local Rushmore chapter by early 1936. That group typically met about once a month in the spring and fall, where it had dinner at a Custer café or another nearby place where food was made available. After dinner the club would usually continue its business meeting and hold a program at one of the member's houses. On January 9, the after-dinner gathering was at Myrle and Francis's home. The subject presented at that meeting's program was "Pan-American Problems and Policies." At the March 5 meeting, "Germany, the National Socialistic State' was the program topic. The final spring meeting was held on May 14. It was guest night, and "about 25 visitors and members" attended to watch a one-act play written and directed by one of the association's members. After a spring break, the group met again on September 24 and decided that some of the fall programs would focus on "Mental Hygiene." The next fall meeting (and last one held before the 1936 general election) occurred at Legion Lake. Dr. Pangborn, the AAUW state president from Spearfish, was the "honored guest." She "addressed the club on the 'History and Purposes of AAUW.'"[94]

PRESIDENT ROOSEVELT MADE A SHORT weekend trip to the Black Hills in the late summer of 1936. At Gutzon Borglum's request, the president agreed to attend the Jefferson-head dedication ceremony at Mount Rushmore during his visit. The special nine-car presidential train arrived in Rapid City about 6:00 p.m. on Saturday, August 29. It was greeted by "huge throngs" that filled the plaza at the train depot and "lined both sides of Main street." After making a few brief remarks about the drought problem, the president was escorted in an "open Packard" automobile to the Alex Johnson Hotel. There he was greeted "by a band of Indian chiefs and sub-chiefs from the Pine Ridge Reservation." Mr. Roosevelt tended to presidential duties that night and made no further public appearances until Sunday morning, when he attended services at the Emmanuel Episcopal Church. After church, he returned to the hotel for a luncheon, and then the presidential party drove to Mount Rushmore for the Jefferson dedication.[95]

The 50-car presidential caravan reached its destination in the early afternoon. About 2,500 people were assembled at the memorial's base near the sculptor's studio when the president arrived. After his open car had been moved near the reviewing stand and positioned so he could comfortably watch the ceremony, Borglum briefly greeted him. Borglum then instructed his daughter Mary Alice to wave an American flag from the stand. When she did so, it told her brother Lincoln (who was standing 1,500 feet above the crowd on the monument's crest) to detonate a dynamite blast that "released 150 tons of granite and strewed the debris at the base of the mountain." Two more blasts followed. Then the 72-foot American flag—the one used in the Washington dedication six years ago—was slowly lifted from Jefferson's head— revealing its features "amidst a burst of applause." Next, flags on top of the mountain that represented Spain and France (prior claimants to this "territory") were lowered. Simultaneously, the 15-star, 15-stripe American flag during Jefferson's presidency was raised above his stone figure. An airplane then circled above the granite sculpture and released 83 parachutes. Each bore a tiny American flag and a small piece of granite taken from the monument.[96]

After the parachute drop, Borglum paid tribute to Doane Robinson and Peter Norbeck for their critical contributions to the Mount Rushmore project. (Those two, together with their wives and other members of the Mount Rushmore National Memorial Commission, were seated on the reviewing stand near the president's car. Unfortunately, Senator Norbeck had "well advanced" cancer of the tongue and jaw by this time, and he could not speak.) Borglum then presented the memorial to the president and told him that "'I want you to dedicate this memorial as a shrine to the country for 100,000 years." The president responded extemporaneously from his car. He said in part: "I am very happy to congratulate all of you not only on what we see today but on what is going to happen in the future at Mount Rushmore." After the ceremony, the president and his family members (sons John and Franklin and daughter-in-law Mrs. James Roosevelt) posed for photos and chatted with Borglum and his family members "for quite a time." The presidential caravan then drove back to Rapid City—passing "hundreds of cheering citizens along the 26-mile route." When he arrived, the president boarded his train and "immediately immersed himself in the business of state."[97]

IN THE *CHRONICLE'S* JUNE 18, 1936 ISSUE, Francis introduced a new column titled "Wayside Notes." It began by stating, "The Chronicle aims to be a community newspaper. We cover local events with no intentional partiality. General editorial comment, while doubtless reflecting the editor's political affiliation, is written with a view to community interest." The column went on to concede that "it is altogether possible that an editorial column may lose its appeal for general community reading if too much of its content seems colored by the personal interest of the editor." Francis's answer to this possibility was to "try a new column which will be more or less political, and frankly so, and to keep personal politics out of the regular editorial column during the current campaign." He added that "there may be considerable of a non-political nature in this column of 'Wayside Notes.' But whatever is here, will be frankly personal. And if you don't like the flavor I'm labelling it so that it need not spoil your enjoyment in reading the balance of the Chronicle."[98]

The "Wayside Notes" column continued to appear in the *Chronicle* through the summer and early fall. It dealt with a variety of topics, such as ways of dealing with the drought, Francis's public challenge to debate his political opponent, Francis's history of advocating water projects for the state, and his views on old-age pension reform. In the column that appeared five days before the general election, Francis wrote: "I AM VERY SORRY that campaign week has occupied so much of my time that it has been impossible to give as much attention to the Chronicle as I would like to have done." He then expressed his gratitude "for the loyalty of the people on the Chronicle staff and all friends of the paper who have assisted in its production during the past few months." The column ended on an optimistic note: "I . . .

believe now we have an opportunity... for a final victory on November 3rd. The outlook is very encouraging, and whatever the outcome I will continue to work for Western South Dakota to the best of my ability."[99]

CHAPTER 12

IF AT FIRST YOU AREN'T ELECTED, TRY, TRY AGAIN

Some men may seek election to congress to right economic wrongs. I feel that urge too. Some men may seek congress for the honor—I am too human to be insensible to that. . . . But one urge that drives me more than anything else—the hope that perhaps I can contribute something to the cause of peace—that there I can be true to the men who—in Woodrow Wilson's words—"were once our comrades and are now gone and have left us under bonds of eternal fidelity."

—Francis Case

The 1926 general election for South Dakota's third district congressman matched incumbent Republican William Williamson against Democrat Arthur Watwood. In late October, the *Hot Springs Star* wrote an editorial that enthusiastically supported Williamson. It presented three reasons why people should vote for him—he had influence with the Coolidge administration; he knew and could serve Hot Springs interests; and he had "won a respected place in Washington." Williamson won the election held on November 2. But the vote was surprisingly close—the margin of victory being just over 2,000 votes. That result prompted Art Brown to write Francis that Williamson "came so near to being defeated this time that I don't believe there's a ghost of a show for him to be elected next time he runs." And given this belief, Brown concluded that "the time is ripe, it seems to me, for an energetic young man, such as Francis H. Case, widely known in Hot Springs and Rapid City, and the entire West-river country to lay his plans to come to Congress in 1928!"[1]

By October 1927, Francis had decided to support Chet Leedom—a former state highway commissioner who now was serving as U.S. Marshall in South Dakota—if Leedom decided to run for the third district congressional seat. Francis therefore sent a letter to Leedom in mid-October that made clear he (Francis) would back Leedom's candidacy if the latter decided to seek Williamson's seat in 1928. That letter also strongly implied that if Leedom chose not to run, Francis might do so himself. One week later, Leedom announced he was a candidate for the job. Francis followed the announcement with an editorial in the *Star*'s November 1 issue. That piece stated "Mr. Williamson is a good congressman, a splendid man" and "if he should be renominated after an open referendum, the Star will be for him[.]" But the editorial also expressed concerns over whether Williamson "was the strongest nominee we can have," contended that the situation "warrants an open party referendum in the primary," and concluded that "Chet Leedom's sombrero in the ring is a good thing for the party."[2]

In November, the *Star* continued to write editorials that discussed the expected contest between Williamson and Leedom. One of those editorials summarized comments about these candidates that appeared in other newspapers throughout the state. Some of those comments favored retaining Williamson, and others supported Leedom. Another *Star* editorial specifically rebutted the charge that "if Hot Springs and Fall River County should support anyone but Williamson, there would be ingratitude without parallel," and it noted Leedom's substantial role in building roads and bridges in Fall River County when he was a state highway commissioner.[3]

By late November, rumors began to circulate that Leedom was going to leave the race in favor of Leslie Jensen—a man who grew up in Hot Springs, fought in the World War, and now served as "collector of internal revenue for South Dakota" in Aberdeen. In response to that rumor, an unknown person from Hot Springs wrote to Leedom and encouraged him to "throw all of your strength to Case" if Leedom decided to end his campaign. One week later, in a confidential letter to Leedom, Francis set forth his own detailed plan to run for the seat if Leedom decided to withdraw. That plan included the assumption that Leedom would support a Case campaign for Congress.[4]

THE 1928 ELECTION WAS CARRIED OUT under a revised primary law. It provided, among other things, that members of each political party in each precinct would hold a meeting on Tuesday, February 14, to nominate three precinct "proposalmen," who in turn would meet on the following Tuesday at the county seat to select three county proposalmen. These three elected delegates would represent the county at the state proposalmen's meeting to be held in Pierre on March 6. At that gathering, state party platforms would be formed, and the proposalmen would "select state party tickets to submit to members of their party at the primary elections." Three weeks later, the precinct proposalmen would convene at their respective county seats and choose the county party tickets. Under the new primary law, independent candidates were allowed to "oppose the regular proposalmen's choice" at the state primary election, which was set to be held on May 22. And the winners in that primary contest would become the "party candidates... in the fall election."[5]

On February 8, Chet Leedom formally withdrew from the race, stating that "were I forced to resign my present position" in order to run for the seat, "it would be impossible for me to assist my two children... to complete their [college] education." Leedom's announcement also noted that "a concerted effort is being put forth by republican ex-servicemen... to secure the nomination for Leslie Jensen," and "should the ex-servicemen be successful in the district, there will be no question about the election of Mr. Jensen." Six days after Leedom withdrew, Republican voters in Fall River County held their precinct-proposalmen elections. Those delegates who favored Jensen won over those who supported Williamson by a "two-to-one vote." One week later, three delegates were selected to represent the county at the upcoming state proposalmen meeting. They were instructed to "'vote and work for the nomination of Leslie Jensen for Congress,'" and "'to use all honorable means to secure his nomination.'"[6]

In an editorial that appeared in the *Star*'s February 28 issue, Francis argued that third district Republicans were entitled to a "referendum upon the representation given by Congressman Williamson." The article began by contending that the voters needed to find out whether Williamson was the best available candidate and to examine his recent activities in Congress. It then noted that "the proposal meetings are not a referendum," and that unorganized counties "have no representation in the proposal meetings." Based on these remarks, the editorial concluded that the May primaries should serve as a "general referendum on the congressional situation," and this was true "regardless of the outcome at the Pierre proposal meeting."[7]

That meeting took place a week later. During those proceedings, the Fall River County proposalmen "'had promise of over 8,000 votes [for Jensen] but it took 9,500 to nominate,'" and several counties "'had been instructed for Williamson before it was known that Jensen would run if nominated.'" Therefore, Jensen's name was not presented to the convention for potential nomination. When it came time to vote for Williamson as the third district congressional nominee, all three of the Fall River and Bennett County delegates passed, as did one delegate from Jackson County and one from Jones County. Nevertheless, Williamson was given the congressional endorsement "without any open opposition except for the passing reported."[8]

Six days after the Pierre meeting, Francis sent a letter to about 30 of his "trusted friends over the district" that stated in part: "With the prospect that Les Jensen will not go into the congressional primary, several people are suggesting that I make the race.... I want your opinion on the matter. Please give it to me straight favorable or unfavorable." Apparently, that same day, Jensen came to Hot Springs and informed Francis that he (Jensen) was not going to run. Over the next two weeks, Francis met with at least a dozen potential backers, Jensen endorsed his candidacy, a Case-for-Congress club was formed (which selected E. B. Adams as chairman, E. R. Murphy as vice-chairman, and O. B. Wallace as secretary), and petitions were signed to place his name on the primary ballot. On March 27, he resigned as commander of the American Legion's Battle Mountain Post—saying that he expected "to enter the race for the republican congressional nomination in the May primaries," and the American Legion constitution prevented him from holding his post while running for political office. And at the Fall River County proposal meeting held that day, the precinct proposalmen—in addition to nominating candidates for county offices—"adopted a resolution endorsing Francis Case as candidate for United States representative to oppose Congressman William Williamson."[9]

ON MARCH 29, FRANCIS FORMALLY ANNOUNCED that he was a candidate for the third-district congressional seat. That announcement was accompanied by a fourfold platform that promised "to attend to those things which Williamson has overlooked." It pledged to purge "the republican party of oil, slush funds, Mellonism and Wall street"; to redeem "the party's faith to the farmers and the tradesmen of the northwest"; to provide "roads, hospitals, schools for today's Indians, who need most, deserve most"; and to grant "not only justice but mercy to disabled veterans for whom the war will never be over; sane defense preparation against future war, conscription of property... [and] life in case of war but taking every possible step to lessen the likelihood of war and to increase the chance of lasting peace."[10]

For the first three weeks in April, the campaign for third district congressman took place mainly through contrasting editorials and articles in the state's newspapers. At least two argued that since "'the first termer [in Congress] accomplishes very little,'" South Dakota should "'return her three congressmen to Washington next fall;'" and one editor predicted that Williamson "will carry every county except Fall River." Others newspapers supported Francis, describing him and his candidacy in positive terms. And one claimed that "'practically all the Indians on the various reservations and a goodly portion of the whites are opposed to Williamson.'" In an editorial written during that period, Francis explained his criticism of Williamson's failure to support the "McMaster resolution," which called for a tariff that would lower excessive rates, establish "a closer parity between agriculture and industry" and therefore help the farmer. The resolution passed the senate, but Williamson voted to table it in the house.[11]

Francis made his first campaign speech at Fort Pierre on April 24. There he accused Williamson of "voting against tax reduction and 'every amendment that promised relief for the small tax payer'." Four days later, he challenged Williamson to a debate, stating that "'I would be very glad to meet him at any point in the district on any date he suggests and share equally with him the cost of the hall to thrash out the issues of this campaign before a public audience.'"[12]

The Case campaign aggressively hit the road after the debate challenge was issued. During the first week in May, Francis, accompanied by two colleagues, travelled 1,400 miles through the district's northern counties. During that trip, he "spoke an average of three times a day" and was "'surprised to see the amount [of support] shown.'" After a short stay at Hot Springs, he returned to the campaign trail the following week. While he was gone, the Case-for-Congress Club sent political ads and other "broadside" literature to district newspapers. In addition, an unnamed campaign committee member wrote a lengthy *Star* editorial. It focused on Francis's connections and contributions to Fall River County, asserted that "Williamson's record is his heaviest liability," and concluded by urging its readers to "VOTE AND WORK FOR CASE NEXT TUESDAY."[13]

By mid-May, Francis had "visited every county in the district," "traveled 6,000 miles," and "put out 45,000 pieces of printed matter." The Case-for-Congress Club officers had also "driven thousands of miles," and others had "given time and energy and funds." And Williamson had agreed to a public debate, which was set to be held at the Rapid City auditorium at 8:00 p.m. on May 17 and chaired by Rapid City attorney George Williams.[14]

THE WILLIAMSON-CASE DEBATE WENT forward as scheduled. Chairman Williams introduced the participants "to the crowd of 700 to 800 people that dared threatening clouds and warning lightning for the expected storm of oratory indoors." By prior arrangement, Williamson was given 30 minutes for his opening statement, Francis allowed 45 minutes in response, and Williamson then given 15 minutes for rebuttal. In his initial remarks, Williamson accused Francis of falsely asserting that he (Williamson) supported a sales tax favored by Secretary of the Treasury Andrew Mellon. Williamson also claimed, among other things, that he was a friend of the farmer, that the present tariff law was "'the fairest tariff law the farmer ever had,'" and that it would be a mistake to "slash the tariff on industry." When it became his turn to speak, Francis "denied having said Williamson voted wrong on the sales tax, but said he had objected to his voting 'No' on the repeal of the automobile tax, and on an amendment which would have cut the tax for small corporations." He claimed the present tariff laws favored industry over agriculture, and he criticized Williamson's unwillingness to do anything to change them. As an example of this unfairness, Francis pointed out that the tariff on aluminum "was 55 percent while that on chickens was only 10 per cent." He also leveled other criticisms against Williamson, including the latter's refusal to support changing the tariff on feldspar and his failure to prevent removal of the Deadwood Assay office and the Rapid City land office. He devoted his last 10 minutes to "a declaration for world peace," where he urged adoption of universal conscription and "attacked the Williamson vote for the Italian debt settlement." That portion of Francis's talk "won loud applause" from the audience."[15]

In rebuttal, Williamson reasserted his charge that Case "had wrongly accused him on the sales tax." And he stated that he voted against the tax cuts because those tax revenues were necessary to pay for anticipated flood and farm relief; that the tariff had not raised the price on aluminum dishes; that the Deadwood Assay office was closed because its cost far exceeded its income; and that he "voted for the Italian debt settlement because some money was better than no money at all." Ten minutes after the debate ended, "a crack of lightning... put out the city lights for a few moments," and "a dash of drenching rain followed." Who won the debate? The reporter who covered it for the *Daily Journal* said: "Nobody knows. Case had more applause than Williamson. A certain percent of this was due to the fact that an oratorical attack is more stirring than a defense. How much that counted nobody knows." *The Daily Deadwood Pioneer-Times* agreed with that assessment. It remarked that "at the close of the debate sentiment was pretty evenly divided, and both men received their share of support in the discussions and arguments which followed."[16]

The primary election was held on Tuesday, May 22. That day was described as "ideal ... for farmers to be in the fields," and "a light rural vote was indicated and expected generally." By 11:00 p.m. that night, Williamson had a lead "of approximately 1,000 votes," although no returns were yet available from 13 counties in the district. The next day, Williamson's lead steadily increased, and Francis conceded victory to his opponent. At noon he wired the following message to Williamson: "'You are the Republican nominee for congress. Congratulations. Good wishes.'" And Williamson replied: "'Congratulations received. Thank you.'" When the final returns were officially compiled from the third district's 24 counties, it was clear that Williamson won a convincing victory. He carried 19 counties, and his vote total was 9,773. Francis, on the other hand, won five counties—Fall River, Harding, Shannon, Todd, and Washabaugh—and received a total of 6,148 votes.[17]

One week after the primary, an article appeared in the *Star* titled "I Mean, 'Thank You'." At the onset, it stated "this is not an editorial: it is just a personal word from Francis Case to his friends." The article frankly admitted that "we got licked" but added that the primary race "was a good fight," and "we have no alibis to offer and want none." It went on to note that "we knew we had a hard job when we started," but "we went out to win." After presenting the votes by county, the piece explained why they "were better in spots than expected ... and worse!" Next, Francis noted that "for myself, I have neither regrets nor pity over the outcome. I saw many friends and found many new ones. It is only for you, that I am concerned. I had the thrill of being in a good scrap; did you?" After reminding its readers of several important issues raised in the campaign, the article concluded: "Our fight was not for men but for certain principles and conditions.... And when the time comes again, --remember what I said in my speeches: 'I expect to be on the firing line for these things all my life. I love South Dakota and I am for my friends.'"[18]

In the fall, Francis went on "a week's speaking tour" for the entire Republican ticket. The general election was held on November 6. Candidate Williamson was reelected to his congressional seat over Democrat Arthur Watwood—his same opponent in the previous election. But this time, Williamson won by 7,833 votes—as compared to his 2,030-vote victory over Watwood in 1926. On that same day, the *Star* printed an editorial titled "Let's Get a New Primary Law." It argued that the present law "has destroyed party responsibility" and "costs the state literally hundreds of thousands of dollars."[19]

THE 1929 LEGISLATURE DID PASS a new primary law. It differed from the old law in several respects. One of the "sharpest differences" was that it eliminated proposalmen and all proposal meetings. Instead, it placed "'the nominations for office directly in the hands of the people themselves, at the primary election.'" That election was to be held on the first Tuesday in May in even-numbered years. Each candidate for office was required to file a nominating petition and agree "'to abide by the result of the primary election in regard to his candidacy.'" At that election, party nominations were to be "made for United States senator, representative in Congress, governor, and for all county and legislative offices." In addition, primary voters were to select three delegates to represent their county at the state convention, which would be held at Pierre on a date chosen by each party's central committee. At those conventions, the parties would "'nominate all the state officers except governor, adopt party platforms and elect a state chairman, national committeemen and other party officers.'" Moreover, if no candidate for U.S. senator, congressman, or governor received at least 35 percent of the vote in the primary, the party would choose that nominee at its state convention "'from among the candidates who were voted for at the primary election.'"[20]

On February 4, 1930, Francis announced he would not be a candidate for the third district congressional seat. He thanked his friends for volunteering to work for him in another campaign for Congress; and he explained that all his spare time "'during the past year has been given to promotion of the effort to "Find Oil—or Find Out," believing that the opening of her oil resources is the greatest good fortune in sight for South Dakota.... I am not out of politics because I am an American citizen—but this year the biggest thing in South Dakota is oil.'"²¹

As of 1930, South Dakota was divided into 69 county units. For purposes of "county administration and government," these units were further divided into either organized or unorganized counties. The organized counties (totaling 64) had "a full complement of elected county officials" who were tasked with administering "the affairs of local government." On the other hand, the unorganized counties (totaling five) were attached to an adjoining county "for judicial and other [governmental] purposes" and had "no county seats nor county organization." Those five unorganized counties, and the counties to which they were attached, were Armstrong—attached to Stanley; Shannon—attached to Fall River; Todd—attached to Tripp; Washabaugh—attached to Jackson; and Washington—attached to Pennington. All five "were included in the various Indian Reservations" located west of the Missouri River: Armstrong in the Cheyenne River Reservation; Todd in the Rosebud Reservation; and Shannon, Washabaugh, and Washington in the Pine Ridge Reservation.²²

In its April 25 issue, the *Argus-Leader* reported that, according to S. D. Attorney General M.Q. Sharpe, "persons living in unorganized counties cannot vote at the May 6 primary election." That ruling reaffirmed a previous one made in 1924, where the attorney general's office concluded that "the statutes relating to elections in unorganized counties did not authorize holding of a party primary or provide any machinery for such election." The next day, Francis protested Sharpe's decision as being "contrary to the practice of the 1924, 1926 and 1928 primaries, regardless of prior rulings" and "in disregard to the new primary law and to the session laws of 1923." And he said that he would "at once institute proceedings to preserve the hitherto recognized right of voters in . . . unorganized counties, to take part in the primary election and further to secure representation in the state party conventions."²³

Legal action soon followed. On April 28, Francis, and several others, represented by Clifford Wilson, secured a temporary writ of mandamus that required the Pennington County auditor to supply ballots and conduct a primary election in unorganized Washington County. The writ was made permanent on May 2, thereby ensuring that a Washington County primary would go forward. In addition, Francis joined others in a mandamus proceeding brought in Tripp County that sought to compel a primary election in unorganized Todd County. Although the judge there issued a temporary mandamus order earlier in the week, he refused to make the order permanent after conducting a hearing on May 3. Meanwhile, the Fall River County auditor announced that a primary election would be held in Shannon County regardless of the legal rulings, since he had already printed and partially distributed ballots there before the attorney general issued his late-April decision. And the Jackson County auditor decided to ignore Sharpe's ruling and to provide primary ballots to attached Washabaugh County.[24]

On May 6, three unorganized counties (Shannon, Washington, and Washabaugh) cast votes in the primary. With respect to the other two (Todd and Armstrong), the auditors in Tripp and Stanley counties chose not to provide ballots for an election in their attached counties. And shortly after the primary was held, the Jackson County auditor—who had furnished ballots for the Washabaugh County election—"decided not to count them out of deference to the attorney general's opinion[.]" On the other hand, the Shannon and Washington county primary votes were tallied, and the results were sent to the secretary of state in Pierre. But the state canvassing board, charged with totaling the returns "from the various county auditors," refused to count these votes because there was "some question" as to their "legality." So, despite Francis's efforts to ensure that unorganized counties be allowed to participate in the 1930 primary, no votes from any of the five unorganized counties were counted in that election.[25]

E. B. ADAMS, L. D. STONECYPHER, AND FRANCIS were the three delegates chosen to represent Fall River County at the Republican State Convention held in Pierre on May 20. Whereas all 64 organized counties in the state sent three delegates, the five unorganized counties did "not participate." As a member of the platform committee, Francis proposed a plank that addressed the unorganized-counties-voting-in-the-primary issue. It read:

> 'We believe that electors residing in the unorganized counties of the State deserve the right to participate fully in the primary elections. We welcome their fellowship in the Republican party, and if any change in the laws be needed to provide for their participation in all primary and general elections, we pledge the efforts of the party to secure the same.'

In the early afternoon, the convention delegates unanimously voted to include this plank, along with 13 others, in the party platform.[26]

Another task for the convention was to nominate a candidate for governor. Five gubernatorial hopefuls entered the May 6 primary election. Gladys Pyle, the current secretary of state, finished in first place, outdistancing her nearest rival by 1,610 votes and receiving 28.3 percent of all votes cast. But as noted above, the 1929 primary law required that if no party's candidate for governor received at least 35 percent of the total vote, the nomination for that office must be made at the party convention. Balloting for the governorship began at 1:40 p.m. Brooke Howell, who finished third in the primary contest, led the pack on four of the first six ballots. But Pyle (whom Francis supported) made steady gains and was in first place on seven roll call votes as the process continued into the afternoon. Finally, on the twelfth ballot, Howell withdrew from the race and threw his support to Warren Green. Green finished last in the May primary and was low man on the convention's first ballot. But he "gained some strength on each roll call," and with Howell's backing, he was nominated for governor on the twelfth ballot.²⁷

On November 4, Francis printed a statement in the *Weekly Star* that indicated his voting preferences for the general election held that day. He began by saying, "'I shall vote the entire Republican ticket, Tuesday except on attorney general.'" His statement went on to criticize Sharpe for disclosing the results of the latter's banking investigation just before the election, and Francis argued that doing so created "'suspicion and undermined public confidence in sound institutions.'" He added that Sharpe's ill-timed public disclosure was "'on a par with the misjudgment he displayed in ruling that unorganized counties could not take part in the primary campaign last spring although the new primary law was even more explicit in their favor than the old law under which they had participated for several years.'" He ended by declaring that "'I shall vote for Green for governor and Grigsby for attorney general.'"²⁸

Notwithstanding Francis's voting-preference statement, Sharpe was reelected as attorney general. Green won the governor's race over opponents D. A. McCullough (Democrat) and Helge Tangen (Independent); and Williamson defeated Democratic challenger Theodore B. Werner in the third congressional district contest.²⁹

In his inaugural address to the state legislature, given on January 6, 1931, newly elected Governor Green made several recommendations. One of them was that "our primary election law be amended so that provision is made whereby the legal electors in unorganized counties may participate in the state primary election." Later that month, Representative Clifford Wilson introduced a bill in the House that authorized "primary elections in unorganized counties." The bill passed in the House "without a dissenting vote," the Senate approved it on February 6, and the governor signed it into law three weeks later. Given these developments, the *Weekly Star* declared that "the fight to maintain the rights of electors in unorganized counties to participate in primary elections, begun by the Star last spring, has been won."[30]

AS A RESULT OF THE 1930 CENSUS, South Dakota lost one of its three representatives in Congress. In response, the state legislature passed a congressional reapportionment bill. It divided the state into two districts and made the Missouri River the dividing line between the two. Former districts one and two were now combined into a single District One (the East River district); and former District Three became District Two (the West River district). The reapportionment bill was sent to Governor Green on March 3, 1931, and he signed it into law three days later. This new law was slated to "be in effect during the 1932 political campaign."[31]

Francis played a limited role in that campaign. He did write a long editorial that enthusiastically supported Peter Norbeck in the primary election and printed it in both Custer newspapers; and he spoke at a program for Norbeck held in Rapid City the night before the May 3 primary (which Norbeck overwhelmingly won). In the fall, Francis was "the principal speaker" at a local rally sponsored by the Custer County Republican Committee and the Young Republican League. And on the eve of the November 8 general election, he joined Governor Green and others at the Hot Springs courthouse and spoke in favor of Green's economic policies.[32]

With one notable exception, the 1932 election was a disaster for the South Dakota Republican party. For the first time in the state's history, the Republicans lost every statewide office, including those of governor and attorney general. The Democrats also achieved "overwhelming control" in both houses of the state legislature. On the federal-office level, Democratic candidates ousted incumbent Republicans in both congressional contests, with Fred Hildebrandt winning the race against C. A. Christopherson in the first district and T. B. Werner beating William Williamson in the second district. U.S.

Senator Norbeck provided the one Republican bright spot, as he easily won reelection over four challengers. And finally, "Franklin D. Roosevelt carried the state by a record vote of 183,515, against 99,212 for President Hoover."[33]

ON JANUARY 16, 1934, OVER SIXTY Republican workers "from all parts of Custer County" met and chose five delegates to attend a statewide party rally in Pierre. That gathering—to be held on Lincoln's birthday (February 12)—was expected "to consider a platform and lay plans for the 1934 campaign." Two days after the Custer County meeting, Francis printed an article in the *Chronicle* titled "Timber for a State Platform." There he suggested seven "planks" for consideration at the upcoming Pierre gathering. Those planks consisted of pledges to support the following: a "homestead exemption up to $2,500 valuation for all taxes"; a "reorganization of local governmental units to reduce expenses"; the "abolition of the Occupation Tax on Residents"; sufficient "state aid to rural grade schools"; an "end to new names for old boards" and abolition of "expensive [political] machine offices"; the "abolition of the circle at the head of party columns on the ballot"; and "a State Civil Service code to protect state parks, charitable, penal and educational institutions from unwarranted disruption with a change of administrations."[34]

Over 500 Republicans, including Francis and five others from Custer County, gathered in Pierre on February 12 to seek "republican unification" and "to start the party on a comeback campaign." Although it was originally understood that a party platform would be drafted and candidates would be endorsed at this meeting, "informal conferences" decided the previous night that "no official action should be taken on these matters in advance of the May 1 primary." Accordingly, Francis's proposed seven-plank party platform was not considered. At the rally, several prominent Republican leaders gave rousing speeches, and a resolution was adopted that asked county organizations to get an early start on the 1934 campaign. And although no candidate endorsements were proposed, "considerable sentiment was exchanged on various candidacies" in the hotels and at the city auditorium where the conference was held.³⁵

Two days after the Pierre meeting, Francis formally declared that he was a candidate for "the Republican congressional nomination in the Second South Dakota District." In doing so, he stated, in part, that "'I have decided to be a candidate because of the opportunity a Representative has to work for all of Western South Dakota and because of the faith of friends which I shall do my best to justify.'" His announcement "was accompanied by a nine-point program which he said he would work for if nominated and elected."³⁶

After announcing his candidacy, Francis spent the next several weeks giving speeches at Republican gatherings. On March 23 he spoke at a county rally in Philip "sponsored by the Young Republicans of Haakon county." One night later, he told fifty Young Republicans assembled at Blue Bell Lodge that "there was a special field for the younger members of the party to perform in bringing to the problems of the new day the basic principles of Abraham Lincoln[.]" In mid-April, he appeared at a political meeting in Fort Pierre as "one of the four candidates" seeking the Republican nomination for Congress. There, he explained why he wanted to go to Washington, and he added that "'If you don't like what I say, what I stand for or what you hear about me, vote for one of the other three candidates for the nomination, but let's go out determined to score a smashing victory in November.'" Francis also gave mid-April speeches at Gregory, where he referred to present Democratic congressman Werner as a "'political racketeer,'" at a Lyman County Republican banquet in Kennebec (where rival candidates William Williamson and Dan McCutchen of Belle Fourche also appeared), and at the Murdonga club in Murdo, where he "delivered a very good address on community work[.]"³⁷

Francis also sought endorsements from fellow Republicans to include in his campaign literature and bolster his political profile. His brother Leland obtained a key endorsement from a well-known national figure—retired Major General Smedley D. Butler. Born in 1881 to Quaker parents, Butler "defied his pacifist lineage by joining the Marines just before his 17th birthday." He had a distinguished military career, receiving the Medal of Honor twice and three additional medals for valor. Given the nickname Old Gimlet Eye, he "was known for his leadership and commitment to the welfare of the men under his command." But by the time he retired from the Marines in 1931, he "had come to believe that war—in particular WWI—was really a profitable business for the few and at the expense of thousands of lives," and he "thought of himself as a cog in the imperialist war machine." After his retirement, he "spoke frankly and honestly about his experiences and opinions, and was very popular with the American public."[38]

General Butler's endorsement was garnered in an unusual, and somewhat serendipitous, manner. During the second week in April, Leland took a train from Chicago to Philadelphia to attend the American Academy of Political and Social Science sessions being held there. Butler lived in a Philadelphia suburb (Newton Square), and after conferring with "Smed's" former secretary, Leland decided to visit the suburb on Sunday morning with the hope of arranging an appointment with Butler. When he arrived at Newton Square, Leland went into a store looking for a newspaper, where "a man at the counter turned," and it was "the General himself." After brief introductions, Leland accompanied Butler, his servant's son, and his military companion on a drive to a doctor's office for treatment to the boy's injured hand. The group then returned to Butler's house. While he was in the car and later at the house, Leland explained Francis's views on war and peace, showed Butler a Case campaign circular, and invited the general to come to South Dakota and speak on Francis's behalf. Butler declined the speaking invitation due to prior commitments. But after Leland urged him to write "'something they can use in the newspapers,'" the general "scratched out" with "a stubby pencil" a detailed, enthusiastic endorsement. And he followed up by wiring and mailing messages to Francis that explained why he could not come to South Dakota and included his endorsement.[39]

Francis was delighted to receive Old Gimlet Eye's seal of approval, and he wasted no time making use of it. He printed the complete wired message in the *Chronicle* during the week before the primary election. He also included an excerpted quote in his primary campaign literature—"'Your whole life indicates clearly your preeminent fitness for public service in high office.'" And he employed another quote from the Butler endorsement in a *Daily Journal* political advertisement: "'I believe you have the courage to fight this gang of highwaymen to a finish and not by the shadow boxing methods only too prevalent all over the country.'"[40]

Francis made a "fast swing" in the district during the five days before the May 1 primary. It included spending "Thursday... in Rapid City; Friday in the northern hills; Saturday morning at Wasta; Saturday noon at Quinn; Saturday afternoon, Philip; and Saturday night, Winner." On Sunday, he returned to Rapid City and spoke "at a union young people's meeting at the Presbyterian church." Then on the day before the election, he attended rallies and gave speeches in four towns: Newell in the morning, Whitewood in the afternoon, and Custer and Hot Springs that night.[41]

The next day, South Dakota held its primary election. A total of 25,705 votes were spread among the four candidates seeking the Republican congressional nomination in the second district. The final vote count was William Williamson—7,780, Dan McCutchen—6,864, Francis Case—6,380, and Earl Hammerquist (from Farmingdale in Pennington County)—4,681. Although Williamson clearly won the primary, he did not receive 35 percent of the votes cast. So, in accordance with the 1929 primary law, the Republican candidate for that office would be chosen at the state party convention. On the Democratic side, incumbent congressman Theodore Werner easily won his primary for the Second District seat. He beat his single opponent—attorney John T. Milek from Sturgis—by more than a two-to-one margin and received almost 69 percent of the vote.⁴²

The Republican state convention was scheduled to be conducted "in the house chamber at the capitol" at Pierre on May 29. A few weeks before it was held, the Case campaign prepared a memorandum addressed "To the Delegates, Republican State Convention, Second Congressional District." That document, titled **THINK ABOUT NOVEMBER** in bold letters, contended that "the purpose of the 35 per cent law is to help a party by giving it a chance to deliberate and select a true majority candidate who can stand the blaze in a hard fight." It went on to argue, again using bold letters, that **"the supreme test of a candidate is how he runs where he is known best TOGETHER WITH the home counties of all his opponents."** Using the May 1 primary voting results, the memo demonstrated that when the votes for each candidate's home county were tabulated and compared to the votes the other candidates received in that county, Francis was the clear winner. To bolster the point, the memo then repeated the analysis using each candidate's "secondary" home county, and it added those results to that candidate's "home county" votes. Once again, Francis's vote totals were the highest. The memo went on to claim that "on any comparison, where all had the same show, Case stands out head and shoulders," and it concluded that **"Francis Case not only can win but will win."**⁴³

At 11:10 a.m. on May 29, the Republican State Convention was called to order. Soon thereafter, the convention chairman named the platform committee. That committee then met and prepared the party platform, which it submitted to the delegates in mid-afternoon. After "a few changes in wording and addition of a new plank," the convention adopted it. Consisting of 12 planks, the finalized platform was "one of the briefest prepared in recent years." Its "major points" advocated "a flexible tariff to aid agriculture and a revised state taxation system." The platform also recommended "Missouri river diversion for water supply, and development of navigation to reduce freight costs"; "better care for aged Indians, and general improvement of Indian conditions"; "creation of a state constabulary"; "support of 'our entire state educational system' within 'the limit of ... our means'"; cooperation with the federal government in developing an old-age pension program; and undertaking highway development administered "by a non-partisan commission."[44]

After the state platform was adopted, balloting for the second district congressional nomination began. In "order to obtain the district endorsement," the successful candidate needed to receive at least 14,417 votes. (Those votes were distributed among the second district delegates as follows: each county was entitled to send three delegates to the convention, and each delegate cast "the number of votes equal to one-third the number cast in his county at the last general election for the party candidate for governor.") On the first ballot, McCutchen led the pack with 8,994 votes. Francis was a close second, receiving 8,662, and Williamson was barely behind him at 8,572. Hammerquist was a distant fourth at 2,797. The second ballot saw Francis take the lead with 13,954 votes, McCutchen in second with 6,910, Williamson in third with 6,770, and Hammerquist last with 1,196. Finally, the third ballot put Francis well over the top. He garnered 19,423 votes to win the nomination by a comfortable margin. McCutchen stayed in second with 5,608, Williamson finished a distant third with 2,602, and Hammerquist remained in fourth with the same vote total he received in the second round—1,196.[45]

After stopping at Kadoka for Memorial Day, Francis returned to Custer on May 31. There he "issued a statement of appreciation for congratulations and pledges of support" he had received "from everywhere" and from each of the congressional candidates at Pierre. His statement also lauded "the spirit of public service shown by the delegates to the state convention," and he added that "he would make his fall campaign on the republican platform[.]" In separate remarks, Francis thanked the Custer County delegates and others from the county who worked for him during the convention and congratulated him on the outcome. He summed up their contribution by saying "'I was nominated primarily because of the way the home folks stood by me. The vote I got from you who knew me best was what convinced others.'"[46]

IN JUNE AND EARLY JULY, the *Chronicle* reprinted editorial comments from several of the state's newspapers. Those remarks typically congratulated Francis on his nomination victory and explained why he was a qualified and capable candidate. The article from the *Webster Reporter & Farmer*—written by its editor Harold Card—was clearly based on personal knowledge. It said in part:

> As a classmate of Case and later an associate with him on the Rapid City Journal, we believe we can say that we know him as well or better than most folks. He is energetic, able, progressive, fairminded, fearless and honest. These six adjectives cannot be applied to all candidates for office or office holders, but when as in this case they can it is a happy combination.

Other editors described Francis as "a strong candidate" who "will add strength to the republican ticket," a candidate who "is entitled to a high rating," and the candidate who "hit the high point of oratory and enthusiasm" at the convention and "will make a mighty fine congressman."[47]

Francis was encouraged by the support from his fellow newspaper editors. But as the July campaign continued, he observed that "our worst handicap is finances." Beginning in mid-July and continuing into mid-October, he made several written requests for financial help to the Republican National Committee in Washington, D. C. and to the Republican Congressional Committee in Chicago. None of these requests was honored. As a result, the Case campaign was not able to do the amount of political advertising it wanted to or to give financial assistance to the Young Republican Clubs in the second district.[48]

The state Republican campaign was "formally opened" on August 9 with an evening rally at the Lyman County Courthouse in Kennebec. Several Republican leaders—including State Party Chairman Charles S. McDonald, Francis, gubernatorial candidate W. C. Allen, former Attorney General M.Q. Sharpe, and others—gave speeches to a crowd of "approximately 250 persons." And Francis appeared in a variety of other venues during the remainder of August. On the 14th, he was "the headliner" at the golden jubilee celebration in Beresford—a small town located in the southeastern portion of the state. A week later, he attended a Republican political gathering in Mitchell—along with gubernatorial hopeful Allen, state chairman McDonald, and several other Republican candidates running in the fall election. Allen and Francis were together again on August 30, where they spoke at a rally held at the Rapid City municipal auditorium and were given standing ovations from the 2,000 people in attendance. The next day, both gave talks to a Republican rally held during the annual Jones County Fair at Murdo.[49]

On September 1, Francis addressed the Fifth District Farmers Union Convention in Sturgis. Two days later, he gave speeches at Labor Day celebrations in Quinn and Kadoka. By September 10, he had "been in every County since the nominating convention, speaking principally at Fairs, Picnics, etc."; and from that point forward he planned to be "in every County again [before the election] making more direct political speeches."[50]

In early October, Francis received word that his Democratic opponent had publicly challenged him to a debate "on the issues of the congressional campaign." Francis responded by writing a letter to Werner (printed in the *Rapid City Daily Journal*) that formally accepted the challenge and told Werner whom he could contact at Republican headquarters to arrange a time and place for the debate. Werner apparently never followed up on the matter, and no debate was held.[51]

On October 11, Francis addressed a capacity crowd at the community auditorium in Philip, where he gave "specific approval of parts of New Deal legislation and activities," but explained that he would "'be free to look for and guard against impractical or selfish features of [such] legislation[.]'" On that same night, the Pennington County Republican Committee chairman (Walter G. Miser) told a group of West River Republicans at a banquet in Rapid City that "$13,797.17 of South Dakota relief funds had gone to the Gate City Guide, weekly newspaper and printing shop owned by Congressman Theodore B. Werner[.]" Commenting on this allegation in an interview the next day, Werner "had nothing to say other than that the checks referred to were received for services rendered." Francis had a different response. In an evening speech at Edgemont, he informed an "attentive audience" of the situation and said that "politicians who talk about the money changers and point their fingers at somebody in Wall Street to hide their own pirating are the double dealers who undermine the best possibilities of the national recovery program. They betray the trust of their party and all people should unite to unload them."[52]

Francis's willingness to concede that some New Deal ideas were sound caught the attention of the *Daily Journal*. In an October 12 editorial titled "Campaign Funds," it posited that the Republican leaders' "task has been to differentiate between the 'New Deal' which represents the national hope and the 'New Deal' which represents the Democratic interpretations of that hope." It went on to observe that

> Francis Case, candidate for congress, has reduced the position of liberal Republicans in South Dakota to ten words which

adequately represents the feeling of a large proportion of thinking voters. Says Mr. Case: 'Keep the good in the New Deal; drop the bad.' Mr. Case has come very close to the kernel of the issue in this election.

Francis continued the approach described in the "Campaign Funds" article as the race entered its final stages.[53]

During the last six days before the election, he again teamed up with Allen to campaign together. On Halloween night, they made a joint appearance in Hot Springs. That rally was described as an "overflowing homecoming for Case and a welcome for Allen[.]" The two left town early the following morning and made stops at Pringle, Custer, and Hermosa before arriving in Rapid City around noon. There, they met a large car caravan, which escorted them to the Alex Johnson Hotel, where they gave talks at a luncheon held in their honor. That evening, both spoke "to a crowd that packed" the American Legion Hall in Belle Fourche. The next day, Allen and Francis called on Republican supporters in Spearfish and went to Philip "to keep a speaking engagement." Allen then "turn[ed] back eastward" to finish his campaign. Francis came back to Rapid City on November 3 to appear at a "Black Hills rally," where he was the principal speaker; and Leslie Jensen spoke on Allen's behalf at that event. Finally, on the night before the election, Francis closed his campaign with a speech at a Republican rally in Deadwood, whereas Allen made his "final pleas for votes" at Aberdeen—his home town.[54]

THE EARLY RETURNS FOR THE November 6 election indicated that Francis and Werner were in a "seesaw battle" for the second district congressional seat, as "the lead switched several times during the tabulation." But when the final returns were all counted, Werner won the election by 3,362 votes, having received 35,467 to Francis's 32,105. Out of the 24 counties in the district, Werner won 17 and

Francis won 7. And "with Werner's victory, the democrats recorded a clean sweep, naming the governor, congressman in the first district, and the entire state ticket." The gubernatorial and first congressional district races were not close, as the incumbent governor Tom Berry defeated William C. Allen by 52,751 votes (172,228 to 119,477), and incumbent congressman Fred H. Hildebrandt beat his challenger C.A. Christopherson by 38,102 votes (122,932 to 84,830). In sum, "no Republican won a single major election—the only time in the history of the state."[55]

Two days after the election, Francis issued a statement to the press about the outcome. He began by wishing Werner well in his work to bring New Deal benefits into the district. Next, he thanked the "'Republicans in Western South Dakota,'" who "'put up a real fight and lost the score but not the game.'" Then he asserted that "'our candidates were up against the buzz-saw. We inherited ill-will. We had to combat mistaken notions about our position and about relief. We had no campaign chest and the Democrats had a big one.'" And he ended on a hopeful note: "'This work must go on. America must find the way between the abuses of the old order and the excesses of the new—and will.'" After seeing Francis's post-election comments, Peter Norbeck reportedly said that "it was the best statement he ever read from a defeated candidate."[56]

Francis received many letters that congratulated him on a well-run campaign, lamented the results, and encouraged him to stay in politics. These included correspondence from Harold Card, who extended "hearty congratulations on the splendid race you made against Werner," and said that Francis had the "right to feel mighty proud . . . , particularly in comparison with the rest of the ticket." And Art Brown wrote that he "could hardly believe" Werner had won, that "the people of the West River country made a serious mistake," and that someday Francis "will be going to Congress and then some!" [57]

In answer to the many letters he received after the election, Francis printed a four-page response addressed to "Dear Friend." He began by repeating his post-election statement to the press cited above. He then emphasized that "the hardest part about losing is the thought of the friends who worked so loyally," and "I do thank you every one." Next, he expanded upon the points made in his prior press statement by providing a detailed analysis of the congressional race and the campaign in general. Then he included a sampling of suggestions from people who wanted to achieve more Republican success in the future. Francis ended by encouraging his followers to "think and talk citizenship and politics and good government freely"; and he advised them that "if this letter... stirs you to write me again, I'll boil the ideas that come, into a round robin and send them to the [county] chairmen over the state." Immediately after he read the "Dear Friend" letter, Leland wrote to his brother: "Your little pamphlet... is, in my opinion a gem. It salvages strengths, including morale, and keeps you at the helm so far as Republican opinion is concerned."[58]

IN A LETTER TO HIS BROTHER dated November 29, 1935, Francis discussed several topics, including the likely Republican candidates for president and vice-president in the 1936 election. Regarding his own political ambitions, he noted he was "receiving considerable encouragement and may throw my hat in again, if I can find any way out satisfying Myrle that it is the thing to do. I believe I will try it." Less than two months later, he wrote a detailed, five-page letter to his father on "the question of politics." There, he analyzed several issues, including how various Republican presidential hopefuls would fare in South Dakota and the likely Republican and Democratic candidates for governor and second district congressman. With respect to the governorship, he concluded Leslie Jensen would be a formidable candidate. And he added that "personally, I'd prefer to be governor than congressman—at least the next two years, and especially from this district." Considering the congressional seat, Francis remarked that he had "far more urging to run for congress this year than I had two years ago—but I also know that some good party members are hesitant to say anything." He noted that "Paul Martin announced a year ago—on a pro-Roosevelt ticket," that William Williamson and Leslie Jensen were possible "real candidates," and that "Jensen would be harder to beat than anyone else I can think of right now." Francis concluded his politics discussion by saying

> there is another issue which, whatever place I am, I'll bring in, whether congress or what not. And it concerns something that is the most important thing in public life as far as I am concerned. It is a constitutional amendment... to restore to the people the right to decide when we send troops abroad for war.... I think you know that since the war I have felt more deeply on the subject of war and peace than ever before—but even before that, I had said that the one goal of my life would be to do something to lessen the likelihood of war and to increase the likelihood of peace, especially in this hemisphere so that the European balance of power idea might not be set up to harass generations to come in this world.[59]

Shortly after Francis's January 19, 1936, letter to his dad, several Republicans made it known that they would join Paul Martin, Hot Springs attorney, in seeking the nomination for second-district congressman. And another prominent Republican decided to run for governor. William Williamson publicly entered the congressional race during the last week in January. On February 6, Francis announced he was a candidate for that office, as did Henry Jacobsen, a Butte County Commissioner from Castle Rock. That night, Leslie Jensen revealed he would seek the gubernatorial nomination. Four days later, Loyson G. Troth, a farmer and rancher in Lyman County and former state secretary of agriculture, entered the congressional contest. And finally, on February 18, Henry Atwater, mayor of Sturgis and "long time active republican," threw his hat into the congressional-candidate ring. The Republican field was now set—with six candidates running for the West River congressional seat and one vying for governor.[60]

Six days after he announced his candidacy, Francis issued a statement that outlined his campaign platform. Titled "'Our Job is to Re-Establish Opportunity as the Birthright of Every American,'" the document advocated establishing a publicity program for the state's natural resources; protecting "American markets for American workers at American prices"; providing "respectable old-age pensions, NOW—not when the victims of recent cruel years are dead"; continuing "relief work... while it is needed, and ALSO open the door to private employment"; achieving "international monetary stabilization"; and supplementing "national defense with the universal service act to make war involving America unprofitable for anyone, anywhere, anytime."[61]

Francis's platform also criticized the Roosevelt administration. It claimed that a "New Deal mistake is the idea that a political handout is an adequate substitute for a regular job and that a successful business is crooked." It also accused Democratic "opponents" of offering "more dizzy tunes, more vote-baiting, more waste, more political racketeering and ultimate autocracy." Finally, the statement ended by presenting a suggestion—and challenge—to Western South Dakota voters: "We, of all people, ought to see that the mission of America is to maintain the ideal of government as the servant of its citizens and not their taskmaster. Whatever districts of limited horizon may say, Western South Dakota will proclaim the spirit of an unbeaten, onward-looking people."[62]

Francis engaged in limited campaigning during March. The latter half of that month, he visited McLaughlin on the Standing Rock Reservation, where the local newspaper noted he had "many friends in this part of the country" who would support him in the primary. On March 27, he and fellow congressional candidate Paul Martin spoke to between 400 and 500 American Indians on the Pine Ridge Reservation. Martin talked about bank failures, the social security act, and pension plans; whereas Francis told the crowd it could benefit from dams, better roads, and wood from the Black Hills. He also "urged that each reservation elect one man who would be contact officer... who would keep posted on regulations and know the routine of making claims."[63]

The Case primary campaign ramped up its activity in April. In a speech given at Deadwood on the 2nd, Francis touted development of nonmetallic ores (feldspar and bentonite) and gold in the Black Hills; and he advocated creating a mining commissioner and establishing a U.S. Bureau of Mines station in the Hills. Four days later, he proposed a three-fold program "to ensure American neutrality and to keep the United States out of foreign wars." That program, presented on the 19th anniversary of America's entry into the World War, called for:

> 1. Adoption of the American Legion's Universal Draft Law to make capital and industry liable to conscription in case of war.
>
> 2. National defense under unified command 'strong enough to protect America from attack by land, sea or air.'
>
> 3. A constitutional amendment permitting a popular vote before the United States is committed to war 'on foreign soil.'[64]

On the same day that Francis announced the above "three-fold program," the South Dakota secretary of state's office "officially entered" ten Republicans and six Democrats for the "eight major political nominations" to be decided by the state's May 5 primary election. There was no intraparty contest for governor, as the Democratic incumbent Tom Berry sought a third term without party opposition, and Leslie Jensen was the only Republican to file a nominating petition. Because six men sought the Republican nomination for second district congressman, lots were drawn to determine the order they would appear on the primary ballot. Troth was chosen and therefore listed first. Lots for the remaining five were drawn in the following order: Martin, Williamson, Atwater, Jacobsen, and Case. Since there were a half dozen potential nominees, newspapers predicted that the "final decision in this republican contest probably rests with the party state convention as it is considered doubtful if any of the six candidates can poll the required 35 per cent of the total votes in the primary."[65]

A few days after appearing as the principal speaker at a Republican rally in Wasta, Francis made two speeches over WNAX radio in Yankton. The first, given on April 19 and titled "The Unknown Soldier Amendment," was described as "a non-partisan, non-political talk" and dealt "with the question of national defense and world peace." The next day, Francis returned to the studio and presented a speech on "The American Way Out." In that talk, he derided the New Deal spending policies as the "Red Ink Way," and he concluded that such policies thwarted ambition and resulted in government dependency. His answer to that approach was the "American Way Out," which he said was to "provide relief when and where it is needed without any strings attached" and to "encourage thrift, encourage industry, [and] encourage resources such as we have here in Western South Dakota[.]"[66]

After the Yankton radio talks, Francis made some political appearances on the Rosebud Reservation and was "enthusiastic over the outcome." He then returned to Custer to catch up on campaign correspondence and other matters. His final primary-campaign push began on April 27, when E. J. "Hook" Phares and he left town for a "swing to the northern part of the district." The next day he gave an address at Pierre on KGFX radio (content unknown). The following few days included campaign stops in Corson, Perkins, and Harding counties, and he ended the week with some "important meetings" in Lawrence and Pennington counties.[67]

At Francis's prior request and expense, newspapers in Rapid City, Lead, and Deadwood all ran the identical political ad in their May 2 editions. It was titled "For Congress," included a "head shot" photograph of Francis, and listed six short phrases that described "His Program." In addition, the May 2's *Rapid City Daily Journal* contained a full page devoted to political advertisements for both Republican and Democratic candidates seeking local, state, and national offices. The most prominent ad, "Inserted and Paid for by Rapid City Friends of Francis Case," cited facts to support its pitch that their candidate was "The Best Vote-Getter" and would be "The Best Congressman." The three papers also ran the following ad at Francis's request and payment: "**Case for Congress**—Last in order on the ballot but first choice for the job. Mark your ballot for Francis Case for Congress." This ad appeared in the *Daily Journal* and *Daily Call*'s May 4 editions, whereas the *Pioneer-Times* inserted it on May 5: primary-election day.[68]

Francis scored a resounding victory in the primary. He received 10,104 votes out of 25,605 cast—giving him 39.5 percent of the vote and thereby achieving the nomination without having to seek it at the Republican convention. The other five candidates' order of finish and their vote totals were Williamson, 6,048; Atwater, 4,272; Martin 2,264; Troth, 1,507; and Jacobsen, 1,410. Out of the 20 organized counties, Francis won 16, Williamson 2 (Jackson and Ziebach), Atwater 1 (Meade), and Jacobsen 1 (Butte). Francis also won all 5 unorganized counties except Armstrong, which did not participate in the primary. On the Democratic side, Werner easily defeated John T. Milek—a candidate he had beaten in the two previous primaries. Werner received 71.3 per cent of the 16,544 votes cast and won every county except Haakon.[69]

Francis received many letters that congratulated him on his victory. They came from his relatives, friends, and those involved in his campaign. His immediate reactions to the victory were set forth in the *Chronicle*'s May 7 edition. There, in separate articles, he thanked his supporters in Custer County for their vote, the *Chronicle* staff for regularly getting the paper out while he was away campaigning, and the editors of other South Dakota newspapers for their "generous" comments on "the recent congressional primary election."[70]

ON JUNE 1, THE "PARTY'S CANDIDATES for the four major offices"—Jensen, governor; Chandler Gurney, Sioux Falls, U.S. senator (elected in the primary over one opponent); Karl Mundt, Madison, first district congressman (unopposed in the primary); and Francis—came to Pierre on the eve of the Republican state convention. There, they met with other party members in "preliminary conferences" and "aided in platform deliberations." During those talks, the 15-member platform committee considered "300 suggested planks and topics for planks."[71]

The next day, about 300 Republicans attended the convention in the capitol's house chamber. In addition to nominating the nine candidates for state positions below governor, the delegates elected Harlan Bushfield (from Miller) as state party chairman and Harvey Jewett, Jr. (from Aberdeen) as national committeeman. They also adopted the party platform, which had been pared down to 22 planks but still contained "several thousand words." Among other things, it included farm planks that called for a tariff to protect American commodities from foreign competition, lower interest rates on farm loans, government research to increase the market for farm products, and the elimination of politics in federal farm financing. Other planks advocated adequate federal government relief to be locally administered "independent of politics," elimination of politics from educational institutions, support for the state's "Indian population," and balanced federal and state budgets. The platform also recognized the "right of employees to self-organization," it favored federal laws that aided "aged citizens" and "others physically disabled," and it advocated legislation that would make it mandatory "to conscript wealth as well as man power in time of war" and "regulate the munitions industry." Finally, it pledged to reduce state taxes, recommended "fair trade legislation and enforcement of anti-trust laws," and favored eliminating the state highway commission and substituting "a qualified engineer" in its place. The *Journal* reported that during the convention, Francis was a "hard worker" who "aided in platform work and in general activities, helping to align party facilities for the fall campaign[.]"[72]

The Republican National Convention was held in Cleveland, Ohio, from June 9 through 12. On the night of June 11, the delegates nominated Alfred M. Landon, governor of Kansas, as their presidential candidate for 1936. The next day, Colonel Frank Knox, publisher of the *Chicago Daily News* in Illinois, was chosen as the vice-presidential nominee. The national ticket was now set and ready to begin "a mighty drive to unseat the new deal."[73]

During the latter part of June, Francis spoke at an Old Settlers picnic in Corson County. He also "drove over parts of 15 counties west of the Missouri River" and "saw 900 miles of dry weather and its results." On June 26, he came back to Pierre. In a brief speech made there, he described the "drouth" (or drought) conditions in the West River counties and proclaimed they were "as bad as anyone has said." Three days later, he met with fellow candidates Jensen, Mundt, and Gurney and state party chairman Bushfield in Huron, where the group devised a program "to provide relief for immediate needs in the drouth situation, and to reduce the effects of dry seasons in the future." All five meeting participants signed a written statement that explained the program in detail, and all five pledged to support it.[74]

On July 18, Francis attended the Annual Farm Picnic at Newell. The program included an address by Congressman Werner, acrobatic exhibitions, a magician's act, a baseball game, 4-H club presentations, a "horseshoe pitching contest, children's contests, a dance and tours about the farm." Before he went to this event, Francis had been assured that the gathering was "nonpolitical." Nevertheless, during his

If At First You Aren't Elected, Try, Try Again

speech, Werner repeatedly referred to his "opponents" and "devoted several minutes to a direct personal attack" on Francis. Two days later, Francis issued a public challenge to debate Werner at "one or several points in the district." When asked if he would accept the challenge, Werner replied: "'I'm not concerned in his candidacy and refuse to engage in school boy methods... I am attempting to serve my constituents and haven't time to engage in a debate with Case at any time during my campaign.'" After he learned about this response, Francis said: "'Werner's refusal to debate was expected. He throws his rocks and runs: That isn't even good schoolboy stuff.... The voters will pass their own verdict on a candidate who fights sham battles with imaginary issues and false statements.'"[75]

As he did during the 1934 congressional campaign, Francis made a written appeal for financial support to Chester Bolton, Chairman of the Republican Congressional Committee. He also wrote to Carl Bachman, chairman of that committee's western division, wherein he stated that "all we need is enough funds to get our message to the people and we can win this district." And Harvey Jewett, Jr., South Dakota's member of the Republican National Committee, supported Francis's efforts to obtain national committee campaign funds. Unlike in 1934, these appeals were successful, as Francis subsequently received a $1,000 contribution from the national congressional committee. He donated half of that amount to the Republican state committee.[76]

MARY, HERBERT, AND CAROL CASE came out to the Black Hills some time during the summer of 1936. In early September, Carol and one of her friends were "rusticating" in "the shack" outside of Custer—most likely the cabin Carol had built on her "Dusty" mining claim in 1933. Herbert suddenly arrived and told her that Francis needed someone to come to his office "that day" to "take care of his campaign correspondence." Carol "came right in," and she worked for her brother for the remainder of the campaign. She began by typing letters that he wrote, but soon she was sending out literature and answering correspondence on his behalf. She also did some separate campaigning on her own in letters to her friends that asked for their vote. And she kept Francis apprised of the Custer campaign operation while he was on the road.[77]

On Sunday afternoon, September 6, about 300 people gathered in Hot Springs' Kidney Springs Park for an open-air meeting of the town's Townsend Old Age Pension Club. The high school band began the program with a 30-minute concert. Then John Mueller, Sr., the band leader's father, made some brief comments. Next, Paul Martin, the club's president (who opposed Francis in the 1936 primary) introduced Francis as the featured speaker. During his talk, he said: "I am for and will actively support old age pension legislation based on a sales or transaction tax... that will bring now and not delay deserved independence and freedom from worry to our aged people and help to restore opportunity to youth." He also acknowledged "the great contribution Dr. Townsend has made" regarding proposed old age pension legislation. But he disagreed with Townsend's recent demand to set the minimum pension payment at $200 a month, arguing that "it would be better to start at a figure that will provide security yet which we are sure can be paid and build that up as times improve." He ended his remarks by assuring the crowd that "when the cause of old age pensions needs a friend, I'll be on the job[.]"[78]

During the next week, General Smedley Butler was in Denver, where he attended and spoke at the Veterans of Foreign Wars' national convention. Friends had persuaded him to visit and make appearances in "the Black Hills and the Rosebud country" on his return trip east, and Francis greeted him when he arrived in Hot Springs on Sunday morning, September 20. After Butler paid "his respects to comrades at Battle Mountain Sanitarium and the State Soldiers home," he, Francis, and others toured the Black Hills. That trip included stops at Legion

Lake, the Needles, and Mount Rushmore. The tour ended when the group reached Rapid City in the afternoon.[79]

That evening, "Old Gimlet Eye" was the guest of honor at an informal dinner held in the Alex Johnson Hotel. Several veterans and others were present. Serving as toastmaster, Francis introduced Butler and "told something of his background and record." The general responded by recalling several of his war-time experiences in China, France, and Haiti. The dinner guests and other ex-servicemen then escorted Butler to the municipal auditorium, where over 1,500 people were gathered to hear him speak. His address, titled "American Ideals," stressed that "'Americanism is staying at home and minding our own business.'" He added that "'there may be an opportunity soon to practice that doctrine,'" because another world war will inevitably occur "'just as soon as Hitler has enough trained reserves.'" Butler's speech was well received, and the crowd frequently interrupted him with applause.[80]

The next day, Butler and Francis travelled to Winner, where they attended a Case-for-Congress rally that evening. Addressing a large crowd, the general gave "an emphatic endorsement" of Francis's candidacy, noting that "the Custer publisher would stand on his own feet and fight for the things he believed right." He also remarked that "'If you send a lot of worms to Congress, someone is bound to walk on them. They won't step on Case.'" During his speech, Francis concentrated mostly on explaining his proposed "Unknown Soldier" amendment. Sometime after the Winner rally, the Case campaign prepared a four-page brochure that highlighted the connection between Butler and Case on war-and-peace issues. It contained an expanded version of the article about Butler's Black Hills/Winner visit that appeared in the *Chronicle*'s September 24 issue; a summary of Francis's current program on war and peace; Butler's endorsement given to Francis in 1934; and the proposed "Unknown Soldier" amendment with an accompanying explanation of its scope and purpose.[81]

FRANCIS'S CAMPAIGN IN OCTOBER CONCENTRATED on two main activities—giving talks over the radio and speaking at Republican rallies held throughout the district. His radio presentations began at station KFYR in Bismarck, North Dakota, where he spoke in the morning and early afternoon on October 5. In the first talk, he posited that there are two kinds of congressmen in Washington—representatives and rubber stamps—and Werner fell into the latter category. He described his opponent as an "order-taker," a "servant of the bosses higher up," and a mere "clerk"; and he gave several specific examples of how Werner handled various political issues versus how a "true representative" would have dealt with them. It is not known what topic Francis discussed during his afternoon speech.[82]

In mid-October, Francis gave four speeches over WNAX radio—two on the 13th and two on the 14th. In the first, made in the afternoon, he reviewed the state's political and economic history, pointed out abuses in New Deal programs, and stated that Gurney, Jensen, Mundt and he wanted "to make this a good young man's country again." That evening, he reviewed Werner's voting record in Congress after making clear that his review "will have nothing to do with personalities, but will be strictly and solely items from the record of congressional voting as compiled by the research bureau of the Republican congressional campaign committee." Early the next day, Francis's topic was "You and the Next War." There he expounded on the horrors of war, lamented that "another world war is in the making," and noted that he stood for adequate national defense, universal service, strict limitations on American munition sales, and adoption of the "Unknown Soldier" amendment. His final radio speech at Yankton, given in the early afternoon, was on the subject "America and Me." In that talk, he criticized the current New Deal administration and pointed out its similarities to "the feudal system, centuries ago." He then explained how the Republican platform and Republican candidates proposed to support the American farmer.[83]

Francis returned to KFYR Bismarck to give two more radio speeches on October 26—one in the morning and the other in the early afternoon. It also appears that he gave a final talk over KGFX at Pierre two days later. One of the speeches presented at Bismarck was titled "The End of the Road in One-Man Government." It was basically an expanded version of the you-and-the-next-war talk given at Yankton on the 14th. In the only other speech located, most likely given at Bismarck, he spoke "about the smoke screen that the desperate New Dealers are trying to raise in a final effort to save themselves in South Dakota." He then summarized many of the proposals that were included in his formal campaign announcement, in the Republican Party platform, and in his previous campaign speeches.[84]

The second major campaign activity—appearing at rallies and giving speeches—became more frequent in October. On the same day he made the radio speeches in Bismarck on the 5th, Francis gave a talk in Dupree—the Ziebach County seat situated on the Cheyenne River Reservation. The next morning, he spoke at Little Eagle on the Standing Rock Reservation. Six days later, he campaigned at St. Francis on the Rosebud Reservation. Shortly after his radio presentations in Yankton, he made four campaign stops on October 16—two in Gregory County, one in Tripp County, and one in Jackson County. The following day, he visited a small town in Mellette County and four villages on the Rosebud Reservation. In those speeches, Francis typically emphasized selected points made in his radio addresses and presumably discussed his proposals to help the American Indians when he spoke to them.[85]

Francis returned to the Black Hills for speaking engagements during the next week. On the night of October 20, Jensen and he headlined a Lawrence County Republican rally at Deadwood, where Francis criticized the acting U.S. Postmaster General William Howes for campaigning on Werner's behalf, despite "'regulations forbidding political activity by people in the postal service.'" He repeated that criticism two nights later at a Republican gathering in Creighton—a small community in northeastern Pennington County. The next evening, in a speech at Hot Springs, he called for the "'setting up of different standards for government.'" He concluded his October speaking campaign with three appearances on the Cheyenne River Reservation—Isabel on the 26th (after the Bismarck radio talks), and La Plant and the Cheyenne Agency on the 27th; and one in the Black Hills—Custer on the 30th.[86]

In the final countdown prior to the election, Francis's campaign ran political advertising that appeared in several West River newspapers. For example, an ad proclaiming that he was "The Right Man for Congress," and featuring several quotes from his campaign, was published in the *Isabel News* on October 30. That same ad appeared the next day in the *Lead Daily Call, Deadwood Pioneer-Times,* and *Black Hills Weekly*. The *Rapid City Daily Journal* published it on November 2, and the *Burke Gazette* did so on an unknown date. In addition, the *Daily Journal* ran two large ads paid for by the Young Republican Congressional Campaign Committee. The first one, appearing in the paper's October 31 edition, pictured Francis shaking hands with Smedley Butler and contained the text of Francis's end-of-the-road speech given at Bismarck five days earlier. The second ad was printed in the November 2 edition. It contained copies of relief checks that were issued to Werner's newspaper and printing shop in late 1933, and it claimed that Werner violated federal regulations that provided a congressman "shall not profit or benefit... from business with the government[.]"[87]

On the day before the election, Francis made two last-minute campaign appearances. At noon, Gladys Pyle and he attended a rally in Spearfish, where he stated he would "'vote to repeal the present so-called security act, with its tax on wages, and to substitute a pay-as-you-go true old age pension that would begin at once.'" That evening, Samuel McKelvie, former governor of Nebraska, and Francis addressed "about a two-thirds full republican house" at Rapid City's municipal auditorium. After months of strenuous campaigning, his political fate was now up to the voters.[88]

THE VOTERS DID NOT DISAPPOINT. They elected Francis in a close race. Out of 67,361 total votes cast, he received 34,812 to Werner's 32,549—giving him a 2,263-vote margin of victory. Francis carried 14 counties to Werner's 10. So, he won the election with 51.7 percent of the vote. In other races, Chandler Gurney lost the U.S. senate race to W. J. Bulow 135,461 to 141,509 (and Independent Arthur Bennett garnered 12,816 votes); F. H. Hildebrandt prevailed over Karl Mundt for first district congressman 110,829 to 108,259; and Leslie Jensen won the governorship by beating Tom Berry 151,659 to 142,255.[89]

On a nationwide basis, the 1936 election was a debacle for the Republican Party. Contrary to the *Literary Digest*'s flawed polling results that predicted Landon would win the presidency (*see* Chapter 7, note 40), Franklin Roosevelt was reelected in a historic landslide. He received 27,476,673 votes out of the 45,357,120 total cast, giving him 60.6 percent of the popular vote. Out of the 48 United States, he won 46, with Landon winning only Maine and Vermont. That translated into 523 votes in the Electoral College for Roosevelt and eight for his opponent. In South Dakota, FDR won 54 percent of the 296,452 votes cast. The Republicans lost 15 seats in the 435-seat U.S. House of Representatives, reducing their total there from 103 to 88 members. Francis was one of only two Republicans in the country to defeat an incumbent Democratic congressman (the other was from the 13th District in Ohio). In the U.S. Senate, the Republicans lost nine seats, reducing their numbers from 25 to 16. Finally, with respect to governorships, the GOP could take some small comfort in the fact that at least it did not lose more ground. Only eight states had Republican governors after the 1934 election. Aided by Les Jensen's win—they kept that same number in 1936.⁹⁰

Francis received many congratulatory letters on his victory. They came from a variety of sources, including E. B. Adams (written with confidence four days before the election), Walter Travis (Western Director of the state Republican Service League and Treasurer of the Young Republican Congressional Campaign Committee), M.Q. Sharpe (who Francis had publicly opposed for state attorney general in the 1930 election), Chet Leedom (whose support Francis unsuccessfully sought in the 1928 congressional primary election), John Milek (Werner's opponent in the 1932, 1934, and 1936 Democratic primaries), Karl Mundt, O. W. Coursey, James Blue Bird (Chairman of the Native American Church of South Dakota), Leland, Chester Bolton, and several others.⁹¹

Shortly after the election outcome was determined, both Francis and Werner thanked their supporters in their respective newspapers. In the *Chronicle*'s November 5 edition, Francis wrote that he was "deeply indebted to those... for their loyalty and encouragement thru the steps that have led to this point." On that same day, an article titled "Congressman Werner's Statement" appeared in the *Gate City Guide*. There, Werner thanked "the friends who stood by me" and stated: "I fought the best fight that I knew, and I have the approbation of my own conscience in the fact that every blow I dealt in this campaign was clean and above the belt." His statement did not congratulate Francis on winning the election.⁹²

Francis also sent several telegrams to people who had provided important help in his campaign. On November 4, he wired this message to Leland: "Apparently they fell for whatever it was. Thanks your help." The next day, additional telegrams, with brief messages, were wired to Harry Kehm, Chairman of the South Dakota Republican Service League: "Your organization clicked especially Travis Sincerest thanks"; to Harlan Bushfield, Republican State Chairman: "Sincerest thanks for your counsel courage cooperation and hard work"; to General Smedley D. Butler: "You tamed the Rosebud and we won"; and to Governor Les Jensen: "You are a great old fullback More power to you." In the weeks that followed, Francis wrote several letters to those who worked for his election to Congress. And after working almost three months in his office, Carol began her return trip to Chicago in late November, with an interim stop at the Case home in Mankato.[93]

Apart from receiving and producing a significant volume of post-election correspondence, Francis travelled to several out-of-town gatherings in November. During the week after the election, he went to a meeting at Brookings, where county authorities "from over the state" talked about the farm program they desired for 1937. He also met with the Livestock Protection Association in Rapid City. On November 16, he, Myrle, Jane, and family dog Woof took a four-day trip to Denver, where Francis visited the regional forest service headquarters to discuss the Civilian Conservation Corps (CCC) and federal highway programs. The next week he investigated the Belle Fourche irrigation project's additional water needs by attending the district directors quarterly meeting at Newell and inspecting the nearby Orman Dam and surrounding area.[94]

IN ADDITION TO TAKING CARE of her daughter, Myrle participated in two local activities before the family left for Washington. On November 12, she served as one of five judges in a Custer High School declamatory contest that featured oratorical, dramatic, and poetry sections. One contestant was chosen from each section to represent the school in the district contest held at Hot Springs the next week. There, each Custer winner competed against students from six other West River schools, and each won third place in her or his respective section. Two weeks after returning from the Denver trip with her family, Myrle attended the American Association of University Women's

December meeting at Mrs. Hobart Gates's house, where she presented reviews of two books that studied mental hygiene.⁹⁵

With respect to his newspaper operations, Francis made up his mind in October that he would sell *The Hill City News* "if a proper sale could be arranged." Following the election, he received letters of interest from potential buyers and conducted negotiations with Waldon Lee, a Haakon County employee from Philip. Lee ultimately agreed to buy the paper, the sale was finalized on November 28, and it was publicly announced six days later. As for the *Chronicle*, Francis decided that while he was away in Washington, the paper would retain its current, six-member staff; and that Carl Sundstrom, whom his boss described as "the young man who ha[s] been very loyal and faithful," would act as foreman and general manager.⁹⁶

On the night before his fortieth birthday, the Custer Commercial Club held a "public birthday reception" for Francis. Several friends and admirers from Custer, its surrounding community, and Rapid City attended. The program featured music from the high school band and songs by the boy's glee club, a female soloist, and the Wind Cave CCC quartet. Then Custer's mayor Eric Heidepriem and representatives from "various civic groups" gave "generous tributes" to Francis, who responded by expressing his appreciation for the event and stating "it was his desire to render 'a service as American and non-partisan as the crowd is here tonight.'"⁹⁷

Two days later, on December 10, Francis, Myrle, and Jane (and apparently Woof) left Custer by car to begin their journey to Washington, D. C. When they arrived in Rapid City, Myrle and Jane got on a train to Mitchell, whereas Francis met that night with a group from Rapid City and Hill City to discuss "water conservation in the area." The next day he drove to Wanblee (in Jackson County) and talked about American Indian problems with members of the Pine Ridge and Rosebud reservations. After spending that night in Philip, he travelled north to Eagle Butte (on the border between Ziebach and

Dewey counties) to confer "with Indians from the Cheyenne River and Lower Standing Rock reservations on conditions there." The Case family reunited at Mitchell on the 14th and then drove to Mankato to see Francis's parents. After arriving, they also visited Esther and Raymond Sunderman near Le Sueur, who by that time had added two children to their family: Dale Llywellyn, born on January 6, 1933; and Marilyn Claire, born on December 11, 1935. Concluding their Minnesota visit, the east-bound travelers left for Chicago.[98]

In late November, Leland began planning a banquet to honor Francis when he passed through Chicago. That event took place at the Georgian Hotel in Evanston on the night of December 18. About 75 guests attended, including Leland, Carol, and "other relatives"; former professors Dr. Ernest H. Hahne, Dr. William D. Schermerhorn, and others; and people with present or past ties to Custer or Rapid City. Former Illinois Attorney General Oscar Carlson served as toastmaster, and Fred Sargent, president of the Chicago and Northwestern Railroad, gave the "principal talk." For entertainment, radio singer Robert Morris, son of Reverend and Mrs. Clay Morris of Hot Springs, "appeared in cowboy costume" and "sang two songs that nearly made all South Dakotans homesick." Dr. Hahne introduced Francis, gave him a gigantic fish hook as "the proper implement for work in Washington," and "recalled Case's victory in a national oratorical contest when a student at Dakota Wesleyan[.]" Francis responded with a speech explaining how he won the election, and he "punctuated his discussion of campaign tactics by giving credit to several former professors who were present."[99]

After leaving Chicago, the Cases ran into icy roads east of Fort Wayne, Indiana, turned south to Marietta, Ohio, crossed the Ohio River into West Virginia, and experienced considerable snow until they got over the Allegheny Mountains. Late one night near the end of their trip, Francis picked up a newspaper at a gas station and learned that Senator Norbeck had died. After the family reached Washington,

Francis sent a telegram to Mrs. Norbeck. It said: "'The Senator's love and devoted work for South Dakota is a subject of universal comment here.'"[100]

When the Case family got to Washington on or about December 21, they moved into a furnished apartment that had been "rented by correspondence." They soon decided it did not suit their needs, went house hunting, and located a furnished house for rent in nearby Arlington, Virginia, before the congressional term began on January 3.[101]

Meanwhile, back in South Dakota, an important event occurred in Carol's life. Sometime after she attended the banquet for Francis in Evanston, she travelled back to the Black Hills. And on the day after Christmas, she married Bertin Goddard, a 40-year-old, divorced lawyer who practiced law in Hot Springs and had served as Fall River County judge from 1930 to 1935. Her sister Joyce, a justice of the peace, officiated the marriage in Hot Springs.[102]

While they were still living in the apartment, Francis parked his car overnight on Rhode Island Avenue. On December 30, he received a "traffic violation notice ... for parking between 2:00 and 8:00 a.m. at 1400 Rhode Island Avenue NW." On January 2, he sent a letter to the Inspector in Charge of Traffic at the Metropolitan Police Department. That letter enclosed the traffic ticket and the following "statement of facts."

> I have been in the city about a week or ten days and have been living at the Miramar Apartments. I had parked the car at approximately the same spot for four or five nights on the suggestion of some one there in the lobby who said that the 'No parking between 2:00 and 8:00 a.m.' was a snow regulation, so if snow was on the ground it could be cleared. As you know there has been no snow and other carswere parking there, so I assumed it was all right,—Nothing to the contrary being said until I received this notice.

Francis followed the above explanation with this request: "In view of the fact it was a misunderstanding of the regulations and since the offense will not be repeated, . . . [is it] possible that this matter may be waived for a new person out of the state. Whatever your disposition in the matter is, it will be cheerfully accepted."[103]

On the day before Congress convened and Francis was sworn in, the traffic inspector acknowledged receipt of the letter, summarized the violation, and stated, "You are advised that this traffic violation notice will be cancelled and you can therefore consider the incident closed." Francis's approach to his traffic-ticket situation was simple but effective: he set forth the facts in a clear and straightforward way, provided persuasive reasons why the offense could be waived, but agreed to "cheerfully" accept the traffic department's decision in the matter. A similar approach would serve him well in handling the vastly more important and complicated issues he would face during his long and consequential career in Congress.[104]

EPILOGUE

Francis went on to serve seven terms in the U.S. House of Representatives. The voters continued to reelect him by wide margins. In 1938, he faced a familiar opponent: former Congressman Werner. Francis easily prevailed in that election, garnering 61.4 percent of the vote (41,335 to 25,932). He won all the second district's 24 counties. Werner did not run against him again. The 1938 election also produced two additional Republican victories for federal office, as Chan Gurney was elected to the U.S. Senate and Karl Mundt won the first-district House seat.[1]

Francis won five House elections in the 1940s by even greater margins than in 1938. In 1940, he received 66.1 percent of the vote, followed by 71.8 percent in 1942, 69.0 percent in 1944, 73.6 percent in 1946, and 65.9 percent in 1948. Between 1938 and 1948, his six-election-average portion of the vote was 68 percent, and he never faced a primary challenge for his party's nomination in any of those six contests.[2]

Four months after Francis took his seat in Congress, he applied for a commission in the U.S. Marine Corps Reserve. His application was accepted, and he became a captain in the Reserve in May 1937. He requested that he be assigned to active duty a few months before the United States entered World War II, on the day Congress declared war (December 8, 1941), and again in July 1942. The Marine Corps

Commandant responded by telling Francis that his requests were "very gratifying to me but I have always felt that the services you are rendering as a Member of Congress are of far greater importance to the war effort than a tour of active duty in the Marine Corps would be[.]" In April 1947, after "having attained the age of fifty," Francis was transferred to the Marines Honorary Retired List. One month later, he was temporarily promoted to major, and that promotion became permanent in November. He remained on the Honorary Retired List until at least 1951, and he proudly supported the Marine Corps for the rest of his life.³

Work on Mount Rushmore continued during the early years of Francis's tenure in Congress. Lincoln's head was dedicated on September 17, 1937, and Roosevelt's on July 2, 1939. Gutzon Borglum died on March 6, 1941, when the monument was almost completed. It was left to his son Lincoln to finish the work, which he did during the summer and early fall of that year. Francis continued to be a "Rushmore enthusiast" who was "dedicated to the cause." In 1937, he cooperated with the National Park Service "in securing a $50,000 appropriation" for the project. The following year, he helped ensure House passage of a bill that, among other things, authorized a $300,000 appropriation for the monument's completion.⁴

During Francis's first term in Congress, he served on four committees: Mines and Mining, Indian Affairs, Claims, and Irrigation and Reclamation. At the beginning of his second term, he was assigned to "'the powerful Appropriations Committee'"—a position he retained during the entire time he was a House member. Service on that committee was "exclusive" when the appointment was made, so he had to give up his previous committee assignments. The Appropriations Committee named for 1939-40 included 15 Republicans and 25 Democrats. The Committee's basic purpose was to rule on "all bills that appropriate money except those for private claims or pensions." It typically met once a week "to receive bills which are worked up by its subcommittees following days or weeks of hearings." Francis served on two of those subcommittees: Independent Offices Appropriations and War Department Appropriations. The former prepared the bills for "between 40 and 50 Independent agencies of the government." The latter formulated two bills—the Civil Functions Bill, which involved "the work of the Army Engineers in Flood Control and Rivers and Harbor improvements," and "the regular bill for the Military Establishment." Serving on the Appropriations Committee gave Francis "more leverage with executive departments," and it put him "in a better position to work for the funding of projects for South Dakota."[5]

ON APRIL 6, 1945, FRANCIS ATTENDED the dedication of a new Veteran's Facility at Fort Meade near Sturgis, South Dakota. He played a major role in converting that old military post into a modern, 720-bed neuro-psychiatric hospital. The next day, his and Myrle's son (Francis, Jr.) was born in Rapid City. On April 10, the baby exhibited "a very rare condition and trouble." Francis, accompanied by a nurse, decided to take his newborn on a train to Rochester, Minnesota, for "a special examination and possible emergency operation." But before they arrived there, the baby died in the morning on April 11. In his newsletter written in late April, Francis described that tragic event and said: "It is impossible for me to express fully what the sympathy and thoughtful kindnesses of friends have meant to Mrs. Case, Jane and myself in this time. We have learned something of the kinship with others that comes from sorrow."[6]

In June, the seven-member House Subcommittee on War Department Appropriations planned a special mission to "review financing of... [the United States'] overseas operations," and to "study ways to expedite return of soldiers from overseas." That mission began on August 16—the day after Japan "announced its intention to surrender" and thus bring the Second World War to an end. Over the next 38 days, Francis and his six fellow congressmen covered 36,300 miles in a C-54 cargo plane. They visited over 60 military installations in Hawaii, Australia, the Pacific Islands, Egypt, Iran, India, China, Italy, Germany, France, and England before returning to Washington on September 23. Francis and George Mahon, a Democrat from Texas and subcommittee member, drafted a report based on the congressmen's studies and observations made during their "round-the-world trip." That report was presented to President Truman at the White House on October 1. Among its conclusions and recommendations were that "the world-wide networks of airways, landing fields, weather and traffic control facilities established during the war should be conserved"; that "China offers the largest and most fruitful single field in the world for United States foreign trade"; that a commission should be immediately created "to study all phases of atomic power"; and that the demobilization program for Army personnel overseas "must be expedited."[7]

Two years later, Francis was asked to serve on a House Select Committee on Foreign Aid. That committee—which became known as the "Herter Committee" because Christian Herter, Republican congressman from Massachusetts, became its leader—had 19 members who were chosen "from 15 major House Committees." Its purpose was "to get the facts on which Congress is expected to make important decisions next winter on foreign aid." The committee was broken down into five subcommittees: Finance, Austria-Germany, France-Belgium-Holland-Luxembourg, Italy-Greece-Trieste, and Agriculture. Francis was made chairman of the Austria-Germany subcommittee, which included four other congressmen and two consultants. It was to be headquartered in Frankfurt, Germany.[8]

The Herter Committee sailed for England and arrived in early September, 1947. Francis and his subcommittee then went on to Germany, where they did their "principal work." After spending about a month investigating the situation in Europe, the Herter Committee returned to Washington and presented the various subcommittee findings to Congress. Francis wrote most of the Austria-Germany subcommittee report. It recommended that the practice of dismantling industrial plants in West Germany be stopped, and it observed that an "economically healthy Germany would provide a bulwark against Communist encroachment." It also "questioned the soundness of the European Recovery Program" (better known as the Marshall Plan because Secretary of State George Marshall introduced it in a speech that summer) because the program apparently did not allot enough money for Germany.[9]

FRANCIS ACCOMPLISHED MANY THINGS WHILE he was a West River congressman. During his first term, he obtained funds to build Sheridan Lake (south and west of Rapid City) as a Civilian Conservation Corps project. In 1939, he and Senator Burton Wheeler, a Democrat from Montana, co-sponsored the so-called Case-Wheeler Act, which set up "water conservation projects... in several western states." Under that act, Francis brought two irrigation projects to his state: the Angostura on the Cheyenne River (south of Hot Springs), and Deerfield Dam on Rapid Creek (west of Rapid City).[10]

Francis and Senator Chan Gurney "actively promoted" building an Army Air Corps base in South Dakota. Two days after the United States entered the Second World War, Rapid City was "selected as one of the seven sites in the nation for immediate construction of air bases." It became known as Weaver Army Air Base and was later renamed Ellsworth Air Force Base. During that same time frame, Francis, through his work and contacts on the War Department Subcommittee, ensured that an ammunition depot, together with a new town named Provo, were built in his district—25 miles southeast of Hot Springs.[11]

Francis's most significant contribution to the war effort began on March 28, 1942, when the House passed his amendment to the Sixth Supplemental Defense Bill. That amendment denied "use of funds in the bill to make 'final' payment to a war contractor until after he filed a certificate of actual costs" and agreed to a "flat 6 percent profits limitation" on those costs. The Senate, after making some adjustments, passed a similar amendment, and both House and Senate then agreed on a version that dropped the six-percent-profits limit but required a "renegotiation of price when costs showed it to be excessive." That version was sent to the White House and signed into law. After the so-called "Renegotiation Statute" had been in effect for about a year, Francis offered an amendment to an Army appropriation bill. His amendment, which was accepted, expanded the Renegotiation Statute's coverage to two government agencies that dealt in war contracts but were not subject to the original act.[12]

After the war was over, Francis received a letter from Secretary of War Robert Patterson. It said, among other things, that "'refunds in contract renegotiation as of November 15, 1946 have reached... slightly over $10 billion'" and "the savings to the government were, of course, far greater than are revealed by the figures. This is due to the fact that the presence of renegotiation influenced many contractors to reduce their prices in forward contracts.'" [13]

Two years after the V. A. Hospital was established at Fort Meade, Francis "led the way to secure" the Black Hills National Cemetery on the "grounds of the old Fort Meade military reservation." The cemetery opened in 1948. As it continued to develop during the following year, he correctly predicted that "as time goes on, more and more, South Dakota veterans and their wives—or husbands as the case may be—will be interred in this cemetery which has an unusual setting with the pine-covered mountains in the background and will have perpetual care."[14]

IN ADDITION TO FOCUSING ON military-related projects, Francis expended considerable time and effort in developing and advancing a water-management plan for the Missouri River Basin. Based on his and others' input, Congress passed the Flood Control Act of December 1944. This act was based on the Pick-Sloan plan, which called for "the conservation, control, and use of water resources in the entire Missouri River Basin." Among other things, it authorized the federal government to build five large "rolled-earth, multipurpose dams" across the Missouri River. Four of those dams were to be in South Dakota (Gavins Point, Randall, Big Bend, and Oahe) and one in North Dakota (Fort Garrison). The act also provided for the "construction of dams and reservoirs on certain western tributaries of the Missouri River... to provide irrigation, flood control and silt detention[.]" By early 1948, construction funds had been provided for Randall Dam, and funds to complete plans and specifications for Oahe Dam had been obtained.[15]

Francis's concern for the American Indians in his district was reflected in efforts to "compensate them for damages and losses caused by the federal government." In 1937 and again in 1939, he introduced an "indemnity bill 'to liquidate the liability' of the United States for the massacre at Wounded Knee [on the Pine Ridge Reservation] in 1890." Although the House Committee on Indian Affairs approved the bill in 1939, it failed to reach the House floor for a vote. He had more success in securing legislation he described as "Indian welfare acts." Those included passage of the Pony Claims Bill, which permitted "reimbursing several hundred Sioux Indians for ponies seized by the Army years ago"; legislation that provided "payments of Sioux treaty benefits," and acts that mandated "refunds of taxes illegally collected" on certain American Indian lands.[16]

On January 29, 1946, Francis introduced a labor/management bill "in an attempt to do something about strikes and industrial disputes generally." The bill soon became known as the Case Labor Bill. Its overall purpose "was to prevent... strikes and lock-outs affecting the public interest that are called without warning," and it sought "to settle industrial disputes without interruption of production and employment and without force or violence." After five days of debate, the bill passed the House with "a dozen amendments" in early February. It then went to the Senate, and "debate on the Case bill... continued both in the public sector and in Congress for the next three months." Finally, after adding several "restrictive features" to the bill, the Senate passed its rewritten version, the House adopted that version, and the bill was sent to the president for his signature.[17]

Francis wrote a letter to President Truman dated June 1 that explained the bill's objectives and urged him not to veto it. But Truman, who had received conflicting advice from many different sources, ultimately decided to exercise his veto power. The House immediately "voted 255 to 135 to override the veto, five short of the 260 to 130 that would have been necessary for passage without his signature." One year later, Congress made another attempt to implement labor/management legislation. Known as the Taft-Hartley Bill, it contained many of the Case bill's features and added others. Congress passed the revised bill over the president's veto in June 1947. Commenting on these developments, Francis wrote that "the 'Case Labor Bill,... although vetoed by the President, established the public demand for democratic reforms in labor relations and was the fore-runner of the Taft-Hartley Act of 1947."[18]

In 1949, Francis became a member of the Committee on Un-American Activities. His work on that committee included attending hearings on "communist infiltration of labor unions to sabotage key industries" and "legislation to compel reluctant heads of executive agencies to fire persons known to be security risks." In 1950, he, along with fellow committee members Richard Nixon of California and Francis Walter of Pennsylvania, were named to a special subcommittee charged with revising the so-called Mundt-Nixon bill to register communists. That bill had passed the House, but not the Senate, in the previous Congress. Francis made subtle changes in the bill's language intended "to prevent its wording and content from violating constitutional guarantees." The revised bill passed both the House and Senate, and it became law over President Truman's veto. Known as the Internal Security Act, it required, among other things, that "Communist-action" organizations and their members must register with the U.S. Attorney General, whereas "Communist-front" organizations need only register their officers. The U.S. Supreme Court upheld the act's constitutionality in 1961.[19]

ON FEBRUARY 21, 1950, FRANCIS publicly announced that he was a candidate for the Senate seat currently held by two-term incumbent Chan Gurney. Francis decided to seek that office because "he realized that he had obtained as much authority and power in the House as he could realistically expect" and "he had found the workload, as a member of the House Committee on Appropriation, increasingly burdensome." In the Republican primary election held on June 6, he beat Gurney by getting 58 percent of the vote (59,314 to 42, 823). John A. Engle, an attorney from Avon, was his Democratic opponent in the general election that fall. Francis won that contest in convincing fashion, receiving 160,670 votes to Engel's 90,692. By garnering 63.9 percent of the vote, he received the "largest percentage ever polled in a senatorial race" in South Dakota.[20]

Soon after Congress convened in January 1951, Francis revealed his Senate committee assignments. He was appointed to the Committee for the District of Columbia, which had jurisdiction over the nation's capital city. As its "ranking minority member," he also became an ex-officio member of "the Appropriations sub-committee for the District." In addition, he was put on "a so-called major committee: Public Works." That committee primarily dealt with bills concerning "Roads, Flood Control, Post offices and other federal buildings." Soon after it was organized, he was "assigned to a special subcommittee on 'Roads.'"[21]

Two years later, the Republicans became the majority party in both the Senate and House, and Francis's committee assignments expanded and increased. He was appointed chairman of the District of Columbia Committee; and he became a high-ranking member on the Public Works Committee, chairman of its Roads subcommittee, and one of three ex-officio members "on the Appropriations Committee for River and Flood Control appropriations." He also was assigned to the Armed Services Committee, which handled "all legislation related to the several branches of the Armed Forces—Navy, Air [Force], Army and Marine Corps." In March, he was named to the newly-formed, three-member Standing Subcommittee on Real Estate and Military Construction.[22]

Francis remained on the Public Works and Armed Services Committees for the remainder of his Senate career. He left the District of Columbia Committee after Congress adjourned in 1954 but rejoined that committee in 1959. And throughout his time as a senator, he was appointed to other committees that dealt with specific issues.[23]

DURING A MEETING WITH U.S. Postmaster General Jesse Donaldson in the fall of 1951, Francis proposed that the federal government issue a postage stamp that featured the Mount Rushmore National Memorial. He pointed out that August 10, 1952, would be the silver anniversary of the monument's dedication in 1927; and it would be appropriate if an "anniversary stamp" first went on sale during a celebration of Rushmore's twenty-fifth year. In early December, Francis got word that Donaldson was "seriously considering" the stamp proposal. Francis and Republican Congressman E. Y. Berry—who had been elected to the former's House seat in 1950—then "led a campaign" to get stamp approval from the Post Office Department. Their efforts were rewarded, and they received notice in early January that the stamp would be produced and ready to go on sale in conjunction with the August celebration at the monument. By mid-May, the three-cent stamp's design had been finalized. It was medium green in color, it prominently displayed the memorial in the upper half of the vertical, rectangular stamp, and it showed a mother and boy in the lower right-hand corner—"looking intently at the heroic figures on the mountain." One month later, Donaldson announced that 110 million stamps would be initially printed.[24]

When it opened on the morning of August 11, the Keystone Post Office began the first-day sale of Mount Rushmore commemorative stamps. A few hours later, an estimated 5,000 people assembled at the monument to celebrate its silver anniversary. Francis led off the speakers' program by recalling the project's history and praising its sculptor. Regarding the latter, he said: "It took love of country, indomitable determination, knowledge of history and the ways of men in the world of affairs in addition to artistic excellence and engineering skill to make this Great American Memorial. Gutzon Borglum had them all." Later in the program, Francis introduced some of the "distinguished guests" on the speakers' platform, including Congressman Ben Jensen of Iowa, "governor and Mrs. Sigurd Anderson, Senator and Mrs. Karl Mundt, Congressman and Mrs. E. Y. Berry, Mrs. Case and others." During his talk, Senator Mundt gave his interpretation of why Borglum decided to make Washington, Jefferson, Roosevelt, and Lincoln "the subjects for the four granite portraits on the mountain." South Dakota Governor Anderson also paid tribute to the sculptor and the men he chose to honor.[25]

On February 19, 1954, Francis, Congressman Berry, Senator Mundt, and John Boland, Sr.—president of the Mount Rushmore National Memorial Society—appeared before the House Appropriations Subcommittee for the U.S. Department of the Interior. At that meeting, Boland outlined the Society's proposed program to make improvements "at the national shrine," and Francis presented the Society's request for a $500,000 appropriation that would be used for the needed construction projects. Those included "an amphitheater, trails, walks and overlooks, a service road, a concession building... a dormitory" and related items. The total cost for the project would be $569,500. Francis explained that the Memorial Society would contribute $69,500 of that amount, and it would repay the remaining $500,000 to the U.S. Treasury over a 20-year period. The House subcommittee subsequently approved the program, dividing the government's "cash advance into two parts, $250,000 this year and a like amount next year." In early May, Francis presented the same proposal to the Senate appropriations subcommittee for the Interior Department. That subcommittee also approved it. By mid-June, the Memorial Society's proposal had passed both the House and the Senate and become law, so $250,000 was available for use at the monument on July 1. In a December article that reviewed Francis's congressional accomplishments, the *Rapid City Daily Journal* noted that "more than two-thirds of the money spent on Rushmore Memorial was appropriated after Case went to Congress."[26]

Francis also continued his interest in the Missouri River Basin project after he entered the Senate. In the fall of his first year there, he announced that the Senate and House appropriations committees had agreed to provide $2,000,000 to start construction of the Gavins Point Dam on the Missouri River. In addition, those committees appropriated $3,770,000 for the Oahe Dam and $32,699,000 for the Randall Dam—where construction was already well underway. Less than three years later, he noted that President Eisenhower was scheduled to push a button in Washington, D. C. "to set the power flowing from the first of the generators in Randall Dam." In May 1954, he gave examples of progress made in "harnessing" some of the Missouri River's western tributaries: "Angostura Dam on the Cheyenne River has been completed, together with its irrigation system. Shadehill Dam on the Grand River is in operation for flood control. Pactola Dam on Rapid Creek provides flood control, municipal and air base water supply, and irrigation."[27]

Epilogue

IN FEBRUARY 1950, JOSEPH MCCARTHY, a Republican senator from Wisconsin, "rose to prominence by falsely claiming to have a list of 205 known Communists working at the U.S. State Department." Two years later, he refused to appear before the Senate Subcommittee on Privileges and Election, which was investigating him on six charges that primarily involved misusing federal funds or using his official position to enhance his own finances. In 1953, as chairman of the Permanent Investigations Subcommittee, McCarthy subpoenaed witnesses, held hearings, and made "wild accusations against those who he perceived as disloyal, many of whom lost their jobs and reputations." In February 1954, he accused the U.S. Army of improperly promoting a Communist within its ranks, and he "brazenly insulted General Ralph Zwicker and his counsel" in a televised hearing watched by eight million viewers.[28]

On July 30, Senator Ralph Flanders, a Republican from Vermont, introduced a senate resolution that proposed "to censure Senator McCarthy." During the next week, a senate select Committee of Six was appointed "to whom the Resolution of Censure and all proposed amendments should be referred for investigation and report." The committee's three Republicans were Utah's Arthur Watkins (chairman), Frank Carlson of Kansas, and Francis. Its three Democrats were Edwin C. Johnson— Colorado, John Stennis—Mississippi, and Sam J. Ervin—North Carolina. Although Francis "reluctantly accepted the appointment," he "was instrumental" in the committee's organization. It adopted his motion that the hearings not be televised or taped, and it accepted his suggested candidate for its legal counsel. He served as secretary when the committee met in executive session. On August 31, it held the first of its nine public hearings. During those proceedings, McCarthy was not permitted to use "his old tactic of grabbing the initiative and confusing the issue." Francis "took an active role" in the hearings, and one reporter "called him the toughest member in dealing with McCarthy, and the one most impervious to McCarthy's insults." The committee's report, issued on September 27, unanimously recommended that McCarthy be censured on two counts: "for contempt of the Senate and refusal to appear before the Subcommittee on Privileges and Election"; and for "his 'reprehensible' treatment of General Zwicker."[29]

The Senate decided not to address the McCarthy matter until after the November 2 elections. In the meantime, Francis's office received a "tremendous amount of pro-McCarthy mail"—not only from South Dakotans but from the entire nation. This public pressure may have contributed to his expressed second thoughts about signing the select committee's report, and he proposed "that McCarthy offer a formal apology to the Senate and the charges be forgiven." That idea received no support from any of the committee members—or from McCarthy. A few days later, Francis announced that, based on newly-obtained evidence of an Army "cover-up," he now opposed censuring McCarthy based on his abuse of General Zwicker. Several senate leaders agreed with his position, and Chairman Watkins was persuaded to substitute the Zwicker count for a new one that condemned McCarthy "for his attacks on the Watkins Committee."[30]

The debate on the McCarthy charges began on November 29. It was "bitter and often intemperate." Finally, on December 2, the Senate "voted to condemn McCarthy on two counts—abuse of the Subcommittee on Privileges and Election and abuse of the Watkins Committee." The roll-call vote was 67-22, with all Democrats voting against McCarthy and the Republicans "almost evenly divided." Francis "voted for the first count . . . but voted "present" for the second."[31]

AFTER FRANCIS BECAME A SENATOR, he stated that "a demand for more roads in South Dakota had a lot to do with my first running for Congress. Through the years, better and safer roads have been a major interest." When he was chairman of the Public Works Subcommittee on Roads in 1954, he was able to act upon that interest. That year, he "handled" the Federal Highway Act in the Senate, which provided one billion dollars for highways in the United States. Two years later, he played a significant role in creating the Federal Highway Act of 1956, which was described as "the largest program for road-building in the history of this or any other country," and the "major impetus" to the interstate highway system. That legislation authorized federal money to build primary, secondary, and urban roads, plus interstate highways, throughout the country. Francis, through his own bills and amendments to bills proposed by others, was responsible for several features of the new law.[32]

IN EARLY 1956, THE SENATE was considering whether to pass a bill that would exempt independent natural-gas producers from federal rate control. The bill had considerable support among the senators, and President Eisenhower had indicated he favored it. But on Friday, February 3, while the bill was being debated on the senate floor, Francis announced that "he had rejected a $2,500 campaign contribution from an individual who was interested in the passage of the bill, and that the offer had changed his position from probable support to opposition." He told his colleagues that he objected to "'doing something so valuable to those interested in natural gas that they advance huge sums of money as a downpayment, so to speak, on the profits they expect to harvest.'" The following Monday, the Senate passed a resolution that established a four-man select committee to investigate what became known as the "natural gas incident." It also passed the bill by a 53 to 38 vote.[33]

The natural gas incident sparked considerable interest with the public. Francis's senate speech "had all Washington agog," and "the press carried headline stories about the bribe attempt in the major newspapers followed by feature stories and cartoons on the bill, its sponsors, and Case." When the bill went to the White House, the president received conflicting advice on whether to sign it. After "thorough study of all the pertinent facts and exhaustive discussions," he vetoed the bill; and he explained his reasons for doing so in a message to Congress that stated in part:

> I am unable to approve H. R. 6645... This I regret because I am in accord with its basic objectives. Since the passage of this bill, a body of evidence has accumulated indicating that private persons, apparently representing only a very small segment of a great and vital industry, have been seeking to further their own interests by highly questionable activities. These include efforts that I deem to be so arrogant and so much in defiance of acceptable standards of propriety as to risk doubt among the American people concerning the integrity of governmental processes.
>
> * * *
>
> I believe I would not be discharging my own duty were I to approve this legislation before the activities in question have been fully investigated by the Congress and the Department of Justice. To do so under such conditions... would be a disservice both to the people and to their Congress. Accordingly, I return H. R. 6645 without my approval.[34]

On April 7, the Senate Select Committee assigned to investigate the incident "reported its conclusion that though "there was neither a bribe nor an intent to bribe,... this is a case of irresponsibility run riot,' and that the purpose of the gift to Case was to influence his vote." Two and a half months later, a federal grand jury indicted the Superior Oil Company and two of its lawyers—John M. Neff and Elmer Patman—on conspiracy charges related to the incident. On December 14, Neff and Patman were each fined $2,500 and given one-year suspended jail sentences after pleading guilty to failing to register as lobbyists, and "the Superior Oil Company was fined $5,000 for 'aiding and abetting' this failure." And despite the president's "call for corrective legislation, the Congress did not pass another gas bill" because, according to him, "the issue was too 'hot.'"[35]

In late 1955, Francis began to organize his reelection-to-the-Senate campaign. He had no challenger in the June 1956 Republican primary. Despite his overwhelming Senate victory in 1950, he "seemed vulnerable" in the 1956 election. His participation in the McCarthy affair and his public exposure of the natural gas incident turned some voters against him. But the main source of his vulnerability appeared to be Eisenhower's unpopular agricultural policies, although Francis had not consistently supported them. Those policies became the main issue in his fall campaign, and he "nearly became a victim of the farm revolt." He beat his Democratic opponent—Kenneth Holum, a farmer from Groton—by only 4,620 votes (147,621 to 143,001). His margin of victory was 1.6 percent, making this the closest election in his congressional career.[36]

FRANCIS'S INTEREST IN WATER RESOURCES was not confined to controlling the Missouri River and its tributaries. During his last year in the House, and throughout his time in the Senate, he studied the possibilities of producing rain by seeding clouds with silver iodide or dry ice (frozen carbon dioxide) so that the "particles of mist that make up a cloud" would condense and "fall as drops of rain or flakes of snow." Convinced that increasing rainfall or modifying clouds could potentially have significant implications "for national defense as well as for agriculture and industry," Francis presented a bill in Congress that created a National Advisory Committee on Weather Control. That committee was "charged with trying to bring together the results of laboratory experiments and field projects and to develop dependable guiding principles for cloud modification." President Eisenhower signed the bill that created the committee in 1953. Less than a year later, he approved legislation that appropriated funds for its operation. After submitting a report to the president at the end of

1957, the committee went out of existence. Believing that its weather modification studies should continue, Francis introduced a bill that put "weather research activities" under the National Science Foundation's (NSF's) jurisdiction. The bill became law in July 1958, and the NSF, along with other government agencies, continued to do weather research.[37]

In addition to his efforts to control the weather, Francis also looked to another source of producing usable water. Thus, in 1952, he sponsored a bill in the Senate that became law. Known as the Saline Water Act, its primary purpose was "to stimulate and organize research in demineralizing sea water and brackish water." (Brackish water is generally defined as water with a salt content of more than fresh water but less than sea water. It "can occur naturally as brackish groundwater in subsurface saline aquifers" or "as surface water due to natural erosion." Some agricultural irrigation practices and mining activities generate "drainage waters that are highly brackish.") Three years later, Congress extended the Saline Water Act. And in 1958, the president signed a bill—cosponsored by Francis and Senator Clint Anderson of New Mexico—that provided "for the construction of five saline water demonstration plants ... [that] will convert sea or brackish water into fresh water." A site selection committee later determined that brackish water plants would be in Webster, South Dakota and Roswell, New Mexico; and salt water plants were to be situated in San Diego, California, Freeport City, Texas, and an unknown site on the East Coast. Congress appropriated funds for the Webster plant in May 1960. The newsletter that made the announcement also included this personal note: "Sen. And Mrs. Case are pleased as punch with their first grandchild, a 7-pound 7-ounce girl born to their daughter Jane (Mrs. Allen Commander) on May 16. The grand-daughter has been named Catherine Case Commander."[38]

In accordance with the plan originally conceived in the Flood Control Act of 1944, dam construction on the Missouri River continued from the mid-to-late 1950s. In 1958, Congress passed, and the president signed, a massive, omnibus water-resources bill that covered projects in the Missouri River Basin and throughout the United States. While the bill was making its way through Congress, Francis successfully added an amendment that reserved "for South Dakota 50 per cent of the electrical power to be generated by Big Bend Dam when it is constructed." About two years later, his office provided a "progress report" on the four Missouri River dams in the state. It noted, among other things, that construction was "just getting underway" at Big Bend and "first power is to be on line in July 1964"; that Oahe was expected to be 68 percent complete by next year and "first power on the line [is] set for July 1962"; that Ft. Randall was "placed in full operation in 1956"; and that Gavins Point "has been completed for several years," and last year about 1.75 million people visited "the fine, constant-level Lewis and Clark Lake formed by this dam." When the Big Bend Dam site was dedicated on May 29, 1960, Francis declared that "we have come full circle in the dream for the Missouri River development that took form just 20 years ago."[39]

One of Francis's amendments to the Federal Highway Act of 1956 increased the interstate highway system from 40,000 to 41,000 miles. Under the original 40,000-mile plan, South Dakota was allotted 512 miles for the highway that would become Interstate 90 and run from east to west across the entire state. Francis indicated that the additional 1,000 miles were "needed to make connections in various parts of the country," and he gave examples of necessary routes in Oregon, Utah, Colorado, and the Dakotas. Coordinating his efforts with Robert Kerr—Oklahoma's Democratic senator and fellow Public Works Committee member—Francis arranged to have the north-south highway (Interstate 29) extend from Sioux Falls to Fargo, North Dakota; and a bypass (Interstate 229) constructed at Sioux Falls. This scheme added 166 miles to South Dakota's interstate system. (Senator Kerr also garnered significant "new" interstate miles for his home state.)

Senator Hubert Humphrey, Democrat from Minnesota, wanted the north-south highway extension to pass through the western side of his state, but the Case-Kerr proposal prevailed over the Minnesota option.[40]

As previously stated, Francis served two separate "stints" on the District of Columbia Committee while he was in the Senate. In his first four years, he was a committee member from 1951 through 1952 and committee chairman from 1953 through 1954. After he decided not to return to the committee in 1955 "because of increasing duties on the Armed Service[s] and Public Works Committees," the local Washington newspapers called attention to the committee's major accomplishments under his leadership. They included providing a "305 million dollar public works bill for rebuilding city facilities" and "better tools for law enforcement, a modern business corporation law, district government reorganization and a continuation of the fight for home rule and national representation." Francis returned to the committee in early 1959 and was one of its members for the next three years. During that time, his most important contribution to the District was "authorship of the constitutional amendment" that gave its residents "three electoral votes for President and Vice-President." This provision, which became the 23rd Amendment to the U.S. Constitution, was ratified on March 29, 1961. When he left the committee in January 1962, Francis said: "I have given a good deal of time to District matters—because I am interested in the problems of the Capital."[41]

Francis's concern for his Native American constituents continued after he became a U.S. Senator. Sometime in 1950, he "saw at Oglala on the Pine Ridge the worst fire-trap cellar being used for a school that I have seen anywhere." He demanded an investigation of the situation, and its results convinced the Bureau of Indian Affairs Commissioner Dillon Myer "that a new school was a 'must.'" Its construction began in June 1953 and was completed about a year later. In August 1954,

Francis announced that the Bureau of Indian Affairs was planning a "three-year program to improve 267 miles of roads" located on eight of South Dakota's nine American Indian Reservations (Flandreau was not included). Authority for this project was derived from a provision that Francis included in the 1954 Federal Highway Act. Four years later, he authored a law that reimbursed "the Crow Creek Indians for loss of lands to the Fort Randall Dam Reservoir"; and he, along with bill cosponsor Senator Mundt, produced a law that paid "the Standing Rock Sioux Tribe damages and rehabilitation costs for loss of land to the Oahe Dam Reservoir."[42]

IN MID-MARCH 1962, FRANCIS was taken to nearby Bethesda Naval Hospital for "what was described as a mild heart involvement following an earlier bout with the flu." He spent two weeks there before returning to the office. At the end of his newsletter dated April 2, he added a personal note: "To the many, many friends who have sent either directly or through others their 'get well' greetings while I was in the hospital, my sincere thanks. Your messages were helpful and it is good to be 'on the job' again."[43]

By early 1961, he had decided to seek a third term in the Senate. Unlike the 1956 election, he had an opponent in the primary—South Dakota current attorney general, former speaker of the house and former lieutenant governor A. C. Miller. Francis did "virtually no campaigning in the primary" and "made only a few personal appearances in the state" after experiencing health problems in March. Miller "ran as an ultra-conservative Republican." Francis won the June 5 primary in decisive fashion. He received 83.5 per cent of the vote (57,583 to 11,414), whereas Miller "failed to carry a single county outside of his home county of Lyman."[44]

As he had done after his hospital stay in March, Francis ended his June 18 newsletter with a personal note. This one said: "Thank you, everyone, for whatever interest you may have taken in the primary election of June 5, 1962. I trust that in every respect the results may contribute to responsible and representative government." Three days later, after giving a speech on stockpile disposals to his fellow senators, "he expressed some discomfiture and a doctor was summoned to the Republican cloakroom off the Senate floor." Shortly thereafter, Francis felt better and went to his office to work on a speech he expected to deliver that night. But he began "suffering extreme discomfort" in the early evening, and he was taken to Bethesda Naval Hospital about 7:00 p.m. After he arrived there, Myrle and Jane were "summoned to his bedside." They left later that evening "upon being advised his pulse was better and he was resting." Although "doctors reported his progress through the night was satisfactory," his condition "suddenly worsened" that morning, and he died of a heart attack at 9:19 a.m.[45]

Three hours later, the Senate "met briefly... to hear a formal announcement of death" given by Senator Mundt. Then the Senate "adjourned for the day out of respect for its deceased member." On Sunday afternoon, June 24, 500 people, including "scores of senators and Government officials," attended memorial services for Francis at the Metropolitan Memorial Methodist Church in Washington. The Reverend Edward G. Latch, the church's pastor, eulogized Francis and read two messages received by the Case family—one from President Kennedy and the other from the poet Robert Frost. Then the Chaplin of the Senate—Reverend Frederick Brown Harris—gave the closing prayer, and six Marine pallbearers rolled the casket out of the church.[46]

Francis's body was flown to Rapid City Sunday night after the memorial services. On Monday and Tuesday morning, it lay in state at the Behrens Funeral Home, where "thousands of friends, constituents, and well-wishers paid their last respects." The funeral was held at the First Methodist Church on Tuesday afternoon. About 1,000 people crowded into the church, and another 200 "lined the street in the church vicinity." Those attending the service included Myrle and Jane; Francis's four siblings and several family relatives; a delegation from Washington, headed by Vice President Lyndon B. Johnson, that included 12 senators and two representatives; South Dakota Governor Archie Gubbrud and "most state officials"; and eleven members of Francis's senatorial staff. The six pallbearers were all from the Black Hills. Twelve honorary pallbearers, from throughout the state, were also named prior to the funeral. The church's pastor, Reverend Robert H. Wagner, officiated the service and gave the eulogy. The Reverend Dr. Edwin R. Garrison (from Aberdeen) "read scripture passages and offered the pastoral prayer." Vice President Johnson and Iowa Senator Jack Miller made brief statements praising their former colleague. After the service, Francis was buried in Mountain View Cemetery next to his infant son. The Custer Masonic Lodge performed the graveside rites, with Robert Benton officiating. Then Lyndon Johnson "extended his condolences to the immediate family at the gravesite."[47]

MOST OF THE OBITUARIES AND editorials written after Francis's death emphasized his contributions to South Dakota and the nation as well as his personal qualities. But a few of them recalled the "little things" he did for people that showed he "kept the common touch." The *Lead Daily Call* noted that he "was never too busy to answer an inquiry, regardless of its triviality for he had a great awareness of the importance of small matters to the questioner"; and he somehow found time "to fly hundreds of miles to attend the funeral of an employee, to answer a schoolchild's letter, [and] to stop to explain a particular piece of legislation." The *Custer County Chronicle* cited other examples of "'little' unpublicized acts" that he handled: "a draft hardship case, a dispute with some Government agency, the encouragement of some young man or woman in a difficult time, help in securing a pension for someone, [and] assistance in clearing an Indian claim." One such little act that was publicized and ultimately benefitted several young men occurred in 1954. Mrs. Carl B. Hoy of Vermillion, whose son Richard was a cadet at West Point, wrote

Francis a letter that asked why butter was not served there instead of oleomargarine. Francis presented this inquiry in a letter to the Army's adjutant general, and arrangements were subsequently made whereby the cadet mess was provided with "surplus butter instead of oleo."[48]

On July 25, 1962, the Senate suspended its legislative business "in order that memorial addresses may be delivered on the life, character, and public service of the Honorable Francis Case[.]" Fifty senators (28 Republicans and 22 Democrats) gave remarks about their former colleague. Those comments generally recalled highlights of his life before he entered the Senate, their experiences working with him on various Senate committees, his legislative accomplishments, and their thoughts about him as a person. Five Democrats alluded to his handling of the "natural gas incident" as an illustration of his courage and integrity. A sampling of quotations from these tributes shows the deep respect and admiration Francis engendered from his fellow senators.[49]

Illinois Republican and Minority Leader Everett McKinley Dirksen said, "there was upon him the mark of greatness, because he felt his debt to the past, because he so fully discharged his obligation to the present, and because he had a deep sense of trusteeship to the future." Mississippi Democrat John Stennis remarked that "Senator Case, with all of his ability and talent, was one of the most modest men I have ever known." Maine's Republican senator—Margaret Chase Smith—noted "there was never a more sincere, dedicated, and painstaking person[.]" Recalling their time together on the Public Works Committee, Oregon Democrat Wayne Morse stated, "he was our leader in connection with all road legislation. He deserves a great share of the approval ... for the establishment and expansion of the Interstate Highway System." And Democrat Richard B. Russell, who had served in the Georgia House of Representatives for 10 years and the U.S. Senate for 30 years, said, "I have spent the greater part of my adult life in legislative work ... [and] have come in contact with many legislators, ... but in all that period and among all those acquaintances

I have never known a more conscientious, a more thorough, or more courageous legislator than Francis Case."⁵⁰

If Francis had lived, his opponent for the fall election would have been George McGovern. McGovern had previously served two terms in Congress (from January 3, 1957 to January 3, 1961) as the representative for South Dakota's First District, had unsuccessfully run against Karl Mundt for the state's other senate seat in 1960, and had been appointed by President Kennedy as director of the Food for Peace Program on January 20, 1961. On July 9, 1962, the Republican State Central Committee met in Pierre and chose Joe Bottum—current state lieutenant governor from Rapid City—to run against McGovern in the fall; and that day Governor Gubbrud appointed Bottum to serve out the remainder of Francis's term. The November election was very close, as McGovern won by 597 votes out of 254,319 cast.⁵¹

IN A 1959 NEWSLETTER, FRANCIS stated that "Randall Dam has created a magnificent reservoir, useful for power, flood control, irrigation, boating, fishing and a longer waterway than Big Bend and Lewis and Clark [lakes] combined." Named the Fort Randall Reservoir, this body of water extended up the Missouri River from Pickstown to Chamberlain for 111 miles, and it had a shoreline of 575 miles. A few days after Francis died, Republican Congressman Ben Reifel, who was elected to represent South Dakota's First District in 1960, sought to honor the late senator by drafting federal legislation that would change the reservoir's name to "Lake Case." In addition, he suggested that a future bridge that would span the reservoir—originally designated as the Platte-Winner Bridge—be renamed "The Francis Case Memorial Bridge." Senator Mundt and Representative Berry submitted similar resolutions in Congress concerning the reservoir, and they joined the suggestion that the state highway department should name the Platte-Winner Bridge after Francis. When he submitted these proposals, Representative Reifel said: "There are countless projects all across South Dakota for which Francis Case was primarily responsible, but he was particularly identified with these two."[52]

Both proposals were implemented. Largely due to Mundt's efforts in the Senate and Reifel's in the House, the bill to change the reservoir's name to Lake Francis Case (instead of "Lake Case") passed both houses of Congress in the summer of 1963, and President Kennedy signed the bill into law on August 16. It stated in part: "The Fort Randall Reservoir in the State of South Dakota shall be known as Lake Francis Case in honor of the late Senator of South Dakota, who was so very instrumental in the development of the Missouri River Basin program."[53]

On July 17, 1962, a groundbreaking ceremony for the future Platte-Winner Bridge took place near the bridge site (14 miles west of Platte on the Fort Randall Reservoir). During that event, Harold Schuler—Francis's chief South Dakota assistant—told the audience how Francis secured a $4.5 million appropriation for the bridge in a bill that President Eisenhower signed into law in 1960; and Governor Gubbrud said he hoped to return after the bridge was built to dedicate it to Francis's memory. The state highway department "assumed jurisdiction for administration, design and construction" of the bridge, and original plans called for its completion in 1964. But unforeseen fluctuations in the reservoir level, defective pilings that had to be repaired, and other factors delayed the project's completion until the fall of 1966. When finished, the bridge was 5,665 feet long, making it "the longest bridge between the Mississippi River and the West Coast."[54]

The bridge was dedicated as the Francis Case Memorial Bridge on September 27, 1966, and the South Dakota legislature officially adopted that name during its next session. An estimated 12,000 people attended the ceremony, including "dignitaries" such as Secretary of the U.S. Department of the Interior Stewart Udall (who gave the dedicatory address), Under Secretary of Interior Kenneth Holum

(Francis's opponent in the 1956 Senate election), Senator McGovern, former Governor Gubbrud, and current Governor Nils Boe. Myrle and her sister Bess Graves were also there. During his remarks, Secretary Udall "called the big bridge a 'spendid example of new modern highway transportation[.]'" After his speech, Myrle and former Governor Gubbrud "cut the ribbon which officially opened the new bridge to traffic[.]" Then "state and federal dignitaries rode across the bridge in antique cars ... and many hardy individuals walked across the bridge and back."[55]

In addition to the "renaming" activities, three new buildings in the Black Hills were named to honor Francis during the two years following his death. The first was the Case Auditorium in Hot Springs. This $405,000 structure was "a combination gymnasium-auditorium for the school's and community's use and an armory to be used by Company B, 109th Engineers" of the South Dakota National Guard. A dedication ceremony was held at the new auditorium on November 18, 1962. T. E. McColley, president of the Hot Springs Board of Education, presided over the program, which included a dedicatory address by Governor Gubbrud. Myrle and Jane were among the honored guests. The second building was an elementary school in Sturgis. It had four classrooms and a multi-purpose room. The school board accepted a citizens-committee recommendation to name it the Francis Case Building. Its name—and those of three other schools—was formally announced at the high school baccalaureate services held on May 19, 1963. Myrle and Jane attended the announcement ceremony, where Myrle "was presented with a large spray of carnations." That night they took the flowers to the Case graves at the Rapid City cemetery. The third building was also an elementary school—designated for the Douglas School System at Ellsworth Air Force Base. The students voted to name it the Francis Case Building. It was constructed for $556,441 and contained 26 classrooms. An open house was held there on November 8, 1964, during which Francis's life was commemorated. Joyce Wilson and Carol Goddard were among the estimated 750 visitors who toured the building that day.[56]

After seeking and obtaining Myrle's permission, Senator McGovern introduced a joint resolution in the Senate on August 8, 1963, that would name a new bridge in Washington, D. C. the "Francis Case Memorial Bridge." Senator Mundt cosponsored the resolution. Four days later, Congressman Reifel introduced a similar resolution in the House. The bridge, which crossed "the Washington Channel of the Potomac River on Interstate 95," was 1,312 feet long and six lanes wide. It was completed on July 31, 1962, and cost $9.2 million.[57]

The Senate passed the joint resolution in August 1964, but the House District of Columbia committee did not clear it for a House vote. In the next Congress, McGovern again presented his joint resolution in the Senate, and Reifel submitted his slightly different version in the House, with E. Y. Berry acting as cosponsor. After a "little flap" between the House and Senate, the McGovern proposal was agreed upon by both houses, sent to the White House, and signed by President Johnson on September 25, 1965.[58]

The Francis Case Memorial Bridge was formally dedicated on April 20, 1966. More than 100 people attended the ceremony held near the bridge, including Myrle; Jane—with her husband James Williams and young daughters Catherine and Julia; Joyce; Leland and Josephine; Carol; Esther; and several other family members. Many "close friends and fellow-workers" were also present. After the United States Army Band played the national anthem, the Reverend Dr. Edward G. Latch (who conducted the memorial service in Washington two days after Francis's death) gave the invocation. The master of ceremonies—Brigadier General C. M. Duke—then greeted the crowd, introduced distinguished guests, and read a tribute to Francis from Representative Reifel. Remarks by Representative Berry and addresses by Senators Mundt and McGovern followed. They spoke about Francis's life and congressional career, and they emphasized his contributions to the District of Columbia. After McGovern finished his dedicatory address, Myrle unveiled a large bronze plaque that would "be placed on the bridge in the near future." It read: "Francis Case Memorial Bridge—named in honor of Francis Case—1896-1962—Newspaper Editor-Congressman, Senator from South Dakota, Chairman of the Senate Committee on the District of Columbia during the 83rd Congress."[59]

AS NOTED IN CHAPTER 2, Francis won the McRoberts Oratorical Contest two days before he graduated from high school in 1914. Early on in his winning speech, he said that "deep in the heart of every true man, there slumbers a desire to be somebody, to do something that will carry the remembrance of his name beyond his own lifetime." Francis embraced that desire, and he fulfilled it.[60]

PHOTOS, MAPS, AND OTHER IMAGES

Leland D. Case and Edith H. Grannis, eds., *New Hampshire to Minnesota: Memoirs of Samuel Higbee Grannis (1839-1933)*

Armenia Jane Lewis and Samuel H. Grannis, who were married on June 2, 1867.

Herbert L. Case Papers

Herbert Case and Mary E. Case on their wedding day—August 28, 1894.

Author's Collection

Francis Case, circa 1898.

Carol Case Goddard Collection

Grandma Grannis holding Carol at the parsonage in Swaledale, Iowa, 1903. Francis (on left), Joyce, and Leland are standing behind them.

Carol Case Goddard Collection

Left to right, Leland, Carol, Francis, and Joyce in Christmas photo, 1905.

Photos, Maps, and Other Images 399

Case Ranch Collection

Francis as an "agent" for *The Saturday Evening Post* in Marathon, Iowa, December 1907.

Case Ranch Collection

Frank and Mary A. Case's "Golden Wedding Picture" taken on their 50th anniversary, March 25, 1908. Those present in the photo, and their relationship to the guests of honor, are: back row, left to right: De Witt Brown (grandson), Frank L. Brown (grandson), Warren J. Brown (son-in-law), Herbert L. Case (son), Ora S. Durr (grandson-in-law); third row, left to right: Inez Durr (granddaughter), Lewis Brown (grandson), Joyce Case (granddaughter), Hattie R. Brown (daughter); second row, left to right: Mrs. Frank Brown (granddaughter-in-law), Mary A. Case, Frank Case, Mary E. Case (daughter-in-law), Francis Case (grandson); "childrens' row," left to right: Harry Brown (great grandson), Carol Case (granddaughter), Leland Case (grandson), Daphne Durr (great granddaughter), and Esther Case (granddaughter).

Carol Case Goddard Collection

The Case family at their South Dakota homestead near Bear Butte in 1910. Left to right: Carol, Francis, Joyce, Mary E. (seated in front of Joyce), Esther, Leland, and Herbert. Peggy, the pet dog, is next to Leland.

TRACK SQUAD

First Row, Left to Right: Cotterton. Cruickshank. Bower. Nielsen, Manager. Fay. Hoehn. Sjolander
Second Row, Left to Right: Collinge, Captain. Williams. Hoon. Sweet, Coach. Burke. Whitman. Carney.
Third Row, Left to Right: Harlow. Case.

The Scoop, Author's Collection

The 1912 Sturgis High School track team. Upon seeing this photo, Mary A. wrote in her diary that "Francis' picture in a bunch of boys with just short breeches not pretty."

The Patee '14, Helen Magee Collection

The Hot Springs High School football team, 1913. Back row, left to right: Francis, Carl Hunter, Coach Fred Ingle, Ray Williams, Dean Eastman; second row, left to right: Herbert Kime, George Miller, Bill Dudley, Leonard March, John Murray; front row, left to right; John Volin, Harry Marty, George Leach (holding football), Rupert Gillespie, Verne Scott, and Ross Magowan.

Annual Staff

Rupert Gillespie	Editor-in-Chief
Marie Magowan	Associate Editor
Harry Marty	Business Manager
Fulton Dudley	Assistant Business Manager
George Leach	Athletic Department
Vern Scott	Assistant, Athletic Department
Francis Case	Literary Department
Dee Petty	Joke Department
John Volin	Cartoons
Rolf Kime	Class of '15
Roy Williams	Class of '16
Tom Miller	Class of '17

The Patee '14, Helen Magee Collection

The Hot Springs High School yearbook staff, 1914.

Carol Case Goddard Collection

Back row, left to right: Francis, Herbert, Leland; front row, left to right: Samuel H. Grannis, Armenia Grannis, Mary E., and Frank Case in Hot Springs, circa 1914.

Carol Case Goddard Collection

The Case family in front of the Hot Springs Methodist Church during the Christmas holidays, 1915. Left to right: Joyce, Francis, Esther (in front of Francis), Mary E., Herbert, Carol, and Leland.

The Tumbleweed MCMXVII, Case Ranch Collection

Dakota Wesleyan state debate champions for 1916. Top photos—Affirmative Team: left to right, Elmer Lushbaugh, Myron Brink, and Francis; bottom photos—Negative Team: left to right, Harold Card, Frank Petrie, and Frank Leffert.

Photos, Maps, and Other Images 407

Case Ranch Collection

Mohonk Conference attendees outside the Mohonk Mountain House resort in New York on May 18, 1916. Top photo includes the whole group; bottom photo shows, within that group, left to right: William Howard Taft, Francis, and William Jennings Bryan.

Carol Case Goddard Collection

The Case brothers, July 1917.

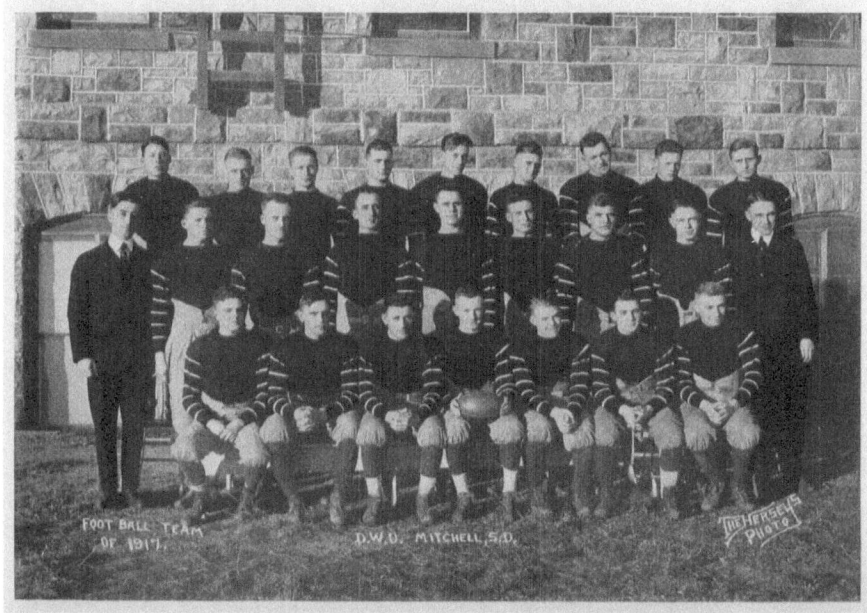

The Tumbleweed 1919, Case Ranch Collection

The Dakota Wesleyan football team, 1917. Francis is in the back row, far right, coach Ray McLean is in the second row, far left, and Harold Card is in the second row, third from the right.

The Tumbleweed 1919, Case Ranch Collection

Page from the Wesleyan yearbook recounting Francis's and Lloyd Rising's oratorical accomplishments.

Carol Case Goddard Collection

Dakota Wesleyan graduate, May 1918.

Case Ranch Collection

Private Francis Case, United States Marine Corps.

Case Ranch Collection

Section 5, Company D, USMC, Mare Island, California. Two drill instructors are standing by lamp posts slightly in front of the first row. The other two instructors are in the first row—Francis is fourth from the left, and the remaining instructor is sixth from the left. The photograph was taken on August 29, 1918.

Case Ranch Collection

Dan Brummitt, editor of *The Epworth Herald*, in an undated photograph. According to Francis, "Dr. Brummitt and I get on together like the wind and leaves in autumn."

Carol Case Goddard Collection

Francis on commencement day at Northwestern University, 1920.

The Abingdon Religious Education Texts
David G. Downey, General Editor
CHRISTIAN CITIZENSHIP SERIES   NORMAN E. RICHARDSON, Editor

HANDBOOK OF CHURCH ADVERTISING

BY

FRANCIS H. CASE

THE ABINGDON PRESS
NEW YORK   CINCINNATI

Author's Collection

Title page for *Handbook of Church Advertising*, published on March 3, 1921.

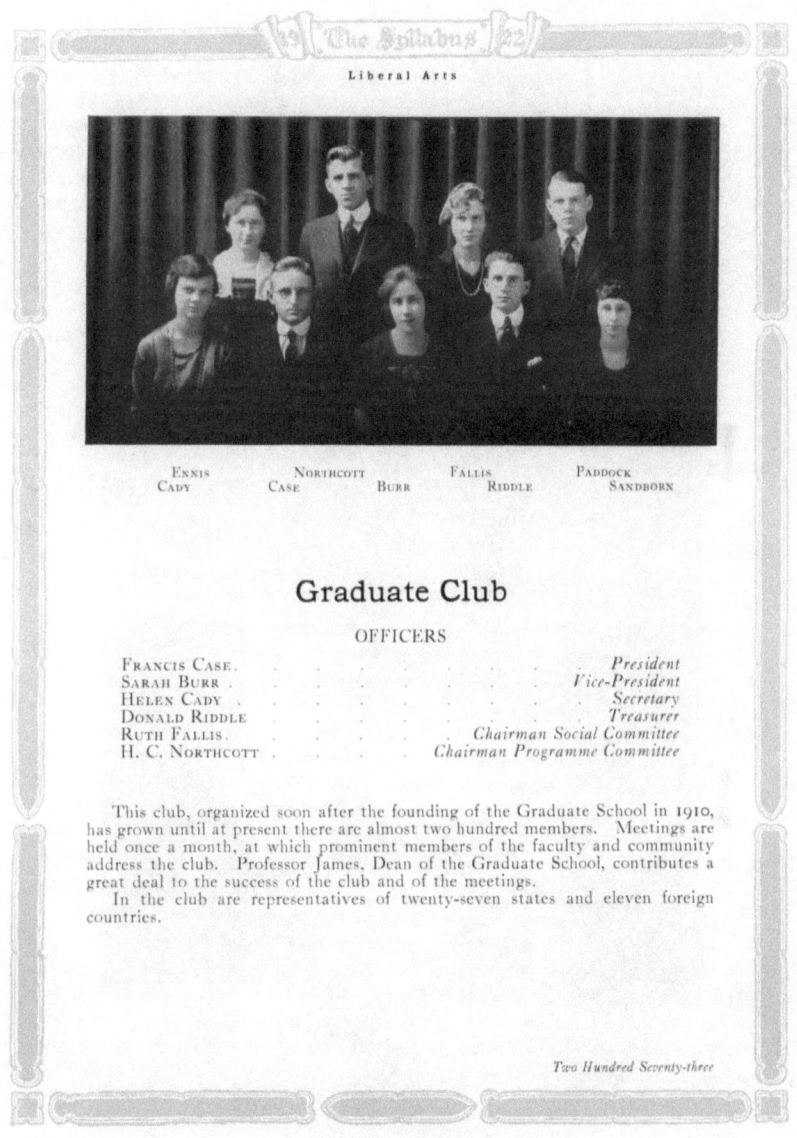

The Syllabus 1922, Case Ranch Collection

Page from Northwestern University yearbook that describes the Graduate Club and pictures its officers, 1922.

The Syllabus 1922, Case Ranch Collection

Art Brown as a college student at Northwestern, 1922.

Photos, Maps, and Other Images 419

The Tumbleweed 1923, Dakota Wesleyan Archives

Myrle Graves's junior-class photo with accompanying text in Dakota Wesleyan yearbook, 1922.

The Tumbleweed 1923, Dakota Wesleyan Archives

Dakota Wesleyan Science Club. Myrle is in the front row, third from the right.

Case Ranch Collection

Myrle, circa 1924.

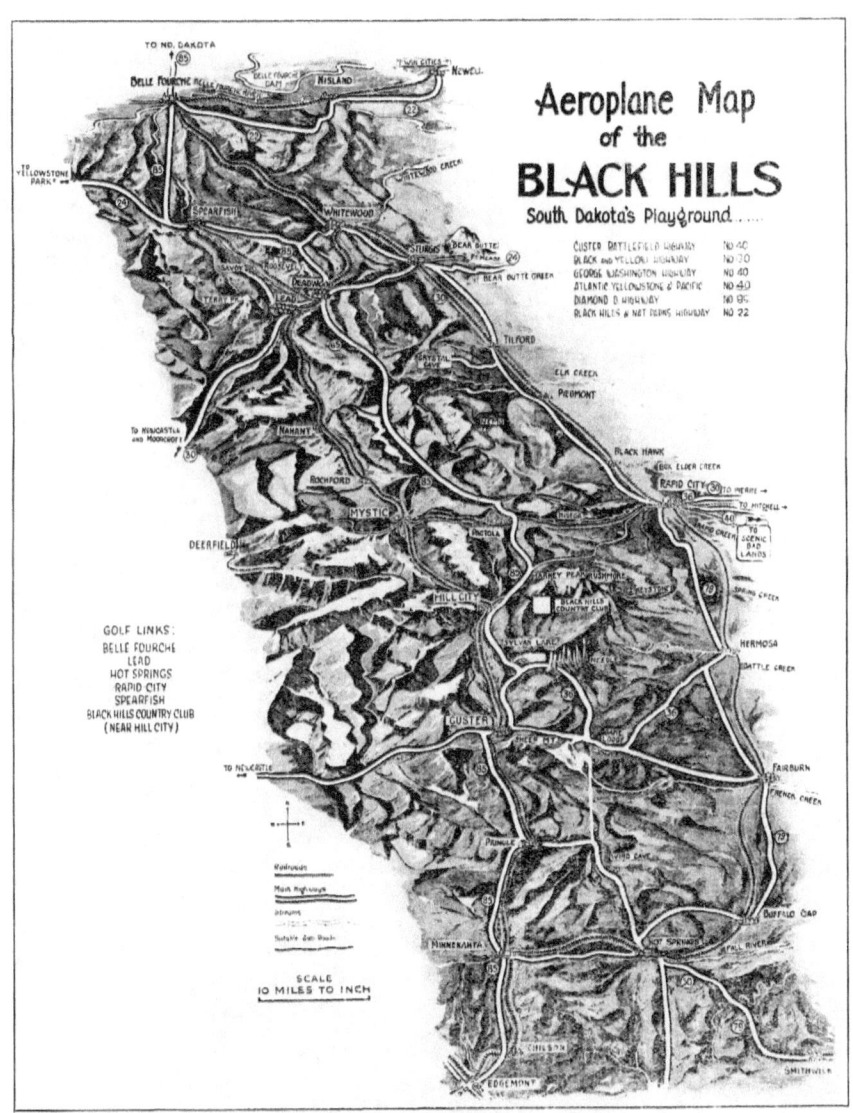

Tourist News, Carol Case Goddard Collection

Map of the Black Hills that appeared in the first issue of *Tourist News*, May 21, 1926.

Case Ranch Collection

Mrs. Francis Case on her honeymoon in late summer, 1926.

Helen Magee Collection

Badger Clark in the Black Hills, circa 1926.

Pat Roseland Collection

President Calvin Coolidge celebrates his fifty-fifth birthday at the State Game Lodge on July 4, 1927. First Lady Grace is seated in the foreground.

Photos, Maps, and Other Images 425

Rapid City Journal

President Coolidge addresses the crowd at the "second dedication" of Mount Rushmore on August 10, 1927. Sculptor Gutzon Borglum, with arms folded, looks on.

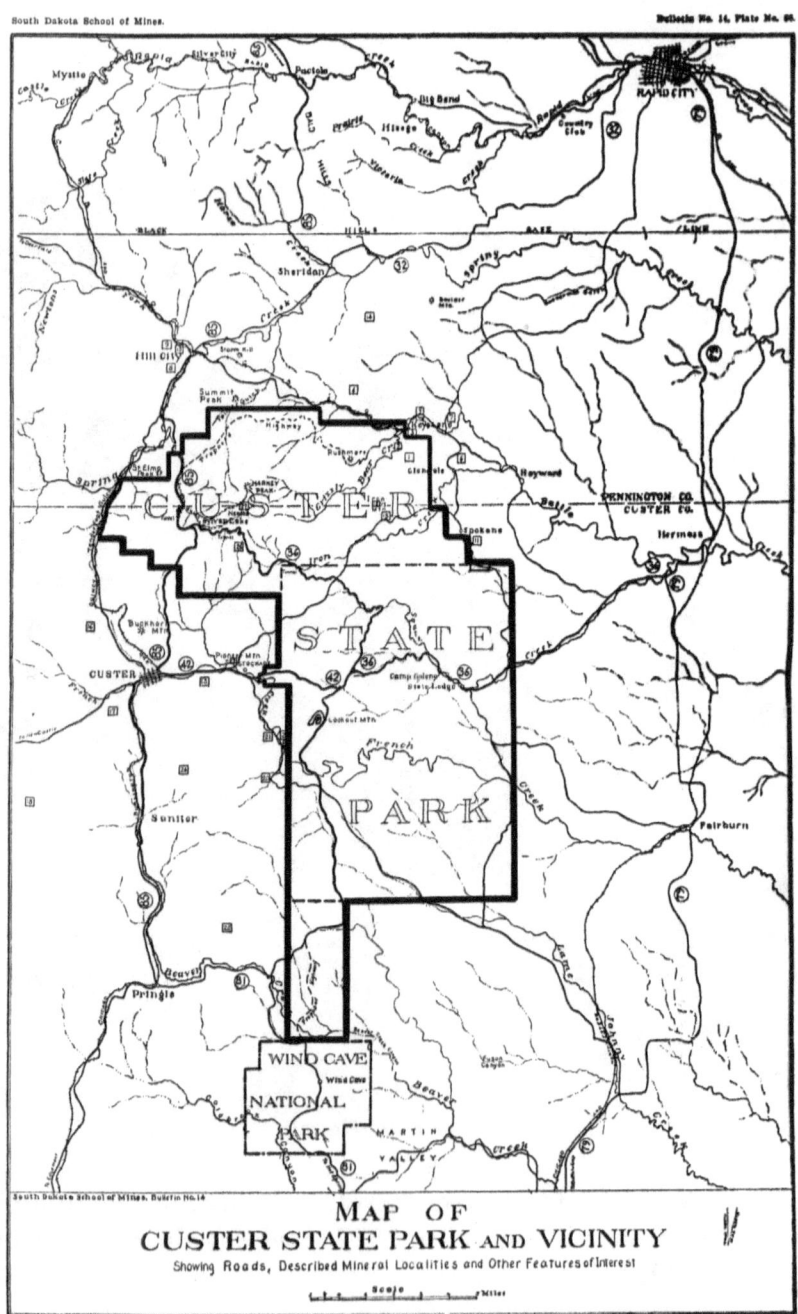

Cleophas C. O'Harra and Joseph P. Connolly, *The Geology, Mineralogy, and Scenic Features of Custer State Park, South Dakota*, Author's Collection

Map showing the location and boundaries of Custer State Park after it was expanded in January 1925.

Case Ranch Collection

Francis's cabin in Custer State Park, August 1927. Standing at the doorway are Francis, his mother Mary, and her three grandchildren—Allen, Lois, and Dorothy Wilson.

First page of *The Hot Springs Evening Star* "Extra" that announces the oil strike made on January 10, 1929.

Case Ranch Collection

Cover of the *Mount Rushmore National Memorial "Jefferson Number"* published in July 1931. Francis edited this booklet and secured its advertisements.

South Dakota 1936

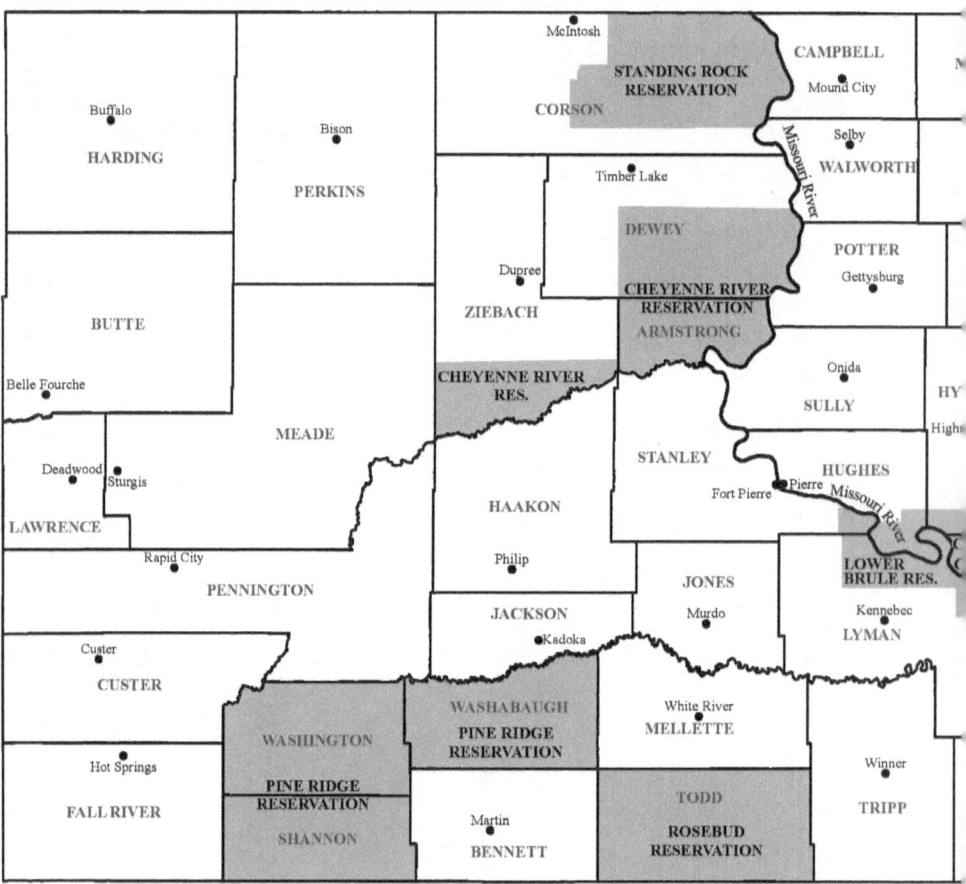

Map showing South Dakota's American Indian Reservations, Counties, and County Seats as of 1936.

Case Chronicles

HOME EDITION — Custer, S. D. February, 1935 — Vol. I, No. 1.

LIFE BEGINS AT TWO A. M.

2:00 a. m. Night Club
6:00 a. m. Breakfast
9:00 a. m. "Coffee"
10:00 a. m. Ablutions
12:00 M. Dinner
3:00 p. m. "Coffee"
6:00 p. m. Supper
9:00 p. m. Lunch
Plenty of entertainment before and after each meal.

SPORTS

Catch-as-catch-can is the only recognized hold. Try-outs have begun for the weight events, using celluloid rattles.

Neighborhood News

A joint shower was given Myrle Case and Ann Gates by members of their bridge club two months ago. The Cases and Gates live two doors apart.

Within an hour of two weeks after Jane Case came, Janet Gates arrived. Janet weighs 6 lbs. 2 oz, and bears considerable resemblance to her near twin.

Chronicles

Published—Not Too Often

Myrle Graves Case
Francis H. Case
            Co-Editors
Woof Wigglesworth
           Chief Barker

Entered as First Class Mail Matter, generally.
Subscriptions, Impossible.

Mother's Page

Everybody asks about her and then proceeds to give the baby all the attention.
(Editorial note: Father isn't even asked about.)

ANIMALS

Woof, the wire-haired terrier who has had a monopoly of attention for almost two years, instead of being jealous as expected, has asserted a proprietary interest in the new baby.

The first day, she refused to leave the room the baby was in. She still insists on being present when the baby is awake and is always the first to hear her move.

During bath time, Woof looks on in fascination, but some disgust. Her actions seem to say, "What a job! I could do better with my tongue."

MUSIC

Critics are baffled by the sparing use of vocal ability.
Notes are soprano. Technique good, but enunciation offers room for improvement.

MARKETS

Plenty of bids. No quotations given.

WEATHER

Damp, with occasional showers.

EXTRA! Population Up ½

Jane Marie Case arrived at 4:30 p. m., Sunday, February 10, 1935, to make a 50 per cent increase in the family of Mr. and Mrs. Francis Case of Custer, South Dakota.

The young lady made her first appearance in the Black Hills Methodist Hospital at Rapid City. Her first public appearance was a sunshiny day, February 22, when she motored to Custer to make her permanent home.

Good neighbors, friends and relatives had prepared a housewarming for her with dresses, caps, stockings, coats, blankets etc., for some weeks in advance.

The young lady is quiet and reserved but has expressed satisfaction with all arrangements and notices more of them each day.

She weighed 6 pounds and 14 ounces when born, and began gaining the day she was a week old. Her hair, black at birth, is now a soft brown and long enough to wear ribbons. Her eyes are a warm brown.

Auntie Irma Weyler and daughter "Biji" are frequent visitors. Little Jane will owe Aunt Irma much for a good start.

Carol Case Goddard Collection

The *Case Chronicles* announces Jane Marie Case's birth and describes her first week at home.

Photos, Maps, and Other Images 433

Aberdeen American-News

Francis and the *Custer County Chronicle* staff in front of the Chronicle office, July 1936.

Aberdeen American-News

Francis, 17-month-old daughter Jane, and Woof Wigglesworth in front of the Case home in Custer, July 1936.

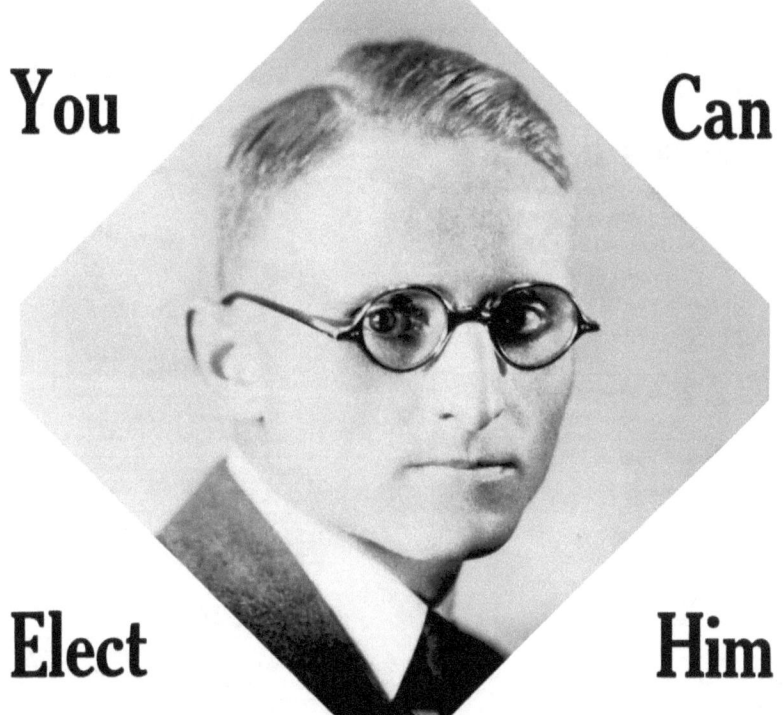

Primary campaign poster, 1928.

The Right Man for Congress

Francis H. Case

of Custer, Newspaper Editor, Community Builder

DEPENDABLE and CAPABLE

Has Ideas and Gets Results

A Ready and Forceful Speaker

An Earnest Student; A Tireless Worker

FOR CONGRESS—VOTE FOR FRANCIS H. CASE

Ask for a Republican Ballot
Primary Election, Tuesday, May 1st.

Vote for One, Representative in Congress.

☐ EARL HAMMERQUIST

☒ FRANCIS H. CASE

☐ WILLIAM WILLIAMSON

☐ DAN McCUTCHEN

Case will always be "on the job" for the welfare of the people and the development of Western South Dakota.

Case - for - Congress
Second South Dakota District
Republican Ticket, Primaries, May 1, 1934

Francis H. Case, of Custer
Newspaper Editor and Community Builder

"OLD DAYS are gone. But life goes on. And, out of today's distress, men must fashion better things. Health, play and schools for children. Dreams and opportunities for youth. Competence and happiness for adulthood. And an approach to old age without fear or dread.

"These are 'life, liberty and the pursuit of happiness', today. What will be the Republican party's part in this? Exactly what we give toward it. Fair Taxes. Better Markets. Security. A Square Deal. Peace. Development of Natural Resources. All these if we will!

"Surely in Western South Dakota. We are of the last frontier, but we live in the new day. We weigh East and West. Our people are the sons and daughters of pioneers. We understand the destiny of America.

"This is no ordinary election. Men must say whether we shall accept makeshifts and lose hard-won liberties or whether we shall build with the strength and sense God has given us. The West-River is a young country. Our 'Best is Yet to Be!' "

"Your whole life indicates clearly your preeminent fitness for public service in high office."—Major General Smedley D. Butler.

STANDS FOR "THE SQUARE DEAL"
AND A NEW DAY IN AMERICAN POLITICS

Carol Case Goddard Collection

Front and back pages of 1934 primary campaign brochure.

For Congressman
VOTE FOR
FRANCIS CASE
(HEHAK HEMAZA)

CASE'S INDIAN PROGRAM

1. An Indian will be selected as one of my Secretaries in Washington to help give you REAL Service.

2. I will work for a "Service" officer on each Reservation to be chosen by the Members of the Reservation.

3. Active cooperation with Ralph Case in getting settlement of the Black Hills claims and other suits now pending.

4. Every possible assistance in getting Indian farms restocked with cattle, horses, pigs and chickens.

5. Encouragement for our schools and help in placing Indian young people in real jobs.

6. Development of homes for the aged Indians at the Agencies.

REPUBLICAN PARTY

Vote for One, United States Senator

☐ C. A. CHRISTOPHERSON

☐ CHANDLER GURNEY

Vote for One, Representative in Congress

☐ LOYSON G. TROTH

☐ PAUL E. MARTIN

☐ WILLIAM WILLIAMSON

☐ HARRY P. ATWATER

☐ HENRY JACOBSEN

☒ FRANCIS CASE

Author's Collection

Front page of 1936 primary campaign circular that includes "Case's Indian Program."

Case and Werner campaign cards used
for the general election, 1936.

Photos, Maps, and Other Images

Rapid City Journal

Francis and General Smedley ("Old Gimlet Eye") Butler shaking hands on September 20, 1936.

Hot Springs Evening Star

Front page of Hot Springs newspaper declares Republicans Jensen and Case are elected while Democrats' "New Deal Landslide Sweeps Entire Country."

ACKNOWLEDGMENTS

In 1955, my older sister Sally, younger sister Shelley, and I went to our great uncle's ranch near Custer to ride a horse. It is my first memory of Francis Case. Our grandmother Joyce drove us there from Hot Springs, and great "Aunty Carol" accompanied the group. We children each took turns riding a small, black-and-white pony. I remember being impressed by Francis's kindness, patience, and attention to the safety of his young riders.

About 50 years later, I came across a book that contained tributes to Francis. It was prepared shortly after he died in 1962. In that book, his U. S. Senate colleagues, members of the U. S. House of Representatives, several newspaper editors, and others describe the late senator's life and character. Reading those accounts made me want to learn more about him.

At roughly the same time, I had decided to write about my dad Allen's World War II service in Algeria, Italy, and Austria. Francis makes a brief appearance in that book. About a month after the Japanese surrendered, dad and he met in Paris, attended meetings at the Palace of Versailles, and then went to London together. He is also mentioned in my next book, which recounted uncle Phil Saunders's war experience in China. There, short passages talk about Francis's membership in the South Dakota congressional delegation that invited President

Eisenhower to visit the Black Hills in 1953, and his narrow senate re-election victory in 1956. These glimpses of Francis's life, and a few conversations with his daughter Jane, rekindled and reinforced my desire to explore that life in detail, and then to write this book. I am deeply indebted to several sources and many people who helped me achieve that goal.

Regarding secondary sources, Richard R. Chenoweth's "Francis Case: A Political Biography," which appears in *South Dakota Historical Collections*, provided an excellent overall history of Francis's family, his early life, and his political career. For general background material about the Case family and its early days in Iowa and South Dakota, the following books were also consulted and relied upon: *New Hampshire to Minnesota: Memoirs of Samuel Higbee Grannis (1839-1933)*, edited by Leland D. Case and Edith E. H. Grannis; the Fall River County Historical Society's *Fall River County Pioneer Histories*; and Jarvis Harriman's *The Man from the Hills: A Biography of Leland Davidson Case*. James D. McLaird's *The Dakota Wesleyan University Memory Book 1885-2010* included useful information about university life while Francis and Leland were college students. To get an understanding of important developments and events that occurred in the Black Hills before and while Francis lived there, the following books were most helpful: Herbert S. Schell's *History of South Dakota*; Jessie Y. Sundstrom's *Pioneers and Custer State Park: A History of Custer State Park and Northcentral Custer County*; Seth Tupper's *Calvin Coolidge in the Black Hills*; Rex Alan Smith's *The Carving of Mount Rushmore*; and *The WPA Guide to South Dakota*, compiled and written by the Federal Writers' Project of the Works Progress Administration.

In addition to the books listed above (and others), I also relied upon printed magazine articles and several materials obtained from the internet. Those sources were mostly used to supplement and expand upon topics addressed in the narrative.

Acknowledgments

The previously mentioned materials were essential to my overall understanding of Francis's life and times. But the heart of this book was drawn from primary, contemporaneous sources. They included diaries, letters, telegrams, newspapers, Case family scrapbooks, old photographs, high school and college yearbooks, and military records. Those items were in many places, and there are dozens of people who assisted me in finding and procuring them.

Thanks to the late Charles Cochran, a well-known Custer resident and a board member of that town's 1881 Courthouse Museum, who purchased the Case family papers at the Carol Goddard estate auction and then donated those papers to the museum. Thanks to Jane Case, for getting the museum's permission to loan those papers to me so I could use them in preparing this book. And finally, thanks to Ralph Kelley who, when he was a boy, helped his father build the Case ranch house. Ralph and I loaded the voluminous papers (which were later organized into six Bankers Boxes) into my car for transport from the Case ranch to my home in July 2015. These materials, which have been collectively designated as the Carol Case Goddard Collection, were an invaluable source of family letters, telegrams, and photographs; Francis's correspondence with others; papers pertaining to the Cases' interest in gold mining; a 1909 South Dakota map; information regarding Francis's political campaigns; and other miscellaneous documents.

After conducting a preliminary review of the Carol Case Goddard Collection, I returned to the Case Ranch in late August 2018. Spending two long days there, I surveyed materials stored in five large cartons. These included Francis's college yearbooks and college newspaper; records and photos of Francis as a U. S. Marine; issues of *The Epworth Herald* during the time he worked for that publication; family letters and photographs; his personal file on Mount Rushmore; and scrapbooks that contained newspaper clippings, Francis's speeches, correspondence, and other useful items. I also conducted an extensive interview with Jane, where she shared many memories about her parents. Late during the second day, while searching for additional documents in a small, separate building known as the "south cabin," we fortunately came upon an old black travel bag. It contained Mary Antoinette Case's daily diaries for the years 1881 to mid-1917. These provided an unexpected resource for learning about the early Case years—especially while the family lived in Iowa. And Jane kindly allowed me to take them and a selected portion of the above-described materials back to Minnesota.

In between that initial visit and the fall of 2023, I have conducted numerous further interviews with Jane—in person and over the phone, visited her at the ranch on many occasions, obtained further documents and photographs from her, and got her signature authorizing release of Francis's military records. Throughout the entire book research-and-writing process, she has provided valuable assistance, and she has become a great friend.

Another critical resource for the book was the George and Eleanor McGovern Library at Mitchell. I first met Laurie Langland—the Dakota Wesleyan University Archivist and Archivist for the Dakotas Conference of the United Methodist Church—on a brief stop there in July 2017. During that session, she gave me an overview of the Francis H. Case Collection and a quick tour of the library. The next day she emailed me a detailed, 174-page "Descriptive Inventory" of that collection and sent links to other resources.

Three multi-day visits to the McGovern Library followed between 2018 and 2020. On those occasions, Laurie had files ready for me when I arrived, retrieved other files requested after starting the research, and called my attention to sources that I otherwise would have missed. During and after the second and third visits, she made copies of hundreds of pages and identified each document's file. In 2022, I made two additional research requests by phone and follow-up emails. As a result of the McGovern Library research, I obtained copies of

Acknowledgments

congressional newsletters prepared by Francis and his staff. Those served as the primary documents used to write the book's Epilogue. That research also produced letters among the Case family; information on Francis's career in the Marines and his entry into the newspaper business; materials related to his political campaigns; and miscellaneous correspondence on several subjects. And thanks to Laurie's efforts, I also was provided with at least four books that were helpful, was given copies of Leland D. Case and Harold W. Card interview transcripts, discovered who won a debate between Wesleyan and the School of Mines, and obtained scanned photos of Myrle Graves when she was a college student. My sincere thanks to Laurie for all the help she provided during the book's research process.

I am also grateful to Lori J. Terrill—Special Collection Librarian and Archivist at the Leland D. Case Library for Western Historical Studies at the Black Hills State University in Spearfish. During my two-day session there in early July 2020, Lori produced files, photographs, and scrapbooks for my review and made copies of items requested. The next day, she scanned and emailed photos and a pamphlet that described Frank Case's homemade liniment. That visit yielded critical correspondence and newspaper articles that were not located in other places.

Contemporary newspaper articles were an important source of information for this book. Some of these were found in the sources mentioned above. In addition, electronic newspaper archives—located at http://newspapers.com, https://chroniclingamerica.loc.gov, and http://www.newspaperarchive.com—were extensively relied upon for access to newspapers published in South Dakota and elsewhere. But none of those sites presently contains the Hot Springs or Custer newspapers created near or during the time Francis published them. Fortunately, most of those papers are on microfilm at the South Dakota State Archives in Pierre. In addition, the relevant Custer issues are available at that paper's current office in Custer.

My physical newspaper research began at the *Chronicle* office during August 2018. Charley Najacht, the *Chronicle*'s publisher at the time, gave me free rein to examine old issues, which were bound in books that each contained a year's worth of papers. Although mainly focused on researching another subject during that session, I did get a good sense of the *Chronicle*'s newspaper archive and located some useful articles from the 1920s.

In July, 2020, I resumed newspaper research at the South Dakota State Archives, where I concentrated on reading old newspapers published in Custer, Sturgis, and Hot Springs. My thanks go to Ken Stewart, Research Room Administrator, who set up the visit and retrieved the microfilm rolls before I arrived; and to Kimberly Smith, Librarian, and Sara Casper, Government Archivist, who showed me how to operate the microfilm-reader machine. Two weeks later, Nichole Hosette, Digital Archivist, told me that the state archives will loan its newspaper microfilm to local libraries. That knowledge led to conducting broader, more comprehensive Hot-Springs-and-Custer-paper research at the R. H. Stafford Library in Woodbury, Minnesota. The research was done over 15 days in September, 2020, and an additional eight days in December, 2021. Thanks to Nicole, Kimberly, and Halley Hair at state archives, for making those microfilm loans, and thanks to Liz Gonzales, Stafford's Librarian, for accepting them. Additional thanks to Liz, staff member Janet Poff, and other staffers, for arranging unlimited access to their library's microfilm reader.

Researching the Custer papers continued in 2022. In June, I made a second trip to the state archives. My gratitude is extended to Kevin DeVries, who had become the Research Room Administrator, and to Kimberly Smith. Both assisted me in researching and copying relevant *Chronicle* articles during that session. In July and September, I returned to the *Chronicle* office for one-day visits to tie up loose ends and do research on Custer papers published during 1931 to 1933 that had "Black Hills" in their titles. I am grateful to Jerry Lenander, Owner;

Jason Ferguson, General Manager; Jeanne Fuerstenberg, Circulation/Bookkeeper; Jay Gismondi, Graphic Design; Lori Thorson; and Charity Wessel, for welcoming me, setting me up in the back room, and accommodating me all day while they produced their weekly paper.

Finally, regarding newspaper research, I owe special thanks to Matthew T. Reitzel, Manuscript/Photo Archivist at the state archives. While this book was being written, Matthew conducted five discrete research projects. In each, he found exactly what I was looking for, and he often supplemented those findings with additional helpful articles. And apart from newspaper articles, he also located and sent me several old South Dakota maps that were essential when determining the state's American Indian Reservation boundaries as they existed in 1936.

Grateful acknowledgment is extended to several other people who made significant contributions to this book. They include my cousin Jane Saunders Mauss, who supplied the photo of a very young Francis; Jim Sword, Hot Springs attorney, who sent me many Case-related items not found elsewhere; Dr. Sam Herley, Curator of the South Dakota Oral History Center at the University of South Dakota, who provided an audio recording and partial written transcript of an interview with Leland D. Case conducted in 1973; and Valesha Hooper, Expert Archives Technician at the National Archives, National Personnel Records Center in St. Louis, Missouri, who supervised the location, reproduction, and mailing of Francis's military personnel file.

I also thank Toni Moore, Sturgis Public Library, and Leona Schroeder and Guy Edwards, Jr., members of the Sturgis & Meade County Historical Society, for providing a copy of the 1912 Sturgis High School yearbook; and South Dakota Cabin Owners Association members Angela and Karl Leggate, for giving me a tour of the cabin that Francis owned in Custer State Park, during which I admired the original cobblestone fireplace, examined the icebox that Francis used, and, with Karl's help, measured the original floor's dimensions.

Additionally, thanks to my sister Suzan Wilson Spates and her husband Ken, for sending me a copy of the letter that Herbert Case wrote to his parents on the day his daughter Joyce was born; Lee Stroshine, Librarian and Archivist at the Sturgis Public Library, for helping me research the Sturgis elementary school named after Francis; Pat Roseland and Katie Roseland, Rapid City, for providing the photo of President Coolidge taken on his 55th birthday; and Peggy Johnson and Jeff Gillitzer at Pointmap, Inc. in Roseville, for producing a map of South Dakota that shows the American Indian Reservations, counties, and county seats as of 1936.

Apart from the few photo scans mentioned above, the remaining images for this book had to be scanned, and many needed to be restored. I am grateful to Emma Rivers and Andy Concha at Image Up Creative Services in Rapid City; Julia Takemura Sears, Chris Fure, and Chaela Solberg at Memories Renewed in Fridley, Minnesota; and Thom Abbott at Fast Foto Film Lab in Bloomington, Minnesota, for scanning those remaining photos, the maps, and the other images, and for handling the original photos (or, in some cases, the old books, fragile picture frames, and original newspaper clippings that contained them) with expert care. Thanks to Emma Rivers and Brad Fox at Fast Foto Film Lab, for restoring photos—some of which had significant damage. And added thanks to Emma, for finding a creative way to highlight William Howard Taft, Francis, and William Jennings Bryan in a group photo; and to Brad, for restoring most photos, two of the three maps, and a majority of other images that appear in the book.

I also acknowledge the following people who granted permission to use certain copyrighted images. Thanks to Brett Nachtigall, publisher of the *Fall River County Herald-Star* in Hot Springs, for allowing me to use images of the *Hot Springs Evening Star*'s front page; to Michelle Gullett, News Archives and Licensing Manager at Lee Enterprises in Omaha, Nebraska, for granting me a non-exclusive license to reproduce historic *Rapid City Journal* photos of Calvin Coolidge and

Francis Case; and to Pat Roseland, for granting permission to use a photo of Calvin Coolidge.

For her assistance and support during the thinking, writing, and publishing phases of this work, I am profoundly grateful to my wife Kris. As the book was created, she patiently acted as a sounding board and trusted advisor when I needed another opinion on issues that arose. She also helped me edit and proofread the manuscript—and choose the book's cover and its interior design. And thanks to our daughter Casey, for solving technological problems that were encountered while preparing the manuscript.

The talented and dedicated professionals at AuthorImprints in Encinitas, California, transformed the manuscript and accompanying items into this book, and they managed its publication. Thanks to Angela Haddon, for designing the cover; and to Kerri Esten and Manon Wogahn, for creating the interior layout, implementing multiple changes to the manuscript during the production process, finalizing the book, and setting up accounts for its distribution. My gratitude is also extended to others who performed specific jobs essential to the book's creation. Thanks to Emery Howe, for editing, proofreading, and, in some cases, improving the book's many footnotes; to Paula Fitzgerald, for carefully proofreading the main text and making it conform to professional standards; and to Louisa Emmons, for preparing the thorough and detailed index. Finally, a special thanks to David Wogahn—AuthorImprints founder and president—for supervising and assisting his team's work; for coordinating and managing the tasks performed by Emery, Paula, and Louisa; and for keeping me well informed and engaged throughout the entire book production process.

This book is dedicated to Jane Case—and to my beloved late cousin, Phillip Carl Saunders, who encouraged and supported this project from the very beginning.

NOTES

The archives and collections used in creating this book are listed below. Their shorthand descriptions are employed in the Photos, Maps and Other Images section and in the notes that follow.

Archives of the Dakotas Conference of the United Methodist Church, George and Eleanor McGovern Library, Dakota Wesleyan University, Mitchell, South Dakota (hereinafter noted as Archives of the Dakotas Conference).

Archives of the South Dakota Oral History Center, University of South Dakota, Vermillion, South Dakota (hereinafter noted as South Dakota Oral History Center).

Carol Case Goddard Collection, 1881 Courthouse Museum, Custer, South Dakota (hereinafter noted as Carol Case Goddard Collection).

Case Papers, Jane Case Ranch, Custer, South Dakota (hereinafter noted as Case Ranch Collection).

Dakota Wesleyan University Archives, George and Eleanor McGovern Library, Dakota Wesleyan University, Mitchell, South Dakota (hereinafter noted as Dakota Wesleyan Archives).

Francis H. Case Collection, Dakota Wesleyan University Archives, George and Eleanor McGovern Library, Dakota Wesleyan University, Mitchell, South Dakota (hereinafter noted as Francis H. Case Collection).

Francis Higbee Case Military Records, National Archives, National Personnel Records Center, St. Louis, Missouri (hereinafter noted as FHC Records, National Archives, NPRC).

Helen Magee Collection, Hot Springs Public Library, Hot Springs, South Dakota, http://www.hotspringspubliclibrary.com (hereinafter noted as Helen Magee Collection).

Herbert L. Case Papers, Leland Davidson Case Library for Western Historical Studies, Black Hills State University, Spearfish, South Dakota (hereinafter noted as Herbert L. Case Papers).

PROLOGUE

1. "Got Inspiration to Be an Orator from Bryan," *Mankato Free Press* (Mankato, MN), March 18, 1946.

CHAPTER 1. EARLY LIFE IN IOWA

The quotation at the beginning of the chapter is from a diary kept by Francis's grandmother—Mary A. Case. The entry, made on July 18, 1903, was her description of Francis when he was six years old.

1. "Mrs. F. L. Case Dead," *Hot Springs Weekly Star* (Hot Springs, SD), August 31, 1917); "Total Population for Iowa's Incorporated Places: 1850-2000," p. 4, accessed September 7, 2020, https://www.iowadatacenter.org/datatables/PlacesAll/plpopulation18502000.pdf (hereinafter *Population for Iowa's Incorporated Places*).
2. "Mrs. F. L. Case Dead," *Hot Springs Weekly Star*; Mary A. Case, diary from Clear Lake, IA, entry under printed heading "Cash Account. August.," 1898, Case Ranch Collection (hereinafter *MAC Diary*).
3. "History of Clear Lake," accessed August 26, 2020, http://www.cityofclearlake.com/pview.aspx?id= 2087&catid=0; "Mrs. F. L. Case Dead," *Hot Springs Weekly Star*; *MAC Diary*, 1881, *passim*, February 22, 1897, April 24, 1899, October 8, 13, 1901, November 19, 1902; "Dr. F. L. Case & Son's 'Out-O-Sight' Liniment," box 5, file 6, Herbert L. Case Papers; "Iowa, Marriages, 1890–1992," s.v. "Hattie R. Case & Warner J. Brown," *Myheritage.com*.
4. "License," Deacon's credentials for Herbert L. Case, May 27, 1889, box 6, file 3, Carol Case Goddard Collection; *Fall River County Pioneer Histories* (Fall River, SD: Fall River County Historical Society, 1976), p. 52 (hereinafter *Fall River Histories*).
5. "Funeral Held for Rev. Case," *Mankato Free Press* (Mankato, MN), October 11, 1956 (hereinafter *Funeral Held for Rev. Case*); *MAC Diary*, June 13, 14, 1893.
6. Bennett Mitchell, *History of the Northwest Iowa Conference: 1872–1903* (Sioux City, IA: Perkins Bros. Company, 1904), pp. 200–1, 312 (hereinafter Mitchell, *History of the Northwest Iowa Conference*); Population for Iowa's Incorporated Places, p. 14.
7. *MAC Diary*, February 19, March 27, May 29, July 3–6, 1894, Case Ranch Collection.

8. Leland Davidson Case and Edith E. H. Grannis, eds., *New Hampshire to Minnesota: Memoirs of Samuel Higbee Grannis (1839–1933)* (Tucson, AZ: self-published, 1962), pp. 27, 40–41, 53-58, 59, 74, 147–48 (hereinafter Case and Grannis, eds., *SHG Memoirs*).
9. Ibid., pp. 87, 90, 93, 96; *Fall River Histories*, p. 52.
10. Herbert L. Case to Mary Grannis, July 27, 1894, box 6, file 1, Carol Case Goddard Collection; *MAC Diary*, August 8, 9, 1894, Case Ranch Collection.
11. H. L. & M. E. Case to Francis and the other children, December 9, 1949, box 2, file 10, Herbert L. Case Papers; *MAC Diary*, August 27, 28, 1894; *Funeral Held for Rev. Case*.
12. *MAC Diary*, August 29-September 11, 1894.
13. Mitchell, *History of the Northwest Iowa Conference*, p. 312; *Funeral Held for Rev. Case*; H. L. & M. E. Case to Francis and the other children, December 9, 1949; *MAC Diary*, October 11, 1894, February 9, July 4, 13, 1895; H. L. Case to Mr. & Mrs. F. L. Case, July 4, 1895, in author's possession.
14. "Deacon Certificate," October 6, 1895, Deacon's Credentials for Herbert L. Case, box 6, file 3, Carol Case Goddard Collection; Mitchell, *History of the Northwest Iowa Conference*, p. 312. Lake Mills's population increased from 604 in 1890 to 1,293 in 1900. See *Population for Iowa's Incorporated Places*, p. 13.
15. H. L. & M. E. Case to Francis and the other children, December 9, 1949, and Herbert Case to Carol, April 11, 1933, box 2, file 6, Herbert L. Case Papers; *Population for Iowa's Incorporated Places*, pp. 13, 14, 21; *MAC Diary*, December 9, 1896.
16. *MAC Diary*, March 17, 19, May 30, 1897.
17. "Elder Certificate," September 26, 1897, Deacon's Credentials for Herbert L. Case, box 6, file 3, Carol Case Goddard Collection; *MAC Diary*, September 25, 26, 1897.
18. "Certificate of Baptism," February 6, 1898, carton A, Case Ranch Collection; Mitchell, *History of the Northwest Iowa Conference*, p. 99.
19. *MAC Diary*, May 17–25, October 5, 1898.
20. Ibid., October 24–27, December 27–28, 1898, February 6–9, 1899, May 22–24, June 13–15, August 1–5, 12–16, 18–21, September 26, October 4–5, 1899.
21. Ibid., May 3, 8, July 4–6, October 2, 1900; Leland Davidson Case, interview by John Watterson, Hot Springs, SD, July 19, 1973. Research data obtained through the archives of the South Dakota Oral History Center, on behalf of the Department of Native Studies at University of South Dakota, Vermillion, SD. SDOHP #851 (hereinafter LDC Interview, July 19, 1973, South Dakota Oral History Center). Leland's claim that he increased Wesley's population by one percent was exaggerated, as 730 people lived there in 1900. See *Population for Iowa's Incorporated Places*, p. 26.

22. *MAC Diary*, October 6–7, 25, November 27, 1900.
23. Ibid., December 21, 24, 1900.
24. Ibid., March 7, 8, 11–16, 18–21, 26, April 4, July 3, 1901.
25. Ibid., May 1–2, 14, 28, June 6, 8–9, July 4–5, 28, August 3–9, September 30, October 25–26, 1901, February 27, May 9–10, June 17–18, July 18–19, August 7, September 30, 1902.
26. Ibid., October 5, 7, 1902.
27. Herbert Case to Carol, April 11, 1933, box 2, file 6, Herbert L. Case Papers; *MAC Diary*, April 12, 1903; H. L. & M. E. Case to Francis and the other children, December 9, 1949.
28. Mother to Francis, April 11, 1921, box 6, file 9, Carol Case Goddard Collection.
29. "Certificate of Award," May 14, 1903, in author's possession.
30. *MAC Diary*, July 18–21, August 8, September 10, September 23, 1903.
31. Ibid., October 12, November 17, 1903; *Population for Iowa's Incorporated Places*, p. 22.
32. *MAC Diary*, December 29–31, 1903, January 1–2, 1904; Case and Grannis, eds., *SHG Memoirs*, p. 148.
33. *MAC Diary*, January 24, February 24, 1904. Whooping cough, also known as pertussis, is "an acute, highly contagious bacterial infection," which "commonly affects infants and young children." This disease gets its name from the high-pitched "whoop" sound that occurs "when individuals attempt to inhale." The sound is produced from the inflamed and swollen "laryngeal structures (voice box) that vibrate when there is a rapid inflow of air during inspiration." Unfortunately for the Case children, neither antibiotics nor a vaccine to treat or prevent whooping cough was available when they contracted the disease. See Melissa Conrad Stöppler, "Whooping Cough (Pertussis)," MedicineNet, accessed October 16, 2020, http://www.medicinenet.com/pertussis/article.htm.
34. *MAC Diary*, January 14, 27, March 17, 20, 21, May 9, June 10, 14, 16, 18, August 24, 1904.
35. Ibid., October 5, November 19–23, 1904.
36. "Billy Sunday," accessed March 14, 2020, http://www.u-s-history.com/pages/h3877.html; "Billy Sunday Time Line," accessed March 14, 2020, www.billysunday.org/timeline3.html; New World Encyclopedia, s.v. "Billy Sunday," accessed March 14, 2020, www.newworldencyclopedia.org/entry/Billy Sunday.
37. "Billy Sunday," http://www.u-s-history.com/pages/h3877.html; New World Encyclopedia, "Billy Sunday."
38. New World Encyclopedia, "Billy Sunday."

39. "Billy Sunday," http://www.u-s-history.com/pages/h3877.html; New World Encyclopedia, "Billy Sunday."
40. "Billy Sunday," http://www.u-s-history.com/pages/h3877html; New World Encyclopedia, "Billy Sunday."
41. "Billy Sunday," http://www.u-s-history.com/pages/h3877html; New World Encyclopedia, "Billy Sunday."
42. New World Encyclopedia, "Billy Sunday."
43. Ibid.
44. Ibid.
45. Ibid.; "Billy Sunday Time Line," http://www.billysunday.org/timeline3.html.
46. *MAC Diary*, entry under printed heading "Memoranda" dated February 27, 1904, January 13, 18, 22, 24, 25, 1905.
47. Ibid., February 25, March 2, 5, 30, April 9, entry under printed heading "Bills Payable. December," 1905.
48. Ibid., June 16, 20, July 2, 1905. Diphtheria "is an infectious disease caused by bacteria that usually produce exotoxins that damage human tissue." Its initial symptoms "are flu-like but worsen to include fever, swallowing problems, hoarseness, enlarged lymph nodes, coughing, and shortness of breath." The disease's "most notable feature" is the "formation of a thick gray substance called a pseudomembrane over the nasal tissues, tonsils, larynx, and/or pharynx." This substance "sticks to tissues and may obstruct breathing." If left untreated, "the pseudomembrane can extend into the larynx and trachea and obstruct the airway," and "this can be life threatening and lead to death." Diphtheria "was "once a major cause of illness and death among children." It is now preventable by a vaccine and is treatable with antibiotics, either separately or in combination with a diphtheria antitoxin, but such measures were not available in 1905. See Charles Patrick Davis, "Diphtheria," MedicineNet, accessed October 16, 2020, http://www.medicinenet.com/diphtheria_facts/article.htm; "History of Diphtheria," History of Vaccines, accessed October 16, 2020, http://www.historyofvaccines.org/timeline/diphtheria; W. A. Adedeji, "The Treasure Called Antibiotics," *Annals of Ibadan Postgraduate Medicine* 14, no. 2 (2016), accessed October 28, 2020, https://www.ncbi.nlm.nih.gov/pmc/articles/PMC5354621/.
49. Herbert Case to Carol, April 11, 1933, box 2, file 6, Herbert L. Case Papers.
50. *MAC Diary*, October 4, 20, December 9, 13–16, 28, 1905.
51. Ibid., January 20, February 25, May 23, entry under printed heading "Cash Account July" dated March 12, 1906.
52. Ibid., July 25–30, August 3, 1906; Mary E. Case to "Dear Ones at Home" [Armenia and Samuel Grannis], November 3, 1906, box 6, file 3, Carol Case Goddard Collection.

53. *MAC Diary*, July 4, 25, 27, 28, 30, August 1, 1907. When Billy Sunday died many years later, Francis printed the following notice in his newspaper: "BILLY SUNDAY, famed baseball player who became a great evangelist, is dead. There was one thing about Billy Sunday—you could not hear and then forget him. He had a message." See "Float of the Street," *Custer County Chronicle* (Custer, SD), November 14, 1935.
54. *MAC Diary*, October 3, 1907; "Preview of a Senator," *Saturday Evening Post*, November 13, 1954. Marathon is about 85 miles southwest of Clear Lake and 18 miles west of Plover. Its 1910 population was 532. See *Population for Iowa's Incorporated Places*, p. 15.
55. *MAC Diary*, December 20, 1907; Case and Grannis, eds., *SHG Memoirs*, p. 149.
56. *MAC Diary*, January 5, February 9, 16, March 18–22, 1908.
57. Ibid., March 23-24, 1908.
58. Ibid., entry under printed heading "Memoranda," March 25, 1908; Golden Wedding Picture, carton B, Case Ranch Collection.
59. *MAC Diary*, March 26-28, 1908.
60. "Preview of a Senator," *Saturday Evening Post*; Francis H. Case to Dr. F. L. Case, April 4, 1908, carton B, Case Ranch Collection.
61. *MAC Diary*, July 26, September 18, 21, 30, 1908. The Chautauqua meeting referred to in this paragraph was an outgrowth of the "Chautauqua Movement," which has been described as a "popular U. S. movement in adult education that flourished during the late 19th and early 20th centuries." In 1874, John H. Vincent and Lewis Miller founded the Chautauqua Lake Sunday School Assembly in western New York. It began as a program that trained Sunday-school teachers and workers, but it gradually expanded "to include general education, recreation, and popular entertainment." The original Assembly's success "led to the founding of many similar 'chautauquas' throughout the United States patterned after the original institution." By 1900, "there were hundreds of 'tent' chautauquas and nearly 150 independent chautauquas with permanent lecture halls[.]" See *Encyclopedia Britannica Online*, s.v. "Chautauqua Movement," accessed May 19, 2022, http://www.britannica.com/topic/chautauqua-movement.
62. *MAC Diary*, October 20, 27, November 3, 7, 1908; Doris Kearns Goodwin, *The Bully Pulpit: Theodore Roosevelt, William Howard Taft, and the Golden Age of Journalism* (New York: Simon & Schuster, 2013), pp. 501, 555–56. Taft "carried twenty-nine of the forty-six states, beating Bryan by over a million and a quarter votes." Ibid., p. 556.
63. *MAC Diary*, December 18, 1908.
64. Ibid., May 21, entries under printed headings "Cash Account August" (dated May 18) and "Cash Account September" (dated May 24), 1909. Mary A. continued to admire and respect Billy Sunday for the rest of her life. Her diaries recorded where and when his meetings were held, the number of

converts he made, and the dollar amounts of contributions he received. She also noted several instances where she read his sermons or other family members read them to her. See, *e.g.*, *MAC Diaries*, November 7, 16, 1910, entry under printed heading "Addresses," 1911, March 1, 1912, February 27, November 3, 1914, January 24, February 6, 9, 10, 16, 21, March 2, 29, April 16, May 28, December 18, 1915, January 30, April 11, 1916, January 21, 28, February 9, and March 25, 1917.

65. Ibid., August 13-20, 1909; "Sturgis saloon was first Methodist meeting place," *Sturgis Tribune* (Sturgis, SD), April 12, 1972; South Dakota Conference of the Methodist Church Historical Committee, *Circuit Riders of the Middle Border: A History of Methodism in South Dakota* (Sioux Falls, SD: Midwest Beach, 1965), p. 72; *Funeral Held for Rev. Case*; Richard R. Chenoweth, "Francis Case: A Political Biography," in *South Dakota Historical Collections* (Pierre, SD: State Publishing Company, 1978), p. 296; Jarvis Harriman, *The Man from the Hills: A Biography of Leland Davidson Case* (Tucson, AZ: Westerners International, 1994), p. 7; LDC Interview, July 19, 1973, South Dakota Oral History Center.

CHAPTER 2. MOVE TO SOUTH DAKOTA

The quotation at the beginning of the chapter is from an oration that Francis presented on May 26, 1914.

1. Mary A. Case, diary from Clear Lake, IA, August 31, 1909, Case Ranch Collection (hereinafter *MAC Diary/CL*); Jarvis Harriman, *The Man from the Hills: A Biography of Leland Davidson Case* (Tucson, AZ: Westerners International, 1994), pp. 1–2 (hereinafter Harriman, *The Man from the Hills*).
2. *MAC Diary/CL*, September 9, 10, 17, 1909; Harriman, *The Man from the Hills*, p. 4; *Fall River County Pioneer Histories* (Fall River, SD: Fall River County Historical Society, 1976), p. 52 (hereinafter *Fall River Histories*). The population of Sturgis in 1910 was 1,739. See United States Census Bureau, "Statistics for South Dakota" (Washington, DC: 1913), p. 581, accessed November 11, 2020, http://www2.census.gov/library/publications/decennial/1910/abstract/supplement-sd.pdf (hereinafter *Statistics for South Dakota*).
3. Harriman, *The Man from the Hills*, pp. 2–3.
4. "Sturgis saloon was first Methodist meeting place," *Sturgis Tribune* (Sturgis, SD), April 12, 1972; Leland Davidson Case, interview by Robert Webb, Mitchell, SD, April 23, 1972, transcript, Francis H. Case Collection (hereinafter LDC Interview, April 23, 1972, Francis H. Case Collection); Harriman, *The Man from the Hills*, p. 5.
5. "Sturgis saloon was first Methodist meeting place," *Sturgis Tribune*.

6. Leland Davidson Case, interview by John Watterson, Hot Springs, S. Dak., July 19, 1973. Research data obtained through the archives of the South Dakota Oral History Center, on behalf of the Department of Native Studies at University of South Dakota, Vermillion, S. Dak. SDOHP #851 (hereinafter LDC Interview, July 19, 1973, South Dakota Oral History Center); Harriman, *The Man from the Hills*, p. 7.
7. Francis Case to Myrle and Jane, February 17, 1948, carton A, Case Ranch Collection; *MAC Diary/CL*, April 4, 1910. It is very likely that Francis won his silver medal in the "Declamatory Contest" held annually at Sturgis High School. See the discussion of that contest later in this chapter.
8. *Fall River Histories*, p. 53; "Bear Butte State Park," accessed November 11, 2020, http://www. visitrapidcity.com/parks/bear-butte-state-park; LDC Interview, April 23, 1972, Francis H. Case Collection. Bear Butte is a small mountain that lies close to the Black Hills. It was formed from volcanic, igneous rock that pierced the earth's surface several million years ago. The Lakota people call it "Matˇhó Pahá," meaning "Bear Mountain," because its profile resembles a sleeping bear. The Cheyenne people have named it "Noahvose." Historic Native American leaders, including Red Cloud, Crazy Horse, and Sitting Bull, all visited "Bear Mountain" to pray. Bear Butte continues to be "a place of pilgrimage for Indians throughout the United States and Canada," and "vision quests, sweat lodges, and other ceremonies are frequently held on the mountain." See Lori Erickson, "The Sacred Mountain of Bear Butte in South Dakota," *Spiritual Travels*, accessed November 11, 2020, http://www.spiritual travels.info/spiritual-sites-around-the-world/north-america/the-sacred-mountain-of-bear-butte/; "Bear Butte State Park," South Dakota Game, Fish, and Parks, accessed November 11, 2020, https://gfp.sd.gov/parks/detail/bear-butte-state-park/.
9. LDC Interview, April 23, 1972, Francis H. Case Collection. Congress passed the Homestead Act in 1862. It provided that any adult who was a citizen (or intended to become one) and who "had never borne arms against the U.S. Government" could file a claim for 160 acres of surveyed government land. These claimants "were required to 'improve' the plot by building a dwelling and cultivating the land." They were entitled to this property, "free and clear" after residing there for five years and paying a small registration fee. Title to the plot could also be obtained after the claimant had lived there for six months, made trivial improvements, and paid the government $1.25 per acre. After the Civil War ended, Union soldiers "could deduct the time they had served from the residency requirements." Claims that were "not 'proved up' (meaning that the homesteaders on them did not complete the ownership requirements and receive title to the property) were known as relinquishments." When the claim was relinquished, "it reverted back to the active control of the U. S. government, and "most relinquishments were opened back up to homesteading." They "generally commanded prices ranging from $50 to $400." See Act of May 20, 1862 (Homestead Act), Pub. L. No. 37-64, 12 Stat. 392 (1862), accessed November 13, 2020, https://

www.archives.gov/milestone-documents/homestead-act; "Frequently Asked Questions," Homestead National Historical Park, National Parks Service, accessed November 13, 2020, http://www.nps.gov/home/faqs.htm; Herbert S. Schell, *History of South Dakota* (Lincoln: University of Nebraska Press, 1961), p. 173 (hereinafter Schell, *History of South Dakota*).

10. LDC Interview, April 23, 1972, Francis H. Case Collection.
11. Mary E. Case to "Dear ones all at home" [Armenia and Samuel Grannis], July 4, 1910, box 6, file 6, Carol Case Goddard Collection.
12. Ibid. Fort Meade was "the army post located between Bear Butte and Sturgis that had been founded during the Indian Wars." See Harriman, *The Man from the Hills*, p. 10. A potato race is a race in which each runner attempts to retrieve a series of potatoes or other small objects one at a time.
13. Mary E. Case to "Dear ones all at home" [Armenia and Samuel Grannis], July 4, 1910; Richard R. Chenoweth, "Francis Case: A Political Biography," in *South Dakota Historical Collections* (Pierre, SD: State Publishing Company, 1978), p. 296(hereinafter Chenoweth, "Francis Case,"); Harriman, *The Man from the Hills*, pp. 8–9.
14. Harriman, *The Man from the Hills*, pp. 9–10; "Francis Case Is Crusader Of South Dakota Politics," *Aberdeen American-News* (Aberdeen, SD), August 23, 1936.
15. Harriman, *The Man from the Hills*, pp. 10–13; LDC Interview, April 23, 1972, Francis H. Case Collection.
16. Harriman, *The Man from the Hills*, p. 14; Chenoweth, "Francis Case," p. 296.
17. Harriman, *The Man from the Hills*, pp. 4, 13.
18. Chenoweth, "Francis Case," p. 296; LDC Interview, April 23, 1972, Francis H. Case Collection; Harriman, *The Man from the Hills*, p. 14; Francis Case to Myrle and Jane, February 17, 1948, carton A, Case Ranch Collection.
19. South Dakota Conference of the Methodist Church Historical Committee, *Circuit Riders of the Middle Border: A History of Methodism in South Dakota* (Sioux Falls, SD: Midwest Beach, 1965), p.74; Harriman, *The Man from the Hills*, p. 14; Schell, *History of South Dakota*, p. 257.
20. *MAC Diary/CL*, May 31, June 1–7, 1911.
21. Mary E. Case to "Dear ones all at home" [Armenia and Samuel Grannis], July 4, 1910; *MAC Diary/CL*, June 8–14, 1911.
22. *MAC Diary/CL*, June 15–20, 22, 1911.
23. Ibid., June 23, 24, 1911.
24. Harriman, *The Man from the Hills*, p. 12.
25. Sturgis High School, *The Scoop* (Lead, SD: 1912), pp. 7–12, 16 (page citations are to PDF version); Francis Case to Myrle and Jane, February 17, 1948.
26. *The Scoop*, 1912, pp. 7, 9, 10, 16, 18.

27. Ibid., p. 19; Harriman, *The Man from the Hills*, p. 18; "Deadwood Girl Will Go to Vermillion," *Daily Deadwood Pioneer-Times* (Deadwood, SD), March 30, 1912; "Girl Wins High School Contest," *Mitchell Capital* (Mitchell, SD), April 4, 1912; *MAC Diary/CL*, April 26, 1912. Francis is incorrectly identified as "Miss Frances Case" in the two newspaper articles noted here.
28. *The Scoop*, 1912, p. 24; *MAC Diary/CL*, March 6, 1912; "Deadwood Wins B. H. Championship," *Daily Deadwood Pioneer-Times* (Deadwood, SD), May 25, 1912.
29. Harriman, *The Man from the Hills*, pp. 14–15; LDC Interview, April 23, 1972, Francis H. Case Collection; *Statistics for South Dakota*, p. 576; Herbert L. Case to Francis H. Case, memorandum, November 2, 1932, box 2, file 6, Herbert L. Case Papers; Herbert L. Case, report to Annual Conference of the Black Hills Mission, August 6, 1913, file: Case, Herbert Llywellyn, 1871–1956, Archives of the Dakotas Conference.
30. Harriman, *The Man from the Hills*, p. 15–16; Harold W. Card, interview by Robert Webb, Webster, SD, May 27, 1972, transcript, Francis H. Case Collection (hereinafter HWC Interview, May 27, 1972, Francis H. Case Collection).
31. *Fall River Histories*, p. 53; Harriman, *The Man from the Hills*, p. 15; Violet Miller Goering, *Dakota Wesleyan University: Century I* (Freeman, SD: Pine Hill Press, 1996), pp. 11, 37 (hereinafter Goering, *Dakota Wesleyan University*); "Sacrifice, Service and Greatness," Dakota Wesleyan University, accessed November 20, 2020, http://www.dwu.edu/about-dwu/why-dwu/dwu-history; Dakota Wesleyan University, *Nineteen Hundred Thirteen Tumbleweed* (Mitchell, SD: 1912), p. 85 (hereinafter *1913 Tumbleweed*).
32. Goering, *Dakota Wesleyan University*, p. 36; "Student Record [Student Enrollment] Dakota University," pp. 196, 197, Dakota Wesleyan Archives; *1913 Tumbleweed*, p. 98.
33. *1913 Tumbleweed*, pp. 73–74, 131–34, 137, 141–43; "Academy Has Commencement," *Mitchell Capital* (Mitchell, SD), June 11, 1914.
34. *MAC Diary/CL*, October 16, 17, November 28, December 14, 23–25, entry under printed heading "Cash Account February," 1912; Donald C. Vodden, grave marker, Black Hills National Cemetery, Sturgis, Meade County, South Dakota, digital image s.v. "Donald C. Vodden," *FindaGrave.com*.
35. *MAC Diary/CL*, January 17, April 3, 17, 18, 23, May 31, July 16, August 11, 1913; "Montana Bishop Succumbs in Wisconsin," *Butte Miner* (Butte, MT), April 2, 1916; Herbert L. Case, report to Annual Conference of the Black Hills Mission, Archives of the Dakotas Conference; *Fall River Histories*, p. 53; Chenoweth, "Francis Case," p. 297.
36. *Statistics for South Dakota*, p. 577; Lee Case, *Lee's Official Guide Book to the Black Hills and The Badlands* (Sturgis, SD: The Black Hills and Badlands Association, 1949) pp. 89–90; "The Story of Hot Springs," Black Hills Visitor, accessed November 24, 2020, http;//www.blackhillsvisitor.com/learn/

about-hot-springs/. "Minnekahta," is a Sioux Indian word that means "warm waters." See Case, *Lee's Guide*, p. 89.

37. *Fall River Histories*, p. 53; *Hot Springs Schools: 101 Years* (Hot Springs, SD: Star Print, 1983), pp. 4–5 (hereinafter noted as *Hot Springs Schools*); "Local News Notes," *Mitchell Capital* (Mitchell, SD), September 11, 1913; Friends of the Library, Methodist Church, pp. 8, 9, binder 145, Helen Magee Collection, accessed November 25, 2020; Herbert L. Case to Francis H. Case, memorandum, November 2, 1932, box 2, file 6, Herbert L. Case Papers; Hot Springs High School, *The Patée "14"* (Hot Springs, SD: 1914), p. 1I, Patee/1914/1915/1916, binder 130 (hereinafter *Patée 1914*), Helen Magee Collection, accessed November 23, 2020. Patee is the French word for buffalo. The Patee was chosen as the first school emblem in 1913 but replaced by the Bison in 1919. Since 1920, the school's athletic teams have been known as the Bison. Red and white were the high school's original colors. In 1922, these were replaced by royal blue and white. See *Hot Springs Schools*, p. 5.
38. *Patée 1914*, p. 1E.
39. Ibid., pp. 1D, 1L, 1AB, 1AC; "Hot Springs," *Mitchell Capital* (Mitchell, SD), June 4, 1914.
40. *Patée 1914*, p. 1Z.
41. Ibid.
42. *MAC Diary/CL*, October 2, 5–10, 12, 14–18, 1913.
43. *Fall River Histories*, p. 53; *Hot Springs Schools*, p. 2; Harriman, *The Man from the Hills*, p. 16.
44. *MAC Diary/CL*, October 26, 28, 31, November 1, 2, entry under printed heading "Bills Payable. January.," 1913; *Fall River Histories*, p. 53.
45. *MAC Diary/CL*, November 24, 27, December 5, 7, 9, 13, 15, 17–19, 21–23, 1913; "Spray of the Springs," *Hot Springs Weekly Star* (Hot Springs, SD), November 28, 1913.
46. *MAC Diary/CL*, December 24, 1913; "Spray of the Springs," *Hot Springs Weekly Star* (Hot Springs, SD), January 2, 1914; "Senator Case Recalls Highlights of Badger Clark's Life in Hills," *Rapid City Daily Journal* (Rapid City, SD), September 29, 1957.
47. *MAC Diary/CL*, December 25, 26, 29, 30, 1913.
48. *MAC Diary/CL*, December 19, entries under printed heading "Calls," 1913; Mary A. Case, diary from Hot Springs, SD, January 2, 3, March 31, May 5, 26, 1914, Case Ranch Collection (hereinafter *MAC Diary/HS*).
49. *MAC Diary/HS*, January 9, 13–17, 19, 24, February 5, 9, March 1, 11, 13–17, 22, 25–26, April 2, 5, 7, 16–17, 19, May 5, 7, 9, 11, 17–18, 27, 30–31, 1914.
50. "Nineteen Will Graduate," *Hot Springs Weekly Star* (Hot Springs, SD), May 22, 1914; Katie Hunhoff, "The Old Swimming Hole," *South Dakota*

Magazine, accessed December 1, 2020, http://www.southdakotamagazine.com/cascade-falls; *Patée 1914*, p. 1H.
51. "Nineteen Will Graduate," *Hot Springs Weekly Star*; Scott Gerloff, *Hot Springs Architectural Guide* (Historic Preservation Commission, 1979); *Hot Springs Schools*, p. 17.
52. "Nineteen Will Graduate," *Hot Springs Weekly Star*; St. Luke's Episcopal Church, p. 8, binder 146, Helen Magee Collection, accessed December 2, 2020; *Patée 1914*, pp. 1I, 1J,1K, 1AB; "Hot Springs," *Mitchell Capital* (Mitchell, SD), June 4, 1914.
53. "Case Wins in Oratory," *Hot Springs Weekly Star* (Hot Springs, SD), May 29, 1914; Francis Case, "The Blazed Trail" (speech), May 13, 1914, Black Scrapbook 1914-1943, carton E, Case Ranch Collection.
54. "Case Wins in Oratory," *Hot Springs Weekly Star*.
55. "Nineteen Will Graduate," *Hot Springs Weekly Star*; *Hot Springs Schools*, pp. 16-17; "Hot Springs," *Mitchell Capital* (Mitchell, SD), June 4, 1914; "Class Breakfast," *Hot Springs Weekly Star* (Hot Springs, SD), June 5, 1914.
56. *MAC Diary/HS*, June 29, 1914; LDC Interview, July 19, 1973, South Dakota Oral History Center; "Fine New Roads," *Hot Springs Weekly Star* (Hot Springs, SD), July 3, 1914; "Misleading Reports," *Hot Springs Weekly Star* (Hot Springs, SD), July 17, 1914; "Personal Glimpses of Republican Candidates," *Custer County Chronicle* (Custer, SD), October 29, 1936; Helen Magee to George D. Coder, October 23, 1973, Wind Cave, p. 16, binder 108, Helen Magee Collection, accessed July 1, 2020. Wind Cave National Park was created by Congress and President Theodore Roosevelt in 1903. Its original size was about 11,000 acres. The park was named for Wind Cave, which was discovered in 1881. By 1914, "no less than 100 miles and 3,000 rooms . . . [had] been explored" in the cave, and guided tours were available for members of the public. See "Wind Cave National Park Time Line," National Park Service, accessed December 2, 2020, http://www.nps.gov/wica/learn/historyculture/wica-time-line.htm; "Ho! For the Black Hills," *Custer Weekly Chronicle* (Custer, SD), July 11, 1914; Wind Cave, pp. 23, 31, binder 108, Helen Magee Collection; *MAC Diary/HS*, July 13, 1914.
57. *MAC Diary/HS*, July 2, 5, 12, 13, 19, 26, August 2, 4, 7–9, 16, 24, 31, September 12, 13, 1914.

CHAPTER 3. COLLEGE CAREER AT DAKOTA WESLEYAN BEFORE AMERICA ENTERED THE WORLD WAR

The quotation at the beginning of the chapter is from Francis's oration titled "The Modern Paradox." It was presented in 1916.

1. Richard R. Chenoweth, "Francis Case: A Political Biography," in *South Dakota Historical Collections* (Pierre, SD: State Publishing Company, 1978), p. 298; Violet Miller Goering, *Dakota Wesleyan University: Century*

I (Freeman, SD: Pine Hill Press, 1996), p. 36 (hereinafter Goering, *Dakota Wesleyan University*); James D. McLaird, *The Dakota Wesleyan University Memory Book 1885-2010* (Mitchell, SD: Dakota Wesleyan University, 2010), p. 51 (hereinafter McLaird, *DWU Memory Book*); Francis Case to Frank Farley, July 24, 1926, file cabinet 45, new drawer 179/old drawer 184, box 2, file: Miscellaneous Correspondence 2-F-G file, Francis H. Case Collection.

2. Harold W. Card, interview by Robert Webb, Webster, SD, May 27, 1972, transcript, Francis H. Case Collection (hereinafter HWC Interview, May 27, 1972, Francis H. Case Collection); Herbert L. Case, report to Annual Conference of the Black Hills Mission, August 6, 1913, file: Case, Herbert Llywellyn, 1871–1956, Archives of the Dakotas Conference; Mary A. Case, diary from Hot Springs, SD, entry under printed heading "Addresses," 1914, Case Ranch Collection (hereinafter noted as *MAC Diary*).

3. McLaird, *DWU Memory Book*, p. 52; "Wesleyan Students Well Organized," *Phreno Cosmian* (Mitchell, SD), June 2, 1915, Dakota Wesleyan Archives (hereinafter *Phreno Cosmian*).

4. McLaird, *DWU Memory Book*, pp. 52, 71, 72; Dakota Wesleyan University, "Wesleyan Orators," *The Tumbleweed: MCMXVII* (Mitchell, SD: 1916), carton B, Case Ranch Collection (hereinafter *1917 Tumbleweed*).

5. "Daedalians Initiate," *Phreno Cosmian*, February 25, 1915, Dakota Wesleyan Archives.

6. Dakota Wesleyan University, *Nineteen Hundred Thirteen Tumbleweed* (Mitchell, SD: 1912), p. 121 (hereinafter *1913 Tumbleweed*). Daedalus was a master craftsman, architect, and artist in Greek mythology, who was credited with the invention of carpentry and carpenter's tools, the creation of many works of sculpture, and the construction of the mythical Labyrinth of King Minos as well as the wings Daedalus and his son Icarus used to escape Minos's prison. See Andrew Stewart, *One Hundred Greek Sculptors, Their Careers and Extant Works* (New Haven, CT: Yale University Press, 1990), Perseus Digital Library, http://www.perseus.tufts.edu/hopper/text?doc=Perseus:text:1999.04.0008:part=2:chapter=1:section=1.

7. "Thalian-Daedalian Annual Banquet," *Phreno Cosmian*, March 4, 2015, carton B, Case Ranch Collection.

8. "Frost Expelled; Not in Weather," *Mitchell Capital* (Mitchell, SD), May 20, 1915.

9. *MAC Diary*, May 20, 21, 23, 24, 1915. Yellowstone National Park was created in 1872 when president Ulysses S. Grant signed its implementing legislation. It is "the oldest, one of the largest, and probably the best-known national park in the United States;" and it "includes the greatest concentration of hydrothermal features in the world." The park is situated in three states—mostly in northwestern Wyoming and partially in southern Montana and eastern Idaho. Shaped like a box, its original size was 2,142,720 acres. The supposition that Francis worked at buildings or on roads is based on the following circumstances. First, by 1915, several

substantial structures had been built in the park, including a hotel and Fort Yellowstone at Mammoth Hot Springs and the Old Faithful Inn in the Upper Geyser Basin. Francis may have performed work at one or more of these buildings. Second, when he reported for work in late May, the park's roads "were rough and very hazardous." Earlier that year, the Secretary of the Interior had authorized private automobiles to enter Yellowstone, beginning on August 30. These facts suggest the roads needed to be improved in the summer of 1915 to accommodate anticipated automobile traffic. Third, the U. S. Army ran the park from 1886 to 1918, making it unlikely that his summer job would have involved park administration or management. See "Birth of a National Park," National Parks Service, accessed December 10, 2020, http://www.nps.gov/yell/historyculture/yellowstoneestablishment.htm; Kenneth Pletcher, *Encyclopedia Britannica Online*, s.v. "Yellowstone National Park," accessed December 10, 2020, http://www. britannica.com/place/Yellowstone-National-Park; "Yellowstone Park," *Hot Springs Weekly Star* (Hot Springs, SD), February 19, 1915; "Cody Will Celebrate Admission of Autos," *Custer Weekly Chronicle* (Custer, SD), June 19, 1915; "Yellowstone National Park's First 130 Years," accessed December 8, 2020, http://web.archive.org/web/20120414205203/http://windowsintowonderland.org/history/army&nps/page17.htm.

10. *MAC Diary*, September 18, 19, 1915; "Spray of the Springs," *Hot Springs Weekly Star* (Hot Springs, SD), September 24, 1915; "Editorial Staff," *Phreno Cosmian*, October 14, 1915, *1917 Tumbleweed*, carton B, Case Ranch Collection. The school newspaper's title—*The Phreno Cosmian*—comes from Greek words meaning "Mind of the World."

11. "Classes Hold Social Events," *Phreno Cosmian*, October 14, 1915, "Sophomores Entertained," *Phreno Cosmian*, November 4, 1915; *1917 Tumbleweed*, carton B, Case Ranch Collection.

12. "Daedalians Win Loving Cup," *Phreno Cosmian*, December 16, 1915, carton B, Case Ranch Collection.

13. "Prof. Elmer Wilds Gives Loving Cup," *Phreno Cosmian*, October 21, 1915, "Daedalians Win Loving Cup," *Phreno Cosmian*, December 16, 1915; *1917 Tumbleweed*, carton B, Case Ranch Collection.

14. "Daedalians Given Wilds Trophy," *Phreno Cosmian*, January 13, 1916, carton B, Case Ranch Collection.

15. *MAC Diary*, December 25, 1915; Methodist Church, p. 81, binder 145, Helen Magee Collection, accessed December 12, 2020; Mary E. Case to Mrs. R. W. Monkman, January, 1916, box 4, file 8, Carol Case Goddard Collection.

16. *MAC Diary*, December 31, 1915, January 1, 4, 1916; Mary E. Case to Mrs. R. W. Monkman, January, 1916; Leland Davidson Case and Edith E. Grannis, eds., *New Hampshire to Minnesota: Memoirs of Samuel Higbee Grannis (1839-1933)* (Tucson, AZ: self-published, 1962), p. 148. "Watch Night" is a "Christian religious service held on New Year's Eve." The service

typically consists of "a vigil to reflect upon the year past and to contemplate the one to come." It usually begins sometime between 7:00 and 10:00 P.M. and ends at midnight. See *Encyclopedia Britannica Online*, s.v. "Watch Night," accessed December 12, 2020, http://www.britannica.com /topic/ Watch-Night.

17. "Thalian-Daedalian Annual Banquet," *Phreno Cosmian*, January 20, 1916, Editorial, *Phreno Cosmian*, February 3, 1915 [sic; 1916], carton B, Case Ranch Collection.
18. Editorial, *Phreno Cosmian*, February 3, 1915 [*sic*; 1916], "Case Wins Peace Contest," *Phreno Cosmian*, February 10, 1916, carton B, Case Ranch Collection; HWC Interview, May 27, 1972, Francis H. Case Collection.
19. "Debaters Are Hard at Work," *Phreno Cosmian*, February 10, 1916, carton B, Case Ranch Collection.
20. "Local Prohibition Oratorical Held," *Phreno Cosmian*, March 2, 1916, carton B, Case Ranch Collection.
21. "Wesleyan Wins State Championship for Second Consecutive Year," *Phreno Cosmian*, March 9, 1916, "Debate Champions for 1916," *Phreno Cosmian*, April 6, 1916, carton B, Case Ranch Collection.
22. "Wesleyan Wins State Championship for Second Consecutive Year" and "Debaters Are Entertained," *Phreno Cosmian*, March 9, 1916, carton B, Case Ranch Collection.
23. "Wesleyan Wins Peace Contest," *Phreno Cosmian*, April 6, 1916, carton B, Case Ranch Collection.
24. "Local Prohibition Oratorical Held," *Phreno Cosmian*, March 2, 1916, "Card Places Second in State Peace [*sic*]," *Phreno Cosmian*, April 20, 1916, carton B, Case Ranch Collection.
25. "Dakota Wesleyan Man Wins Interstate Peace Contest," *Phreno Cosmian*, May 11, 1916, carton B, Case Ranch Collection; "Francis Case Winner," *Hot Springs Weekly Star* (Hot Springs, SD), May 12, 1916; *MAC Diary*, May 5, 6, 1916, Case Ranch Collection.
26. "Initiate Platform Artists," *Mitchell Capital* (Mitchell, SD), May 18, 1916; "Pi Kappa Delta Forensic Society," *Phreno Cosmian*, April 6, 1916, carton B, Case Ranch Collection. Pi Kappa Delta is a national honorary society formed in 1913 "for the purpose of promoting interest in intercollegiate forensic activities." Wesleyan's "forensic men" had petitioned the national society for membership in the spring of 1915. The petition was granted, and on December 3, seven charter members and two honorary faculty members were officially initiated into the Dakota Wesleyan chapter. Students were required to have represented their school in an intercollegiate forensic event in order to become members. The Pi Kappa's symbol is a fraternity key—"jeweled in a manner that instantly tells the member's standing in the society." Wesleyan was proud to be "the only school in the state to boast of such an organization." See "Pi Kappa Delta Chapter Formed," *Phreno Cosmian*,

December 16, 1915, "Pi Kappa Delta Forensic Society," *Phreno Cosmian*, April 6, 1916, carton B, Case Ranch Collection.
27. "Local and Personal," *Mitchell Capital* (Mitchell, SD), May 18, 1916; *MAC Diary*, May 19, 1916; *The World Book Encyclopedia*, (1992), s.v. "Niagara Falls"; Tobey Grumet Segal, "The Mohonk Mountain House in the Catskills: A Family Nature Retreat," *New York Family*, June 25, 2019, http://www.newyorkfamily.com/mohonk-mountain-house-new-york/; "Mohonk History," Mohonk Mountain House, accessed December 21, 2020, http://www.mohonk.com/history/mohonk-history/.
28. "Historical Note," Lake Mohonk Conference on International Arbitration Records (DG 054), Swarthmore College Peace Collection, https://archives.tricolib.brynmawr.edu/resources/scpc-dg-054; *Encyclopedia Britannica Online*, s.v. "William Howard Taft," accessed December 21, 2020, http://www.britannica.com/biography/William-Howard-Taft; *Encyclopedia Britannica Online*, s.v. "William Jennings Bryan," accessed December 21, 2020, http://www.britannica.com/biography/William-Jennings-Bryan.
29. Charles F. Howlett, "The Evolution of Peace Education in the United States from Independence to the World War I Era," in *Encyclopedia of Peace Education*, ed. Monisha Bajaj (Charlotte, NC: Information Age Publishing, 2008), accessed December 21, 2020, https://www.tc.columbia.edu/epe/epe-entries/Howlettevolution21May09.pdf, p. 5.
30. HWC Interview, May 27, 1972, Francis H. Case Collection; Francis Case, "The Modern Paradox" (Richmond, VA: Peace Association of Friends in America, 1916), p. 3 (hereinafter Case, *Modern Paradox*), Black Scrapbook 1914-1943, carton E, Case Ranch Collection.
31. "Wesleyan Man Wins High Honor," *Mitchell Capital* (Mitchell, SD), May 25, 1916; "Got Inspiration to Be an Orator from Bryan," *Mankato Free Press* (Mankato, MN), March 18, 1946.
32. Case, *Modern Paradox*, pp. 3–6.
33. Ibid., pp. 7–8.
34. "National Honors Captured by Dakota Wesleyan Orator," *Phreno Cosmian*, May 25, 1916, carton B, Case Ranch Collection; "Got Inspiration to Be an Orator from Bryan," *Mankato Free Press*; "Wesleyan Man Wins High Honor," *Mitchell Capital*.
35. Mohonk Conference photograph, 1916, Case Ranch Collection.
36. "At Mohawk [sic], New York," *Hot Springs Weekly Star* (Hot Springs, SD), May 19, 1916; "Got Inspiration to Be an Orator from Bryan," *Mankato Free Press*; "Case is Given Big Ovation," *Phreno Cosmian*, June 1, 1916, Dakota Wesleyan Archives.
37. "Annual Student Election Held" and "Case is Given Big Ovation," *Phreno Cosmian*; "Case Is Given a Big Ovation," *Mitchell Capital* (Mitchell, SD), June 1, 1916.
38. HWC Interview, May 27, 1972, Francis H. Case Collection.

39. "Bible Study and Student Life," *Phreno Cosmian*, June 8, 1916, "Student Organizations," *Phreno Cosmian*, September 28, 1916, carton B, Case Ranch Collection; "Local Notes," *Mitchell Capital* (Mitchell, SD), July 6, 1916; "Lake Geneva and the Four Year Program" and "Resolution Adopted By 1916 Geneva Conference," *Phreno Cosmian*, November 2, 1916, carton B, Case Ranch Collection.
40. "Local Notes," *Mitchell Capital*; Herbert L. Case to Francis H. Case, July 7, 1916, p. 29, "People C," binder 064, Helen Magee Collection, accessed June 25, 2020; *MAC Diary*, July 8-13, 15, 16, 1916.
41. *MAC Diary*, July 16, 17, September 2, 3, 8, 1916; Herbert L. Case to Francis H. Case, July 7, 1916, p. 29; W. N. McCoun to Francis Case, November 19, 1936, box 2, file 9, Carol Case Goddard Collection.
42. "Student Organizations," "Christian Societies," and "Editorial Staff," *Phreno Cosmian*, September 28, 1916, carton B, Case Ranch Collection; "Local Notes," *Mitchell Capital* (Mitchell, SD), September 28, 1916.
43. "Dr. Gilliland Made Acting President" and "Dr. Allen Delivers Opening Address," *Phreno Cosmian*, September 21, 1916, carton B, Case Ranch Collection.
44. "South Dakota News," *Mobridge News* (Mobridge, SD), October 5, 1916; "Methodist Conference at Watertown," *Herald-Advance* (Milbank, SD), October 6, 1916; *MAC Diary*, September 25, 30, October 1, 1916; United States Census Bureau, "Statistics for South Dakota" (Washington, DC: 1913), p. 579, accessed November 11, 2020, http://www2.census.gov/library/publications/decennial/1910/abstract/supplement-sd.pdf.
45. *MAC Diary*, October 7, 9, 11-14, 1916.
46. "Football," *1917 Tumbleweed*; McLaird, *DWU Memory Book*, p. 74.
47. "New Yorker Is Elected Coach," *Mitchell Capital* (Mitchell, SD), August 24, 1916; "University Notes," *Phreno Cosmian*, February 17, 1916, "Coach J. C. Loman" and "Football Prospects Becoming Brighter," *Phreno Cosmian*, September 21, 1916, carton B, Case Ranch Collection.
48. "Wesleyan Wins Against Madison," *Phreno Cosmian*, October 5, 1916, "Nebraska Defeats Local Methodists," *Phreno Cosmian*, October 12, 1916, carton B, Case Ranch Collection.
49. "Coyotes Defeat Blue and White," *Phreno Cosmian*, October 19, 1916, "Morningside Romps Plucky Dakotans," *Phreno Cosmian*, November 2, 1916, carton B, Case Ranch Collection.
50. Francis to Homefolks, November 5, 1916, file: Case, Francis, Dakota Wesleyan Archives.
51. "Huron Avenges Past Defeats," *Phreno Cosmian*, November 23, 1916, carton B, Case Ranch Collection.

52. "Madison Normal Wins Second Game," *Phreno Cosmian*, November 30, 1916, "Yankton Wins from Wesleyan," *Phreno Cosmian*, December 7, 1916, carton B, Case Ranch Collection.
53. Editorial, *Phreno Cosmian*, December 7, 1916, carton B, Case Ranch Collection.
54. Editorial and "All Conference Denominational Teams," *Phreno Cosmian*, December 7, 1916, carton B, Case Ranch Collection; "Huron Claims College Title," *Mitchell Capital* (Mitchell, SD), November 30, 1916.
55. "Honors Awarded Football Men" and "Annual Banquet for Gridiron Braves," *Phreno Cosmian*, December 14, 1916, carton B, Case Ranch Collection; "Will Banquet Football Men," *Mitchell Capital* (Mitchell, SD), November 30, 1916.
56. Francis to Homefolks, November 5, 1916; "Academy Oratorical," *Phreno Cosmian*, May 3, 1917, carton B, Case Ranch Collection.
57. "Debate Schedule Announced," *Phreno Cosmian*, October 5, 1916, "Daedalians Champs in Society Debates," *Phreno Cosmian*, January 11, 1917, carton B, Case Ranch Collection.
58. "Deputation Work Important," *Phreno Cosmian*, November 2, 1916, "Gospel Teams Busy in Vacation," *Phreno Cosmian*, January 11, 1917, carton B, Case Ranch Collection.
59. "Dr. Schermerhorn Elected President," *Phreno Cosmian*, December 14, 1916, "Schermerhorn Accepts Chair," *Phreno Cosmian*, January 11, 1917, "Our New President," *Phreno Cosmian*, February 8, 1917, "New President Addresses Students," *Phreno Cosmian*, March 22, 1917, "Dr. Schermerhorn to Boost for Students," *Phreno Cosmian*, March 29, 1917, "Schermerhorn Here for Commencement," *Phreno Cosmian*, May 23, 1917, carton B, Case Ranch Collection.
60. "Wesleyan Academy Teams Win Title in Triangle," *Phreno Cosmian*, January 18, 1917, carton B, Case Ranch Collection.
61. Francis to Homefolks, January 28, 1917, Francis to Mother, February 18, 1917, box 1, file 7, Carol Case Goddard Collection.
62. "Nebraska and South Dakota Methodists Debate Tonight," *Phreno Cosmian*, March 1, 1917, "Wesleyan Wins 3-0 Over Nebraska Trio" and "Society Notes," *Phreno Cosmian*, March 8, 1917, carton B, Case Ranch Collection.
63. "University Notes," *Phreno Cosmian*, March 1, 1917, "Postponed State Quadrangle Tonight," *Phreno Cosmian*, March 22, 1917, "Wesleyan State Forensic Champion," *Phreno Cosmian*, March 29, 1917, carton B, Case Ranch Collection.
64. "Regulations Governing Academy Oratorical Contest for the Case Trophy," Dakota Wesleyan Forensic Board Minutes, 1916-1924, Dakota Wesleyan Archives.

65. "Prep Declamation Held This Month," *Phreno Cosmian*, March 8, 1917, "Todnem Gets First in Prep Oratorical," *Phreno Cosmian*, March 29, 1917, "Academy Oratorical," *Phreno Cosmian*, May 3, 1917, carton B, Case Ranch Collection.
66. "Y.M.C.A.," *Phreno Cosmian*, March 8, 1917, "Society Notes," *Phreno Cosmian*, March 22, 1917, "Y.M.C.A. Elects New Set of Executives," *Phreno Cosmian*, March 29, 1917, "Y.M.C.A. Starts New Year Today," "Deputation Work a Real Experience" and "Big Opportunities for a College Man in Boy's Work," *Phreno Cosmian*, April 26 [*sic*; April 5], 1917, "Deputation Team Visits Spencer," *Phreno Cosmian*, May 23 [*sic*; May 24], 1917, carton B, Case Ranch Collection; Francis to Home Folks, May 13, 1917, box 6, file 3, Carol Case Goddard Collection.

CHAPTER 4. DAKOTA WESLEYAN AFTER WAR DECLARED

The quotation at the beginning of the chapter is from a letter Francis wrote to his "Homefolks" dated May 23, 1917.

1. "Students Should 'Hold Steady'" and "Military Drill Starts at Once," *Phreno Cosmian* (Mitchell, SD), April 26, 1917, "Attention," *Phreno Cosmian*, May 10, 1917, carton B, Case Ranch Collection (hereinafter *Phreno Cosmian*).
2. Young Men's Christian Association, "'For the Boys Over There,'" The 1918 United War Work Campaign, accessed January 11, 2021, http://unitedwarwork.com/groups/young-mens-christian-association/; "Army Y.M.C.A. Will Look After Comforts of Soldiers" (article reprinted from *The Lawrentian*), *Phreno Cosmian*, May 23 [*sic*; May 24], 1917.
3. Francis to Home Folks, May 23, 1917, box 6, file 3, Carol Case Goddard Collection; Raymond P. Kaighn to Francis H. Case, May 26, 1917, cabinet 45, new drawer 179/old drawer 184, box 1, file: Misc. Corresp. 1917–1928, 2 of 5, Francis H. Case Collection.
4. "Student Election to Be Held Friday," *Phreno Cosmian*, April 26, 1917, "Wesleyan Host to College Pressmen," *Phreno Cosmian*, May 10, 1917, "College Pressmen Form Organization," *Phreno Cosmian*, May 16 [*sic*; May 17], 1917.
5. "Pi Kappa Delta Forensic Fraternity," *Phreno Cosmian*, May 3, 1917, "College Frat Men Hold Initiation Feast," *Phreno Cosmian*, May 23 [*sic*; May 24], 1917.
6. Francis to Papa, July 27, 1917, file: Case, Francis, Dakota Wesleyan Archives; Mary A. Case, diary from Hot Springs, SD, June 1–4, 1917, Case Ranch Collection (hereinafter *MAC Diary*).
7. Francis Case to Raymond P. Kaighn, June 30, 1917, Richard H. Edwards to Francis Case, July 3, 1917, cabinet 45, new drawer 179/old drawer 184, box 1, file: Misc. Corresp. 1917–1928, 2 of 5, Francis H. Case Collection.

8. "Biographical Sketch: Francis Higbee Case," January 1945, carton C, Case Ranch Collection; Francis to Papa, July 27, 1917; Francis Case to Rev. Charles M. Donaldson, July 21, 1920, box 2, file 23, Carol Case Goddard Collection.
9. *MAC Diary*, June 17, 20, July 11, 23, 27, 1917; "Spray of the Springs," *Hot Springs Weekly Star* (Hot Springs, SD), August 3, 1917; "Mrs. F. L. Case Dead," *Hot Springs Weekly Star* (Hot Springs, SD), August 31, 1917; Francis to Dad, August 31, 1918, cabinet 45, new drawer 179/old drawer 184, box 1, file: Reverend Herbert L. Case, Francis H. Case Collection.
10. "Dakota Wesleyan Has Splendid Opening" and "Football Men at It," *Phreno Cosmian*, September 20, 1917, "New English Teacher Is Live Wire," *Phreno Cosmian*, September 27, 1917, "Wilds Goes to Platteville," *Phreno Cosmian*, October 4, 1917.
11. "Y.M. Leadership Changes," *Phreno Cosmian*, September 20, 1917, "Y.M.C.A.," *Phreno Cosmian*, September 27, 1917.
12. "Your Paper" and "Getting Acquainted," *Phreno Cosmian*, September 20, 1917.
13. Harold W. Card, interview by Robert Webb, Webster, SD, May 27, 1972, transcript, Francis H. Case Collection; Leland Davidson Case, interview by Robert Webb, Mitchell, SD, April 23, 1972, transcript, Francis H. Case Collection; Francis to Homefolks, November 17, 1917, box 1, file 7, Francis H. Case to James A. James, March 11, 1921, box 2, file 14, Carol Case Goddard Collection; Dakota Wesleyan University, *The Tumbleweed: MCMXVII* (Mitchell, SD: 1916), *The Tumbleweed: 1919* (Mitchell, SD: 1918) (hereinafter *1919 Tumbleweed*), carton B, Case Ranch Collection.
14. "Athletic Board After New Coach," *Phreno Cosmian*, February 1, 1917, "McLain [sic] To Be D. W. Coach Next Year," *Phreno Cosmian*, April 26, 1917, "Mt. Union College Man to Coach Here," *Phreno Cosmian*, May 10, 1917, "Football Men at It," *Phreno Cosmian*.
15. "Football Men at It," *Phreno Cosmian*, "Pepper Fest for Football Friday," *Phreno Cosmian*, September 27, 1917, "Saturday Starts Football Season," *Phreno Cosmian*, October 4, 1917, "Doping the Conf. Championship," *Phreno Cosmian*, November 1, 1917.
16. "Wesleyan Tromps on Lutherans," *Phreno Cosmian*, October 11, 1917.
17. "Wesleyan Ties Up Trinity," *Phreno Cosmian*, October 18, 1917, "Wesleyan Warriors Weigh," *Phreno Cosmian*, November 1, 1917.
18. "North'n Normal Gets Score," *Phreno Cosmian*, October 25, 1917.
19. "Blue and White Scrap Maroons" and "Doping the Conf. Championship," *Phreno Cosmian*, November 1, 1917.
20. "Methodists Legislate at Pierre," *Phreno Cosmian*, October 4, 1917; "Home Purchased by Hospital for Nurses," *Rapid City Daily Journal* (Rapid City, SD), October 5, 1917; "Methodist Conference," *Rapid City Daily Journal* (Rapid City, SD), October 7, 1917; "The Daily Journal," *Rapid City Daily*

Journal (Rapid City, SD), November 4, 1917; *Fall River Pioneer Histories* (Fall River, SD: Fall River Historical Society, 1976), pp. 52–53.

21. "The Daily Journal," *Rapid City Daily Journal* (Rapid City, SD), November 4, 1917; Jarvis Harriman, *The Man from the Hills: A Biography of Leland Davidson Case*, (Tucson, AZ: Westerners International, 1994), p. 18; "Box Elder," *Rapid City Daily Journal* (Rapid City, SD), December 7, 1917; "Annual Meeting of Hospital Board Held," *Rapid City Daily Journal* (Rapid City, SD), December 23, 1917. Rapid City is located 43 miles south and east of Spearfish. Rapid's 1920 population was 5,777. See: United States Census Bureau, "Fourteenth Census of the United States, State Compendium: South Dakota," (Washington, DC: 1925), p. 8, accessed January 19, 2021, http://www2.census.gov/prod2/decennial/documents/06229686v38-43ch3.pdf.

22. "10,000 Parade Mitchell for Liberty Loan," *Mitchell Capital* (Mitchell, SD), October 25, 1917; "Wesleyan Boosts Liberty Bonds," *Phreno Cosmian*, November 1, 1917; Francis to Homefolks, November 17, 1917. "A Liberty Bond is a debt obligation issued by the U.S. Department of the Treasury in conjunction with the Federal Reserve. Also known as a Liberty Loan, it was a war bond, issued in four installments in 1917–18 as a means to finance the U.S.' participation in World War I and the Allied war effort in Europe." See James Chen and Troy Segal, "Liberty Bond," Investopedia, accessed January 22, 2021, http://www.investopedia.com/terms/l/liberty-bond.asp.

23. "Blue and White Scrap Maroons," *Phreno Cosmian*, "Rierson's [sic] Drop Kick Defeats Sioux Falls," *Phreno Cosmian*, November 8, 1917.

24. "Wesleyan Beats Miners 13-6" and "University Notes," *Phreno Cosmian*, November 15, 1917.

25. "Wesleyan Battles Presbyterians 0-0," *Phreno Cosmian*, November 22, 1917, "Great Grid Battle Goes to Yankton 19-13, *Phreno Cosmian*, December 6, 1917, "Wesleyan Warriors Are Some Bunch," *Phreno Cosmian*, January 17, 1918.

26. "Great Grid Battle Goes to Yankton 19-13," *Phreno Cosmian*; Francis Case to Mrs. H. L. Case, telegram, November 29, 1917, box 6, file 6, Carol Case Goddard Collection.

27. "Harkness Pilot of 1918 Squad," *Phreno Cosmian*, December 6, 1917, "There Were Some Good Fights," "A Worth While Season," and "Annual Grid Banquet Given Team," *Phreno Cosmian*, January 17, 1918.

28. Francis to Papa, December 9, 1917, file: Case, Francis Higbee, 1896–1962, Archives of the Dakotas Conference; "McLean Picks Conf. Eleven," *Phreno Cosmian*, December 13, 1917, "Mythical Elevens Are Chosen," *Phreno Cosmian*, January 17, 1918.

29. Francis to Papa, December 9, 1917.

30. "Delta Rho Society Gets Second Debate," *Mitchell Capital* (Mitchell, SD), December 20, 1917; "Kappas Winners Society Debates," *Phreno Cosmian*, January 10, 1918.

31. Francis to Homefolks, January 27, 1918, box 1, file 7, Carol Case Goddard Collection; "Night School for Civil Service," *Phreno Cosmian*, November 15, 1917, "Night School is Proving Success," *Phreno Cosmian*, December 6, 1917, "Wesleyan Would Help Win War," *Phreno Cosmian*, January 10, 1918.
32. Francis to Homefolks, January 27, 1918.
33. "Wesleyan Would Help Win War," *Phreno Cosmian*; "The American Home Guard in the 20th Century," May 26, 2017, https://www.worldhistory.us/military-history/the-american-home-guard-in-the-20th-century.php; James D. McLaird, *The Dakota Wesleyan University Memory Book 1885-2010* (Mitchell, SD: Dakota Wesleyan University, 2010) p. 80; Lon Fort to Francis Case, order, January 17, 1918, box 1, file 14, Carol Case Goddard Collection.
34. Francis to Homefolks, January 27, 1918; "Kenneth West Is Shot Returning from Guard Duty," *Phreno Cosmian*, January 31, 1918.
35. "Kenneth West Is Shot Returning from Guard Duty," "Just Personal," and "'In the Shadow'," *Phreno Cosmian*, January 31, 1918.
36. "Old Line Goes to Rising," *Phreno Cosmian*, January 17, 1918, "Rising Adds an Interstate Victory—D.W.U.'s Best Year" and "Wesleyan Wins State Champ.," *Phreno Cosmian*, April 25, 1918; *1919 Tumbleweed*.
37. "Dakota State News," *Forest City Press* (Forest City, SD), January 24, 1918; Francis to Homefolks, January 27, 1918; Editorial, *Phreno Cosmian*, February 7, 1918. Rising went on to show that his victory was no fluke. On February 14, he won the state contest at Huron against four other contestants. On April 5, the western division contest was held at Mitchell. Orators representing six states—North Dakota, South Dakota, Missouri, Nebraska, Kansas, and Iowa—entered the competition. Rising finished third, which meant he did well enough to advance to the final competition. Two weeks later, the top three western division orators (representing Missouri, North Dakota, and South Dakota) met the top three from the eastern division (representing Minnesota, Indiana, and Illinois) in Topeka, Kansas, to decide the overall winner. (The other three states in the eastern division were Wisconsin, Michigan, and Ohio.) Rising, who "was stronger than at any previous contest in which he appeared," won first place and received the gold medal from the Old Line Oratorical Association. When word of his victory got back to the Wesleyan student body, "their enthusiasm knew no bounds." Plans were immediately made for a reception at which Rising would be presented with a loving cup. See "Wesleyan Orator Carries Off First Honors in State Old Line Contest," *Phreno Cosmian*, February 21, 1918, "Wesleyan Orator Places in Old Line Divisional," *Phreno Cosmian*, April 11, 1918, "Rising Adds an Interstate Victory—D.W.U.'s Best Year," *Phreno Cosmian*.
38. "Adelphians Win Academy Debate," *Phreno Cosmian*, January 10, 1918, "Wesleyan Academy Teams Win Duel with Yankton," *Phreno Cosmian*, January 31, 1918, "'Preps' Win Yankton Dual Debates," *Phreno Cosmian*, April 25, 1918.

39. "'Defiant Reform'," *Phreno Cosmian*, February 7, 1918, "Not a Joke," *Phreno Cosmian*, Febuary 21, 1918.
40. "Wesleyan Would Help Win War," *Phreno Cosmian*, "Wesleyan Men 'With the Colors'" and "Annual Patriotic Fetes Tomorrow," *Phreno Cosmian*, February 21, 1918, "Service Flag of 126 Stars Dedicated on Patriotic Day," *Phreno Cosmian*, February 28, 1918.
41. "Berry '16 Gives Life for Country's Cause," *Phreno Cosmian*, February 21, 1918, "Service Flag of 126 Stars Dedicated on Patriotic Day," *Phreno Cosmian*.
42. "Service Flag of 126 Stars Dedicated on Patriotic Day," *Phreno Cosmian*.
43. "Senior Class Pushing Play," *Phreno Cosmian*, January 31, 1918, "Some Senior Play, 'Met,' Tuesday," *Phreno Cosmian*, March 7, 1918, "Senior Class Prove to Be Real Actors," *Phreno Cosmian*, March 21, 1918.
44. "Forensic Battles Are Arranged," *Phreno Cosmian*, September 27, 1917, "Five Colleges Fight for Forensic Fame Tonight," *Phreno Cosmian*, March 14, 1918, "Wesleyan is State Forensic Champion," *Phreno Cosmian*, March 21, 1918.
45. "Wesleyan vs. Morningside," *Phreno Cosmian*, March 21, 1918, Wesleyan Wins Dual Forensic Battle" and "University Notes," *Phreno Cosmian*, March 28, 1918.
46. "Wesleyan Wins Dual Forensic Battle," *Phreno Cosmian*, "Wesleyan Wins Dual Debate from Morningside College," *Phreno Cosmian*, April 25, 1918.
47. "Preps Contend in Oratorical" and "Francis Case Turns Out Prep Champions," *Phreno Cosmian*, April 25, 1918.
48. "Endowment Campaign Work Starting," *Phreno Cosmian*, April 11, 1918, "Endowment Campaign Launched Sunday," *Phreno Cosmian*, May 3 [*sic*; May 2], 1918; Francis Case to Rev. Charles M. Donaldson, July 21, 1920, box 2, file 23, Francis to Mother, April 24, 1918, box 1, file 7, Carol Case Goddard Collection.
49. "Coach McLain [*sic*] Enters Army," *Phreno Cosmian*, April 18, 1918, "College Press Meet Highly Successful," *Phreno Cosmian*, May 3 [*sic*; May 2], 1918.
50. "Pi Kappa Delta Has Annual Banquet," *Phreno Cosmian*, April 25, 1918.
51. "Exams Blue Penciled as a War Measure," *Phreno Cosmian*, May 3 [*sic*; May 2], 1918.
52. Editorial and "Endowment Campaign Launched Sunday," *Phreno Cosmian*, May 3 [*sic*; May 2], 1918.
53. "College War Year Nears End; Twenty-One Graduates," *Phreno Cosmian*, May 3 [*sic*; May 2], 1918. Wesleyan's 1918 college graduating class included 14 women and seven men: Leona Lloyd Burr, Harold William Card, Margaret Irene Card, Francis H. Case, Nettie Ruth Goodrich, Edith Flossie Holmes, Lila Gladys Kehm, Lillie Louise Kunkle, Walter William Ludeman, Lynas Elmer Lushbaugh, Mayme Pauline Miles, Anna McKay, Mildred

Prisch, Lloyd Harrison Rising, Edna A. Radabaugh, Ward Henry Stieber, Elma Kathleen Swartz, Lloyd Gilman Thompson, Matilda Tartleton, Mildred Calfree Test, and Ethel Nina Zeller. See also *1919 Tumbleweed*.
54. Francis to Mother, April 24, 1918; Francis H. Case to David M. Rogers, August 13, 1921, box 1, file 14, Carol Case Goddard Collection; "Neighborhood News," *Mitchell Capital* (Mitchell, SD), May 30, 1918.

CHAPTER 5. BECOMING A MARINE

The quotation at the beginning of the chapter is from a letter Francis wrote to his "Homefolks" dated June 4, 1918.

1. Francis to Homefolks, January 27, 1918, box 1, file 7, Carol Case Goddard Collection.
2. Francis Case to David M. Rogers, August 13, 1921, box 1, file 14, Carol Case Goddard Collection; Leland Davidson Case, interview by Robert Webb, Mitchell, SD, April 23, 1972, transcript, Francis H. Case Collection (hereinafter LDC Interview, April 23, 1972); "The Daily Journal," *Rapid City Daily Journal* (Rapid City, SD), June 5, 1918.
3. LDC Interview, April 23, 1972.
4. Ibid.
5. Francis to Homefolks, June 4, 1918, box 5, file 5, Carol Case Goddard Collection; United States Marine Corps Enlistment Form, June 4, 1918, file no. 121882, FHC Records, National Archives, NPRC.
6. "Mare Island, CA [USMC]," The Military Yearbook Project, accessed March 6, 2020, https://militaryyearbookproject.org/references/base-histories/general-histories/mare-island-ca; Matt Hevezi, "Mare Island was first California boot camp," Leatherneck forums, August 22, 2006, http://www.leatherneck.com/forums/showthread.php?33786 (hereinafter Hevezi, "Mare Island"). Mare Island was originally named Isla de la Plana by a Spanish explorer in 1775. It got its current name in 1835 when, according to legend, "a ferry carrying men and livestock ran into bad weather." The weather conditions caused some of the livestock to jump overboard. Most of the animals drowned, but a few of them made it to shore. Among the surviving animals was a white mare that belonged to General Mariano Vallejo—the Mexican comandante for Northern California. He renamed the island after his horse (Ibid.).
7. Francis to Homefolks, June 4, 1918; *Service Record Book of Case, Francis H.*, pp. 1-3 (hereinafter *Service Record Book*), United States Marine Corps Enlistment Form, June 4, 1918, FHC Records, National Archives, NPRC.
8. "The Daily Journal," *Rapid City Daily Journal*, (Rapid City, SD), July 6, 1918 and September 25, 1918; Francis to Mother, August 20, 1918, box 1, file 7, Carol Case Goddard Collection.

9. Francis to Mother, August 20, 1918.
10. Ibid.; "Extra and Special Duty Details," *Service Record Book*, p. 15.
11. Francis to Dad, August 31, 1918, cabinet 45, new drawer 179/old drawer 184, box 1, file: Reverend Herbert L. Case, Francis H. Case Collection; "Instructors & men, Sec 5 Co D—USMC—Mare Is. Calif," photograph, August 29, 1918, blue/gray notebook labelled "Francis," carton B, Case Ranch Collection.
12. Robert J. Smith, "The U. S. Army and the Great Influenza Pandemic of 1918," *On Point: The Journal of Army History* 25, no. 2 (2019): 18–19 (hereinafter Smith, "Great Influenza Pandemic"); John M. Barry, "Journal of the Plague Year," *Smithsonian Magazine*, November 2017, p. 36 (hereinafter Barry, "Plague Year").
13. Barry, "Plague Year," pp. 36, 37, 39; Jay Hilotin, "'Spanish flu' 1918 vs Covid-19," slide 5, http://www.gulfnews.com/special-reports/Spanish-flu-1918-vs-covid-19-1.1582445160581 (hereinafter Hilotin, "Spanish Flu"); Smith, "Great Influenza Pandemic," p. 19.
14. Smith, "Great Influenza Pandemic," p. 21; Barry, "Plague Year," p. 42.
15. Smith, "Great Influenza Pandemic," pp. 18–19; Barry, "Plague Year," pp. 34, 36, 37, 41.
16. Smith, "Great Influenza Pandemic," pp. 19–20.
17. Smith, "Great Influenza Pandemic," pp. 20–21; Barry, "Plague Year," p. 36.
18. Barry, "Plague Year," pp. 36–37; Smith, "Great Influenza Pandemic," p. 21.
19. Barry, "Plague Year," pp. 37–39.
20. Smith, "Great Influenza Pandemic," pp. 22, 25; Barry, "Plague Year," p. 41.
21. Barry, "Plague Year," p. 41, Hilotin, "Spanish Flu," slide 33.
22. Karie Youngdahl, "The 1918-19 Spanish Influenza Pandemic and Vaccine Development," History of Vaccines, September 26, 2018, https://web.archive.org/web/20210126132602/https://historyofvaccines.org/content/blog/vaccine-development-spanish-flu ; (hereinafter Youngdahl, "Vaccine Development"); Barry, "Plague Year," pp. 34, 36, 37; Hilotin, "Spanish Flu," slide 15; Carol R. Byerly, "The U.S. Military and the Influenza Pandemic of 1918-1919," *Public Health Reports* 125, no. S3 (2010), https://www.ncbi.nlm.nih.gov/pmc/articles/PMC2862337/.
23. Francis to Mother, October 6, 1918, box 1, file 8, Carol Case Goddard Collection.
24. Ibid.; Francis to Mother et al, October 8, 1918, box 1, file 7, Carol Case Goddard Collection; "Small Arms Record," *Service Record Book*, p. 16; Hevezi, "Mare Island." The term "butts" in Francis's October 8 letter refers to the mounds of earth behind targets on a shooting range.
25. Herbert L. Case to Carrie Matthews, October 22, 1918, box 2, file 2, Herbert L. Case Papers.

26. Francis to Esther, November 1, 1918, box 1, file 7, Carol Case Goddard Collection.
27. Ibid. Note that Francis referred to getting "three vaccine shots" in his description of measures the Marines took to prevent the flu. It is likely this was a vaccine made from bacilli (a class of bacteria) that was taken from sick individuals and killed by heat. It was administered in three doses "given 48 hours apart." That vaccine did not prevent the Spanish flu because, as we now know, "influenza . . . [is] in fact caused by a virus, not a bacterium." At best, the vaccine may have "reduced the attack rate of pneumonia after viral influenza infection," but even this conclusion is in doubt. See Youngdahl, "Vaccine Development."
28. Francis to Mother, November 21, 1918, box 1, file 7, Carol Case Goddard Collection; Harold W. Card, interview by Robert Webb, Webster, SD, May 27, 1972, transcript, Francis H. Case Collection.
29. Francis to Mother, Thanksgiving Day [November 28], 1918, box 1, file 7, Carol Case Goddard Collection.
30. Francis to Mother and all, December 8, 1918, box 1, file 8, Carol Case Goddard Collection.
31. Francis to Homefolks, December 22, 1918, box 1, file 7, Carol Case Goddard Collection.
32. Ibid.
33. Commanding Officer, Company D to Adjutant and Inspector, Headquarters, Washington, D.C., memorandum for discharge order, December 30, 1918, FHC Records, National Archives, NPRC; "Extra and Special Duty Details," p. 15, "Professional and Conduct Record of Case, Francis H.," p. 4, Offenses Committed form, p. 10, *Service Record Book*; Honorable Discharge certificate, January 15, 1919, carton B, Case Ranch Collection; Good Conduct Medal certificate no. 45570, January 15, 1921, FHC Records, National Archives, NPRC.
34. "The Daily Journal," *Rapid City Daily Journal* (Rapid City, SD), January 21, 1919; "The Daily Journal," *Rapid City Daily Journal* (Rapid City, SD), February 1, 1919.

CHAPTER 6. RETURN TO ALMA MATER

The quotation at the beginning of the chapter is taken from the *Phreno Cosmian*, March 6[, 1919] issue.

1. "High School Commencement This Week," *Rapid City Daily Journal* (Rapid City, SD), June 9, 1918; "President Gage Talks to High School Class," *Rapid City Daily Journal* (Rapid City, SD), June 14, 1918; "The Daily Journal," *Rapid City Daily Journal* (Rapid City, SD), September 25, 1918; Francis to Mother, August 20, 1918, box 1, file 7, Carol Case Goddard Collection.

Notes

2. Francis to Mother, August 20, 1918, Francis to Mother, October 6, 1918, box 1, file 8, Carol Case Goddard Collection; "Go to War, Go to College, Says Uncle Sam," *Rapid City Daily Journal* (Rapid City, SD), August 13, 1918.
3. "Wesleyan to Adopt Quarter System," *Phreno Cosmian* (Mitchell, SD), March 7, 1918, carton B, Case Ranch Collection (hereinafter *Phreno Cosmian*); "Wesleyan University Postpones Opening," *Rapid City Daily Journal* (Rapid City, SD), September 1, 1918.
4. "Free College Training at Dakota Wesleyan U.," *Rapid City Daily Journal* (Rapid City, SD), September 6, 1918.
5. Ibid.; "Colleges in State Offer Training to Young Men," *Rapid City Daily Journal* (Rapid City, SD), September 10, 1918; "Tuesday Day When Colleges Enter Service," *Rapid City Journal* (Rapid City, SD), September 28, 1918; James D. McLaird, *The Dakota Wesleyan University Memory Book 1885-2010* (Mitchell, SD: Dakota Wesleyan University, 2010), pp. 80–81 (hereinafter McLaird, *DWU Memory Book*).
6. Francis to Mother, October 6, 1918, Leland to Folks, December 1, 1918, box 4, file 10, Carol Case Goddard Collection; McLaird, *DWU Memory Book*, p. 81; "Wesleyan Loses to Vermillion," *Phreno Cosmian*, December 12, 1918.
7. McLaird, *DWU Memory Book*, pp. 81, 86; Leland to Folks, December 1, 1918.
8. "Wesleyan Warriors Are Some Bunch," *Phreno Cosmian*, January 17, 1918, "Wesleyan Loses to Vermillion," *Phreno Cosmian*, "Dakota Wesleyan's Gold Stars." and "Wesleyan Men Who Entered Service," *Phreno Cosmian*, February 27[, 1919].
9. "Y.M. Leadership Changes," *Phreno Cosmian*, September 20, 1917, "New Stars Added to Service Flag," *Phreno Cosmian*, December 12, 1918, "Dakota Wesleyan's Gold Stars.," *Phreno Cosmian*.
10. "Plan to Disband S.A.T.C. Dec 24," *Phreno Cosmian*, December 12, 1918, "S.A.T.C. Comes to Close Dec. 21" and "Officials Explain Early Disbanding," *Phreno Cosmian*, January 2, 1919.
11. Editorial, *Phreno Cosmian*, December 12, 1918.
12. "Society Pledges," *Phreno Cosmian*, December 19, 1918, "Freshman Class Holds Election," *Phreno Cosmian*, January 2, 1919.
13. "Company, Attention!" *Phreno Cosmian*, December 19, 1918, "S.A.T.C. Comes to Close Dec. 21," *Phreno Cosmian*.
14. "Wesleyan to Adopt Quarter System," *Phreno Cosmian*, "Dr. Adelbert Semans Addresses Students," *Phreno Cosmian*, January 2, 1919, "Wesleyan Opens Phillips Hall," *Phreno Cosmian*, January 9, 1919; Leland to Folks, December 1, 1918, Leland to Folks, January 6, 1919, Leland to Folks, January 28, 1919, box 4, file 10, Carol Case Goddard Collection.

15. Jarvis Harriman, *The Man from the Hills: A Biography of Leland Davidson Case* (Tucson, AZ: Westerners International, 1994), p. 22; "About *The Mitchell Gazette* (Mitchell, S.D.), 1913–1935," Chronicling America, https://www.chroniclingamerica.loc.gov/lccn/sn2001063105/; Leland to Folks, January 28, 1919; "Editorial Staff," *Phreno Cosmian*, January 2, 1919, "Editorial Staff," *Phreno Cosmian*, February 27[,1919].
16. "'Will Have Debates' Says Forensic Board," *Phreno Cosmian*, January 9, 1919.
17. "Daedalians Hold Initiation" and "Mrs. Laura E. Ruth Chief Yeoman in Navy [sic]," *Phreno Cosmian*, January 9, 1919. Due to a printer's error, the story on Coach McLean's possible return to Wesleyan appears under the above title, and the story about Mrs. Ruth (a Wesleyan alumna) is under the title "Coach Ray McLean May Return Here."
18. "Collegiate Debate Questions Chosen," *Phreno Cosmian*, January 23, 1918 [sic; 1919].
19. "Francis Case to Coach Debate at U" and "Prexie Speaker at Simpson College," *Phreno Cosmian*, January 30, 1919, "Annual Intersociety Debates Ruled Out" and "University Notes," *Phreno Cosmian*, February 5 [sic; February 6], 1919; E. M. Burch to Francis, January 21, 1919, box 2, file 5, Carol Case Goddard Collection.
20. "Thalian-Daedalians Enjoy Sleigh Ride," *Phreno Cosmian*, February 13, 1919.
21. Francis to Mother and all, February 16, 1919, box 1, file 7, Carol Case Goddard Collection; "Coach Gives Rousing Pep Speech in Chapel," *Phreno Cosmian*, February 13, 1919, "Wesleyanites Defeat Greyhounds 28 to 10," *Phreno Cosmian*, February 20[, 1919].
22. "Adelphians Carry Off Debate Honors," *Phreno Cosmian*, February 20[, 1919], "University Notes," *Phreno Cosmian*, May 29, 1919; Francis to Mother, February 21, 1919, box 1, file 7, Carol Case Goddard Collection.
23. "Wesleyan's Gold Star Men," Editorial, "Lest We Forget," "To the Service Flag," "Dakota Wesleyan's Gold Stars.," and "Wesleyan Men Who Entered Service," *Phreno Cosmian*, February 27[, 1919], "A Correction," *Phreno Cosmian*, March 6[, 1919].
24. "Thirteen Men Try Collegiate Debate," *Phreno Cosmian*, March 6[, 1919].
25. "Girls Show Up Well for Coming Debates," *Phreno Cosmian*, March 6[, 1919], "Sophomore Girls in Debate Try Outs," *Phreno Cosmian*, March 13, 1919, "Frosh in Forensics," *Phreno Cosmian*, March 20, 1919.
26. Francis to Homefolks, March 24, 1919, box 4, file 10, Carol Case Goddard Collection.
27. Ibid.; *Phreno Cosmian* (Freshman Souvenir Edition), March 20, 1919.
28. "Coach Ray L. McLean Loses Life in Germany," *Phreno Cosmian*, April 3, 1919.

29. Francis to Miss Esther Case, March 30, 1919, box 6, file 6, Carol Case Goddard Collection; "D.W.A. Victor Over Huron and Yankton," *Phreno Cosmian*, April 10, 1919, "Academy in Forensics," *Phreno Cosmian*, May 29, 1919.
30. "Frosh-Soph Co-eds Battle in Debate," *Phreno Cosmian*, April 3, 1919, "Freshmen Win in Debate Tryouts," *Phreno Cosmian*, April 10, 1919, "Girls' Debate Ends in Victory for Yankton," *Phreno Cosmian*, May 8, 1919; Dakota Wesleyan University, *The Tumbleweed: 1919* (Mitchell, SD: 1918), carton B, Case Ranch Collection.
31. Francis to Carol, April 12, 1919, box 6, file 6, Carol Case Goddard Collection.
32. Francis to Mother and All, April 20, 1919, Leland to folks, April 20, 1919, box 4, file 10, *Carol Case Goddard Collection*.
33. "College Debate Questions Chosen," *Phreno Cosmian*, "Debate Season Opens Saturday Night in Dual with Morningside," *Phreno Cosmian*; "Morningside Wrests Double Victory from Wesleyanites Saturday Night," *Phreno Cosmian*, May 1, 1919.
34. "Sophomore Class Roll," *Phreno Cosmian*, March 13, 1919, "Debate Season Opens Saturday Night in Dual with Morningside," *Phreno Cosmian*; Francis to Homefolks, April 26, 1919, carton 1, box 7, Carol Case Goddard Collection.
35. "Morningside Wrests Double Victory from Wesleyanites Saturday Night." *Phreno Cosmian*.
36. "Sophomore Class Roll," *Phreno Cosmian*, "Morningside Wrests Double Victory from Wesleyanites Saturday Night," *Phreno Cosmian*, "Dakota Wesleyan, Yankton and Huron Vie for State Debate Championship," *Phreno Cosmian*, May 8, 1919, "Wesleyan Makes a Great Record for College in a War Year," *Phreno Cosmian*, June 19, 1919.
37. "Memorial Drive of Locust Trees to Be Main Feature of Arbor Day," *Phreno Cosmian*, April 24, 1919, "Annual Tree Plant Made Big Occasion" and "Wesleyan Victorious Over Baseball Rivals," *Phreno Cosmian,* May 8, 1919, "Arbor Day Memorial," *Phreno Cosmian*, May 29, 1919.
38. "Co-eds Clash in Collegiate Debate," *Phreno Cosmian*, May 1, 1919, "Girls' Debate Ends in Victory for Yankton," *Phreno Cosmian*, May 8, 1919.
39. "Academy Senior Play Memorial for School," *Phreno Cosmian*, April 24, 1919, "Fourth Year Preps Make Hit on Stage," *Phreno Cosmian*, May 22, 1919, "Prexy Announces Faculty Changes," *Phreno Cosmian*, May 29, 1919.
40. "Academy Senior Play Memorial for School," *Phreno Cosmian*, "Fourth Year Preps Make Hit on Stage," *Phreno Cosmian*, "Senior Academy Play" and "Senior Academy Presents Memorial," *Phreno Cosmian*, May 29, 1919.
41. "Case Announces Prep Oratorical Trophy," *Phreno Cosmian*, March 6[, 1919], "Preps Engage in Oratory Clash," *Phreno Cosmian*, June 12, 1919.

42. "Profs Much in Demand for Commencements," *Phreno Cosmian*, June 19, 1919; Francis to Mother, Esther, Carol, and Grandpa, June 14, 1919, box 4, file 3, Carol Case Goddard Collection.
43. "Flu Takes Life of Ada Ferguson," *Phreno Cosmian*, December 19, 1918, "Former Wesleyanite Loses Life in France" and "Flu Causes Death of Former Student," *Phreno Cosmian*, April 24, 1919, "75 People Awarded Diplomas at Thirty Third Commencement" and "Wesleyan Makes Great Record for College in War Year," *Phreno Cosmian*, June 19, 1919.
44. "Wesleyan Conference Champ," *Phreno Cosmian*, March 20, 1919, "Wesleyan Victorious Over Baseball Rivals," *Phreno Cosmian*, May 8, 1919, "Baseball Year Ends with Final Victory," *Phreno Cosmian*, May 15, 1919, "Wesleyan Wins in Hot Contest," *Phreno Cosmian*, May 29, 1919, "Baseball Locals Lose to Alexandria 11-5," *Phreno Cosmian*, June 5, 1919, "Wesleyan Makes Great Record for College in War Year," *Phreno Cosmian*.
45. Francis H. Case to Charles H. Denby, Jr., November 18, 1921, box 1, file 10, Carol Case Goddard Collection; "Several Professors to Graduate Schools," *Phreno Cosmian*, June 19, 1919; Francis to Father, July 15, 1919, box 4, file 3, Carol Case Goddard Collection.

CHAPTER 7. GRADUATE SCHOOL AND TRADE PAPER JOB IN THE WINDY CITY

The quotation at the beginning of the chapter is taken from a letter from Francis to Dr. Brummitt dated August 15, 1920.

1. Case to Merrill J. Holmes, September 25, 1919, box 2, file 16, Francis to Homefolks, March 28, 1920, box 2, file 33, Carol Case Goddard Collection.
2. *Encyclopedia of Cleveland History*, s.v. "Epworth League," accessed March 25, 2021, http://www.case.edu/ech/articles/e/epworth-league; "Where the Epworth League Got Its Name," *Epworth Herald* (Chicago, IL), October 9, 1920, carton B, Case Ranch Collection (hereinafter *Epworth Herald*); New York Annual Conference of the United Methodist Church, "The Epworth Herald, Dec 2009," accessed March 24, 2021, http://www.nyac.com/theepworthheralddec2009; "The Place of the Junior League in the Church" and "The What and Why of the Junior League," *Epworth Herald*, May 22, 1920; Dan B. Brummitt, *The Efficient Epworthian: Being "Epworth League Methods" Revised—Expanded—Rewritten* (New York: The Methodist Book Concern, 1914), p. 40 (hereinafter Brummitt, *The Efficient Epworthian*); "High Lights of the General Secretary's Report," *Epworth Herald*, May 15, 1920.
3. "The Epworth Herald, Dec 2009," accessed March 24, 2021, http://www.nyac.com/theepworthheralddec2009; "We Have Fifteen Thousand New Friends," *Epworth Herald*, January 24, 1920; Brummitt, *The Efficient Epworthian*, title page, pp. 277, 365.

4. "The Epworth Herald," *Epworth Herald*, January 3, 1920, "Whose Paper is This Anyway? Yours? Prove It!," *Epworth Herald*, June 19, 1920.
5. Francis to Mother and all, November 9, 1919, box 1, file 7, Carol Case Goddard Collection; "High Lights of the General Secretary's Report," *Epworth Herald*.
6. J. A. James to Dean Wigmore, November 11, 1919, Frederic B. Crossley to Francis H. Case, December 16, 1919, box 1, file 10, Francis Case to Fred M. Dille, December 5, 1919, box 2, file 23, Coursey to Case, December 19, 1919, Francis to Coursey, December 26, 1919, box 3, file 1, Carol Case Goddard Collection.
7. Francis to Papa, Mama, Joyce, Carol, Esther, Leland, and Grandpa, December 22[, 1919], box 1, file 7, Carol Case Goddard Collection.
8. Ibid.
9. Francis to Coursey, December 26, 1919; "Professor Hahne," *Phreno Cosmian* (Mitchell, SD), April 18, 1918, "Burch Takes Prexy's Old Chair at Garrett," *Phreno Cosmian*, May 3, 1918, carton B, Case Ranch Collection (hereinafter *Phreno Cosmian*); Northwestern University, *The Syllabus 1922* (Evanston, IL: 1921) pp. 176–77, 404 (hereinafter *Syllabus 1922*), carton B, Case Ranch Collection.
10. Francis to Papa, December 30, 1919, box 1, file 8, Carol Case Goddard Collection.
11. Brandrup & Nettleton to Whom It May Concern, March 13, 1915, box 1, file 21, Joyce to Francis, August 24, 1921, box 2, file 24, Carol Case Goddard Collection; "Spray of the Springs," *Hot Springs Weekly Star* (Hot Springs, SD), April 2, 1915 and September 24, 1915; Mary A. Case, diary from Hot Springs, SD, June 13, 27, July 4, September 4, 10, October 12, 1916 (hereinafter *MAC Diary*), Case Ranch Collection.
12. "Local Notes," *Mitchell Capital* (Mitchell, SD), November 2, 1916; "Mrs. F. L. Case Dead," *Hot Springs Weekly Star* (Hot Springs, SD), August 31, 1917; "The Daily Journal," *Rapid City Daily Journal* (Rapid City, SD), January 18, 1918; "University Notes," *Phreno Cosmian*, January 31, 1918; "Business College for South Dakotans," *Daily Argus-Leader* (Sioux Falls, SD), April 3, 1919; "The Daily Journal," *Rapid City Daily Journal* (Rapid City, SD), May 8, 1919; *Fall River County Pioneer Histories* (Fall River, SD: Fall River County Historical Society, 1976), p. 53 (hereinafter *Fall River Histories*); "Nettleton Commercial College," *Daily Argus-Leader* (Sioux Falls, SD), August 27, 1919.
13. "Joyce Wilson Was First 'Woman of Year'," *Hot Springs Star* (Hot Springs, SD), October 18, 1978; Leland Davidson Case and Edith E. H. Grannis, eds., *New Hampshire to Minnesota: Memoirs of Samuel Higbee Grannis (1839-1933)* (Tucson, AZ: Self-published, 1962), p. 151 (hereinafter Case and Grannis, eds., *SHG Memoirs*); *Fall River Histories*, p. 284; "Wilson-Case Marriage Occurred Yesterday," *Rapid City Daily Journal* (Rapid City,

SD), January 22, 1920; Unidentified and undated newspaper article titled "Marriages," box 1, file 21, Carol Case Goddard Collection; "Shower for Bride-Elect," *Daily Argus-Leader* (Sioux Falls, SD), August 21, 1919; "Shower for Miss Case," *Daily Argus-Leader* (Sioux Falls, SD), August 23, 1919.

14. "Shower for Bride-Elect," *Daily Argus-Leader*; Francis to Mother, Joyce, et al, Sunday evening [January 11, 1920], Box 1, File 7, Unidentified and undated newspaper article titled "Marriages;" Mary E. Case, "Details of the Wedding," undated, box 1, file 21, Carol Case Goddard Collection; "Wilson-Case Marriage Occurred Yesterday," *Rapid City Daily Journal*.
15. , Francis Case to "Bill," January 31, 1920, box 2, file 28, Case to Merrill J. Holmes, September 25, 1919, box 2, file 16, Francis to My Dear Valentine [Carol], February 17, 1920, box 1, file 14, Carol Case Goddard Collection.
16. Francis to Homefolks, March 28, 1920, box 1, file 14, Carol Case Goddard Collection.
17. Francis to "Sis" [Carol], April 3, 1920, box 5, file 1, Carol Case Goddard Collection; *Epworth Herald*, April 3 and April 10, 1920.
18. Francis Case to J. P. Jenkins, April 25, 1920, box 2, file 14, Francis H. Case to Matthew D. Smith, May 13, 1920, box 2, file 32, Schermerhorn to Francis Case, May 24, 1920, box 2, file 21, Carol Case Goddard Collection.
19. "The Daily Journal," *Rapid City Daily Journal* (Rapid City, SD), June 10, 1920; Francis Case to C. V. Gilliland, June 9, 1920, box 2, file 15, Norman E. Richardson to Christian F. Reisner, May 26, 1920, box 2, file 38, Francis Case to My Dear Sir, November 3, 1920, box 1, file 14, Carol Case Goddard Collection.
20. Schermerhorn to Francis Case, July 1, 1920, Schermerhorn to Francis Case, July 27, 1920, Francis Case to W. D. Schermerhorn, July 11, 1921, box 2, file 21, Carol Case Goddard Collection.
21. Christian F. Reisner to P. S. Flores, July 17, 1920, box 2, file 38, Carol Case Goddard Collection; United Methodist Publishing House, "History," accessed April 17, 2021, http://www.umph.org/Who-Are-We/History; "The Epworth Herald," *Epworth Herald*, January 3, 1920; Invoices, Methodist Book Concern, June 22 and 24, 1920, box 2, file 8, Caroline B. Auteurieth to Mr. Case, June 21, 1920, Francis H. Case, to Christian F. Reisner, June 26, 1920, Christian F. Reisner to Francis H. Case, June 28, 1920, Francis H. Case to Christian F. Reisner, July 6, 1920, Caroline B. Auteurieth to Francis H. Case, July 7, 1920, Francis H. Case to Christian F. Reisner, July 13, 1920, box 2, file 38, Francis Case to Norman E. Richardson, August 27, 1920, box 2, file 28, Francis H. Case to David C. Downey, August 30, 1920, box 2, file 23, Carol Case Goddard Collection.
22. Dan B. Brummitt to E. H. Forkel, June 26, 1920, Francis Case to Dr. Brummitt, August 15, 1920, box 1, file 14, Dan B. Brummitt to Case, August 18[, 1920], box 3, file 2, Carol Case Goddard Collection.

23. "Francis H. Case, Assistant Editor," *Epworth Herald*, September 18, 1920; Francis H. Case to "Bill," December 7, 1920; Carol Case Goddard Collection.
24. "The Daily Journal," *Rapid City Daily Journal* (Rapid City, SD), September 12, 1920; "Dr. F. L. Case, 87, Dies Suddenly in Minnesota," *Rapid City Daily Journal* (Rapid City, SD), September 10, 1924; *Fall River Histories*, p. 53; HLC to Francis, October 6, 1920, H L Case to Francis, May 25, 1921, box 2, file 33, Grandpa Case to Francis, February 1, 1921, H L Case to Francis and Leland, March 22, 1921, Francis H. Case to Frank L. Case, June 23, 1921, box 1, file 13, H L Case to Francis, July 17, 1921, box 4, file 10, Carol Case Goddard Collection.
25. Jarvis Harriman, *The Man from the Hills: A Biography of Leland Davidson Case* (Tucson, AZ: Westerners International, 1994), p. 23; Leland Davidson Case, interview by Robert Webb, Mitchell, SD, April 23, 1972, transcript, Francis H. Case Collection.
26. "South Dakota Student Receives High Honor," *Rapid City Daily Journal* (Rapid City, SD), December 7, 1920; "Graduate Club," *Syllabus 1922*, p. 273; Francis Case to Peter C. Lutkin, December 7, 1920, P. C. Lutkin to Francis H. Case, December 9, 1920, box 2, file 37, Francis H. Case to Fellow Student, March 18, 1921, box 2, file 14, Carol Case Goddard Collection.
27. Francis H. Case to "Bill," December 7, 1920; Mother to Francis H. Case, December 9, 1920, box 5, file 2, Francis Case to Harrison A. Schmitt, January 12, 1921, box 2, file 32, Francis H. Case to Dr. Reisner, December 30, 1920, box 2, file 38, Carol Case Goddard Collection; Case and Grannis, eds., *SHG Memoirs*, pp. 148–49.
28. Francis to Carol, January 24, 1921, box 5, file 2, Carol Case Goddard Collection.
29. H. L. Case to Francis H. Case, February 20, 1921, box 1, file 15, Leland to Brother, February 20, 1921, box 4, file 10, Carol to Francis, February 21, box 5, file 4, Punkins [Esther] to Francis, February 22, 1921, box 2, file 22, Carol Case Goddard Collection; "Louise Wood in the New York, U.S., Arriving Passenger and Crew Lists (including Castle Garden and Ellis Island), 1820-1957;" "Louise Woods [*sic*]," 1910 United States Census, Sheldon, Iroquois County, Illinois; "Louise Wood," 1920 United States Census, Sheldon, Iroquois County, Illinois "Louise Wood digital image s.v. "Louise Wood," *Ancestry.com*; *Syllabus 1922*, pp. 256-57, 279, 309; Agnes Wright Spring (Mrs. Archer T.), ed., "Pi Phis in the Public Eye," *The Arrow: Official Publication of the Pi Beta Phi Fraternity* 40, no. 3 (March 1924): 586.
30. Francis to Carol, March 13, 1921, Francis to Punkins [Esther], March 13, 1921, Mother to Francis, partial letter, date unknown but apparently written in March, 1921, box 6, file 9, Leland to Francis, August 19, 1921, box 4, file 10, Carol Case Goddard Collection.
31. Francis Case to Ethel Owen, January 17, 1921, Ethel Owen to Francis H. Case, January 19, 1921, E. Owen to Francis H. Case, February 11, 1921,

Francis H. Case to Arthur F. Stevens, February 21, 1921, box 2, file 37, Francis Case to Christian F. Reisner, February 25, 1921, box 2, file 38, Papa HLC to Francis, March 3, 1921, box 2, file 33, Carol Case Goddard Collection.

32. Ethel Owen to Francis H. Case, March 4, 1921, box 2, file 37, Carol Case Goddard Collection; Francis H. Case, *Handbook of Church Advertising* (New York: The Abingdon Press, 1921) (hereinafter *Handbook*); "Christian Advocate (Nashville [Tenn.]) 1853-1940," Library of Congress, accessed Sept 1, 2023, https://www.loc.gov/item/sn93062956; "Books and Periodicals," *Christian Advocate* (Nashville, TN), March 18, 1921. Noting that it was "an important historical work," a company named FB & c Ltd. in London, England recently published the *Handbook* in paperback under the company's registered trademark Forgotten Books. The *Handbook* is currently available on the Forgotten Books website to read online or as an e-book, and paperback and hardcover versions are available on Amazon.

33. Francis H. Case to Arthur F. Stevens, May 26, 1921, box 2, file 37, Carol Case Goddard Collection; "Among the New Books," *Pacific Christian Advocate* (Portland, OR), June 22, 1921.

34. W. D. Schermerhorn to Francis Case, April 11, 1921, Francis Case to W. D. Schermerhorn, April 13, 1921, box 2, file 21, Harold to Case, April 30, 1921, box 2, file 25, Carol to Francis, May 22, 1921, box 5, file 4, Joyce to Francis, May 17, 1921, box 2, file 22, Francis to Homefolks, May 23, 1921, box 1, file 7, Carol Case Goddard Collection; Case and Grannis, eds., *SHG Memoirs*, p. 151.

35. Francis to Homefolks, May 23, 1921.

36. Ibid., Joyce to Francis, June 14, 1921, box 2, file 22, Francis H. Case to Guy, November 25, 1921, box 2, file 27, Carol Case Goddard Collection; *Fall River Histories*, pp. 42-43; "Francis H. Case Gives University Address Sunday," *Phreno Cosmian*, June 9, 1921, file: Case, Francis, Dakota Wesleyan Archives.

37. Francis to Homefolks, May 23, 1921, box 1, file 7, Francis Case to W. D. Schermerhorn, July 11, 1921, box 2, file 21, Francis Case to Wade Crawford Barclay, June 14, 1921, box 3, file 2, Carol Case Goddard Collection.

38. Francis H. Case to Clarence V. Gilliland, July 8, 1921; Francis Case to W. D. Schermerhorn, July 11, 1921, box 2, file 21, Francis Case to N. E. Richardson, August 25, 1921, box 34, file 2, George M. Smith to F. M. Case, April 29, 1921, Francis H. Case to George M. Smith, April 30, 1921, box 2, file 32, Francis Case to Professor Eliot, July 22, 1921, box 2, file 23, Walter B. Niles to Mr. Case, September 2, 1921, box 2, file 36, Mother to Francis, July 2, 1921, Mother to Francis, August 8, 1921, box 6, file 9, Carol Case Goddard Collection.

39. Francis H. Case to Clarence V. Gilliland, July 8, 1921; Dan B. Brummitt to Charles E. Guthrie, July 23, 1921, Dan B. Brummitt to Mr. Allen, August 4, 1921, box 3, file 2, Carol Case Goddard Collection.

40. E. Owen to Norman E. Richardson, August 17, 1921, box 2, file 37, Francis Case to N. E. Richardson, August 25, 1921, box 2, file 34, Carol Case Goddard Collection. *The Literary Digest* was founded by two former Lutheran ministers—Isaac K. Funk and Adam W. Wagnalls—in 1890. It was a weekly news magazine that emphasized "opinion articles and an analysis of news events." In 1916, it "conducted a national survey of voter preferences [for president] by "mailing out millions of post cards and counting the returns." Armed with these results, the *Digest* correctly predicted that Woodrow Wilson would be elected president of the United States. By the early 1920s, "with a circulation of more than 1,000,000," the magazine was regarded as "something of an American institution." It continued to conduct presidential polls and "'went on to successfully call the next four elections.'" Those polls generated substantial newspaper coverage, which in turn increased the magazine's readership. In 1936, the *Digest* "'set out to launch its most ambitious poll ever.'" It sent out over ten million postcards to "'*Literary Digest* subscribers, people on automobile registration lists, and names in telephone directories, of which 2.4 million were returned.'" The responses led the magazine to predict that "'Republican candidate Alfred Landon would defeat Franklin Roosevelt, receive 57 percent of the popular vote, and carry thirty-two states in the Electoral College.'" Instead, "'Roosevelt won by a landslide, commanding 61 percent of the popular vote and winning in all but two states.'" The poll's methodology was "'heavily flawed'" because "'the sample was biased toward Republican-leaning voters who could afford telephone service, cars, and magazine subscriptions.'" In addition, "'the volunteers who tabulated the results were not carefully trained, which introduced additional error into the calculations.'" The *Digest* "was completely discredited because of the poll," which led to its subsequent downfall. It merged with another magazine in 1938, "only to fail soon after." See *Encyclopedia Britannica Online*, s.v. "Magazine Publishing," accessed May 4, 2021, http://www.britannica.com/topic/publishing/Magazine-publishing; "The Literary Digest," Vintage Magazine Shoppe, accessed May 4, 2021, http://www.vmshoppe.com/catalog/the-literary-digest/; *American Government and Politics in the Information Age* (Minneapolis: University of Minnesota Libraries, 2011), chap. 7.3, https://open.lib.umn.edu/americangovernment/chapter/7-3-polling-the-public/.
41. Francis Case to N. E. Richardson, August 25, 1921; "'Selling' Religion," *The Literary Digest*, August 20, 1921, pp. 28-29.
42. "Francis H. Case's Book on Church Publicity Praised by Famous Periodical," *Evanston News-Index*, (Evanston, IL), September 6, 1921; Christian F. Reisner to Francis H. Case, September 24, 1921, box 2, file 38, Carol Case Goddard Collection.
43. *Syllabus 1922*, p. 224; "Acacia History," accessed May 8, 2021, http://www.acacia.org/history; Francis H. Case to A. W. Harris, April 29, 1922, box 2, file 24, Leland to Francis, April 8, 1921, box 4, file 10, Carol Case Goddard

Collection; Chris Kavan, "Moments in Acacia History: First Recharter," accessed May 8, 1921, http://www.acacia.org/moments.

44. *Syllabus 1922*, pp. 179, 224; Francis to Harold, May 30, 1922, cabinet 45, new drawer 179/old drawer 184, box 2, file: Newspaper and Politics, Miscellaneous, Francis H. Case Collection.
45. Hall to Case, August 14, 1921, Francis H. Case to A. W. Harris, April 29, 1922, box 2, file 24, Case to Art, September 3, 1921, box 2, file 33, Carol Case Goddard Collection.
46. Francis H. Case to J. A. James, September 23, 1921, box 2, file 14, Schermerhorn to Francis Case, September 27, 1921, box 2, file 21, Dan BB to Case, October 10, 1921, box 3, file 2, Carol Case Goddard Collection.
47. Francis Case to H. E. Luccock, September 29, 1921, box 2, file 37, Dan BB to Case, October 10, 1921, box 3, file 2, Francis to Carol, October 27, 1921, box 6, file 9, Carol Case Goddard Collection.
48. Francis to Carol, September 16, 1921, Francis to Carol, October 27, 1921, Mother to Francis, November 29, 1921 (received), box 6, file 9, Carol Case Goddard Collection.
49. Mother to Francis, November 29, 1921 (received); Francis Case to John F. Way, December 22, 1921, box 2, file 34, Francis H. Case to Arthur F. Stevens, December 26, 1921, The Methodist Book Concern to Francis H. Case, "Copyright and Royalty Memorandum," July 31, 1921, box 2, file 37, Carol Case Goddard Collection; *Fall River Histories*, p. 53.
50. Mother to Francis, January 4 and 8, 1922, box 2, file 34, Carol Case Goddard Collection.
51. Francis Case to O. W. Coursey, January 10, 1922, box 3, file 1, Carol Case Goddard Collection; Francis to Dad, January 29, 1922, cabinet 45, new drawer 179/old drawer 184, box 1, files: Reverend Herbert L. Case, Francis H. Case Collection.
52. Francis to Carol, January 6, 1921 [sic; 1922], box 4, file 4, Francis Case to O.W. Coursey, January 10, 1922, box 3, file 1, Carol Case Goddard Collection.
53. Francis to Dad, January 29, 1922.
54. Ibid.; Francis H. Case to J. F. Way, February 9, 1922, cabinet 45, new drawer 179/old drawer 184, box 2, file: Miscellaneous Correspondence, Francis H. Case Collection; Francis H. Case to Dean J. A. James, memorandum, September 23, 1921, box 2, file 14, Francis H. Case to H. F. Harrington, January 9, 1922, box 2, file 24, H. F. Harrington, to Francis H. Case, January 12, 1922, box 1, file 10, Francis Case to O.W. Coursey, January 10, 1922, box 3, file 1, Carol Case Goddard Collection.
55. Herbert L. Case to Francis H. Case, telegram, March 25, 1922, box 2, file 33, Mother to Francis, postcard, March 26, 1922, Mother to Francis, postcard, March 27, 1922, box 2, file 34, Herbert L. Case to Francis, March 27, 1922, box 2, file 33, Mother to "My dear boy," undated, box 2, file 34,

Herbert L. Case to Francis H. Case, telegram, March 28, 1922, box 2, file 33, Carol Case Goddard Collection; Case and Grannis, eds., *SHG Memoirs*, pp. 101, 147.

56. Case to Bernie Brereton, February 24, 1922, Bernie to Friend Case, March 14, 1922, box 3, file 2, Case to Card, February 27, 1922, box 2, file 25, Francis H. Case to C. W. Downey, February 27, 1922, box 2, file 23, Harold to Francis, March 1, 1922, box 2, file 27, Francis Case to Ora G. Durr, March 11, 1922, box 2, file 33, Carol Case Goddard Collection; Francis to Harold, April 29, 1922, cabinet 45, new drawer 179/old drawer 184, box 2, file: Newspaper and Politics, Miscellaneous 1922, Francis H. Case Collection.

57. Papa to Francis, March 15, 1922, Papa to Francis, March 18, 1922, box 2, file 33, Mother to Francis, undated, box 2, file 34, Carol Case Goddard Collection.

58. Francis to Harold, April 29, 1922, Card to Case, May 3[, 1922], Harold to Francis, undated, Card to Francis, May 13, 1922, Francis to Harold, May 13, 1922, Francis to Harold, May 16, 1922, H.W.C. to Case, May 18, 1922, Francis to Harold, May 26, 1922, Francis to Harold, May 30, 1922, cabinet 45, new drawer 179/old drawer 184, box 2, file: Newspaper and Politics, Miscellaneous 1922, Francis H. Case Collection; Francis to Dad, May 11, 1922, box 2, file 33, Carol Case Goddard Collection.

59. Lewis Schuster to Francis Case, May 26, 1922, box 2, file 34, John F. Way to Francis H. Case, May 26, 1922, box 2, file 32, L. Guy Brown to Francis, April 24, 1922, L. Guy to Case, May 31, 1922, box 2, file 27, Carol Case Goddard Collection; "Wesleyan Will Have New Head," *Daily Argus-Leader* (Sioux Falls, SD), March 8, 1922; "New Wesleyan President," *Herald-Advance* (Milbank, SD), March 29, 1922.

60. Francis to Harold, April 29, 1922, Francis to Harold, May 13, 1922, Francis to Harold, May 30, 1922, cabinet 45, new drawer 179/old drawer 184, box 2, file: Newspaper and Politics, Miscellaneous 1922, Francis H. Case Collection; Case to Guy, March 1, 1922, box 2, file 27, Lewis Schuster to Francis Case, box 2, file 34, Carol Case Goddard Collection; Violet Miller Goering, *Dakota Wesleyan University: Century I* (Freeman, SD: Pine Hill Press, 1996), p. 46; "New President Assumes Duties," *Daily Argus-Leader* (Sioux Falls, SD), June 8, 1922.

61. Francis to Harold, April 29, 1922, Card to Case, May 3[, 1922], Harold to Francis, Saturday afternoon, [May 6, 1922], Francis to Harold May 13, 1922, Francis to Harold, May 30, 1922, cabinet 45, new drawer 179/old drawer 184, box 2, file: Newspaper and Politics, Miscellaneous 1922, Francis H. Case Collection.

62. Francis to Dad, May 11, 1922, box 2, file 33, Carol Case Goddard Collection; Francis to Harold, May 13, 1922, Harold to Case, Wed. afternoon, [June 21, 1922], Francis to Harold, June 23[, 1922], cabinet

45, new drawer 179/old drawer 184, box 2, file: Newspaper and Politics, Miscellaneous 1922, Francis H. Case Collection.
63. Francis to Harold, June 23[, 1922].
64. Ibid.; HWC to Francis, June 28, 1922, box 2, file 25, Carol Case Goddard Collection; Francis H. Case to Joseph Gossage, June 30, 1922, F. W. Meyers to Mr. Case, July 7[, 1922], Mrs. Gossage to Mr. Case, July 14[, 1922], Alice Gossage to Francis H. Case, undated, F. W. Meyers to Friend Case, July 29[, 1922], cabinet 45, new drawer 179/old drawer 184, box 1, files: Misc. Corresp. 1917–1928 1 of 5, Francis H. Case Collection.
65. *Rapid City Daily Journal* (Rapid City, SD), August 15, 1922; Francis Case to Journal People, August 21, 1922, Alice Gossage to Mr. Case, August 24[, 1922], cabinet 45, new drawer 179/old drawer 184, box 1, files: Misc. Corresp. 1917–1928 1 of 5, Francis H. Case Collection.
66. Francis to Carol, Mother, et al, August 28[, 1922], box 4, file 4, Carol Case Goddard Collection; Francis Case to Hahn, August 28[, 1922], Hahn to Francis Case, telegram, August 29, 1922, cabinet 45, new drawer 179/old drawer 184, box 1, file: Misc. Corresp. 1917–1928 5 of 5, Francis H. Case Collection.
67. "The Daily Journal," *Rapid City Daily Journal* (Rapid City, SD), September 6, 1922; Francis to Art, August 29, 1922, Francis Case to Dr. Harris (partial letter), September 6, 1922, Francis H. Case to Dr. Jenkins, September 20, 1922, cabinet 45, new drawer 179/old drawer 184, box 1, file: Misc. Corresp. 1917–1928 3 and 5 of 5, Francis H. Case Collection.

CHAPTER 8. RAPID CITY NEWSPAPERMAN AND INVOLVED CITIZEN

The quotation at the beginning of the chapter is from a letter that Ernest Hahne wrote to Francis dated September 18, 1922.

1. Case to Hahne, September 14, 1922, cabinet 45, new drawer 179/old drawer 184, box 1, file: Misc. Corresp. 1917–1928 5 of 5, Francis H. Case Collection.
2. Hahn to Case, September 18, 1922, Case to Hahn, September 24, 1922, Francis H. Case to Paul R. Flint, September 26, 1922, Francis to Bernie, October 5, 1922, cabinet 45, new drawer 179/old drawer 184, box 1, files: Misc. Corresp. 1917–1928 4, 1, and 5 of 5, Francis H. Case Collection; Francis to Dad, (letter undated but accompanying envelope postmarked September 26, 1922), box 4, file 4, Carol Case Goddard Collection.
3. Francis Case to Bernie, October 6, 1922, Art Brown to Francis Case, October 24, 1922, cabinet 45, new drawer 179/old drawer 184, box 1, files: Misc. Corresp. 1917–1928 5 and 2 of 5, H. L. Harrington to Francis L. [*sic*] Case, October 21, 1922, cabinet 45, new drawer 179/old drawer 184, box 2, file: Misc. Corresp. 1922, Francis H. Case Collection.

4. "Daily Guide Bows to Rapid People," *Rapid City Daily Journal* (Rapid City, SD), November 9, 1922; "The Rapid City Daily Guide (Rapid City, SD) 1922-1924," Library of Congress, accessed June 21, 2021, https://www.loc.gov/item/sn97065819/.
5. "Journal Announces Additions to Staff," *Rapid City Daily Journal* (Rapid City, SD), December 12, 1922; "Ye Black Hills Eds Discuss the Work," *Rapid City Daily Journal* (Rapid City, SD), November 14, 1922.
6. "Sturgis Has Community Thanksgiving Services," *Rapid City Daily Journal* (Rapid City, SD), December 3, 1922; "The Daily Journal," *Rapid City Daily Journal* (Rapid City, SD), December 2, 1922; Earl R. Bovee to Francis, October 21, 1922, cabinet 45, new drawer 179/old drawer 184, box 1, file: Misc. Corresp. 1917–1928 2 of 5, Francis H. Case Collection.
7. "Agreement" with attached "Statement of Agreed Policies," December 7, 1922, box 1, file 10, Carol Case Goddard Collection.
8. Ibid.
9. "Journal Announces Additions to Staff," *Rapid City Daily Journal*; "The Daily Journal," *Rapid City Daily Journal* (Rapid City, SD), December 19, 1922, "Additional Local," *Rapid City Daily Journal* (Rapid City, SD), June 22, 1923. Harold was unable to join the *Journal* until June because he previously agreed to fulfill coaching and part-time teaching duties at Tyndall High School for the 1922-1923 school year. See HWC to Francis, [May 24, 1922], Francis H. Case to Harold W. Card, telegram, May 26, 1922, cabinet 45, new drawer 179/old drawer 184, box 2, file: Newspaper and Politics, Miscellaneous 1922, Francis H. Case Collection; O.W. Coursey to Case, July 4, 1922 with attached article titled "H.W. Card Will Edit Tyndall Newspaper" from unidentified newspaper, box 3, file 1, Carol Case Goddard Collection.
10. Francis to Carol, December 13, 1922, box 4, file 4, Carol Case Goddard Collection; Bernie to Case, September 30, 1922, Charles M. Stuart to Francis H. Case, December 26, 1922, Francis to Mother, December 31, 1922, cabinet 45, new drawer 179/old drawer 184, box 1, files: Misc. Corresp. 1917–1928 1 and 5 of 5, Reverend Herbert L. Case, Francis H. Case Collection; Hahne to Case, December 26, 1922, cabinet 45, new drawer 179/old drawer 184, box 2, file: Misc. Corresp. 1922, Francis H. Case Collection.
11. "City in Brief," *Rapid City Daily Journal* (Rapid City, SD), January 7, 1923; "'Legion Look for Action and Achievement,' Halley," *Rapid City Daily Journal* (Rapid City, SD), January 4, 1923; "City, area deaths," *Rapid City Journal* (Rapid City, SD), March 4, 1986; "Press Association Honors Local Men," *Rapid City Daily Journal* (Rapid City, SD), January 23, 1923; Membership cards, box 1, file 16, Carol Case Goddard Collection. In March 1919, members of the American Expeditionary Force met in Paris and held the first American Legion caucus. Two months later, the group's draft preamble and constitution were approved at a caucus in St. Louis, and the

organization adopted "The American Legion" as its official name. Congress chartered The American Legion "as a patriotic veterans organization" in September. Its first convention was held in Minneapolis in November. There, its Constitution and preamble were adopted, and it was decided to locate the national headquarters in Indianapolis. The Legion has focused "on service to veterans, servicemembers and communities," and it "evolved from a group of war-weary veterans of World War I into one of the most influential nonprofit groups in the United States." See "History," American Legion, accessed June 11, 2021, https://www.legion.org/history. The International Association of Lions Clubs was established at Chicago and Dallas, Texas, in 1917. It adopted the name and symbol "Lions" because "the lion stood for strength, courage, fidelity and vital action." The group has been described as "a large International association composed of representative business and professional men who feel an interest in the welfare and progress of their city and community." The clubs "are non-political, non-sectarian and non-secret organizations[.]" The Association truly became "international" in 1920, when it granted a charter to a club in Windsor, Canada. At that time, Lions Club membership in the United States totaled 6,400, and clubs were active in 23 states. A Lions Club was formed in Rapid City in mid-November, 1921. See Paul Martin, *We Serve: A History of the Lions Clubs* (Washington, DC: Regnery Gateway, 1991) pp. 5-9; "Association Name and Symbol," Lions International, accessed June 23, 2021, http://www.web.archive.org/web/20180924184128/http:/www.lionsclubs.org/EN/who-we-are/mission-and-history/association-name-symbol.php; "Lions to Invade Rapid City," *Rapid City Daily Journal* (Rapid City, SD), November 10, 1921; "Making History Every Day," Lions International, accessed June 11, 2021, http://www.lionsclubs.org/en/discover-our-clubs/interactive-timeline; "The Daily Journal," *Rapid City Daily Journal* (Rapid City, SD), November 29, 1921. Finally, the Masonic Lodges are based on and guided by the concept of Freemasonry, which has been described as "the teachings and practices of the secret fraternal (men only) order of Free and Accepted Masons, the largest worldwide secret society." The first Freemasonry Grand Lodge was founded in England in 1717. Freemasonry contains many characteristics of a religion, and its teachings emphasize morality, charity, and obedience to the law. In Anglo-Saxon countries, including the United States, "membership is drawn largely from among white Protestants." In most lodges, "Freemasons are divided into three major degrees—entered apprentice, fellow of the craft, and master mason." See *Encyclopedia Britannica Online*, s.v. "Freemasonry," accessed June 11, 2021, http://www.britannica.com/topic/order-of-Freemasons.

12. "Methodist Auxiliary Selects Fine Comedy," *Rapid City Daily Journal* (Rapid City, SD), March 25, 1923; "Dad 'Turns Trick' in Auxiliary Play," *Rapid City Daily Journal* (Rapid City, SD), March 29, 1923; "This is Some Sort of Publicity Stunt for 'Turning Trick'," *Rapid City Daily Journal* (Rapid City,

SD), March 31, 1923; "See These People Turn the Trick at Elks' Tomorrow," *Rapid City Daily Journal* (Rapid City, SD), April 1, 1923.
13. "Citizens and Veterans Join in Observance of Nation's Memorial Day," *Rapid City Daily Journal* (Rapid City, SD), May 31, 1923.
14. Ibid.; "In Flanders Fields Summary & Analysis," LitCharts, accessed June 14, 2021, http://www.litcharts.com/poetry/john-mccrae/in-flanders-fields.
15. "Harold Card Will Bring His Bride," *Rapid City Daily Journal* (Rapid City, SD), June 13, 1923; HWC to Francis, [May 24, 1922], cabinet 45, new drawer 179/old drawer 184, box 2, file: Misc. Corresp. 1922, Francis H. Case Collection; "Journal Announces 2 Changes in Staff," *Rapid City Daily Journal* (Rapid City, SD), June 10, 1923.
16. "Harold Card Will Bring His Bride," *Rapid City Daily Journal*; "Additional Local," *Rapid City Daily Journal* (Rapid City, SD), June 22, 1923; "Thrifty Ladies Look at Page 2 Before Buying," *Rapid City Daily Journal* (Rapid City, SD), June 30, 1923.
17. "Journal Announces 2 Changes on Staff," *Rapid City Daily Journal*; Leland Davidson Case, interview by Robert Webb, Mitchell, SD, April 23, 1972, transcript, Francis H. Case Collection (hereinafter noted as LDC Interview, April 23, 1972); "The Daily Journal," *Rapid City Daily Journal* (Rapid City, SD), May 9, 1922.
18. "Wesleyan Alumni to Have Magazine," *Rapid City Daily Journal* (Rapid City, SD), July 18, 1923.
19. Art to Francis, undated, Art to Francis, July 29, 1923, Art to Francis, August 2, 1923, Art to Francis, August 4[, 1923], Art to Francis, August 15, 1923, cabinet 45, new drawer 179/old drawer 184, box 2, file: Miscellaneous Correspondence 2-A-B, Francis H. Case Collection.
20. "Mr. Gossage Returns from Eastern Trip," *Rapid City Daily Journal* (Rapid City, SD), August 18, 1923; Art to Francis, August 15, 1923; Francis to Art, August 21, 1923, cabinet 45, new drawer 179/old drawer 184, box 1, file: Misc. Corresp. 1917–1928 1 of 5, Francis H. Case Collection.
21. Art to Francis, August 4[, 1923], Art to Francis, August 15, 1923; Art to Francis, August 23, 1923, cabinet 45, new drawer 179/old drawer 184, box 1, file: Misc. Corresp. 1917–1928 5 of 5, Francis H. Case Collection; Francis to Art, August 21, 1923; "Local Notes," *Rapid City Daily Journal* (Rapid City, SD), September 5, 1923.
22. Art to Francis, August 2, 1923; LDC Interview, April 23, 1972; "The Daily Journal," *Rapid City Daily Journal* (Rapid City, SD), February 25, 1923 and September 11, 1923.
23. LDC Interview, April 23, 1972; Jarvis Harriman, *The Man from the Hills: A Biography of Leland Davidson Case* (Tucson, AZ: Westerners International, 1994), pp. 25, 26.

24. Francis to Grandpa Grannis, October 23, 1923, box 1, file 10, Carol Case Goddard Collection; "Daily Guide Bows to Rapid People," *Rapid City Daily Journal*.
25. "Local Notes," *Rapid City Daily Journal* (Rapid City, SD), November 10, 1923; "Little News Items," *Evening Republic* (Mitchell, SD), November 12, 1923; "Miners Will Break Bread Among Lions," *Rapid City Daily Journal* (Rapid City, SD), December 11, 1923; "Gadski Elected to Captain Mines," *Rapid City Daily Journal* (Rapid City, SD), December 12, 1923; "Legion Makes Plans for Big Music Comedy," *Rapid City Daily Journal* (Rapid City, SD), September 29, 1923; "Legion Signs to Red Cross 100 Per Cent," *Rapid City Daily Journal* (Rapid City, SD), October 25, 1923; "Legion's Show Draws Crowd Three Nights," *Rapid City Daily Journal* (Rapid City, SD), November 10, 1923.
26. "Local Notes," *Rapid City Daily Journal* (Rapid City, SD), December 27, 1923; "South Dakota, U.S. Marriages, 1905-2017," s.v. "Arthur Reed Brown" (December 25, 1923), *Ancestry.com*.; "The Daily Journal," *Rapid City Daily Journal* (Rapid City, SD), December 28, 1923.
27. Francis H. Case to Grandpa Grannis, January 15, 1924, box 1, file 10, Carol Case Goddard Collection.
28. "Guide Suspends Daily Publication," *Rapid City Daily Journal* (Rapid City, SD), February 12, 1924, "As Others See Us," *Rapid City Daily Journal* (Rapid City, SD), March 2, 1924; "Murdo Coyote," Mondo Times, accessed June 22, 2021, http://www.mondotimes.com/1/world/us/41/8805/24785; "The Rapid City Daily Guide (Rapid City, SD) 1922-1924," Library of Congress, https://www.loc.gov/item/sn97065819/.
29. "Local Notes," *Rapid City Daily Journal* (Rapid City, SD), February 26, 1924; "He Made Them Read," *Rapid City Daily Journal* (Rapid City, SD), March 2, 1924; "Hill City," *Rapid City Daily Journal* (Rapid City, SD), March 8, 1924; "Newspaper Information: Hill City News," South Dakota State Historical Society, accessed June 22, 2021, https://www.history.sd.gov/archives/Newspaperinfo.aspx?ID=97065850.
30. "Homer Surbeck Wins in Oratory," *Rapid City Daily Journal* (Rapid City, SD), January 12, 1924; Francis H. Case to Grandpa Grannis, January 15, 1924; "Radio Program Is Miners' Own," *Rapid City Daily Journal* (Rapid City, SD) March 11, 1924.
31. "Huron Wins from Mines in Debate By 2 To 1 Decision," *Rapid City Daily Journal* (Rapid City, SD) March 18, 1924; "Miners Lose Hard Fought Word Tilt to Aberdeen Trio" and "Local Notes," *Rapid City Daily Journal* (Rapid City, SD), March 22, 1924; "Columbus Wins Over Rapid City Debaters," *Daily Argus-Leader* (Sioux Falls, SD), March 24, 1924; "Important Notice," Wesleyan Alumnal Association, box 6, file 8, Carol Case Goddard Collection; "Miners Drop Second Debate to Wesleyan," *Rapid City Daily Journal* (Rapid City, SD), March 25, 1924.

32. "Scenic High Closes Successful Year," *Rapid City Daily Journal* (Rapid City, SD), May 25, 1924; "Twenty-Eight Graduated at Indian School," *Rapid City Daily Journal* (Rapid City, SD), May 31, 1924.
33. "Lions Club Plans Clean Up at Park," *Rapid City Daily Journal* (Rapid City, SD), May 22, 1924; "Knowles Tells of Game Preservation," *Rapid City Daily Journal* (Rapid City, SD), June 11, 1924; "Local Lions Leave for Convention at Omaha," *Rapid City Daily Journal* (Rapid City, SD), June 22, 1924.
34. "Lions Gather at Omaha Next Week," *Rapid City Daily Journal* (Rapid City, SD), June 19, 1924; "S. F. Lions Back from Omaha," *Daily-Argus Leader* (Sioux Falls, SD), June 27, 1924; "How Lions Roared in Omaha Will Be Topic of Luncheon," *Rapid City Daily Journal* (Rapid City, SD), July 1, 1924; "Colorado – Multiple District 6," Golden Lions Club, accessed June 23, 2021, https://web.archive.org/web/20210811181919/https://www.goldenlionsclub.org/pdf/CO20Lions-History.pdf; "Touchstone Story: The Parade," Lions International, July 20, 2016, http://www. lionsclubs.org/it/node/11521.
35. Francis H. Case, ed., *Advertising the Church: Suggestions by Church Advertisers* (New York: Abingdon Press, 1925), unnumbered Contents page (hereinafter Case, *Advertising the Church*); Francis H. Case, *Handbook of Church Advertising* (New York: Abingdon Press, 1921), pp. 3-5; "Advertising the Church," cabinet 45, new drawer 179/old drawer 184, box 1, file: Personal corresp. 1925, Francis H. Case Collection.
36. Case, *Advertising the Church*, p. 11; copy of *Advertising the Church*, Francis H. Case Collection.
37. "Dr. F. L. Case, 87, Dies Suddenly in Minnesota," *Rapid City Daily Journal* (Rapid City, SD), September 10, 1924; "Iowa Pioneer Dies at Son's Home in Mankato," *Star Tribune* (Minneapolis, MN), September 11, 1924; Francis to Carol, September 10, 1924, box 6, file 8, Carol Case Goddard Collection.
38. "Coolidge Club is Formed Here," *Rapid City Daily Journal* (Rapid City, SD), February 24, 1924. History.com Editors, "Calvin Coolidge," accessed June 25, 2021, http://www.history.com/topics/us-presidents/calvin-coolidge.
39. FHC to Hahne, September 20, 1924, box 2, file 37, Statement of Traveling Expenses for Francis Case, October 1 to November 3, 1924, box 2, file 31, Carol Case Goddard Collection; C. E. Coyne, *Official Election Returns for South Dakota: General Election November 4, 1924* (Pierre, SD: Hipple, 1924), p. 6, accessed June 25, 2021, http://www.sdsos.gov/elections-voting/assets/historicalelectiondata/1924G.pdf (page citations are to PDF version). From 1913 to 1931, South Dakota had three U. S. congressional districts. The first consisted of counties situated in the southeast and central parts of the state, the second was comprised of counties in the north-central and northeast portions, and the third included the counties located west of the Missouri River. As a result of the 1930 census, the state lost one of its seats. The third district had therefore "vanished" by the 1932 campaign and election. It became the second district, while the first was expanded to include

all counties east of the Missouri River. (The second district's boundaries eventually moved further east due to population changes and redistricting requirements mandated by the U.S. Supreme Court.) Finally, South Dakota lost its second district as a result of the 1980 census, and since 1982 it has had only one district that covers the entire state. See Tom Lawrence, "South Dakota once had three congressional districts. Then it had two. Now it has one. Here's how we lost two of them," *The South Dakota Standard*, April 10, 2020, http://www.sdstandardnow.com/home/south-dakota-once-had-three-congressional-seats-then-it-had-two-now-it-has-one-heres-how-we-lost-two-of-them; Randy McDaniel, "There Was a Time South Dakota Elected Three Congressmen," *KXRB*, June 29, 2016, https://web.archive.org/web/20160630173012/http://www.kxrb.com/south-dakota-once-had-three-congressional-districts/; "River Line Bill Signed By Green," *Hot Springs Weekly Star* (Hot Springs, SD), March 10, 1931; Christine Barbour and Gerald C. Wright, *Keeping the Republic: Power and Citizenship in American Politics*, 4th ed. (Washington, DC: CQ Press, 2009), p. 295.

40. "G.O.P. Speakers to Invade West River Country" and "Coolidge-Dawes Sentiment Growing in Western Section Says Republican Chairman," *Rapid City Daily Journal* (Rapid City, SD), September 28, 1924; "Elections," in *2005 South Dakota Legislative Manual*, p. 11-12, accessed June 25, 2021, http://www.sdsos.gov/elections-voting/assets/ElectionsReturnsPre1972.pdf (hereinafter *Election Statistics*, page citations are to PDF version).

41. Francis Case to John F. Way, October 23, 1924, box 2, file 13, Carol Case Goddard Collection; "Case and McMillan to Speak for G.O.P.," *Rapid City Daily Journal* (Rapid City, SD), October 31, 1924; Joyce to Mother, November 2 and 5, 1924, box 6, file 8, Carol Case Goddard Collection.

42. "State Sure for G.O.P. Is Prediction," *Rapid City Daily Journal* (Rapid City, SD), November 4, 1924; Joyce to Mother, November 2 and 5, 1924, box 6, file 8, Carol Case Goddard Collection; *Election Statistics*, p. 11; Dave Leip, "1924 Presidential Election Results-South Dakota," *Dave Leip's Atlas of U.S. Presidential Elections*, accessed June 28, 2021, http://www.uselectionatlas.org (hereinafter *Dave Leip's Atlas*); Francis H. Case to John F. Way, November 10, 1924, box 2, file 13, *Carol Case Goddard Collection*. President Coolidge "convincingly won" the 1924 presidential general election. He received 54 percent of the nationwide popular vote, which "gave him a majority in 35 states [including South Dakota] and almost 72 percent of the electoral college votes." His Democratic opponent—John Davis—garnered just 29 per cent of the popular vote. He won 12 states, which resulted in 26 percent of the electoral-college votes. Finally, LaFollette, who finished second to Coolidge in South Dakota, got only 17 percent of the popular vote nationwide, although he did win his home state of Wisconsin. That meant he received 13 of the 531 votes cast in the electoral college. See "Distribution of votes in the 1924 US presidential election," *Statista*, accessed June 25, 2021, http://www.statista.com/statistics/1056541/distribution-votes-1924-us-presidential-election/; "1924 Presidential General Election Results," *Dave*

Leip's Atlas. Voter percentage figures have been rounded off to the nearest whole percentage point.

43. "S.D. Lawmakers Settle Down to Sixty Day Grind" and "Tax Revision to Aid Agriculture Urged by Gunderson," *Daily Argus-Leader* (Sioux Falls, SD), January 6, 1925; Francis to Little Lady [Myrle Graves], January 6, 1925, red scrapbook, carton C, Case Ranch Collection.

44. "Gov. Gunderson Greets Citizens of South Dakota," *Daily Argus-Leader* (Sioux Falls, SD), January 7, 1922; Francis to Little Lady [Myrle Graves], January 6, 1925.

45. Francis to Little Lady [Myrle Graves], January 6, 1925.

46. "Local Notes," *Rapid City Daily Journal* (Rapid City, SD), November 10, 1923; "Little News Items," *Evening Republic* (Mitchell, SD), November 12, 1923; Francis to Carol, September 10, 1924, box 6, file 8, Carol Case Goddard Collection; Francis to Little Lady [Myrle Graves], January 6, 1925.

47. "Famous Mrs. Fair Two Nights with An All-Star Cast," *Rapid City Daily Journal* (Rapid City, SD), February 22, 1925; "'France Was Never Like This,' Famous Mrs. Fair," *Rapid City Daily Journal* (Rapid City, SD), February 25, 1925; "Home Talent Play Wins Success in Its First Showing," *Rapid City Daily Journal* (Rapid City, SD), February 27, 1925; "'Famous Mrs. Fair,' Second Night, Wins More Plaudits," *Rapid City Daily Journal* (Rapid City, SD), February 28, 1925.

48. "'Mrs. Fair' To Play on Lyceum Tonight," *Rapid City Daily Journal* (Rapid City, SD), February 26, 1925; "Home Talent Play Wins Success in Its First Showing," *Rapid City Daily Journal*; "'Famous Mrs. Fair,' Second Night, Wins More Plaudits," *Rapid City Daily Journal*.

49. "Agreement," May 28, 1925, box 1, file 10, Carol Case Goddard Collection; "Art Brown Takes Washington Job," *Rapid City Daily Journal* (Rapid City, SD), May 3, 1925.

50. Francis to Carol, May 11, 1925, box 1, file 15, Carol Case Goddard Collection.

51. "Card and Case Sell Holdings in the Journal," *Rapid City Daily Journal* (Rapid City, SD), May 29, 1925; "Journal Celebrates 80th Year Here: Birth In 'Hay Camp' Dates to Jan. 5, 1878," *Rapid City Daily Journal* (Rapid City, SD), January 5, 1958; "Agreement," May 28, 1925.

52. "'A. G.' Reviews Fifty Years of Journal History," *Rapid City Daily Journal* (Rapid City, SD), February 18, 1928; "Change in Management of Sioux Falls Press," *Daily Argus-Leader* (Sioux Falls, SD), June 18, 1925; "Good Luck, Mr. Mitchell," *Daily Argus-Leader* (Sioux Falls, SD), June 19, 1925; "State's Oldest Editor Retires," *Daily Argus-Leader* (Sioux Falls, SD), June 23, 1925; "The Daily Journal," *Rapid City Daily Journal* (Rapid City, SD), July 1, 1925; "Journal Completes 75 Years of Reporting Area News," *Rapid City Daily Journal* (Rapid City, SD), January 4, 1953; "Journal Celebrates 80th Year Here: Birth In 'Hay Camp' Dates to Jan. 5, 1878," *Rapid City Daily Journal*.

53. "Belle Fourche Plans Welcome for Sunshiners," *Daily Argus-Leader* (Sioux Falls, SD), May 14, 1925; "Agreement," June 5, 1925, box 2, file 31, Carol

Case Goddard Collection; "Tri-State Round Up," *Rapid City Daily Journal*, (Rapid City, SD), July 2, 1925.

54. "National Klan to Enter 500 Horses in Belle Parade," *Rapid City Daily Journal* (Rapid City, SD), April 19, 1925; "Belle Fourche Makes Big Plans for Annual Rodeo," *Rapid City Daily Journal* (Rapid City, SD), April 26, 1925; "Selling 75,000," *Rapid City Daily Journal* (Rapid City, SD), May 5, 1925; "Belle Fourche Ready for Klan" and "Eighth Annual Tri-State Roundup Opens Tomorrow," *Rapid City Daily Journal* (Rapid City, SD), July 1, 1925; "Many Places for Folks to Celebrate July 4th," *Daily Argus-Leader* (Sioux Falls, SD), July 2, 1925.

55. "More Locals," *Rapid City Daily Journal* (Rapid City, SD), July 1, 1925; Francis Case to Mr. J. S. Smith, July 8, 1925, "Round Up Program Sales Record" (undated), Francis Case to Mrs. Baird, July 8, 1925, Mrs. Baird to Francis Case, July 17, 1925, box 2, file 31, Francis to Carol, July 14, 1925, box 1, file 14, Carol Case Goddard Collection.

56. "Crowds Leave Belle Fourche," *Daily Argus-Leader* (Sioux Falls, SD), July 6, 1925; "Thousands Saw Great Roundup and Klan Meet," *Daily Argus-Leader* (Sioux Falls, SD), July 7, 1925.

57. "Thousands Saw Great Roundup and Klan Meet," *Daily Argus-Leader*; "Klan Procession Attracts Audience as it Passes," *Rapid City Daily Journal* (Rapid City, SD), July 8, 1925.

58. "Thousands Saw Great Roundup and Klan Meet," *Daily Argus-Leader*; "Klan Procession Attracts Audience as it Passes," *Rapid City Daily Journal*.

59. Mankato High School Commencement program, January 20, 1922, box 1, file 18, Mother to Francis, [March, 1922], Mother to Francis, Sunday. P. M. [May 14, 1922], box 2, file 34, Francis to Carol, December 13, 1923, box 4, file 4, Carol Case Goddard Collection; "Additional Local," *Rapid City Daily Journal* (Rapid City, SD), April 4, 1923; Leland Davidson Case and Edith E. H. Grannis, eds., *New Hampshire to Minnesota: Memoirs of Samuel Higbee Grannis (1839-1933)* (Tucson, AZ: Self-published, 1962), p. 151 (hereinafter Case and Grannis, eds., *SHG Memoirs*).

60. Mother to Carol, [June 2, 1923], Assistant Secretary & Registrar (signature not legible) to Carol Case, July 16, 1923, Mabel Cole to Carol Case, July 19, 1923, Notice of Furlough, September 12, 1923 and January 3, 1924, Joyce to Carol, October 28, 1923, box 6, file 10, H. L. Case to Carol, May 21, 1924, box 6, file 8, Carol Case Goddard Collection; "Local Notes," *Rapid City Daily Journal* (Rapid City, SD), September 15, 1923; "Milwaukee, Wisconsin, U.S., Births, 1839–1911," s.v. "Ralph Frederick Albert Himmelhoch," 1920 United States Census, Milwaukee, Milwaukee County, Wisconsin, digital image s.v. "Ralph Himmelhoch," *Ancestry.com*.

61. Mother to Carol, [May 16, 1924], Florence Hunt to Miss Case, September 5, 1924, Francis to Carol, September 10, 1924, Jos. Milligan to Ralph, December 28, 1924, Ralph Himmelhoch to Milton J. Foreman, March 16, 1927, box 6, file 8, Carol Case Goddard Collection; "Local Notes," *Rapid*

City Daily Journal (Rapid City, SD), June 5, 1924; "More Locals," *Rapid City Daily Journal* (Rapid City, SD), July 25, 1924.
62. Francis to Carol, September 10, 1924, box 6, file 8, Leland to Carol, March 15, 1925, box 4, file 10, Francis to Carol, April 9, 1925, Leland to Carol, April 24, 1925, box 5, file 6, Francis to Carol, May 11, 1925, box 1, file 15, Carol Case Goddard Collection; "Minnesota Official Marriage System, 1850-2019," s.v. "Ralph Frederick Himmelhoch" (March 18, 1925), *Ancestry.com*.
63. Francis to Carol, July 14, 1925, box 1, file 14, Carol Case Goddard Collection; Case and Grannis, eds., *SHG Memoirs*, p. 151.
64. Francis to Mater et al, July 29[, 1925], cabinet 45, new drawer 179/old drawer 184, box 2, file: Miscellaneous Correspondence 2–Case, Francis H. Case Collection; "Local Notes," *Rapid City Daily Journal* (Rapid City, SD), August 7, 1925; Francis Case to Bronson, August 11, 1925, box 2, file 31, Carol Case Goddard Collection.
65. "Case Brothers Buy Hot Springs Paper" and "Paper Incorporates," *Rapid City Daily Journal* (Rapid City, SD), September 5, 1925.

CHAPTER 9. HOT SPRINGS NEWSPAPERMAN AND BLACK HILLS PROMOTER—THE EARLY YEARS

The quotation at the beginning of the chapter is from an editorial Francis wrote in *The Rapid City Daily Journal* titled "Just Personal." It appeared in the May 29, 1925 issue.

1. Francis to Carol, Sunday, [September 13, 1925], box 1, file 7, Francis to Leland, September 24, 1925, box 2, file 31, Francis to Dad and all, September 25, 1925, box 1, file 10, Carol Case Goddard Collection; "Hot Springs to Have Semi-weekly News" and "The New Star Company," *Hot Springs Star* (Hot Springs, SD), October 1, 1925; Francis Case, "My Days with the Hot Springs Star," May 1963, H. S. Star/Times Herald Early Newspapers, pp. 31-33, binder 046, Helen Magee Collection, accessed June 29, 2020 (hereinafter "My Days with the Hot Springs Star," Helen Magee Collection).
2. Francis to Dad and all, September 25, 1925; Blackstone Institute to Francis H. Case, November 9, 1925, cabinet 45, new drawer 179/old drawer 184, box 2, file: Misc. Correspondence 1925, Francis H. Case Collection; Leland to Francis, September 21, 1925, box 2, file 31, Carol Case Goddard Collection; "Gets Prominent Place in University Paper," *Hot Springs Star* (Hot Springs, SD), October 8, 1925.
3. "Hot Springs to Have Semi-weekly News" and "The New Star Company," *Hot Springs Star*.
4. "Hot Springs to Have Semi-weekly News," *Hot Springs Star*.

5. "The New Star Company," *Hot Springs Star*.
6. "Go to Rushmore," *Rapid City Daily Journal* (Rapid City, SD), September 30, 1925; "Rushmore Mountain to Be Dedicated Tomorrow to Colossal Statues of America's Great Men; Proposed Memorial Will Be Largest in World," *Daily Argus-Leader* (Sioux Falls, SD), September 30, 1925; Francis to Carol, October 4, 1925, box 1, file 16, Carol Case Goddard Collection.
7. Rex Alan Smith, *The Carving of Mount Rushmore* (New York: Abbeville Press, 1985), pp. 108–09 (hereinafter Smith, *Carving Mount Rushmore*); "Go to Rushmore," *Rapid City Daily Journal*; "Rushmore Mountain to Be Dedicated Tomorrow to Colossal Statues of America's Great Men; Proposed Memorial Will Be Largest in World," *Daily Argus-Leader*.
8. Smith, *Carving Mount Rushmore*, p. 110; "Rushmore Duly Dedicated," *Custer Weekly Chronicle* (Custer, SD), October 10, 1925.
9. Smith, *Carving Mount Rushmore*, p. 110; "Unveil Washington Statue October 1,'26," *Rapid City Daily Journal* (Rapid City, SD), October 2, 1925; "Rushmore Duly Dedicated," *Custer Weekly Chronicle*.
10. Herbert S. Schell, *History of South Dakota* (Lincoln: University of Nebraska Press, 1961), pp. 265–69, 388 (hereinafter Schell, *History of South Dakota*); Smith, *Carving Mount Rushmore*, pp. 46, 84, 111; "Unveil Washington Statue October 1,'26," *Rapid City Daily Journal*; "Rushmore Duly Dedicated," *Custer Weekly Chronicle*; United States House of Representatives, "MARTIN, Eben Wever," accessed August 18, 2021, https://history.house.gov/People/Listing/M/MARTIN,-Eben-Wever-(M000176)/.
11. Smith, *Carving Mount Rushmore*, pp. 111-12; "Unveil Washington Statue October 1,'26," *Rapid City Daily Journal*.
12. Francis to Carol and Ralph, November 28, 1925, box 5, file 6, Carol Case Goddard Collection; Francis to Leland, December 21, 1925, cabinet 45, new drawer 179/old drawer 184, box 2, file: Miscellaneous Correspondence 2–Case, Francis H. Case Collection.
13. "New Officers Named for Commercial Club," *Hot Springs Star* (Hot Springs, SD), January 26, 1926; "Hot Springs Commercial Club Elects Officers," *Rapid City Daily Journal* (Rapid City, SD), January 28, 1926.
14. "An Announcement and an Opportunity," *Hot Springs Star* (Hot Springs, SD), February 2, 1926; Francis to Leland, February 23, 1926, cabinet 45, new drawer 179/old drawer 184, box 2, file: Miscellaneous Correspondence 2–Case, Francis H. Case Collection; "To the Johnsons," *Hot Springs Star* (Hot Springs, SD), March 23, 1926.
15. "Employee or Officer, Public is Interested Says Libel Suit Jury," *Hot Springs Star* (Hot Springs, SD), November 30, 1926; "Highway Jobs to Bates, Shade," *Daily Argus-Leader* (Sioux Falls, SD), January 7, 1925; "Shade Will Take State Park Job," *Rapid City Daily Journal* (Rapid City, SD), May 23, 1925.

16. "Jury Convicts A. W. Ewert," *Daily Argus-Leader* (Sioux Falls, SD), February 12, 1926; Schell, *History of South Dakota*, p. 279.
17. "Ewert, Gunderson, Norbeck," *Hot Springs Star* (Hot Springs, SD), February 16, 1926; Schell, *History of South Dakota*, p. 279.
18. "South Dakota Politics," *Hot Springs Star* (Hot Springs, SD), February 16, 1926.
19. "The Criticism of Shade" and "South Dakota Politics," *Hot Springs Star* (Hot Springs, SD), March 2, 1926.
20. "Col Shade Sues Hot Springs Star," *Rapid City Daily Journal* (Rapid City, SD), March 11, 1926; "Col. Shade Asks Star for $15,000," *Hot Springs Star* (Hot Springs, SD), March 16, 1926; "Employee or Officer, Public is Interested Says Libel Suit Jury," *Hot Springs Star*; Francis to Dad, March 29, 1926, cabinet 45, new drawer 179/old drawer 184, box 2, file: Miscellaneous Correspondence 2–Case, Francis H. Case Collection.
21. "Summer White House Urged in State Park," *Hot Springs Star* (Hot Springs, SD), March 30, 1926; Hot Springs Kiwanis club to Senator Peter Norbeck, telegram, March 30, 1926, cabinet 45, new drawer 179/old drawer 184, box 2, file: Miscellaneous Correspondence 1926, Francis H. Case Collection.
22. "Coolidge Asked to Black Hills," *Daily Argus-Leader* (Sioux Falls, SD), April 1, 1926; "A Column for Everybody," *Daily Argus-Leader* (Sioux Falls, SD) June 10, 1927.
23. "Hope President May Make Visit," *Daily Argus-Leader* (Sioux Falls, SD), April 8, 1926; United States House of Representatives, "SANDERS, Everett," accessed August 25, 2021, https://history.house.gov/People/Listing/S/SANDERS,-Everett-(S000034)/#biography.
24. "Wright to Go to Washington to Urge Visit," *Rapid City Daily Journal* (Rapid City, SD), April 9, 1926; "Wright Has Hope Coolidge to Come," *Rapid City Daily Journal* (Rapid City, SD), April 10, 1926; Francis H. Case to Representative William Williamson, night letter, April 15, 1926, cabinet 45, new drawer 179/old drawer 184, box 2, file: Miscellaneous Letters 1926, Francis H. Case Collection; "A Column for Everybody," *Daily Argus-Leader*.
25. "S.D. Delegation Invites Coolidge," *Rapid City Daily Journal* (Rapid City, SD), April 19, 1926; United States Congress, "McMASTER, William Henry," accessed August 26, 2021, https://bioguide.congress.gov/search/bio/M000563; United States House of Representatives, "CHRISTOPHERSON, Charles Andrew," accessed August 26, 2021, https://history.house.gov/People/Listing/C/CHRISTOPHERSON,-Charles-Andrew-(C000384)/; United States House of Representatives, "JOHNSON, Royal Cleaves," accessed August 26, 2021, https://history.house.gov/People/Listing/J/JOHNSON,-Royal-Cleaves-(J000173)/; Schell, *History of South Dakota*, p. 333; Williamson to Case, April 26, 1926, cabinet 45, new drawer 179/old drawer 184, box 2, file: Miscellaneous Letters 1926, Francis H. Case Collection.

26. Francis Case to Congressman Williamson, April, 29, 1926, cabinet 45, new drawer 179/old drawer 184, box 2, file: Miscellaneous Letters 1926, Francis H. Case Collection; William Kelly, "Calvin Coolidge's Indelible Vacation to the Black Hills," White House Historical Association, August 13, 2017, http://www.whitehousehistory.org/calvin-coolidges-indelible-vacation-to-the-black-hills.
27. "Shade's Resignation Is Reported Asked," *Daily Capital Journal* (Pierre, SD), April 5, 1926; "What Others Say," *Hot Springs Star* (Hot Springs, SD), April 13, 1926; "Newspaper Information: Evening Huronite," South Dakota State Historical Society, accessed August 30, 2021, http://www.history.sd.gov/archives/NewspaperInfo.aspx?ID=99062806.
28. "Shade Will Resign Job in State Park," *Daily Capital Journal* (Pierre, SD), May 21, 1926; "Meyers Says No Trouble with Chief," *Rapid City Daily Journal* (Rapid City, SD), May 22, 1926.
29. "Shade to Quit Park July 1, Says Pierre" and "Cutting Apron Strings," *Hot Springs Star* (Hot Springs, SD), May 25, 1926.
30. Francis to Della Brown, May 22, 1926, cabinet 45, new drawer 179/old drawer 184, box 2, file: Miscellaneous Correspondence 2–A–B, Francis to Dad, May 28, 1926, cabinet 45, new drawer 179/old drawer 184, box 2, file: Miscellaneous Correspondence 2–Case, Francis H. Case Collection; *Tourist News* (Hot Springs, SD), May 21, 1926, box 5, file 9, Carol Case Goddard Collection; "Johnsons Return," *Hot Springs Star* (Hot Springs, SD), June 29, 1926.
31. "Commercial Club Gets 3 to 6 Requests Daily on Roads, Hills, Town," *Hot Springs Star* (Hot Springs, SD), May 25, 1926; Francis to Dad, May 28, 1926.
32. Francis to Dad, May 28, 1926.
33. "Dennison of Vermillion to Superintend State Park," *Times-Herald* (Hot Springs, SD), July 2, 1926; "Shade Leaves for West Coast," *Rapid City Daily Journal* (Rapid City, SD), July 6, 1926; "Col. Shade Leaves for California Trip," *Hot Springs Star* (Hot Springs, SD), July 13, 1926.
34. Francis to Dad, March 29, 1926; Francis to Carol & Ralph, August 18, 1926, box 1, file 7, *Carol Case Goddard Collection*.
35. Wedding announcement, August 19, 1926, Jim Dolliver to Francis, September 7, 1926, black scrapbook, 1914–1943, carton E, Case Ranch Collection; "Society News," *Rapid City Daily Journal* (Rapid City, SD), August 21, 1926; "Weddings," *Hot Springs Star* (Hot Springs, SD), August 24, 1926; Francis H. Case, "Record of Marriage," August 19, 1926, registered no. 1367, certificate no. 113584, South Dakota Department of Health, Pierre, SD.
36. Photo card, "Keystone Hotel—McCook, Nebraska," hotel bill, "The Cosmopolitan," August 23, 1926, black scrapbook, 1914–1943, carton E, Case Ranch Collection; Francis Case to Dr. W. D. Engle, October 12,

1926, cabinet 45, new drawer 179/old drawer 184, box 2, file: Miscellaneous Correspondence 2–E, Francis H. Case Collection.

37. "Grand Lake, Colorado," accessed September 3, 2021, http://www.grandlakecolorado.com; "Recreation," Town of Grand Lake, accessed September 4, 2021, http://www.townofgrandlake.com/community/page/recreation; "Grand Lake," accessed September 3, 2021, http://www.visitgrandcounty.com/explore/towns/grand-lake; Photograph of Corner Cupboard, black scrapbook, 1914–1943, carton E, Case Ranch Collection; "Corner Cupboard," Grand Lake Area Historical Society, accessed September 3, 2021, http://www.grandlakehistory.org/wp-content/uploads/2020/10/CORNER-CUPBOARD.pdf.

38. Art and Della to Francis, August 23, 1926, cabinet 45, new drawer 179/old drawer 184, box 1, file: Personal Corresp. 1926–Newspaper, Francis H. Case Collection; Joyce and Cliff to Mr. and Mrs. Francis H. Case, telegram, August 25, 1926, poem signed by members of the Hot Springs Publishing Company staff, congratulations-on-marriage letters, black scrapbook, 1914–1943, carton E, Case Ranch Collection; A. W. Harris to Case, May 11, 1922, box 1, file 10, Carol Case Goddard Collection; Jarvis Harriman, *The Man from the Hills: A Biography of Leland Davidson Case* (Tucson, AZ: Westerners International, 1994), pp. 29–30; Leland to Francis, September 27[, 1926], cabinet 45, new drawer 179/old drawer 184, box 2, file: Miscellaneous Letters 1927, Francis H. Case Collection.

39. "Elections," in *2005 South Dakota Legislative Manual*, p. 11-12, accessed June 25, 2021, http://www.sdsos.gov/elections-voting/assets/ElectionsReturnsPre1972.pdf (page citations are to PDF version); Peter Norbeck to Case, November 6, 1926, cabinet 45, new drawer 179/old drawer 184, box 1, file: Misc. Corresp. 1917–1928 5 of 5, Francis H. Case Collection.

40. "Judge Miser Leaves Circuit Court Bench," *Hot Springs Star* (Hot Springs, SD), November 16, 1926; "Employee or Officer, Public is Interested Says Libel Suit Jury," *Hot Springs Star*.

41. "Shade Loses His Action for Libel," *Rapid City Daily Journal* (Rapid City, SD), November 26, 1926; "Employee or Officer, Public is Interested Says Libel Suit Jury," *Hot Springs Star*.

42. "Shade-Star Case to Jury on Wednesday," *Hot Springs Star* (Hot Springs, SD), November 23, 1926; "Employee or Officer, Public is Interested Says Libel Suit Jury," *Hot Springs Star*.

43. "Employee or Officer, Public is Interested Says Libel Suit Jury," *Hot Springs Star*.

44. "Shade-Star Case to Jury on Wednesday," *Hot Springs Star*; "Shade Case Ordered to Jury Today," *Rapid City Daily Journal* (Rapid City, SD), November 24, 1926; "Employee or Officer, Public is Interested Says Libel Suit Jury," *Hot Springs Star*.

45. "Shade Loses His Action for Libel," *Rapid City Daily Journal*; "Employee or Officer, Public is Interested Says Libel Suit Jury," *Hot Springs Star*.
46. "Employee or Officer, Public is Interested Says Libel Suit Jury," *Hot Springs Star*.
47. J. A. Stanley to Case, November 26, 1926, cabinet 45, new drawer 179/old drawer 184, box 2, file: Miscellaneous Letters 1926, H. L. Case to Joyce and Francis and Clifford and ALL, November 29, 1926, Art to Francis, December 2, 1926, cabinet 45, new drawer 179/old drawer 184, box 1, file: Personal Corresp. 1926–Newspaper; Coursey to Case, November 26, 1926, John F. Way to Francis, November 30, 1926, George J. Miller to Friend Francis, December 23, 1926, cabinet 45, new drawer 179/old drawer 184, box 1, file: Misc. Corresp. 1917–1928 5 of 5, Francis H. Case Collection; Hot Springs High School, *The Patée '14*, pp. 1Y, 1Z, Patee/1914/1915/1916, binder 130, Helen Magee Collection, accessed November 23, 2020; "Employee or Officer, Public is Interested Says Libel Suit Jury," *Hot Springs Star*.
48. Francis Case to James M. Stewart, December 20, 1926, cabinet 45, new drawer 179/old drawer 184, box 1, file: Misc. Corresp. 1917–1928 5 of 5; Francis Case to Millard Scott, April 20, 1927, cabinet 45, new drawer 179/old drawer 184, box 2, file: Miscellaneous Correspondence 2–S, Francis H. Case Collection.
49. "A Column for Everybody," *Daily Argus-Leader* (Sioux Falls, SD), June 10, 1927; Seth Tupper, *Calvin Coolidge in the Black Hills* (Charleston, SC: The History Press, 2017), pp. 27–28 (hereinafter Tupper, *Coolidge in Hills*).
50. "My Days with The Hot Springs Star," Helen Magee Collection; Tupper, *Coolidge in Hills*, pp. 28, 29.
51. "Vision of White House in Black Hills During Summer Coming True," *Hot Springs Star* (Hot Springs, SD), May 24, 1927.
52. Francis Case to W. H. King, telegram, May 24[, 1927], Francis Case to Calvin Coolidge, telegram, May 24[, 1927], Francis Case to Peter Norbeck, night letter, May 24[, 1927], cabinet 45, new drawer 179/old drawer 184, box 2, file: Miscellaneous Correspondence 2–Misc., Francis H. Case Collection.
53. "President Comes to Hills June 16," *Custer Weekly Chronicle* (Custer, SD), June 4, 1927; Tupper, *Coolidge in Hills*, p. 30; "A Column for Everybody," *Daily Argus-Leader*; Leland Davidson Case, interview by Robert Webb, Mitchell, SD, April 23, 1972, transcript, Francis H. Case Collection (hereinafter LDC Interview, April 23, 1972).
54. "Leave It to The Hills," *Hot Springs Star* (Hot Springs, SD), June 14, 1927; Tupper, *Coolidge in Hills*, pp. 41–42; "President and Mrs. Coolidge at Custer Park," *Custer Weekly Chronicle* (Custer, SD), June 18, 1927; "Editor's Absence Blocks Plans for Times-Herald," *Times-Herald* (Hot Springs, SD), June 17, 1927; 1910 United States Census, Mitchell, Davison County, South Dakota,

digital image s.v. "Myrle L. Graves," *Ancestry.com*; Francis Case to Dan B. Brummitt, July 22, 1927, cabinet 45, new drawer 179/old drawer 184, box 2, file: Miscellaneous Letters 1927, Francis H. Case Collection. Badger Clark's poem, "Leave It to The Hills," is reproduced in its entirety below:

> Best leave the Hills to do the entertaining
> Of those two Coolidge folks from Washington.
> We Hillers are some short on social training
> To do things in the style they've seen 'em done.
> The highbrows with their saying wise or funny,
> The diplomats with all their savoir faire,
> The silk-pajama outfit with their money
> Have entertained that presidential pair.
> Feted and feasted them beyond all countings
> And flattered them with all applausive breath—
> In fact, dear folks, they've fled to these yere mountings
> Because they're nearly entertained to death.
> Let's leave it to the Hills; our peaks and canyons
> Can do the social stuff to heart's content.
> Once, say the Sioux, they had gods for companions,
> So they're quite equal to a President.
> A mountain trail knows all of fascination;
> The pine's old song can gladden and beguile;
> A mountain creek, for charming conversation,
> Can beat the fairest debutante a mile.
> Oh yes, we'll give our guests a hearty howdy,
> But spare them much human fuss and frills.
> For even Washington is cheap and dowdy
> Beside the entertainment of the Hills.

55. Tupper, *Coolidge in Hills*, pp. 42-46.
56. Tupper, *Coolidge in Hills*, pp. 55, 57, 62. For detailed and entertaining accounts describing the president's first day of trout fishing, including how his success was guaranteed when, prior to his arrival, his South Dakota hosts secretly stretched wire netting across the stream under bridges located two miles apart; planted old, fat, tame trout who had spent their entire lives at the Spearfish fish hatchery eating ground liver or ground horse meat; and reserved the two-mile, fenced-off creek section "for presidential fishing only," see Tupper, *Coolidge in Hills*, pp. 49–54 and Smith, *Carving Mount Rushmore*, pp. 142, 145–47.
57. Tupper, *Coolidge in Hills*, p. 128; Kelly, "Calvin Coolidge's Indelible Vacation."
58. Tupper, *Coolidge in Hills*, pp. 125, 128, 129.
59. Ibid., pp. 15–16, 110–11, 129–130.

60. Tupper, *Coolidge in Hills*, pp. 92–94, Smith, *Carving Mount Rushmore*, pp. 142, 144.
61. Tupper, *Coolidge in Hills*, pp. 99–104; Smith, *Carving Mount Rushmore*, pp. 150–53.
62. Smith, *Carving Mount Rushmore*, pp. 153–54; Tupper, *Coolidge in Hills*, pp. 104–05.
63. Tupper, *Coolidge in Hills*, p. 130; "President's Party Will Visit Hot Springs" and "Program for Coolidge Day in Hot Springs," *Hot Springs Star* (Hot Springs, SD), August 16, 1927; Francis to Carol, Sunday, [August 14, 1927], box 4, file 2, *Carol Case Goddard Collection*.
64. "My Days with The Hot Springs Star," Helen Magee Collection; History.com Editors, "Calvin Coolidge," accessed June 25, 2021, http://www.history.com/topics/us-presidents/calvin-coolidge; "Day, Coolidge's Townsman Says Much Imagination Shown in Stories of Him," *Hot Springs Star* (Hot Springs, SD), August 23, 1927; "Coolidges Enjoyed Stay at Hot Springs," *Daily Deadwood Pioneer-Times* (Deadwood, SD), August 20, 1927.
65. Tupper, *Coolidge in Hills*, p. 131; "L'Envoi," *Hot Springs Star* (Hot Springs, SD); September 6, 1927; "An Unwritten Despatch," *Hot Springs Star* (Hot Springs, SD), October 11, 1927.
66. Tupper, *Coolidge in Hills*, p. 131; Carl H. Loocke, *Scouting in the Black Hills* (Custer, SD: The Chronicle Shop, 1935), pp. 37–39.
67. "L'Envoi," *Hot Springs Star*.
68. "Hills People Bid Goodbye to Coolidge," *Daily Argus-Leader* (Sioux Falls, SD), September 9, 1927; Tupper, *Coolidge in Hills*, p. 131.
69. Cleophas C. O'Harra and Joseph P. Connolly, *The Geology, Mineralogy, and Scenic Features of Custer State Park, South Dakota* (Rapid City: South Dakota School of Mines, 1926), pp. 15–16 (hereinafter O'Harra and Connolly, *Geology of Custer State Park*); Badger Clark, *Custer State Park: Black Hills of South Dakota* (Pierre, SD: Game, Fish and Parks Commission, n.d.), pp. 4–5; Act of Mar. 12, 1919, 1919 S.D. Sess. Laws ch. 165, 151.
70. O'Harra and Connolly, *Geology of Custer State Park*, pp. 15-16; Act of Mar. 21, 1921, 1921 S.D. Sess. Laws ch. 188.
71. Act of Mar. 21, 1921, 1921 SD Sess. Laws ch. 188; O'Harra and Connolly, *Geology of Custer State Park*, p. 116.
72. O'Harra and Connolly, *Geology of Custer State Park*, p. 17, plate 59, "Geological Map of Custer State Park and Vicinity."
73. "Growing Pains," *Times-Herald* (Hot Springs, SD), April 16, 1926.
74. "Custer State Park," *Hot Springs Star* (Hot Springs, SD), May 4, 1926; "Colonel Shade's Bequest," *Hot Springs Star* (Hot Springs, SD), August 3, 1926.
75. "Norbeck Urges Bill for Park," *Rapid City Daily Journal* (Rapid City, SD), June 27, 1927; "Governor Won't Veto Budget Bill in Entirety," *Rapid City*

Daily Journal (Rapid City, SD), July 2, 1927; 1927 S.D. Special Sess. Laws ch. 12.

76. "Two South Dakota Poets," *Daily Argus-Leader* (Sioux Falls, SD), January 11, 1927; Jessie Y. Sundstrom, *Pioneers and Custer State Park: A History of Custer State Park and Northcentral Custer County* (Custer, SD: Self-published, 1994), pp. 140, 142 (hereinafter noted as Sundstrom, *Pioneers and Custer State Park*).

77. Francis to Carol, Sunday, [August 14, 1927], box 4, file 2, Carol Case Goddard Collection; Francis Case to Dan B. Brummitt, July 22, 1927, cabinet 45, new drawer 179/old drawer 184, box 2, file: Miscellaneous Letters 1927, M. E. Nystrom to Francis H. Case, January 24, 1928, cabinet 45, new drawer 179/old drawer 184, box 2, file: Miscellaneous Correspondence 2–N & O, Francis Case to Lloyd E. Rising, February 13, 1928, cabinet 45, new drawer 179/old drawer 184, box 2, file: Miscellaneous Letters 1928, Francis H. Case Collection; Sundstrom, *Pioneers and Custer State Park*, pp. 87, 128; "History of Our Cabin....#23" (Gering, NE: South Dakota Cabin Owners Association, 2005); photograph of cabin taken August 1927, carton C, Case Ranch Collection; site visit to cabin conducted on July 2, 2022.

78. College transcript, Esther Case, issued by State Teachers College, Mankato, MN, November 5, 1928, college transcript, Esther Case, issued by Gustavus Adolphus College, St. Peter, MN, November 5, 1928, box 5, file 7, Francis to Carol, Sunday, [August 14, 1927], box 4, file 2, Carol Case Goddard Collection.

79. Harold to Francis, October 30[, 1927], cabinet 45, new drawer 179/old drawer 184, box 2, file: Newspaper and Politics Miscellaneous 1922–1934, Francis H. Case Collection; "Eyes of Three Counties Set On Contest Buick-Aspiring Candidates," "Rules and Regulation," "Get Your Friends to Help You!," and "Schedule of Votes and Subscription Price," *Hot Springs Star* (Hot Springs, SD), November 1, 1927.

80. "Introducing Star, Times-Herald's Buick Aspiring Candidates" and "Good Morning Candidates!," *Hot Springs Star* (Hot Springs, SD), November 8, 1927; "Ruth Kipp Leads List of Candidates for the Buick," advertisements, *Hot Springs Star* (Hot Springs, SD), November 15, 1927; "Will Your Subscription Count? Look at the List," *Hot Springs Star* (Hot Springs, SD), November 22, 1927; "Ruth Kipp Maintains Lead As First Period Is Closed," advertisements, *Hot Springs Star* (Hot Springs, SD), November 29, 1927; "Just One Week From Saturday, The Great Campaign Will Close," *Hot Springs Star* (Hot Springs, SD), December 6, 1927; "Here's Three Go-Getters Hard to Beat for Ability," advertisements, and "It Won't Be Long Now Saturday Nite The End," *Hot Springs Star* (Hot Springs, SD), December 13, 1927; "Alcesta Murphy Awarded Prize Buick Sedan Saturday Night," *Hot Springs Star* (Hot Springs, SD), December 20, 1927.

81. "Alcesta Murphy Awarded Prize Buick Sedan Saturday Night," *Hot Springs Star*; "To the Public," *Hot Springs Star* (Hot Springs, SD), December 20, 1927; "The Northwest Post (Belle Fourche, Butte County, S.D.) 1902-193?," Library of Congress, accessed October 19, 2021, https://www.loc.gov/item/sn97065724/.
82. "Star Starts New Home on Middle Lot Midway Between Upper and Lower Town," *Hot Springs Star* (Hot Springs, SD), November 1, 1927.
83. Francis to Carol, November 16[, 1927], box 4, file 2, Carol Case Goddard Collection; "Readers Take an Interest in Work at New Star Building," *Hot Springs Star* (Hot Springs, SD), November 29, 1927; "Star Moving to New Home," *Hot Springs Star* (Hot Springs, SD), December 27, 1927; Francis Case to Wayne George, December 20, 1928, cabinet 45, new drawer 179/old drawer 184, box 2, file: Miscellaneous Correspondence 2–F–G, Francis H. Case Collection.
84. "My Days with the Hot Springs Star," Helen Magee Collection.

CHAPTER 10. HOT SPRINGS NEWSPAPERMAN AND BLACK HILLS PROMOTER—THE LATER YEARS

The quotation at the beginning of the chapter is taken from an article titled "A Personal Word." It appeared in the April 21, 1931 issue of the *Hot Springs Weekly Star*.

1. Francis to Hall, June 18, 1928, cabinet 45, new drawer 179/old drawer 184, box 2, file: Miscellaneous Correspondence 2–H, Francis H. Case Collection.
2. Ibid.; "Announcing the Evening Star," *Hot Springs Star* (Hot Springs, SD), September 25, 1928; Francis Case to Wayne George, December 20, 1928, cabinet 45, new drawer 179/old drawer 184, box 2, file: Miscellaneous Correspondence 2–F–G, Francis H. Case Collection; "About Us," Associated Press, accessed January 7, 2022, http://www.ap.org/about; *Encyclopedia Britannica Online*, s.v. "Associated Press," accessed January 7, 2022, http://www.britannica.com/topic/Associated-Press.
3. McCambridge to Francis Case, September 15, 1928, box 5, file 9, Carol Case Goddard Collection; "Announcing the Evening Star," *Hot Springs Star* (Hot Springs, SD), September 25, 1928; "Hot Springs Star," *Hot Springs Star* (Hot Springs, SD), October 9, 1928; "The Hot Springs Weekly Star," *Hot Springs Weekly Star* (Hot Springs, SD), November 20, 1928.
4. "Local Golfers Play Annual Handicap Tourney Match," *Hot Springs Star*, (Hot Springs, SD), September 25, 1928; "Ben Potts Captures Silver Cup of Country Club Handicap Tourney," *Hot Springs Star*, (Hot Springs, SD), November 6, 1928.
5. "Ben Potts Captures Silver Cup of Country Club Handicap Tourney," *Hot Springs Star*.

6. M. M. Oppegard to Francis H. Case, October 29, 1928, box 5, file 9, Carol Case Goddard Collection; "Star Records Smashed!!," *Hot Springs Weekly Star* (Hot Springs, SD), December 4, 1928; "Badger Clark Joins Star Staff," *Hot Springs Weekly Star* (Hot Springs, SD), December 18, 1928.
7. "Local Notes," *Rapid City Daily Journal* (Rapid City, SD), December 21, 1928; "Pioneer Dakotan Succumbs While Fishing Sunday," *Queen City Mail* (Spearfish, SD), September 6, 1935; "D. Wayne George Dies--Rites Held Here Wednesday," *Queen City Mail* (Spearfish, SD), July 21, 1955; "The Sundance Times (Sundance, Crook County, Wyo.) 1926-Current," Library of Congress, accessed January 10, 2022, https://www.loc.gov/item/sn92067069/; Francis Case to Wayne George, December 20, 1928, D. Wayne George to Francis Case, January 4, 1929, cabinet 45, new drawer 179/old drawer 184, box 2, file: Miscellaneous Correspondence 2–F–G, Francis H. Case Collection.
8. "Big OIL Strike in Red Canyon Hole," *Hot Springs Evening Star* (Hot Springs, SD), January 11, 1929, "Evening Star Turns Morning Star to Tell World of the Oil Well," *Hot Springs Weekly Star* (Hot Springs, SD), January 15, 1929; "Announcing the 'Hills Oil Review'," *Hot Springs Weekly Star* (Hot Springs, SD), January 22, 1929.
9. "Well Flowing at Noon Today," "Take This Trip to Red Canyon," and "Evening Star Turns Morning Star to Tell World of the Oil Well," *Hot Springs Weekly Star* (Hot Springs, SD), January 15, 1929.
10. "Announcing the 'Hills Oil Review'," *Hot Springs Weekly Star*; Advertisement, "Now Ready Number Three of The Black Hills Oil and Mining Review," *Hot Springs Weekly Star* (Hot Springs, SD), May 7, 1929; "Senate, Too, Passes Bills To Exempt Oil and Mining," *Hot Springs Weekly Star* (Hot Springs, SD), February 26, 1929; "Bulow Put Pen to Bettelheim Bill 43," *Hot Springs Weekly Star* (Hot Springs, SD), March 5, 1929; "What Oil Means," *Hot Springs Weekly Star* (Hot Springs, SD), April 9, 1929; "Curtailed Oil Production and Fall River County," *Hot Springs Weekly Star* (Hot Springs, SD), April 30, 1929; "10 Million From 640 Acres," *Hot Springs Weekly Star* (Hot Springs, SD), October 1, 1929; Advertisement, "OIL Men," *Hot Springs Weekly Star* (Hot Springs, SD), January 29, 1929; Advertisement, "New County Maps . . . And Oil Lease Blanks," *Hot Springs Weekly Star* (Hot Springs, SD), May 14, 1929. For the numerous articles that address the various oil companies' exploration efforts and geologists' reports during 1929, see *Weekly Star* issues published between January 29 and December 31 in that year.
11. "Two More Development Companies Incorporate," *Rapid City Daily Journal* (Rapid City, SD), May 14, 1929; "Will Pool Stocks and Royalties," *Hot Springs Weekly Star* (Hot Springs, SD), November 26, 1929; Advertisement, "Western Securities, Inc. . . . Announces a Limited Offering of Stock at Par," *Hot Springs Weekly Star* (Hot Springs, SD), December 24, 1929.

12. "Start Tomorrow On Barker Dome," *Hot Springs Weekly Star* (Hot Springs, SD), May 14, 1929; Advertisement, "We're Off!," *Custer Weekly Chronicle* (Custer, SD), May 23, 1929; "Visitors Watch Drill at Barker; Now In Redbeds," *Hot Springs Weekly Star* (Hot Springs, SD), July 2, 1929; "Black Hills Pete's Well No. 1 Comes In With Heavy Gas Flow," *Hot Springs Weekly Star* (Hot Springs, SD), December 10, 1929.
13. "Barker Well Hits a Flow of Commercial Oil at 1328 Ft." and "'All South Dakota Forward'," *Hot Springs Weekly Star* (Hot Springs, SD), December 31, 1929.
14. "Hot Springs Celebrates Burn Oil from New Well," *Custer Weekly Chronicle* (Custer, SD), January 9, 1930; "Hot Springs to Have 'Oil Exchange'; Office at Evans," *Hot Springs Weekly Star* (Hot Springs, SD), January 7, 1930; "New Business Reflects Local Oil Find" and advertisement, "The Oil Exchange," *Hot Springs Weekly Star* (Hot Springs, SD), January 14, 1930.
15. "Oil Exchange Gets Inquiries From a Number of States," *Hot Springs Weekly Star* (Hot Springs, SD), February 4, 1930; "Geologist For Lion Oil Goes Over Structures," *Hot Springs Weekly Star* (Hot Springs, SD), March 4, 1930; "Increasing Oil Activity Gets Big Play" and "B. H. Pete Gives Out His Report," *Hot Springs Weekly Star* (Hot Springs, SD), March 12, 1930; "Strong Rapid Group Enters Field," *Hot Springs Weekly Star* (Hot Springs, SD), March 18, 1930; "Geologic Report on the Barker," *Hot Springs Weekly Star* (Hot Springs, SD), March 25, 1930; "Country Club Well Spudded In," *Hot Springs Weekly Star* (Hot Springs, SD), April 1, 1930; "This Well Is To Be Called Rockford '1'," *Hot Springs Weekly Star* (Hot Springs, SD), May 20, 1930; "Black Hills Pete Spuds in Rockford Well No. 1," *Hot Springs Weekly Star* (Hot Springs, SD), June 17, 1930; "Rockford Well By 600 Feet Before Two Weeks Have Passed; July 20 Aim," *Hot Springs Weekly Star* (Hot Springs, SD), July 1, 1930; "Reports Indicate Growth For Western Securities In First Year of Operation," *Hot Springs Weekly Star* (Hot Springs, SD), July 8, 1930.
16. "Red Canyon Title Litigation Is Settled," *Hot Springs Weekly Star* (Hot Springs, SD), March 25, 1930; "Morgans of Minneapolis Will Put Red Canyon on Pump; Drill Others," *Hot Springs Weekly Star* (Hot Springs, SD), August 5, 1930; "Morgan Interests Develop Red Canyon" and "With Rockford at Oil, B.H.P. Starts 3rd Well in Barker Field," *Hot Springs Weekly Star* (Hot Springs, SD), August 19, 1930.
17. "Black Hills Petroleum Negotiating For Renewed Work At Barker Early in Spring," *Hot Springs Weekly Star* (Hot Springs, SD), January 13, 1931; "Osage Crude Drops From $1.65 to 50 Cents in 6 Months," *Hot Springs Weekly Star* (Hot Springs, SD), March 17, 1931; Advertisement, "Give a Thought to the Growing OIL DISTRICT around Hot Springs," *Hot Springs Weekly Star* (Hot Springs, SD), August 19, 1930; "Drilling Will Be Resumed On Country Club Well Within Few Days, Grandbouche Says," *Hot Springs Weekly Star* (Hot Springs, SD), April 7, 1931.

Notes 509

18. Leland Davidson Case, interview by Robert Webb, Mitchell, SD, April 23, 1972, transcript, Francis H. Case Collection.
19. "Commercial Club Talks Passion Play," *Hot Springs Weekly Star* (Hot Springs, SD), December 18, 1928; "New Chamber Faces Bright 1929," *Hot Springs Weekly Star* (Hot Springs, SD), January 22, 1929.
20. "Dozen Subjects to Be Discussed at Greater South Dakota Congress," *Daily Argus-Leader* (Sioux Falls, SD), January 17, 1929; "Speakers Arrive for Greater S.D. Congress," *Daily Argus-Leader* (Sioux Falls, SD), January 21, 1929; "'Coordinating' State Congress Opens 4-Day Meet," *Rapid City Daily Journal* (Rapid City, SD), January 22, 1929.
21. "'Coordinating' State Congress Opens 4-Day Meet," *Rapid City Daily Journal*; "Summer Cabins Bring Residents," *Hot Springs Weekly Star* (Hot Springs, SD), January 29, 1929. In August 1927, State Secretary of Agriculture Louis Crill suggested a more ambitious plan for private cabins in Custer State Park than the one Francis presented to the Greater South Dakota Congress. As the *Hot Springs Star* reported then, Crill said "There is room for the building of 10,000 cabins in the State Park alone and have none of them on the main highways to obstruct the view of the natural scenery. At a rental of $10.00 annually for each site, it will be seen that this would bring an annual revenue of $100,000 to the State Park, and it will not be many years until it is a self supporting activity of our state." See "What They Say," *Hot Springs Star* (Hot Springs, SD), August 30, 1927.
22. "Figure Over 1000 On Congress Registration," *Rapid City Daily Journal* (Rapid City, SD), January 25, 1929; "Congress Adopts Resolutions Directing Progress" and "The Daily Journal," *Rapid City Daily Journal* (Rapid City, SD), January 26, 1929.
23. "Remarks of Hon. Peter Norbeck of South Dakota in the Senate of the United States," (Washington, DC: U. S. Government Printing Office), February 22, 1929, box 1, file 12, Carol Case Goddard Collection; Rex Alan Smith, *The Carving of Mount Rushmore* (New York: Abbeville Press, 1985), pp. 174–77 (hereinafter Smith, *Carving Mount Rushmore*).
24. Smith, *Carving Mount Rushmore*, pp. 177–182; "Keystone Man, in Sioux Falls, Enthusiastic Over Mining, Scenic Possibilities in Hills," *Daily Argus-Leader* (Sioux Falls, SD), June 16, 1929.
25. Francis to Leland, April 24, 1929, H. S. Star/Times Herald Early Newspapers, p. 25, binder 046, Helen Magee Collection, accessed June 29, 2020; "Hot Springs News Makes Initial Appearance," *Lead Daily Call* (Lead, SD), August 20, 1928; "Edgemont to Have a New Newspaper," *Rapid City Daily Journal* (Rapid City, SD), December 31, 1922.
26. "Announcing the 'Hills Oil Review'," *Hot Springs Weekly Star*, (Hot Springs, SD), January 22, 1929; Advertisement, "Now Ready Number Three of The Black Hills Oil and Mining Review," *Hot Springs Weekly Star* (Hot Springs, SD), May 7, 1929; "A New Field for The News," *Hot Springs Evening Star*

(Hot Springs, SD), May 23, 1929; "Hot Springs, Edgemont Papers Merge with Oil Publication," *Daily Argus-Leader* (Sioux Falls, SD), May 25, 1929.

27. "U. S. Offers Ground for Vacation Homes," *Daily Argus-Leader* (Sioux Falls, SD), May 18, 1929.
28. "Cabin Sites Cost But $10 A Year in The Black Hills," *Custer Weekly Chronicle* (Custer, SD), May 30, 1929; Advertisement, "Build a summer cabin," *Custer Weekly Chronicle* (Custer, SD), May 23, 1929; "Build Summer Nest in The Hills—Klock," *Hot Springs Evening Star* (Hot Springs, SD), June 11, 1929.
29. "Charm of Black Hills Draws Interested Visitors from Everywhere; Summer Cabins Are Decorated with Products of Forest and Plains," *Daily Argus-Leader* (Sioux Falls, SD), June 29, 1929.
30. Jessie Y. Sundstrom, *Pioneers and Custer State Park: A History of Custer State Park and Northcentral Custer County* (Custer, SD: Self-published, 1994) pp.140–41; "Badger Clark Builds His Home in the State Park," *Hot Springs Weekly Star* (Hot Springs, SD), October 29, 1929.
31. Francis to Carol, August 20, 1929, box 6, file 4, Carol Case Goddard Collection; "Discussing Plans for Annual Camp," *Rapid City Daily Journal* (Rapid City, SD), April 19, 1928; "Church Camp In Black Hills Attracts Many People," *Daily Argus-Leader* (Sioux Falls, SD), August 11, 1928; "About Pactola," Silver City Historical Society, accessed January 20, 2022, https://web.archive.org/web/20211202073729/http://www.silvercitysd.com/Pactola.html; "Methodist Camp to Open Monday," *Rapid City Daily Journal* (Rapid City, SD), July 25, 1929; "Institute Work Opens At Methodist Camp," *Rapid City Daily Journal* (Rapid City, SD), July 29, 1929; "Republican Hills Leaders Gather," *Rapid City Daily Journal* (Rapid City, SD), September 25, 1929; "Bronson Again Named Head Associated Clubs," *Rapid City Daily Journal* (Rapid City, SD), November 9, 1929.
32. "Locals," *Rapid City Daily Journal* (Rapid City, SD), December 26, 1929; R. P. Williams to Major General Commandant, memorandum, May 12, 1937, FHC Records, National Archives, NPRC; R. McC. Pate to All Reserve Officers, memorandum, October 1, 1946, Francis Case to Captain MacArthur H. Manchester, April 19, 1947, cabinet 31, new drawer 121/old drawer 126, box 1, file: Marine Corps (Reserve), Francis H. Case Collection.
33. Esther to Carol, [April 27, 1928], box 5, file 7, Carol Case Goddard Collection; Francis Case to Hall, June 18, 1928, cabinet 45, new drawer 179/old drawer 184, box 2, file: Miscellaneous Correspondence 2–H, Francis H. Case Collection.
34. Mother to Carol, [undated but envelope postmarked October 27, 1928], box 5, file 7, Carol Case Goddard Collection.
35. Mother to Carol, [February 6, 1929], Mother, Esther and Dorothy to Joyce, June 16, 1929, Esther to Francis, Leland, Joyce and all, June 20, 1929, box 6, file 4, Carol Case Goddard Collection; "'Things to Wear for Those Who

Care'," *Brainerd Daily Dispatch* (Brainerd, MN), January 14, 1926; "Help Wanted—Women," *Minneapolis Tribune* (Minneapolis, MN), April 7, 1930.
36. Mother and Esther to Mrs. Ralph Himmelhoch, telegram, September 6, 1929, Esther to Carol and Ralph, November 13, 1929, The Old Lady [Esther] to Old Man [Leland], [January 22, 1930], box 6, file 4, Carol Case Goddard Collection; "Mankato Daily Free Press (Mankato, Minn.) 1887-1931," Chronicling America, accessed January 24, 2022, https://chroniclingamerica.loc.gov/lccn/sn83016588.
37. The Old Lady [Esther] to Old Man [Leland], [January 22, 1930]; Herbert L. Case to Leland, January 15, 1930, box 4, file 10, Carol Case Goddard Collection.
38. "Social and Personal," *Hot Springs Weekly Star* (Hot Springs, SD), February 25, 1930; Leland Davidson Case and Edith E. H. Grannis, eds., *New Hampshire to Minnesota: Memoirs of Samuel Higbee Grannis (1839-1933)* (Tucson, AZ: Self-published, 1962), pp. 24, 47, 49, 79; H. L. Case to Leland, February 17, 1930, box 6, file 5, Carol Case Goddard Collection.
39. Francis to Carol, May 10, 1930, box 1, file 7, Francis to Grandpa, Edith and Mamie, January 21, 1931, box 2, file 17, Carol Case Goddard Collection; "Star Dust," *Hot Springs Weekly Star* (Hot Springs, SD), June 3, 1930; "Hot Springs Goes Forward!," *Hot Springs Weekly Star* (Hot Springs, SD), March 24, 1931.
40. "Star to Install High Speed Newspaper Press, to Serve Growing List" and advertisement, "The Hot Springs Weekly Star and The Hot Springs Evening Star Will Give Away an Automobile," *Hot Springs Weekly Star* (Hot Springs, SD), February 4, 1930.
41. "Star Announces $3,500 Contest," advertisement, "Join the Hot Springs Evening Star---and---The Weekly Star's Subscription Campaign Today," and advertisement, "PICK YOUR PRIZE," *Hot Springs Weekly Star* (Hot Springs, SD), February 11, 1930; Advertisement, "DO YOU WANT?," *Hot Springs Weekly Star* (Hot Springs, SD), February 25, 1930.
42. "Star Announces $3,500 Contest," *Hot Springs Weekly Star*.
43. Advertisement, "Let Your Name be Placed Here—OPPORTUNITY IS YOURS IF YOU WILL BUT GRASP IT NOW!! It is FREE—It is YOURS Awaits Any Man, Woman, Boy or Girl," *Hot Springs Weekly Star* (Hot Springs, SD), February 18, 1930; "Wire-Wheel Deluxe Marquette for Star's Big Contest Shipped," "'Doers' Are the Ones Who Get the Prizes of Life," "Here's the Truth; You Should Try," advertisement, "Are You Capitalizing Your Spare Time?," "More the Merrier in the Star's Big Contest," and advertisement, "DO YOU WANT?," *Hot Springs Weekly Star* (Hot Springs, SD), February 25, 1930; "Four Special Prizes are Announced for Saturday," *Hot Springs Weekly Star* (Hot Springs, SD), March 4, 1930; "Here's Another $25 Special; Note This Ardmore Winner," *Hot Springs Weekly Star* (Hot Springs, SD), March 12, 1930; "The Faithful Wore Green on the 17th; and Somebody Will Wear an Auto on April 12," *Hot Springs Weekly Star* (Hot

Springs, SD) March 18, 1930; "Mary Jones Wins Week's Cash Prizes," *Hot Springs Weekly Star* (Hot Springs, SD), March 25, 1930; "Race Enters Final Week Mrs. A. W. Fellows Wins $25," *Hot Springs Weekly Star* (Hot Springs, SD), April 8, 1930.

44. "Here's a Mark to Shoot at, One $25 Cash Prize This Week," *Hot Springs Weekly Star* (Hot Springs, SD), April 1, 1930; "Race Enters Final Week Mrs. A. W. Fellows Wins $25," *Hot Springs Weekly Star*; "Town and Country Divide Prizes," *Hot Springs Weekly Star* (Hot Springs, SD), April 15, 1930.

45. Advertisement, "Progress . . . . . Vision - - -," *Hot Springs Weekly Star* (Hot Springs, SD), March 12, 1930; "Town and Country Divide Prizes," *Hot Springs Weekly Star*; Sketch of Goss Comet, *Hot Springs Weekly Star* (Hot Springs, SD), April 22, 1930; "Star Dust," *Hot Springs Weekly Star* (Hot Springs, SD), June 3, 1930.

46. "Citizens' Military Training Camp photograph album, MSS.10.02, Butler Center for Arkansas Studies, Arkansas Studies Institute, accessed February 2, 2022, https:// cdm15728.contentdm.oclc.org/digital/collection/findingaids/ id/5393; Carole Stobke, "Citizens Military Training Camps (CMTC)," *Genea-Musings*, April 10, 2019, http://www.genea musings.com/2019/04/guest-post-citizens-military-training.html (hereinafter Stobke, "Citizens Military Training Camps"); "The C. M. T. C. Camps," *Daily Argus-Leader* (Sioux Falls, SD), March 13, 1930.

47. "C. M. T. Camps For 5,000 This Season," *Hot Springs Weekly Star* (Hot Springs, SD), March 12, 1929; "Editorial Comment," *Hot Springs Weekly Star* (Hot Springs, SD), April 16, 1929.

48. "The C. M. T. C. Camps," *Daily Argus-Leader*; "Those Wanting to Attend the C. M. T. C. Camps, Act Now," *Hot Springs Weekly Star* (Hot Springs, SD), April 8, 1930; "Local Men Prepare to Attend Summer Camps," *Rapid City Daily Journal* (Rapid City, SD), May 29, 1930; "State CMTC, Organized Reserves Have Big Year In 1931—Colonel True Gives Information on Work," *Daily Argus-Leader* (Sioux Falls, SD), January 17, 1932.

49. "C. M. T. C. Quota from Fall River County Can Go to Fort Snelling; But Apply Now," *Hot Springs Weekly Star* (Hot Springs, SD), April 7, 1931; "H. R. Slocum Is Appointed C. M. T. C. Chairman for County," *Hot Springs Weekly Star* (Hot Springs, SD), December 8, 1931. The CMTC program continued until 1940. According to some sources, it was a disappointment, at least with respect to its goal of producing commissioned officers. To support that argument, it has been pointed out that although "nearly 400,000 men attended at least on year of the program" during its existence, only about 5,000 completed the required four-year course in consecutive summers, enlisted in the Army, and became commissioned second lieutenants after graduating from Officer's Candidate School. See Stobke, "Citizens Military Training Camps."

50. "U. S. Memorial at Rushmore Is of Gigantic Size," *Daily Argus-Leader* (Sioux Falls, SD), May 18, 1930; "Plans Completed for Rushmore Event," *Daily Argus-Leader* (Sioux Falls, SD), June 28, 1930; "2,500 Attend Rushmore Ceremonies," *Daily Argus-Leader* (Sioux Falls, SD), July 5, 1930.
51. "Plans Completed for Rushmore Event," *Daily Argus-Leader*; "2,500 Attend Rushmore Ceremonies," "Half Million Year's Existence Is Seen for Rushmore Memorial," and "Rushmore Sidelights," *Daily Argus-Leader* (Sioux Falls, SD), July 5, 1930.
52. "Plans Completed for Rushmore Event," *Daily Argus-Leader*; "2,500 Attend Rushmore Ceremonies" and "Rushmore Sidelights," *Daily Argus-Leader*; Smith, *Carving Mount Rushmore*, pp. 211, 213; *Mount Rushmore National Memorial: Jefferson Number*, (Washington, DC: Committee on Design and Publicity, Mount Rushmore National Memorial Commission, 1931), p. 7 (hereinafter *Jefferson Number*), carton C, Case Ranch Collection.
53. Smith, *Carving Mount Rushmore*, pp. 213–14.
54. Chambers Kellar to Francis H. Case, July 17, 1930, box 3, file 3, Francis to Dad and Mother, July 25, 1930, box 1, file 7, Carol Case Goddard Collection; "Hot Springs," *Rapid City Daily Journal* (Rapid City, SD), September 5, 1930.
55. Herbert L. Case to Joyce, Francis, Leland and Carol, October 28, 1930, Herbert L. Case to Francis and Myrle, October 28, 1930, box 2, file 17, Carol Case Goddard Collection.
56. Francis to Mother, November 20, 1930, Herbert L. Case to Francis, December 11, 1930, Mother to Francis, undated, box 2, file 17, Francis to Carol and Ralph, January 20, 1931, box 6, file 5, Carol Case Goddard Collection.
57. Francis to Mother, January 20, 1931, box 2, file 17, Carol Case Goddard Collection; Myrle to Francis, [February 3 and 5, 1931], red scrapbook, carton C, Case Ranch Collection.
58. "Star Acquires a New Chief" and "A Personal Word," *Hot Springs Weekly Star* (Hot Springs, SD), April 21, 1931.
59. "The Daily Argus Leader," *Daily Argus-Leader* (Sioux Falls, SD), April 17, 1931; "The Pioneer Times," *Deadwood Pioneer Times* (Deadwood, SD), April 17, 1931; "Evening Huronite," *Evening Huronite* (Huron, SD), April 23, 1931.
60. "Dinner Honoring Norbeck Offered," *Rapid City Daily Journal* (Rapid City, SD), April 16, 1931; "State Chamber to Promote Aviation," *Evening Huronite* (Huron, SD), April 17, 1931; "News of Our Neighbors: Hot Springs," *Rapid City Daily Journal* (Rapid City, SD), April 21, 1931.
61. "Society," *Rapid City Daily Journal* (Rapid City, SD), May 1, 1931; "Odd Fellows," Independent Order of Odd Fellows, accessed February 16, 2022, http://www.odd-fellows.org/about/odd-fellows/; "Rebekahs," Independent Order of Odd Fellows, accessed February 16, 2022, http://www.odd-fellows.

org/about/rebekahs; "Farewell Dinner Given for Madera," *Rapid City Daily Journal* (Rapid City, SD), April 28, 1931.
62. "Francis Case Speaker," *Daily Argus-Leader* (Sioux Falls, SD), April 5, 1931; "Gann Valley Grads Hear Francis Case," *Evening Huronite* (Huron, SD), May 27, 1931; *South Dakota Map*.
63. Francis Case to Carol, June 3, 1931, box 1, file 7, Carol Case Goddard Collection.
64. "Governor and Mrs. Green Spend Week End Resting and Fishing at Blue Bell," *Hot Springs Weekly Star* (Hot Springs, SD), June 23, 1931; "Report of Committee on Publicity and Design (from May 8, 1931 to Oct. 17, 1931)," (hereinafter *Publicity and Design Report*), carton C, Case Ranch Collection; "Alco Gravure Inc.," accessed February 17, 2022, http://www.usa.com/frs/alco-gravure-inc-110001809491.html.
65. Jarvis Harriman, *The Man from the Hills: A Biography of Leland Davidson Case* (Tucson, AZ: Westerners International, 1994) pp. 39–40 (hereinafter noted as Harriman, *The Man from the Hills*).
66. Ibid., 41–42.
67. Ibid., 44, 46, 68; Dad to Leland, July 3, 1931, Dad to Leland, July 13, 1931, box 2, file 5, Herbert L. Case Papers. Rotary International "is the worldwide association of all Rotary clubs." Paul Harris, a Chicago attorney, formed the first such club in 1905 when "he invited three men to meet with him one evening for fellowship," and they discussed supporting "each other in their careers." The group became known as the Rotary Club from its "original practice of rotating the meeting place among the members' office locations." By 1910, Rotary Clubs existed in 14 American cities. In January 1911, the magazine which eventually became *The Rotarian* appeared. Ten years later, the clubs had spread to six continents. According to its website, Rotary International today is "a global network of 1.4 million neighbors, friends, leaders, and problem-solvers who see a world where people unite and take action to create lasting change;" and its mission is to "provide service to others, promote integrity, and advance world understanding, goodwill, and peace through our fellowship of business, professional, and community leaders." See *The World Book Encyclopedia*, (1992), s.v. "Rotary International;" Harriman, *The Man from the Hills*, pp. 44–45; "Our History," Rotary International, accessed February 18, 2022, http://www.rotary.org/en/about-rotary/history; "Who We Are," Rotary International, accessed February 18, 2022, http://www.rotary.org/en/about-rotary.
68. Harriman, *The Man from the Hills*, p. 50; "Sturgis," *Rapid City Daily Journal* (Rapid City, SD), August 12, 1931.
69. *Publicity and Design Report*; "Rushmore Book for 1931 Here," *Rapid City Daily Journal* (Rapid City, SD), July 28, 1931; "Exchange Expressions," *Lead Daily Call* (Lead, SD), August 11, 1931.

70. *Publicity and Design Report*; "Alco Gravure, Inc.;" "Rushmore Book for 1931 Here," *Rapid City Daily Journal*.
71. "Mt. Rushmore Brochure for This Year is Out," *Lead Daily Call* (Lead, SD), August 1, 1931; *Jefferson Number*, passim; "Rushmore Booklet Is Released," *Hot Springs Weekly Star* (Hot Springs, SD), August 4, 1931.
72. John A. Boland to Francis, August 1, 1931, John A. Boland to Francis, October 17, 1931, carton C, Case Ranch Collection; *Publicity and Design Report*; "Custer Chronicle Sold," *Daily Argus-Leader* (Sioux Falls, SD), September 11, 1931.

CHAPTER 11. BACK TO THE NEWSPAPER BUSINESS, AND PURSUIT OF OTHER INTERESTS

The quotation at the beginning of the chapter is from the *Custer Weekly Chronicle*, September 17, 1931 issue.

1. Federal Writers' Project of the Works Progress Administration, *The WPA Guide to South Dakota* (St. Paul, MN: Minnesota Historical Society Press, 2006), p. 301 (hereinafter Federal Writers' Project, *WPA Guide*); "History of Custer," accessed March 9, 2022, http://www.custer.govoffice.com/history; U. S. Department of Commerce, *Fifteenth Census of the United States: 1930,* vol. 1: *Population* (Washington, DC: United States Government Printing Office, 1931), p. 1026.
2. "Custer Chronicle Sold," *Daily Argus-Leader* (Sioux Falls, SD), September 11, 1931; "Case Buys Custer Chronicle from Trent," *Rapid City Daily Journal* (Rapid City, SD), September 11, 1931; "Francis Case Buys the Custer Chronicle," *Lead Daily Call* (Lead, SD), September 11, 1931; "'What South Dakota Makes, Makes South Dakota," *Custer Weekly Chronicle* (Custer, SD), September 17, 1931.
3. *Black Hills News* (Custer, SD) September 19, 1931; "A New Field for the News," *Hot Springs Evening Star* (Hot Springs, SD), May 23, 1929.
4. *Black Hills News* (Custer, SD), September 19, 26, and October 3 through December 19, 1931; *Custer Weekly Chronicle* (Custer, SD), September 17, 24, and October 1 through December 24, 1931.
5. "The Rapid City Daily Journal," *Rapid City Daily Journal* (Rapid City, SD), September 12, 1931; "The Daily Argus-Leader," *Daily Argus-Leader* (Sioux Falls, SD), September 22, 1931; "The Iroquois Chief (Iroquois, SD), 1888-1953," Library of Congress, accessed March 16, 2022, https://www.loc.gov/item/sn00065133/; "In a Good Town," *Custer Weekly Chronicle* (Custer, SD), October 1, 1931.
6. "South Dakota Board of Regents Information," RocketReach, accessed March 8, 2022, http://www.rocketreach.co/south-dakota-board-of-regents-profile_b5dd1f07f42e4bd2; "Guy Harvey Will Be Secretary for Board of Regents," *Daily Argus-Leader* (Sioux Falls, SD), October 17, 1931.
7. "Francis H. Case Chosen Regent," *Daily Argus-Leader* (Sioux Falls, SD), September 25, 1931; "Editor of Chronicle Named to State Board of Regents," *Custer Weekly Chronicle* (Custer, SD), October 1, 1931; "Case

to Speak Here Thursday," *Phreno Cosmian* (Mitchell, SD), May 15, 1934, file: Case, Francis, Dakota Wesleyan Archives; John F. Way to Francis Case, November 12, 1924, box 2, file 31, Carol Case Goddard Collection; "The Daily Argus-Leader," *Daily Argus-Leader* (Sioux Falls, SD), September 28, 1931; "State Press Comment," *Deadwood Pioneer-Times* (Deadwood, SD), September 29, 1931; "Evening Huronite," *Evening Huronite* (Huron, SD), October 6, 1931.

8. "Guy Harvey Will Be Secretary for Board of Regents," *Daily Argus-Leader* (Sioux Falls, SD), October 17, 1931; "News of Our Neighbors: Custer," *Rapid City Daily Journal* (Rapid City, SD), November 20, 1931; "Past Presidents of BHSU," Black Hills State University, accessed March 17, 2022, https://www.bhsu.edu/President/Past-Presidents; "News of Our Neighbors: Sturgis," *Rapid City Daily Journal* (Rapid City, SD), November 25, 1931.

9. "Regents Hold Meeting Here," *Daily Argus-Leader* (Sioux Falls, SD), February 19, 1932; "Faculties Given Board Approval," *Daily Argus-Leader* (Sioux Falls, SD), February 20, 1932; "Case in Attendance at Board of Regent Confab," *Rapid City Daily Journal* (Rapid City, SD), March 31, 1932; "Case Estimates Salary Savings," *Rapid City Daily Journal* (Rapid City, SD), April 11, 1932.

10. "Regents to Meet at Mines Next Friday," *Rapid City Daily Journal* (Rapid City, SD), November 16, 1932; "Regents Leave After Budget Session Here," *Rapid City Daily Journal* (Rapid City, SD), November 21, 1932.

11. "School Consolidation Report Nearly Ready," *Lead Daily Call* (Lead, SD), December 19, 1932; "Elections," in *2005 South Dakota Legislative Manual*, p. 13, accessed June 25, 2021, http://www.sdsos.gov/elections-voting/assets/ElectionsReturnsPre1972.pdf (page citations are to PDF version); "Education Issue Has High Place on S.D. Calendar," *Daily Argus-Leader* (Sioux Falls, SD), January 6, 1933.

12. "Regents Place 7 Recommendations Before Governor," *Rapid City Daily Journal* (Rapid City, SD), January 13, 1933.

13. "Wells Is Regent, Replacing Case," *Rapid City Daily Journal* (Rapid City, SD), January 17, 1933; "Case Replaced by Democrat, Board Regents," *Weekly Pioneer Press* (Deadwood, SD), January 19, 1933.

14. "Mine Men Start New Organization," *Rapid City Daily Journal* (Rapid City, SD), June 13, 1931; "Prepare for Next Meeting Mining Assn.," *Deadwood Pioneer-Times* (Deadwood, SD), September 20, 1931; "Mining Association to Meet; and Committees Are Named," *Custer Weekly Chronicle* (Custer, SD), October 1, 1931.

15. "Talk of Oil and Mineral Problems," *Rapid City Daily Journal* (Rapid City, SD), October 3, 1931; "Lively Session of Mining Assn. Held, Newcastle," *Deadwood Pioneer-Times* (Deadwood, SD), October 4, 1931.

16. "New Type Face for Chronicle," *Custer Weekly Chronicle*, (Custer, SD), October 1, 1931; Advertisement, "The Garlock Theater and The Chronicle Join in Offering You During November a Free Theatre Ticket with Your Chronicle Subscription," *Custer Weekly Chronicle* (Custer, SD), November 12, 1931; Advertisement, "Pathfinder: The Time-Tested News Weekly Right from Washington, D.C. is now offered to you along with Your Chosen Home Paper," *Custer Weekly Chronicle* (Custer, SD), November 26, 1931.
17. "BLACK HILLS Weekly Chronicle," *Black Hills Weekly Chronicle* (Custer, SD), December 26, 1931; "Custer County Chronicle," *Custer County Chronicle* (Custer, SD), December 31, 1931; *Custer County Chronicle* (Custer, SD), March 3, 1932.
18. "Property Changes Hands at Custer," *Rapid City Daily Journal* (Rapid City, SD), January 14, 1932; Francis to Carol, July 3, 1932, box 1, file 7, Carol Case Goddard Collection.
19. "Float of the Street," *Custer County Chronicle* (Custer, SD), March 24, 1932.
20. "Green Declares He'll 'Fight' for Black Hills Posts," *Custer County Chronicle* (Custer, SD), April 14, 1932.
21. "Custer Men Plead Hills' Timber Cause" and "Float of the Street," *Custer County Chronicle* (Custer, SD), April 21, 1932.
22. "Float of the Street," *Custer County Chronicle* (Custer, SD) August 11, 1932; "7,800 Black Hills Posts are Purchased by State," *Custer County Chronicle* (Custer, SD), December 22, 1932.
23. "List Contracts for Road Work," *Rapid City Daily Journal* (Rapid City, SD), September 9, 1932; "Many Get Work Through Roads," *Rapid City Daily Journal* (Rapid City, SD), September 16, 1932; "Other Editors," *Rapid City Daily Journal* (Rapid City, SD) November 15, 1932.
24. "Other Editors," *Rapid City Daily Journal*; "The Black Hills Weekly archives," *Newspapers.com*, accessed August 4, 2022, http://www.newspapers.com/paper/the-black-hills-weekly/3644/.
25. *Black Hills Chronicle* (Custer, SD), May 14, 1932; *Black Hills Chronicle* (Custer, SD), May 21, 1932; *Black Hills Chronicle* (Custer, SD), June 11, 1932; *Black Hills Chronicle* (Custer. SD), October 8, 1932; *Black Hills Chronicle* (Custer, SD), October 15, 1932.
26. "Memorial Day Program," *Custer County Chronicle* (Custer, SD), May 26, 1932; "Custer Prepares for Observances," *Rapid City Daily Journal* (Rapid City, SD), May 27, 1932; "Memorial Day Observance is Given by Many," *Custer County Chronicle* (Custer, SD), June 2, 1932.
27. Francis to Carol, July 3, 1932, box 1, file 7, Carol Case Goddard Collection.
28. "Building of Lake at Legion Park Will Provide Jobs for Needy Men," *Custer County Chronicle* (Custer, SD), September 22, 1932; Jessie Y. Sundstrom, *Pioneers and Custer State Park: A History of Custer State Park and Northcentral Custer County* (Custer, SD: Self-published, 1994), p. 131 (hereinafter Sundstrom, *Pioneers and Custer State Park*); *Encyclopedia Britannica Online*,

s.v. "Reconstruction Finance Corporation," accessed February 25, 2022, http://www.britannica.com/topic/Reconstruction-Finance-Corporation; "Governor Green Sees Lake Job," *Custer County Chronicle* (Custer, SD), December 1, 1932.

29. "Governor Green Sees Lake Job," *Custer County Chronicle*; "Dirt Work is Done for Dam of Legion Lake," *Custer County Chronicle* (Custer, SD), February 23, 1933; "Legion Lake in State Park Begins to Fill," *Custer County Chronicle* (Custer, SD), March 30, 1933; "Custer Workers Get Most of R.F.C. Funds at Lake," *Custer County Chronicle* (Custer, SD), May 11, 1933.
30. "Proposal of 'Lake Pershing' for New Lake Draws Plenty of Fire," *Custer County Chronicle* (Custer, SD), April 6, 1933.
31. Ibid.
32. "Chips and Splinters," *Black Hills Chronicle* (Custer, SD), April 15, 1933.
33. "And Still the Names Come—from Anne to Ponderosa; from Radium to Crow Dog," and ballot, "A Name for the New Lake," *Custer County Chronicle* (Custer, SD), April 20, 1933; Ballot, "A Name for the New Lake," *Custer County Chronicle* (Custer, SD), April 27, 1933; "Crow Dog, Legion Lake, Bear Track Lead in Preferences Expressed for New Lake in Custer State Park," *Black Hills Chronicle* (Custer, SD), April 29, 1933. The 41 names on the April 27 ballot were: Pussy Willow Lake, Custer Lake, Lake Lakota, Lake Galena, Peace Lake, Kinnikinic Lake, Lake Nevin, Rainbow Lake, Sunset Lake, Sioux Lake, Lake Teresa, Lake Albien, Lake Booth, Lake Peterson, Lake Tubbs, Lake Evans, Lake Ponderosa, Lake Anne, Lake Tallent, Lake Pershing, Legion Lake, Lake of the Woods, Lake Sans Arc, Crow Dog Lake, Bear Track Lake, Pine Lake, Lake Pondora, Lake Depression, Lake Coolidge, McClelland Lake, Granite Lake, Mica Lake, Lariat Lake, Lake Calamity, Lake Argonne, Bellau [sic] Woods Lake, Lake Norbeck, Wounded Knee, Radium Lake, Paul's Lake, and Doughboy Lake.
34. "'Legion Lake' Leaps to Lead as Best Name," *Black Hills Chronicle* (Custer, SD), May 6, 1933.
35. "And Still the Names Come—from Anne to Ponderosa; from Radium to Crow Dog," *Custer County Chronicle*; "New Legion Lake in Custer Park Dedicated Sunday," *Rapid City Daily Journal* (Rapid City, SD), June 12, 1933.
36. "National Guard Encampment Is Opened Today," *Rapid City Daily Journal* (Rapid City, SD), June 10. 1933; "New Legion Lake in Custer Park Dedicated Sunday," *Rapid City Daily Journal*; "New Legion Lake in Custer State Park Is Dedicated with Ceremonies Yesterday," *Lead Daily Call* (Lead, SD), June 12, 1933; "Legion Dedicates New Lake at Mt. Coolidge Camp," *Custer County Chronicle* (Custer, SD), June 15, 1933.
37. "Chronicle Opens Huge Subscription Drive," advertisement: "The Custer County Chronicle and The Black Hills Chronicle Announce a Subscription Drive, Open to Men, Women and Children.," "Rules and Regulations of

the Subscription Campaign," "Subscription Price and Vote Schedule of the Custer County Chronicle or Black Hills Chronicle," and "Combination Rate for Both Papers," *Custer County Chronicle* (Custer, SD), September 29, 1932; "Our Subscription Drive," *Black Hills Chronicle* (Custer, SD), October 1, 1932.

38. "Drive for New Readers Officially Opens Today," *Custer County Chronicle* (Custer, SD), October 6, 1932; "Voting Begins Now," *Custer County Chronicle* (Custer, SD), October 13, 1932; "Voting Begins Now," *Black Hills Chronicle* (Custer, SD), October 15, 1932; "Vote Standings," *Custer County Chronicle* (Custer, SD), October 20, 1932; "Vote Standings," *Black Hills Chronicle* (Custer, SD), October 22, 1932; "First Period Vote Offer Ends Next Saturday Night," "Vote Standings," and advertisement, "ATTENTION . . . . Candidates and Readers!," *Custer County Chronicle* (Custer, SD), October 27, 1932; "Daily Honor Roll Period In 'Drive' Starts Saturday" and "Vote Standings," *Custer County Chronicle* (Custer, SD), November 3, 1932; "Subscription Drive Ends One Week From Saturday" and "Vote Standings," *Custer County Chronicle* (Custer, SD), November 10, 1932; "Vote Standings," *Custer County Chronicle* (Custer, SD), November 17, 1932.

39. "Subscription Drive Ends Saturday Night at Nine" and advertisement, "Two Days Left!!," *Custer County Chronicle* (Custer, SD), November 17, 1932; "Subscription Drive Ends with Distribution of Awards" and "Judges Statement," *Custer County Chronicle* (Custer, SD), November 24, 1932.

40. Herbert L. Case to Rev. J. W. Mettam, March 19, 1931, Herbert L. Case to Julia Babcock, February 22, 1932, box 2, file 5, Herbert L. Case Papers; Mother to Carol, [January 22, 1932], box 6, file 5, Carol Case Goddard Collection.

41. Leland to Mother & Dad, June 10, 1932, box 5, file 2, Herbert Case to Carol, box 1, file 18, Carol Case Goddard Collection.

42. Herbert L. Case to Leland Davidson Case, November 10, 1932, Herbert L. Case to Delbert Clithero, December 6, 1932, box 2, file 6, Herbert L. Case Collection; Leland Davidson Case and Edith E. H. Grannis, eds., *New Hampshire to Minnesota: Memoirs of Samuel Higbee Grannis (1839-1933)* (Tucson, AZ: Self-published, 1962), p. 152 (hereinafter Case and Grannis, eds., *SHG Memoirs*).

43. "Prominent South Haven Woman Dies," *News-Palladium* (Benton Harbor, MI), January 7, 1933; "Custer City News," *Custer County Chronicle* (Custer, SD), February 9, 1933; Case and Grannis, eds., *SHG Memoirs*, pp. 116–17.

44. "Custer City News," *Custer County Chronicle* (Custer, SD), February 9, 1933; "Social and Personal," *Custer County Chronicle* (Custer, SD), May 25, 1933; "Custer," *Rapid City Daily Journal* (Rapid City, SD), May 31, 1933; "Social and Personal," *Custer County Chronicle* (Custer, SD), June 1, 1933.

45. "Street Float," *Custer County Chronicle* (Custer, SD), March 23, 1933.

46. Herbert S. Schell, *History of South Dakota* (Lincoln: University of Nebraska Press, 1961), pp. 146–48, 374 (hereinafter Schell, *History of South Dakota*); Gary Hoover, "A Real Goldmine: The Homestake Story," *American Business History*, August 1, 2021, http://www.americanbusinesshistory.org/a-real-goldmine-the-homestake-story/.

47. "Much Gold Being Mined in Custer County Streams," *Deadwood Pioneer-Times* (Deadwood, SD), May 13, 1931; "Great Strides Are Being Made in Mining in Black Hills Area," *Custer Weekly Chronicle* (Custer, SD), May 14, 1931; "$2,000 in Gold Daily Taken from Hills by Placers," *Hot Springs Weekly Star* (Hot Springs, SD), August 4, 1931; "Black Hills Reports Modern Gold Booms," *Daily Argus-Leader* (Sioux Falls, SD), September 21, 1931.

48. "Lode vs. Place[r] Mining," Wells Historical Society and Museum, accessed April 9, 2022, https://wellshistoricalsociety.ca/sketch/lode-vs-place-mining/; "Two More Giant Placers Pocket the Town," *Custer County Chronicle* (Custer, SD), July 14, 1932. For detailed descriptions and discussions of the various placer-and-lode-mining methods, *see* Schell, *History of South Dakota*, pp. 144–148; *Encyclopedia Britannica Online*, s.v. "Mining," accessed May 25, 2020, https://www.britannica.com/technology/mining; U.S. Environmental Protection Agency, Office of Wastewater Management, "Hardrock Mining Overview," accessed May 22, 2020, https://www3.epa.gov/npdes/pubs/overview.htm.

49. United States Department of Agriculture, *Anatomy of a Mine from Prospect to Production* (Ogden, UT: United States Department of Agriculture, Forest Service, 1995), pp. 7–10, 15–16, accessed April 9, 2022, https://www.fs.usda.gov/rm/pubs_int/int_gtr035.pdf. (page citations are to PDF version); Notice of Claim by FHC, June 28, 1934, Exemption Claim by Francis H. Case, July 1, 1936, box 1, file 11, Carol Case Goddard Collection.

50. "$50,000 Placer Mining Plant To be in Operation in Spring," *Black Hills News* (Custer, SD), October 3, 1931; "Dr. Roos Reports Growing Work in Mining Prospects," *Custer Weekly Chronicle* (Custer, SD), November 26, 1931; "Placer Mining Revival Inspires Brilliant Number B.H. Engineer," *Black Hills Weekly Chronicle* (Custer, SD), January 9, 1932; "1932 Promises to be Banner Year for Mining Growth in the Hills," *Custer County Chronicle* (Custer, SD), January 14, 1932; "Two More Large Placers Now Underway," *Custer County Chronicle* (Custer, SD), June 30, 1932; "Two More Giant Placers Pocket the Town," *Custer County Chronicle* (Custer, SD), July 14, 1932; "Eureka Moves Two Machines on to Placers," *Black Hills Chronicle* (Custer, SD), October 15, 1932; "Minneapolis Men Prospect Placers," *Black Hills Chronicle* (Custer, SD), January 28, 1933; "Gold Mining Is Way Out Denver Mining Man Says," *Custer County Chronicle* (Custer, SD), February 2, 1933; Placer Location Notice: Dusty Placer claim, April 22, 1933, Lode Location Notice: Carol's Castle Lode claim, April 22, 1933, box 5, file 10, Carol Case Goddard Collection.

51. "Social and Personal," *Custer County Chronicle* (Custer, SD), July 27, 1933; Hot Springs High School, *The Bison* (Hot Springs, SD: 1939); Lode Location Notice: Dusty Lode claim, August 3, 1933, Lode Location Notice: Eleventh Hour Lode claim, August 10, 1933, box 5, file 10, Carol Case Goddard Collection; "Social and Personal," *Custer County Chronicle* (Custer, SD), August 17, 1933; Case and Grannis, eds., *SHG Memoirs*, p. 152.

52. "File Papers," *Rapid City Daily Journal* (Rapid City, SD), May 6, 1933; Exemption Claim: Acacia Mining Company, July 1, 1936, box 1, file 14, Lode Location Notice: Early Day Lode claim, May 16, 1933, Lode Location Notice: Contact Lode claim, May 26, 1933, Lode Location Notices: Democrat Lode claim nos. 1-6, June 9, 1933, box 4, file 9, Carol Case Goddard Collection; "Custer City News," *Custer County Chronicle* (Custer, SD), September 28, 1933.

53. Wikitree, s.v. "James Francis Michaud (1905-1986)," accessed April 15, 2022, http://www.wikitree.com/wiki/Michaud-2249; Time sheet for Ira Michaud, June and July, 1933, Francis H. Case to P. D. Troughton, July 13, 1933, Francis H. Case to Frank Cottrell, August 17, 1933, box 4, file 9, Carol Case Goddard Collection.

54. Northwestern University, *The Syllabus 1922* (Evanston, IL: 1921) p. 224; Francis Case to C. E. Conn, April 2, 1934, Francis Case to Oza Amos, April 2, 1934, Francis to Morris, April 2, 1934, Francis to Morris, April 2, 1934 (second letter), file 1, box 11, Carol Case Goddard Collection.

55. "Custer City News," *Custer County Chronicle* (Custer, SD), December 28, 1933; "Weylers Purchase Paper; Move to Belle Fourche," *Custer County Chronicle* (Custer, SD), August 1, 1935; Morris to Francis, April 19, 1934, Francis to Morris, June 9, 1934, C. E. Conn to Francis H. Case, June 24, 1934, box 1, file 11, Carol Case Goddard Collection.

56. Notice of Claim by FHC, June 28, 1934, Francis Case to Palmer Hubbard and Francis Michaud, June 28, 1934, box 1, file 11, Receipt, Register of Deeds for Custer County to Francis Case, July 3, 1934, box 4, file 9, Morrie to Francis, July 7, 1934, Francis to Morrie, July 9, 1934, box 1, file 11, Carol Case Goddard Collection.

57. Francis to Morrie, July 9, 1934; "Custer City News," *Custer County Chronicle* (Custer, SD), July 19, 1934; Lode Location Notice: Dusty Hour Lode claim, July 12, 1934, Placer Location Notice: Sawdust Placer claim, box 5, file 10, Carol Case Goddard Collection.

58. "News of Custer City," *Custer County Chronicle* (Custer, SD), July 26, 1934; "Custer City News," *Custer County Chronicle* (Custer, SD), August 30, 1934.

59. Exemption Claim by Francis H. Case, July 1, 1936, box 1, file 11, Exemption Claim by Acacia Mining Company, Francis H. Case, President, July 1, 1936, box 1, file 14, Carol Case Goddard Collection.

60. "News of Custer City," *Custer County Chronicle* (Custer, SD), July 18, 1935; Lode Location Notice: Sawdust No. 1 Lode claim, July 14, 1935, Lode

Location Notice: Sawdust Lode II, July 31, 1935, Lode Location Notice: Sawdust Lode II (amendment), August 17, 1935, Lode Location Notice: Skipper Lode claim, September 14, 1935, Placer Location Notice: Saturday Nite Placer claim, September 14, 1935, box 5, file 10, Carol Case Goddard Collection.

61. Francis Case to C. E. Conn, April 2, 1934; Richard R. Chenoweth, "Francis Case: A Political Biography," in *South Dakota Historical Collections* (Pierre, SD: State Publishing Company, 1978), p. 303; Lode Claim Location Certificate: Zigzag IV Lode claim, June 21, 1945, Lode Location Notice: Bed Rock Mica Lode claim, July 1, 1940, box 5, file 10, Carol Case Goddard Collection.

62. "CCC Brief History," Civilian Conservation Corps Legacy, accessed March 9, 2022, http://www.ccclegacy.org/CCC_Brief_History.html; Sundstrom, *Pioneers and Custer State Park*, pp. 152–53.

63. "CCC Camps in South Dakota," CCC Museum of South Dakota, accessed April 19, 2022, http://www.southdakotaccc.org/camps.php; Sundstrom, *Pioneers and Custer State Park*, p. 153; "Narrows," CCC Museum of South Dakota, accessed April 19, 2022, http://www. southdakotaccc.org/camp.php?camp-name=SP-3-Narrows.

64. Fred Heidepriem, W. A. Nevin, Francis H. Case, and Scovel Johnson to C. W. Robertson, box 1, file 12, Carol Case Goddard Collection; "Two New Lakes Assured in Custer State Park," *Custer County Chronicle* (Custer, SD), June 15, 1933.

65. "Two New Lakes Assured in Custer State Park," *Custer County Chronicle*; "Doran," CCC Museum of South Dakota, accessed April 19, 2022, http://www.southdakotaccc.org/camp.php?camp-name=SP-2-Doran; "New Park Lake East of Custer Starts to Fill," *Custer County Chronicle* (Custer, SD), May 3, 1934; Francis H. Case to Tracy Dawson & Locke, June 13, 1935, transfer files, box 1, file: Miscellaneous 1934–1938 pt. 2, Francis H. Case Collection.

66. "Float of the Street," *Custer County Chronicle* (Custer, SD), June 14, 1934; "Building of Dam for Large Lake in State Park Nears Completion," *Daily Argus-Leader* (Sioux Falls, SD), February 22, 1934.

67. "Ask Designs for Sylvan Lake Hotel," *Rapid City Daily Journal* (Rapid City, SD), October 19, 1935; "New Lakes to Get New Names," *Custer County Chronicle* (Custer, SD), October 24, 1935; "Nine New Lakes Constructed in Hills Recently," *Rapid City Daily Journal* (Rapid City, SD), November 12, 1934; "Filling of New Lakes Will Mean Skating Ponds for Winter Sports," *Custer County Chronicle* (Custer, SD), November 15, 1934; "Float of the Street," *Custer County Chronicle* (Custer, SD), July 11, 1935; "Custer is Thankful for the Building This Year," *Custer County Chronicle* (Custer, SD), November 21, 1935; Francis Case to Senator Peter Norbeck, June 13, 1935, transfer files, box 1, file: Miscellaneous 1934–1938 pt. 2, Francis H. Case Collection.

Notes

68. "Two New Lakes Assured in Custer State Park," *Custer County Chronicle*; Cleophas C. O'Harra and Joseph P. Connolly, *The Geology, Mineralogy, and Scenic Features of Custer State Park, South Dakota* (Rapid City: South Dakota School of Mines, 1926), plate 60, "Map of Custer State Park and Vicinity"; "Pine Creek," CCC Museum of South Dakota, accessed April 18, 2022, http://www.southdakotaccc.org/camp.php?camp-name=SP-1-Pine-Creek; "Plans Sylvan Lake Hotel Under Way," *Lead Daily Call*, (Lead, SD), October 19, 1935.

69. "Lodge," CCC Museum of South Dakota, accessed April 19, 2022, http://www.southdakotaccc.org/camp.php?camp-name=SP-4-Lodge; Sundstrom, *Pioneers and Custer State Park*, pp. 156–59; "Filling of New Lakes Will Mean Skating Ponds for Winter Sports," *Custer County Chronicle*; "CCC's Transform Scarred Mud and Underbrush into Spot of Beauty," *Rapid City Daily Journal* (Rapid City, SD), April 8, 1935.

70. "CCC's Transform Scarred Mud and Underbrush into Spot of Beauty," *Rapid City Daily Journal*; "Ask Designs for Sylvan Lake Hotel," *Rapid City Daily Journal*; "Plans Sylvan Lake Hotel Under Way," *Lead Daily Call*; "New Lakes to Get New Names," *Custer County Chronicle*.

71. Sundstrom, *Pioneers and Custer State Park*, pp. 159–160; "Narrows," CCC Museum of South Dakota; "Custer Camp's Name Changed," *Rapid City Daily Journal* (Rapid City, SD), April 8, 1935; Francis H. Case to Captain R. R. Glenn, June 11, 1935, transfer files, box 1, file: Miscellaneous 1934–1938 pt. 2, Francis H. Case Collection.

72. Sundstrom, *Pioneers and Custer State Park*, pp. 160–61.

73. "Doran," CCC Museum of South Dakota, accessed April 19, 2022, http://www.southdakotaccc.org/camp/php?camp-name=SP-2-Doran; "Pine Creek," CCC Museum of South Dakota, accessed April 18, 2022, http://www.southdakotaccc.org/camp/php?camp-name=SP-1-Pine-Creek; "Lodge," CCC Museum of South Dakota; "Narrows," CCC Museum of South Dakota; Lisa Thompson, "Civilian Conservation Corps (CCC) (1933)," The Living New Deal, accessed April 23, 2022, http://www.livingnewdeal.org/glossary/civilian-conservation-corps-CCC-1933/; Sundstrom, *Pioneers and Custer State Park*, pp. 161-62.

74. "Around the West-River: Late News from a Great Growing Empire," *Rapid City Daily Journal* (Rapid City, SD), May 19, 1933; "Custer City News, *Custer County Chronicle* (Custer, SD), May 25, 1933; "Around the West River: Late News from a Great Growing Empire," *Rapid City Daily Journal* (Rapid City, SD), May 27, 1933; *Fall River County Pioneer Histories* (Fall River, SD: Fall River County Historical Society, 1976), p. 284.

75. "Custer County Chronicle," *Custer County Chronicle* (Custer, SD), August 31, 1933; *Custer County Chronicle* (Custer, SD), August 1, 1935.

76. Advertisement, "We'll Trade with You . . . . . . ," *Custer County Chronicle* (Custer, SD), September 21, 1933.

77. "News of Custer City," *Custer County Chronicle* (Custer, SD), October 5, 1933; Advertisement, "Potatoes Are Cheaper," *Custer County Chronicle* (Custer, SD), October 19, 1933.
78. "Answers to Frequently Asked Questions About Native Peoples," Native American Rights Fund, accessed April 26, 2022, http://www.narf.org/frequently-asked-questions/; Linda Darus Clark, "Sioux Treaty of 1868," National Archives, accessed April 28, 2022, http://www.archives.gov/education/lessons/sioux-treaty; "The Founding of Standing Rock Sioux Tribe," Standing Rock Sioux Tribe, accessed April 26, 2022, http://www.standingrock.org/about/; Schell, *History of South Dakota*, pp. 135–36, 138–39; *Encyclopedia of the Great Plains*, s.v. "United States v. Sioux Nation of Indians," by Mark R. Scherer, accessed April 26, 2022, http://www.plainshumanities.unl.edu/encyclopedia/doc/egp.law.050. For more than 100 years, the Sioux have sought to reclaim the Black Hills. In 1920, they brought a lawsuit in the Court of Claims, alleging "that the government had taken the Black Hills without just compensation in violation of the Fifth Amendment." That suit was ultimately dismissed in 1942. Beginning in 1946, the Sioux reasserted their arguments before the congressionally-created Indian Claims Commission. That body ruled in favor of the Sioux tribes and held they were entitled to $17.5 million, without interest. On appeal, the Court of Claims again dismissed the tribes' claim, holding that it was barred by the 1942 decision. In 1978, Congress authorized a new review of the claim, despite the earlier court rulings that had rejected it. This time, the Court of Claims held "that the government had indeed acted in bad faith in taking the Black Hills and that the Sioux were entitled to $17.1 million in damages, plus interest from 1877." The United States Supreme Court affirmed this decision in 1980. But the Sioux tribes have refused to accept the money judgment (which has now grown to "well beyond" a billion dollars with accrued interest). Instead, they have continued efforts to reclaim portions of the Black Hills. See *Encyclopedia of the Great Plains*, s.v. "United States v. Sioux Nation of Indians;" "United States v. Sioux Nation of Indians," *Oyez.org*, accessed April 26, 2022, http://www.oyez.org/cases/1979/79-639; "Why the Sioux Are Refusing $1.3 Billion," PBS NewsHour, August 24, 2011, http://www.pbs.org/newshour/arts/north_america-july-dec11-blackhills_08-23.
79. "Indian Country," United States Attorney's Office, District of South Dakota, accessed March 11, 2022, http://www.justice.gov/usao-sd/Indian-country; "The Founding of Standing Rock Sioux Tribe," Standing Rock Sioux Tribe; "Lower Brule Sioux Tribe Traditional Territory," Kul Wicasa Oyate, accessed April 26, 2022, http://www.lowerbrulesiouxtribe.com/lower-brule-territory; Schell, *History of South Dakota*, p. 222, 246 (map), 247, 316 (map), 329; *Encyclopedia Britannica Online*, s.v. "Wounded Knee Massacre," accessed March 30, 2023, http://www.britannica.com/event/Wounded-Knee-Massacre.
80. Schell, *History of South Dakota*, p. 253; Federal Writers' Project, *WPA Guide*, pp. 22–3, 28. In February 1887, the U. S. Congress passed the Dawes Allotment or Severalty Act (Allotment Act). It provided that American Indian reservation land would be distributed among individual Native Americans

"with the aim of creating responsible farmers in the white man's image." The act authorized the president "to grant each household head 160 acres with smaller tracts to single men, women and children." (The Sioux Agreement of 1889 increased those authorized allotments to "320 acres to the head of the family and 160 acres for all other members of the household.") By the Allotment Act's terms, the government held these "allotments" in trust for 25 years, after which it would remove the trust status and issue the American Indian owner full title to the land. The act also provided that any lands that remained after allotments were made to Native Americans—referred to as "unallotted" or "surplus" lands—would become available for public sale to white settlers. That provision applied to all five western South Dakota reservations created in 1889, and it collectively reduced their total land area by more than half between 1904 and 1913. The Allotment Act failed to "mak[e] the Indians self-supporting," and it did not free them "from the guardianship of the Indian Bureau." Moreover, the allotment policy "drastically reduced the amount of lands owned by tribes." In response to these shortcomings, Congress passed the Indian Reorganization Act of 1934. Among other things, that act "specifically prohibited further allotting of lands and restored remaining surplus lands to tribal ownership at the discretion of the Secretary of the Interior." See Schell, *History of South Dakota*, pp. 246 (map), 316 (map), 328, 329, 333; *Encyclopedia Britannica Online*, s.v. "Dawes General Allotment Act," accessed December 21, 2022, http://www.britannica.com/topic/Dawes- General-Allotment-Act; "Native American Ownership and Governance of Natural Resources," United States Department of the Interior, Natural Resources Revenue Data, accessed December 19, 2022, https:revenuedata.doi.gov/how-revenue-works/native-american-ownership-governance/.

81. Federal Writers' Project, *WPA Guide*, pp. 23, 202, 232–33, 270, 332, 340–41; "Cheyenne River Sioux Reservation," Aktá Lakota Museum and Cultural Center, accessed April 27, 2022, https://web.archive.org/web/20211023200805/http://aktalakota.stjo.org/site/News2?page=NewsArticle&id=8653; "Indian Country," United States Attorney's Office, District of South Dakota. Both the Rosebud and Pine Ridge reservations lost a considerable amount of land due to the public-sale-of-surplus-lands feature of the Allotment Act (see note 80 above). Under the Sioux Agreement of 1889, the Rosebud encompassed Gregory, Tripp, Mellette, and Todd counties. But by opening the lands "to white settlement" in all but the latter county between 1904 and 1911, the "actual closed boundaries" had been reduced to Todd County only. Despite that official boundary designation, Francis sometimes referred to any of these four counties as being in "Rosebud country" or simply in "the Rosebud." With respect to Pine Ridge, Bennett County had been included in its boundaries set in 1889. But Bennett was excluded from the Pine Ridge Reservation in 1911, when that county was declared to be "surplus lands" and opened to

public settlement. See Schell, *History of South Dakota*, pp. 246 (map), 253–55, 316 (map); Federal Writers' Project, *WPA Guide*, p. 322.
82. "Indian Country," United States Attorney's Office, District of South Dakota; Federal Writers' Project, *WPA Guide*, pp. 23, 28; Schell, *History of South Dakota*, p. 92.
83. "Custer City News," *Custer County Chronicle* (Custer, SD), August 2, 1934; "Sioux Indians Make Chronicle Editor Chief," *Custer County Chronicle* (Custer, SD), August 9, 1934.
84. "South Dakota: Flandreau Reservation," Partnership with Native Americans, accessed April 26, 2022, http://www.nativepartnership.org/site/PageServer?pagename=PWNA_Native_Reservations_Flandreau; "History," Flandreau Santee Sioux Tribe, accessed April 26, 2022, http://www.fsst-nsn.gov/history; Federal Writers' Project, *WPA Guide*, pp. 23, 28.
85. "Births," *Custer County Chronicle* (Custer, SD), February 14, 1935; *Case Chronicles*, February, 1935, box 1, file 7, Carol Case Goddard Collection; "Float of the Street," *Custer County Chronicle* (Custer, SD), April 4, 1935.
86. C L Breckenridge to Mrs. Francis H Case, telegram, February 12, 1935, Bess to Myrle, [February 12, 1935], Dorothy to Myrle, December [*sic*; February] 11, 1935, Dan B. to Francis, March 21, 1935, box 2, file 22, Carol Case Goddard Collection; "The Christian Advocate (New York), 1866-1938 [Online Resource]," Library of Congress, accessed December 14, 2022, http://www.loc.gov/item/2007233809/; "Society & Club," *Custer County Chronicle* (Custer, SD), May 30, 1935; "The Colome Times (Colome, Tripp County, S.D.) 1909-19??," Library of Congress, accessed May 5, 2022, http://www.loc.gov/item/sn97065702/; "Float of the Street," *Custer County Chronicle* (Custer, SD), April 4, 1935; Leland to Francis, March 3, 1935, Art Brown to Francis, May 1, 1935, transfer files, box 1, file: Miscellaneous 1934-1938 pt. 2, Francis H. Case Collection.
87. Alfred J. Booth to Lieutenant Francis Higbee Case, memorandum, February 18, 1935, transfer files, box 1, file: Miscellaneous 1934-1938 pt. 1, R. McC. Pate to All Reserve Officers, memorandum, October 1, 1946, cabinet 31, new drawer 121/old drawer 126, box 1, file: Marine Corps (Reserve), Francis H. Case Collection.
88. "Custer," *Rapid City Daily Journal* (Rapid City, SD), December 22, 1933; "Custer," *Rapid City Daily Journal* (Rapid City, SD), March 16, 1934; "Society & Club," *Custer County Chronicle* (Custer, SD), April 18, 1935; "Society & Club," *Custer County Chronicle* (Custer, SD), May 30, 1935.
89. "News of Custer City," *Custer County Chronicle* (Custer, SD), July 18, 1935; Lode Location Notice: Sawdust No. 1 Lode Claim, July 14, 1935, box 5, file 10, Carol Case Goddard Collection; "News of Custer City," *Custer County Chronicle* (Custer, SD), August 22, 1935.
90. "Custer Enjoys Building Boom for Businesses," *Custer County Chronicle* (Custer, SD), May 30, 1935; "Chronicle's New Home," *Custer County*

Chronicle (Custer, SD), August 15, 1935; "Custer is Thankful for the Building This Year," *Custer County Chronicle* (Custer, SD), November 21, 1935.

91. "Weylers Purchase Paper; Move to Belle Fourche," *Custer County Chronicle* (Custer, SD), August 1, 1935.
92. "S.D. Hopes for Cold Wave End—Hill City Hit by Fire," *Rapid City Daily Journal* (Rapid City, SD), January 23, 1936; "Hare to Print News in Custer," *Rapid City Daily Journal* (Rapid City, SD), January 24, 1936; "Carrying On," *Rapid City Daily Journal* (Rapid City, SD), January 25, 1935; "News of Custer City," *Custer County Chronicle* (Custer, SD), January 30, 1936; "Hare Sells Hill City News to Case, Carrier," *Rapid City Daily Journal* (Rapid City, SD), April 16, 1936; Advertisement, "Select Your Candidates; BE SURE TO VOTE," *Rapid City Daily Journal* (Rapid City, SD), May 2, 1936; Francis Case to Lyle L. Mariner, November 27, 1936, box 2, file 20, Francis Case to Frank Carrier, November 28, 1936, box 1, file 10, Carol Case Goddard Collection; "Philip Man Buys Hill City News," *Rapid City Daily Journal* (Rapid City, SD), December 4, 1936.
93. Francis to Dad, January 19, 1936, Leland to Francis, March 8, 1936, transfer files, box 2, file: Personal 1934-1938, Francis H. Case Collection.
94. "Society and Club Notes," *Custer County Chronicle* (Custer, SD), February 20, 1936; "Society and Club," *Custer County Chronicle* (Custer, SD), March 12, 1936; "Society and Club Notes," *Custer County Chronicle* (Custer, SD), May 14, 1936; "Society and Club Notes," *Custer County Chronicle* (Custer, SD), October 1, 1936; "Society and Club Notes," *Custer County Chronicle* (Custer, SD), October 22, 1936. In 1881, Marion Talbot, who later became the College of Women's Dean at the University of Chicago, and Ellen Swallow Richards, the first woman to earn a college chemistry degree, met in Boston with fifteen other alumnae from eight colleges and founded an organization that would later become known as the American Association of University Women. That association sought "the betterment of women's lives and their personal growth." It also believed that "a greater number of college-educated women would be of benefit to society in general." See "Our History," American Association of University Women, accessed May 7, 2022, http://www.aauw.org/about/history/; *Encyclopedia Britannica Online*, s.v. "American Association of University Women," accessed May 7, 2022, http://www.britannica.com/topic/American-Association-of-University-Women.
95. "Roosevelt Acclaimed by Huge Crowds in His Two Day Sojourn Here," *Gate City Guide* (Rapid City, SD), September 3, 1936; "F. R. Sends Protest to Spain Following Mt. Rushmore Talk," *Rapid City Daily Journal* (Rapid City, SD), August 31, 1936; Rex Alan Smith, *The Carving of Mount Rushmore* (New York: Abbeville Press, 1985) p. 311 (hereinafter Smith, *Carving Mount Rushmore*).

96. "Roosevelt Acclaimed by Huge Crowds in His Two Day Sojourn Here," *Gate City Guide*, "F. R. Sends Protest to Spain Following Mt. Rushmore Talk," *Rapid City Daily Journal*.
97. "F. R. Sends Protest to Spain Following Mt. Rushmore Talk," *Rapid City Journal*; Smith, *Carving Mount Rushmore*, pp. 312, 313; "President Roosevelt's Speech at Mt. Rushmore Dedication" and "Roosevelt Acclaimed by Huge Crowds in His Two Day Sojourn Here," *Gate City Guide* (Rapid City, SD), September 3, 1936.
98. "Wayside Notes," *Custer County Chronicle* (Custer, SD), June 18, 1936.
99. "Wayside Notes," *Custer County Chronicle* (Custer, SD), July 2, 1936; "Wayside Notes," *Custer County Chronicle* (Custer, SD), July 23, 1936; "Wayside Notes," *Custer County Chronicle* (Custer, SD), August 20, 1936; "Wayside Notes, *Custer County Chronicle* (Custer, SD), September 10, 1936; "Wayside Notes," *Custer County Chronicle* (Custer, SD), October 29, 1936.

CHAPTER 12. IF AT FIRST YOU AREN'T ELECTED, TRY, TRY AGAIN

The quotation at the beginning of this chapter is taken from a radio broadcast Francis made at Bismarck, North Dakota, on October 26, 1936.

1. "Encourage Williamson," *Hot Springs Star* (Hot Springs, SD), October 26, 1926; "Elections," in *2005 South Dakota Legislative Manual*, p. 12, accessed October 24, 2021, http://www.sdsos.gov/elections-voting/assets/ElectionsReturnsPre1972.pdf (hereinafter *Election Statistics*; page citations are to PDF version); Art to Francis, [November 25, 1926], cabinet 45, new drawer 179/old drawer 184, box 2, file: Misc. Letters 1927, Francis H. Case Collection.
2. Francis to Chet, October 18, 1927, cabinet 45, new drawer 179/old drawer 184, box 2, file: Misc. Letters 1927, Francis H. Case Collection; "U. S. Marshall to Enter Race for Congress," *Rapid City Daily Journal* (Rapid City, SD), October 25, 1927; "Chet Leedom's Sombrero," *Hot Springs Star* (Hot Springs, SD), November 1, 1927.
3. "Mr. Williamson, Mr. Leedom," *Hot Springs Star* (Hot Springs, SD), November 15, 1927; "Debunking That Ghost," *Hot Springs Star* (Hot Springs, SD), November 29, 1927.
4. Unknown writer to Chet, November 30, 1927, Francis to Chet, December 7, 1927, cabinet 45, new drawer 179/old drawer 184, box 2, file: Misc. Letters 1927, Francis H. Case Collection; "Hats Uneasy as Time for Voting Nears," *Hot Springs Star* (Hot Springs, SD), February 7, 1928.
5. "Election This Year Under Revised Primary Law," *Rapid City Daily Journal* (Rapid City, SD), January 14, 1928.
6. "Declares Concerted Movement on to Back Jensen," *Rapid City Daily Journal* (Rapid City, SD), February 8, 1928; "Delegates to Favor Jensen Are Elected,"

Hot Springs Star (Hot Springs, SD), February 14, 1928; "Republicans Elect Three for L. Jensen," *Hot Springs Star* (Hot Springs, SD), February 21, 1928.
7. "Entitled to a Referendum," *Hot Springs Star* (Hot Springs, SD), February 28, 1928.
8. "Echoes from Politicians with Shrinking and Expanded Halos," *Hot Springs Star* (Hot Springs, SD), March 13, 1928; "Endorsement of Williamson is Refused; Case Announces," *Hot Springs Times-Herald* (Hot Springs, SD), March 30, 1928.
9. Francis Case to B. J. Hubbard, March 12, 1928, cabinet 45, new drawer 179/ old drawer 184, box 2, file: Misc. Letters 1927, Francis H. Case Collection; Francis Case to Wm. J. Bordeaux, March 12, 1928, box 1, file 17, Carol Case Goddard Collection; "Case Resigns As Post Commander," *Rapid City Daily Journal* (Rapid City, SD), March 27, 1928; "State Senate and House Candidates Nominated," *Rapid City Daily Journal* (Rapid City, SD), March 28, 1928; "Endorsement of Williamson is Refused; Case Announces," *Hot Springs Times-Herald*.
10. "Case Announces He Is Candidate," *Daily Argus-Leader* (Sioux Falls, SD), March 29, 1928; "Out in the Open," *Daily Argus-Leader* (Sioux Falls, SD), March 30, 1928.
11. "Congressional Nomination Fights Which Promise to Hold Stage in Campaign are Forging to Front," *Rapid City Daily Journal* (Rapid City, SD), April 6, 1928; "If This Be Democratic," *Hot Springs Star* (Hot Springs, SD), April 17, 1928; "As Others See the Campaign," *Hot Springs Star* (Hot Springs, SD), April 24, 1928.
12. "Case Makes First Campaign Speech," *Rapid City Daily Journal* (Rapid City, SD), April 25, 1928; "Case Speaks Again on Road Allotment Fund," *Rapid City Daily Journal* (Rapid City, SD), April 28, 1928.
13. "Case Optimistic After North Trip," *Rapid City Daily Journal* (Rapid City, SD), May 7, 1928; "Case Warns of Power Trust," *Rapid City Daily Journal* (Rapid City, SD), May 11, 1928; Case-For-Congress Club to unnamed recipient, May 11, 1928, box 1, file 6, Carol Case Goddard Collection; Advertisement, "Vote For FRANCIS H. CASE for Congress" and "Our County's Opportunity," *Hot Springs Star* (Hot Springs, SD) May 15, 1928.
14. Francis Case to Those Fine Friends Who Signed My Petition of Nomination, undated, box 1, file 6, Carol Case Goddard Collection; "Williamson and Case Here for Debate Tonight," *Rapid City Daily Journal* (Rapid City, SD), May 17, 1928.
15. "Williamson and Case Hold Verbal Battle Here," *Rapid City Daily Journal* (Rapid City, SD), May 18, 1928; "Williamson and Case Have Crowd," *Evening Huronite* (Huron, SD), May 18, 1928; "Andy, Aluminum, Williamson," *Hot Springs Star* (Hot Springs, SD), January 31, 1928.

16. "Williamson and Case Hold Verbal Battle Here," *Rapid City Daily Journal*; "Williamson and Case Engage in a Debate," *Daily Deadwood Pioneer-Times* (Deadwood, SD), May 19, 1928.
17. "Northern Hills Give Williamson Early Lead in Race," *Hot Springs Star* (Hot Springs, SD), May 22, 1928; "Williamson and Christopherson Win Primaries," *Rapid City Daily Journal* (Rapid City, SD), May 23, 1928; "I Mean, 'Thank You'," *Hot Springs Star* (Hot Springs, SD), May 29, 1928; Gladys Pyle, comp., *Official Election Returns for South Dakota: Primary Election May 22, 1928*, (Pierre, SD: Hipple, 1928), p. 7, http://www.sdsos.gov/elections-voting/assets/historicalelectiondata/1928P.pdf (page citations are to PDF version).
18. "I Mean, 'Thank You'," *Hot Springs Star*.
19. "Francis Case Won't Oppose Williamson," *Daily Argus-Leader* (Sioux Falls, SD), February 1, 1930; *Election Statistics*, p. 12; "Let's Get a New Primary Law," *Hot Springs Star* (Hot Springs, SD), November 6, 1928.
20. "Explains New Primary Law," *Lead Daily Call* (Lead, SD), February 26, 1929; "Proposalman Eliminated; Candidates Are Chosen by Petition," *Hot Springs Star* (Hot Springs, SD), February 18, 1930.
21. "Case Says Oil Not Politics for Him This Year," *Hot Springs Star* (Hot Springs, SD), February 4, 1930.
22. "Only Organized Counties Will Be Represented," *Daily Argus-Leader* (Sioux Falls, SD), May 14, 1930; Little Thunder v. State of South Dakota, 518 F.2d 1253 (8th Cir. 1975), https://law.resource.org/pub/us/case/reporter/F2/518/518.F2d.1253.74-1967.html; "Primary Question Taken to Court," *Todd County Tribune* (Mission, SD), May 1, 1930; "Unorganized County Question Up Again," *Daily Deadwood Pioneer-Times* (Deadwood, SD), January 23, 1923; Workers of the Writers' Program of the Work Projects Administration in the State of South Dakota, *South Dakota Place-Names: Part 1 State, County, and Town Names* (Vermillion: University of South Dakota, 1940), pp. 3, 5, 16, 17, 19.
23. "Residents In Unorganized Counties Cannot Vote in Primary May 6," *Daily Argus-Leader* (Sioux Falls, SD), April 25, 1930; "Protest is Made on Legal Ruling," *Daily Argus-Leader* (Sioux Falls, SD), April 26, 1930; "Battle on for Unorganized Counties," *Hot Springs Weekly Star* (Hot Springs, SD), April 29, 1930.
24. "Ballots for Washington, Shannon," *Hot Springs Weekly Star* (Hot Springs, SD), April 29, 1930; "Fight Their Behalf Wins in Test Case," *Hot Springs Weekly Star* (Hot Springs, SD), May 6, 1930; "Voting Seen in Two Unorganized Counties," *Daily Argus-Leader* (Sioux Falls, SD), May 6, 1930.
25. "Lesson On New Primary Law," *Evening Huronite* (Huron, SD) May 2, 1930; "South Dakota Goes to the Polls," *Hot Springs Weekly Star* (Hot Springs, SD), May 6, 1930; "Voting Seen in Two Unorganized Counties," *Daily Argus-Leader*; "Votes in Unorganized Counties Not to Count," *Evening*

Huronite (Huron, SD), May 10, 1930; "Gunderson Gains Another County," *Daily Argus-Leader* (Sioux Falls, SD), May 16, 1930.

26. "Only 28 of 192 Delegates to State G.O.P. Convention," *Daily Argus-Leader* (Sioux Falls, SD), May 14, 1930; "Republican Hosts Start Gathering for Convention," *Rapid City Daily Journal* (Rapid City, SD), May 17, 1930; "Unorganized Counties to Have a Voice," *Hot Springs Weekly Star* (Hot Springs, SD), February 10, 1931; "The Republican Platform," *Daily Argus-Leader* (Sioux Falls, SD), May 23, 1930; "Pyle Takes Lead on Sixth Ballot," *Daily Argus-Leader* (Sioux Falls, SD), May 20, 1930.

27. *Election Statistics*, p. 12; "Pyle Takes Lead on Sixth Ballot," *Daily Argus-Leader*; "Republicans Complete State Ticket," *Daily Argus-Leader* (Sioux Falls, SD), May 21, 1930.

28. "Sharpe Handles Dynamite as If It Were Confetti: Vote for Grigsby," *Hot Springs Weekly Star* (Hot Springs, SD), November 4, 1930.

29. "Official Vote by Counties," South Dakota Secretary of State, accessed June 8, 2022, http://www.sdsos.gov/elections-voting/assets/historicalelectiondata/1930G.pdf, p. 9 (page citations are to PDF version); *Election Statistics*, p. 13.

30. "Green Asks Solons for Public Economy and More Equitable Taxation," *Daily Argus-Leader* (Sioux Falls, SD), January 6, 1931; "List More Bills in Legislature," *Rapid City Daily Journal* (Rapid City, SD), January 23, 1931; "Unorganized Counties to Have a Voice," *Hot Springs Weekly Star*; "Governor Signs 22 New Laws For South Dakota," *Rapid City Daily Journal* (Rapid City, SD), February 25, 1931.

31. "State Splits at Missouri on Congress," *Hot Springs Weekly Star* (Hot Springs, SD), March 3, 1931; "River Line Bill Signed by Green," *Hot Springs Weekly Star* (Hot Springs, SD) March 10, 1931. For further discussion of the state's congressional reapportionment history, see Chapter 8, note 39.

32. "Norbeck Needs You---Now!," *Custer County Chronicle* (Custer, SD), April 28, 1932; "Norbeck Needs You---Now!," *Black Hills Weekly Chronicle* (Custer, SD), April 30, 1932; "Norbeck Meeting Attracts Crowd," *Rapid City Daily Journal* (Rapid City, SD), May 3, 1932; *Election Statistics*, p. 13; "Around the West-River," *Rapid City Daily Journal* (Rapid City, SD), October 15, 1932; "Crowd Hears Green Talk at Springs," *Rapid City Daily Journal* (Rapid City, SD), November 7, 1932.

33. Herbert S. Schell, *History of South Dakota* (Lincoln: University of Nebraska Press, 1961), p. 283; *Election Statistics*, p. 13.

34. "Republicans Pick Five Delegates" and "Float of the Street," *Custer County Chronicle* (Custer, SD), January 18, 1934.

35. "Republicans Gather at Pierre in Numbers," *Custer County Chronicle* (Custer, SD); "Republican Auxiliary Plan Is Defeated," *Rapid City Daily Journal* (Rapid City, SD), February 12, 1934; "Republicans Convene at Pierre;

McDonald Issues Party Warning," *Daily Argus-Leader* (Sioux Falls, SD), February 12, 1934.
36. "Francis Case in Congress Race," *Rapid City Daily Journal* (Rapid City, SD), February 14, 1934; "Case Enters Race for Seat in House," *Custer County Chronicle* (Custer, SD), February 15, 1934. Francis's nine-point program he pledged to work for if sent to Congress is reproduced below:

> 1. Better markets for South Dakota producers—farmers, ranchers, miners and laborers in every industry.
> 2. National Recovery, regardless of partisan politics, and not forgetting the common school system.
> 3. A nation-wide constabulary equipped to stamp out organized crime.
> 4. Thrift in public finances.
> 5. Enough government regulation to insure "a square deal"—and no more—to all business, large or small, and to the consumer as well.
> 6. Application of Civil Service principles to the selection of staffs for Civil and Public Works administration.
> 7. The American system of a representative government—"of, by and for ALL the people" and against party profiteering in the name of government and against tyranny by any man, board or bureau.
> 8. PEACE—by staying out of foreign wars, maintenance of adequate defense and fair treatment for the nation's soldiers.
> 9. Development of the natural resources in South Dakota.

37. "Fifty Attend Young Republicans Meeting" and "News of Custer City," *Custer County Chronicle* (Custer, SD), March 29, 1934; "Francis Case Speaks in Gregory Section," *Custer County Chronicle* (Custer, SD), April 12, 1934; "Case of Custer Pleads for Republican Revival," *Rapid City Daily Journal* (Rapid City, SD), April 18, 1934; "Float of the Street," *Custer County Chronicle* (Custer, SD), April 19, 1934.
38. Leland to Francis, April 17, 1934, transfer files, box 1, file: Butler, Smedley 1934-1936, Francis H. Case Collection; "Major General Smedley Butler," Americans Who Tell the Truth, accessed June 9, 2020, https://americanswhotellthetruth.org/portraits/major-general-smedley-butler.
39. Leland to Francis, April 17, 1934, S.D. Butler to Francis H. Case, April 15, 1934, transfer files, box 1, file: Butler, Smedley 1934-1936, Francis H. Case Collection; "General Smedley Butler Wires Best Wishes to Case; Declares Exploiters' Hold Must Be Broken," *Custer County Chronicle* (Custer, SD), April 26, 1934.
40. "General Smedley Butler Wires Best Wishes to Case; Declares Exploiters' Hold Must Be Broken," *Custer County Chronicle*; Campaign brochure, "Case-for-Congress," carton C, Case Ranch Collection; Political advertisement, "Speech! Speech! Speech! Hear Francis H. Case Candidate for Congress," *Rapid City Daily Journal* (Rapid City, SD), April 26, 1934.

41. "Republicans to Meet Monday Night at Custer," *Custer County Chronicle* (Custer, SD), April 26, 1934; "Record Crowd Attends Republican Rally Here," *Custer County Chronicle* (Custer, SD), May 3, 1934.
42. "Primary Election Has Attention of State and County," *Rapid City Daily Journal* (Rapid City, SD), May 1, 1934; Myrtle Morrison, comp., *Official Election Returns for South Dakota: Primary Election May 1, 1934* (Pierre, SD: Hipple, 1934), pp. 4, 5, http://www.sdsos.gov/elections-voting/assets/historicalelectiondata/1934P.pdf (page citations are to PDF version).
43. "Date Is Set for Republican State Convention on May 29," *Rapid City Daily Journal* (Rapid City, SD), May 10, 1934; "Think About November," memorandum, May 12, 1934, transfer files, box 1, file: Congressional Committee/Congressional Campaign Com. 1934–1936, Francis H. Case Collection.
44. "Case Wins Congressional Nomination," *Rapid City Daily Journal* (Rapid City, SD), May 29, 1934; "G.O.P. Urges Fight for Liberty," *Daily Argus-Leader* (Sioux Falls, SD), May 29, 1934.
45. "Date Is Set for Republican State Convention on May 29," *Rapid City Daily Journal*; "G.O.P. Urges Fight for Liberty, *Daily Argus-Leader*.
46. "Case Gets Many Congratulations on Victory at Pierre" and "'The Home Folks Did It'," *Custer County Chronicle* (Custer, SD), May 31, 1934; "Case Expresses His Appreciation," *Rapid City Daily Journal* (Rapid City, SD), June 1, 1934.
47. "A Few From the Flower Garden," *Custer County Chronicle* (Custer, SD), June 21, 1934; "A Few From the Flower Garden," *Custer County Chronicle* (Custer, SD), June 28, 1934; "A Few From the Flower Garden," *Custer County Chronicle* (Custer, SD), July 5, 1934.
48. Francis H. Case to Chester C. Bolton, July 17, 1934, Francis H. Case to Henry P. Fletcher, July 18, 1934, Henry P. Fletcher to Francis H. Case, July 26, 1934, Francis H. Case to Leo E. Allen, September 10, 1934, Leo E. Allen to Francis H. Case, September 12, 1934, transfer files, box 1, file: Congressional Committee/Congressional Campaign Com. 1934–1936, Francis H. Case Collection; Chester C. Bolton to Francis H. Case, October 15, 1934, Chester C. Bolton to Francis H. Case, October 16, 1934, box 2, file 10, Francis Case to the Publisher Addressed, undated, box 1, file 6, Henry P. Fletcher to Francis H. Case, November 20, 1934, box 2, file 31, Carol Case Goddard Collection.
49. "G.O.P. Campaign Opens Thursday," *Daily Argus-Leader* (Sioux Falls, SD), August 7, 1934; "State G.O.P. Drive Opens in Kennebec," *Rapid City Daily Journal* (Rapid City, SD), August 10, 1934; Bill Kaye to Case, July 26, 1934, transfer files, box 1, file: Headquarters 1934–1936, Francis H. Case Collection; "Beresford Makes Elaborate Plans for Jubilee Celebration Next Week," *Daily Argus-Leader* (Sioux Falls, SD), August 10, 1934; "Allen Expands Relief Issues," *Daily Argus-Leader* (Sioux Falls, SD), August 22, 2022; "Ruden to Speak on G.O.P. Program," *Rapid City Daily Journal* (Rapid

City, SD), August 28, 1934; "Allen Pleads for State Economy At Republican Rally," *Rapid City Daily Journal* (Rapid City, SD), August 31, 1934; "Many Politicians to Talk at Annual Fair at Murdo," *Daily Argus-Leader* (Sioux Falls, SD), August 29, 1934.

50. "News of Custer City," *Custer County Chronicle* (Custer, SD), September 6, 1934; Francis H. Case, to Leo E. Allen, September 10, 1934, transfer files, box 1, file: Congressional Committee/Congressional Campaign Com. 1934–1936, Francis H. Case Collection; "Farmers Union Hold Convention at Sturgis," *Custer County Chronicle* (Custer, SD), September 13, 1934.
51. "Case Ready to Debate Werner," *Rapid City Daily Journal* (Rapid City, SD), October 4, 1934; Harlow & family to Francis, October 22, 1934, box 2, file 10, Carol Case Goddard Collection.
52. "Case Asks for More Power to Local Groups," *Custer County Chronicle* (Custer, SD), October 11, 1934; "Reveals Funds Paid to Gate City Guide," *Lead Daily Call* (Lead, SD), October 12, 1934; "Case Criticizes Special Favors," *Rapid City Daily Journal* (Rapid City, SD), October 13, 1934.
53. "Campaign Formula," *Rapid City Daily Journal* (Rapid City, SD), October 12, 1934; "Tammany Out Nov. 6, Case Says" and "'America Must Find the Way Between the Old Freedoms and the New Prohibitions'," *Custer County Chronicle* (Custer, SD), November 1, 1934.
54. "Allen Makes Big Hit with the Indians," *Lead Daily Call* (Lead, SD), November 1, 1934; Geo. H. Henry to Francis Case, October 29, 1934, box 2, file 10, Carol Case Goddard Collection; "W.C. Allen Tells Hills Where He Stands On Roads," *Rapid City Daily Journal* (Rapid City, SD), November 1, 1934; "G.O.P. Plans Final Rally," *Rapid City Daily Journal* (Rapid City, SD), October 27, 1934; "Allen and Case Speak at Belle," *Rapid City Daily Journal* (Rapid City, SD), October 30, 1934; "Speakers Cover State in Final Campaign Fight," *Daily Argus-Leader* (Sioux Falls, SD), November 1, 1934; "Allen Is Called 'State-Minded'," *Daily Argus-Leader* (Sioux Falls, SD), November 2, 1934; "Lawrence Co. G.O.P. to Hold Rally Tonight," *Lead Daily Call* (Lead, SD), November 5, 1934; "South Dakota Voters Braced for Election," *Deadwood Pioneer-Times* (Deadwood, SD), November 5, 1934.
55. "Demos Make Clean Sweep," *Rapid City Daily Journal* (Rapid City, SD), November 7, 1934; "Werner Takes Congress Race," *Custer County Chronicle* (Custer, SD), November 8, 1934; Myrtle Morrison, comp., *Official Election Returns for South Dakota: General Election November 6, 1934* (Pierre, SD: Hipple, 1934), pp. 2, 4, http://www.sdsos.gov/elections-voting/assets/historicalelectiondata/1934GeneralReturns.pdf (page citations are to PDF version); Richard R. Chenoweth, "Francis Case: A Political Biography," in *South Dakota Historical Collections* (Pierre, SD: State Publishing Company, 1978), p. 314.
56. "'We Lost the Score but Not the Game'," *Custer County Chronicle* (Custer, SD), November 8, 1934; Charles H. Whiting to Francis H. Case, November 12, 1934, box 2, file 31, Carol Case Goddard Collection.

57. Harold to Francis, undated, Art Brown to Francis, November 9, 1934, box 2, file 31, Carol Case Goddard Collection.
58. Francis H. Case to Dear Friend, November 19, 1934, box 2, file 31, Carol Case Goddard Collection; Leland to Francis, November 24, 1934, transfer files, box 1, file: Miscellaneous 1934–1938 pt.2, Francis H. Case Collection.
59. Francis to Leland, November 29, 1935, Francis to Dad, January 19, 1936, transfer files, box 2, file: Personal 1934-1938, Francis H. Case Collection.
60. "Paul Martin Announces Candidacy for Congress," *Custer County Chronicle* (Custer, SD), January 24, 1935; "Williamson Enters Congressional Race," *Custer County Chronicle* (Custer, SD), January 30, 1936; "Case to Run for Congress," *Rapid City Daily Journal* (Rapid City, SD), February 6, 1936; "Case Candidate for Republican Congress Post," *Lead Daily Call* (Lead, SD), February 6, 1936; "Jensen Announces Governor Candidacy," *Rapid City Daily Journal* (Rapid City, SD), February 7, 1936; "Troth Announces in Congress Race," *Rapid City Daily Journal* (Rapid City, SD), February 10, 1936; "Atwater Out for Congress," *Rapid City Daily Journal* (Rapid City, SD), February 18, 1936; "Asks That Williamson and Case Take Stand," *Rapid City Daily Journal* (Rapid City, SD), February 26, 1936.
61. "Case Outlines Campaign Plans," *Rapid City Daily Journal* (Rapid City, SD), February 12, 1936; "'Our Job is to Re-establish Opportunity as the Birthright of Every American,'" *Custer County Chronicle* (Custer, SD), February 13, 1936.
62. "Case Outlines Campaign Plans," *Rapid City Daily Journal*; "'Our Job is to Re-establish Opportunity as the Birthright of Every American,'" *Custer County Chronicle*.
63. Francis to Leland, March 12, 1936, transfer files, box 2, file: Personal 1934-1938, Francis H. Case Collection; "They Say . . . You May Not Agree; Not Always Do We," *Custer County Chronicle* (Custer, SD), March 26, 1936; "Case Criticized Bill for Indians," *Rapid City Daily Journal* (Rapid City, SD), March 28, 1936.
64. "Case Advocates Bureau of Mines Station in Hills," *Lead Daily Call* (Lead, SD), April 3, 1936; "Case Would Submit War Move to Vote," *Rapid City Daily Journal* (Rapid City, SD); Newspaper clipping, "Case Urges 3-Fold Plan to Insure U. S. Neutrality," undated, box 1, file 17, Carol Case Goddard Collection.
65. "Entry Into Primary Election Contest for Nominations Is Completed; All Petitions In," *Lead Daily Call* (Lead, SD), April 6, 1936; "Candidates Draw Lots for Places," *Rapid City Daily Journal* (Rapid City, SD), April 7, 1936; "16 Candidates Out for Major Political Jobs," *Weekly Pioneer-Times* (Deadwood, SD), April 9, 1936.
66. "Alien Workers Scored by Case," *Rapid City Daily Journal* (Rapid City, SD), April 17, 1936; "Case to Speak Over WNAX Sunday-Monday," *Custer County Chronicle* (Custer, SD), April 16, 1936; "Case Urges 3-Fold Plan

to Insure U. S. Neutrality"; "Case Assails 'Red Ink' Way," *Rapid City Daily Journal* (Rapid City, SD), April 20, 1936; "Portion of Radio Address Over WNAX Monday April 20th By Francis Case," *Custer County Chronicle* (Custer, SD), April 23, 1936. No copy or summary of "The Unknown Soldier Amendment" speech has been located. The text of that proposed amendment appears below:

"ARTICLE _____

The right to declare war ABROAD is hereby restored to the people.

1. The Congress shall not declare war, except the territory of the United States be actually invaded or attacked, until a proposal for a declaration of war shall have been approved by a majority of those voting in a special national election in which all citizens over the age of eighteen years may participate.

2. The President as Commander-in-Chief of the Army and Navy shall not send armed expeditionary forces in excess of 25,000 men more than 500 miles beyond the territory of the United States except in movement between portions of that territory, until after such a declaration of war by the people.

3. The Congress shall provide for carrying out the provisions of this article by appropriate legislation."

See "Smedley Butler Urges Americans to Stay Out of European Wars," campaign brochure, undated, cabinet 45, new drawer 179/old drawer 184, box 2, file: Miscellaneous Correspondence 2–Misc., Francis H. Case Collection.

67. Francis to Perry, April 25, 1936, Francis to Haver, April 26, 1936, box 2, file 5, Francis to Chan, April 26, 1936, box 5, file 3, Carol Case Goddard Collection; "Round About Town," *Custer County Chronicle* (Custer, SD), April 30, 1936.

68. "Case Urges 3-Fold Plan to Insure U. S. Neutrality"; Political advertising, "For CONGRESS," *Rapid City Daily Journal* (Rapid City, SD), May 2, 1936; Paid political advertising, "FOR CONGRESS," *Lead Daily Call* (Lead, SD), May 2, 1936; "FOR CONGRESS," *Deadwood Pioneer-Times* (Deadwood. S. Dak.), May 2, 1936; "Select Your Candidates; BE SURE TO VOTE," *Rapid City Daily Journal* (Rapid City, SD), May 2, 1936; "Case for Congress," *Rapid City Daily Journal* (Rapid City, SD), May 4, 1936; Political advertising, "CASE FOR CONGRESS," *Lead Daily Call* (Lead, SD), May 4, 1936; "CASE FOR CONGRESS," *Deadwood Pioneer-Times* (Deadwood, SD), May 5, 1936.

69. Myrtle Morrison, comp., Official Election Returns for South Dakota: Primary Election May 5, 1936 (Pierre, SD: Hipple, 1936), pp. 4, 5, http://www.sdsos.gov/elections-voting/assets/historicalelectiondata/1936P.pdf (page citations are to PDF version); *Election Statistics*, pp. 13, 14.

Notes 537

70. Irma to Francis and Pud [Myrle], undated, O.W. Coursey to Francis H. Case, May 6, 1936, Herbert L. Case to Francis, May 7, 1936, Mother to Francis, undated, Arthur A. Juhnke to Francis, undated, Harlan J. Bushfield to Francis Case, May 7, 1936, Harold to Francis, May 8, 1936, transfer files, box 1, file: Congratulations and support after primaries 1936, Francis H. Case Collection; "Thank You," "Loyalty Beyond Price," and "Thank You, All," *Custer County Chronicle* (Custer, SD), May 7, 1936.
71. "Candidates Talk Over Plans Prior to State Meeting," *Rapid City Daily Journal* (Rapid City, SD), June 1, 1936; *Election Statistics*, p. 14; "Few Ballots Required to Perfect Candidate List at State Meeting," *Rapid City Daily Journal* (Rapid City, SD), June 3, 1936.
72. "Few Ballots Required to Perfect Candidate List at State Meeting," *Rapid City Daily Journal*; "South Dakota Republican Party Platform, 1936," *Custer County Chronicle* (Custer, SD), June 11, 1936; "At Convention," *Rapid City Daily Journal* (Rapid City, SD), June 3, 1936.
73. "Convention Starts Tonight," *Rapid City Daily Journal* (Rapid City, SD), June 9, 1936; "Landon and Knox Are Chosen," *Rapid City Daily Journal* (Rapid City, SD), June 12, 1936.
74. "Round About Town," *Custer County Chronicle* (Custer, SD), June 25, 1936; "Case Says Farmers Doing What They Can for Selves," *Rapid City Daily Journal* (Rapid City, SD), June 26, 1936; "Wayside Notes" and "Republican Candidates Set Forth 7-Point Relief Program on Drouth," *Custer County Chronicle* (Custer, SD), July 2, 1936.
75. "Newell Scene of Annual Fete Today," *Rapid City Daily Journal* (Rapid City, SD), July 18, 1936; "Werner Turns Down Challenge by Case," *Rapid City Daily Journal* (Rapid City, SD), July 20, 1936; "Wayside Notes," *Custer County Chronicle* (Custer, SD), July 23, 1936.
76. Francis Case to Chester C. Bolton, July 13, 1936, Harvey to Francis, July 17, 1936, Harvey Jewett, Jr. to Carl Bachmann, July 17, 1936, Francis Case to Chester C. Bolton, July 29, 1936, Francis Case to Harvey Jewett, Jr., July 29, 1936, transfer files, box 1, file: Congressional Committee/ Congressional Campaign Com. 1934–1936, Francis H. Case Collection; "Roosevelt Spent $1,800 in State," *Rapid City Daily Journal* (Rapid City, SD), December 1, 1936.
77. "Many Attend Jensen Day at Hot Springs," *Custer County Chronicle* (Custer, SD), September 17, 1936; Francis to Karl E. Mundt, September 11[, 1936], Francis to Judge E. Y. Berry, September 18[, 1936], transfer files, box 1, file: Miscellaneous 1934–1938 pt.1, Francis H. Case Collection; Francis Case by Carol Case to George Whirlwind Soldier, October 2, 1936, Francis Case by Carol Case to Luke Gilberts, October 2, 1936, box 5, file 3, Secretary to Francis Case to J. H. Flannery, October 3[, 1936], box 2, file 20, Carol to Francis, October 13, 1936, box 5, file 4, Carol Case, Secretary to Francis Case to Ben C. Horse, October 14[, 1936], box 5, file 3, Carol to Ada, October 15[, 1936], Carol Case to Mr. and Mrs. Lloyd E. Sutherland,

October 15[, 1936], Carol Case to Mr. and Mrs. Arthur Galbraith, October 15[, 1936], box 2, file 20, Carol Case to Mrs. Eleanor A. Wright, October 28[, 1936], box 2, file 6, Carol Case Goddard Collection.

78. "Case Speaks for Old Age Pensions," *Rapid City Daily Journal* (Rapid City, SD), September 8, 1936; "Wayside Notes," *Custer County Chronicle* (Custer, SD), September 10, 1936.
79. "Smedley Butler Will Speak at Rapid Sunday," *Custer County Chronicle* (Custer, SD), September 17, 1936; "Butler Enroute to Hills Today," *Rapid City Daily Journal* (Rapid City, SD), September 19, 1936; "Butler Declares Hitler Bringing on Another War," *Rapid City Daily Journal* (Rapid City, SD), September 21, 1936.
80. "Butler Declares Hitler Bringing on Another War," *Rapid City Daily Journal*; "Smedley Butler Urges Americans to Stay Out of European Wars," *Custer County Chronicle* (Custer, SD), September 24, 1936.
81. "Butler Urges Case's Election at Winner," *Rapid City Daily Journal* (Rapid City, SD), September 22, 1936; "Smedley Butler Urges Americans to Stay Out of European Wars," *Custer County Chronicle*; "Smedley Butler Urges Americans to Stay Out of European Wars," campaign brochure, Francis H. Case Collection.
82. "Paid Notices," *Rapid City Daily Journal* (Rapid City, SD), October 3, 1936; "KFYR. Bismarck. 8:00 A.M., Monday, October 5, 1936," speech, box 1, file 9, Carol Case Goddard Collection.
83. "City Items," *Rapid City Daily Journal* (Rapid City, SD), October 12, 1936; "A Young Man's Country, Again," speech, box 1, file 9, Carol Case Goddard Collection; "WNAX #2. 10/13/36 How Mr. Werner Voted," speech, transfer files, box 2, file: Talks, Francis H. Case Collection; "Talk #3 – WNAX - !0/14/36," speech, and "WNAX. . . 4.," speech, box 1, file 9, Carol Case Goddard Collection.
84. "Francis Case Speaks Over Bismarck and Pierre," *Custer County Chronicle* (Custer, SD), October 22, 1936; Mary to Herbert, postcard, [October 27, 1936], box 2, file 20, Carol Case Goddard Collection; Political advertising, "The Most Important Message That Has Come Out of This Campaign," *Rapid City Daily Journal* (Rapid City, SD), October 31, 1936; Speech, untitled and undated, transfer files, box 2, file: Talks, Francis H. Case Collection.
85. "Two Independents Qualify in State," *Rapid City Daily Journal* (Rapid City, SD), October 5, 1936; Francis Case to William Long Feather, October 2[, 1936], Francis Case by Carol Case to Felix Crazy Bull, October 2[, 1936], box 5, file 3, P. J. Dunn to J. F. Frame, October 14, 1936, P. J. Dunn to L. E. Goodwin, October 14, 1936, P. J. Dunn to J. H. Fryberger, October 14, 1936, P. J. Dunn to C. E. Kell, October 14, 1936, P. J. Dunn to Perry Greek, October 14, 1936, box 2, file 20, Carol Case Goddard Collection; "Case Scores House of 'Rubber Stamps'," *Rapid City Daily Journal* (Rapid City, SD), October 17, 1936. Sometime before the primary, Francis had set forth

his "Indian Program" in a separate campaign circular that was distributed to several of his American Indian contacts throughout the district. The program was described in six numbered paragraphs:

> "1. An Indian will be selected as one my Secretaries in Washington to help give you REAL service.
> 2. I will work for a 'Service' officer on each Reservation to be chosen by the Members of the Reservation.
> 3. Active cooperation with Ralph Case in getting settlement of the Black Hills claims and other suits now pending.
> 4. Every possible assistance in getting Indian farms restocked with cattle, horses, pigs and chickens.
> 5. Encouragement for our schools and help in placing Indian young people in real jobs.
> 6. Development of homes for the aged Indians at the Agencies."

See "For Congressman Vote for Francis Case (Hehak Hemaza)," campaign circular, undated, in author's possession.

86. "GOP Rally at Deadwood Was Well Attended," *Lead Daily Call* (Lead, SD), October 21, 1936; "Case Criticizes Howes' Activity," *Rapid City Daily Journal* (Rapid City, SD), October 23, 1936; "Case Pleads for Change in Policy," *Daily Capital-Journal* (Pierre, SD), October 24, 1936; "Case Hits Alleged Discrimination in Federal Road Grants," *Rapid City Daily Journal* (Rapid City, SD), October 27, 1936; Francis Case by Carol Case to Luke Gilberts, October 2[, 1936], box 5, file 3, Carol Case Goddard Collection; "Rallies to Wind Up Campaign In The County," *Custer County Chronicle* (Custer, SD), October 29, 1936.

87. Newspaper clippings and political advertising, box 2, file 20, Carol Case Goddard Collection; Political advertising, "The Right Man for Congress," *Lead Daily Call* (Lead, SD), October 31, 1936; Political advertising, "The Right Man for Congress," *Deadwood Pioneer-Times* (Deadwood, SD), October 31, 1936; Political advertising, "The Right Man for Congress," *Rapid City Daily Journal* (Rapid City, SD), November 2, 1936; Political advertising, "The Most Important Message That Has Come Out of This Campaign," *Rapid City Daily Journal* (Rapid City, SD), October 31, 1936; Political advertising, "'Bringing Home the Bacon'," *Rapid City Daily Journal*, (Rapid City, SD), November 2, 1936.

88. "Case And Pyle Will Speak in Spearfish Monday," *Lead Daily Call* (Lead, SD), October 30, 1936; "Case Speaks of Werner, Pension," *Rapid City Daily Journal* (Rapid City, SD), November 2, 1936; "City Items," *Rapid City Daily Journal* (Rapid City, SD), November 3, 1936; "Sam McKelvie to Speak Here Soon," *Rapid City Daily Journal* (Rapid City, SD), October 24, 1936; "Major Rallies Are Held Here," *Rapid City Daily Journal* (Rapid City, SD), November 3, 1936.

89. Myrtle Morrison, comp., Official Election Returns for South Dakota: General Election November 3, 1936 (Pierre, SD: Hipple, 1936), pp. 2, 3, 4, 6, http://www.sdsos.gov/elections-voting/assets/historicalelectiondata/1936G.pdf (hereinafter *S.D. Official Election Returns 1936,* page citations are to PDF version). Francis won the following counties: Butte, Corson, Custer, Fall River, Haakon, Harding, Jackson, Jones, Lawrence, Lyman, Meade, Mellette, Shannon (unorganized), and Washabaugh (unorganized); whereas Werner prevailed in Bennett, Dewey Gregory, Pennington, Perkins, Stanley, Tripp, Ziebach, Todd (unorganized), and Washington (unorganized).

90. *Encyclopedia Britannica Online,* s.v. "United States Presidential Election of 1936," accessed June 17, 2020, http://www.britannica.com/event/United-States-presidential-election-of-1936; *S.D. Official Election Returns 1936,* p. 5; United States House of Representatives, "74th Congress (1935–1937)," accessed November 17, 2022, https://history.house.gov/Congressional-Overview/Profiles/74th/; United States House of Representatives, "75th Congress (1937–1939)," accessed November 17, 2022, https://history.house.gov/Congressional-Overview/Profiles/75th/; Art Brown, "Former South Dakotan Writes About Our 'Freshman Congressman'," essay, undated, p. 1, transfer files, box 2, file: Case Political Ads-Speeches-Clippings, Francis H. Case Collection; United States Senate, "United States Senate Party Division," accessed November 17, 2022, http://www.senate.gov/history/partydiv.htm; Encyclopedia of the Great Depression, s.v. "Election of 1934," by Howard W. Allen, accessed November 17, 2022, https://encyclopedia.com/economics/encyclopedias-almanacs-transcripts-and-maps/election-1934; "Governors: Net Gain of 5 for The Democrats," *CQ Almanac 1974,* 30th ed. (Washington, DC: Congressional Quarterly, 1975), pp. 850–51.

91. E. B. Adams to Francis H. Case, October 30, 1936, box 2, file 6, Walter Travis to Francis Case, November 5, 1936, box 2, file 9, M. Q. Sharpe to Francis Case, November 5, 1936, Chet Leedom to My Dear Boy [Francis], November 5, 1936, John T. Milek to Francis Case, November 6, 1936, box 2, file 1, Karl E. Mundt to Francis, November 6[, 1936], box 1, file 6, Coursey to My dear Congressman Case, November 7, 1936, box 2, file 9, James Blue Bird to Francis Case, November 12, 1936, box 5, file 3, Leland to Francis, November 16, 1936, box 4, file 10, Chester C. Bolton to Francis Case, November 18, 1936, box 2, file 8, Carol Case Goddard Collection; Francis Case To The Newspaper Addressed, 1936, black scrapbook 1914–1943, carton E, Case Ranch Collection.

92. "Thank You," *Custer County Chronicle* (Custer, SD), November 5, 1936; "Congressman Werner's Statement," *Gate City Guide* (Rapid City, SD), November 5, 1936.

93. Francis to Leland Davidson Case, telegram, November 4, 1936, box 2, file 1, Francis Case to Harry Kehm, telegram, November 5, 1936, Francis Case to Harlan Bushfield, telegram, November 5, 1936, Francis Case to General Smedley D. Butler, telegram, November 5, 1936, Francis Case to Governor Les Jensen, telegram, November 5, 1936, box 2, file 20, Harry C. Kehm

and Claude A. Hamilton to Francis Case, November 5, 1936, Francis Case to E. B. Adams, November 13[, 1936], box 2, file 6, Francis Case to Karl E. Mundt, November 14[, 1936], box 2, file 9, Francis Case to Robert Audiss, November 16, 1936, box 2, file 6, Francis to Leland, November 20, 1936, box 4, file 10, Carol Case to Wilbert Hain, November 25, 1936, box 2, file 20, Francis Case to J. F. Frame and Lee Goodwin, December 3, 1936, box 1, file 6, Carol Case Goddard Collection.

94. "Round About Town," *Custer County Chronicle* (Custer, SD), November 19, 1936; Francis to Leland, November 20, 1936, box 4, file 10, Francis H. Case Collection; "Case Birthday Party Planned," *Rapid City Daily Journal* (Rapid City, SD), December 7, 1936; "Congressman-Elect Case to Be Given Reception Tonight," *Lead Daily Call* (Lead, SD), December 8, 1936.

95. "Students Place in Declam Contest," *Custer County Chronicle* (Custer, SD), November 26, 1936; "Society and Club Notes," *Custer County Chronicle* (Custer, SD), December 10, 1936.

96. Lyle L. Mariner to Francis Case, November 6, 1936, box 2, file 20, Leonard Ellin to Francis Case, November 12, 1936, box 2, file 4, Francis Case to Frank Johnson, November 20, 1936, box 2, file 9, Francis Case to Lyle L. Mariner, November 27, 1936, box 2, file 20, Francis Case to Frank Carrier, November 28, 1936, box 1, file 10, Carol Case Goddard Collection; "Philip Man Buys Hill City News," *Rapid City Daily Journal* (Rapid City, SD), December 4, 1936; "Regular Staff to Manage Chronicle," *Custer County Chronicle* (Custer, SD), December 10, 1936.

97. "Case Birthday Party Planned," *Rapid City Daily Journal*; "Many Attend Reception for Francis Case," *Custer County Chronicle* (Custer, SD), December 10, 1936.

98. "Cases Leave for Capital Today," *Custer County Chronicle* (Custer, SD), December 10, 1936; Francis Case to Capt. W. A. Ross, November 20, 1936, Francis Case to Col. A. Neves, November 23, 1936, box 1, file 6, Carol Case Goddard Collection; "Congressman-Elect Case to Be Given Reception Tonight," *Lead Daily Call*; "Water Conservation Discussed at Meet," *Rapid City Daily Journal* (Rapid City, SD), December 11, 1936; "Francis Case Visiting Here on Way to Washington, D. C.," *Mankato Free Press*, (Mankato, MN) December 16, 1936; Leland Davidson Case and Edith E. Grannis, eds., *New Hampshire to Minnesota: Memoirs of Samuel Higbee Grannis (1839-1933)* (Tucson, AZ: Self-published, 1962), p. 153.

99. Leland to Francis, November 25, 1936, box 4, file 10, Carol Case Goddard Collection; "Case Credits NU Teachers for Victory," *Evanston Daily News-Index* (Evanston, IL), December 19, 1936; "Wayside Notes," January 4, 1937, lime-green scrapbook, carton C, Case Ranch Collection.

100. "Wayside Notes," January 4, 1937.

101. Ibid.

102. *Fall River County Pioneer Histories* (Fall River, SD: Fall River County Historical Society, 1976), pp. 99, 100; Carol Case Goddard, "Record of Marriage," December 26, 1936, registered no. M-384, certificate no. 188771, South Dakota Department of Health, Pierre, SD.
103. Francis Case to Benjamin A. Lamb, January 2, 1937, transfer files, box 2, file: Personal 1934–1938, Francis H. Case Collection.
104. "Wayside Notes," January 4, 1937; Benj. A. Lamb to Hon. Francis Case, January 4, 1937, transfer files, box 2, file: Personal 1934–1938, Francis H. Case Collection.

EPILOGUE

1. Goldie Wells, comp., *Official Election Returns for South Dakota: General Election November 8, 1938* (Pierre, SD: Hipple, 1938), p. 5, accessed January 6, 2023, http://www.sdsos.gov/elections-voting/assets/historicalelectiondata/1938G.pdf (page citations are to PDF version); "Elections," in *2005 South Dakota Legislative Manual*, p. 15, accessed December 10, 2022, http://www.sdsos.gov/elections-voting/assets/ElectionsReturnsPre1972.pdf (hereinafter *Election Statistics*, page citations are to PDF version).
2. *Election Statistics*, pp. 15-18.
3. R. P. Williams to Major General Commandant, memorandum, May 12, 1937, Leland Davidson Case to Commandant of the Marine Corps, December 1, 1981, Multiple Purpose Correspondence Form, unknown author to Leland Davidson Case, January 8, 1982, FHC Records, National Archives, NPRC; "Interview Memo," Francis Case call to Gen Holcomb, December 8, 1941, Francis Case to Lieutenant General Thomas Holcomb, July 2, 1942, T. Holcomb to Mr. Case, July 7, 1942, R. McC. Pate to All Reserve Officers, memorandum, October 1, 1946, R. McC. Pate to Captain Francis H. Case, memorandum, January 20, 1947, E. J. Snell to Captain Francis H. Case, memorandum, January 28, 1947, Lemuel C. Shepherd Jr. to Captain Francis H. Case, memorandum, April 14, 1947, Francis Case to Captain MacArthur H. Manchester, April 19, 1947, Captain Francis H. Case to Commandant of the Marine Corps, memorandum, April 25, 1947, A. A. Vandegrift to Major Francis H. Case, memorandum, May 28, 1947, James Forrestal to Major Francis H. Case, memorandum, June 24, 1947, A. A. Vandegrift to Major Francis H. Case, memorandum, November 20, 1947, W. A. Reaves to Major Francis H. Case, memorandum, December 13, 1947, Major Francis H. Case to Director, Ninth Marine Corps Reserve District, memorandum, December 17, 1947, Melvin J. Maas to Francis Case, January 8, 1948, Francis Case to Colonel Melvin J. Maas, February 10, 1948, Noel C. Gregory to Major Francis H. Case, memorandum, March 15, 1951, file cabinet 31, new drawer 121/old drawer 126, box 1, file: Marine Corps (Reserve), Francis H. Case Collection.

4. Rex Alan Smith, *The Carving of Mount Rushmore* (New York: Abbeville Press, 1985), pp. 324–25, 330, 333, 340–48, 369–72, 386, 397–98; "Western South Dakota and Washington," newsletter, May 27[, 1937], cabinet 1, new drawer 1/old drawer 1/2, box 1, Francis H. Case Collection.
5. Richard R. Chenoweth, "Francis Case: A Political Biography," in *South Dakota Historical Collections* (Pierre, SD: State Publishing Company, 1978), p. 318 (hereinafter Chenoweth, "Francis Case"); "Washington & Western South Dakota," newsletter, January 23, 1939, "Your Affairs in Washington," newsletter, October 14, 1940, cabinet 1, new drawer 1/old drawer 1/2, box 1, Francis H. Case Collection.
6. "Notes from Washington," newsletter, April 24, 1944, "Washington Report," newsletter, April 26, 1945, "Report from Washington," newsletter, February 9, 1948, cabinet 1, new drawer 1/old drawer 1/2, box 1, Francis H. Case Collection; Harlan A. Walker to Francis Case, April 14, 1945, box 2, file 12, Carol Case Goddard Collection.
7. "News Release," August 18, 1945, "Notes from the Pacific," newsletters, released September 6, 13, and 20, 1945, "Washington Report," newsletter, September 27, 1945, "Report from Washington," newsletter, October 4, 1945, cabinet 1, new drawer 1/old drawer 1/2, box 1, Francis H. Case Collection.
8. "Overseas Report," newsletter, September 2, 1947, cabinet 1, new drawer 1/old drawer 1/2, box 1, Francis H. Case Collection.
9. Ibid.; Chenoweth, "Francis Case," p. 364; "The Marshall Plan: Design, Accomplishments, and Significance," Congressional Research Service, accessed January 13, 2023, http://www.everycrsreport.com/reports/R45079.html.
10. "Your Affairs in Washington," newsletter, September 2, 1940, "Report from Washington," newsletter, February 9, 1948, cabinet 1, new drawer 1/old drawer 1/2, box 1, Francis H. Case Collection; Chenoweth, "Francis Case," p. 319.
11. Chenoweth, "Francis Case," p. 328; "Notes from Washington," newsletter, December 15, 1941, "Notes from Washington," newsletter, January 19, 1942; "Report from Washington," newsletter, February 9, 1948, "Francis Case Reports from Washington, D. C.," newsletter, June 29, 1953, cabinet 1, new drawer 1/old drawer 1/2, box 1, Francis H. Case Collection.
12. "Notes from Washington," newsletter, April 6, 1942, "Notes from Washington," newsletter, April 27, 1942, "Notes from Washington," newsletter, June 28, 1943, "Notes from Washington," newsletter, February 21, 1944, cabinet 1, new drawer 1/old drawer 1/2, box 1, Francis H. Case Collection.
13. "Report from Washington," newsletter, December 12, 1946, cabinet 1, new drawer 1/old drawer 1/2, box 1, Francis H. Case Collection.

14. Paul Higbee, "Stories Beneath the Stones," *South Dakota Magazine*, November/December 2017, http://www.southdakotamagazine.com/stories-beneath-the-stones; "Washington Report," newsletter, November 24, 1947, "In Congress with Case," newsletter, March 29, 1949, cabinet 1, new drawer 1/old drawer 1/2, box 1, Francis H. Case Collection.
15. "Report from Washington," newsletter, May 15, 1944, "Notes from Washington," newsletter, December 14, 1944, "Report from Washington," newsletter, February 9, 1948, "From the Office of Senator Francis Case," newsletter, May 5, 1954, cabinet 1, new drawer 1/old drawer 1/2, box 1, Francis H. Case Collection; United States Bureau of Reclamation, "Pick Sloan Missouri Basin Program," accessed April 3, 2023, http://www.usbr.gov/projects/index.php?id=380; Chenoweth, "Francis Case," pp. 319–22.
16. Chenoweth, "Francis Case," p. 324; David W. Grua, *Surviving Wounded Knee: The Lakotas and the Politics of Memory* (New York: Oxford University Press, 2016), pp. 93–4, 171–72, 174; "Your Affairs in Washington," newsletter, March 25, 1940, "Washington Report," newsletter, July 5, 1945, "Report from Washington," newsletter, February 9, 1948, cabinet 1, new drawer 1/old drawer 1/2, box 1, Francis H. Case Collection.
17. "Report from Washington," newsletter, January 31, 1946, "Report from Washington," newsletter, February 8, 1946, "Washington Report," newsletter, February 21, 1946, cabinet 1, new drawer 1/old drawer 1/2, box 1, Francis H. Case Collection; Chenoweth, "Francis Case," pp. 347–48, 353–54.
18. Chenoweth, "Francis Case," pp. 354–56, 358–59; "Report from Washington," newsletter, June 13, 1946, "Washington Report," newsletter, May 17, 1947, "Report from Washington," newsletter, February 9, 1948, cabinet 1, new drawer 1/old drawer 1/2, box 1, Francis H. Case Collection.
19. "Congressional Report," newsletter, August 7, 1950, "Congressional Report," newsletter, August 28, 1950, "Congressional Report," newsletter, September 4, 1950, "Senator Francis Case Reports," newsletter, June 12, 1961, cabinet 1, new drawer 1/old drawer 1/2, box 1, Francis H. Case Collection; Major Acts of Congress, s.v. "Communist Control Act of 1954," by Carl Auerbach, accessed March 21, 2023, https://www.encyclopedia.com/history/encyclopedias-almanacs-transcripts-and-maps/communist-control-act-1954.
20. Chenoweth, "Francis Case," pp. 370, 376, 378; *Election Statistics*, p. 18.
21. "Francis Case Reports," newsletter, January 18, 1951, "Francis Case Reports," newsletter, January 27, 1951, cabinet 1, new drawer 1/old drawer 1/2, box 1, Francis H. Case Collection.
22. "Francis Case Reports," newsletter, January 12, 1953, "Francis Case Reports," newsletter, January 19, 1953, "Francis Case Reports," newsletter, January 26, 1953, "Francis Case Reports," newsletter, February 23, 1953, "Francis Case Reports," newsletter, March 16, 1953, "Francis Case Reports from the Senate," newsletter, February 14, 1955, cabinet 1, new drawer 1/old drawer 1/2, box 1, Francis H. Case Collection.

23. "Francis Case Reports from Washington, D. C.," newsletter, January 10, 1955, "Report from the Senate," newsletter, January 14, 1957, "Report from the Senate," newsletter, January 21, 1957, "Senator Francis Case Reports," newsletter, February 2, 1959, "Senator Francis Case Reports," newsletter, May 4, 1959, "Francis Case Reports," newsletter, January 25, 1960, "Senator Francis Case Reports," newsletter, April 10, 1961, "Senator Francis Case Reports," newsletter, May 15, 1961, "Senator Francis Case Reports," newsletter, January 22, 1962, cabinet 1, new drawer 1/old drawer 1/2, box 1, Francis H. Case Collection.
24. "Report from the Office of Francis Case," newsletter, December 9, 1951, "Francis Case Reports from Washington DC," newsletter, January 10, 1952, "Francis Case Reports from Washington DC," newsletter, May 12, 1952, "Francis Case Reports," newsletter, June 16, 1952, cabinet 1, new drawer 1/old drawer 1/2, box 1, Francis H. Case Collection; "To Issue Postage Stamp Featuring Mt. Rushmore," *Mobridge Tribune* (Mobridge, SD), January 17, 1952; "Mt. Rushmore Memorial's 25th Year to Be Celebrated," *Daily Argus-Leader* (Sioux Falls, SD), August 10, 1952.
25. "Mt. Rushmore Memorial's 25th Year to Be Celebrated," *Daily Argus-Leader*; "Borglum's Masterpiece," speech, carton C, Case Ranch Collection; "Rushmore Draws Praise from Lawmakers, Postal Officials On Anniversary," *Rapid City Daily Journal* (Rapid City, SD), August 11, 1952; "Silver Anniversary for Mount Rushmore" and "Rushmore Bulwark Against Communism," *Rapid City Daily Journal* (Rapid City, SD), August 12, 1952; "Inspiration in Mt. Rushmore; Tourists Crowd Black Hills, One of Nature's Fairylands," *Daily Argus-Leader* (Sioux Falls, SD), August 15, 1952.
26. "Francis Case Reports from Washington, D. C.," newsletter, February 8, 1954, "Francis Case Reports from Washington, D. C.," newsletter, February 22, 1954, "Francis Case Reports from Washington, D. C.," newsletter, May 10, 1954, "Francis Case Reports from Washington, D. C.," newsletter, June 14, 1954, cabinet 1, new drawer 1/old drawer 1/2, box 1, Francis H. Case Collection; "Master Plan for Rushmore Approved; Officers Elected," *Rapid City Daily Journal* (Rapid City, SD), February 14, 1954; "Improvements Asked At Mount Rushmore," *Rapid City Daily Journal* (Rapid City, SD), February 21, 1954; "Case Asks Funds for Rushmore," *Daily Argus-Leader* (Sioux Falls, SD), May 6, 1954; "Let's Have a Testimonial Dinner for Francis Case," *Rapid City Daily Journal* (Rapid City, SD), December 13, 1954.
27. "Report from the Senate," newsletter, October 15, 1951, "Report from the Senate," newsletter, October 22, 1951, "Francis Case Reports from Washington, D. C.," newsletter, February 1, 1954, "From the Office of Senator Francis Case," newsletter, May 5, 1954, cabinet 1, new drawer 1/old drawer 1/2, box 1, Francis H. Case Collection.
28. Jesse Greenspan, "How Eisenhower Secretly Pushed Back Against McCarthyism," *History.com*, March 4, 2020, http://www.history.com/news/dwight-eisenhower-joseph-mccarthy-red-scare; Tom Wicker, *Shooting Star:*

The Brief Arc of Joe McCarthy (Orlando, FL: Harcourt, 2006), pp. 126, 139, 140 (hereinafter Wicker, *Shooting Star*); Chenoweth, "Francis Case," pp. 392, 395.

29. Dwight D. Eisenhower, *Mandate for Change: 1953-1956* (Garden City, NY: Doubleday, 1963), p. 329 (hereinafter Eisenhower, *Mandate for Change*); "Francis Case Reports from Washington, D. C.," newsletter, August 9, 1954, cabinet 1, new drawer 1/old drawer 1/2, box 1, Francis H. Case Collection; Wicker, *Shooting Star*, 175-78; Chenoweth, "Francis Case," pp. 393, 395.
30. Eisenhower, *Mandate for Change*, p. 329; Chenoweth, "Francis Case," pp. 396–97; Wicker, *Shooting Star*, pp. 180–81.
31. Eisenhower, *Mandate for Change*, pp. 330, 599; Chenoweth, "Francis Case," pp. 398; Wicker, *Shooting Star*, pp. 182–83.
32. "Francis Case Reports from Washington, D. C.," newsletter, March 22, 1954, "Francis Case Reports from the U. S. Senate," newsletter, April 4, 1955, "Report from the Senate," newsletter, June 25, 1956, cabinet 1, new drawer 1/old drawer 1/2, box 1, Francis H. Case Collection; Chenoweth, "Francis Case," p. 416. Francis was responsible for the following features included in the Federal Highway Act of 1956:

    1. Definite increase of the funds for the Primary and Secondary Systems along with the Interstate in order to have a more balanced system. 2. Exemption of gasoline used on the farms from the federal gas tax for highways. 3. Establishment of a 20 per cent transfer clause so that any state can "tailor" its funds for primary, secondary or urban, according to its special need. 4. Increase in the matching ratio for federal[/state] share on the Interstate System [from 60/40 to 90/10]. 5. Establishment of "contract authority" and increase of funds for roads on federal lands, so that the government's own areas were not neglected in road-building. 6. Recognition of the cost of relocating rural telephone and electric lines when state law permits. 7. Cooperation between state and federal government in "pre-determining" wage rates when contracts are advertised.

    The 1956 Congress also accepted Francis's amendment to increase the interstate system from 40,000 to 41,000 miles. See "Report from the Senate," newsletter, June 25, 1956, "Senator Francis Case Reports," newsletter, June 26, 1961, cabinet 1, new drawer 1/old drawer 1/2, box 1, Francis H. Case Collection.
33. Marian D. Irish and James W. Prothro, *The Politics of American Democracy*, 5th ed. (Englewood Cliffs, NJ: Prentice-Hall, 1971), pp. 280–81; Chenoweth, "Francis Case," pp. 399, 401–02, 404.
34. Eisenhower, *Mandate for Change*, pp. 555–56; Chenoweth, "Francis Case," p. 401.
35. Eisenhower, *Mandate for Change*, p. 556.
36. *Election Statistics*, p. 19; Chenoweth, "Francis Case," pp. 419, 421–25.

37. "Francis Case Reports from Washington DC," newsletter, August 17, 1953, "Francis Case Reports to South Dakota from the Senate in Washington, D. C.," newsletter, June 28, 1954," "Senator Francis Case Reports," newsletter, July 7, 1958, "Senator Francis Case Reports," newsletter, July 28, 1958, "Senator Francis Case Reports," newsletter, April 18, 1961, cabinet 1, new drawer 1/old drawer 1/2, box 1, Francis H. Case Collection; "All About Dry Ice—And Its Many Uses," *dryiceInfo.com*, accessed April 10, 2023, http://www.dryiceinfo.com.

38. "Francis Case Reports from Washington, DC," newsletter, August 17, 1953, "Francis Case Reports from the U. S. Senate," newsletter, April 25, 1955, "Senator Francis Case Reports," newsletter, August 18, 1958, "Senator Francis Case Reports," newsletter, August 26, 1958, "Senator Francis Case Reports," newsletter, June 15, 1959, "Senator Francis Case Reports," newsletter, February 29, 1960, "Senator Francis Case Reports," newsletter, May 23, 1960, cabinet 1, new drawer 1/old drawer 1/2, box 1, Francis H. Case Collection; S. Gray, R. Semiat, M. Duke, A. Rahardianto, and Y. Cohen, "Seawater Use and Desalination Technology," in *Treatise on Water Science* vol. 4, ed. Peter Wilderer (Elsevier, 2011), https://www.sciencedirect.com/science/article/pii/B9780444531995000774.

39. "Senator Francis Case Reports," newsletter, June 30, 1958, "Senator Francis Case Reports," newsletter, August 26, 1958, "Senator Francis Case Reports," newsletter, January 26, 1959, "Senator Francis Case Reports," newsletter, March 28, 1960, "Francis Case Reports," newsletter, June 6, 1960, cabinet 1, new drawer 1/old drawer 1/2, box 1, Francis H. Case Collection.

40. "Senator Francis Case Reports," newsletter, February 9, 1959, "Senator Francis Case Reports," newsletter, July 6, 1960, "Francis Case Reports," newsletter, June 26, 1961, cabinet 1, new drawer 1/old drawer 1/2, box 1, Francis H. Case Collection; T. W. Sneed, comp., *Summary of Legislative Activities: Committee on Public Works, United States Senate, Eighty Fourth Congress* (Washington, DC: United States Government Printing Office, 1956), p. II; "How South Dakota 'Stole' an Interstate," *Argus Leader* (Sioux Falls, SD), June 28, 1981; "Historian: Interstate 29 Benefits South Dakota," *Black Hills Pioneer* (Spearfish, SD), April 23, 2018.

41. "Report from Washington," newsletter, July 23, 1951, "Francis Case Reports from Washington DC," newsletter, January 17, 1952, "Francis Case Reports from Washington DC," newsletter, January 31, 1952, "Senator Francis Case Reports," newsletter, February 2, 1959, "Senator Francis Case Reports," newsletter, March 2, 1959, cabinet 1, new drawer 1/old drawer 1/2, box 1, Francis H. Case Collection; "Case Commended for Work in Washington," *Daily Argus-Leader* (Sioux Falls, SD), January 26, 1955; "Sen. Francis Case, In Congress 25 Years," *Washington Post* (Washington, DC), June 23, 1962; *Memorial Services Held in the Senate and House of Representatives of the United States, Together with Remarks Presented in Eulogy of Francis H. Case* (Washington, DC: United States Government Printing Office, 1962), p. 53 (hereinafter *Francis Case Memorial Addresses*); Christine Barbour and Gerald

C. Wright, *Keeping the Republic: Power and Citizenship in American Politics*, 4th ed. (Washington, DC: CQ Press, 2009), p. 931.
42. "Francis Case Reports from Washington, D.C.," newsletter, July 20, 1953, "From the Office of Senator Francis Case," radio release, August 2, 1954, "Senator Francis Case Reports," newsletter, August 26, 1958, cabinet 1, new drawer 1/old drawer 1/2, box 1, Francis H. Case Collection.
43. "Senator Case Is Hospitalized," *Washington Post* (Washington, DC), June 22, 1962; "Death Takes Senator Case," *Rapid City Daily Journal* (Rapid City, SD), June 22, 1962; "Senator Francis Case Reports to South Dakota," newsletter, April 2, 1962, cabinet 1, new drawer 1/old drawer 1/2, box 1, Francis H. Case Collection.
44. Chenoweth, "Francis Case," pp. 427–28; "Case, Nauman Win Top State Contests," *Rapid City Daily Journal* (Rapid City, SD), June 6, 1962; "Death of Case Ends 25 Years in House, Senate," *Sioux Falls Argus-Leader* (Sioux Falls, SD), June 22, 1962; *Election Statistics*, p. 20.
45. "Senator Francis Case Reports to South Dakota," newsletter, June 18, 1962, cabinet 1, new drawer 1/old drawer 1/2, box 1, Francis H. Case Collection; "Senator Francis Case Of South Dakota Dies," *Evening Star* (Washington, DC), June 22, 1962; "Heart Attack Fatal to Sen. Case," *Daily Republic* (Mitchell, SD), June 22, 1962; "Senator Francis Case Died This Morn," *Daily Capital Journal* (Pierre, SD), June 22, 1962.
46. "Memorial Services Sunday for Senator Francis Case," *Washington Star* (Washington, DC), June 23, 1962; *Francis Case Memorial Addresses*, pp. 11-15; "Notables Attend Services Here for Senator Case," *Washington Post* (Washington, DC), June 25, 1962, "Thousands of Friends Pay Last Respects to Sen. Case," *Daily Plainsman* (Huron, SD), June 25, 1962.
47. "Thousands Pay Last Respects to South Dakota's Sen. Case," *Lead Daily Call* (Lead, SD), June 25, 1962; "Senator's Funeral Scheduled Tuesday, Body Flown Home," *Pierre State News* (Pierre, SD), June 25, 1962; "Pallbearers Are Named for Case," *Sioux Falls Argus-Leader* (Sioux Falls, SD), June 23, 1962; "Humble, Powerful Pay Last Respects to Case," *Rapid City Daily Journal* (Rapid City, SD), June 26, 1962; "State Pays Last Tribute to Senator," *Rapid City Daily Journal* (Rapid City, SD), June 27, 1962; "Nation's Leaders, Friends Pay Final Tribute to Case," *Sioux Falls Argus-Leader* (Sioux Falls, SD), June 27, 1962; *Francis Case Memorial Addresses*, p. 43. In addition to Lyndon Johnson, the Washington delegation that attended the services included Republican senators Karl E. Mundt (South Dakota), Bourke Hickenlooper and Jack Miller (Iowa), Milton Young (North Dakota), Frank Carlson (Kansas), J. Glen Beall (Maryland), Roman Hruska (Nebraska), John Sherman Cooper (Kentucky), and J. Caleb Boggs (Delaware); Democratic senators John Stennis (Mississippi), Howard W. Cannon (Nevada), and Quinton Burdick (North Dakota); and Republican representatives E. Y. Berry and Ben Reifel (South Dakota). The six pallbearers were Martin Kothe, L. M.

Test and Charles Endicott—Custer, Charles Whiting and E. F. Gronert—Rapid City, and John Mueller—Hot Springs. Honorary pallbearers included Harold Card—Webster, Leslie Jensen—Hot Springs, John Griffin—Sioux Falls, Dr. F. E. Manning—Custer, Jarvis Davenport—Sturgis, Leo Temmey—Huron, Clinton Richards—Deadwood, R. P. Harmon—Belle Fourche, Walter Travis—Watertown, A. M. Eberle—Brookings, George Toft—Mitchell, and Henry Schmitt—Aberdeen. Members of Francis's senatorial staff at the funeral were Loren Carlson, Harold Schuler, Art Juhnke, Ed Johnson, Caroline Greek, Dick Bowen, Don Arnold, Mae Aaberg, Nettie Savage, Mabel Connell, and Bob Seaman. Francis's body was transferred to and interred at the Black Hills National Cemetery on December 3, 1981. Francis, Jr. (whose body was transferred) and Myrle (who died on December 4, 1989) are also buried there. See "Vice President Heads Delegation to Case Funeral," *Daily Plainsman* (Huron, SD), June 26, 1962; "Pallbearers Are Named for Case," *Sioux Falls Argus-Leader*; "Humble, Powerful Pay Last Respects to Case," *Rapid City Daily Journal*; "State Pays Last Tribute to Senator," *Rapid City Daily Journal*; National Cemetery Administration, "Black Hills National Cemetery: An Introduction," accessed March 7, 2023, http://www.cem.va.gov/docs/legacy/BlackHillsNationalCemeteryLessonPPT.pdf, slide no. 8; Francis Higbee Case, grave marker, Black Hills National Cemetery, Sturgis, Meade County, South Dakota, digital image s.v. "Francis Higbee Case," *FindaGrave.com*; "Today's Obituaries," *Rapid City Journal* (Rapid City, SD), December 6, 1989.

48. "The Backlog," *Lead Daily Call* (Lead, SD), June 25, 1962; "Nor Long Remember," *Custer County Chronicle* (Custer, SD), June 28, 1962; "Letter from a S.D. Mother Brings Butter to W. Point," *Daily Argus-Leader* (Sioux Falls, SD), March 27, 1954; "West Point Cadets to Eat Butter Now," *Daily Plainsman* (Huron, SD), March 28, 1954.

49. *Francis Case Memorial Addresses*, Contents, pp. 17, 31, 59, 60, 65, 73.

50. Ibid., pp. 35, 38, 41, 56, 62; United States Senate, "Everett McKinley Dirksen: A Featured Biography," accessed September 5, 2023, http://www.senate.gov/senators/FeaturedBios/Featured_Bio_Dirksen.htm; United States Congress, "STENNIS, John Cornelius," accessed September 5, 2023, https://bioguide.congress.gov/search/bio/S000852; United States Senate, "Margaret Chase Smith: A Featured Biography," accessed September 5, 2023, http://www.senate.gov/senators/FeaturedBios/Featured_Bio_SmithMargaret.htm; United States Senate, "Wayne L. Morse: A Featured Biography," accessed September 5, 2023, http://www.senate.gov/senators/Featured_Bio_Morse.htm; United States Congress, "RUSSELL, Richard Brevard, Jr.," accessed September 5, 2023, https://bioguide.congress.gov/search/bio/R000536.

51. United States House of Representatives, "MCGOVERN, George Stanley," accessed April 21, 2023, https://history.house.gov/People/Listing/M/McGOVERN,-George-Stanley-(M000452)/; "Bottum Named Case's Replacement; Tapped for November Ballot," *Sioux Falls Argus-Leader* (Sioux Falls, SD), July 10, 1962; *Election Statistics*, pp. 19, 20, 21.

52. "Senator Francis Case Reports," newsletter, April 27, 1959, cabinet 1, new drawer 1/old drawer 1/2, box 1, Francis H. Case Collection; *Congressional Record*, 88th Cong., 1st session, p. 10668; *Election Statistics*, p, 20; "Honors for Case Sought by Reifel," *Sioux Falls Argus-Leader* (Sioux Falls, SD), June 26, 1962; "'Lake Case' Move Starts in Congress," *Sioux Falls Argus-Leader* (Sioux Falls, SD) June 28, 1962.

53. "Reifel Introduces First Legislation," *Rapid City Daily Journal* (Rapid City, SD), January 10, 1963; "Mundt Bills Would Honor Case Memory," *Daily Plainsman* (Huron, SD), January 13, 1963; "Reservoirs Named for Case, Sharpe," *Rapid City Daily Journal*, (Rapid City, SD), August 16, 1963; Ben Reifel to Myrle G. Case, July 23, 1963, Ben Reifel to Myrle Case and Jane, August 26, 1963 (enclosure), brown scrapbook, carton C, Case Ranch Collection.

54. *Francis Case Memorial Addresses*, pp. 181-84; "Event Signals Start of New Bridge in S.D.," *Sioux Falls Argus-Leader* (Sioux Falls, SD), July 18, 1962; "Completion Date for Francis Case Bridge Delayed," *Rapid City Daily Journal* (Rapid City, SD), March 30, 1963; "S.D. Road Record Set," *Sioux Falls Argus-Leader* (Sioux Falls, SD), December 24, 1964; "Udall Speaker for Dedication of S.D. Bridge," *Daily Republic* (Mitchell, SD), August 24, 1966; "Platte-Winner Bridge Dedication Marks End of Frustrating Project," *Daily Plainsman* (Huron, SD), September 25, 1966.

55. "Udall Sees Bright Future for State in Dedicatory Remarks," *Daily Republic* (Mitchell, SD), September 28, 1966; *Congressional Record*, 89th Cong., 2nd Session, p. 23283; "Unanimity Marks Action of Solons," *Sioux Falls Argus-Leader* (Sioux Falls, SD), January 28, 1967; "Legislature at a Glance," *Sioux Falls Argus-Leader* (Sioux Falls, SD), February 2, 1967.

56. Dedication program: Case Auditorium, November 18, 1962, box 1, file 18, Carol Case Goddard Collection; "Governor Gives Address at Dedication Ceremony," *Hot Springs Star* (Hot Springs, SD), November 22, 1962; "This Old School House," *In Touch* 4, no. 4 (April/May 2008), p. 6, "This Old School House," *In Touch* 6, No. 1 (August-October, 2009), p. 6; Sixty Fifth Annual Sturgis High School Baccalaureate and Commencement Program, May 19 and May 23, 1963, brown scrapbook, carton C, Case Ranch Collection; phone interview with Jane Case on May 1, 2023; Robert R. Spelts to Mrs. Francis Case, March 25, 1963, brown scrapbook, "Francis Case Building Open House," program, November 8, 1964, red scrapbook, carton C, Case Ranch Collection; "Francis Case Open House Draws 750," *Rapid City Daily Journal* (Rapid City, SD), November 9, 1964.

57. George McGovern to Mrs. Case, July 2, 1963, George McGovern to Mrs. Case, July 11, 1963, George McGovern to Mrs. Case, August 12, 1963, Hon. Ben Reifel, "The Francis Case Memorial Bridge" (excerpt from the *Congressional Record*), August 12, 1963, brown scrapbook, carton C, Case Ranch Collection; "Congressmen Want New Bridge Named in Honor of Sen. Case," *Rapid City Daily Journal* (Rapid City, SD), August 13, 1963;

"Wash. Bridge May Be Named for Senator Case," *Sioux Falls Argus-Leader* (Sioux Falls, SD), August 11, 1964; "Dedication Ceremonies of the Francis Case Memorial Bridge," program, April 20, 1966, carton B, Case Ranch Collection.
58. "Berry Urges Early Action on Case Bill," *Sioux Falls Argus-Leader* (Sioux Falls, SD), May 14, 1965; "Francis Case Bridge Finally a Reality," *Rapid City Daily Journal* (Rapid City, SD), September 27, 1965; "Dedication Ceremonies of the Francis Case Memorial Bridge."
59. "Francis Case Bridge Dedicated," *Rapid City Daily Journal* (Rapid City, SD), April 20, 1966; "Dedication Ceremonies of the Francis Case Memorial Bridge;" "Case Name Will Be Remembered," *Rapid City Daily Journal* (Rapid City, SD), April 21, 1966; "Case Memorial Bridge Is Dedicated in Washington," *Hot Springs Star* (Hot Springs, SD), April 28, 1966.
60. Francis Case, "The Blazed Trail," speech, May 13, 1914, black scrapbook, 1914–1943, carton E, Case Ranch Collection.

INDEX

Pages referencing photos, maps, and other images are in italics.

A

"A Cowboy's Prayer" (Clark), 226
Acacia House and fraternity, 158, 161, 162, 167, 292
Acacia Mining Company, 291–294
Adams, E. B., 216, 239, 319, 327, 356
Adelphians, the, 35, 126
Advertising the Church (Case), 184–185
"All of a Sudden Peggy" (Denny), 94–95
Alleger, C. N., 234
Allen, Eugene, 64
Allen, W. C., 337, 339, 340
American Association of University Women, 309–310, 357–358, 527n94
"American Ideals" (Butler), 351
American Legion Lake Committee, 280
Amphictyons, the, 35, 126
Anderson, Clint, 380
Andrus, W. B., 176
Angostura Dam, 367, 374
Anson, Adrian ("Cap"), 13
Appropriations Committee (U.S. Congress), 364–365
Arnold, W. R., 122–123
Associated Commercial Clubs of the Black Hills, 252
Associated Royalties, 242, 243

Athenians, the, 35

B

Bakewell, R. C., 216, 218
Barker oil wells, 242–244
Battle Mountain Sanitarium
  Calvin Coolidge tours, 226
  chaplain at, 155
  Clifford Wilson as employee at, 145
  General Smedley Butler greets comrades at, 350
  yearly revenue for community, 245
Battle of Little Big Horn, 302
Bear Butte State Park, 458n8
Bell, Bert, 275
Berry, E. Y., 372, 373, 387, 390, 548–549n47
Berry, John, 94
Berry, Tom, 274, 340
Bethesda Naval Hospital, 383, 384
Big Bend Dam, 381
Black Hills Chronicle, 279, 284–285, 301
Black Hills College, 39
Black Hills Mining and Industrial Association, 274–275
Black Hills News, 249, 270, 276, 290
  . see also *Black Hills Weekly Chronicle*
Black Hills Oil and Mining Review, 241, 248–249

Black Hills Petroleum Company (BHP), 242, 244
. see also Barker oil wells
Black Hills Weekly Chronicle, 276, 279
Boland, John, 267–268, 373
Borglum, Gutzon
  death of, 364
  gives addresses at Mount Rushmore, 202–203, 224, 261, 311
  meets President Franklin Roosevelt, 311
  President Coolidge gives appointments to personal friends of, 248
  President Coolidge presents drill bits to, 224–225
  proposed statues at Mount Rushmore to be carved by, 201
  at Washington dedication at Mount Rushmore, 261
  writes article for "Jefferson Number" booklet, 268
Bottum, Joe, 387
Bovee, family of Ezra, 27, 30–31
brackish water, 380
brackish water plants, proposed locations of, 380
Brink, Myron, 52, 54, *406*
Bronson, R. L., 192–193, 197, 208
Brown, Art
  and Della Kjelmyr, 177–179, 180
  extracurricular activities of, 174, 180
  Francis Case on, 158
  at the *Rapid City Daily Journal*, 170–171, 173, 176
  at Northwestern University, 1922, *418*
  on staff of Nation's Business, 191
Brown, Della Kjelmyr, 177–179, 180, 186, 191
Brown, Grace, 305
Brown, Hattie Case (aunt), 4
Brummit, Dan
  on *Case Chronicles*, 307
  confidence in work of Francis Case, 159
  as editor, 141, *414*
  Francis Case on, 144
  offers assistant editor position to Francis, 147
  temporarily turns over *Herald* to Francis, 155–156
  . see also Epworth Herald
Bryan, William Jennings, 19, 21, 58, 59, 60, 61, *407*
Bulow, William, 215, 219, 241, 242, 246, 260, 355
Bunt, Richard, 81, 84, 86
Burch, Ernest, 143
Butler, Smedley D., 332–333, 350, 351, *439*

C

Camp Doran, 296–297, 300
Camp Funston, 106, 108
Camp Lodge, 298–299, 300
Camp Narrows, 299–300
Camp Pine Creek, 298, 300
Campbell, Wright E., 202
Card, Harold W.
  classmate of Francis at Dakota Wesleyan Academy, 34–35
  on Dakota Wesleyan University debate teams, 52, 54, 70, 73, 95, 96, *406*
  on Dakota Wesleyan University football team, 66, 67, 82, 84, 85, 86, *409*
  delivers commencement address, 183
  in Eighth Annual Convention and Oratorical Contest, 56
  extracurricular activities while at Rapid City, 180
  Francis rooms with family of, 48
  honorary pallbearer at Case funeral, 548-549n47
  initiated into Pi Delta Kappa, 57

Index

involvement in YMCA, 62–63, 64, 70, 80
as lifelong friend of Francis Case, 34
marriage of, 176
at Quantico, 105
and *Rapid City Daily Journal*, 172
trading brushes for chickens, 62
Carlson, Frank, 375, 548–549n47
Case, Caroline Mary ("Carol") (sister). *see* Himmelhoch, Caroline Mary Case ("Carol") (sister)
Case, Duwane Davidson (uncle), 3, 79
Case, Esther Josephine (sister). *see* Sunderman, Esther Josephine Case (sister)
Case, Francis Higbee
  at Acacia House and fraternity, 158, 161, 162, 167
  at Acacia Mining Company, 291–294
  accomplishments as congressman, 367–368
  accuses Postmaster William Howes of illegal campaigning, 353–354
  accuses Werner of federal regulations violations, 354
  accuses Werner of misappropriating funds, 338
  in "All of a Sudden Peggy," 94–95
  at All-State Forensic Quadrangular meet, 73
  "The American Way Out" speech by, 345
  announces candidacy for US representative, 319, 331, 342
  at annual intersociety debates, 51–52, 70, 89
  appeals for campaign financial support, 336–337, 349
  as Army reservist, 252, 307
  and Associated Press, 238
  at Associated Royalties and United Oil, 242

and authorship of provision that became 23rd Amendment to U.S. Constitution, 382
banquet to honor, 359
baptism of, 8
becomes member of Standing Rock Sioux, 304–305
birth and death of son, 365
birth of, 7
birth of daughter Jane Marie Case, 305–306, *432*
and Black Hills Mining and Industrial Association, 274–275
"The Blazed Trail," oratorical contest, 42–43
with brother and sisters at Christmas, *398*
with brother Leland, *408*
builds cabin in Custer State Park, 231–232, *427*
buys home in Custer, 276
buys interest in *Hot Springs Star*, 199
in campaign for third district congressman, 1928, 320–321
Case and Werner campaign cards, *438*
and *Case Chronicles*, 305–306, *432*
and Case Labor Bill, 369–370
celebrates Christmas, 1919, 143–144
as chairman of Public Works Subcommittee on Roads, 376–377
characterizes opponent Theodore Werner, 352
childhood of, 27, 28, *396, 397, 398, 399, 400, 401*
and Citizens Military Training Camps (CMTC), 258–260
concern for American Indians, 369, 382–383
constructs new headquarters for Star Publishing, 234–235
with daughter Jane and Woof, 1936, *434*
death of, 384

Case, Francis Higbee cont'd
  on death of Billy Sunday, 456n53
  delivers Memorial Day address at Custer ceremonies, 279–280
  delivery of commencement addresses, 136, 183, 265, 300
  demands investigation of Indian School, 382
  on developing dependable guiding principles for cloud modification, 379
  on District of Columbia Committee, 372, 382
  earns monogram letter in football, 69
  editing and advertising of "Jefferson Number," 267, *429*
  election statistics as member of House and Senate, 1938–1962, 363, 371, 379, 383
  "The End of the Road in One-Man Government" speech, 353
  on establishing U.S. Bureau of Mines station, 344
  on exempting independent natural-gas producers from federal rate control, 377–378
  experiences shaping political career of, 1, 28–29, 61
  as Fall River County delegate at Republican State Convention, 327–328
  family journeys to Washington, D.C., 358–360
  family rents house in Arlington, Virginia, 360
  in "The Famous Mrs. Fair," 189–190
  and Federal Highway Act of 1956, 546n32
  findings in report to President Truman on overseas operations, 365–366
  funeral of, 384–385, 548–549n47
  future plans in letter to father, 87–89
  General Smedley Butler endorses, 332–333
  granddaughter Catherine Case Commander born, 380
  health of, 83, 104–105, 383–384
  and *Hill City News*, 309, 358
  honeymoon of, 214–215
  in Hot Springs Commercial Club, 204, 212
  at Hot Springs High School as student, 37–38
  and *Hot Springs Star*, 263–264
  on House Select Committee on Foreign Aid (Herter Committee), 366–367
  at inauguration of E.D. Kohlstedt as seventh president of Dakota Wesleyan, 165
  Indian Program of, 346, *437*, 538–539n85
  inducted into Pi Kappa Delta, 57
  initiates summer White House project, 207–208
  in intercollegiate debate, 1918, 95–96
  interest in pursuing law, 142, 147, 149, 197, 200, 239, 263
  interest in water resources, 379–381
  involvement in YMCA, 70, 74
  laws and bills to reimburse Native Americans, 369, 383
  lawsuit of M. L. Shade against Star Publishing and, 216–219
  legally challenges denial of vote to unorganized counties, 325–326
  in letter to father on question of politics, 341–342
  letter to sister Carol on her 16th birthday, 131
  marries Myrle Graves, 214
  at meeting of Townsend Old Age Pension Club, 350
  as member of Committee of Six in McCarthy affair, 375–376

Index 557

as member of Committee on Un-American Activities, 370–371
as member of House Appropriations Committee, 364–365, 371
and Missouri River Basin project, 368–369, 374
in National Peace Contest, 58–60, *407*
and National War Work Council (NWWC), 76, 78
on the New Deal, 338, 343, 345
and newspaper proposal, 163–164, 165
nine-point program of, 331, 532n36
nominated at 1934 Republican State Convention, 335–336
obituaries and editorials written in honor of, 385–386
in official general election returns of 1936, 540n89
oratorical contests of, 32–33, 42–43, 53–54, 55–56, 56–57, 58–61, 92–93, *407, 410*
organizational memberships of, 174, 489–490n11
outlines 1936 campaign platform, 343
parking violation of, 360–361
participates in Hot Springs Country Club golf tournament, 238–239
participation in athletics, 33, 38, 66–68, 81–83, 85–87, *402, 403, 409*
participation in extracurricular activities, 37–38, 41, 51, 90, *404*
participation in intercollegiate debates, 54–55, 72–73, 95–96, 131–133, *406*
participation in inter-society debates, 51–52, 70, 89
participation in Lions Club, 174, 183–184
at *The Phreno Cosmian*, 51, 61, 76

persons attending funeral of, 384–385, 548–549n47
platform for 1928 primary, 319–320
platform for 1936 primary, 343
political rally at Lyman County Courthouse, 337
primary campaign brochure, 1934, *436*
primary campaign circular, 1936, *437*
primary campaign poster, 1928, *435*
program to ensure American neutrality and keep U.S. out of foreign wars, 344
promotes building Army Air Corps base in South Dakota, 367
promotes building of summer homes in Black Hills, 246, 288
proposal to change name Ft. Randall Reservoir in honor of, 387–388
proposes stamp of Mount Rushmore National Memorial, 372–373
on Public Works Committee, 372, 382
publishes and sells souvenir programs, 192–194
purchases *Custer Weekly Chronicle*, 269–270
purchases *Hot Springs Star*, 199
purchases *Times-Herald*, 197
in Rapid City Coolidge Club, 185–186
recommended for position in Washington, DC, 147
registers to read law, 200
relationship with grandparents, 41, 44, 77
relationships with women, 151–152, 159, 160, 166, 173–174, 213
religious devotion of, 8, 11, 72, 77
in results of 1928 primary election, 322–323
in results of 1934 election, 339–340
in results of 1936 election, 355–356

Case, Francis Higbee   cont'd
  in results of 1936 primary election, 346
  in results of 1950 election, 371
  in results of 1950 primary election, 371
  in results of 1956 election, 379
  in results of 1962 primary election, 383
  role in approval of construction projects at Mount Rushmore, 373–374
  role in Black Hills National Cemetery, 368
  role in developing and advancing water management, 368–369
  role in Renegotiation Statute, 367–368
  selling *Saturday Evening Post* magazine, 19, 20–21, *399*
  Senate committee assignments of, 371–372, 383
  service in Home Guard, 90–91
  at South Dakota Board of Regents of Education, 271–274
  at South Dakota College Press Association, 76–77
  at South Dakota Republican State Committee's Western Division, 186
  speaks at Greater South Dakota Congress, 245–246
  sponsors Saline Water Act bill, 380
  at Sturgis High School as student, 31–32
  summer school at Garrett Bible Institute, 148
  supports building of summer homes in Custer State Park, 288
  trading brushes for chickens, 62
  in "Turning the Trick," 174–175
  The Unknown Soldier Amendment proposed by, 345, 351, 535–536n66
  various congressional committees of, 364–365, 371
  views on acceptable traits of young women, 151–152
  views on social side of politics, 188–189
  at Western Securities, Inc., 242
  in Williamson-Case debate,1928, 321–322
  at Wind Cave National Park, 44, 454n56
  writes letter to family on choosing active service, 101–102
  at XLNT Boarding Club, 80–81
  at Yellowstone National Park, 50, 463–464n9
  in YMCA, 62–63, 64
  . see also *Black Hills News*; *Black Hills Weekly Chronicle*; Case, Myrle Graves (wife); *Custer County Chronicle*; *Custer Weekly Chronicle*; Dakota Wesleyan Academy; Dakota Wesleyan University; *Epworth Herald*; Graves, Myrle (girlfriend); *Handbook of Church Advertising* (Case); *Hot Springs Star*; Mare Island (CA); Northwestern University; *Rapid City Daily Journal*; Star Publishing Company; *Times-Herald*; *Tourist News*; U.S. Marine Corps
Case, Francis Llywellyn ("Frank") (paternal grandfather)
  50th wedding anniversary of, 20, *400*
  birth of, 3
  death of, 185
  declining health, death, and funeral of wife, 77–79
  moves with Herbert and Mary E. to Mankato, 150
  selling of bibles by, 41, 44
  sells "Out-O-Sight" Liniment, 3–4, 12, 150

Index

veterinary practice of, 3–4, 12, 41, 44
Case, Hattie, 3, 8, 38, 40, *400*
. see also Brown, Hattie Case (aunt)
Case, Herbert Llywellyn (father)
  acquires additional preaching stations, 26
  appointed Superintendent of Cheyenne River District of Dakota Conference, 33
  assists at Rapid City Deaconess Hospital, 112
  attends Ministers' Week, 285–286
  becomes Deacon, 7
  birth of, 3
  circuit ministry of, 22, 28–29, 33
  on coming to pulpit from boxcar, 24
  and dangerous incidents in Sturgis, 25–26
  as hospital field secretary, 83–84
  moves family to Black Hills of South Dakota, 23–25
  moves family to land claim, 26–27
  moves with Mary E. and Frank Case to Mankato, 150
  ordained as elder, 7
  parsonage in Sturgis, 25
  as pastor for Congregational Church, 285–286
  as pastor in Hot Springs, South Dakota, 37
  pastoral assignment in Everly, Iowa, 7
  pastoral assignment in Klemme, Iowa, 6
  pastoral assignment in Lake Mills, Iowa, 7
  pastoral assignment in Ledyard, Iowa, 4
  pastoral assignment in Marathon, Iowa, 19
  pastoral assignment in Plover, Iowa, 17
  pastoral assignment in Renwick, Iowa, 6
  pastoral assignment in Sanborn, Iowa, 11
  pastoral assignment in Swaledale, Iowa, 9
  pastoral assignment in Wesley, Iowa, 8
  pastoral assignments in South Dakota, 33–34, 65
  performs daughter Joyce's wedding ceremony, 146
  performs daughter Esther's wedding ceremony, 254–255
  purchases house for parents, 39
  pursues gold mining claims, 294
  sells life insurance, 150
  at Upper Iowa University, 4, 6
  wedding of, 5–6, *395*
Case, James Francis (uncle), 3, 79
Case, Jane Marie (daughter), 305–307, 308, 309, 357, 358, 380, 384, 389, 390, *434*
Case, Josephine Altman ("Joan") (sister-in-law), 266
Case, Joyce Armena. see Wilson, Joyce Armena Case (sister)
Case, Leland Davidson (brother)
  at Associated Royalties and United Oil, 242
  baptism of, 10
  birth of, 8
  and brother, *408*
  with brother and sisters at Christmas, *398*
  buys interest in *Hot Springs Star*, 199
  childhood sicknesses of, 9, 12
  and Daedalian Literary Society, 122, 124
  and debate team at Dakota Wesleyan University, 127–128, 131–133
  elected to Forensic Board, 122
  enlists in Students' Army Training Corps (SATC), 119

Case, Leland Davidson   cont'd
  enrolls at Macalester College, 150–151
  gives banquet to honor Francis Case, 359
  graduates from high school, 117
  on Hot Springs oil boom, 245
  interest in *Hot Springs Star* and *Times-Herald*, 200
  at *Rapid City Daily Journal*, 176, 177
  at *Lead Daily Call*, 179
  marriage of, 267
  at *The Mitchell Gazette*, 123
  purchases *Times-Herald*, 197
  recalls Alice Gossage, 177
  recalls dangerous incidents in Sturgis, 25–26
  relates car mishap on way to taking brother to enlist in Marines, 102–103
  retirement from *Hot Springs Star*, 263–264
  at *The Rotarian*, 266, 514n67
  secures political endorsement of General Smedley Butler for Francis, 332–333
  in Students' Army Training Corps (SATC), 117–118
  at Tri-State Roundup, 193
  working in Paris, 215
Case, Mary Antoinette Davidson ("Mary A.") (paternal grandmother)
  50th wedding anniversary of, 20, *400*
  admiration for Billy Sunday, 16, 17–18, 19
  birth of, 3
  declining health, death, and funeral of, 77–79
Case, Mary Ellen Grannis ("Mary E.") (mother)
  character of, 5
  disapproval of drinking alcohol, 27
  graduates from Mankato State Normal School, 5
  wedding of, 6, *395*
Case, Myrle Graves (wife)
  at bedside of gravely ill husband, 384
  birth and death of son, 365
  burial of mother, 222
  buys home in Custer, 276
  at ceremonies dedicating public buildings to husband, 389
  in Contract Study Club, 307–308
  death and burial of sister, 287
  death and funeral of father, 287–288
  at dedication of Francis Case Memorial Bridge (Washington, D.C.), 390, 391
  family members employed at *Chronicle*, 292
  at funeral service of husband, 384
  gives birth to Jane Marie Case, 305–306
  grand-daughter Catherine Case Commander born, 380
  on honeymoon, 214–215, *422*
  marries Francis Case, 214
  as member of American Association of University Women (AAUW), 309–310
  presents reviews of two books on mental hygiene, 357–358
  at ribbon cutting of Francis Case Memorial Bridge (South Dakota), 389
  serves as judge in Custer High School contest, 357
  takes care of sick father, 261–263
Case Auditorium, 389
Case Chronicles, 305–306, *432*
Case family
  at Associated Royalties and United Oil, 242
  attendance at camp meetings, 18

Index

attends dedication of Francis Case Memorial Bridge (Washington, D.C.), 390
bicycle of, 18
boys provide meat for, 28
celebration of July 4, 1911, 31
children of Herbert and Mary A. at Christmas, 1905, *398*
chores of children in, 28
digging wells during drought, 28, 30–31
home schooling of children, 29
at Hot Springs Methodist Church during Christmas holidays, 1915, *405*
life on the claim, 27–30
move by Frank and Mary A. to Hot Springs, 38–39
pastimes and recreation of, 11, 28
photo taken by itinerant photographer, 29, *401*
religious devotion of, 4, 11, 12, 20
source of clothing, 25
at South Dakota homestead, 29, *401*
on trading Francis's sister for farm and pony, 10
tragedies experienced by, 3
various visits of, 4–5, 6, 7, 8–10, 11–12, 16, 18, 20, 21
visit from Frank and Mary A. to Herbert's family in Sturgis, 30–31
visit from Samuel and Armenia Grannis to Herbert's family in Hot Springs, 44, *405*
Case Labor Bill, 369–370
Center Lake and dam, 298–299
Chandler, L. W., 177, 182
Chautauqua Movement, 456n61
Chenoweth, Richard, 294
Citizens Military Training Camps (CMTC), 258–260, 512n49
Civilian Conservation Corps (CCC), 295–296, 357, 367
Clark, Charles ("Badger")

in Black Hills, circa 1926, *423*
cabins of, 231, 251
as good friend of Francis Case, 40
joins staff of *Hot Springs Evening Star*, 239
nominates name for lake at Custer State Park, 281–282
poems by, 221, 226, 502–503n54
President Coolidge requests meeting with, 226
Clionians, the, 35
cloud modification, 379
Cobb, Ty, 13
Committee of Six, 375
communist/communism, 370–371, 375
Contract Study Club, 307–308
Coolidge, Calvin
in 1924 election results, 187, 494n42
accepts invitation to Black Hills, 221
celebrates fifty-fifth birthday, 223, *424*
chooses not to run for reelection in 1928, 223
delegation of Sioux Indians honors, 223–224
four-gun salute to, 283
at Mount Rushmore, 224–225, *425*
requests meeting with Hezron Day, 226
trout fishing, 222, 503n56
visit to Yellowstone National Park, 226
visits Black Hills of South Dakota, 221–228
Coolidge, Grace, 219, 223, *424*
Coolidge Day, 225–226
Cowalski, Clarence, 233
Cox, Professor, 143
Crill, Louis, 245–247, 509n21
Custer, George Armstrong, 269
Custer Commercial Club, 358

Custer County Chronicle
  Francis and staff in front of Chronicle office, 1936, *433*
  incorporates *Black Hills Chronicle*, 301
  Irma and Laurence Weyler employed at, 292
  lists proposed names for lake in Custer State Park, 282, 518n33
  moves to new home, 308
  offers subscriptions for potatoes or cut wood, 301
  prints Butler's endorsement of Francis Case, 333
  publishes five-point program for Custer County, 288
  stories on gold-mining in Black Hills, 290
  subscription drive, 284-285
  "Wayside Notes" column introduced into, 312
  . see also *Custer Weekly Chronicle*

Custer State Park
  Badger Clark nominates name for lake at, 281–282
  Blue Bell Lodge in, 246, 265, 308, 331
  cabins of Badger Clark in, 231, 251
  campaign to name lake at, 281–283, 518n33
  Civilian Conservation Corps (CCC) camps at, 296, 298, 299
  construction of dams and lakes at, 280–281, 296–297, 298–299
  dedication of Lake Legion at, 283–284
  expansion of, 228, 229
  four-gun salute to President Coolidge at, 283
  Francis supports building of summer homes in, 246, 288
  law passes to centralize administration of, 230
  map showing location and boundaries after expansion, *426*
  matters related to cabin site leases, 229, 231
  origins of, 228
  State Game Lodge in, 209–210, 217, 220–223, 227, 231, 246, 298, *424, 426*
  State Secretary of Agriculture's plan for private cabins in, 509n21
  Times-Herald publishes editorial critical of superintendency of, 229–230

Custer Weekly Chronicle
  dimensions, price, and format of, 270
  improvements to, 275–276
  promotes building of summer cabins, 250
  renamed *Custer County Chronicle*, 276
  stories on gold-mining in Black Hills, 290
  . see also *Custer County Chronicle*

D

Daedalian Literary Society, 49, 51–52
Daedalus, 463n6
Daily Argus-Leader, 249–251
Dakota Wesleyan Academy
  Academy Oratorical Contest, 73–74, 96, 135–136
  debate teams win third consecutive championship, 137
  Francis Case as debate coach for, 69, 71
  Francis Case as student at, 34–35
  Harold Card as student at, 34–35
  inter-academy debates, 93, 129–130
  inter-society debates, 126
  literary societies, 35, 126
  presentation of "What Would a Gentleman Do?" 135
Dakota Wesleyan University

Index

annual inter-society debates, 70, 89
annual spring festival, 50
Arbor Day celebration, 1919, 134
commencement week, 1918, 98
dedications of service flags, 94, 121, 137
E. D. Kohlstedt becomes president of, 164–165
final examinations eliminated, 1918, 97–98
football season, 1915, 65
football season, 1916, 65–68
football season, 1917, 81–83, 84–86, *409*
football season, 1918, 120
Francis Case as debate coach and school recruiter at, 125, 126–127
Francis Case presents "In Defense of the Younger Generation" address at, 155
Francis Case resigns from Board of Trustees of, 272
Francis's and Lloyd Rising's oratorical accomplishments at, *410*
graduating class of 1918, *411*, 473–474n53
history of, 34
intercollegiate debates and oratorical contests, 1919, 124–125
literary societies, 48
Myrle Graves's junior class photo in yearbook of, *419*
presentation of faculty members, 1917, 79
Science Club, *419*
Spanish flu (1918 pandemic) at, 119–120
speeding up of spring term, 1918, 90
state debate champions, 1916, *406*
Students' Army Training Corps (SATC) at, 118–119, 121–122, 123
student killed, 91–92, 94

tryouts for men's intercollegiate debate teams, 1919, 127–128
tryouts for women's intercollegiate debate teams, 1919, 128
wins South Dakota Conference Collegiate Championship, 1919 (in basketball), 137
women's intercollegiate team chosen, 130–131
. *see also Phreno Cosmian* (Dakota Wesleyan University newspaper)
dam construction for Missouri River Basin Project, 368–369, 374, 380–381
d'Argent, Edward J., Rev., 42
Davidson, Mary Antoinette ("Mary A."). *see* Case, Mary Antoinette Davidson ("Mary A.") (paternal grandmother)
Davis, John, 187
Dawes, Charles, 186
Dawes Allotment or Severalty Act (Allotment Act). *see* Native Americans
Day, Hezron, 226
Deerfield Dam, 367
Delta Rho, 51, 52, 70, 89
"Democracy in Action" (Case), 92
Dennison, J. C., 213
Dillon, Chester, 65
diphtheria, 16–17, 262, 455n48
Dirksen, Everett McKinley, 386
"dog town," 30
Dolliver, Robert H., 22
Donaldson, Jesse, 372–373
Duke, C. M., 390
Dunn, Olin V., 137

E

Eastman, Charles, 43
Edgemont Express, 248
Eighth Annual Lions International Convention, 183–184

Eisenhower, Dwight, 374, 377–378, 379, 388
Emergency Conservation Work (ECW) Act, 295
"emigrant" car, 23
Epworth Herald
  history of, 140–141
  increase in subscriptions to, 160–161
  job at, 141, 147, 149–150, 156
  liaison officer hired, 161–162
  monthly column by Francis, 182
  offices of, 142–143, 144
  . *see also* Brummit, Dan
Epworth League, 140
  . *see also Epworth Herald*
Erskine, C. D., 202
Ervin, Sam J., 375
Ewert, Adolf W., 205–206

F

Federal Highway Act of 1956 (and amendments), 377, 381–382, 546n42
Ferguson, Ada, 137
Fetzner, Frank, 281
Flanders, Ralph, 375
Flavin, George, 191
Flood Control Act of 1944, 369, 380–381
Francis Case Building, 389–390
Francis Case Memorial Bridge (South Dakota), 388–389
Francis Case Memorial Bridge (Washington, D.C.), 390
Freemasonry, 489–490n11
Frost, Robert, 384
Ft. Randall Dam and Reservoir, 374, 381, 383, 388

G

Gage, Harold, 120, 121
Gage, Harry, 117
Garrett Bible Institute, 71, 148, 164
Gavins Point Dam, 374, 381

General Custer expedition, 269, 288, 302
Getchall, Albert, 106
Gideon, C. C., 217
Gilliland, C. V., 64, 91, 94, 121
Goddard, Bertin, 360
Goddard, Caroline Mary Case ("Carol") (sister), 360
gold, Black Hills discovery of
  boom town claim, 289
  during General Custer expedition, 269, 288, 302
  and Homestake Mining Company, 289
  methods of mining gold, 289
  mining activities authorized, 290
  resurgence in gold-mining activity in 1931, 289
  working claims by Case family, 291–294
Goodrich, Ruth, 135
Gossage, Alice, 167, 172, 177, 192
Gossage, Joseph, 167, 172, 178, 183–184, 192
Grannis, Armenia Jane Lewis (maternal grandmother), 5, 162–163, *394, 397*
Grannis, Mary Ellen ("Mary E."). *see* Case, Mary Ellen Grannis ("Mary E.") (mother)
Grannis, Samuel Higbee (maternal grandfather)
  death and funeral of, 287
  grain and coal business of, 5, 150
  marriage of, 5, *394*
  serves in Civil War, 5
Graves, John (father-in-law), 231, 261–262
Graves, Myrle (girlfriend)
  attends Dakota Wesleyan homecoming festivities, 180
  circa 1924, *420*
  Francis expresses affection for, 189

Index   565

junior class photo in Dakota
   Wesleyan University yearbook,
   419
at Tri-State Roundup, 193
. *see also* Case, Myrle Graves (wife)
Greater South Dakota Congress,
   245–247
Green, Warren
   appoints Francis to South Dakota
      Board of Regents of Education,
      272–274
   and funding of dam at Custer State
      Park, 280
   inaugural address of, 328–329
   nominated for governor, 327–328
   on "post pile" editorial in *Custer
      County Chronicle*, 277
"Growing Pains" (editorial), 229–230
Gunderson, Carl
   1925 inaugural address and reception
      of, 187–188
   loses general election of 1926, 215
   and rumors about resignation of M.
      L. Shade, 211
   and scandal involving M. L. Shade,
      205–207
   speaking engagements of, 186
   wires President Coolidge to visit
      Black Hills, 208
Guthrie, Charles E., 142, 156

H

Hahne, Ernest, 143–144, 167,
   169–170, 359
Hamilton, J. W., 10
Handbook of Church Advertising (Case)
   follow-up volume to, 184
   review by *Literary Digest* on,
      156–157
   publication of, 152–153
   publisher of, 149
   royalty check from publication of,
      160
   title page for, *416*

Hansen, Ethel, 32
Harkness, Kenneth, 86, 87, 120
Harris, Frederick Brown, 384
Harvey, Guy, 274
Hawley, Harold, 216
Hazzard, J. Charles, 123–124
Hearst, George, 288–289
Hehaka Hemaza (Iron Horn Elk), 305
Herter Committee, 366–367
Hesketh, S. Edna, 189
Heumphreus, M. W., 291
Hibbard, Palmer, 291, 292–293
Hill City News, 182, 309, 358
Himmelhoch, Caroline Mary Case
   ("Carol") (sister)
   assists Francis Case in campaign
      correspondence, 349–350
   birth of, 10
   with brothers and sister at Christmas,
      398
   childhood sicknesses of, 12, 16–17
   graduates from high school, 195
   higher education of, 195, 196
   locates and works gold claims,
      290–291, 293
   marital problems of, 286
   marriage of, 196
   relationship with Ralph
      Himmelhoch, 195, 196
   returns to Mankato after marital
      breakup, 286–287
   at Vogue School of Design and
      Institute of Art, 286–287, 291
   . *see also* Goddard, Caroline Mary
      Case ("Carol") (sister)
Himmelhoch, Ralph (brother-in-law)
   marital problems of, 286
   relationship and marriage to Carol
      Case, 195–196
   takes Francis on tour of his law
      offices, 265
Hoffman, Donald, 52
Homestake Mining Company, 289
Homestead Act of 1862, 458–459n9

homesteaders, 24, 25, 29
Hoover, Herbert, 248, 330
Horse Thief Lake and dam, 298
Hot Springs Chamber of Commerce, 245
Hot Springs Commercial Club, 220, 221, 245
. see also Hot Springs Chamber of Commerce
Hot Springs Country Club's Sixth Annual handicap golf tournament, 238–239
Hot Springs Evening Star
  announces oil strike, *428*
  Badger Clark joins staff of, 239
  control and management change, 263
  converted to daily newspaper, 238
  front page on Jensen and Case victory, *440*
  promotes private home building in Black Hills, 250
  reports oil strike by Red Canyon Oil Well, 240–241
Hot Springs High School, 37–38, 41–44, 145, 300, *403*, *404*, 461n37
Hot Springs News, 248
Hot Springs Oil Exchange, 243
Hot Springs Star
  articles on rural credit funds scandal, 205–207
  on centralized superintendency of Custer State Park, 230
  changes name to *Hot Springs Weekly Star*, 238
  construction of new headquarters for *Times-Herald* and, 234–235
  subscription contest at, 232–234
  unites with *Times-Herald*, 200
  . see also Hot Springs Weekly Star
Hot Springs Weekly Star
  Hot Springs Star changes name to, 238

  plan for financing new newspaper press by holding subscription contest, 255–258
  promotes Citizens Military Training Camps (CMTC), 258–259
  reports on oil development in 1931, 244–245
  stories about oil developments, 241
Howe, Elizabeth, 281
Howell, Brooke, 327
Howes, William, 353–354
Hoy, Carl B., Mrs., 385–386
Hurley, Steve, 226–227

I
"In Flanders Fields" (McCrae), 175–176
Indian Program, *437*, 538–539n85
influenza vaccine, 476n27
  . see also Spanish flu (1918 pandemic)
Intercollegiate Peace Association (IPA), 58
Internal Security Act, 371

J
Jenkins, John, 98
Jensen, Leslie, 317–319, 339, 341, 342, 344, 347, 348, 352, 353, 355, 357, 548–549n47
Johnson, A. T., 199, 201, 204, 207, 212
Johnson, Cora B., 199, 201, 204, 207, 212
Johnson, Edwin C., 375
Johnson, Florence, 190
Johnson, Lyndon B., 385, 390, 548–549n47
Jones, Hilton, 51

K
Kappa Pi Phi, 70, 89
Kennedy, John, 384, 387, 388
KFYR radio station, 352, 353
KGFX radio station, 353

Index

Kipp, Ruth, 233
Kjelmyr, Della. *see* Brown, Della Kjelmyr
Knights of the Ku Klux Klan (KKK), 193, 194–195
Knox, Frank, 348
Kohlstedt, E. D., 164
Krusen, Wilmer, 109–110

L

labor and management legislation, 370
LaFollette, Robert, 186, 187
Lake Mohonk Conference on International Arbitration, 58, *407*
Landon, Alfred M., 348
Latch, Edward G., 384, 390
Latham, W. E., 248
"Leave It to the Hills" (Clark), 221, 502–503n54
Lee, George E., 248
Lee, Haldon, 358
Leedom, Chet, 316–318, 356
Leffert, Frank, 54, *406*
Legion Lake. *see* Custer State Park
Lenker, C. B., 280, 283
Lewis, Armenia Jane. *see* Grannis, Armenia Jane Lewis (maternal grandmother)
Lewis and Clark Lake, 381
Liberty Bonds (Liberty Loans), 84, 471n22
Lions Club, 174, 183–184, 489–490n11
locally employed men (LEM), 295
Loman, James C., 65–66, 81
Loocke, Carl, Rev., 203
Ludeman, Walter, 54, 73, 89, 95
Lushbaugh, Elmer, 54, 72, 77, 95, *406*
Lysen, Irene, 176

M

Madera, Roy, 265
"Man to Man" (Case), 53–54
Manuel, Moses, 288–289

maps, *421, 426, 430–431*
Mare Island (CA), 474n6
. *see also* U.S. Marine Corps
Martin, Ewert W., 202
Masonic Lodges, 489–490n11
McCarthy, Joseph, 375–376
McColley, T. E., 389
McCrae, John, 175
McCullough, D. A., 328
McDonald, Charles S., 259, 337
McGovern, George, 387, 389, 390, 391
McLean, Ray L., 81, 97, 124, 129, 137, *409*
McMaster, W. H., 186, 187, 188
McRoberts Oratorical Contest, 42–43, 391
Methodist Black Hills Mission, 22
Methodist Book Concern, 149, 156–157
Methodist Episcopal Church, 4, 20, 83
. *see also Epworth Herald*; Epworth League
Meyers, F. W., 166–168, 170, 178–179
Michaud, Francis, 291, 292–293
Michaud, Ira, 291–292
Milek, John T., 334
Miller, George, 219, *403*
Miller, Lauritz, 216
Milton Literary Society, 37–38
Miser, Walter G., 338
Missouri River Basin project, 368–369, 374, 380–381, 388
Mitchell, Charles Bayard, 98
Mohonk Mountain House, 57
Morgan Holding Company, 244
Morse, Wayne, 386
Mount Coolidge, 223
Mount Rushmore
    approval of construction projects at, 373–374
    Francis Case and dignitaries at silver anniversary of, 373
    initial dedication of, 201–203

Mount Rushmore *cont'd*
  Jefferson dedication at, 311
  law creates Rushmore National
    Memorial Commission, 247–248
  Lincoln dedication at, 364
  President Coolidge at second
    dedication of, 224–225, *425*
  Roosevelt (Theodore) dedication at, 364
  U.S. postal stamp of, 372–373
  visit by President Franklin Roosevelt, 310–311
  Washington dedication at, 260–261
Mount Rushmore National Memorial Commission, 267–268
Mundt, Karl, 347, 348, 352, 355, 356, 363, 373, 383, 384, 387, 388, 389, 390, 548–549n47
Mundt-Nixon bill, 370–371
Murphy, Alcesta, 233
Myer, Dillon, 382

N

National Advisory Committee on Weather Control, 379
National Forest Service, 296
National Park Service, 296, 364
National War Work Council (NWWC), 75–76
Native Americans
  1868 Treaty of Fort Laramie, 302
  Allotment Act, 524–526nn80–81
  Battle of Little Big Horn, 302
  Black Horse (Sioux Indian Chief), 203
  Cheyenne River Reservation, 303, 354, 359
  Chief Grey Eagle, 305
  and Civilian Conservation Corps (CCC) program, 295
  concern of Francis Case for, 369, 382–383
  construction of Indian School, 382
  Crow Creek Reservation, 304, 383
  in discussion of "Rapid Indians" athletes, 38–39
  Flandreau Reservation, 305
  graduation address at Rapid City Indian School, 183
  Great Sioux Reservation, 302–303
  Hunkpapa tribe, 304
  Indian Program of Francis Case, 437, 538–539n85
  Indian Reorganization Act of 1934, 524–525n80
  Itazipco (Sansarc) tribe, 303
  laws and bills to reimburse, 369, 383
  Lower Brule Reservation, 303
  Lower Yanktonai tribe, 304
  map of South Dakota's American Indian Reservations, Counties, and County Seats as of 1936, *430–431*
  Mdewakanton tribe, 305
  Miniconjou tribe, 303
  Oglala tribe, 303
  Oohenonpa tribe, 303–304
  Pine Ridge Reservation, 303, 310, 343–344, 358
  Pony Claims Bill, 369
  Rosebud Reservation, 303, 345, 353, 358
  Sicangu tribe, 303
  Sihasapa tribe, 303, 304
  Sioux Agreement of 1889, 302, 524–526nn80–81
  Sioux Nation, 303–304, 524n78
  Sisiton tribe, 304
  Sisseton Reservation, 304
  Standing Rock Reservation, 303, 304, 344, 353, 359, 383
  United States v. Sioux Nation of Indians, 524n78
  Upper Yanktonai tribe, 304
  Wahpekute tribe, 305
  Wahpeton tribe, 304
  Yankton Reservation, 304
  Yankton tribe, 304
Neff, John M., 378

Nettleton, George, 145
Nixon, Richard, 370
Norbeck, Peter
  creates informal committee to explore land acquisition, 296
  death of, 359–360
  introduces bill to centralize administration of Custer State Park, 230
  and Mount Rushmore project, 202, 224, 225, 311
  reelection to U.S. Senate, 215
  and rural credit funds scandal, 205
  and summer White House project, 208, 210, 219, 220, 221, 223
  testimonial dinner for, 264
Northwestern University
  Acacia House and fraternity, 158, 161, 162, 167, 292
  commencement day at, *415*
  Francis Case as graduate student at, 137–138, 151, 158, 162
  Francis Case completes Master's degree at, 147–148
  Graduate Club and officers at, *417*
Nystrom, M. E. ("Monty"), 231

O

Oahe Dam and Reservoir, 374, 381, 383
O'Harra, Cleophas C., 260, 268, 272
oil discovery and exploration in South Dakota, 240–245
"Our Job is to Re-Establish Opportunity as the Birthright of Every American" (Case), 343
"Out-O-Sight" Liniment, 3–4, 12, 150

P

Patman, Elmer, 378
Payne, Mark, 65
Pershing, John J., 110
phaeton, 39

Phreno Cosmian (Dakota Wesleyan University newspaper), 51, 61, 64, 68–69, 76, 80–81, 91–92, 93, 98, 127, 128–129
Pi Kappa Delta, 57, 77, 97, 465–466n26
Pick-Sloan plan, 369
Petrie, Frank, 54, 72, *406*
Proffitt, W. E., Mrs., 37
Pyle, Gladys, 327, 354

R

racial discrimination, 38–39
Rapid City Daily Journal
  acquiring loan for, 169–170
  daily routine at, 169
  division of work at, 179
  on events preceding 1924 national election, 186
  exploring investing in, 166–168
  Harold Card and Francis Case sell ownership interests in, 191–192
  new officers take charge of, 192
  role of Art Brown in, 173, 179
  role of Francis Case in, 172, 179
  role of Harold Card in, 172, 176, 179, 192
  role of L. W. Chandler in, 177
  role of Leland Case in, 177
  role of W. B. Andrus in, 173
  signed and written agreement of purchase, 172–173
  turnover of employees at, 176
  . see also Gossage, Alice; Gossage, Joseph
"Rapid Indians," 38–39
Reconstruction Finance Corporation (RFC), 280–281
Red Canyon Oil Well, 240, 244
Reifel, Ben, 387–388, 389, 390, 548–549n47
Republican National Convention, 1936, 348

Republican State Convention, 1934, 334–335
Republican State Convention, 1936, 347–348
Richards, Ellen Swallow. *see* American Association of University Women
Richardson, Norman E., 148, 149, 153, 156–157
Rising, Lloyd, 92, 95, *410*, 472n37, 473–474n53
Roberts, W. J., 42
Robinson, Billy Doane, 261
Robinson, Doane, 202, 225, 260–261, 268
Rockford No. 1 (oil well), 244
Roosevelt, Franklin D., 294–296, 310–312, 330, 355
Rotary Club, 514n67
Rushmore Mountain. *see* Mount Rushmore
Rushmore National Memorial Commission, 247–248
Russell, Richard B., 386–387

S

Saline Water Act, 380
salt water plants, proposed locations of, 380
Schermerhorn, William D.
  advice at onset of World War, 75
  announces recruitment of Home Guards, 90–91
  at dedication of Wesleyan service flag, 121
  gives baccalaureate sermon for commencement week, 1918, 98
  as graduation commencement speaker, 136
  as president of Dakota Wesleyan University, 70–71
  resigns Wesleyan presidency, 164
School of Mines, 111, 182, 227
Seaman, William, 51, 52
Shade, M. L.
  advocates for centralized administration of Custer State Park, 230
  rumored resignation of, 211
  in rural credit funds scandal, 205–207
  as supervisor for construction of dam that created Center Lake, 298–299
  trial in lawsuit against Francis Case and Star Publishing Company by, 205–207, 216–219
Shadehill Dam, 374
Sharpe, M. Q., 325, 328, 337
Sheridan Lake, 367
Sioux City, Iowa, 4, 66, 82, 132
Smith, Margaret Chase, 386
South Dakota
  1910 drought in, 27, 29
  1934 Republican State Convention, 334–335
  1936 Republican State Convention, 347–348
  Board of Regents of Education, 271
  Civilian Conservation Camps (CCC) in, 296–300
  congressional districts of, 493–494n39
  development of potential oil resources in, 241–245
  discovery of gold in Black Hills of, 269, 288–294, 302
  irrigation projects of, 367
  legislature passes congressional reapportionment bill, 329
  legislature passes new primary law, 1929, 324
  map of Black Hills, *421*
  map showing South Dakota's American Indian Reservations, Counties, and County Seats as of 1936, *430–431*
  oil discovery and exploration in, 240–245

problem of voting in unorganized counties of, 325–326
promotion of private home building in Black Hills of, 246, 249–250, 509n21
results of 1932 election in, 329–330
results of 1934 primary election in, 333–334
results of 1936 election in, 355–356, 540n89
State Fish and Game Commission of, 281
State Highway Commission of, 277–279
State Senate and House invite President Coolidge to Black Hills, 219
South Dakota Debating League, 95
South Dakota International Prohibition Association Eighth Annual Convention and Oratorical Contest, 56
South Dakota School of Mines. *see* School of Mines
Spalding, A. G., 13
Spanish flu (1918 pandemic)
among Allied nations, 108–109
at Dakota Wesleyan University, 119–120
demographic overview of, 107
initial wave of, 108–109
possible origins of, 107–108
second wave of, 109–111
statistics from, 106, 110–111
symptoms of, 107
third wave of, 108–109
. *see also* influenza vaccine
"Spartacus to the Gladiators" (Case), 32–33
Spearfish Normal, 32
Spoonts, Lorine Jones, 268
Stanley, John A., 217, 218
Star Publishing Company

buys subscription list of *Hot Springs News* and *Edgemont Express*, 248–249
construction of addition to, 255
construction of new headquarters for, 234–235
employment of Esther Case at, 232
Hot Springs Star and *Times-Herald* unite, 200
oil exploration coverage at, 241–242
publication rights to *Tourist News* and *Black Hills Oil and Mining Review* transferred, 248–249
role of Francis Case in, 199
subscription contest at, 232–234
trial in lawsuit of M. L. Shade against Francis and, 207, 216–218
. *see also Hot Springs Evening Star; Hot Springs Star; Hot Springs Weekly Star; Times-Herald*
State Fish and Game Commission, 281
Stennis, John, 375, 386, 548–549n47
Stockade Lake and dam, 296–297
Stonecypher, L. D., 327
strikes and industrial disputes, 369–370
Students' Army Training Corps (SATC), 117–119, 121
summer White House project, 207–210, 219–221
Sunday, William Ashley ("Billy")
declining health and death of, 15–16, 456n53
early life of, 12–13
Francis Case on death of, 456n53
marriage of, 14
ministry of, 14–15, 21–22
professional baseball career of, 13
views on politics and temperance, 15
Sunderman, Esther Josephine Case (sister)
birth of, 19
education of, 232

Sunderman, Esther Josephinee cont'd
gives birth to Charles Leland Sunderman, 262
gives birth to Dale Llywellyn Sunderman, 359
gives birth to Marilyn Claire Sunderman, 359
Mankato Daily Free Press, 253–254
marriage of, 254–255
at Star Publishing, 232, 252–253
Sunderman, Raymond (brother-in-law), 254–255, 262, 359
Sundstrom, Carl, 358
Sundstrom, Jessie, 300
Superior Oil Company, 378
Surbeck, Homer, 182

T

Tacy, Thomas O., 37, 41, 43
Taft, William Howard, 19, 21, 58, 61, *407*
Taft-Hartley Bill, 370
Talbot, Marion. *see* American Association of University Women
Tangen, Helge, 328
Thalians, the, 49–50, 124
The American Legion, 489–490n11
"The American Way Out" (Case), 345
The Black Hills Chronicle, 282–283, 284–285
"The Blazed Trail" (Case), 42–43
The Christian Advocate, 153, 307
"The End of the Road in One-Man Government" (Case), 353
"The Famous Mrs. Fair" (play), 189–190
The Literary Digest, 156–157, 355, 485n40
"The Modern Paradox" (Case), 57, 58–60, 61–62
The Pathfinder, 275–276
The Rapid City Daily Guide, 171, 179–180, 181–182

"The Renaissance from War" (Rising), 92
The Saturday Evening Post, 19, 20–21, *399*
The Unknown Soldier Amendment, 345, 351, 535–536n66
Thompson, Helen Amelia ("Nell"), 14, 15
Times-Herald
construction of new headquarters for *Hot Springs Star* and, 234–235
converted into daily newspaper, 238
enlargement of, 204
publishes editorial critical of Custer State Park, 229–230
subscription contest at, 232–234
unites with *Hot Springs Star*, 200
. see also *Hot Springs Evening Star*
Tourist News, 212, 248–249, *421*
Trent, C. W., 269–270
Trimble, John B., 8
Tri-State Roundup, 192, 194
Troth, Loyson G., 268
True, John, 259
Truman, Harry, 366, 370–371
"Turning the Trick" (play), 174–175

U

Udall, Stewart, 388
United Oil, 242
U.S. Marine Corps
applies for commission in reserves of, 363–364
awarded Good Conduct Medal, 115–116
boot camp experience in, 104–105
government discharges Marines stationed at Mare Island (CA), 115
physical examination for, 103
Private Francis Case, USMC, *412*
receives honorable discharge from, 113

Index

response to Spanish flu (1918 pandemic) at Mare Island (CA), 111, 113–114
Section 5, Company D, USMC, Mare Island, (CA), *413*
signs oath of allegiance to United States, 104
training facility at Mare Island (CA), 104
U.S. Public Health Service, 110
U.S. Supreme Court, 371

W

Walter, Francis, 370
war bonds. *see* Liberty Bonds (Liberty Loans)
"Watch Night" (Christian religious service), 53, 464–465n16
Watkins, Arthur, 375
Watkins Committee, 376
Weaver Army Air Base (Ellsworth Air Force Base), 367
Wells, Will, 274
Werner, Theodore
  accused of federal regulations violations by Case, 354
  Case and Werner campaign cards, *438*
  creator and editor of *The Rapid City Daily Guide*, 171
  dislike of Francis Case, 275
  and Francis Case at political event, 348–349
  loses elections to Francis Case, 355, 363
  wins congressional seat against Francis Case, 339–340
  wins primary for congressional seat, 334
Wesley, Charles, 140
Wesley, John, 140
West, Carroll ("Cal"), 79–80, 121, 127
West, Kenneth, 91–92, 94
Western Securities, Inc., 242, 243

"What Would a Gentleman Do?" (play), 135
Wheeler, Burton, 367
Whiting, Charles H., 291, 548–549n47
whooping cough, 12, 454n33
Wigglesworth, Woof, 306, 307, 309, 357, 358, *432*, *434*
Wigmore, J. H., 142
Wilcox, Morris, 292, 293
Wilds, Elmer, 52, 76, 77, 79
Williamson, William
  in 1924 general election, 186, 187
  in 1926 general election, 215, 316–317
  in 1928 general election, 323
  in 1930 general election, 328
  in 1932 general election, 329
  appointed to Rushmore National Memorial Commission by President Herbert Hoover, 248
  invites President Coolidge to Black Hills, 208–210
  in results of 1928 primary election, 322–323
  in results of 1934 primary election, 333–334
  in results of vote for congressman at 1934 Republican State Convention, 335
  in Williamson-Case debate, 1928, 321–322
  writes article for "Jefferson Number" booklet, 268
Wilson, Clifford (brother-in-law)
  at Associated Royalties and United Oil, 242
  biographical information about, 145–146
  Francis Case registers to read law with, 200
  introduces House bill to authorize primary elections in organized counties, 328–329

Wilson, Joyce Armena Case   cont'd
  represents Francis Case and Star
    Publishing in lawsuit, 216
  represents Francis Case in legal
    challenge to bring votes to
    unorganized counties, 325–326
  shares importance of Red Canyon oil
    strike, 214
  at Western Securities, Inc., 242
Wilson, Joyce Armena Case (sister)
  birth of, 6
  with brothers and sister at Christmas,
    398
  childhood sickness of, 9
  and children quarantined for
    diphtheria, 262
  as corporate treasurer of *Times-
    Herald*, 197
  as faculty member of Nettleton
    Commercial College, 145
  gives birth to Allen Grannis Wilson,
    154
  gives birth to Dorothy Joyce Wilson,
    197
  gives birth to Lois Arlene Wilson,
    195
  as instructor at Mankato
    Commercial College, 145
  love of playing piano, 23–24, 28
  officiates marriage of sister Carol,
    360
  as student at Dakota Wesleyan
    Academy, 34–35, 37
  as student at Dakota Wesleyan
    University, 37, 40, 44
  as student at Mankato Commercial
    College, 49, 144
  as student at South Dakota State
    College, 144–145
  wedding of, 146
  at Wilson Law Office, 253
Wind Cave National Park, 44, 462n56
WNAX radio station, 247–248, 345,
  352
Wood, Louise, 152, 159
Wood, Winnette Lindamood, 137
World War, 15, 75, 84, 111, 120, 174,
  175, 189, 205, 279, 281, 295, 305,
  317, 332, 344
  . see also Citizens Military Training
    Camps (CMTC); National War
    Work Council (NWWC); Spanish
    flu (1918 pandemic)
World War II, 300, 363, 365, 367
Wounded Knee Massacre, 202–203,
  369

Y
Yellowstone National Park, 50, 226,
  463–464n9
YMCA (Young Men's Christian
  Association), 63, 75–76
  . see also West, Carroll ("Cal")
Young, Charles, 10

Z
Zwicker, Ralph, 375, 376

www.ingramcontent.com/pod-product-compliance
Lightning Source LLC
Chambersburg PA
CBHW031358290426
44110CB00011B/197